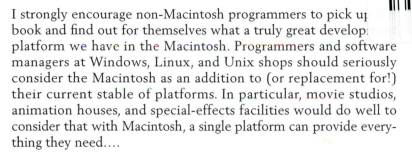

I strongly encourage non-Macintosh programmers to pick up this book and find out for themselves what a truly great development platform we have in the Macintosh. Programmers and software managers at Windows, Linux, and Unix shops should seriously consider the Macintosh as an addition to (or replacement for!) their current stable of platforms. In particular, movie studios, animation houses, and special-effects facilities would do well to consider that with Macintosh, a single platform can provide everything they need....

—from the foreword by Philip J. Schneider
R&D Engineer, Industrial Light + Magic

Finally, the book I've wanted for years is here! As a graphics programmer, I appreciate the clear explanations of how Quartz has packaged the state of the art for mere mortals. As a Cocoa programmer, I appreciate the clear explanation of which [Quartz] facilities...Cocoa is already leveraging. This will become a well-thumbed resource for all graphics programmers on Mac OS X, whether or not they're using Cocoa, Carbon, or porting code from another platform.

—Dr. Michael B. Johnson
Pixar Animation Studios

I've been using Quartz since the first release of Mac OS X, and this book covers it all! Great advice, good sample code—it's the book to have if you want to learn everything about Quartz.

—Stephane Marcouiller
SDE, Microsoft Corporation

Not only do the authors of *Programming with Quartz* have a superb understanding of their subject matter, but they have conveyed their knowledge in a clear, concise, and readable manner. *Programming with Quartz* has saved me quite a bit of time on my first major Quartz project, and its more general lessons on graphics programming techniques and concepts will prove valuable when using any modern graphics API.

—Josh Aas
Software Engineer, Mozilla Corporation

Even after implementing several features using Quartz, I still learned things from this book that I did not know. For example, the chapter on handling PDF images is very thorough in its descriptions and the issues it raises. I wish I had this chapter when I implemented this feature. The book is very well written and covers many complex topics in 2D graphics clearly and at a level appropriate for all programmers. *Programming with Quartz* continues Apple's tradition of producing excellent documentation for its developers.

—Ron Ullmann
Macintosh Business Unit, Microsoft Corporation

Programming with Quartz

2D and PDF Graphics in Mac OS X

David Gelphman
Bunny Laden

ELSEVIER

AMSTERDAM • BOSTON • HEIDELBERG • LONDON
NEW YORK • OXFORD • PARIS • SAN DIEGO
SAN FRANCISCO • SINGAPORE • SYDNEY • TOKYO

Morgan Kaufmann Publishers is an imprint of Elsevier

Senior Editor	Tim Cox
Publishing Services Manager	Simon Crump
Project Manager	Elisabeth Beller
Assistant Editor	Rick Camp
Editorial Assistant	Jessica Evans
Cover Design	Laurie Anderson
Cover Image	© Digital Vision/Getty Images (photographer, Chris Knapton)
Text Design	Rebecca Evans
Composition	Nancy Logan
Technical Illustration	Dartmouth Publishing, Inc.; Apple
Copyeditor	Yonie Overton
Proofreader	Jennifer McClain
Indexer	Steve Rath
Interior and Cover Printer	Transcontinental Interglobe

Morgan Kaufmann Publishers is an imprint of Elsevier.
500 Sansome Street, Suite 400, San Francisco, CA 94111

Library of Congress Cataloging-in-Publication Data
Application submitted.

ISBN 13: 978-0-12-369473-7
ISBN 10: 0-12-369473-6
For information on all Morgan Kaufmann publications,
visit our website at *www.mkp.com* or *www.books.elsevier.com*.

Printed in Canada

05 06 07 08 09 5 4 3 2 1

To my friend, colleague, and manager of many years, who fosters a great working environment, inspires me with his creativity and hard work, and provides top-notch technical assistance and advice.

To Mac developers, who will bring Quartz alive in innovative ways.

Contents

Chapter 3

Using Quartz 2D in Cocoa

Chapter 4

Using Quartz 2D in Carbon

Chapter 5

The Quartz Coordinate System and Coordinate Transformations

Chapter 6

Drawing with Paths

Chapter 7

Color, Alpha Transparency, and the Quartz Graphics State   147

Chapter 8

Data Providers and Data Consumers   185

Foreword

The typical day-to-day experience of most programmers consists of what is euphemistically known as "maintenance" (that is, fixing mistakes in existing code) or, if their karma is particularly good, the occasional opportunity to add new features to an existing library or application. While these activities (particularly the latter) can be rewarding in their own ways, the programmer is always constrained in some fashion by the requirement of compatibility with the existing code base, with other existing libraries and applications, or with old file formats. While civilians (i.e., nonprogrammers) often fantasize about winning the lottery, the equivalent for many programmers is the rare opportunity to create a new library from scratch, without the constraints that often frustrate their desires to extend and improve an existing library.

The advent of Mac OS X provided engineers at Apple with the opportunity (and challenge) to start afresh. Apple wisely chose to bring forward those parts of the original "toolbox" (APIs, in non-Apple speak) in the form of the Carbon interface—this allowed the existing application base to be ported to Mac OS X in a relatively painless fashion. However, Apple also recognized the tremendous opportunity afforded them by the fact that new Mac OS X APIs needn't be backward compatible; they could start from scratch without being so constrained and could take advantage of new technologies, hardware capabilities, and the lessons learned over many years of providing libraries and services to application developers.

With Quartz 2D, Apple's engineers have gone far beyond merely meeting that challenge and have produced an API that is simply spectacular. Here's a thought experiment: close your eyes and imagine you've been given the opportunity to write a modern 2D graphics API from the ground up—what would be on your wish list? Certainly you'd want it to be device- and resolution-independent. You'd want sophisticated color management—the ability to use a variety of color spaces, including calibrated color—and you'd certainly want to support transparency and blending. You'd want sophisticated handling of text: layout, fonts, and Unicode support. You'd want to be able to take advantage of widely used file formats and libraries (such as QuickTime, JPEG, PostScript, EPS, and PDF) but be independent of these as much as possible. You'd want it to be easy to do easy things, like draw a circle or a box, and you'd want it to be as easy as possible to do very complex things (for example, by providing a manageable interface to inherently complex functionality such as with color management or bitmap file formats). You'd want the API to be clean, consistent, elegant, and orthogonal so programmers could create more of the incredible applications the Macintosh is justifiably known for. You'd also want it to be blazingly fast to give users the best possible experience. Quartz 2D fulfills all those wishes and much more.

The best API in the world isn't going to go very far without adequate documentation. At the very least one needs a reference manual, and Apple's have historically been quite good. Reference manuals are not intended to teach programmers the how and why of using an API, and so one can find for almost any API a number (often a large number) of books that purport to be tutorial in nature. I don't need to offer more than the observation that such books tend to be highly variable in their value, to put it as diplomatically as possible. This is lamentable but understandable; the task of describing a rich and powerful API is certainly one of the most difficult in technical writing.

The authors of the book you now hold in your hands have met the challenge of describing Quartz 2D in a simply spectacular fashion: this is unquestionably one of the best API books I've ever encountered. The Quartz 2D API's elegance, clarity, and power is mirrored beautifully by the authors' presentation: easy things are easy to understand, while complex functionality is explained in as straightforward a fashion as possible. Many API how-to books fall down most dramatically in their use of code examples—either they are much too shallow or much too arcane or, worst of all, they will attempt to guide the reader through the entire development cycle of a contrived application. Not so with this book— indeed, the examples here are, well, exemplary; they're chosen to guide the reader from complete naiveté to mastery and are explained in such a way that the application programmer understands *why* and not just *how*. This book has two other great strengths. First, as with many APIs, Quartz 2D provides several ways of accessing the library's functionality, and the authors go to great effort to explain the often subtle differences in the approaches and provide clear guidelines to the programmer for choosing the right approach. Second, the authors have provided a liberal dose of advice on best practices: tidbits of information regarding how to use the API correctly, which may not necessarily be obvious even to experienced programmers.

The authors, in the preface that follows, have nicely described the goals and organization of the book and have provided a broad overview of some of Quartz 2D's functionality (that is, what makes it such a great API), so I won't belabor that here. Read the book! They also describe the intended audience, but since I have an opinion here and the imprimatur to state it, I will belabor that aspect. The Macintosh is so widely regarded for its "ease of use" that this phrase has almost become a cliché. The Macintosh has been wildly successful in the artistic, musical, and publishing communities. Both of these phenomena have led to the view among many non-Macintosh programmers that the Macintosh is not a serious machine for business or science, much less an appealing platform for hardcore programming. I love the Macintosh for its ease of use, its "it just works" nature, the beauty and elegance of its user interface, and the awesome applications available for it, but, even with all of this, I believe the Macintosh's greatest strength lies in its APIs—they are simply the best in the business.

The Macintosh is inarguably the best platform for users, but it is also the best platform for developers as well. By using Quartz 2D in the Carbon or Cocoa framework, developers can create the sorts of interactive applications for which the Mac is famous, and with much greater ease than on other platforms. But since Quartz 2D is not by its nature tied to either of these frameworks, programmers can take advantage of the tremendous power of the API in command-line applications written in C and C++. Quartz 2D also has Python bindings for the great majority of its functionality, allowing programmers to simultaneously take advantage of Python and Quartz 2D. The authors don't specifically mention it, but it would be possible to write an interactive application with a GUI in either X11 or Python and use most of the functionality of Quartz 2D.

In light of all this, I strongly encourage non-Macintosh programmers to pick up this book and find out for themselves what a truly great development platform we have in the Macintosh. Programmers and software managers at Windows, Linux, and Unix shops should seriously consider the Macintosh as an addition to (or replacement for!) their current stable of platforms. In particular, movie studios, animation houses, and special-effects facilities would do well to consider that with Macintosh, a single platform can provide everything they need: 3D applications (e.g., Maya and LightWave 3D), 2D applications (e.g., Adobe Photoshop), compositing (Shake), digital video editing (Final Cut Pro), and so on, as well as the best platform for developing in-house 3D and 2D applications. Let Quartz 2D and this wonderful book show you the possibilities.

Philip J. Schneider
R&D Engineer
Industrial Light + Magic
October 2005

Preface

This book describes the Quartz 2D graphics and imaging system in Mac OS X and explains how to use the Quartz 2D application programming interface (API). With the Portable Document Format (PDF) at the core of its imaging model, Quartz 2D is a breakthrough technology for two-dimensional (2D) graphics on personal computers. Quartz 2D provides the support you'd expect for graphics primitives like lines, curves, rectangles, arbitrary paths, and images. It also supports features such as translucency, layers, shadows, and a host of other sophisticated effects. Not only can you create PDF documents, but you can draw and dissect existing ones.

The Quartz 2D implementation is fast and easy to use. In addition to 2D-drawing and PDF support, Quartz 2D reads, displays, and writes a wide variety of bitmap image formats.

Color management is built into Quartz. Quartz 2D works behind the scenes with ColorSync technology to make sure ICC color profiles are respected. Applications can use calibrated color spaces as well as device color spaces.

Quartz 2D drawing can be sent to a printer, captured to a PDF file, or rendered to an offscreen bitmap just as easily as it can be drawn to the display. That's because drawing destinations are treated as abstractions. Applications can focus on the drawing and let the system handle the process of rendering the content to a specific destination.

Our Objective

This book is intended to familiarize developers with the capabilities of Quartz 2D and to get them programming Quartz graphics in their applications. The book describes how best to use Quartz 2D and gives numerous code examples to show how to accomplish many of the drawing tasks possible with Quartz 2D.

Any of the following will benefit from reading this book:

- New Mac OS X developers who want to get started with 2D graphics in Mac OS X.

- Longtime Mac OS developers who have used the Carbon framework and want to add powerful new drawing capabilities, support PDF documents, and improve the quality of the graphics in their applications.

- Cocoa programmers who want to understand and more fully exploit the power of the Quartz 2D graphics system that sits underneath the Cocoa graphics API.

- UNIX developers interested in the graphics capabilities in Mac OS X. Many UNIX developers utilize and are familiar with PostScript. Quartz 2D is a natural fit for these developers.

- Web developers who want to create dynamic content using Quartz 2D.

- Anyone interested in powerful 2D graphics systems.

The book takes a practical, hands-on approach by promoting the best practices for using Quartz 2D. It also shows how to ensure compatibility with various versions of Mac OS X.

This book discusses Quartz 2D in a manner that is independent of any higher-level application frameworks. The code examples work in both the Carbon and Cocoa frameworks and can also be used in command line tools that are not linked to either of these frameworks. The focus of this book is on Quartz 2D and not on details about the Cocoa and Carbon frameworks.

The Quartz 2D API reference is available at no cost from the Apple Developer Connection website (*http://developer.apple.com*), so this book does not duplicate the reference. Instead, this book focuses on the concepts of Quartz 2D and on using the API to accomplish lots of interesting and useful graphics tasks. The Quartz 2D reference is an important complement to the book.

Outline

The chapters in this book cover a wide variety of graphics topics, including drawing line art graphics, using and creating bitmap images, drawing text, and drawing, creating, and parsing PDF documents. The following descriptions outline the primary programming topics addressed by each chapter. The outline may help you decide which chapters are most important for a particular programming task and which chapters, if any, you can skip.

- "Introducing Quartz 2D" (page 1) discusses the lineage of the Quartz 2D drawing library, gives an overview of its capabilities, and provides information about what kinds of software can take advantage of Quartz 2D.

- "Quartz 2D Drawing Basics" (page 15) introduces the API, shows the sorts of graphical output that is produced by Quartz 2D, and provides code samples to help developers get started.

- "Using Quartz 2D in Cocoa" (page 45) gives step-by-step instructions for creating an application in Xcode that uses the Cocoa framework and Quartz 2D functions. The finished result is an application that draws Quartz graphics in a Cocoa window.

- "Using Quartz 2D in Carbon" (page 65) gives step-by-step instructions for creating an application in Xcode that uses the Carbon framework and Quartz 2D functions. The finished result is an application that draws Quartz graphics in a Carbon window.

- "The Quartz Coordinate System and Coordinate Transformations" (page 83) describes the coordinate system in terms of user space and device space, then shows how working in abstract user space makes it easy to manipulate graphics objects.

- "Drawing with Paths" (page 103) discusses path properties and geometries, shows how to use Quartz functions to create and draw paths, discusses the parameters that affect the way Quartz fills and strokes paths, describes path-based clipping, and provides information on anti-aliasing and pixel alignment.

- "Color, Alpha Transparency, and the Quartz Graphics State" (page 147) provides conceptual information on color and color spaces, shows how to use color spaces, gives details on alpha transparency, and describes the parameters associated with the graphics state.

- "Data Providers and Data Consumers" (page 185) introduces the Quartz objects that abstract data management and shows how to use them to read data from and write data to various destinations.

- "Drawing Images" (page 203) describes information related to bitmap images (including image formats), shows how to read bitmap data from and write bitmap data to various sources, shows how to draw bitmap images, and introduces image utility functions.

- "Image Masking" (page 263) defines the objects that can be used as masking agents and shows how to use these agents to achieve a variety of effects. This includes drawing with image masks, masking an image with an image mask or masking colors, and clipping drawing with an image mask.

- "Text" (page 289) provides information about the low-level text drawing Quartz provides and introduces some of the application framework text-drawing APIs that are built on top of Quartz and can be used as an alternative.

- "Creating Bits" (page 345) discusses using the bitmap graphics context to create a rasterized representation of Quartz drawing for exporting to external file formats and for copying on screen. It also shows how to use CGLayer objects for caching graphics.

- "Opening and Drawing PDF Documents" (page 397) describes the basic attributes of PDF documents and shows how to use Quartz to work with and draw existing PDF data.

- "Creating and Examining PDF Documents" (page 435) provides details about creating new PDF documents from Quartz drawing and how to parse existing PDF documents to examine their contents.

- "Advanced Drawing Features" (page 481) discusses creating and drawing Quartz patterns, drawing graphics with shadows, compositing objects as a group using transparency layers, and defining and drawing Quartz shadings.

- "Supporting PostScript and EPS Data" (page 565) describes using PostScript and encapsulated PostScript (EPS) data as source data for onscreen drawing and printing.

- "Performance and Debugging" (page 593) discusses the programming practices that achieve good performance. It also presents techniques for debugging drawing problems, including tips about some of the most common problems developers encounter.

- "Creating Quartz Tools and Python Scripts" (page 631) discusses using Quartz from command line tools or other code that does not present a user interface. It introduces the Quartz Python bindings that allow creation of Python scripts that use Quartz to create graphics or process PostScript or PDF documents.

Conventions and Assumptions

As of the writing of this book, there have been five major releases of Mac OS X, beginning with Mac OS X version 10.0 through the latest version, Mac OS X version 10.4 (Tiger). This book treats the functionality available in Mac OS X version 10.1 (Puma) as the baseline feature set available in Quartz and other parts of Mac OS X. If there is no specific designation about a given API or feature, assume that it is available in all versions of Mac OS X starting with Puma.

Because Quartz is a technology that is expanded and refined with each OS release, many features have been added since Puma. In this book, Quartz API and other OS features that are only available in a release subsequent to Puma are indicated as such. For example, if a given feature is only available in Mac OS X version 10.2 (Jaguar) or later versions, it is called out as "available in Jaguar and later versions" (or "introduced in Jaguar"). For a section where all the concepts and programming APIs discussed in that section are only available in a version after Puma, an icon (10.3 ▶) representing the version number appears in the left margin. Every feature introduced in a given OS version is available in all sub-sequent versions, so the designation of a given OS version indicates that the feature is available beginning with that version and is available in all subsequent versions.

Table 1 provides the release name for each Mac OS X version. This table also supplies the approximate release date since many developers use this information to help decide which versions of the OS to support. As you read the book, you can always refer to this table if it is unclear as to which OS version a given release name corresponds.

Table 1 Cat Names and Mac OS X Version Numbers

Release Name	Mac OS X Version	Release Date
Cheetah	10.0	March 2001
Puma	10.1	September 2001
Jaguar	10.2	August 2002
Panther	10.3	October 2003
Tiger	10.4	April 2005

In a number of places, this book discusses development tools such as Xcode and Interface Builder or debugging tools such as Quartz Debug. In each case, unless specially called out, the version of the tool under discussion is that provided as part of the developer tools shipped with Tiger.

This book does not cover techniques developers can use to determine which version of Mac OS X is currently executing. Instead, the recommended approach is to test for the specific capability of interest, typically by testing for the availability of the symbol of the function of interest. The discussion in "Creating Color Spaces by Name (Jaguar)" (page 164), the code in Listing 7.5 (page 165), and the references of "Color, Alpha Transparency, and the Quartz Graphics State" (page 147) cover the typical way that you perform runtime testing of the capabilities of the OS.

Source Code

All the code examples from this book are contained in a single file download available from Morgan Kaufmann's website at *www.mkp.com/companions/0123694736*.

In most cases the code examples are supplied as Xcode projects, except for the example Python scripts, which are stand-alone files. The download package includes a README file that describes its contents and how to compile and use them.

The code examples in this book are, for the most part, window-system and application-framework agnostic. You can use the code in Carbon applications, Cocoa applications, and UNIX tools. In many cases, the code can be adapted for use with the Python scripting language.

Because some of the code examples use features available only in Tiger and later versions, they can be compiled only on Tiger or a release subsequent to Tiger. Most of the code would build and run just fine on Mac OS X version 10.3 (Panther), but compilation of code that uses Tiger features, even when used conditionally, requires building on Tiger. Most of the examples will run properly on Jaguar and later versions.

The Apple Developer Connection (ADC) Reference Library contains code samples for Quartz 2D and a variety of other graphics and imaging technologies—printing, Core Image, OpenGL, and so forth. See *http://developer.apple.com/samplecode/GraphicsImaging*.

Header Files

Quartz 2D functionality is provided by the Application Services umbrella framework, which contains two subframeworks that together make up Quartz 2D. To use Quartz 2D, you must link to the Application Services framework or another framework such as the Carbon or Cocoa framework that links to the Application Services framework.

Most of the header files for Quartz 2D are available in the `CoreGraphics.framework` directory. The full path to the header files is

```
/System/Library/Frameworks/ApplicationServices.framework/Frameworks/
CoreGraphics.framework/Headers
```

The `ImageIO.framework` is the part of Quartz 2D that supports reading and writing image files. It is implemented as a subframework of the Application Services framework. The full path to the `ImageIO.framework` header files is

```
/System/Library/Frameworks/ApplicationServices.framework/Frameworks/
ImageIO.framework/Headers
```

A list of the header files that contain the functions discussed in a given chapter appears at the end of that chapter.

Quartz Technologies

Quartz encompasses many technologies, including the Quartz 2D drawing library, the Quartz Compositor, Quartz Services, Core Image, Core Video, PDF Kit, and Quartz Composer. This book focuses on using the Quartz 2D drawing library to develop software for Mac OS X. The Quartz Compositor is discussed only as it relates to how to get the best performance when drawing with Quartz 2D (see "The Quartz Compositor" (page 594)). The other Quartz technologies aren't discussed other than the short introduction that follows but may be of interest to anyone developing graphics software. Links to Apple documentation about these technologies are in the section "See Also" at the end of this Preface.

The **Quartz Compositor** is part of the windowing system in Mac OS X and as such relates to drawing performance. Applications do not interact directly with the Quartz Compositor but do so instead through the application frameworks that are built on top of the window system. Applications draw content into the windows provided by the application frameworks. The Quartz Compositor is responsible for mixing that content onto the screen. The flexibility of the Quartz Compositor is responsible for the powerful Exposé feature introduced in Panther. (Exposé provides access to any open window with just one keystroke.)

Quartz Services manages displays and supports remote operation of the Macintosh user interface; it does not provide drawing capabilities. The display management portion of Quartz Services can determine how many displays are attached to a computer and can change the configuration of one or more displays—two tasks that game developers and developers of other applications that run in full-screen mode find useful. The remote operation capabilities of Quartz Services allow specialized applications, such as Apple Remote Desktop and Timbuktu, to control the user interface remotely and obtain the screen raster data for remote viewing.

The Quartz technologies discussed next are available only in Tiger and later versions.

Core Image is an image processing framework that, when possible, uses programmable graphics hardware to provide near real-time image processing capabilities. Core Image has a number of built-in image processing filters. Compositing, color adjustment, distortion, and geometry filters are a few of the categories of filters that are available. Core Image also provides an architecture that allows the creation of custom filters. The Core Image framework is designed to work well with Quartz 2D, enabling you to apply Core Image filter effects to Quartz 2D images.

Core Video provides support for processing QuickTime movie data with Core Image filters or OpenGL rendering. In addition, it provides timing services that can coordinate any type of drawing to the refresh rate of a display. Core Video is new to Tiger but is also available on Panther when QuickTime 7 is installed.

PDF Kit is a high-level framework built on top of the PDF capabilities available in Quartz 2D. PDF Kit is a framework designed to allow easy display and navigation of PDF documents in Cocoa applications. It supports easy use of PDF features that are not directly supported by Quartz 2D, such as links, annotations, and text search. It also supports adding annotations to existing PDF documents.

Quartz Composer is a powerful visual programming tool that allows processing and rendering of graphical data without writing any code. It allows the exploration and integration of the graphics technologies available in Mac OS X, such as Quartz 2D, Core Image, Core Video, QuickTime, and OpenGL, together with other technologies such as MIDI Services and RSS. Compositions created in Quartz Composer can stand alone or be integrated into an application.

See Also

The Quartz development mailing list (quartz-dev) is an excellent place to discuss programming issues with other developers using Quartz 2D and other Quartz technologies. To subscribe to the mailing list, sign up at *http:// lists.apple.com/mailman/listinfo/quartz-dev*.

The ADC Reference Library provides a wealth of information about the Quartz technologies discussed in this chapter.

Quartz Services Reference documents the APIs available in Quartz Services:

> *http://developer.apple.com/documentation/GraphicsImaging/Reference/ Quartz_Services_Ref/index.html*

You can find more information on the Core Image framework in these documents:

- *Core Image Programming Guide* provides conceptual information about Core Image and how to use it:

  http://developer.apple.com/documentation/GraphicsImaging/Conceptual/ CoreImaging/index.html

- *Core Image Reference* is the API reference for Core Image:

  http://developer.apple.com/documentation/GraphicsImaging/Reference/ CoreImagingRef/index.html

Information about Core Video is available in these documents:

- *Core Video Programming Guide* introduces Core Video concepts and how to apply them:

  http://developer.apple.com/documentation/GraphicsImaging/Conceptual/ CoreVideo/index.html

- *Core Video Reference* provides a complete reference to the Core Video API:

  http://developer.apple.com/documentation/GraphicsImaging/Reference/ CoreVideoRef/index.html

Information about PDF Kit is available in these documents:

- *PDF Kit Programming Guide* provides conceptual information about PDF Kit and shows how to program with it:

  http://developer.apple.com/documentation/GraphicsImaging/Conceptual/ PDFKitGuide/index.html

- *PDF Kit Reference* provides a complete reference to the PDF Kit API:

  http://developer.apple.com/documentation/GraphicsImaging/Reference/ PDFKit_Ref/index.html

Information about Quartz Composer is available in these documents:

- *Quartz Composer Programming Guide* shows how to create compositions with Quartz Composer and how to play compositions in a Cocoa-based application:

  http://developer.apple.com/documentation/GraphicsImaging/Conceptual/ QuartzComposer/index.html

- *Quartz Composer Reference* is the reference documentation for the Quartz Composer API:

  http://developer.apple.com/documentation/GraphicsImaging/Reference/ QuartzComposerRef/index.html

Quartz Composer is installed as part of the Developer SDK for Tiger. It is installed in the directory

```
/Developer/Applications/Graphics Tools/
```

Acknowledgments

Many people were instrumental in the development of this book. This book would not have been possible without the encouragement and support of our Apple colleagues in Quartz engineering and technical publications. We'd also like to thank the many technical reviewers, both inside and outside of Apple, whose thoughtful suggestions improved the quality of the content. Those reviewers outside of Apple include Eric Blanpied, André Mazzone, Nick Nallick, Matthew Peterson, Philip Schneider, and Ken Turkowski. The folks at Morgan Kaufmann made the process a smooth one due to the efforts of Tim Cox, Elisabeth Beller, Jessie Evans, and Richard Camp. Finally, grateful thanks go to Leslie Johnson for her support during the writing of this book.

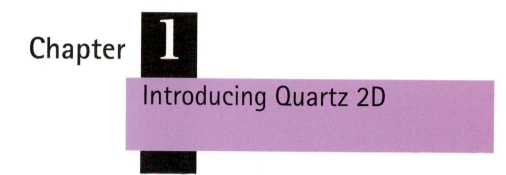

Chapter 1

Introducing Quartz 2D

The Apple Mac OS X operating system contains a powerful 2D graphics imaging library called Quartz. A large part of what gives the Mac OS X user interface the rich look that it has is the use of Quartz drawing by the Aqua user interface and the built-in application toolkits.

The Quartz 2D drawing library allows applications to draw text, curves and shapes, images, and Portable Document Format (PDF) documents in amazingly flexible ways. This rich drawing library supports drawing graphics to an onscreen window or an offscreen bitmap and creating new PDF documents or PostScript output data.

Quartz 2D is also known as Core Graphics, which is frequently abbreviated as CG. Quartz is a term aimed at consumers, whereas Core Graphics is known to many programmers. The Quartz 2D technology is implemented primarily in the Apple Core Graphics framework (ApplicationServices.framework/Frameworks/CoreGraphics.framework), so it's important that you equate one term with the other. All Quartz 2D function calls use the prefix CG. In this book, the terms Quartz, Quartz 2D, and Core Graphics are synonymous with "Quartz 2D drawing library" unless stated otherwise.

A Bit of History

The history of Quartz is partly told by the story of the evolution of graphics programming on the Macintosh computer, starting with the Mac's introduction in 1984. While not strictly necessary to understand Quartz itself, its history provides insight into its power and what you can accomplish with it. There are two main players in this story—the graphics capabilities provided by the Macintosh and the breakthrough graphics applications created for the early Mac. As is the case with most evolutionary processes, outside influences—Adobe, Aldus, the NeXT programming environment, and a number of key individuals—played pivotal roles in this story.

The graphics system on the Macintosh in its initial incarnation in 1984 was borrowed from the graphics system created for the Apple Lisa computer. Bill Atkinson designed and wrote the initial QuickDraw graphics programming library that was the cornerstone for all drawing done on the Macintosh display. QuickDraw was a pixel-oriented graphics system with a 16-bit, integer-based coordinate system. Initially, it had little support for color. These may seem like significant limitations today, but at the time QuickDraw was an amazing advance for graphics on a personal computer. Compare the typical user interface of a computer before QuickDraw graphics on the left in Figure 1.1 with that using QuickDraw graphics on the right.

Equally important in the early days of the Macintosh was MacPaint—the signature graphics application program that gave the Macintosh its immediate designation as a platform for creating graphics. Written by Bill Atkinson, this program was the first among a series of innovative graphics applications that ran on the Macintosh platform. MacPaint was a painting program for creating 1-bit-deep, black-and-white graphics, which was essentially what QuickDraw supported in its early days. Figure 1.2 shows the MacPaint program running on an early Macintosh computer, and Figure 1.3 shows a drawing done with MacPaint.

MacDraw was the second major new graphics application for the Macintosh that took graphics to a new level. It was an object-based graphics drawing program rather than a pixel painting program like MacPaint. A user could build a drawing by choosing one or more predefined shapes or creating a shape from a series of lines. Solid and pattern fills were available to enhance the image. Figure 1.4 shows MacDraw with an example drawing.

Figure 1.1 Graphics before (left) and after (right) QuickDraw

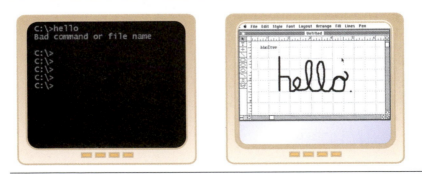

Figure 1.2 MacPaint running on an early Macintosh computer

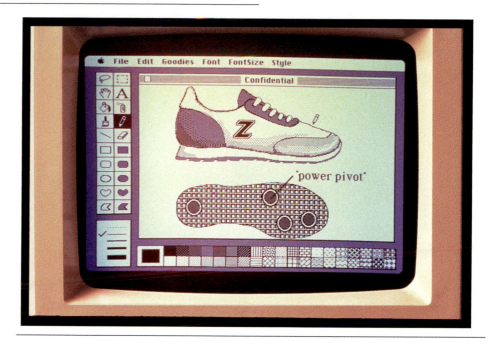

Figure 1.3 A drawing done with MacPaint

Figure 1.4 MacDraw running on an early Macintosh computer

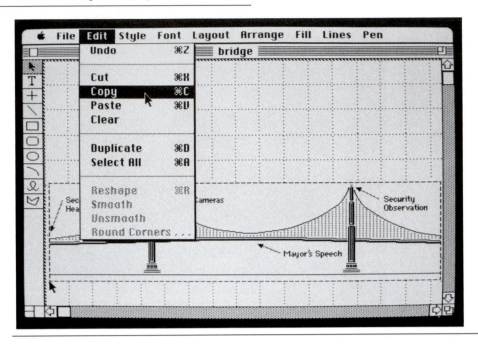

In 1985, Apple Computer and Adobe Systems paired up to create the Apple LaserWriter printer, the next fundamental advance of graphics on the Macintosh. This was the first printer to incorporate the PostScript language developed by Adobe. Prior to the LaserWriter printer, the detailed onscreen graphics created by a Mac could only be printed to low-resolution dot matrix printers. The LaserWriter printer, with its 300 dots per inch (dpi) output, high-quality typography, and laser printer sharpness was an enormous boost to the appeal of the Mac. Figure 1.5 is a photograph of a Macintosh and the original LaserWriter printer.

The true power of the LaserWriter printer was more than just the fact that it could impressively print QuickDraw graphics. The LaserWriter printer used the PostScript programming language and imaging model, a much more versatile graphics system than Apple's QuickDraw.

The superiority of PostScript became apparent when Aldus Corporation introduced the PageMaker application program for the Mac. By generating PostScript for printing, PageMaker achieved results that far exceeded any other program on the Macintosh at the time. The Macintosh, PageMaker, and the LaserWriter were the tools that began the desktop printing revolution. When Linotype Corporation introduced PostScript-based typesetters that could produce output exceed-

Figure 1.5 The Macintosh and the original LaserWriter printer

ing 2400 dpi, users were able to produce true professional print quality with PageMaker, a Macintosh computer, and a high-resolution PostScript output device.

Adobe Systems took the next huge step to advance graphics applications on the Macintosh platform when it introduced the Adobe Illustrator application in early 1987. The Illustrator application allowed users to draw impressive line art graphics with precise curves and lines and place those together with text. The artistic beauty of what could be drawn with the Illustrator program was the best on any personal computer to date. Figure 1.6 shows one of the early Illustrator drawings. The Illustrator application didn't use QuickDraw for its graphics but instead relied on a drawing engine based on Adobe PostScript software.

Also in early 1987, Apple introduced the Macintosh II, the first color Macintosh computer. The QuickDraw drawing library was extended to allow drawing in color and was renamed Color QuickDraw. Color QuickDraw greatly expanded the capabilities of the Macintosh system software for drawing but it didn't fundamentally change the drawing model of QuickDraw, which continued to be a pixel-oriented drawing system based on integer coordinates.

Soon after the introduction of the Macintosh II, Fractal Software (later changed to Fractal Design) pushed the envelope for graphics on the Macintosh with the introduction of the ImageStudio application. ImageStudio was the first Macintosh program for editing grayscale images that were produced by scanners, and it could also be used as a grayscale pixel painting program. This was a precursor of things to come on the Macintosh platform.

The next major graphics advance on the Macintosh occurred when the little-known BarneyScan image editing program was acquired by Adobe Systems and renamed Adobe Photoshop. After it shipped in 1990, Photoshop quickly became

Figure 1.6 A drawing done with the Adobe Illustrator application

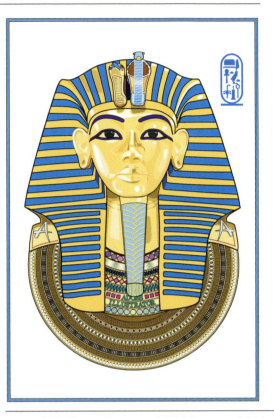

the industry standard for image editing on personal computers. When Photoshop later introduced layers, it utilized the technique of alpha compositing. Alpha compositing, formalized by Porter and Duff in 1984, allows the transparency of graphics to be controlled by the user. With alpha compositing, graphics drawn on top of other graphics can be translucent to expose graphics layers underneath. At the time, alpha compositing wasn't available in QuickDraw, and the PostScript imaging model only supported the drawing of opaque graphics on top of other graphics.

Meanwhile developments elsewhere were at work shaping the long-term history of Macintosh graphics. In 1988 Adobe Systems introduced "The Display Post-Script System," better known as Display PostScript. Display PostScript was an implementation of the Adobe PostScript interpreter with extensions to make it more suitable for use as an interactive graphics programming library. NeXT, the company started by Apple cofounder Steve Jobs, was the first to license it. The

NeXT implementation of Display PostScript added the ability to draw with alpha compositing.

The huge selling point of Display PostScript was the power of PostScript graphics. The integration of Display PostScript on the NeXT computer meant that developers for the platform had that power at their fingertips. Because of the popularity of PostScript printers, the notion of WYSIWYG (What you see is what you get) was taken to another level beyond that on any other platform. A disadvantage of Display PostScript was that programming it sometimes required in-depth understanding of the arcane PostScript language.

As the Macintosh matured, it became clear that a more modern graphics subsystem than QuickDraw was necessary for the platform. Major third-party developers such as Adobe, Aldus, Fractal Design, and Quark were using much more powerful graphics libraries in their software than Apple had built into the Macintosh. Many of these graphics libraries were built on the PostScript imaging model. To produce high-quality graphics for the Macintosh, developers now had to write their own graphics routines since the capabilities provided by the Macintosh platform were lagging the state of the art, much of which was driven by PostScript.

Over time Adobe realized that Display PostScript wasn't going to take over the world. But Adobe had ideas on how some of the benefits of PostScript could be brought to users. Adobe began to focus on the fact that a PostScript page description of text and graphics had excellent potential as an archival form and many users were using it as such. While not editable, a PostScript page description could reproduce the visual form of the graphics and text. However, using PostScript to archive graphics required a PostScript interpreter to view the graphics. Adobe had only limited success in licensing Display PostScript, which caused Adobe to pursue another form for PostScript graphics.

Adobe created an easily parseable form of a graphics description that didn't utilize the programmability of the PostScript language but instead utilized its underlying imaging model. Adobe created the Portable Document Format (PDF) specification based in part on the Adobe Illustrator file format and using an imaging model based on the PostScript language. In 1993, Adobe introduced Adobe Acrobat and the PDF document format.

In 1996, Apple bought NeXT, bringing Steve Jobs, the NeXTStep operating system with Display PostScript, and a new team of graphics programmers to Apple. The PostScript imaging model in Display PostScript was still a powerful 2D graphics imaging model, but by that time the landscape had changed.

With its unsurpassed imaging model, PDF had become an industry standard for distributing documents. For Mac OS X, Apple created its own graphics library based on the PDF imaging model, enhancing it in various ways, including the support of alpha transparency. In addition to alpha compositing, this graphics library supports anti-aliasing, which produces higher-quality results on low-resolution output devices such as screen displays.

Apple calls the implementation of this graphics library Core Graphics internally and uses the name Quartz 2D publicly. Quartz has virtually all the imaging power of PostScript and PDF while adding significant enhancements, greatly increasing the capabilities of the graphics system available to third-party software developers writing for the Macintosh. These and other features are discussed throughout the book.

Quartz 2D Overview

The Quartz 2D imaging model is based on the PDF imaging model. The PDF imaging model itself is based on the PostScript imaging model, which has proved to be a robust drawing model that is highly capable of describing complex drawing as well as document pages that contain text and images. The additional features added by the PDF imaging model combined with those uniquely added by Quartz add up to a flexible, high-quality library for graphics programming. The capabilities and quality of the graphics system available on the Mac OS X platform now approach that previously available in only the most advanced applications. By learning graphics programming with Quartz 2D, you will be able to harness the power of the Quartz imaging model.

The Quartz coordinate system is extremely flexible. Coordinates are specified as floating-point values, and the coordinate system itself can be manipulated to produce complex results with minimal effort from the programmer. For example, you can rotate the entire coordinate system rather than recalculating a drawing so that it appears rotated. A great deal of the power of the Quartz drawing model is that it is resolution- and device-independent. Applications do not need to pay attention to the details of the output device; they draw their graphics independent of the resolution, color characteristics, and other details of the drawing destination. The Quartz drawing library takes care of mapping coordinates, matching colors, converting pixel formats, and handling other device issues.

The Quartz drawing model supports just about any kind of 2D drawing—text, complex line art containing curves and shapes, sampled images, and PDF documents themselves, as shown in Figure 1.7 and Figure 1.8. Content can be rotated, clipped through a text mask, and transformed in a number of ways. In addition, alpha transparency is a built-in feature.

Figure 1.7   Basic elements of Quartz drawing

Simple and complex line art

Simple and complex text

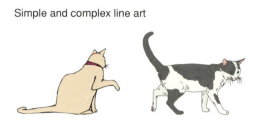

Come to the party for the cats!

Come to the party for the cats

Complex raster image and photo

Color management is integrated into Quartz; colors can be specified in ways that match results across a wide range of output devices, including printers. Starting with Panther, Quartz can convert PostScript data into PDF files, thus allowing Quartz applications to draw PostScript data the same way they draw PDF data.

Graphics contexts, an important concept in Quartz, represent a destination into which Quartz drawing is rendered. They come in a number of "flavors" including window, PDF, and bitmap. (You'll read more about contexts in "More About Graphics Contexts" (page 41).) You can draw the same drawing to different graphics contexts to capture different representations of the drawing. For example, drawing to a window graphics context causes the Quartz drawing to appear in that window. That same drawing to a PDF graphics context creates a new PDF document that contains the equivalent Quartz drawing. So switching application drawing output from screen to printer or to PDF is as simple as changing the destination graphics context.

The PDF file format is the graphics metafile format for Quartz. Creating a PDF file from Quartz drawing operations fully captures the content of the drawing without down-sampling or performing lossy compression. The PDF document format is also the native spool file format of the printing system. During printing,

Figure 1.8 PDF created by layering images and text

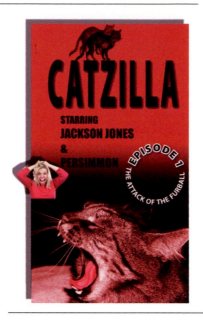

application drawing is captured into a PDF document, which is sent to a print server. The print server handles the conversion of the PDF document into a form appropriate for the destination printer and sends the data to the destination.

What Software Can Use Quartz 2D?

Just about any software that runs in Mac OS X can use Quartz 2D. End-user applications that implement a graphical user interface (GUI) use Quartz, either directly or through the Cocoa or Carbon frameworks, to draw the GUI. UNIX programmers and tool writers use Quartz to create and process graphical data.

Cocoa is an object-oriented application environment designed specifically for developing Mac OS X applications. Quartz is the underlying graphics system used by Cocoa, and in most cases Cocoa provides methods and classes that directly parallel the functions and objects provided by Quartz. Because of this, the concepts of the Quartz drawing model typically translate directly into use of Cocoa drawing facilities.

Although Cocoa developers can use the Objective-C implementation in Cocoa that sits on top of Quartz, using Quartz 2D directly can be beneficial in many situations. Developers who already have a drawing library may find Quartz 2D to be a useful replacement for the lowest-level portions of their drawing library. In such cases, it may make sense to use Quartz 2D directly, even when using Cocoa. Another situation where a Cocoa developer may want to use Quartz directly is when Apple introduces a new feature in Quartz that does not yet have an API in Cocoa. One example of such a feature is Quartz shadings (sometimes called blends). "Cocoa Framework Drawing and Quartz" (page 59) discusses details about when and why Cocoa programmers may want to use Quartz directly instead of the Cocoa drawing API.

The Carbon programming framework is a modernized version of the programming interfaces that developers have used for programming Mac OS since its inception. Carbon is a procedural API that enables C and C++ developers to write applications for Mac OS X. The Carbon framework is also employed by Macintosh developers who want to convert older QuickDraw-based Mac applications to run in Mac OS X.

Applications that replace or enhance their use of QuickDraw with Quartz are able to

- Add support for PDF content.
- Draw with alpha transparency.
- Use a resolution-independent coordinate system and coordinate transformations.
- Take advantage of more powerful graphics primitives.
- Obtain higher-quality imaging, including anti-aliasing.
- Achieve printing output more consistent with that seen onscreen.
- Benefit from efficient reuse of graphical objects, including images.
- Add support for encapsulated PostScript (EPS) file inclusion.
- Perform resolution-independent clipping to shapes.

Applications that don't have a GUI can also use Quartz 2D. Quartz can produce raster data from its drawing and this raster data can then be turned into data files in various file formats. Quartz can create PDF documents that correspond to its drawing, so it can be used to create PDF documents from various data sources. Because of its ability to draw the content of existing PDF documents and create new PDF documents, Quartz makes it easy to add new drawing content to existing PDF documents.

Traditional UNIX tools in compiled programming languages such as C can tap into Quartz raster and PDF capabilities. The bindings added in Panther for the

Python scripting language make it easy to quickly write simple Python scripts to perform interesting tasks. For example, a Python script can process PDF files to add new content, reorder the pages in such a document, and so on.

The use of Quartz from UNIX tools and Python scripts opens up some exciting possibilities for using Quartz in a web-based application that delivers high-quality graphics driven by dynamic content. Again, the abilities of Quartz to produce high-quality raster data or PDF output make it a great tool for producing graphical data. You'll read more about these capabilities as you progress through this book.

Summary

This chapter gives an overview of Quartz, discusses its lineage, and provides some details about Quartz 2D and the software that it's suited for. Quartz has several parts; this book focuses on the Quartz 2D drawing library. Quartz is the result of a 20-year evolution of graphics programming on the Macintosh. It owes a lot of its power to its PostScript and PDF underpinnings. Just about any program, GUI-based or not, can use Quartz 2D.

The rest of this book gets into the nitty-gritty of programming with Quartz. The next chapter gives an introduction to basic drawing using Quartz 2D and provides a number of short code examples to illustrate how drawing is done.

See Also

For in-depth information on the topics discussed in this chapter, see the following:

- *Inside Macintosh: Imaging with QuickDraw*, Apple Computer, Inc., Addison-Wesley, 1994.

- *PostScript Language Reference*, 3rd edition, Adobe Systems, Inc.:

  http://partners.adobe.com/public/developer/en/ps/PLRM.pdf

- Adobe Systems provides all the recent versions of the PDF specification, including versions 1.3 through 1.6. As of this writing the current version is *PDF Reference: Version 1.6*, 5th edition, Adobe Systems, Inc.:

  http://partners.adobe.com/public/developer/pdf/index_reference.html

- "Compositing Digital Images," Thomas Porter and Tom Duff, *Proceedings of the 11th Annual Conference on Computer Graphics and Interactive Techniques,* 1984, pp. 253–259.

You can find more information on the Quartz 2D drawing library in these documents:

- *Quartz 2D Programming Guide* provides conceptual information about Quartz 2D and how to use it:

  http://developer.apple.com/documentation/GraphicsImaging/Conceptual/ drawingwithquartz2d/index.html

- *Quartz 2D Programming Guide for QuickDraw Developers* provides information for developers moving their application drawing from QuickDraw to Quartz 2D:

  http://developer.apple.com/documentation/Carbon/Conceptual/ QuickDrawToQuartz2D/index.html

- *Quartz 2D Reference* is the API reference for Quartz 2D:

  http://developer.apple.com/documentation/GraphicsImaging/Reference/ CGAPI-date.html

Chapter 2

Quartz 2D Drawing Basics

No matter how complex a drawing appears, it's the result of performing a number of basic operations. Paths define shapes. Shapes can be filled, stroked, or both. The painting color can be opaque or have a degree of transparency. Lines can be solid or dashed. Clipping determines which portions of drawing are visible. Drawing can be scaled and otherwise transformed. PDF documents can be treated as a single graphic element but can themselves be arbitrarily complex.

The basic operations available in Quartz produce results that would be difficult to obtain using most other imaging systems. This chapter contains relatively simple examples that illustrate basic drawing operations. Subsequent chapters build on the concepts in these simple examples to show how to achieve more and more complex results.

Quartz Graphics Contexts

Quartz always draws into a graphics context. As described in "Quartz 2D Overview" (page 8), a graphics context is an abstract representation of a drawing destination. A window, a bitmap, and a PDF file are examples of "destinations" that are represented by a graphics context. A Quartz graphics context is an opaque data structure called a `CGContextRef`. The Quartz routines that affect the context all take a `CGContextRef` as a parameter. Quartz has no notion of a "current context"; you always pass a context directly to Quartz functions.

Depending on the task, an application either creates a graphics context or obtains one from a framework (such as when the application draws into a window). "More

About Graphics Contexts" (page 41) gives more details, but to get you started here, these examples assume that a context is provided for drawing. In "Using Quartz 2D in Cocoa" (page 45) and "Using Quartz 2D in Carbon" (page 65), you'll see how to obtain a graphics context for drawing into a window. In later chapters, you'll learn how to create graphics contexts for other, specialized purposes.

Filling a Rectangle

The rectangle is one of the easiest to draw and most commonly used shapes. Consisting of four line segments, the rectangle forms the basis for windows, printed pages, text input fields, and numerous other widgets used in computer user interfaces as well as physical devices. Rectangles are so common that Quartz provides convenience functions to draw them. More complex shapes such as polygons and curved shapes are created by constructing a path. (You'll see how to construct a path later.) This section uses a rectangle-drawing convenience function, CGContextFillRect, so it can focus on the notion of fills and fill colors rather than on how to construct a rectangular shape.

Painting the inside of a shape is called **filling**. The color painted can be a solid color or a pattern that you create. The examples in this chapter specify color in terms of red, green, and blue component values, that is, RGB color. However, you are not limited to painting with RGB colors; Quartz has a number of ways to specify color. "Color, Alpha Transparency, and the Quartz Graphics State" (page 147) discusses the different color models available with Quartz.

When specifying RGB color, values for each component are floating-point values that range between 0.0, meaning the component is absent, to 1.0, meaning the component is present at 100 percent. A primary color contains 100 percent of either red, green, or blue and none of the other two color components. You can adjust the three color components to obtain a wide variety of colors.

The first example performs some very simple drawing, filling a rectangle with a color. The doSimpleRect routine in Listing 2.1 produces the rectangle shown in Figure 2.1.

The routine doSimpleRect first sets the painting color for Quartz to use when filling the rectangle. You pass the context as well as the RGB component values that specify the painting color to the function CGContextSetRGBFillColor. (As promised the code example assumes that a context is provided to the routine.) The example uses (1.0, 0.0, 0.0) for red, green, and blue. The resulting color is pure red because it is 100 percent red and has no green or blue components.

Notice that the function CGContextSetRGBFillColor takes a fourth component value. That value is the **alpha** value, or the opacity of the color that is specified by the other three values. As with the color components, the alpha value can range from 0.0 to 1.0, where 0.0 is totally transparent and 1.0 is completely opaque. The value of 1.0 used in Listing 2.1 means that the paint completely obscures anything underneath it.

Listing 2.1 Filling a rectangle

```
void doSimpleRect(CGContextRef context)
{
  CGRect ourRect;

  // Set the fill color to opaque red.
  CGContextSetRGBFillColor(context, 1.0, 0.0, 0.0, 1.0);

  // Set up the rectangle for drawing.
  ourRect.origin.x = ourRect.origin.y = 20.0;
  ourRect.size.width = 130.0;
  ourRect.size.height = 100.0;
  // Draw the filled rectangle.
  CGContextFillRect(context, ourRect);
}
```

Figure 2.1 The filled rectangle that results from Listing 2.1

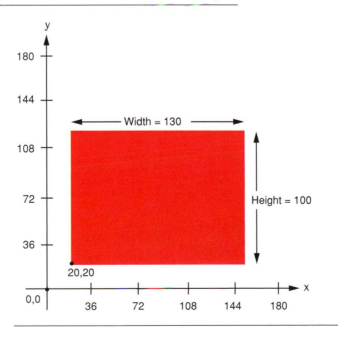

After setting the fill color, the code then sets up a `CGRect` structure to specify the origin and dimensions of the rectangle. A `CGRect` data structure describes a rectangle by its location and size. The coordinates are in the Quartz coordinate system, which is a standard Cartesian coordinate system. The origin is in the lower-left corner of the graphic, with x values increasing to the right and y values increasing up the page. Coordinates in the Quartz coordinate system are specified as floating-point values, and 1 unit does not necessarily correspond to 1 pixel. For now consider each unit as 1 pixel onscreen. "The Quartz Coordinate System and Coordinate Transformations" (page 83) discusses more details.

The function `CGContextFillRect` paints the rectangle passed to it. Quartz defines the origin of a rectangle as the lower-left corner of the rectangle. In this case the rectangle origin is located at x = 20, y = 20. As you can see in Figure 2.1, that is where the lower-left corner appears when filled.

Many graphics systems have a different coordinate system origin and orientation than the Quartz coordinate system. For example, QuickDraw uses a coordinate system with the origin in the top-left corner of the window with increasing y values going down the screen. If that is what you are familiar with and prefer, don't worry; you'll soon see that Quartz functions make it straightforward for you to modify the coordinate system to suit your needs.

Stroking a Rectangle

Painting the border of a shape is called **stroking**. A stroke has a color as well as other attributes, such as width. Similar to the fill color, the stroke color can be defined a number of different ways, but this example uses RGB color. The width of a stroke is specified in standard Quartz coordinate system units using floating-point values; the larger the value, the thicker the stroke.

The line or path that defines any shape is infinitely thin. Quartz paints the stroke so that it straddles the line that defines the shape. Half the stroke is placed on one side of the line defining the shape and the second half of the stroke is placed on the other side. Quartz strokes a curve or line as shown in Figure 2.2. (The

Figure 2.2 Strokes centered on the path

path defining the shape is shown for illustration purposes only; it's not actually painted when the shape is stroked.)

Now take a look at a simple example of stroking a rectangle. The doStrokedRect routine in Listing 2.2 produces the rectangular shape shown in Figure 2.3.

Listing 2.2 Stroking a rectangle

```
void doStrokedRect(CGContextRef context)
{
  CGRect ourRect;
  // Set the stroke color to a light opaque blue.
  CGContextSetRGBStrokeColor(context, 0.482, 0.62, 0.871, 1.0);
  // Set up the rectangle for drawing.
  ourRect.origin.x = ourRect.origin.y = 20.0;
  ourRect.size.width = 130.0;
  ourRect.size.height = 100.0;
  // Draw the stroked rectangle with a line width of 3.
  CGContextStrokeRectWithWidth(context, ourRect, 3.0);
}
```

Similar to the previous example, the routine doStrokedRect first sets the painting color for Quartz to use. Note that the routine sets the color by calling the function CGContextSetRGBStrokeColor instead of CGContextSetRGBFillColor. Quartz

Figure 2.3 The stroked rectangle that results from Listing 2.2

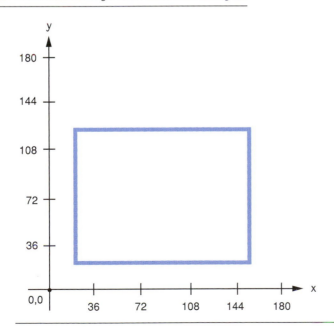

maintains separate colors for filling and for stroking. The function CGContext-SetRGBStrokeColor takes as parameters a graphics context and the RGB component values that define the stroke color. This example uses (0.482, 0.62, 0.871, 1.0) for the red, green, blue, and alpha components to specify a light blue that is fully opaque.

Listing 2.2 creates a rectangle of the same size as that specified in Listing 2.1 (page 17) and then calls the function CGContextStrokeRectWithWidth with the rectangle and a value to specify the stroke width. In this case, the width is 3.0. The line width (specified as a floating-point value) is the number of units wide to paint the stroke.

The Order of Fill and Stroke Operations

The next example takes a closer look at how Quartz strokes shapes. The routine, doStrokedandFilledRect, shown in Listing 2.3, draws the four rectangles shown in Figure 2.4. Each is slightly different from the other. Through these differences you'll explore some of the nuances of stroking.

Listing 2.3 Filled, stroked, and filled-and-stroked rectangles

```
void doStrokedAndFilledRect(CGContextRef context)
{
  // Define a rectangle to use for drawing.
  CGRect ourRect = {{20.0, 220.0}, {130.0, 100.0}};

  // ***** Rectangle 1 *****
  // Set the fill color to a light opaque blue.
  CGContextSetRGBFillColor(context, 0.482, 0.62, 0.871, 1.0);
  // Set the stroke color to an opaque green.
  CGContextSetRGBStrokeColor(context, 0.404, 0.808, 0.239, 1.0);
  // Fill the rectangle.
  CGContextFillRect(context, ourRect);
  // ***** Rectangle 2 *****
  // Move the rectangle's origin to the right by 200 units.
  ourRect.origin.x += 200.0;
  // Stroke the rectangle with a line width of 10.0.
  CGContextStrokeRectWithWidth(context, ourRect, 10.0);
  // ***** Rectangle 3 *****
  // Move the rectangle's origin to the left by 200 units
  // and down by 200 units.
  ourRect.origin.x -= 200.0;
```

```
    ourRect.origin.y -= 200.0;
    // Fill then stroke the rectangle with a line width of 10.0.
    CGContextFillRect(context, ourRect);
    CGContextStrokeRectWithWidth(context, ourRect, 10.0);
    // ***** Rectangle 4 *****
    // Move the rectangle's origin to the right by 200 units.
    ourRect.origin.x += 200.0;
    // Stroke then fill the rectangle.
    CGContextStrokeRectWithWidth(context, ourRect, 10.0);
    CGContextFillRect(context, ourRect);
}
```

The routine doStrokedandFilledRect draws Rectangle 1 just as the code in Figure 2.1 (page 17) draws one—a simple filled rectangle. Prior to drawing Rectangle 2, the code adjusts the origin of the rectangle. In this example, the rectangle origin

Figure 2.4 The rectangles that result from the code in Listing 2.3

Rectangle 1: Filled

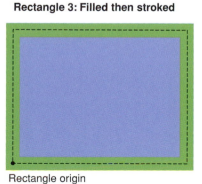

Rectangle origin

Rectangle 2: Stroked

Rectangle origin

Rectangle 3: Filled then stroked

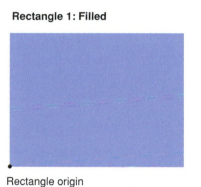

Rectangle origin

Rectangle 4: Stroked then filled

Rectangle origin

moves by 200.0 units in x and leaves the y origin unchanged. The result is that Rectangle 2 is drawn 200 units to the right of Rectangle 1. Unlike Rectangle 1, which is a filled rectangle, Rectangle 2 is a stroked rectangle that's not filled. Similar to the code in Listing 2.2 (page 19), the code draws Rectangle 2 by calling the function `CGContextStrokeRectWithWidth` with the appropriate parameters—a graphics context, a rectangle, and a stroke width. Rectangle 2 uses a thicker stroke than the one drawn by Listing 2.2. Compare the rectangle drawn in Figure 2.3 (page 19) with Rectangle 2 in Figure 2.4 (page 21).

The next two rectangles—Rectangle 3 and Rectangle 4—each have their origins adjusted prior to drawing them. Each rectangle is both filled and stroked. In one case the rectangle is filled then stroked, whereas the other is stroked then filled. The code creates Rectangle 3 by first adjusting its origin –200 units in x (200 units to the left) and –200 units in y (200 units down). Because the code modified the rectangle origin before drawing Rectangle 2, by now moving the origin 200 units horizontally (to the left) prior to drawing Rectangle 3, the rectangle origin is now at the same x position as the original rectangle origin but is now 200 units vertically below the original origin.

The `doStrokedAndFilledRects` routine in Listing 2.3 (page 20) fills Rectangle 3 and then strokes it using a width of 10.0. The result is shown in Figure 2.4. Note that the filled area of Rectangle 3 is smaller than the filled area of Rectangle 1. This is because Quartz centers a stroke on the perimeter of a shape, as shown in Figure 2.2 (page 18). For a stroke width of 10.0, this means 5.0 units of the stroke are outside the shape and 5.0 units are inside (painting over part of the filled area). Recall also that the alpha component of the stroke color is 1.0, meaning that the stroke completely covers over any drawing underneath it.

What happens if the code first strokes and then fills a rectangle? That's what Rectangle 4 illustrates. Before drawing the rectangle, the code adjusts the rectangle origin to the right by 200 units and then uses the same function calls as the ones used for Rectangle 3 but reverses the order of painting operations. Figure 2.4 shows that the width of the stroked line in Rectangle 4 looks thinner than that used for Rectangle 2. Again, Quartz paints half of the stroke on the inside and the other half on the outside. When the code next fills Rectangle 4 with an opaque color, half of the stroke is obscured, making the stroke appear to be thinner than what was specified.

The functions for filling and stroking a rectangle—`CGContextStrokeRectWithWidth` and `CGContextFillRect`—are convenience functions for drawing rectangles. "Drawing with Paths" (page 103) discusses additional convenience routines available in Quartz. Underneath these convenience functions are path construction routines, which will be discussed shortly.

Transforming the Coordinate System

A key part of Quartz is its ability to apply coordinate transformations to drawing. Quartz coordinate transformations can move graphics (translation), change the size of the graphics (scaling), and rotate graphic elements (rotation). These operations can be performed by themselves or can be grouped together to obtain interesting and useful effects.

Translation is a handy way to draw the same shape in two different locations. The example in "The Order of Fill and Stroke Operations" (page 20) draws the same rectangular shape in different locations by adjusting the coordinates of the rectangle itself. You can accomplish the same result by keeping the same rectangle coordinates and instead translating the coordinate system, as shown in Figure 2.5.

The filled square in the figure is first drawn prior to any coordinate transformations and then drawn with the coordinate system translated by 144 units in the x direction and 72 units in the y direction. The rectangle coordinates and the

Figure 2.5 Translation by 144 units in x and 72 units in y

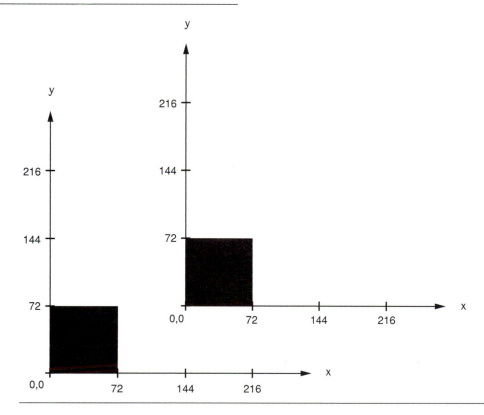

orientation and scale of the coordinate axes are unchanged; only the location of the coordinate origin is changed. The size of a 72-unit square box drawn in the transformed coordinate system is not changed in size, only in location.

The Quartz function `CGContextTranslateCTM` applies a translation to the Quartz coordinate system. You'll see how to use this function in the section "Constructing Quartz Paths" (page 25) as well as in other sections in this chapter. (The term *CTM* in this function and other coordinate transformation functions discussed next is covered in detail in "The Current Transformation Matrix" (page 87).)

Scaling provides a way to uniformly increase or decrease the size of a shape, or to stretch or shrink one dimension of a shape independently from the other dimension. The transformations in Figure 2.6 are both scaling transformations. The origin and orientation of the coordinate axes are unchanged, only the scale is changed. The left side of the figure shows a square transformed by a uniform scale of 2.0 in both the x and y directions. The right side of the figure shows a square transformed nonuniformly by a scale of 1.5 in the x direction and 2.5 in the y direction. In each case, the figure demonstrates the effect of the transformation on a 72-unit square box drawn in the new, transformed coordinate system.

In addition to applying the kind of scaling transformations shown in Figure 2.6, Quartz scaling can flip the coordinate system to create a mirroring effect. For those graphics programmers who are used to drawing in a coordinate system where the origin is in the top-left corner of the drawing canvas with a y coordinate that goes down the canvas, the default Quartz coordinate system can be transformed with a translation and flipped scaling to produce exactly that coordinate system.

The Quartz function `CGContextScaleCTM` applies a scale to the Quartz coordinate system. You'll see how to use this function in the section "Drawing PDF Content" (page 38) later in this chapter.

Rotating the coordinate system is an easy way to rotate a shape instead of recalculating shape coordinates. The transformation in Figure 2.7 is a rotation by 30 degrees. The origin and scale of the coordinate axes are unchanged; the coordinate axes are rotated counterclockwise relative to the untransformed coordinate system.

The Quartz function `CGContextRotateCTM` applies a rotation to the Quartz coordinate system. You'll see how to use this function in the section "Painting with Alpha" (page 30). The rest of the examples in this chapter demonstrate these basic coordinate transformations. "The Quartz Coordinate System and Coordinate Transformations" (page 83) discusses coordinate transformations in much greater depth, including how you can combine multiple transformations to achieve interesting and useful effects.

Figure 2.6 Uniform and nonuniform scaling

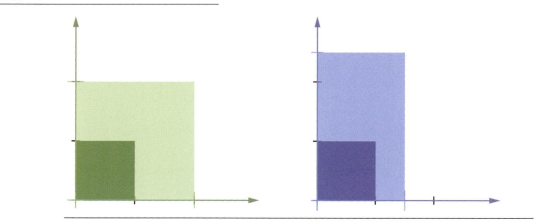

Figure 2.7 Rotation by 30 degrees

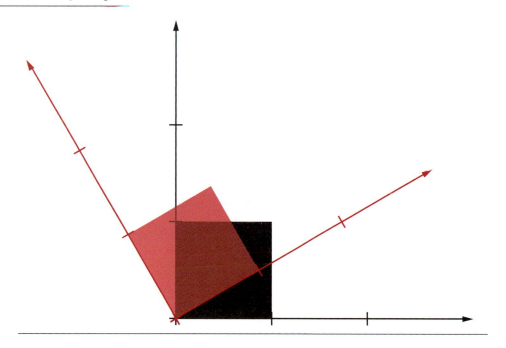

Constructing Quartz Paths

You can draw just about any arbitrary shape in Quartz by constructing a **path**, a sequence of lines and curves that make up a shape, and then performing painting operations on that path. This section shows how to draw the same rectangles shown in Figure 2.4 (page 21) but using path construction functions instead of the convenience functions used to create that figure. In addition, this section uses a Quartz coordinate translation to show how to move the location of drawing without changing the coordinates of the shape.

A path is a mathematical description of the points that make up a sequence of lines and curves. A path is a conceptual entity until it is painted. The sequence of operations needed to draw a shape using paths is

1. Create a path. Define the beginning of a path and use various functions to add lines or curves to the path.

2. Set fill and stroke options such as the color and line width.

3. Paint the path. Painting clears the path from the context. To draw the same shape again, create a new path.

The createRectPath routine in Listing 2.4 shows how to construct a rectangle using a path. The routine doRectPaths draws the same rectangles shown in Figure 2.4 (page 21) but uses the createRectPath routine instead of the Quartz convenience functions.

Listing 2.4 Constructing rectangles using paths

```
void createRectPath(CGContextRef context, CGRect rect)
{
  // Create a path using the coordinates of the rect passed in.
  CGContextBeginPath(context);
  CGContextMoveToPoint(context, rect.origin.x, rect.origin.y);
  // ***** Segment 1 *****
  CGContextAddLineToPoint(context, rect.origin.x + rect.size.width,
              rect.origin.y);
  // ***** Segment 2 *****
  CGContextAddLineToPoint(context, rect.origin.x + rect.size.width,
              rect.origin.y + rect.size.height);
  // ***** Segment 3 *****
  CGContextAddLineToPoint(context, rect.origin.x,
              rect.origin.y + rect.size.height);
  // ***** Segment 4 created by closing the path *****
  CGContextClosePath(context);
}

void doPathRects(CGContextRef context)
{
  // Define a rectangle to use for drawing.
  CGRect ourRect = {{20.0, 220.0}, {130.0, 100.0}};
```

```
// ***** Rectangle 1 *****
// Create the rect path.
createRectPath(context, ourRect);
// Set the fill color to a light opaque blue.
CGContextSetRGBFillColor(context, 0.482, 0.62, 0.871, 1.0);
// Fill the path.
CGContextDrawPath(context, kCGPathFill);  // clears the path
// ***** Rectangle 2 *****
// Translate the coordinate system 200 units to the right.
CGContextTranslateCTM(context, 200.0, 0.0);
// Set the stroke color to an opaque green.
CGContextSetRGBStrokeColor(context, 0.404, 0.808, 0.239, 1.0);
createRectPath(context, ourRect);
// Set the line width to 10 units.
CGContextSetLineWidth(context, 10.0);
// Stroke the path.
CGContextDrawPath(context, kCGPathStroke);  // clears the path
// ***** Rectangle 3 *****
// Translate the coordinate system
// 200 units to the left and 200 units down.
CGContextTranslateCTM(context, -200.0, -200.0);
createRectPath(context, ourRect);
//CGContextSetLineWidth(context, 10.0);  // This is redundant.
// Fill, then stroke the path.
CGContextDrawPath(context, kCGPathFillStroke);  // clears the path
// ***** Rectangle 4 *****
// Translate the coordinate system 200 units to the right.
CGContextTranslateCTM(context, 200.0, 0.0);
createRectPath(context, ourRect);
// Stroke the path.
CGContextDrawPath(context, kCGPathStroke);  // clears the path
// Create the path again.
createRectPath(context, ourRect);
// Fill the path.
CGContextDrawPath(context, kCGPathFill);  // clears the path

}
```

The routine createRectPath shows how to create a path that defines a rectangular shape. It first calls the Quartz function CGContextBeginPath, which replaces any existing path in the context with an empty path. The function CGContext-MoveToPoint establishes the first point on the path and makes that the **current**

point. (Prior to calling CGContextMoveToPoint, an empty path has no starting point.) Next the code calls the function CGContextAddLineToPoint to add a line segment from the existing current point to the point passed to CGContextAdd-LineToPoint. This point becomes the new current point.

So far the rectangle has one side. (Take a look at Segment 1 in Figure 2.8.) The createRectPath adds two more sides by calling the function CGContextAddLineTo-Point two additional times. Each call adds a vertical or horizontal line segment to the path. The fourth side of the rectangle completes the path. To create this side, the code calls the function CGContextClosePath. This function adds a straight line segment from the current point to the initial point on the path. (See Segment 4 in Figure 2.8.)

The createRectPath routine simply creates a rectangular path; it doesn't do any painting. The doPathRects routine in Listing 2.4 (page 26) takes care of that. The doPathRects routine is functionally equivalent to the doStrokedAndFilledRects routine in Listing 2.3 (page 20). Unlike doStrokedAndFilledRects, the doPath-Rects routine needs to use the Quartz routine CGContextDrawPath to actually paint the stroked, filled, and stroked-and-filled paths.

You can refer to Figure 2.4 (page 21) to see what's drawn by the createRect-Path routine. Before drawing Rectangle 1, the code calls the routine create-RectPath to construct a rectangular path for Rectangle 1. Next it sets the fill color by calling the function CGContextSetRGBFillColor. The code paints Rectangle 1 by calling the function CGContextDrawPath with the painting mode

Figure 2.8 Constructing a rectangular path

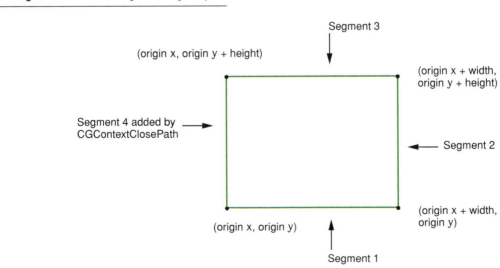

kCGPathFill. This function call also clears the path from the context. To draw another rectangle, the code must create the path again.

In preparation for drawing Rectangle 2, the code first translates the coordinate origin by using the Quartz function CGContextTranslateCTM. This function performs a translation on the Quartz coordinate system as described in "Transforming the Coordinate System" (page 23) and shown there in Figure 2.5. The translation here is +200 units in x and 0 units in y, resulting in a translation of the coordinate origin by 200 units to the right along the x axis. Drawing performed after calling CGContextTranslateCTM takes place in the transformed coordinate system.

Next is a call to the function CGContextSetRGBStrokeColor to set the stroke color. The code then calls the routine createRectPath to construct a rectangular path. It sets the width of the stroke by calling the function CGContextSetLineWidth with the value 10.0. Finally, the code strokes the path by calling the function CGContextDrawPath with the painting mode kCGPathStroke. Unlike the convenience function CGContextStrokeRectWithWidth, when drawing explicitly with paths the line width is set separately from stroking the path.

The code prepares for drawing Rectangle 3 by first calling the function CGContextTranslateCTM to move the origin –200 units horizontally (200 units to the left) and –200 units vertically (200 units down). Note that coordinate transforms are cumulative—a call to CGContextTranslateCTM adjusts the coordinates relative to any previous modifications. In this case, the code already modified the coordinates for Rectangle 2, by moving the origin +200 units horizontally (to the right). The net result of these two calls to CGContextTranslateCTM is that the coordinate origin is now at the same x position as the original coordinate origin but is now 200 units vertically below the original origin.

The code draws Rectangle 3 in the same manner as Rectangle 2 except that it calls the function CGContextDrawPath with the painting mode kCGPathFillStroke. This first performs the fill, painting with the previously set fill color (from Rectangle 1), and then strokes, painting with the previously set stroke color (from Rectangle 2). For Rectangle 3, the code first fills the rectangle and then strokes it to ensure that the portion of the stroke inside the shape covers that portion of the fill inside the shape. This type of fill-then-stroke operation is so common that Quartz defines the special kCGPathFillStroke painting mode used here.

Notice that the code for setting the line width prior to painting Rectangle 3 is commented out because it is unnecessary. Quartz uses the current line width set in the context as the stroke width for a call to CGContextDrawPath with a stroke painting mode. The code already called the function CGContextSetLineWidth to set the line width to 10.0; it would need to call it again only to set the width to a value other than 10.0.

Before drawing Rectangle 4, the code translates the origin to the right by 200 units by again calling the function `CGContextTranslateCTM`. For Rectangle 4, the code creates the path and then strokes it. It creates the path again and fills it. When filling Rectangle 4 with an opaque color, half of the stroke is obscured, making the stroke appear to be thinner than the 10.0 units specified by the line width.

You'll find out more about Quartz paths, how to construct them, and more about filling and stroking paths in "Drawing with Paths" (page 103).

Painting with Alpha

The examples so far paint only with opaque colors. As you'll recall, the opacity or alpha value is the last component supplied as part of a color. The alpha component has a value that ranges from 1.0, meaning fully opaque, to 0.0, meaning completely transparent. Values in between indicate varying degrees of transparency, as shown by the stroke in Figure 2.9.

This section shows how to vary the alpha component to achieve different levels of transparency. It also shows how to transform the coordinate system by rotation to draw a sequence of rectangles rotated relative to one another as shown in Figure 2.10. Each rectangle in the figure is painted with a different shade of red and with an alpha value that decreases with each rectangle drawn.

The `doAlphaRects` routine in Listing 2.5 produces the output shown in Figure 2.10. The code has three parts. Part 1 defines a rectangle location and size and computes the rotation angle required to create a complete circle of rectangles. Note that the rotation angle is calculated in radians because the Quartz function for performing rotation requires angles to be specified in radians, not degrees. (In physics and mathematics, radians are a commonly used measurement of angles— 2π radians is equal to 360 degrees.) The `tintAdjust` variable is computed so that the tint varies over the range from 0.0 to 1.0 for the sequence of rectangles.

Figure 2.9 Example of alpha transparency

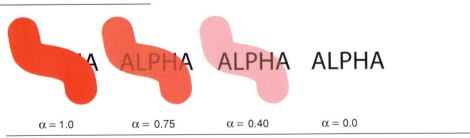

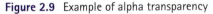

$\alpha = 1.0$ $\alpha = 0.75$ $\alpha = 0.40$ $\alpha = 0.0$

Figure 2.10 Painting rectangles with alpha as drawn using the code in Listing 2.5

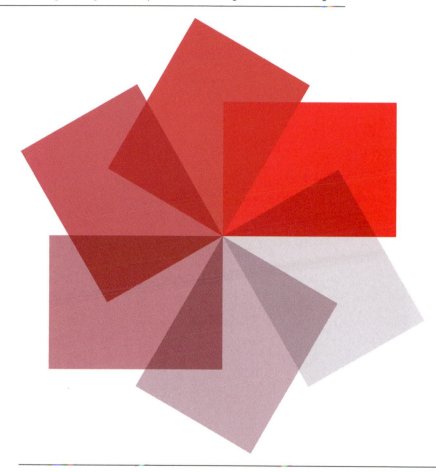

Listing 2.5 Painting with transparent rectangles

```
#include <math.h>
void doAlphaRects(CGContextRef context)
{
  // ***** Part 1 *****
  CGRect ourRect = {{0.0, 0.0}, {130.0, 100.0}};
  int i, numRects = 6;
  float rotateAngle = 2*M_PI/numRects;
  float tint, tintAdjust = 1.0/numRects;
```

```
// ***** Part 2 *****
CGContextTranslateCTM (context, 2*ourRect.size.width,
            2*ourRect.size.height);

// ***** Part 3 *****
for(i = 0, tint = 1.0; i < numRects ; i++, tint -= tintAdjust){
  CGContextSetRGBFillColor (context, tint, 0.0, 0.0, tint);
  CGContextFillRect(context, ourRect);
  CGContextRotateCTM(context, rotateAngle);  // cumulative
  }
}
```

Part 2 of the code calls the function CGContextTranslateCTM to move the coordinate origin to a point that allows the drawing to fall comfortably within the positive quadrant of the coordinate system. Part 3 of the code—the for loop—draws six rectangles, starting with the tint variable set to 1.0 and stepping down each iteration by one-sixth.

The loop performs these tasks:

- Sets the fill color for the context, passing the tint value as a parameter to the function CGContextSetRGBFillColor. The first rectangle uses a completely opaque, red fill. As the tint value varies to 0, the color moves toward black and the fill color is more transparent. The results of the previously drawn rectangle show through more with each subsequent rectangle painted.

- Calls the function CGContextFillRect to paint the rectangle.

- Rotates the coordinate system in preparation for the next iteration through the loop. The function CGContextRotateCTM rotates the coordinate system by a value of rotateAngle. This rotation is centered on the current coordinate origin. Recall that coordinate transformations are cumulative.

The result of this example, as shown in Figure 2.10, is a sequence of rectangles, each of which overlaps the previously drawn rectangle by a small amount. You'll learn more about alpha compositing in "Color, Alpha Transparency, and the Quartz Graphics State" (page 147).

Making Dashed Lines

Quartz can produce strokes other than solid lines of varying widths. This section shows how to make dashed lines using a variety of dash patterns, similar to those shown in Figure 2.11.

Figure 2.11 Dashed and solid strokes as drawn using the code in Listing 2.6

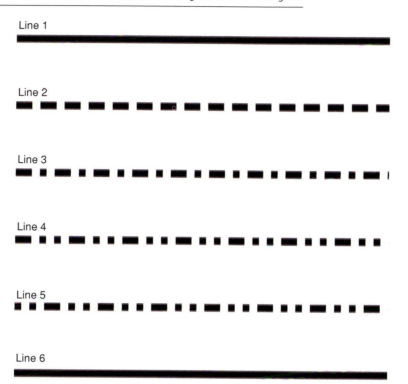

A **dash pattern** consists of a series of floating-point values that alternately specify on and off lengths in Quartz coordinate units. An **on** length is the distance of a painted stroke, whereas an **off** length is the distance for which no painting occurs. All the dashed lines in Figure 2.11 are repeating patterns. Line 2 is a repeating pattern of 12 units on and 6 units off. Line 3 is a repeating pattern of 12 units on, 6 units off, 5 units on, and 6 units off. Line 4 is more complex, using a repeating pattern of 12 units on, 6 units off, 5 units on, 6 units off, 5 units on, and 6 units off.

But what about Line 5? Although it is a dash pattern of short (5 units on, 6 units off), short (5 units on, 6 units off), long (12 units on, 6 units off), it's actually a slightly shifted version of Line 4. Take the dash pattern of Line 4—long (12 units on, 6 units off), short (5 units on, 6 units off), short (5 units on, 6 units off)—but instead of starting the dash pattern with the long dash, start with the first short dash. Then continue painting the dash pattern until you reach the end of the line. When you shift a dash pattern in this manner, you change its phase.

The **phase** of a dash pattern specifies the location, in Quartz coordinate units, to begin a dash pattern. A phase of 0 specifies the start of a dash pattern. Any other phase value specifies a number of units into the dash pattern. For example, the dash used to create Line 4 is 40 units long (12 + 6 + 5 + 6 + 5 + 6). Line 5 is the result of applying the phase value of 18 to that pattern. If you do the math, you'll find that 18 units into the pattern starts the stroke at the first short dash, skipping the first two segments of the dash pattern.

To paint a dash pattern in Quartz, first call the function CGContextSetLineDash to set the dash pattern for the context. Subsequent strokes are painted with the specified line dash. The function takes the following parameters:

- context, the graphics context for which to change the dash pattern.

- phase, the location to begin the dash pattern, which you are an expert with by now!

- lengths[], an array of floating-point values that define a dash pattern. The pattern is a sequence of distances that dashes should be on or off. The first entry in the array is the distance the dash should be on, the next array element specifies the distance the dash should be off, and so on. When the end of the array is reached, Quartz uses the first element of the array to specify the length of the next dash on/off segment.

- count, specifies how many items in the length array should be used. This value must be less than or equal to the number of items in the lengths array.

Note that the code in Listing 2.6 uses the count and phase parameters with a single length array to achieve a variety of effects. The code uses two routines—drawStrokedLine and doDashedLines.

Listing 2.6 Creating dashed strokes

```
void drawStrokedLine(CGContextRef context, CGPoint start, CGPoint end)
{
  CGContextBeginPath(context);
  CGContextMoveToPoint(context, start.x, start.y);
  CGContextAddLineToPoint(context, end.x, end.y);
  CGContextDrawPath(context, kCGPathStroke);
}
void doDashedLines(CGContextRef context)
{
  CGPoint start, end;
  start.x = 20.; start.y = 270.;
  float lengths[6] = { 12.0, 6.0, 5.0, 6.0, 5.0, 6.0 };
```

```
    end.x = 300.; end.y = 270.;
    // ***** Line 1 solid line *****
    CGContextSetLineWidth(context, 5.);
    drawStrokedLine(context, start, end);
    // ***** Line 2 long dashes *****
    CGContextTranslateCTM(context, 0., -50.);
    CGContextSetLineDash(context, 0., lengths, 2);
    drawStrokedLine(context, start, end);
    // ***** Line 3 long short pattern *****
    CGContextTranslateCTM(context, 0., -50.);
    CGContextSetLineDash(context, 0., lengths, 4);
    drawStrokedLine(context, start, end);
    // ***** Line 4 long short short pattern *****
    CGContextTranslateCTM(context, 0., -50.);
    CGContextSetLineDash(context, 0., lengths, 6);
    drawStrokedLine(context, start, end);
    // ***** Line 5 short short long pattern *****
    CGContextTranslateCTM(context, 0., -50.);
    CGContextSetLineDash(context, lengths[0]+lengths[1], lengths, 6);
    drawStrokedLine(context, start, end);
    // ***** Line 6 solid line *****
    CGContextTranslateCTM(context, 0., -50.);
    CGContextSetLineDash(context, 0, NULL, 0);  // Reset dash to solid line.
    drawStrokedLine(context, start, end);
}
```

The drawStrokedLine routine creates a path with its initial point at the start point, adds to the path a line segment from the start point to the endpoint, then strokes the path. The doDashedLine routine in the listing calls drawStrokedLine to draw each of the six lines shown in Figure 2.11.

To draw Line 1, which is a solid line, the code sets the line width and calls the routine drawSrokedLine. Before drawing Line 2, the code calls CGContextSetLine-Dash to set a dash on the context so that subsequent strokes are painted with the specified line dash. It passes the lengths array and a count value of 2 so that Quartz examines only the first two elements of the lengths—that is, 12.0 and 6.0, which specifies a dash pattern of 12 units on then 6 units off. The dash pattern begins at the beginning of the stroked segment. The first 12 units of the path are painted with the stroke color, the next 6 units of the path are not painted, and this sequence is repeated until the end of the stroked path is reached.

The code draws Line 3 by calling the function CGContextSetLineDash with four items in the lengths array. This specifies a dash pattern of 12 units on, 6 units off, 5 units on, and 6 units off; essentially a long-short repeating pattern. The code draws Line 4 in a similar manner but using six items in the lengths array to define the dash pattern.

Recall that Line 5 uses the same pattern as Line 4, but it starts the pattern out of phase by 18 units. This can be accomplished by specifying the phase as the sum of the first two values in the length array (12, 6), or lengths[0]+lengths[1].

Line 6 is a solid line. The code calls the function CGContextSetLineDash, passing NULL for the lengths array and a count of 0. This turns dashing off. You'll find out other ways to affect the way Quartz strokes paths in "Drawing with Paths" (page 103).

Clipping a Drawing

Clipping constrains the drawing to a certain area; Quartz doesn't paint any portion of the drawing that's outside the clipping area. Recall from "Introducing Quartz 2D" (page 1) that a graphics context represents a destination into which Quartz renders. Every graphics context has a clipping area associated with it. For example, when drawing into a window context, drawing is clipped to the content portion of the window; Quartz doesn't draw over the window controls themselves. Quartz and the application toolkits achieve this result by ensuring that the clipping area for a window context is the window content area. When you apply an additional clipping area to a context, Quartz intersects the clipping area you specify with the existing clipping area of the context. Only the intersected portions are visible.

The doClippedCircle routine in Listing 2.7 produces the drawing shown in Figure 2.12. The left side of the figure shows a filled circle over which is drawn a stroked square. The right side of the figure shows the result of using the square as a clipping area for the circle. Now take a closer look at the code that produces this drawing.

Listing 2.7 Clipping a circle

```
#include <math.h>         // for M_PI

void doClippedCircle(CGContextRef context)
{
  CGPoint circleCenter = {150., 150.};
  float   circleRadius = 100.0;
  float   startingAngle = 0.0, endingAngle = 2*M_PI;
  CGRect ourRect = { {65.,65.} , {170., 170.} };
```

```
// ***** Filled Circle *****
CGContextSetRGBFillColor(context, 0.663, 0., 0.031, 1.0);
CGContextBeginPath(context);
// Construct the circle path counterclockwise.
CGContextAddArc(context, circleCenter.x, circleCenter.y, circleRadius,
               startingAngle, endingAngle, 0);
CGContextDrawPath(context, kCGPathFill);

// ***** Stroked Square *****
CGContextStrokeRect(context, ourRect);

// Translate so that the next drawing doesn't overlap what
// has already been drawn.
CGContextTranslateCTM(context,
               ourRect.size.width + circleRadius + 5., 0);
// Create a rectangular path and clip to that path.
CGContextBeginPath(context);
CGContextAddRect(context, ourRect);
CGContextClip(context);

// ***** Clipped Circle *****
CGContextBeginPath(context);
// Construct the circle path counterclockwise.
CGContextAddArc(context, circleCenter.x, circleCenter.y, circleRadius,
               startingAngle, endingAngle, 0);
CGContextDrawPath(context, kCGPathFill);
}
```

The first part of the code defines the circle center, radius, starting angle, and the dimensions of the rectangle, which in this case is a square. Don't worry too much about the values of the rectangle; they have been chosen to make the center of the square coincide with the center of the circle.

Figure 2.12 Clipping a drawing as drawn using the code in Listing 2.7

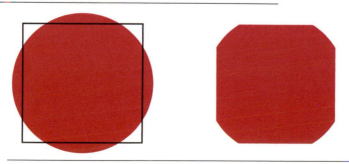

For the left side of Figure 2.12, the doClippedCircle routine first draws a filled circle. It sets the fill color to a dark opaque red and then calls the function CGContextAddArc to create a circular path. You can use this function to create an arc of any radius and angle. This example uses a starting and ending angle that defines a full circle (2π radians). To paint the filled circle, the code calls the function CGContextDrawPath with the kCGPathFill painting mode. Next the code draws the stroked square over the circle. The code doesn't set a stroke color so the stroke is the default color, black. It doesn't set a line width so the width is the default line width of 1 unit. Next the code translates the coordinate system to the right in preparation for drawing the right side of Figure 2.12 by calling the function CGContextTranslateCTM. So far the code hasn't performed any clipping.

Setting up a clipping area requires creating a path to clip to, then calling the function CGContextClip to tell Quartz to constrain drawing to the area inside that path. Now look at how the code in Listing 2.7 (page 36) accomplishes clipping.

First the code creates a new path by calling the function CGContextBeginPath. Then it adds the previously defined square to the path. This is a simple clipping path; a clipping path can be an arbitrary shape. Finally, the code calls the function CGContextClip to tell Quartz that the path it just created is a clipping area. Quartz intersects the supplied path with the existing clip to produce the new clipping area. Now the code draws the filled circle using the same calls it used for the left side of the figure. However, this time only those portions of the circle that fall within the square clipping area are visible.

This example creates a rectangular clipping area by creating a new path, adding a rectangle to it with the function CGContextAddRect, then clipping to that path by calling CGContextClip. Clipping to an arbitrary path requires exactly the same procedure: construct that path using normal path construction functions, then call CGContextClip. In addition to this general method, Quartz provides the convenience routine CGContextClipToRect for clipping to a rectangle specified by a CGRect. This example uses the general method to demonstrate how to do clipping to an arbitrary shape; normally you use the function CGContextClipToRect for rectangular clipping. You'll learn more about clipping in "Drawing with Paths" (page 103) and "Clipping to a Mask (Tiger)" (page 282).

Drawing PDF Content

Because PDF is fundamental to the Quartz imaging system, no introduction to Quartz drawing would be complete without an example of drawing existing PDF content. By combining PDF drawing with Quartz scaling transformations, it is easy to obtain some interesting results.

Drawing a PDF document is simple and straightforward, as shown by the doPDF-Document routine in Listing 2.8, which draws the first page of a PDF document. Figure 2.13 shows the output of this routine.

Listing 2.8 Drawing a PDF page

```
void doPDFDocument(CGContextRef context, CFURLRef url)
{
  CGRect pdfRect;
  CGPDFDocumentRef pdfDoc = CGPDFDocumentCreateWithURL(url);
  if(pdfDoc != NULL){
    // The media box is the bounding box of the PDF document.
    pdfRect = CGPDFDocumentGetMediaBox(pdfDoc, 1);  // page 1
    // Make the destination rect origin at the Quartz origin.
    pdfRect.origin.x = pdfRect.origin.y = 0.;
    CGContextDrawPDFDocument(context, pdfRect, pdfDoc, 1); // page 1

    CGContextTranslateCTM(context, pdfRect.size.width*1.2, 0);
    // Scale nonuniformly, making
    // the y coordinate scale 1.5 times the x coordinate scale.
    CGContextScaleCTM(context, 1, 1.5);
    CGContextDrawPDFDocument(context, pdfRect, pdfDoc, 1);

    CGContextTranslateCTM(context, pdfRect.size.width*1.2,
                pdfRect.size.height);
    // Flip the y coordinate axis horizontally about the x axis.
    CGContextScaleCTM(context, 1, -1);
    CGContextDrawPDFDocument(context, pdfRect, pdfDoc, 1);
    CGPDFDocumentRelease(pdfDoc);
  }else
    fprintf(stderr, "Can't create pdf document for URL\n");
}
```

The doPDFDocument routine takes a reference to a graphics context (CGContext-Ref) and a reference to a CFURL object that specifies the location of a PDF file in the file system.

Note   A CFURLRef is an opaque type that represents a URL defined in the Core Foundation (CF) framework. The CF framework contains a number of data abstractions that can share data between applications. Quartz makes extensive use of this framework.

Quartz uses the opaque data type `CGPDFDocumentRef` to represent a reference to a PDF document. A number of Quartz functions use this data type to obtain information about the document and draw it. The function `CGPDFDocumentCreate-WithURL` creates a `CGPDFDocumentRef` from a `CFURLRef`. If the `CFURLRef` doesn't correspond to a PDF document or the PDF document is corrupt, `CGPDFDocument-CreateWithURL` returns NULL.

After testing to see if the `CGPDFDocumentRef` is NULL, the `doPDFDocument` routine calls `CGPDFDocumentGetMediaBox` to obtain the dimensions of the first page, passing in the `CGPDFDocumentRef` that represents the PDF document and the page number of the page to obtain. The code uses the size of this rectangle to specify the size for Quartz to draw the PDF document. The code first adjusts the rectangle origin to (0,0) so that the graphic is drawn at the origin of the Quartz coordinate system. The call to `CGContextDrawPDFDocument` specifies to draw the first page of the document into the rectangle, scaling as necessary. The page on the left side of Figure 2.13 is the first page of the PDF document at its normal size and orientation.

After drawing the first page of the document, the `doPDFDocument` routine calls the function `CGContextTranslateCTM` to prepare for drawing the PDF document a second time. The amount of x coordinate translation allows enough room for a second drawing of the PDF document to the right of the first. Next the code calls `CGContextScaleCTM` to scale the Quartz coordinate system by a factor of 1 in the x coordinate, which of course performs no scaling in the x coordinate, and 1.5 in the y coordinate. The next call to `CGContextDrawPDFDocument` draws into the scaled coordinate system. As Figure 2.13 shows, the drawing is stretched in the y dimension to 1.5 times the size it was in the previous rendering. In the scaled coordinate system, the length of a unit in the y direction is now 1.5 times as long as it was prior to the scaling. The scale of the x coordinate is unchanged.

Figure 2.13 Drawing a PDF page with scaling as drawn using the code in Listing 2.8

The next call to CGContextTranslateCTM prepares for drawing the PDF document for the final time, with an x translation that leaves enough room between the second and third drawings. The choice for the y translation value is discussed shortly. The next call to the function CGContextScaleCTM scales the Quartz coordinate system by a factor of 1 in the x coordinate and –1 in the y coordinate. In this new coordinate system, the positive x values go to the right and positive y values move *down* the page. The effect of negatively scaling the y coordinate is to flip the coordinate system around the x axis, producing a mirror image. The amount of y translation prior to the scaling is chosen to be the height of the PDF document so that the origin of coordinates is at the top-left corner of the graphic. The effect of scaling the y coordinate by a factor of –1.0 is to maintain the 1.5 scaling set up previously, because calls to CGContext-ScaleCTM are cumulative.

Note The effects of coordinate transformations performed by the functions CGContext-ScaleCTM, CGContextTranslateCTM, and CGContextRotateCTM are cumulative.

The final call to the function CGContextDrawPDFDocument draws the PDF page in the newly transformed coordinate system. The drawing is flipped along the y axis and a unit in the y coordinate is still 1.5 times the length of a unit in x, since scaling transformations are cumulative.

Listing 2.8 (page 39) demonstrates some good coding practices. It uses the same CGPDFDocumentRef to render the document multiple times. In addition to making the code much simpler, reusing the CGPDFDocumentRef has other efficiencies that allow for a much more compact representation of drawing when creating a new PDF document from this sequence of drawing. When the CGPDFDocumentRef is no longer needed, the code calls the function CGPDFDocumentRelease to reclaim any memory and resources associated with the CGPDFDocumentRef. "Quartz Object and Memory Model" (page 599) discusses additional details about these and similar coding practices. You'll find out more about PDF display in "Opening and Drawing PDF Documents" (page 397) and about creation in "Creating and Examining PDF Documents" (page 435).

More About Graphics Contexts

A graphics context is a data type that encapsulates the information Quartz uses to draw to an output "device," such as a window, a PDF file, or a bitmap. The information inside a graphics context includes the graphics drawing parameters and a device-specific representation of the paint on the page.

There are a number of different types of graphics contexts available in Quartz, each with a different purpose. The different types of contexts are

- Window context. This is a graphics context used to draw into a window onscreen. Quartz has no direct creation functions for creating a Window context. Instead, you obtain a window context from the Carbon or Cocoa application frameworks. The next two chapters show how to obtain a window context for each of the application frameworks.

- Bitmap graphics context. A graphics context to draw into a buffer of memory you supply. The bitmap context is described in detail in "Creating Bits" (page 345).

- PDF graphics context. Drawing to a context of this type produces a PDF document that represents the drawing. You can create a PDF context yourself and, in addition, the Mac OS X printing system creates a PDF context that applications draw to in order to print. See "Creating and Examining PDF Documents" (page 435) for more information about the Quartz PDF context.

- PostScript context. Drawing to a context of this type produces a PostScript data stream that represents the Quartz drawing. You can't create this type of context yourself; the printing system creates this type of context as part of printing to PostScript printers.

- GLContext context, available in Panther and later versions. A GLContext is a Quartz context that is created from an OpenGL drawing context. You can use this type of context to perform Quartz 2D drawing to an OpenGL context, allowing you to mix OpenGL and Quartz drawing. Creating and using this context requires knowledge of OpenGL and is beyond the scope of this book.

You can perform the same drawing without regard to the type of context that you are drawing to. You do the drawing and Quartz takes care of converting that drawing into the best representation for the device, or context, into which you are drawing. Device independence is one of the most powerful features of Quartz.

Summary

This chapter discusses basic drawing operations available in Quartz 2D, including filling, stroking, transforming coordinates, drawing paths, using alpha, creating dashed lines, and drawing PDF documents. The order of filling and stroking operations affects the outcome of drawing—the paint applied in the final operation can overlap the previous operation. Quartz provides functions to draw rectangles and arcs, and paths can define arbitrary shapes. Alpha controls the opacity of paint; partly transparent objects let objects underneath show through. The location of objects can be changed either by changing the coordinates at which the object is drawn or by transforming the Quartz coordinate system and then drawing. Transformed coordinates create interesting effects, such as flipping PDF content to create a mirror image.

The next chapter shows how to use the Xcode development environment to create a Quartz application that uses the Cocoa framework. It provides a gentle introduction for those new to Cocoa and shows experienced Cocoa programmers how easy it is to use Quartz 2D directly.

See Also

The header files that contain the structures and functions used in this chapter are

- CGContext.h
- CGGeometry.h
- CGPDFDocument.h

The relevant reference documentation from the ADC Reference Library is

- *CGContext Reference*
- *CGGeometry Reference*
- *CGPDFDocument Reference*

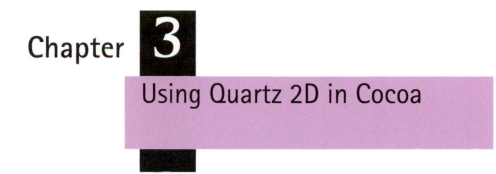

Chapter **3**

Using Quartz 2D in Cocoa

Quartz 2D provides the foundation for Cocoa drawing. Cocoa 2D graphics facilities are built on top of Quartz 2D, and the Cocoa imaging model is that of Quartz 2D. Applications that use the Cocoa framework can use the Cocoa drawing methods that are built on top of Quartz and can call Quartz 2D directly as well. Most of this book discusses using Quartz directly rather than the Cocoa drawing methods that are built on top of Quartz. This chapter is no exception, but you will see how to call Quartz from the Cocoa framework.

Cocoa is a rich object-oriented programming toolkit. Programming in Cocoa requires knowledge of object-oriented programming techniques and the Objective-C language. This chapter does not teach Cocoa programming or discuss object-oriented programming but focuses on how to use Quartz 2D API calls in a Cocoa application and when you might want to use Quartz instead of the Cocoa drawing methods. It discusses the aspects of Cocoa programming that are important when creating an application that performs Quartz drawing. The sample application in this chapter draws the series of alpha composited rectangles shown in Figure 2.10 (page 31).

The first section of this chapter provides a brief overview of Xcode. The next three sections show how to create a Cocoa application in Xcode. Nothing in these sections is specific to drawing with Quartz in Cocoa. Experienced Xcode developers who have written at least one Cocoa application can skip these sections.

The sections "Obtaining a Graphics Context in Cocoa" (page 55) and "Writing the Drawing Code" (page 56) contain Quartz-specific information. For those who have never used the Quartz 2D API directly in Cocoa, these are must-read sections. The section "Cocoa Framework Drawing and Quartz" (page 59) focuses on when a Cocoa application might want to use the Quartz API directly instead of the Cocoa drawing methods.

Xcode Overview

Xcode is a software development environment included with Mac OS X starting with Panther. The Xcode application is part of an integrated suite that brings together tools for writing code, creating user interfaces, compiling, debugging, and managing software projects. Xcode also integrates the Apple Mac OS X reference documentation, making it easy to look up details about the system frameworks. Xcode can create applications that use the Cocoa or Carbon frameworks as well as UNIX command line tools.

Xcode contains an integrated project manager and a built-in source code editor. The project manager makes it easy to pull together the different portions of your application or tool development into a single project. If you don't want to use the Xcode editor, you can use an external code editor of your choosing. The build system uses GCC (Gnu Compiler Collection) tools for compiling and linking projects and a graphical interface to the GDB debugger, providing powerful debugging capabilities.

Some particularly useful features of Xcode are its Zero Link functionality, Fix and Continue, and its integrated distributed build management. With Zero Link, Xcode dynamically links an application at runtime, making the build/run phase of application development much faster. The Fix and Continue capability in Xcode allows you to fix bugs in an application while you are debugging it, then continue, all without rebuilding the application. Xcode also supports distributed build management that builds large software projects using multiple computers on a network. The references at the end of this chapter provide more information on Xcode.

Creating a Cocoa Xcode Project in Tiger

With a little knowledge about Xcode and its features, it's easy to create a Cocoa application. This section shows how to create a project and explains the contents of the project window. This discussion and the associated screen shots are based on Xcode version 2.0 in Tiger. (If you are using a later version of Xcode there may be small differences from what is shown here.)

1. Open Xcode and choose File > New Project.
   A dialog appears similar to that shown in Figure 3.1.

2. Choose Cocoa Application and click Next.

3. Enter a name in the Project Name text field.
   For this project, enter CocoaDrawingShell.

Figure 3.1 Creating a new Cocoa application project in Xcode

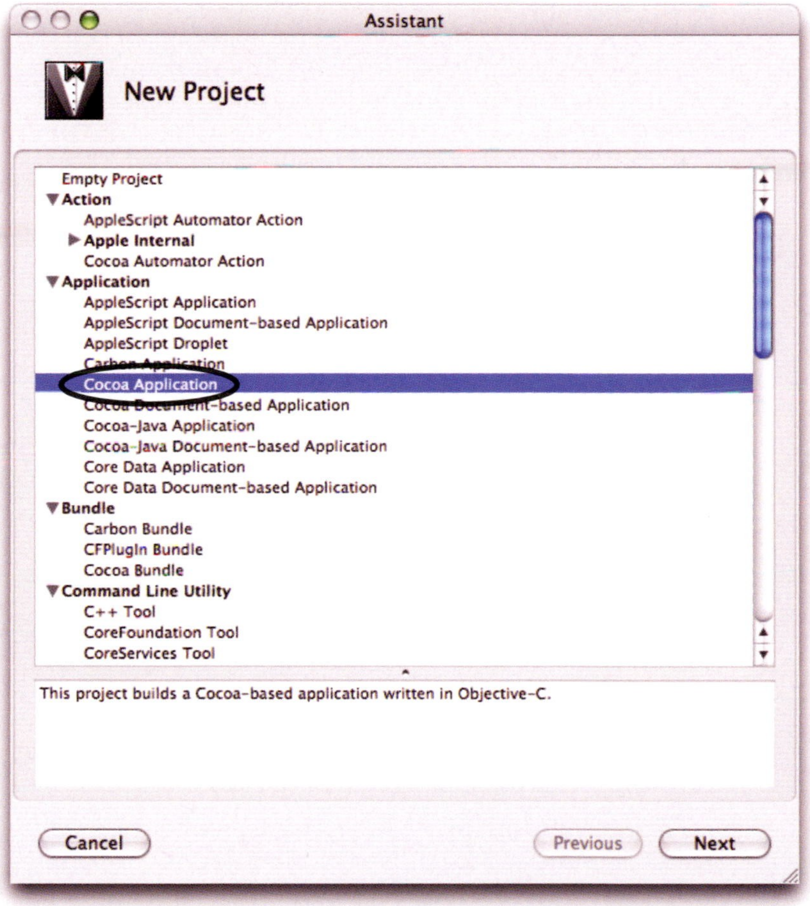

4. Click Choose and select a convenient location on your hard disk. Then click Finish.

When the project opens, a window appears, similar to that shown in Figure 3.2.

The main portion of the project window has two parts: Groups & Files (on the left) and the file list (on the right.) The right side is the list of files used by the project. Xcode adds the AppKit, Cocoa, CoreData, and Foundation frameworks that a Cocoa application requires. It also provides these files:

- CocoaDrawingShell.app is the application that results from building the application. Until the application is built, the file name appears red to signal the file doesn't exist. After you build the application, its name appears in black.

- CocoaDrawingShell_Prefix.pch is the prefix header file for the project. Including your project header files in this file can speed up the compilation of your project. You don't need to modify the contents of this file to build the sample application.

Figure 3.2 The project window in Xcode

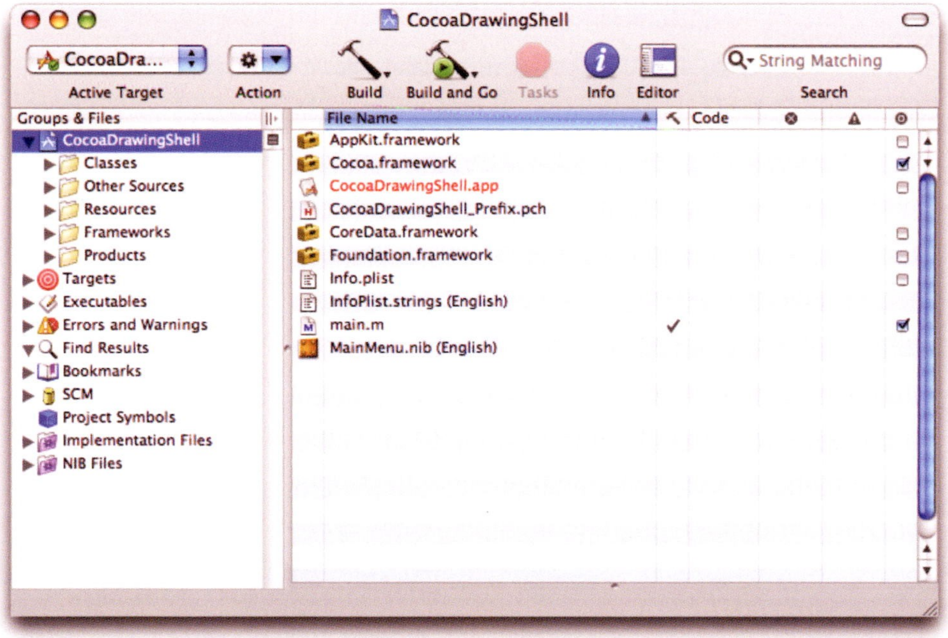

- Info.plist contains the property list for the project. The default contents work well for the sample application.

- InfoPlist.strings contains localized versions of the readable strings in an application. You don't need to modify its contents for the sample application.

- main.m is the code file containing the program's `main` routine. You usually don't make changes to this file.

- MainMenu.nib contains the user interface resources for the application. The icon is characteristic of the Interface Builder application, which you use to create the user interface for a Cocoa application. You will open this file in the next section.

The Groups & Files section of the project window provides a way for you to organize project files. By default, Xcode puts files into the groups shown in the window. The groups are just another way to look at project files. For example, you can also view the MainMenu.nib file name by clicking the disclosure triangle next to Nib Files in the Groups & Files list.

Creating a View in Interface Builder

The Apple Interface Builder application is an integral part of Cocoa application development. Interface Builder is used for adding user interface elements to an application and connecting them to application code. Interface Builder creates user interface data that resides in a nib file. In this section, you open the Main-Menu.nib file provided by Xcode when you created the Cocoa application project. Opening the file in Xcode automatically launches Interface Builder. This discussion and the associated screen shots are based on Interface Builder version 2.5 in Tiger.

1. Double-click the MainMenu.nib file in the file list.

   After Interface Builder launches, several windows appear, similar to those shown in Figure 3.3:

   - A window titled MainMenu.nib, which is a navigational window for organizing and accessing all the items in the nib file.

   - A window titled Window, which is the main application window for the application you are creating. You'll add a view for drawing to this window.

   - A window titled MainMenu.nib - MainMenu, which is the menu bar for the application you are creating. You can add menus and menu items to

Figure 3.3 Interface Builder windows after opening the nib file

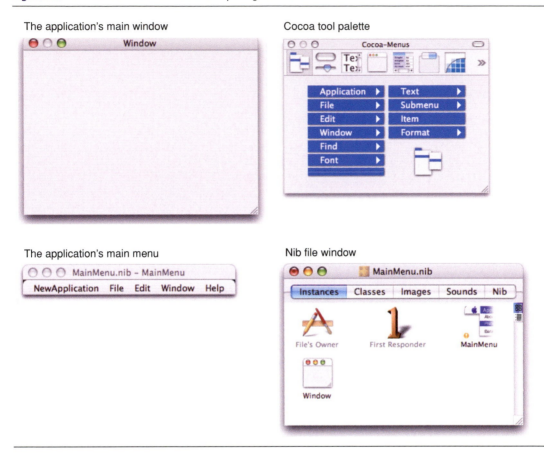

The application's main window

The application's main menu

Cocoa tool palette

Nib file window

this. The sample application does not require any modifications to the menu bar.

- A palette of user interface elements. You navigate through the suite of available interface elements by clicking on the buttons at the top of the palettes. You can hover the pointer over a button to find out which set of elements is associated with that button. Elements are in these groups: menus, controls and indicators, text, windows, data views, container views, graphics views, and controllers.

2. To add a custom view to the application window, click the Containers button on the palette. The Cocoa-Containers panel of the Interface Builder palette is the sixth palette from the left. (See Figure 3.4.) Now drag the CustomView element from the palette to the application window.

Figure 3.4 The Cocoa-Containers palette in Interface Builder

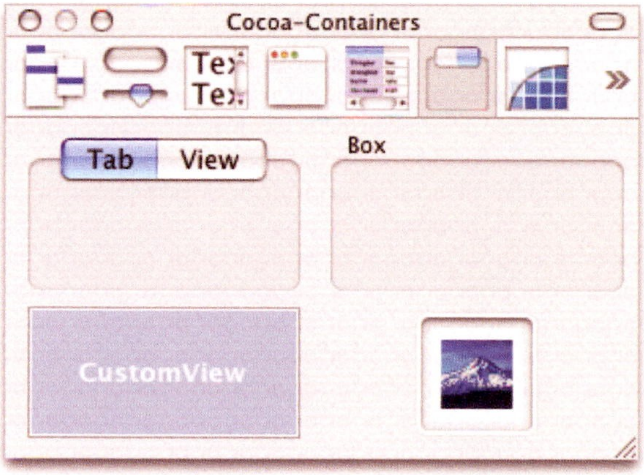

A custom view in Cocoa is a rectangular portion of a window that an application draws into. The view can comprise the entire window or it can be a portion of the window. You'll make the view a portion of the window so that you get a better idea of how views work.

3. Move the CustomView so that it is near the lower-left corner of the window but the lower-left corner of the view is about a half inch to the right and above the lower-left corner of the window.

4. Resize the CustomView by dragging the top-right corner of the view to the top right of the application window, as shown in Figure 3.5.

   The application window in which you placed the CustomView is resizable, but right now the view is not. For the sample application, the view needs to resize when the window resizes. As the window size changes, the lower-left corner of the view should remain fixed relative to the lower-left corner of the window, but the top-right corner of the view should move with the top-right corner of the window. This causes the view to get larger and smaller as the window size changes. You'll next change the view settings so that the view has this behavior.

5. Click inside the CustomView, then choose Tools > Show Inspector (Command-Shift-I).

6. Choose Size from the Inspector window pop-up menu. The Size pane appears and looks similar to that shown in Figure 3.6, except that what you see doesn't have the springs shown in the figure.

52 Chapter 3 Using Quartz 2D in Cocoa

Figure 3.5 The resized view

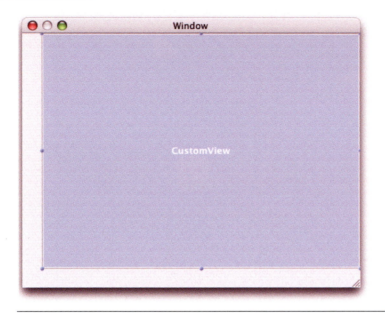

Figure 3.6 The Size pane in the Inspector window for the CustomView

7. In the Autosizing section of the Inspector window, click the horizontal and vertical lines in the interior of the rectangular shape.

When you click a line, its shape changes to a spring. With the springs in place as shown in Figure 3.6, the CustomView resizes as the window sizes but without changing the distance between a corner point of the view rectangle and the corresponding corner of the window.

Now that you've built the interface, you need to connect it to some drawing code.

Connecting the Interface to the Code

The Cocoa class NSView is an abstract class that you subclass to draw view contents and to customize event handling for the view. For the purposes of the sample application, you need to subclass NSView and make it responsible for all drawing into the rectangular area you created with the CustomView interface element in the last section. Interface Builder makes it easy for you to subclass a class and attach the subclass to user interface elements like CustomView. After you attach the subclass, Cocoa automatically calls the drawRect: method associated with this view whenever the view needs to be drawn.

1. In the MainMenu.nib window, click Classes. Then click the custom view in the application window.

Note that the class now chosen in the nib window is NSView.

2. Click so that the nib window is the active window. Then choose Classes > Subclass NSView to create the subclass.

This nib file window and the Classes menu should look similar to Figure 3.7. If the first menu item of the Classes menu isn't Subclass NSView or the item is disabled, make sure you've selected the NSView class in the list of Classes in the nib window and that the nib window is the active window.

At this point, a new class titled MyView appears to the right of NSView in the Classes portion of the nib window. This is the custom class you use to implement drawing in the custom view. Next you must associate this class with the CustomView you added to the window.

3. Click the custom view in the application window. If the Inspector window is not visible, choose Tools > Show Inspector.

Figure 3.7 The Classes menu when the NSView class is selected

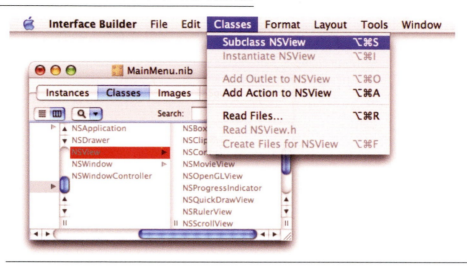

4. In the Inspector window, choose Custom Class from the pop-up menu.

   You see a list of the classes available to assign to the custom view in the application window.

5. Choose MyView from the list of classes; it should be at the top of the list as shown in Figure 3.8.

   Note that the name of the custom view in the application window changes to MyView.

6. In the Classes pane of the MainMenu.nib window, choose the MyView subclass of NSView. Then choose Create Files for MyView from the Classes menu.

   Interface Builder make things easier for you by generating an interface and implementation file for the MyView class. After choosing this menu item, a sheet appears on the nib window. Verify that the directory it is pointing to is the directory for your Xcode project and click the Choose button to generate MyView.h and MyView.m files to add to the project.

Now go back to Xcode and see what the project looks like. Quit Interface Builder, making sure to save your changes.

Figure 3.8 MyView as it appears in the Custom Class list

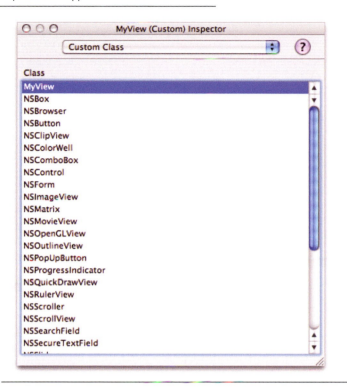

Obtaining a Graphics Context in Cocoa

Before you write the drawing code, it's a good idea to take a look at using a Quartz graphics context for a view in a Cocoa application. "Quartz 2D Drawing Basics" (page 15) introduced the concept of a Quartz graphics context but didn't show how to obtain one.

Although Quartz does not have a notion of a "current context," Cocoa does. Before Cocoa calls your drawing method, it automatically sets the current Cocoa graphics context (NSGraphicsContext) to correspond to the Cocoa view set up in the application window. When your drawing method is called, you obtain the Quartz graphics context by performing these two steps:

1. Send a currentContext message to the class NSGraphicsContext to obtain the current Cocoa NSGraphicsContext.

2. Send a graphicsPort message to the NSGraphicsContext obtained in the first step. The graphicsPort message returns the corresponding CGContextRef.

You can then use this CGContextRef in subsequent Quartz drawing calls. Next you'll look at the actual code to get the graphics context (CGContextRef) and perform the drawing.

Writing the Drawing Code

Interface Builder is well integrated with Xcode. When you created the custom view in Interface Builder you also created two new files MyView.h and MyView.m and added them to the project. You can find the new files in the Other Sources folder in the Groups & Files list in your Xcode project or by looking in the file list for the project, as shown in Figure 3.9.

Double-click the MyView.m file name to see its contents. The file contains two Objective-C methods—initWithFrame: and drawRect:. Focus your attention on the method drawRect:, which looks like this:

```
- (void)drawRect:(NSRect)rect{}
```

Figure 3.9 The project with the new files added by Interface Builder

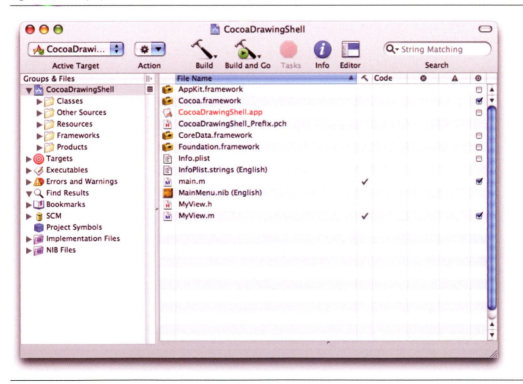

Interface Builder knows that a subclass of NSView needs to implement a drawRect: method to draw the contents of the view. Cocoa implements the NSView abstract class to provide a simple way to perform drawing in the sample application without requiring you to know much about mouse events, window resizing, window visibility, menu choices, and so on. The view you created simply gets told when it is appropriate to draw its contents. Aren't advanced toolkits cool? (See the Cocoa documentation for the Cocoa class NSView for more information on its methods and usage.)

You'll have the application draw the series of alpha composited rectangles that were drawn in Listing 2.5 (page 31) so you can reuse the doAlphaRects routine from that example. The doAlphaRects takes a CGContextRef and draws the rectangles into the context. To draw the alpha rectangles in the view's drawRect: method, you need to obtain the CGContextRef associated with that view.

Listing 3.1 is an updated drawRect: method that draws with Quartz to the context that represents the view. Cocoa calls this method when the view needs to be drawn, supplying an NSRect corresponding to the rectangular area your application draws to. Given the close relationship between Cocoa and Quartz, you shouldn't be surprised that the NSRect data structure is the same as a CGRect data structure. When optimal performance is important, it's a good idea to pay attention to the rectangle that's passed to the drawRect: method. For now, ignore the rect that is passed to the drawRect: method.

Listing 3.1 A Cocoa method that draws using Quartz

```
- (void)drawRect:(NSRect)rect
{
    NSGraphicsContext *nsctx = [NSGraphicsContext currentContext];
    CGContextRef context = (CGContextRef)[nsctx graphicsPort];

    CGContextSetLineWidth(context, 5.0);
    // Draw the coordinate axes.
    CGContextBeginPath(context);
    // First draw the x axis.
    CGContextMoveToPoint(context, -2000., 0.0);
    CGContextAddLineToPoint(context, 2000., 0.0);
    CGContextDrawPath(context, kCGPathStroke);
    // Next draw the y axis.
    CGContextMoveToPoint(context, 0.0, -2000.0);
    CGContextAddLineToPoint(context, 0.0, 2000.0);
    CGContextDrawPath(context, kCGPathStroke);

    doAlphaRects(context);
}
```

The first line in the drawRect: method sends a currentContext message to the class NSGraphicsContext and stores the result in the nsctx variable. Prior to calling the drawRect: method, Cocoa sets the current Cocoa graphics context to that of the view. After obtaining the current Cocoa graphics context, the code sends the graphicsPort message to the NSGraphicsContext stored in nsctx. This returns the Quartz CGContextRef that corresponds to the view.

The next few lines of code draw the coordinate axes. The code strokes two lines corresponding to the x and y axes with a line width of 5 units so they are clearly visible, drawing the x axis from x = -2000.0 to x = 2000.0 and the y axis from y = -2000.0 to y = 2000.0. (These numbers were chosen to be large enough to cover the width and height of a window.) The coordinate origin is where these two lines intersect. The code draws the axes to illustrate how the placement of the CustomView in a window relates to where the drawing is done. You'll take a look at this in the next section.

The last line in the method calls the doAlphaRects routine created previously (shown in Listing 2.5 (page 31)). Simply paste this routine into the MyView.m file immediately before the drawRect: method.

Examining the Drawing Output

You are ready to run the application and check the output. Click the Build and Go button in the Xcode project window. If you are successful, CocoaDrawing-Shell runs and produces the output shown in Figure 3.10. If your project fails to build, click on the Errors and Warnings item in the Groups & Files portion of the project window to show any build errors.

Note that the coordinate axes don't meet in the bottom of the window but at the lower-left corner of the CustomView you created in Interface Builder. Cocoa ensures that the Quartz coordinate origin is at the view origin when it calls the drawRect: method. Recall that you intentionally placed the Custom-View so that it was about a half inch to the right and above the lower-left corner of the window. You could have made the view origin be the lower-left corner of the window; you might want to adjust the view origin for your future applications.

Recall that the code draws the x axis from x = -2000.0 to x = 2000.0 and the y axis from y = -2000.0 to y = 2000.0. Why isn't any portion of the coordinate axes for x < 0 or y < 0 visible? Cocoa sets the Quartz clipping area before calling the view's drawRect: method so that all drawing is clipped to the inside of the view.

Figure 3.10 The output from the CocoaDrawingShell application

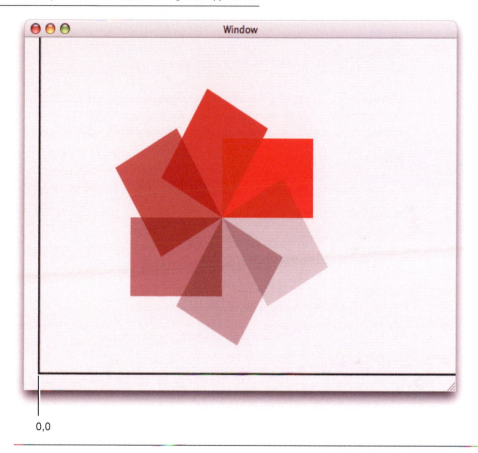

0,0

Cocoa Framework Drawing and Quartz

The Cocoa framework provides a rich set of graphics capabilities, built on top of Quartz. Cocoa provides these through Objective-C classes, as one would expect. In general, the Cocoa graphics capabilities provide a higher level of abstraction than the C-based Quartz graphics API and in many cases are a better match for application drawing. In a sense, the design of the Cocoa graphics classes provide a good "impedance match" with the rest of the Cocoa framework. Many Cocoa applications need only the rich drawing capabilities directly available in Cocoa.

There are many situations where Cocoa provides much higher-level abstractions and capabilities than Quartz does. For example, Quartz has only low-level text drawing capabilities, whereas Cocoa text capabilities provide the ability to work with Unicode text, perform text layout and glyph substitution, and much more. The vast majority of Cocoa applications are better served using Cocoa's text drawing capabilities than using Quartz text drawing directly.

There are several situations where it may be beneficial to use Quartz directly in a Cocoa application:

- Where Cocoa doesn't provide the functionality you need but Quartz does. In this book, you'll see many capabilities in the Quartz API set that are not reflected in the Cocoa drawing API. These capabilities are discussed next.

- Where you need finer control over the way that drawing is performed. In some cases, the Cocoa framework abstractions, while useful for most application drawing, may prevent you from achieving the effect you want.

- Where drawing performance is critical and you've determined that by working with Quartz directly you can achieve a performance benefit you require. Quartz allows more direct control but without the extra support that the Cocoa framework provides. Using Quartz avoids working through another layer.

The primary situation where you might want to use Quartz directly is when there is no corresponding capability with Cocoa drawing methods. Some of the areas where Quartz provides drawing capabilities beyond those available in Cocoa (as of Tiger) are as follows:

- Cocoa has no direct support for most of the features described in "Image Masking" (page 263). For example, there are no Cocoa methods for creating and drawing image masks, masking an image with another image, masking an image with a color, or modifying the clipping area with a mask.

- Cocoa provides support for drawing with patterns that are only created from an NSImage. To draw with patterns that contain arbitrary content (such as line art, text, or image types not supported by NSImage), you must use Quartz directly. "Drawing with Patterns" (page 481) discusses Quartz patterns in depth.

- Cocoa does not provide methods for drawing with CGLayers (see "CGLayers (Tiger)" (page 371)). Cocoa has methods that allow you to cache drawing as a bit-based representation, but by using Quartz CGLayers you can also record drawing as a high-level representation appropriate for drawing multiple times to contexts that are not bit-based.

- Cocoa does not provide methods that draw shadings (see "Drawing with Shadings (Jaguar)" (page 531)). To draw shadings, you must use Quartz directly.

- Cocoa drawing methods do not access Quartz transparency layers. Transparency layers allow the grouping of graphics primitives for purposes of compositing them as a whole rather than as individual elements. To draw with transparency layers, you must instead use the Quartz functions described in "Drawing with Transparency Layers (Panther)" (page 522).

- There is no support in Cocoa for the Quartz blend modes, described in "Blend Modes (Tiger)" (page 170), other than the default Quartz blend mode kCG-BlendModeNormal.

There are some situations where the Cocoa drawing methods have behavior that you might want to avoid:

- Prior to Panther, any NSColor used during PDF generation and printing is treated as completely opaque (alpha = 1).

- Using the NSImage class to draw images can result in the creation of multiple CGImage objects when drawing a given image. This produces larger PDF documents since drawing the same NSImage to a given PDF context multiple times does not produce a single copy of the image data. In addition, JPEG image data is not treated specially by NSImage; therefore, during PDF generation, uncompressed data is written to the PDF document.

- Cocoa's support of PDF documents is more limited than that available in Quartz. Cocoa does not have the ability to work with encrypted documents, either to create them or draw with them. Cocoa provides more limited information about the bounding rectangles of a PDF document and provides none of the PDF document introspection capabilities of Quartz. When creating PDF documents, Cocoa doesn't allow you to add the Author, Title, and other keys available when you use Quartz directly. However, in Tiger, the PDF Kit framework is available to Cocoa applications; this framework provides a rich set of Objective-C classes for drawing and using PDF documents.

- Cocoa's NSImage class has direct support for handling encapsulated PostScript (EPS) data in Panther and later versions by leveraging the PostScript conversion functionality available in Quartz. Note that while PostScript (PS) conversion is available in Cocoa, there is no support for the callbacks available in the Quartz PostScript conversion routines (CGPSConverter). If you need to obtain status, progress, and other messages during EPS/PS conversion, you'll need to use Quartz directly. Prior to Panther, Cocoa has no support for EPS data. If you need to support printing of EPS data on systems prior to Panther, consider using the techniques described in "Printing Source EPS Data" (page 582).

Some developers expect that they may achieve a performance benefit by using the Quartz API rather than Cocoa drawing methods. Because Cocoa drawing is built on top of Quartz drawing, there is some expectation that using Quartz directly is more efficient.

Before drawing the conclusion that you will achieve a significant performance benefit by using Quartz directly, it is a good idea to compare and analyze performance using real-world test cases. As a general rule, the Cocoa implementation on top of Quartz is a relatively thin layer that provides many convenience functions. In addition, it is well matched to and integrated with the programming style of other portions of Cocoa. As just described, the typical benefits achieved by using Quartz directly stem from allowing additional control over how you perform drawing.

Summary

This chapter provides step-by-step instructions for building a Cocoa application that can act as an application shell for working with Quartz 2D. The application uses a custom view that is created in Interface Builder and is a custom subclass of the NSView class. Cocoa calls the drawRect: method of the NSView subclass whenever the contents of the window need to be drawn.

This Cocoa example uses a very small amount of Objective-C—just enough to obtain a Quartz graphics context (CGContextRef) that corresponds to the view in the sample application. Most of the examples in this book use the C language version of the Quartz programming interfaces so that later examples can be used directly in the Cocoa shell application you just created.

See Also

For more information on Xcode and programming Cocoa, see the following:

- Documentation for Xcode and the tools included with the Xcode development environment is available at

  http://developer.apple.com/documentation/DeveloperTools/Xcode-date.html

- *Cocoa Programming for Mac OS X*, Aaron Hillegass, Addison-Wesley, 2nd edition, 2004.

- For a list of the Apple Cocoa documentation (which includes graphics and imaging in Cocoa), see this page of the ADC Reference Library:

  http://developer.apple.com/referencelibrary/Cocoa/index.html

- If you are just getting started with Cocoa, Apple has a useful "getting started" document:

  http://developer.apple.com/referencelibrary/GettingStarted/GS_Cocoa/

Chapter 4

Using Quartz 2D in Carbon

Although you can use the Quartz 2D API just as easily with the Carbon framework as you can with the Cocoa framework, the process of obtaining a graphics context differs depending on which framework you use. The Carbon framework has its origins in the pre–Mac OS X APIs. Originally, Carbon was seen as a bridge between the Mac OS 9 and Mac OS X worlds, but today's Carbon framework is really a collection of C APIs that are used by C and C++ programmers to develop Mac OS X applications. The Carbon framework, unlike Cocoa, provides support for moving older QuickDraw-based applications to Quartz 2D. For that reason, there are two ways to get a Quartz graphics context from the Carbon framework.

The preferable way to obtain a graphics context is to use the HIView subcomponent of HIToolbox. Most of this chapter describes how to set up an HIView and get a graphics context from it. The sections "Setting Up a Carbon Window" (page 68), "Creating an Event Handler" (page 73), and "Examining the Drawing Output" (page 76) contain HIView and Quartz-specific information that works in Jaguar and later versions. If your application must run in versions prior to Jaguar, you instead need to call the QuickDraw functions `QDBeginCGContext` and `QDEndCGContext`, as described in "Using QDBeginCGContext" (page 79).

The first section in this chapter—"Creating a Carbon Xcode Project"—shows how to create a Carbon application in Xcode. Nothing in this section is specific to using Quartz in Carbon. Experienced Xcode developers who have written at least one Carbon application can skip this section. If you haven't used Xcode, you'll want to read this section regardless of which version of Mac OS X your application runs in.

Creating a Carbon Xcode Project

This section creates a Carbon application project using the Xcode version 2.0 development environment in Tiger and explains the contents of a project window. (If you are using a later version of Xcode there may be small differences from what is shown here.) If you haven't used Xcode before, make sure you first read "Xcode Overview" (page 46) in the previous chapter.

1. Open Xcode and choose File > New Project.

   A dialog appears similar to that shown in Figure 4.1.

2. Choose Carbon Application and click Next.

3. Enter a name in the Project Name text field.

   For this project, enter CarbonDrawingShell.

4. Click Choose and select a convenient location on your hard disk. Then click Finish.

   When the project opens, you'll see a window similar to that shown in Figure 4.2.

Figure 4.1 Creating a new Carbon application project in Xcode

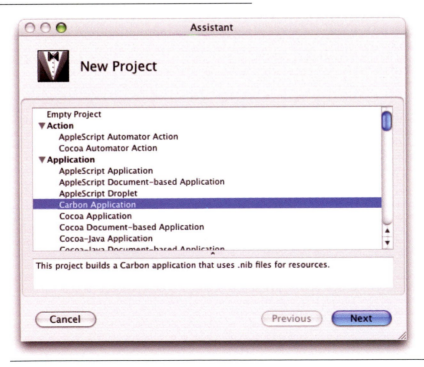

Figure 4.2 The project window in Xcode

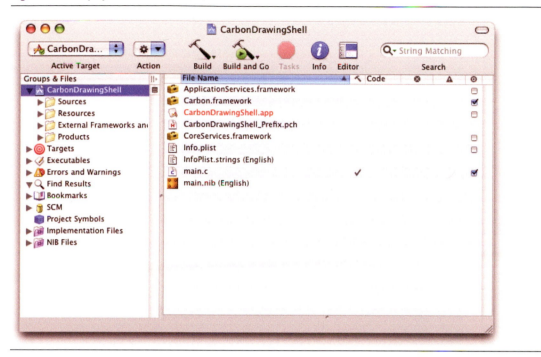

The main portion of the project window has two parts: Groups & Files (on the left) and the file list (on the right). The right side is the list of files needed by the project. Xcode adds the ApplicationServices, Carbon, and CoreServices frameworks needed for a Carbon application. It also provides these files:

■ CarbonDrawingShell.app is the application that results from building the application. Until the application builds, the file name appears red to signal that the file doesn't exist. After you build the application its file name appears black.

■ CarbonDrawingShell_Prefix.pch is the prefix header file for the project. Including your project header files in this file can speed up the compilation of your project. You don't need to modify the contents of this file to build the sample application.

■ Info.plist contains the property list for the project. The default contents work well for the sample application; you don't need to modify this list for the sample application.

■ InfoPlist.strings contains localized versions of the readable strings in an application. You don't need to modify its contents for the sample application.

- main.c contains the code to implement a very simple Carbon application. You'll add code to this file in the section "Creating an Event Handler" (page 73).

- main.nib contains the user interface resources for the application. The icon is characteristic of the Interface Builder application, which you can use to create the user interface for a Carbon application. You open this file in the next section.

The Groups & Files section of the project window provides a way for you to organize project files. By default, Xcode groups files into the groups shown in the window. The groups are just another way to look at project files. For example, you can also view the main.nib file name by clicking the disclosure triangle next to NIB Files in the Groups & Files list.

Setting Up a Carbon Window

Interface Builder provides a graphical way to add user interface elements to a Carbon application instead of adding them programmatically. Interface Builder creates user interface data that resides in a nib file. This section shows how to modify the main.nib file that is provided by Xcode when it creates a Carbon application project. Opening the file in Xcode automatically launches Interface Builder. This discussion and the associated screen shots are based on Interface Builder version 2.5 in Tiger.

1. Double-click the main.nib file in the file list.

   After Interface Builder launches, several windows appear, similar to those shown in Figure 4.3:

   - A window titled main.nib, which is a navigational window for organizing and accessing all the items in the nib file.

   - A window titled Window, which is the main application window for the application you are creating. This is the window you'll use for drawing.

   - A window titled main.nib, which is the menu bar for the application. You can add menus and menu items to this. The sample application requires no modifications to the menu bar.

   - A palette of user interface elements. Click the buttons at the top of the palette to navigate through the suite of available interface elements. Hover the pointer over a button to find out which set of elements is associated with that button. Elements are in these groups: menus, controls, enhanced controls, text-based controls, browsers & tab, and windows.

Figure 4.3 Interface Builder windows after opening the nib file

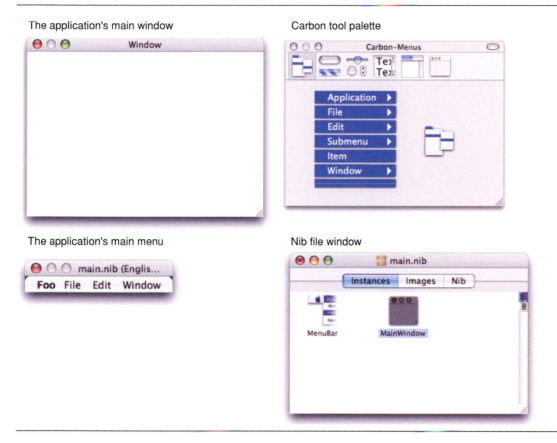

The application's main window

Carbon tool palette

The application's main menu

Nib file window

2. Click the window titled Window. Then choose Tools > Show Inspector or press Command-Shift-I.

3. Choose Attributes from the pop-up menu in the Inspector window, as shown in Figure 4.4. Note that Compositing is on by default. This and the other default settings are exactly what you need; don't make any changes to this pane. If you want, you can resize and reposition the window to suit your application.

Note Compositing windows are available in Jaguar and later versions. This type of window tracks the layered views embedded in it, drawing only when the visible portions of a view need updating.

4. Choose Size from the pop-up menu in the Show Inspector window. Then set the window width to 540 and its height to 440.

Figure 4.4 The Attributes pane in the Inspector window

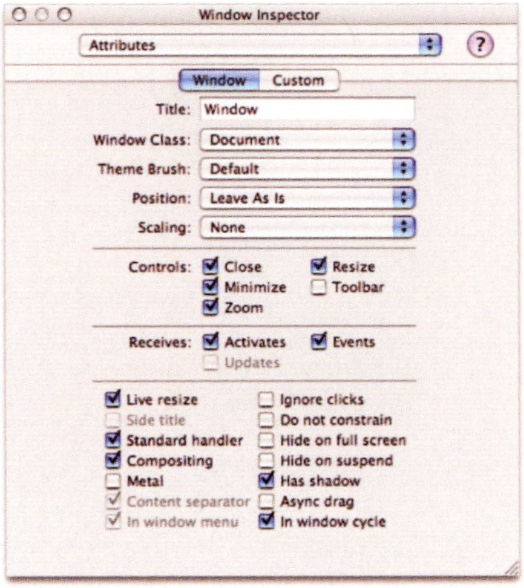

5. Click the Enhanced Carbon Controls button in the tool palette. This is the third button from the left, as shown in Figure 4.5.

6. Drag an HIView object from the palette to the window and position it as shown in Figure 4.6.

   HIViews are object-oriented Carbon Event–based control implementations that work in compositing windows. You'll set up the application so that it draws into the HIView.

7. With the HIView selected, choose Control from the HIView Inspector window's pop-up menu.

8. Type a signature (a four-character sequence) and a unique ID (a 32-bit integer).

   You can use the signature and ID shown in Figure 4.7 (page 72). The only requirement is to make sure the combination is unique. Later you'll access the HIView by using its signature and ID.

9. Now choose the Layout menu in the HIView Inspector window and set the bindings so that the view resizes with its parent window. The settings should match those of Figure 4.8 (page 72).

10. Choose File > Save.

11. Quit Interface Builder and return to Xcode.

Now that you've built the interface, you need to create an event handler that draws into the HIView, as described in the next section.

Figure 4.5 Enhanced Carbon Controls

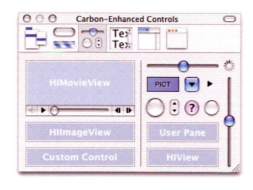

Figure 4.6 An HIView element placed in the window

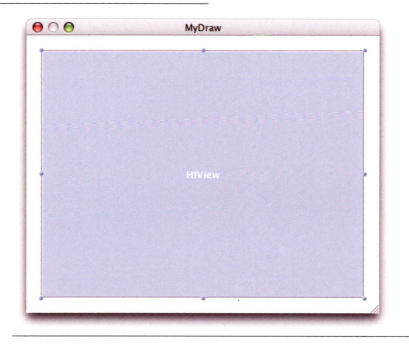

Figure 4.7 The signature and ID entered in the HIView Inspector window

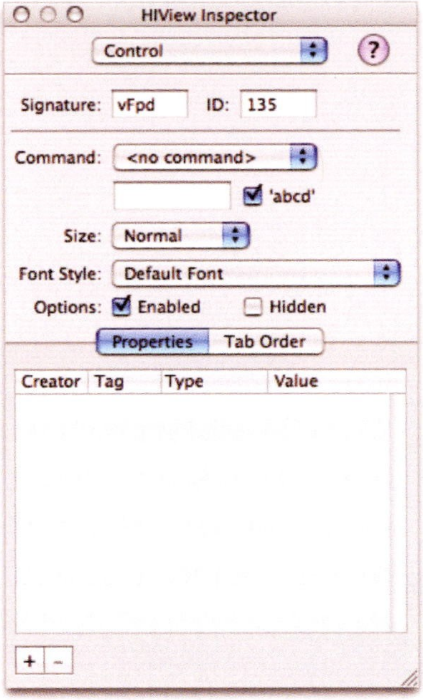

Figure 4.8 Layout bindings for the HIView

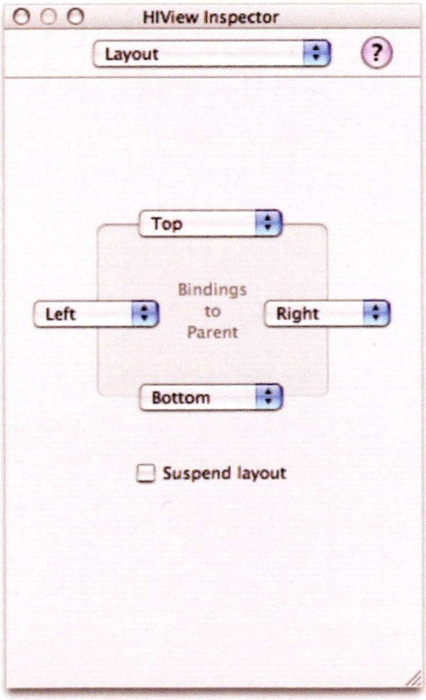

Creating an Event Handler

The Carbon version of the drawing shell application requires a few pieces of C code to connect the normal system window behavior to the drawing code. This section shows how to add code, none of which is specific to Quartz, that does the following:

- Gets the `HIViewRef` associated with the HIView.
- Registers an event handler that will handle drawing for the HIView.
- Takes care of drawing to the HIView embedded in the window.

Double-click the `main.c` file in the Groups & Files list. Take a look at the `main` routine added by Xcode. It contains all the code necessary for a working Carbon application. The code opens the `main.nib` file, creates a window using the attributes you set in Interface Builder, shows the window, and starts the application run loop.

Build and run the project to see that the application opens a window that resizes, has menus that work and that include a command that allows you to quit the application. Of course nothing draws in the application window because you haven't written any drawing code yet.

To make the application useful, you need to write a routine that handles drawing content to the HIView in the window. The custom event handler shown in Listing 4.1 achieves this goal. In a moment, you'll change the application's `main` routine so that the Carbon Event Manager calls the routine `MyDrawEventHandler` in response to a `kEventControlDrawContent` event.

Listing 4.1 An event handler that draws content to a Carbon window

```
OSStatus MyDrawEventHandler (EventHandlerCallRef myHandlerRef,
                EventRef event, void *userData)
{
  OSStatus status = noErr;
  CGContextRef myContext;
  HIRect        bounds;

  // Get the CGContextRef.
  status = GetEventParameter (event,
                kEventParamCGContextRef,
                typeCGContextRef,
                NULL,
```

```
                    sizeof (CGContextRef),
                    NULL,
                    &myContext);
    if(status != noErr){
      fprintf(stderr, "Got error %d getting the context!\n", status);
      return status;
    }

    // Your drawing code can replace what follows.

    // Draw the coordinate axes.
    CGContextSetLineWidth(myContext, 5.0);
    CGContextBeginPath(myContext);
    // First draw the x axis.
    CGContextMoveToPoint(myContext, -2000.0, 0.0);
    CGContextAddLineToPoint(myContext, 2000.0, 0.0);
    CGContextDrawPath(myContext, kCGPathStroke);
    // Next draw the y axis.
    CGContextMoveToPoint(myContext, 0.0, -2000.0);
    CGContextAddLineToPoint(myContext, 0.0, 2000.0);
    CGContextDrawPath(myContext, kCGPathStroke);
    // Now draw the alpha rects.
    doAlphaRects (myContext);
    return status;
}
```

The routine calls GetEventParameter to obtain the Quartz graphics context for the event from the Carbon event passed to the routine. After obtaining the graphics context associated with the HIView, you can perform any Quartz drawing you'd like. Listing 4.1 draws lines that show the origin of the coordinate system. Then it calls doAlphaRects, which is the routine shown in Listing 2.5 (page 31). Copy the doAlphaRects routine to the CarbonDrawingShell application, including the function prototype, to an appropriate location.

You need to update the declarations and the main routine, as shown in Listing 4.2. First, declare constants to represent the signature and ID you assigned to the HIView in Interface Builder. Make sure these match exactly. In the body of the main routine, declare a variable for an HIViewRef. You'll set up the myView variable to reference the HIView.

Next you need to set up an event specification (EventTypeSpec) array for the event class and the kind of events your drawing event handler takes care of. An event handler can handle many events, but for this simple example it handles only one—the kEventControlDraw event. The myViewID variable holds the unique signature-ID values for the HIView.

Xcode supplies all the code that creates a reference for the nib, sets the menu bar, creates a window, and disposes of the nib reference. You need to add the code that gets the `HIViewRef` for the HIView and installs its event handler.

You pass the `HIViewRef` to the Carbon Event Manager function `HIViewInstall-EventHandler`, along with a UPP to your drawing event handler, the number of events it handles, the event specification array, data needed by the handler (which in this case is the `HIViewRef` for the HIView), and `NULL` to indicate that you don't need to obtain the event handler reference. There may be situations for which you'd want to get the event handler reference, but you don't need it for this example.

Listing 4.2 Updated main routine for CarbonDrawingShell

```
// Declare the signature and field ID for the HIView. These must
// match what you assigned to the HIView in Interface Builder.
#define kMyHIViewSignature  'vFpd'
#define kMyHIViewFieldID    135

int main(int argc, char* argv[])
{
  IBNibRef                nibRef;
  OSStatus                err;
  WindowRef               window;
  HIViewRef               myView;
  // Declare the event class and kind for the Carbon event of interest.
  static const EventTypeSpec  kMyEvents[] = { kEventClassControl,
                              kEventControlDraw };
  static const HIViewID       myViewID = { kMyHIViewSignature,
                              kMyHIViewFieldID };

  // Create a reference for the main nib.
  err = CreateNibReference(CFSTR("main"), &nibRef);
  require_noerr(err, CantGetNibRef);

  // Set the menu bar to be the MenuBar from the main nib.
  err = SetMenuBarFromNib(nibRef, CFSTR("MenuBar"));
  require_noerr(err, CantSetMenuBar);

  // Create the MainWindow from the main nib.
  err = CreateWindowFromNib(nibRef, CFSTR("MainWindow"), &window);
  require_noerr(err, CantCreateWindow );
  DisposeNibReference(nibRef);
```

```
    // Get the HIView of the requested ID associated with the window.
    HIViewFindByID( HIViewGetRoot( window ), myViewID, &myView );

    // Install the event handler for the HIView.
    err = HIViewInstallEventHandler(myView,
                NewEventHandlerUPP(MyDrawEventHandler),
                GetEventTypeCount(kMyEvents),
                kMyEvents,
                (void *) myView,
                NULL);
    ShowWindow(window);
    RunApplicationEventLoop();

CantCreateWindow:
CantSetMenuBar:
CantGetNibRef:

    return err;
}
```

Examining the Drawing Output

You are ready to run the application and check the output. Click Build and Go in the Xcode project window. If you are successful, CarbonDrawingShell runs and produces the output shown in Figure 4.9. If your project fails to build, click the Errors and Warnings item in the Groups & Files portion of the project window so that you can examine the build errors.

Compare the drawing in Figure 4.9 with Figure 3.10 (page 59). The drawing produced by the Carbon application is the same as that produced by the Cocoa sample with one exception—the output is flipped. That's because HIView automatically transforms the Quartz context so that the origin of the coordinate system is at the top-left corner of a view instead of at the bottom-left corner. Mac programmers who have used QuickDraw will notice that the HIView coordinate origin and orientation is the same as that used for QuickDraw. The advantage to having the origin at the top left is that the coordinates of objects in a view don't change when the view is resized.

The code in this book assumes the origin is at the lower-left corner, with y values increasing from bottom to top. If you plan to use the CarbonDrawingShell application to try out any of the code in the book, you may want to flip the HIView

Figure 4.9 Rectangles drawn using HIView coordinates

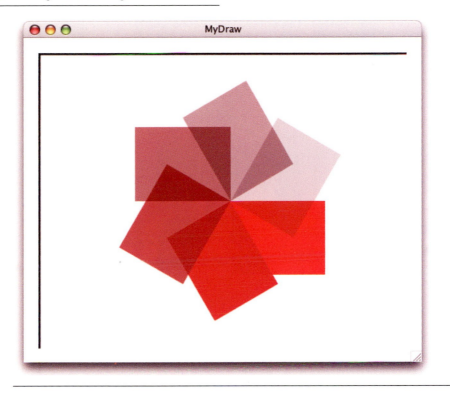

coordinate system to ensure that the drawing is oriented similarly to the figures in the book.

The code in Listing 4.3 transforms the HIView coordinate system to the default Quartz coordinate system. You can simply place this code immediately after the call to `GetEventParameter` to obtain the context and before the drawing code in the drawing event handler. The results will then match the drawing done by the CocoaDrawingShell application and shown in the figures throughout the rest of the book. Figure 4.10 shows the output of the CarbonDrawingShell application after adding the code in Listing 4.3.

Listing 4.3 Code that transforms HIView coordinates to Quartz coordinates

```
HIViewGetBounds((HIViewRef) userData, &bounds);
CGContextTranslateCTM(myContext, 0, bounds.size.height);
CGContextScaleCTM(myContext, 1.0, -1.0);
```

Figure 4.10 Drawing rectangles using Quartz coordinates

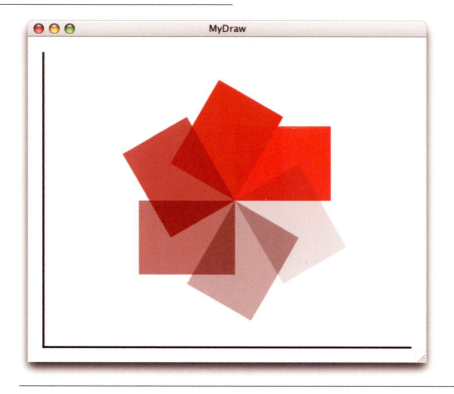

If you choose to use HIView coordinates instead of transforming them to default Quartz coordinates, remember that when you use Quartz to draw text, images, and PDF documents, the content will appear flipped. HIView provides a utility function (`HIViewDrawCGImage`) for drawing Quartz images that you can use instead of calling the Quartz function `CGContextDrawImage`. The HIView function transforms the coordinate system to Quartz coordinates before drawing the image. You'll learn more about drawing text, images, and PDF documents later in the book. The next chapter discusses the Quartz coordinate system in depth and "Drawing Images into a Flipped Coordinate System" (page 210), "Text" (page 289), and "Drawing PDF Documents in a Flipped Coordinate System" (page 408) discuss working in flipped coordinates with Carbon and Cocoa applications.

If you don't see any output in your window after running the application, the most likely cause is that the view control signature and ID that you entered in the Control portion of the HIView Inspector window in Interface Builder (see Figure 4.7 (page 72)) does not match the data you supplied as the `HIViewID` passed to `HIViewFindByID`.

Using QDBeginCGContext

In Puma, compositing windows and the constant kEventParamCGContextRef are not available. This means you can't obtain a Quartz graphics context as described previously in this chapter. In these circumstances, Carbon applications have available a QuickDraw port to draw to. Beginning with Puma, QuickDraw provides functions that allow you to obtain a Quartz context for a QuickDraw port and draw to it.

Note Even when running on Jaguar and later versions, you may have reasons why you can't use compositing HIViews in your application or your code may be invoked in circumstances where you have only a QuickDraw port available to draw to. These are additional situations where you need to use QDBeginCGContext to obtain a Quartz context.

When you aren't using a compositing HIView, you typically create a window and install a window event handler that handles window update events, similar to that shown in Listing 4.4.

You obtain the QuickDraw port for the window by calling the Window Manager function GetWindowPort. To obtain a Quartz graphics context, pass the port and a pointer to a CGContextRef variable to the QuickDraw function QDBeginCGContext, which returns the context for the port. The coordinate system of the context is set to the lower-left corner of the port passed to the function with the y axis going up the drawing canvas. The graphics context is initialized to default values.

After you call QDBeginCGContext, you can call as many Quartz drawing functions as you'd like. Once you call QDBeginCGContext, no QuickDraw drawing can be done to the port passed to QDBeginCGContext until you call QDEndCGContext. When you are done drawing with Quartz, you must call the companion function QDEndCGContext. These functions are always used in pairs to surround Quartz drawing. You can't call QDBeginCGContext a second time without first calling QDEndCGContext. Calling QDEndCGContext passes back the Quartz graphics context and reenables QuickDraw drawing to the port. After you call QDEndCGContext, the context you obtained from QDBeginCGContext is no longer valid and you must not draw to it. To again obtain a context for the port, you must again call QDBeginCGContext. Do not retain the context you obtain from QDBeginCGContext unless you release it before you call QDEndCGContext.

After you call QDBeginCGContext but before a call to QDEndCGContext, only Quartz drawing is allowed. You can't draw to the QuickDraw port supplied to QDBegin-CGContext until you call QDEndCGContext. If you attempt to draw to that port, QuickDraw writes the following message to the console: Ignoring Quickdraw drawing between QDBeginCGContext and QDEndCGContext. This is useful for debugging purposes. During development you may find that some of your QuickDraw drawing is not appearing as you would expect. It's a good idea to check the console log for these messages; their presence indicates that you haven't called QDEndCGContext prior to performing your QuickDraw drawing.

The drawing code in Listing 4.4 produces output similar to that shown in Figure 4.10 (page 78). Note that you need to first erase the content area, removing any previous invalid content. For compositing HIViews, the view system takes care of repairing damage beneath your view, but here you must do that yourself. Without erasing the window to white prior to drawing the content, any previous bits drawn in the window would still be visible. (Of course a typical application would take care to erase and draw only those areas that are invalid and need repainting.)

Note also that you need to call the function CGContextSynchronize after your drawing code and prior to calling QDEndCGContext to indicate that the window context needs to be updated. To improve performance, the Carbon Window Manager keeps track of which portions of the window you've drawn to and marks only those portions as "dirty"; that is, only those portions need to be flushed from the window backing store to the display. When you mix Quick-Draw and Quartz drawing, you need to ensure that the portions that you draw with Quartz are added to the area that is considered dirty; calling CGContextSyn-chronize does this.

An alternative is to call CGContextFlush, which flushes the context drawing immediately to the display. In rare circumstances, it may be necessary to flush the drawing yourself, such as when you are performing an animation. Typically, it is better to call CGContextSynchronize so that as much drawing as possible is collected at once prior to flushing. The pros and cons of each are discussed in "Performance and Debugging" (page 593).

Because of the connection between the QuickDraw port geometry and the Quartz coordinate system, any context you obtain from QDBeginCGContext before a change to window port geometry no longer has the correct coordinate system for the current window. It is important to write your code so that you call QDBeginCGContext *after* any port geometry changes, such as after a window resize.

Listing 4.4 Drawing with Quartz in Puma

```
static void MyHandleWindowUpdate(WindowRef window)
{
  OSStatus err = noErr;
  Rect bounds;
  CGContextRef context = NULL;
  CGrafPtr port = GetWindowPort(window);
  GetWindowPortBounds(window, &bounds);
```

```
err = QDBeginCGContext(port, &context);
if(!err){
  // Calculate the CGRect corresponding to the window bounds
  // expressed in QuickDraw coordinates.
  CGRect portBoundsCGRect = CGRectMake(0, 0,
      bounds.right - bounds.left, bounds.bottom - bounds.top);
  // Set the fill color to opaque white.
  CGContextSetRGBFillColor(context, 1, 1, 1, 1);
  // Fill the window background, erasing any previous content.
  CGContextFillRect(context, portBoundsCGRect);
  // Set the fill color to opaque black.
  CGContextSetRGBFillColor(context, 0, 0, 0, 1);

  // Now draw the desired content.
  CGContextSetLineWidth(context, 5.);
  // Draw the coordinate axes.
  CGContextBeginPath(context);
  // First draw the x axis.
  CGContextMoveToPoint(context, -2000., 0.);
  CGContextAddLineToPoint(context, 2000., 0.);
  CGContextDrawPath(context, kCGPathStroke);
  // Next draw the y axis.
  CGContextMoveToPoint(context, 0., -2000.);
  CGContextAddLineToPoint(context, 0., 2000.);
  CGContextDrawPath(context, kCGPathStroke);

  doAlphaRects(context);

  CGContextSynchronize(context);

  err = QDEndCGContext(port, &context);
}
}
```

Summary

This chapter provides step-by-step instructions for building a Carbon application that can act as a shell for working with Quartz 2D. The application uses an HIView in a window and a Carbon event handler that draws the contents of the HIView whenever it needs to be updated. The HIView coordinate system has an origin located at the upper-left corner of a window, with y values increasing from top to bottom. You can choose to use this coordinate system or you can add a few lines of code to transform HIView coordinates to match the default Quartz coordinate system.

When you draw with Quartz in a Carbon application, it's preferable to use HIViews. If your application must run in Mac OS X versions prior to Jaguar or you have other reasons you cannot take advantage of compositing HIViews, then you need to use the QuickDraw functions QDBeginCGContext and QDEndCG-Context.

The next chapter describes in greater detail the Quartz coordinate system, coordinate transforms, and how to use them.

See Also

For more information on Xcode and programming using the Carbon framework, see the following:

- Documentation for Xcode and the tools included with the Xcode development environment is available at

  http://developer.apple.com/documentation/DeveloperTools/Xcode-date.html

- Carbon "getting started" document from Apple:

  http://developer.apple.com/referencelibrary/GettingStarted/GS_Carbon/

- Carbon documentation from the ADC Reference Library:

  http://developer.apple.com/referencelibrary/Carbon/index.html

For more information on the HIView Toolbox, see the following Apple documents:

- *HIView Programming Guide* discusses the basic concepts behind HIView objects:

  http://developer.apple.com/documentation/Carbon/Conceptual/HIViewDoc/index.html

- *Upgrading to the Mac OS X HIToolbox* provides information on how to move older code to HIView:

  http://developer.apple.com/documentation/Carbon/Conceptual/Upgrading_HIToolbox/index.html

- *HIView Reference:*

  http://developer.apple.com/documentation/Carbon/Reference/HIViewReference/index.html

Chapter 5

The Quartz Coordinate System and Coordinate Transformations

Quartz uses a standard Cartesian coordinate system. By default, the origin is in the lower-left corner of the drawing canvas with x values increasing to the right and y values increasing upwards. Coordinates are floating-point values that represent units in a device-independent coordinate system. An application can draw to a window or a bitmap, a printer, or another output device. Quartz takes care of mapping the coordinates appropriately.

As you've seen in "Quartz 2D Drawing Basics" (page 15), the coordinate system can be transformed by translation, rotation, and scaling operations to achieve a variety of interesting effects with relatively little effort. Quartz also provides additional functions to manage coordinate transformations in a variety of ways. With a more complete understanding of the Quartz coordinate system, coordinate transformations, and the tools Quartz provides, you can greatly increase the capabilities of your application and simplify your usage of Quartz.

User Space and Device Space

Quartz operates in two coordinate spaces: user space and device space. **User space** is an idealized coordinate system that an application draws into. User space coordinates don't necessarily correspond to individual pixel values on any particular output device. User space is abstract; it can be transformed by translation, rotation, and scaling. The origin, orientation, and scale of user space coordinates are not fixed.

Device space is the coordinate system that corresponds to the individual pixels on a specific physical output device, such as a display or printer. The device space coordinate system does not change; for a given device, its origin, orientation, and scale are fixed. The actual origin of the device space coordinate system and its orientation depends on the configuration of the device, as does the distance between each unit. For raster output devices, such as a display or printer, 1 device space unit is 1 pixel value.

The size of 1 unit in user space is dependent on two factors: (1) the initial mapping of user space into device space for the destination device prior to any additional coordinate transformations and (2) any additional coordinate transformations that are applied by the Cocoa or Carbon toolkits plus your own transformations.

The term **default user space** refers to the initial coordinate system set up for a new graphics context. What that graphics context represents determines its initial setup and therefore how many device pixels 1 unit in user space represents. The size of 1 user space unit defaults to the best choice for the type of context. As of Tiger, for a bitmap context and a window context provided by the Cocoa or Carbon toolkits, 1 unit in user space, prior to any transformations, is 1 screen pixel. For a PDF context, the size of a default user space unit is 1/72 of an inch, a unit of measure called a **point**. For a printing context, 1 user space unit is a point, regardless of the resolution of the output device used for printing. This means that for a printing context corresponding to a 300-dpi raster printer, 1 user space unit is 1/72 of an inch, so 72 user space units equals 1 inch or 300 device pixels.

Note   The term *point* has its origins in the printing industry where historically the size of a printer point was approximately 1/72 of an inch. Quartz has adopted the same definition of a point as the PostScript and PDF imaging models with 1 point being exactly 1/72 of an inch.

Figure 5.1 shows the relationship between user space and device space for a typical 300-dpi raster printer. Note that in the figure, the orientation, scale, and origin of user space and device space are each different. The Quartz user space origin is in the lower-left corner of the sheet of paper, with x values increasing to the right and y values increasing up the page. The device space origin for the printer is at the top-left corner of the imageable area of the sheet of paper, with x values increasing to the right and y values increasing down the page. Before any additional transformations, each unit in Quartz user space for a printing context is 1/72 of an inch. Each unit in device space is 1/300 of an inch.

Figure 5.1 User space to device space mapping for a 300–dpi raster printer

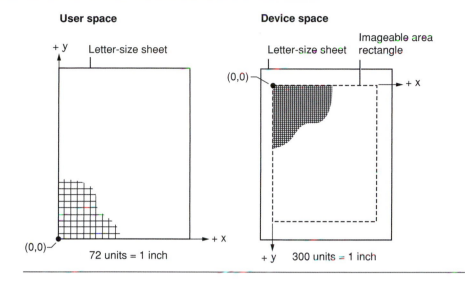

Because Quartz drawing calls take user space coordinates as parameters and the output device coordinates are in device space, Quartz must map all user space coordinates into device space coordinates as part of its rendering. By providing an abstract user space coordinate system and taking care of the mapping of those coordinates onto the output device, Quartz provides a device-independent coordinate system. The coordinate mapping performed by Quartz also provides the flexibility of additional user space transformations, such as the translation, rotation, and scaling of coordinates as seen in the examples in "Quartz 2D Drawing Basics" (page 15).

As of Tiger, the default coordinate system for a window-based context defines 1 unit to be 1 device pixel. However, as Apple moves to a high-resolution user interface, it is highly likely that the relationship between the default user space coordinate system for a window context and the device coordinate system will change. For example, for a 144-dpi display, it would make sense for the default user space coordinate system to have 1 unit equal to 2 device pixels in x and 2 device pixels in y. By providing a user space coordinate system for drawing that is distinct from the device pixels themselves, Quartz makes it straightforward to work in a coordinate system that is not tied to the resolution of the display. The topic of a high-resolution user interface on Mac OS X is an evolving area that is beyond the scope of this book. See "Using Quartz Debug to Explore Resolution Independence" (page 612) for more information about how you can begin preparing your application for a high-resolution user interface while developing with Tiger.

There are some situations where you may want to adjust your drawing coordinates so that they lie on pixel boundaries. See "Aligning User Space Coordinates on Pixel Boundaries (Tiger)" (page 139) for information about why you might want to do this and techniques for performing these adjustments.

Coordinate Transformations

Quartz uses an **affine transformation** to map user space coordinates into device space. Affine transformations preserve the parallelism of lines but not necessarily the length of lines or the angles between nonparallel lines. They can consist of combinations of the translation, scaling, and rotation transformations that are shown in "Transforming the Coordinate System" (page 23).

Transformations can be combined in a variety of ways. The two transformations in Figure 5.2 combine translation and scaling. The difference between the two lies in the order in which these transformations are applied prior to drawing the figure. On both the left and right sides of the figure, the black square is the result of drawing a square that is 72 units on a side. The yellow rectangle on the left side of the figure is the result of first translating by 72 units in x and 36 units in y, then scaling by 2.0 in both x and y, then again drawing a 72-unit square. The blue rectangle on the right side of the figure is the result of first scaling by 2.0 in both x and y, then translating by 72 units in x and 36 units in y, then drawing a 72-unit square. Clearly, the order in which the coordinate transformations are applied affects the final result.

Figure 5.2 Combining translation and scaling transformations

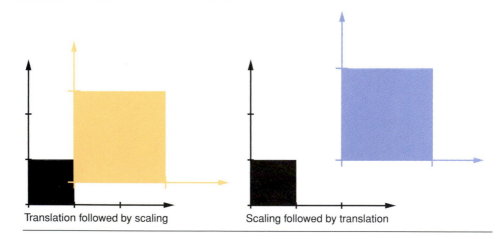

Translation followed by scaling   Scaling followed by translation

Figure 5.3 Combined rotation and scaling transformations

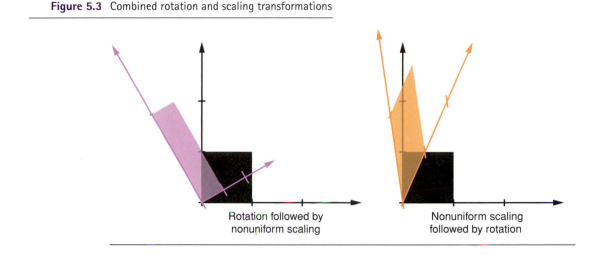

Rotation followed by
nonuniform scaling

Nonuniform scaling
followed by rotation

The two transformations in Figure 5.3 each combine a rotation and a nonuniform scaling. Again the result depends on the order in which the transformations are performed. On both the left and right sides of the figure, the black square is the result of drawing a square that is 72 units on a side. The purple rectangle on the left side of the figure is the result of first rotating by 30 degrees, then nonuniformly scaling the x coordinate by 0.5 and the y coordinate by 2.0, then drawing a 72-unit square. The yellow rectangle on the right side of the figure is the result of first nonuniformly scaling in the x coordinate by 0.5 and the y coordinate by 2.0, then rotating by 30 degrees, then drawing a 72-unit square.

As you can see from the right side of Figure 5.3, the result of performing a nonuniform scaling followed by a rotation is a **skew** (sometimes called a **shear**) to the coordinate axes—they are no longer at a 90-degree angle to one another. "Creating a Skewed Coordinate System" (page 98) describes a skewed coordinate system in more detail and shows an easier way to produce one.

Important Coordinate transformations are not **commutative**—the order in which they are applied affects the final result.

The Current Transformation Matrix

Quartz uses the **CGAffineTransform** data structure to represent an arbitrary Quartz coordinate transformation from one coordinate system to another. The CGAffineTransform that Quartz uses to transform Quartz user space coordinates to device space coordinates is called the **current transformation matrix**, or **CTM**.

The CTM transforms between the user space coordinates supplied to the Quartz path construction and drawing functions and the device space coordinates of the destination output device. The term *current* in the transformation matrix represents the transformation from the *current* user space to device space. At any point in time, you can apply an additional transformation to the current user space and derive a new user space and therefore a new CTM.

The Quartz coordinate transformation functions `CGContextScaleCTM`, `CGContext-TranslateCTM`, and `CGContextRotateCTM` each apply a transform to the CTM, resulting in a new, updated current transformation matrix CTM' that represents the combined results of the specified transform and the CTM at the time the new transform is applied.

The Mathematics of Affine Transforms

This section delves into the mathematics behind the affine transformations that Quartz uses to perform its coordinate transformations. This material is intended for the reader who is familiar with matrix multiplication and comfortable with more advanced mathematical concepts. Knowledge of this level of detail is *not* required for programming Quartz but is provided here for those readers who might benefit from a deeper mathematical understanding of these concepts.

The `CGAffineTransform` data structure represents an arbitrary Quartz coordinate transformation. This data structure consists of six floating-point values: a, b, c, d, tx, and ty. This set of numbers can represent any transformation from one Quartz coordinate system to another.

A general affine transformation from one two-dimensional coordinate system to another can be represented by the following equations:

$$x' = a * x + c * y + t_x$$
$$y' = b * x + d * y + t_y$$

These equations describe how x, y coordinates in an untransformed coordinate system map into x', y' coordinates of a transformed coordinate system. The coefficients a, b, c, d represent scaling and rotation aspects of the coordinate transformation, and the t_x, t_y values represent the translation aspects.

Matrix multiplication conveniently describes the transformation of points from one two-dimensional coordinate system to another. One way of expressing this matrix multiplication is

$$(x'\ y'\ 1) = (x\ y\ 1) \begin{pmatrix} a & b & 0 \\ c & d & 0 \\ t_x & t_y & 1 \end{pmatrix}$$

or

$$Point' = Point \times M_{transform}$$

One of the important properties of affine transformations is that a single matrix can represent a sequence of transformations. For example, two matrices M_1 and M_2, each representing a different transformation, can be concatenated (multiplied) to obtain a single matrix representing the combined result

$$M_{combined} = M_2 \times M_1 \qquad\qquad 5.1$$

where M_1 is the first transformation to apply and M_2 is the second transformation.

Technically, an affine transformation of two dimensions could be represented by a 3x2 matrix instead of a 3x3 matrix with a constant third column. It is a mathematical convenience to consider these transformations as 3x3 matrices and therefore obtain a straightforward way of combining two transformations.

Because the affine transformation matrix M always has the same third column, these transformations can be represented completely by the six other entries: a, b, c, d, t_x, and t_y. These six matrix elements are the data values stored in a Quartz CGAffineTransform data structure.

The translation, scaling, and rotation transformations can each be represented by a 3x3 transformation matrix.

A transformation that performs a translation of t_x in x and t_y in y is represented by the matrix

$$M_{translate} = \begin{pmatrix} 1 & 0 & 0 \\ 0 & 1 & 0 \\ t_x & t_y & 1 \end{pmatrix}$$

A transformation that performs a scaling of s_x in x and s_y in y is represented by the matrix

$$M_{scale} = \begin{pmatrix} s_x & 0 & 0 \\ 0 & s_y & 0 \\ 0 & 0 & 1 \end{pmatrix}$$

A transformation that performs a rotation about the origin by the angle θ is represented by the matrix

$$M_{rotate} = \begin{pmatrix} \cos\theta & \sin\theta & 0 \\ -\sin\theta & \cos\theta & 0 \\ 0 & 0 & 1 \end{pmatrix}$$

A concrete example can help us understand why the order in which transformations are applied is important. Consider combining a translation and scaling matrix to produce one that represents both. By using Equation 5.1 (page 89) you can calculate the matrix for each of the combined effects of the transformations performed in Figure 5.2 (page 86). First, calculate the matrix for the transformation from the left side of the figure, that is, the effect of first translating by 72 units in x and 36 units in y, then scaling by 2 in both x and y. This calculation is

$$M_{translate} = \begin{pmatrix} 1 & 0 & 0 \\ 0 & 1 & 0 \\ 72 & 36 & 1 \end{pmatrix}$$

$$M_{scale} = \begin{pmatrix} 2 & 0 & 0 \\ 0 & 2 & 0 \\ 0 & 0 & 1 \end{pmatrix}$$

$$M_{t,s} = M_{scale} \times M_{translate} = \begin{pmatrix} 2 & 0 & 0 \\ 0 & 2 & 0 \\ 0 & 0 & 1 \end{pmatrix} \begin{pmatrix} 1 & 0 & 0 \\ 0 & 1 & 0 \\ 72 & 36 & 1 \end{pmatrix}$$

$$M_{t,s} = \begin{pmatrix} 2 & 0 & 0 \\ 0 & 2 & 0 \\ 72 & 36 & 1 \end{pmatrix}$$

Now switch the order in which the transformations are applied, first scaling by 2 in both x and y, then translating by 72 units in x and 36 units in y. This calculation is

$$M_{translate} = \begin{pmatrix} 1 & 0 & 0 \\ 0 & 1 & 0 \\ 72 & 36 & 1 \end{pmatrix}$$

$$M_{scale} = \begin{pmatrix} 2 & 0 & 0 \\ 0 & 2 & 0 \\ 0 & 0 & 1 \end{pmatrix}$$

$$M_{s,t} = M_{translate} \times M_{scale} = \begin{pmatrix} 1 & 0 & 0 \\ 0 & 1 & 0 \\ 72 & 36 & 1 \end{pmatrix} \begin{pmatrix} 2 & 0 & 0 \\ 0 & 2 & 0 \\ 0 & 0 & 1 \end{pmatrix}$$

$$M_{s,t} = \begin{pmatrix} 2 & 0 & 0 \\ 0 & 2 & 0 \\ 144 & 72 & 1 \end{pmatrix}$$

The last result is a matrix that represents a translation by 144 units in x and 72 units in y and then scaling by 2 in both x and y. This makes sense. By first scaling the coordinate system so that a unit is twice as long in both x and y and then translating by 72 units in x and 36 units in y, the final translation is 2*72 units in x and 2*36 units in y, relative to the coordinate system prior to applying any transformations.

Saving and Restoring a Coordinate System

As you've seen from many examples, including Figure 5.2 (page 86) and Figure 5.3 (page 87), coordinate system transformations are cumulative. It's easy for you to apply a sequence of transformations to achieve a final result such as rotating and scaling a piece of graphics. But what about a situation where you want to transform some drawing and later want to do some additional drawing that doesn't require those transformations?

One way to undo such transformations is to apply additional transformations that reverse the effects of those already applied. To see what this looks like, examine the code in Listing 5.1 (page 92), which draws the left side of Figure 5.3, the rectangle that was rotated then scaled.

Listing 5.1 Drawing a rotated and scaled rectangle

```
CGRect ourRect = { {0., 0.} , {72., 72.}};
// Draw the unrotated coordinate axes.
drawCoordinateAxes(context);
// Fill the unscaled rectangle.
CGContextFillRect(context, ourRect);

// Rotate the coordinate system by 30 degrees.
CGContextRotateCTM(context, M_PI/6);
// Scale the coordinate system by 0.5 in x and 2.0 in y.
CGContextScaleCTM(context, 0.5, 2.0);
CGContextSetRGBStrokeColor(context, 0.69, 0.486, 0.722, 1.0);
CGContextSetRGBFillColor(context, 0.69, 0.486, 0.722, 0.7);
// Draw the coordinate axes after the transformations.
drawCoordinateAxes(context);
// Fill the rotated and scaled rectangle.
CGContextFillRect(context, ourRect);
```

There should not be anything new to you in Listing 5.1 other than the call to drawCoordinateAxes, a routine that draws the coordinate axes. (Writing this routine is left as an exercise for the reader.) After drawing the axes, the code fills a 72-unit by 72-unit rectangle, then rotates the coordinate system by 30 degrees and scales by 0.5 in x and 2.0 in y. The fill and stroke colors are changed so that the transformed drawing stands out compared to the untransformed drawing. Finally, the code draws the transformed coordinate axes followed by a fill of the 72-unit by 72-unit rectangle.

Attempting to draw the right side of Figure 5.3 (page 87) after the left side is drawn is tricky because the coordinate system is already rotated and scaled. You can get back to the original coordinate system by explicitly undoing the effects of the previous coordinate transformations. This requires first calling CGContextScaleCTM with the values 2.0 in x and 0.5 in y to undo the effects of the previous scaling, then calling CGContextRotateCTM with a value -M_PI/6 to rotate to the previous orientation. At that point, you can draw into the original coordinate system with unscaled and unrotated axes.

The need to transform coordinates and reset back to untransformed coordinates is so great that Quartz provides two useful functions that do this and more. The Quartz function CGContextSaveGState takes a snapshot of the Quartz CTM and other drawing parameters such as the fill and stroke colors and the clipping area. The Quartz function CGContextRestoreGState returns the context to the settings that were in effect at the time CGContextSaveGState was called. Listing 5.2 is the updated code for drawing both the left and right sides of Figure 5.3.

Listing 5.2 Using CGContextSaveGState/CGContextRestoreGState

```
CGRect ourRect = { {0., 0.} , {72., 72.}};
// Draw the coordinate axes with no rotation.
drawCoordinateAxes(context);
// ***** Rectangle 1 *****
CGContextFillRect(context, ourRect);
// Make a snapshot of the CTM and other drawing parameters.
CGContextSaveGState(context);
    // Rotate the coordinate system by 30 degrees.
    CGContextRotateCTM(context, M_PI/6);
    // Scale in x by 0.5 and in y by 2.0.
    CGContextScaleCTM(context, 0.5, 2.0);
    CGContextSetRGBStrokeColor(context, 0.69, 0.486, 0.722, 1.0);
    CGContextSetRGBFillColor(context, 0.69, 0.486, 0.722, 0.7);
    // Draw the coordinate axes after the transformations.
    drawCoordinateAxes(context);
    // ***** Rectangle 2 *****
    CGContextFillRect(context, ourRect);
// Restore the snapshot of the CTM and other drawing parameters.
CGContextRestoreGState(context);
// Now the coordinate system is that before any transformations
// were applied and the fill and stroke colors are also restored.

// Translate to the right for the right side of the drawing.
CGContextTranslateCTM(context, 288., 0.);
drawCoordinateAxes(context);
// ***** Rectangle 3 *****
CGContextFillRect(context, ourRect);
CGContextSaveGState(context);
    // This time perform the scale before rotating.
    CGContextScaleCTM(context, 0.5, 2.0);
    CGContextRotateCTM(context, M_PI/6);
    CGContextSetRGBStrokeColor(context, 0.965, 0.584, 0.059, 1.0);
    CGContextSetRGBFillColor(context, 0.965, 0.584, 0.059, 0.7);
    drawCoordinateAxes(context);
    // ***** Rectangle 4 *****
    CGContextFillRect(context, ourRect);
CGContextRestoreGState(context);
```

The first portion of the code is similar to that in Listing 5.1 except that immediately after drawing Rectangle 1, the code calls CGContextSaveGState. This Quartz function takes a snapshot of the CTM and the stroke and fill painting colors so that they can be restored later. After calling CGContextSaveGState, the code transforms the coordinates and draws the coordinate axes and the second rectangle into the transformed coordinate system. After drawing Rectangle 2, the code calls CGContextRestoreGState, which restores to the snapshot taken by the previous call to CGContextSaveGState. The result is that the CTM (and therefore the coordinate system) returns to its state before the rotation and scaling were applied for drawing Rectangle 2.

The effects of CGContextRestoreGState are apparent when drawing the coordinate axes and Rectangle 3 for the right side of Figure 5.3 (page 87). The axes and Rectangle 3 are not scaled or rotated and are painted in black. Had the code not restored the CTM and drawing colors by using CGContextSaveGState and CGContextRestoreGState, the coordinate axes and Rectangle 3 would have been drawn in the same coordinate system and with the same colors as Rectangle 2 and the axes drawn prior to Rectangle 2.

You might have wondered earlier when you integrated drawing code into applications using the Cocoa and Carbon frameworks why, if coordinate transformations are cumulative, the transformations performed in the drawing routines are not in effect the next time those routines are called to redraw the window/view content when the window size is changed. The reason is that the frameworks use CGContextSaveGState and CGContextRestoreGState to isolate the changes your drawing code makes to the context so that those changes don't affect drawing outside the scope of your drawing code. For example, prior to calling the drawRect: method, Cocoa calls CGContextSaveGState and after the drawRect: method returns, Cocoa calls CGContextRestoreGState to restore the CTM and other drawing parameters that were in effect previously. This effectively isolates the system from changes that you make to the Quartz graphics context in your drawing code.

The Quartz functions CGContextSaveGState and CGContextRestoreGState must be used in pairs; you must call CGContextSaveGState before calling CGContextRestoreGState. You'll learn more detail about these functions in "Color, Alpha Transparency, and the Quartz Graphics State" (page 147), but for now this rule is sufficient.

Affine Transform Convenience Functions

Affine transforms represent arbitrary Quartz coordinate transformations in a compact way. The CGAffineTransform data structure contains all the data needed to describe any affine coordinate transformation. This is especially useful for complex transformations. After you construct a CGAffineTransform, you can apply it with a single call to the Quartz function CGContextConcatCTM, accomplishing what would otherwise take several calls to the rotate, translate, and scale CTM functions. Further, you can repeatedly apply a CGAffineTransform.

You'll see how to accomplish this with a simple example that draws an ellipse. The easiest way to draw an ellipse available in all versions of Quartz is to create a path that is a circle but, prior to creating the path, scale the coordinate system nonuniformly in x and y. The appropriate scale factors depend on the ratio of the major and minor axes of the desired ellipse.

The code in Listing 5.3 uses a CGAffineTransform to draw an ellipse. It first creates a CGAffineTransform that corresponds to a nonuniform scaling transformation of 2.0 in x and 1.0 in y by calling the Quartz function CGAffineTransformMakeScale with the appropriate scaling factors. The code then passes the CGAffineTransform to the function CGContextConcatCTM to apply the transformation to the context. The result in this simple code example is exactly the same as if the call to the function CGContextConcatCTM is replaced with a call to the function CGContextScaleCTM with the scale factors 2.0 in x and 1.0 in y. The output from the simple example is shown in Figure 5.4.

Listing 5.3 Code that draws a simple ellipse

```
CGAffineTransform theTransform = CGAffineTransformMakeScale(2, 1);
CGContextTranslateCTM(context, 100., 100.);
CGContextConcatCTM(context, theTransform);
CGContextBeginPath(context);
CGContextAddArc(context, 0., 0., 45., 0., 2*M_PI, 0);
CGContextDrawPath(context, kCGPathFill);
```

This example shows how to use a CGAffineTransform, but the lines of code needed to perform the transformation can easily be replaced by a single call to the function CGContextScaleCTM. A more interesting example is to repeatedly apply a complex transformation such as that used to create Figure 5.5. The figure is a series of rotated ellipses painted to achieve a blend effect.

Figure 5.4 A simple ellipse

Figure 5.5 Rotated ellipses

To paint one of the rotated ellipses requires code to create an elliptical path that is rotated properly. This means that in addition to scaling nonuniformly to obtain an elliptically shaped path from a circular arc, a rotation is also needed prior to creating the path. Should the scaling operation occur before the rotation or the rotation before the scaling? Recall that Figure 5.3 (page 87) shows the results of applying these two transformations in the different orders. Scaling before rotating produces a skewed coordinate system, as seen in the right side of the figure, and this is not the desired result. To obtain the properly rotated elliptical shape for this scenario, the rotation must precede the scaling.

Now imagine the steps needed to draw a sequence of rotated ellipses. Listing 5.4 rotates and scales the coordinate system prior to creating and painting the path. Because the drawing consists of the same transformed shape drawn multiple times, the same set of coordinate transformations must be applied repeatedly. There is an easier, more efficient way to draw that same shape over and over.

Listing 5.4 Pseudocode for the blended series of rotated ellipses

```
Step 1: Translate to center of first ellipse.
Step 2: Rotate by 45 degrees.
Step 3: Scale by 1, 2.
Step 4: Create path of "circular" arc with center at 0,0.
Step 5: Set the painting color.
Step 6: Paint the path.
Step 7: Return to original coordinate system.
Step 8: Translate to the right for the next ellipse.
Repeat steps 2-8 for the next ellipse.
```

Listing 5.5 contains a doRotatedEllipses routine that draws the blended series of ellipses shown in Figure 5.5. The code is similar to that described in Listing 5.4 but instead uses a CGAffineTransform to make a coordinate transformation that can be applied multiple times. The sequence of transformations to capture with a CGAffineTransform is a rotation followed by scaling. The call to CG-AffineTransformMakeRotation returns a new CGAffineTransform that corresponds to a rotation without any scaling or translation. The function CGAffineTransformScale takes an existing affine transform and x,y scale factors and creates a transform that incorporates the additional scaling. After these two calls, the variable theTransform is an affine transform that corresponds to a rotation followed by scaling. The code applies the affine transform to the current CTM in the context with the Quartz function CGContextConcatCTM. This call is the equivalent of performing the sequence of transformations used to build up the CGAffineTransform.

Listing 5.5 Constructing and applying an affine transform

```
void doRotatedEllipses(CGContextRef context)
{
  int i, totreps = 144;
  float  tint = 1., tintIncrement = 1./totreps;
  // Create a new transform consisting of a 45-degree rotation.
  CGAffineTransform theTransform = CGAffineTransformMakeRotation(M_PI/4);
  // Apply a scale to the transform just created.
  theTransform = CGAffineTransformScale(theTransform, 1, 2);
  // Place the first ellipse at a good location.
  CGContextTranslateCTM(context, 100., 100.);

  for(i=0 ; i < totreps ; i++){
    // Make a snapshot of the coordinate system.
    CGContextSaveGState(context);
      // Set up the coordinate system for the rotated ellipse.
      CGContextConcatCTM(context, theTransform);
      CGContextBeginPath(context);
      CGContextAddArc(context, 0., 0., 45., 0., 2*M_PI, 0);
      // Set the fill color for this instance of the ellipse.
      CGContextSetRGBFillColor(context, tint, 0., 0., 1.);
      CGContextDrawPath(context, kCGPathFill);
    // Restore the coordinate system to that of the snapshot.
    CGContextRestoreGState(context);
    // Compute the next tint color.
    tint -= tintIncrement;
    // Move over by 1 unit in x for the next ellipse.
    CGContextTranslateCTM(context, 1., 0.);
  }
}
```

This example draws a simple blend by repeatedly drawing a shape with some small distance between it and the next shape. In this case the small distance is 1 unit. Choosing the best spacing between the blend elements and the best way to adjust the tint color between shapes requires knowledge of the resolution and characteristics of the destination output device. Quartz offers a better way to draw blends (also called **shadings**), which is discussed in "Drawing with Shadings (Jaguar)" (page 531).

Creating a Skewed Coordinate System

Nonuniform scaling of a coordinate system, followed by a rotation, produces a skew or shear to the coordinate axes, as seen earlier on the right side of Figure 5.3 (page 87). This approach to shearing produces a coordinate system where the axes are not scaled uniformly. This can be corrected by applying additional transformations; however, if the desired result is a coordinate system where the axes are skewed but uniformly scaled, it is easier to apply a single coordinate transformation that produces this result.

Figure 5.6 shows the effects of applying a skew or shear transformation to the default Quartz coordinate system, producing a coordinate system where the x axis is rotated toward the y axis by an angle α relative to the untransformed x axis and the y axis is rotated toward the x axis by an angle β relative to the untransformed y axis. At first glance you might think that the figure is incorrect, because the adjacent sides of the transformed rectangle are not orthogonal to one another and the tick marks on the axes are at an oblique angle to the axes themselves. However, the figure is correct. As with any affine transform, lines that are parallel remain parallel but a skew transformation changes the angle between lines that are not parallel.

One typical use of a skew transformation is to create oblique text, where the β angle is a positive value and the α angle is zero.

A skew transformation where the x axis is skewed by the angle α and the y axis is skewed by the angle β can be represented by the matrix

$$M_{skew} = \begin{pmatrix} 1 & tan\,\alpha & 0 \\ tan\,\beta & 1 & 0 \\ 0 & 0 & 1 \end{pmatrix}$$

Quartz does not have a function specific to applying a skew transformation, but it does provide the function CGContextConcatCTM that allows you to apply an arbitrary affine transform to the CTM. The function CGAffineTransformMake makes it easy to create an arbitrary CGAffineTransform for use with CGContext-

Figure 5.6 A skew transformation

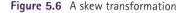

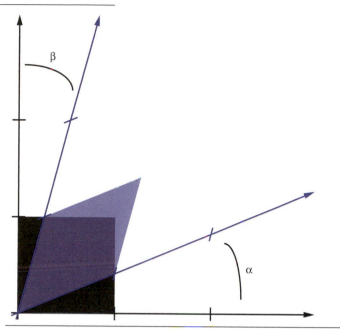

ConcatCTM. The arguments to the function CGAffineTransformMake are the a, b, c, d, tx, and ty values that make up a CGAffineTransform. In the case of a pure skew transformation, the necessary values are a = 1, b = tan(α), c = tan(β), d = 1, and tx = ty = 0.

Listing 5.6 draws the graphic in Figure 5.6 that represents a skew transformation. The code uses a user-supplied routine drawCoordinateAxes to first draw the coordinate axes in the untransformed coordinate system. It then draws a 72-unit rectangle at the Quartz origin. Next the code sets up to draw the skewed coordinate axes and rectangle by creating an affine transform that skews the x axis by the angle α and the y axis by the angle β. It applies that transform to the Quartz coordinate system using the function CGContextConcatCTM. Now it is ready to draw the coordinate axes and rectangle in the skewed coordinate system.

The code next sets the fill and stroke color to a dark blue so that the drawing of the coordinate axes into the transformed coordinate system are a different color than the untransformed drawing. After drawing the coordinate axes, the code changes the fill color to the same shade of blue but with an alpha transparency value of 0.70, then draws the rectangle. This paints a partially transparent rectangle, allowing the untransformed drawing underneath the rectangle to show through.

Listing 5.6   Using a skew transformation to draw Figure 5.6

```
void drawSkewedCoordinateSystem(CGContextRef context)
{
  // alpha is 22.5 degrees and beta is 15 degrees.
  float alpha = M_PI/8, beta = M_PI/12;
  CGAffineTransform skew;
  // Create a rectangle that is 72 units on a side
  // with its origin at (0,0).
  CGRect r = CGRectMake(0, 0, 72, 72);

  CGContextTranslateCTM(context, 144, 144);
  // Draw the coordinate axes untransformed.
  drawCoordinateAxes(context);
  // Fill the rectangle.
  CGContextFillRect(context, r);

  // Create an affine transform that skews the coordinate system,
  // skewing the x axis by alpha radians and the y axis by beta radians.
  skew = CGAffineTransformMake(1, tan(alpha), tan(beta), 1, 0, 0);
  // Apply that transform to the context coordinate system.
  CGContextConcatCTM(context, skew);

  // Set the fill and stroke color to a dark blue.
  CGContextSetRGBStrokeColor(context, 0.11, 0.208, 0.451, 1.0);
  CGContextSetRGBFillColor(context, 0.11, 0.208, 0.451, 1.0);

  // Draw the coordinate axes again, now transformed.
  drawCoordinateAxes(context);
  // Set the fill color again but with a partially transparent alpha.
  CGContextSetRGBFillColor(context, 0.11, 0.208, 0.451, 0.7);
  // Fill the rectangle in the transformed coordinate system.
  CGContextFillRect(context, r);
}
```

Summary

This chapter provides in-depth information about the Quartz coordinate system, coordinate transformations, and the ways that you can use them with Quartz. Applications draw in the user space coordinate system. Quartz transforms user space coordinates into device space coordinates by applying the current transformation matrix (CTM), which is an affine transformation. The user space coordinate system is easily modified by applying additional affine transformations using the Quartz functions `CGContextScaleCTM`, `CGContextTranslateCTM`, `CGContext-RotateCTM`, and `CGContextConcatCTM`. The functions `CGContextSaveGState` and `CGContextRestoreGState` make it easy to save the CTM and other drawing parameters prior to performing coordinate transformations and to then later return to the saved state that existed prior to any transformations. A `CGAffineTransform` data structure provides a convenient way to capture a transformation or a sequence of transformations for repeated use.

With these tools and a greater understanding of the Quartz coordinate system in hand, you're ready to create more complex graphics. The next chapter looks at the details of path construction and the ways Quartz can fill and stroke paths.

See Also

The Quartz coordinate system and its properties are those of the PostScript and PDF imaging models. These are described in the books

- *PostScript Language Reference*, 3rd edition, Adobe Systems Inc.:

  http://partners.adobe.com/public/developer/en/ps/PLRM.pdf

- *PDF Reference: Version 1.6*, 5th edition, Adobe Systems, Inc., and other versions of the PDF specification are available:

  http://partners.adobe.com/public/developer/pdf/index_reference.html

Other good references for discussion of coordinate systems and transformations in 2D computer graphics are

- *Principles of Interactive Computer Graphics*, William M. Newman and Robert F. Sproull, McGraw-Hill, 2nd edition, 1979.

- *Fundamentals of Interactive Computer Graphics*, James D. Foley and Andries Van Dam, Addison-Wesley, 1982.

- *Mathematical Elements for Computer Graphics*, David F. Rogers and J. Alan Adams, McGraw-Hill, 2nd edition, 1989.

The header files that contain the structures and functions used in this chapter are as follows:

- `CGAffineTransform.h` contains the structures and prototypes for the `CGAffineTransform` convenience functions.

- `CGContext.h` contains the prototypes for the CTM transformation routines `CGContextScaleCTM`, `CGContextTranslateCTM`, `CGContextRotateCTM`, and `CGContextConcatCTM`, as well as the functions `CGContextSaveGState` and `CGContextRestoreGState`.

The relevant reference documentation from the ADC Reference Library is

- *CGContext Reference*
- *CGAffineTransform Reference*

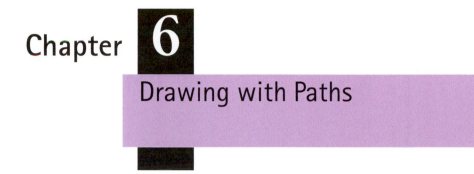

Chapter 6

Drawing with Paths

All Quartz drawing falls into of one of three fundamental categories: line art (graphics that consist of paths that are filled, stroked, or both), sampled images, and text. Understanding how to draw with paths and the way Quartz paints them is a key part of understanding the Quartz imaging model.

Quartz paths are mathematical descriptions. A path can consist of straight-line segments and Bézier curve segments— both quadratic and cubic. Primitive path construction functions add these types of segments to create a path. In addition, Quartz has a number of convenience functions to add path segments for the most common shapes. Paths are constructed separately from painting them. You can fill, stroke, or fill and stroke them. There are a variety of ways to control how Quartz fills and strokes paths; the order of these operations can affect the outcome. In addition to using a path to fill or stroke a shape, paths can define a clipping (or masking) area. In Jaguar and later versions, Quartz allows reusable path objects, making it simpler and more efficient to repeatedly paint a particular shape.

This chapter describes path properties and shows how to use Quartz functions to create, stroke, and fill paths. You'll also see how to perform clipping using paths, work with path objects, and use a variety of utility functions. The chapter also provides a discussion of anti-aliasing and its effect on Quartz rendering.

Properties of Paths

A path consists of a sequence of straight-line and curved segments that are described mathematically. The segments of a path may all be connected or some or all of them may be disconnected. A pair of segments is connected if the segments are defined consecutively and the starting point of the second segment begins at the ending point of the previous segment. The path can represent any shape; the segments making up a path can intersect or cross in arbitrary ways.

A path consists of one or more subpaths. A **subpath** is a sequence of connected segments in the same path. The point where two connected segments in a subpath are connected is a **join**. Other points where path segments in a subpath intersect or cross over one another have no special geometric meaning. A given subpath may be **closed**; that is, the endpoint of a subpath is connected to the starting point of the subpath. If the endpoint of a subpath is not explicitly connected to the starting point of the subpath, the subpath is **open**. The number of segments in a path or subpath has no limit; it can be arbitrarily complex. Figure 6.1 illustrates a number of different path geometries.

Path elements have a direction associated with them. This is important when determining what area is inside of a closed path, as you'll see in "Filling Paths" (page 126). The **direction** of a path element is from the starting point toward the ending point of the path element. In the simple case of a straight-line segment from a starting point to an endpoint, the direction of the path is toward the endpoint.

The Quartz **current point** is the trailing endpoint of the most currently added path segment. Most Quartz functions that add segments to a path begin those segments from the most recently established current point.

You supply user space coordinates to the functions to create a path in the context. Quartz transforms these coordinates into device space coordinates as it adds the path segments to the path.

Figure 6.1 Examples of Quartz paths

Open paths   Closed paths

Multiple subpaths
(open and closed)

Important Changes to the current transformation matrix (CTM) do not affect the coordinates of path segments already added to the current path.

Path Construction Primitives

All paths in Quartz can be constructed using one or more of the following five basic path construction primitive functions, regardless of the complexity of the path.

- CGContextMoveToPoint begins a new subpath in the current path.

- CGContextAddLineToPoint adds a straight line segment to the current path.

- CGContextAddCurveToPoint adds a cubic Bézier curve segment to the current path.

- CGContextAddQuadCurveToPoint adds a quadratic Bézier curve segment to the current path.

- CGContextClosePath ends the current path.

Quartz builds on these five primitives by providing convenience functions to create paths or path segments that correspond to the most common shapes, such as rectangles, arcs, and ellipses. "Path Construction Convenience Functions" (page 111) discusses these in detail.

The first step when constructing a new path, whether constructing it with the path primitive functions or convenience functions, is to discard any existing path with the function CGContextBeginPath. When using the path construction primitives, the next step is to call CGContextMoveToPoint to establish the initial point of the first subpath; this also establishes a current point. You then add segments to the path using the other path construction primitives, as you'll see in a moment. At any time during path construction you can begin a new subpath in the current path that you are constructing by calling CGContextMoveToPoint.

The function CGContextAddLineToPoint adds a straight-line segment from the current point to a new point in user space. The endpoint of this line segment becomes the new current point. Recall that Listing 2.4 (page 26) in "Constructing Quartz Paths" (page 25) constructs a rectangular path using CGContextAddLineToPoint.

The remainder of this section describes the other three path construction primitives—those for constructing cubic and quadratic Bézier curves and for closing subpaths.

Cubic Bézier Curves

Cubic Bézier curves are powerful drawing primitives that allow complex curves to be represented in a relatively compact fashion. These curves are defined by two endpoints together with two additional control points, as shown in Figure 6.2. The cubic Bézier curve in the figure is drawn as a solid line. The curve endpoints are represented by the points P0 and P1. The two control points are represented by C1 and C2. The dotted line segment P0-C1 is tangent to the curve at the endpoint P0. The dotted line segment P1-C2 is tangent to the curve at the endpoint P1.

Points $P(t)$ along a cubic Bézier curve are described by varying the parameter t between 0 and 1 in the equation

$$P(t) = (1 - t)^3 P_0 + 3t(1 - t)^2 C_1 + 3t^2(1 - t) C_2 + t^3 P_1$$

The point at t = 0 is the starting point P0 of the curve and the point at t = 1 is the endpoint of the curve, P1. Bézier curves have the useful property that the quadrilateral that encloses the two endpoints and the two control points contains the

Figure 6.2 Simple cubic Bézier curve

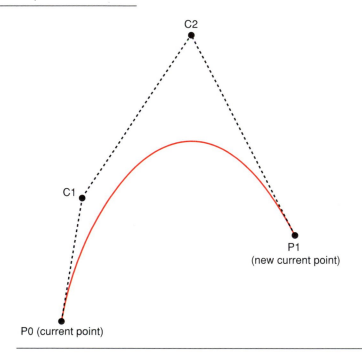

Bézier curve those points define. This means that the smallest rectangle (that is, the bounding rectangle) that encloses the curve endpoints and control points also contains all the points on the curve.

Figure 6.3 shows some of the possible geometries of cubic Bézier curves. As the figure shows, a single cubic Bézier curve can represent a variety of complex curves, including curves that cross over themselves once.

The function `CGContextAddCurveToPoint` adds a cubic Bézier curve segment to a Quartz path. This function takes the following parameters:

- `context`, the graphics context to add the path to.
- `cp1x,cp1y`, the x and y coordinates for the first control point.
- `cp2x,cp2y`, the x and y coordinates for the second control point.
- `p1x,p1y`, the x and y coordinates for the endpoint of the curve.

The starting point of the curve is the current point at the time you call `CGContextAddCurveToPoint`.

Listing 6.1 is a simple example of how to draw with cubic Bézier curves. That code produces the egg-shaped curve shown in Figure 6.4. The doEgg routine in Listing 6.1 uses the points p0 and p1 as the endpoints for the curve path segments and the points c1 and c2 as the control points for the first Bézier segment added to the path. The egg is symmetrically centered on the vertical line between the starting point p0 and the endpoint p1. Because the x coordinate of the endpoints

Figure 6.3 Example cubic Bézier geometries

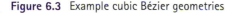

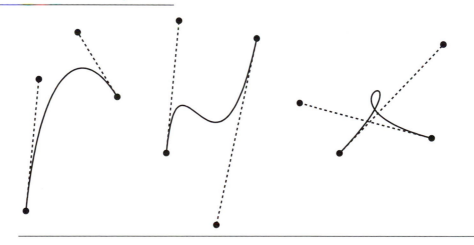

Figure 6.4 The cubic Bézier curves produced by the code in Listing 6.1

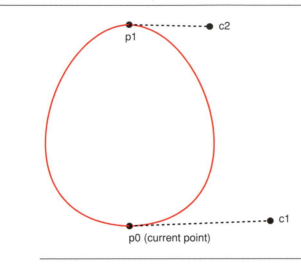

is 0, the code can simply negate the x values of the control points in order to add the second Bézier segment, that for the left side of the egg.

Listing 6.1 Code that produces an egg shape

```
void doEgg(CGContextRef context)
{
  CGPoint p0 = {0., 0.}, p1 = {0., 200.};
  CGPoint c1 = {140., 5.}, c2 = {80., 198.};
  CGContextTranslateCTM(context, 100., 5.);
  CGContextBeginPath(context);

  CGContextMoveToPoint(context, p0.x, p0.y);
  // Create the Bézier path segment for the right side of the egg.
  CGContextAddCurveToPoint(context, c1.x, c1.y, c2.x, c2.y, p1.x, p1.y);
  // Create the Bézier path segment for the left side of the egg.
  CGContextAddCurveToPoint(context, -c2.x, c2.y, -c1.x, c1.y,
                p0.x, p0.y);
  CGContextClosePath(context);
  CGContextSetLineWidth(context, 2);
  CGContextDrawPath(context, kCGPathStroke);
}
```

Using x = 0 for each endpoint illustrates how these curves behave. Start by examining the points defining the cubic Bézier segment corresponding to the right side of the egg. The starting point is (0,0) and the first control point is x = 140, y = 5. The second control point is x = 80, y = 198 and the endpoint is at x = 0, y = 200. Figure 6.4 shows that the lower portion of the egg bulges out further than the upper portion of the egg. This is because the x coordinate of the first control point c1 is larger than the x coordinate of the second control point c2. In this example, the further the control point is in x from the endpoint, the "faster" the curve moves in x away from the endpoint. Recall that the dotted line between the control point and its respective endpoint is tangent to the curve at the endpoint. The closer the y value of each control point is to the y value of its respective endpoint, the flatter the curve is at the point it meets the endpoint.

Quadratic Bézier Curves

A quadratic Bézier curve is another curve drawing primitive available in Quartz. These curves are defined by two endpoints and a single control point, as shown in Figure 6.5. The quadratic Bézier curve itself is drawn as a solid line. The curve endpoints are represented by the points P0 and P1. The control point is represented by the point C. The dotted line segment P0-C is tangent to the curve at the endpoint P0. The dotted line segment P1-C is tangent to the curve at the endpoint P1.

Points $P(t)$ along a quadratic Bézier curve are described by varying the parameter t between 0 and 1 in the equation

$$P(t) = (1 - t)^2 P_0 + 2t(1 - t)C + t^2 P_1$$

The point at t = 0 is the initial point P0 of the curve and the point at t = 1 is the endpoint of the curve, P1. Quadratic Bézier curves have the property that the triangle composed of the two endpoints and the control point encloses the curve those points define. This means that the smallest rectangle (that is, the bounding rectangle) that encloses the curve endpoints and the control point also contains all the points on the curve.

Figure 6.6 shows some of the possible geometries of quadratic Bézier curves. The range of curves that can be represented by a quadratic Bézier is far smaller than what can be represented by a cubic Bézier. The fact that the curve is tangent to the lines connecting each endpoint to the single control point severely restricts the possible geometry. A single quadratic Bézier curve segment cannot cross over itself.

Figure 6.5 A simple quadratic Bézier curve

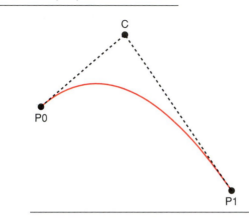

Figure 6.6 Example quadratic Bézier geometries

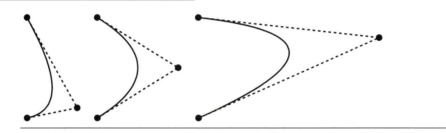

The function `CGContextAddQuadCurveToPoint` adds a quadratic Bézier curve segment to a Quartz path. This function takes the following parameters:

- `context`, the graphics context to add the path to.
- `cpx,cpy`, the x and y coordinates for the control point.
- `p1x,p1y`, the x and y coordinates for the endpoint of the curve.

The starting point of the curve is the current point at the time you call `CGContextAddQuadCurveToPoint`.

Closing Subpaths

Quartz subpaths are either open or closed. A closed subpath has its initial point connected to the last point on the subpath. The function `CGContextClosePath` connects the last point on the subpath with the initial point on the subpath, thereby closing the subpath. If you want to close a subpath, you must call this function even if the initial point and the last point are coincident. If the two points are not coincident, calling CGContextClosePath adds a line segment to the path from the last point on the subpath to the initial point of the subpath.

Path Construction Convenience Functions

While the basic five path construction primitives—CGContextMoveToPoint, CGContextAddLineToPoint, CGContextAddCurveToPoint, CGContextAddQuadCurveToPoint, and CGContextClosePath—allow the construction of any Quartz path, Quartz provides a number of convenience functions to create paths for some of the more common shapes.

The function CGContextAddRect adds a closed rectangular subpath to the current path. The line segments of the rectangle are added in counterclockwise fashion starting with the lower-left corner of the rectangle. Any existing current point is ignored during the creation of this subpath; after its execution the new current point is the origin of the rectangle. You can add multiple rectangles to the current path with one call to the function CGContextAddRects. After this call, the current point is the origin of the last rectangle in the array of rectangles passed to CGContextAddRects.

To add a number of connected line segments at once, you can use the function CGContextAddLines. You supply an array of points and Quartz constructs a new subpath using these points. The first point in the array is the initial point on the subpath. The first line segment is constructed from the initial point to the second point in the array. Each subsequent line segment is constructed from the trailing endpoint of the previous line segment to the next point in the array. The final result is a series of connected line segments. When CGContextAddLines returns, the current point is the last point in the array of points passed to the function. The resulting subpath is open; you must call CGContextClosePath if you want to close it.

You can use the CGContextAddArc function to add arcs and circles to the current path. With appropriate scaling transformations you can use this function to construct ellipses (sometimes called ovals) to a path; see the examples in "Affine Transform Convenience Functions" (page 94). The function CGContextAddArc takes the following parameters:

- context, the graphics context to add the path to.
- centerX,centerY, the x and y coordinates for the center of the circle that defines the arc.
- radius, the radius of the circle that defines the arc.

- startAngle, the starting angle for the arc.

- endAngle, the ending angle for the arc.

- clockwise, the direction along the circle to create the arc. If true, the direction of the arc is clockwise; otherwise it is counterclockwise.

All angles in Quartz are specified in radians. The zero angle is along the positive x axis in Quartz coordinates and positive angles increase counterclockwise.

The convenience function CGContextAddArc adds an arc segment to the current path. The starting point of the arc is defined by the values of centerX, centerY, radius, and startAngle. The ending point of the arc is defined by centerX, centerY, radius, and endAngle. The direction of the arc depends on the value of the clockwise parameter passed to the function. After this function returns, the current point of the current path is the ending point of the arc segment. The resulting subpath is open; you must call CGContextClosePath if you want to close it.

If a current point exists in the path prior to calling CGContextAddArc, Quartz first adds to the path a line segment from the current point to the starting point of the arc, then adds the arc segment. If there is no current point defined in the current path, this function adds only the arc segment to the path.

Figure 6.7 illustrates the behavior of CGContextAddArc. Each of the arc segments in the figure appears as a solid line. For each arc, the point p1 is the starting point of the arc and is at distance r from the center point and at angle θ_1 relative to the x axis. The point p2 is the ending point of the arc and is at distance r from the center point and at angle θ_2 relative to the x axis. The left portion of the figure is

Figure 6.7 Using the CGContextAddArc function

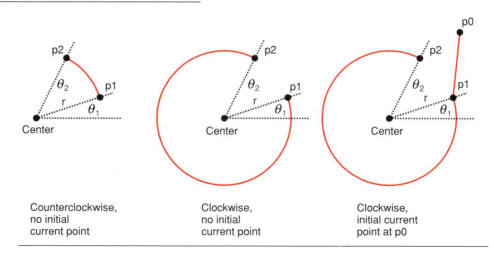

a counterclockwise arc segment drawn from the point p1 to the point p2. Prior to calling CGContextAddArc, the path is empty. The center portion of the figure is the same arc but drawn with the clockwise parameter set to true. The arc again starts at point p1 and ends at point p2, but the arc segment is clockwise. Again, prior to calling CGContextAddArc the path is empty. The rightmost portion of the figure is the same call to CGContextAddArc, but prior to the call, the code uses CGContextMoveToPoint to establish a current point at the point p0. This produces the same result as the center figure but, prior to adding the arc segment starting at point p1, Quartz adds a line segment to the path from p0 to the point p1.

The function CGContextAddArcToPoint provides another way to add an arc segment to a path. The arc segment created by CGContextAddArcToPoint is defined by a radius and two tangent lines. Figure 6.8 shows the geometry involved; the arc segment added by CGContextAddArcToPoint is shown as a solid line. The function CGContextAddArcToPoint takes five parameters—the x and y coordinates of a point p1, the x and y coordinates of a second point p2, and the radius of the arc r. The starting point for constructing the segment added to the path is the point p0, the current point prior to calling CGContextAddArcToPoint. The line from the point p0 to the point p1 and the line from the point p1 to p2 are the two lines tangent to the arc. These lines plus the arc radius r define the arc.

The starting point for the arc segment is the point p1t; at that point the arc is tangent to the line from p0 to p1. The ending point of the arc is the point p2t— the point where the arc is tangent to the line from p1 to p2. If the point p0 is not the same point as the tangent point p1t, the function CGContextAddArcToPoint first adds a line segment to the current path to connect the initial current point to the starting point of the arc segment, then adds the arc segment to the path.

Figure 6.8 The geometry of CGContextAddArcToPoint

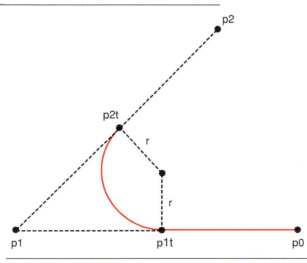

Figure 6.9 Drawing a rounded rectangle

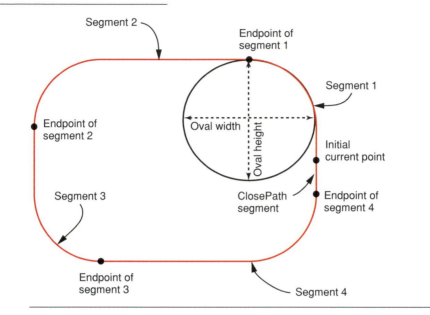

After Quartz adds the arc segment to the path, the new current point is the second tangent point p2t.

If you are a QuickDraw programmer who is familiar with the rounded rectangle shape, you might be wondering how to draw one using Quartz. You can use the function `CGContextAddArcToPoint` to construct the geometry of a rounded rectangle by choosing tangent lines that are the rectangle edges and a radius that is the radius of the corners. Figure 6.9 shows the rounded rectangle produced by the code in Listing 6.2.

The `addRoundedRectToPath` routine in Listing 6.2 adds a new subpath that corresponds to a rounded rectangle to the current path in the context. The doRounded-Rects routine invokes it. The `addRoundedRectToPath` routine is suitable for drawing rounded rectangles similar to those defined by QuickDraw. The rounded corners of rounded rectangles in QuickDraw are defined by an oval that has a width and a height. Note that although the oval width and height are the same in this example, the code works correctly if the oval width and height are not equal.

Listing 6.2 Drawing a rounded rectangle

```
void addRoundedRectToPath(CGContextRef context, CGRect rect, float ovalWidth,
              float ovalHeight)
{
    float fw, fh;
```

```
      // If either ovalWidth or ovalHeight is 0, add a regular rectangle.
      if (ovalWidth == 0 || ovalHeight == 0) {
        CGContextAddRect(context, rect);
      }else{
        CGContextSaveGState(context);
        // Translate to lower-left corner of rectangle.
        CGContextTranslateCTM(context, CGRectGetMinX(rect),
                    CGRectGetMinY(rect));
        // Scale by the oval width and height so that
        // each rounded corner is 0.5 units in radius.
        CGContextScaleCTM(context, ovalWidth, ovalHeight);
        // Unscale the rectangle width by the amount of the x scaling.
        fw = CGRectGetWidth(rect) / ovalWidth;
        // Unscale the rectangle height by the amount of the y scaling.
        fh = CGRectGetHeight(rect) / ovalHeight;
        // Start at the right edge of the rectangle, at the midpoint in Y.
        CGContextMoveToPoint(context, fw, fh/2);
        // ***** Segment 1 *****
        CGContextAddArcToPoint(context, fw, fh, fw/2, fh, 0.5);
        // ***** Segment 2 *****
        CGContextAddArcToPoint(context, 0, fh, 0, fh/2, 0.5);
        // ***** Segment 3 *****
        CGContextAddArcToPoint(context, 0, 0, fw/2, 0, 0.5);
        // ***** Segment 4 *****
        CGContextAddArcToPoint(context, fw, 0, fw, fh/2, 0.5);
        // Closing the path adds the last segment.
        CGContextClosePath(context);
        CGContextRestoreGState(context);
      }
}


void doRoundedRects(CGContextRef context)
{
  CGRect rect = {{10., 10.}, {210., 150.}};
  float ovalWidth = 100., ovalHeight = 100.;
  CGContextSetLineWidth(context, 2.);
  CGContextBeginPath(context);
  addRoundedRectToPath(context, rect, ovalWidth, ovalHeight);
  CGContextSetRGBStrokeColor(context, 1., 0., 0., 1.);
  CGContextDrawPath(context, kCGPathStroke);
}
```

The routine addRoundedRectToPath first makes sure that neither the oval width or the oval height is zero. If either is zero, the code simply adds the rectangle to the current path. For the case where the oval width and oval height are both nonzero, the code first translates to the lower-left corner of the rectangle so that it can work only with the width and height of the rectangle, making the remaining code simpler. The Quartz functions `CGRectGetMinX` and `CGRectGetMinY` return the minimum x and y values of the rectangle. The code uses them to obtain the coordinates for the lower-left corner of the rectangle, the point to which it translates the coordinate origin.

Next the code scales the coordinate system by the oval width and oval height. This ensures that the arc segments that the code constructs are segments of ovals, not circles. After scaling, the oval diameter is 1.0 units in both x and y. The code then recomputes the rectangle width and height to adjust for the scaling just performed. The resulting width and height, fw and fh, can be used in the scaled coordinate system to produce the original width and height of the rectangle.

The function `CGContextMoveToPoint` establishes the initial point of the path at the midpoint of the right edge of the rectangle. The first segment of the rounded rectangle is created by calling `CGContextAddArcToPoint` with the top-right corner point of the rectangle as p1 and the midpoint of the top edge of the rectangle as p2. The radius of the arc is 0.5, which is half the diameter of the oval in the scaled coordinate system. The starting point of Segment 1 is the initial current point and, because the initial current point is not coincident with the first tangent point of the arc, Quartz first adds a line segment from the initial current point to the first tangent point of the arc. Segment 1 does not end at p2 but rather at the point tangent to the arc along the tangent line between p1 and p2, as indicated in the figure.

The function `CGContextAddArcToPoint` constructs Segment 2 by first adding the line segment that connects the trailing endpoint from Segment 1 to the first tangent point of the arc, then adding the arc. The next two calls to `CGContextAdd-ArcToPoint` have a similar result. After adding Segment 4, the current point is at the last point on the arc forming the lower-right corner of the rounded rectangle, as shown in the figure. Finally, the call to `CGContextClosePath` adds the last path segment that connects the endpoint of the arc defining the lower-right corner of the rounded rectangle to the initial point on the path. The resulting path is closed.

Additional Path Convenience Functions (Tiger)

10.4 ▶ Several path construction and painting functions are new to Tiger. The first of these is a set of convenience functions to make it simple to create a path that consists of an ellipse or to fill and stroke an ellipse. The function `CGContextAddEl-lipseInRect` adds to the current path a closed subpath that represents an ellipse.

You supply a `CGRect` that defines the ellipse. The center of the ellipse is the center of the rectangle, and the major and minor axes of the ellipse are defined by the width and height of the rectangle. If the `CGRect` is a square, the path will be a circle. This function does not perform any painting but merely adds the elliptical path to the current path. Figure 6.10 illustrates the relationship between the rectangle passed to `CGContextAddEllipseInRect` and the resulting elliptical path.

Listing 6.3 defines a routine to create elliptical paths. The code first tests whether the Quartz routine `CGContextAddEllipseInRect` is available, and if it is not, the code adds an elliptical path in the same manner that `CGContext-AddEllipseInRect` is defined. It does so by translating to the center of the rectangle, scaling the coordinate system by half the width and height, and then drawing an arc of radius 1 unit to construct the ellipse. The arc is added in the clockwise direction because that is how `CGContextAddEllipseInRect` is defined. The emulation is not a perfect one; it assumes that the current path is not open at the time `myCGContextAddEllipseInRect` is called.

This code can only be built correctly in Tiger and later versions because the symbol `CGContextAddEllipseInRect` is not defined in earlier versions of Quartz. In addition, the build environment variable `MACOSX_DEPLOYMENT_TARGET` must be set to 10.2 or later because the weak linking capability this code relies on is only available in Jaguar and later versions. See the references at the end of this chapter for more information about weak linking and Mac OS X.

Figure 6.10 The elliptical path created by `CGContextAddEllipseInRect`

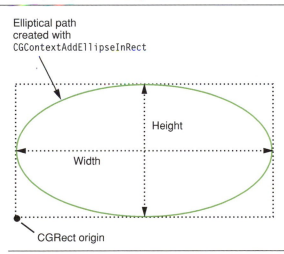

Listing 6.3 Emulating the function CGContextAddEllipseInRect

```
void myCGContextAddEllipseInRect(CGContextRef context, CGRect r)
{
  // If the Quartz built-in function is defined, use it;
  // otherwise use the emulation.
  if(&CGContextAddEllipseInRect != NULL){
    CGContextAddEllipseInRect(context, r);
  }else{
    CGContextSaveGState(context);
      // Translate to the center of the ellipse.
      CGContextTranslateCTM(context,
              CGRectGetMidX(r), CGRectGetMidY(r));
      // Scale by half the width and height of the rectangle
      // bounding the ellipse.
      CGContextScaleCTM(context, r.size.width/2, r.size.height/2);
      // Establish a current point at the first point
      // on the ellipse.
      CGContextMoveToPoint(context, 1, 0);
      // Add a circular arc around the ellipse center.
      CGContextAddArc(context, 0, 0, 1, 0, 2*M_PI, 1);
      CGContextClosePath(context);
    CGContextRestoreGState(context);
  }
}
```

In addition to CGContextAddEllipseInRect, Quartz provides the routines CGContextFillEllipseInRect and CGContextStrokeEllipseInRect. The routine CGContextFillEllipseInRect fills an ellipse defined by the CGRect supplied to it. The routine CGContextStrokeEllipseInRect strokes an ellipse defined by the CGRect supplied to it.

Also added in Tiger is the routine CGContextStrokeLineSegments. This function is useful for stroking a sequence of disconnected line segments in a convenient manner with excellent performance. The function CGContextStrokeLineSegments takes the following parameters:

- context, the graphics context to add the path to.

- points, an array of CGPoint structures. These points define the beginning and ending points of each segment to stroke.

- count, the number of points in the points array. The count argument must be even.

The function CGContextStrokeLineSegments strokes a series of disconnected line segments defined by the points array passed to it. The array element at index 0 is the position of the starting point of the first line segment; the array element at index 1 is the endpoint of that stroked segment. Array element 2 is the starting point of the next stroked segment; array element 3 is the ending point of that segment, and so on. The total number of stroked line segments is count/2.

Stroking Paths

Quartz strokes by painting a line along the path, straddling the path with half the stroke on each side of the path. The stroke follows the trajectory of the path, and the outer edges of the stroke are parallel to the path. After painting the stroke, Quartz sets the path in the context to an empty path.

Several functions stroke paths. For stroking arbitrary shapes, use Quartz path construction functions to create a path that contains one or more subpaths. Then stroke that path using either the function CGContextStrokePath or the function CGContextDrawPath with the painting mode kCGPathStroke. This usage of these two functions is identical, so use the one that suits your taste. Stroking a path can be combined with filling of that path by using the function CGContextDraw-Path with the painting modes kCGPathFillStroke or kCGPathEOFillStroke. These painting modes first fill and then stroke the path. "Filling Paths" (page 126) discusses the difference between Fill and EOFill.

Stroked rectangles don't require any path construction when you use the convenience functions CGContextStrokeRect and CGContextStrokeRectWithWidth (introduced in "Quartz 2D Drawing Basics" (page 15)). These functions create a rectangular path and stroke it. Both of these functions ignore any existing path in the context and, after they execute, the path in the context is empty. The difference between these two functions is that the function CGContextStrokeRect uses the line width parameter that's associated with the graphics state for the context when stroking, and the function CGContextStrokeRectWithWidth uses the line width you explicitly pass when calling it. These functions have no additional side effects; in particular, the line width parameter of the context is not changed by CGContextStrokeRectWithWidth.

Note   Each context has an associated **graphics state** that contains drawing parameters (such as line width, stroke color, and fill color) that affect how Quartz renders graphics. "Color, Alpha Transparency, and the Quartz Graphics State" (page 147) discusses the graphics state in detail and Table 7.1 (page 174) is a table of all the graphics state parameters.

When stroking a path, Quartz uses the current stroke color for the context as the painting color for the stroke. There are a number of additional parameters associated with the graphics state for the context that affect the way Quartz strokes a path. The following subsections discuss each one. In each case, Quartz uses the value of the parameter in the context at the time it strokes the path.

Line Width

The **line width** is the line thickness in user space units that Quartz uses to stroke the path. The Quartz line width parameter in the context is set by the function `CGContextSetLineWidth`. The default line width is 1 unit. Because the line width is specified in Quartz user space units, it is affected by changes to the CTM. The line width is affected by the scaling aspects of the CTM just like path construction is. The current value of the line width and the CTM at the time Quartz performs the stroking determines the thickness of the stroke. Scaling the CTM by a uniform scale factor S prior to stroking produces a line thickness S times thicker than if the scale had not been applied. Nonuniform scaling can produce interesting effects, sometimes unwanted, such as that in Figure 6.11.

The difference between the two ellipses in the figure is the coordinate system at the time Quartz paints the stroke. Ellipse 1 is stroked with a line width of 10 units with no scaling. Ellipse 2 is stroked with a line width of 10 units but with a scaling of 2 in x and 1 in y. This nonuniform scaling produces a thicker line width in the x direction than in the y direction.

The code in Listing 6.4 draws the two ellipses shown in Figure 6.11. To create an elliptical path, the code first scales the coordinate system to obtain the correct major and minor axes of the ellipse. In this example, the ratio of the major and minor axes is 2 in x and 1 in y. Next the code constructs a path that is a circle. The difference between the painting of the two ellipses is the coordinate system at the time the code calls Quartz to paint the stroke. When drawing Ellipse 1, the code calls `CGContextStrokePath` to stroke the path *after* it restores the coordi-

Figure 6.11 Stroking ellipses

Ellipse 1:
Restore before stroke

Ellipse 2:
Stroke before restore

nate system to that in effect prior to scaling for the construction of the elliptical path. When drawing Ellipse 2, the code calls `CGContextStrokePath` to stroke the path *before* it restores the coordinate system.

Listing 6.4 Stroking ellipses

```
void doStrokeWithCTM(CGContextRef context)
{
  CGContextTranslateCTM(context, 150., 180.);
  CGContextSetLineWidth(context, 10);
  // Draw Ellipse 1 with a uniform stroke.
  CGContextSaveGState(context);
    // Scale the CTM so that the circular arc will be elliptical.
    CGContextScaleCTM(context, 2, 1);
    CGContextBeginPath(context);
    // Create an arc that is a circle.
    CGContextAddArc(context, 0., 0., 45., 0., 2*M_PI, 0);
  // Restore the context parameters prior to stroking the path.
  // CGContextRestoreGState does not affect the path in the context.
  CGContextRestoreGState(context);
  CGContextStrokePath(context);

  CGContextTranslateCTM(context, 220., 0.);
  // Draw Ellipse 2 with nonuniform stroke.
  CGContextSaveGState(context);
    // Scale the CTM so that the circular arc will be elliptical.
    CGContextScaleCTM(context, 2, 1);
    CGContextBeginPath(context);
    // Create an arc that is a circle.
    CGContextAddArc(context, 0., 0., 45., 0., 2*M_PI, 0);
    // Stroke the path with the scaled coordinate system in effect.
    CGContextStrokePath(context);
  CGContextRestoreGState(context);
}
```

Line Joins

A **join** defines the point at which two connected segments meet. Quartz treats these connections between path segments specially. The Quartz **line join** parameter controls the way that Quartz joins connected segments. Quartz can apply three different types of joins—miter, round, or bevel—as shown in Figure 6.12. The function `CGContextSetLineJoin` controls the join type and can take as a parameter any one of the values `kCGLineJoinMiter`, `kCGLineJoinRound`, or `kCG-LineJoinBevel`.

Figure 6.12 Types of Quartz line joins

Miter join   Round join   Bevel join

The default is the miter join (kCGLineJoinMiter). For this type of join, Quartz extends the outer edges of the stroke until they meet at an angle, similar to the corner on a picture frame.

For a round join (kCGLineJoinRound), Quartz draws a circular arc around the point where the segments meet. The diameter of this circle is the line width, resulting in a rounded corner.

For a bevel join (kCGLineJoinBevel), Quartz finishes the segments with butt line caps, leaving a notch at the corner. (See the next section "Line Caps" for more discussion of butt line caps.) The resulting notch beyond the segments is filled in with a triangle, resulting in a beveled corner.

When the join style is a miter join, Quartz replaces a miter join with a bevel join if the angle between two connected path segments is too small; this avoids sharp spikes. The **miter limit** determines the angle when a miter join is replaced by a bevel join; it only applies when the Quartz line join is kCGLineJoinMiter. The miter limit is based on the miter length. The **miter length** is the distance between the point where the inner edges of the stroke intersect and the point where the outer edges of the stroke intersect. Figure 6.13 illustrates the miter length. If the ratio of the miter length and the line width exceeds the miter limit, Quartz replaces a miter join with a bevel join.

The ratio between the miter length and the line width is expressed in terms of the angle θ between the two segments:

$$miterlimit = \frac{miterlength}{linewidth} = \frac{1}{sin\frac{\theta}{2}}$$

The default Quartz miter limit is 10. This value causes miter joins to be replaced by beveled joins when the angle between the segments is less than about 11 degrees. A larger miter limit allows the miter length to be larger, that is, allows larger spikes. Figure 6.14 shows the results of the miter limit. In the lower portion of the figure, the miter limit is the default value of 10. As the angle between the two connected path segments gets smaller, the miter join is replaced by a beveled join. The upper portion of the figure shows a large miter limit with a small angle between the two connected path segments; the sharp spike is the

Figure 6.13 The miter length

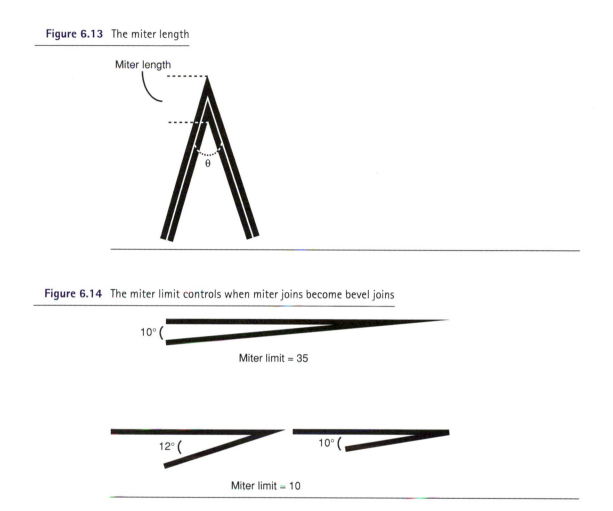

Figure 6.14 The miter limit controls when miter joins become bevel joins

result of a large miter length. Although the function CGContextSetMiterLimit adjusts the miter limit, the default value is appropriate for most applications.

Line Caps

An endpoint of an open subpath is a point that is not connected to any other point in the subpath. A subpath has two endpoints if it is open and no endpoints if it is closed. Quartz treats the endpoints of an open subpath specially. It applies one of three types of **line cap**—butt, square, or rounded—as shown in Figure 6.15. The white lines in the figure represent the path being stroked. Calling the function CGContextSetLineCap with one of the three possible values (kCGLineCap-Butt, kCGLineCapSquare, or kCGLineCapRound) changes the line cap setting.

Figure 6.15 Quartz line caps

Butt line cap   Square line cap   Rounded line cap

Figure 6.16 Stroking open subpaths (left) and closed subpaths (right)

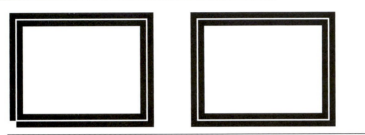

The butt line cap (kCGLineCapButt) is the default. Quartz stops the stroke at the endpoint of the open path segment and squares off the end. There is no projection beyond the end of the path.

The square line cap (kCGLineCapSquare) is sometimes called a projected line cap. Quartz projects the stroke beyond the endpoint by one-half the line width and squares off the end of the stroke.

When the line cap is a round line cap (kCGLineCapRound), Quartz paints a semi-circular arc at each endpoint. The diameter of the arc is the line width.

Because Quartz applies the line cap to the endpoints of an open path, you need to be sure to close a path that you want treated as closed, as evident in Figure 6.16. The white line in each graphic in the figure represents the unstroked path. The graphic on the left is a path whose starting point is in the lower-left corner of the graphic, with line segments created counterclockwise around the shape. The last line segment is added so that its endpoint coincides with the starting point of the path, but the path is not explicitly closed prior to stroking the path. The graphic on the right of the figure is created in exactly the same manner except, prior to calling CGContextStrokePath to stroke the path, it is closed by calling CGContextClosePath.

Note that the lower-left corner of each graphic is different. In the graphic on the left (which is not explicitly closed), the endpoints are each treated with the current line cap, and are drawn with the line cap set to the default value, kCGLine-CapButt. The stroke is painted up to each endpoint and is squared off at the endpoint. This leaves a notch at the point where the two endpoints are located.

The graphic on the right is the same path, but it is closed prior to stroking. This means that the starting and ending points of the path are connected. Because the path is closed, Quartz applies a line join at that point just like each of the other corners where the path segments are joined. To ensure that a subpath is stroked as a closed subpath, you must close the subpath by calling the function CGContextClosePath.

Line Dash

As introduced in "Making Dashed Lines" (page 32), the **line dash** parameter controls whether the stroke is a solid line or a sequence of dashes. The function CGContextSetLineDash specifies the line dash as a sequence of dash-on and -off segments together with a phase parameter that specifies how far into the dash sequence to begin the dash when Quartz paints the stroke.

Quartz treats each subpath within a path independently; the phase and dash pattern are restarted at the beginning of each subpath. Stroking with a dash has behavior similar to stroking without a dash. The current line join parameter of the context controls the way Quartz paints joins of connected path segments, and the current line cap parameter controls the way Quartz paints the endpoints of each open subpath.

The current line cap parameter of the context also determines the way Quartz paints the ends of each dash-on segment. At each end of every dash-on segment, Quartz applies the current line cap. Figure 6.17 illustrates this behavior. Each of the lines in the figure is drawn with a line width of 5 units and a line dash of 12 units on, 12 units off. The gray lines in the figure represent the path being stroked. The only difference between each stroked path in the figure is that the Quartz line cap is changed prior to stroking.

Figure 6.17 Dashing with different line caps

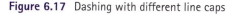

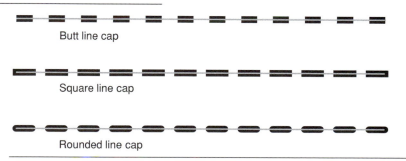

Butt line cap

Square line cap

Rounded line cap

When dashing with a butt line cap, the dash-on and dash-off segments in the figure are each of the same length because the dash-on and dash-off segments themselves are the same length and the butt line cap begins and ends at the endpoint of each dash-on segment. When drawing the same dash pattern with a square (or projected) line cap, the stroke at the end of each dash segment projects an additional amount equal to half the stroke width. Each dash-on segment has the same treatment as the subpath endpoints. When drawing the same dash pattern with a rounded line cap, the ends of each dash segment are rounded just like the stroke at the beginning and ending points of the subpath.

Filling Paths

Filling a path means to paint the interior of the path. Quartz uses the current fill color of the context to paint the path. After painting the path, Quartz sets the path in the context to an empty path. For simple shapes, it is intuitively obvious what the interior of the path is. When filling more complex shapes that cross over themselves or paths that have multiple subpaths, the interior of the path is not immediately obvious. Quartz defines two distinct rules to determine the interior of a path. You choose which rule to apply when filling a path—the nonzero winding number rule or the even-odd rule.

The **nonzero winding number rule** takes into account the direction of the path segments that make up the path. To determine whether a point is in the interior of a path, Quartz conceptually constructs a ray from that point out to infinity. It counts the number of times the ray intersects the path where the path travels from right to left and subtracts that count from the number of times the ray intersects the path where the path goes left to right. The resulting number is the **winding number**, and if the winding number is nonzero, the point is in the interior of the path. If a path segment coincides with the ray chosen or is tangent to it, another ray is chosen; the direction of the ray is arbitrary.

For a simple shape such as a rectangle, the nonzero winding number rule is simple: a ray to infinity from any point inside the rectangle crosses the path of the rectangle once and the winding number is computed to be 1; that point is inside. For a point outside the rectangle, the ray either does not intersect the rectangle or it crosses the path defining the rectangle twice, once in each direction, and the resulting winding number is 0; that point is outside.

Figure 6.18 shows some geometries that are more complex. The shapes on the left and center of the figure are each drawn as two subpaths but with a significant difference. The inner rectangular path of the shape on the left is constructed in the opposite direction as the outer rectangular path of that shape. The two rectangular subpaths comprising the center shape are each drawn in the same direc-

Figure 6.18 Nonzero winding number rule fill

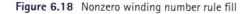

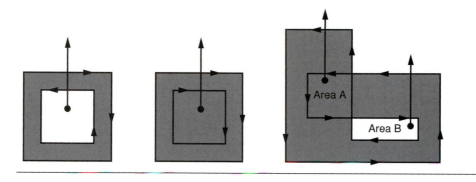

tion. The winding number fill rule treats these shapes differently. For the shape on the left, a ray outward from any point inside the inner rectangle crosses the path from right to left once and from left to right once, yielding a winding number of zero. This means that the points inside the inner rectangle are *outside* the path and are not painted. For the shape in the center where the two paths are constructed in the same direction, a ray drawn from the center of the inner rectangle crosses the path twice in one direction and zero times in the other, yielding a winding number of two. Therefore, for this shape, the points inside the inner rectangle are *inside* the path and are painted.

The shape on the right of the figure is a single connected path that intersects itself, producing two areas where the notion of the interior of the shape is not obvious. For a point inside Area A, the ray shown in the figure crosses right to left twice and does not cross left to right, producing a winding number of 2, meaning those points are inside the path. For a point inside Area B, the ray shown in the figure crosses right to left once and left to right once, yielding a winding number of zero. Points inside Area B are therefore outside the path.

If you forget whether the nonzero winding number fill rule is "zero means inside" or "nonzero means inside," consider the simple example of a circle or a rectangle where you intuitively know what is inside. Applying the rule in those cases makes it clear that "nonzero means inside."

The second fill rule available in Quartz is the **even-odd fill rule**. For this rule, the direction of the path segments is unimportant. To determine whether a point is in the interior of a path using the even-odd fill rule, Quartz conceptually constructs a ray from that point out to infinity. It counts the number of times the ray intersects the path. If the number of intersections is odd, the point is inside the path. If the number of intersections is even, the point is outside the path. The even-odd fill rule is rarely used. Its use is typically confined to emulating another graphics model such as QuickDraw, which uses the even-odd fill rule.

Figure 6.19 shows the even-odd fill rule applied with some more complex geometries. Again, the inner rectangular path of the rectangular shape on the left is constructed in the opposite direction as the outer rectangular path of that shape. The two rectangular subpaths comprising the shape in the center are each drawn in the same direction. However, since the even-odd fill rule doesn't consider the direction of the path, the two shapes are filled identically. A ray to infinity from the center of the shape crosses the path twice, an even number; thus, the center of the shape is outside the path. The shape on the right is also painted differently with the even-odd fill rule than with the winding number rule. For a point inside Area A, the ray shown in the figure crosses the path twice, an even number, meaning those points are outside the path. For a point inside Area B, the ray shown in the figure also crosses the path twice; points inside Area B are therefore outside the path.

If you forget whether the even-odd fill rule is "even means inside" or "odd means inside," consider the simple example of a circle or a rectangle where you intuitively know what is inside. Applying the rule in those cases makes it clear that "odd means inside."

There are several ways you can draw filled shapes using Quartz. For filling arbitrary shapes, use the Quartz path construction functions to create a path (containing one or more subpaths) and fill that path using the nonzero winding number rule by using the function CGContextFillPath or the function CGContextDrawPath with the painting mode kCGPathFill. To fill the current path using the even-odd fill rule, you can use the function CGContextEOFillPath or the function CGContextDrawPath with the painting mode kCGPathEOFill.

Stroking a path can be combined with filling by using the function CGContextDrawPath with the painting mode kCGPathFillStroke to use the nonzero winding number fill rule or the painting mode kCGPathEOFillStroke to use the even-odd fill rule. These painting modes first fill, then stroke the path.

Figure 6.19 Even-odd fill

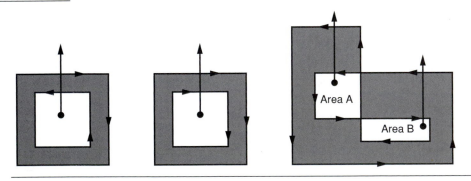

Regardless of the fill rule applied, to fill an open subpath, Quartz must implicitly close it prior to filling. Operations that fill a path implicitly close all open subpaths prior to filling. Operations that both fill and stroke only implicitly close the path for the filling portion of the operation; the stroke portion of the operation is applied without closing any open subpaths that exist. If you want the path to be closed prior to stroking, you must explicitly close it with `CGContextClosePath`.

Quartz has convenience functions for filling rectangles. The function `CGContextFillRect` allows you to fill a specified rectangle without performing any explicit path construction. The function `CGContextFillRects` allows you to fill a specified *array* of rectangles without any explicit path construction. These functions ignore any current path in the context and, after they return, the current path in the context is empty. Quartz uses the nonzero winding number fill rule when filling rectangles with these convenience functions.

Quartz does not supply an "erase rectangle" function because Quartz has no notion of a "background" color or an erase color. To achieve this result, you first set the fill color to the color you want to erase with and then call `CGContextFillRect`.

Quartz does provide the specialized function `CGContextClearRect`, which should not be confused with an erasing operation. Information about the function `CGContextClearRect` is in "Erasing and Clearing a Context" (page 351).

Clipping with Paths

Every Quartz context has a current **clipping area**—the area into which Quartz can draw. Any drawing that lies outside this clipping area does not appear; only those portions inside the clipping area are painted. Drawing is **clipped** to the clipping area in the context.

Quartz provides two ways to perform clipping. The first is based on paths. In Tiger and later versions, Quartz also allows clipping to image masks. The discussion here is limited to clipping to paths. See "Clipping to a Mask (Tiger)" (page 282) for a discussion of clipping to masks.

For path-based clipping, conceptually Quartz produces the clipping area by intersecting a sequence of paths. With this type of clipping, the clipping area is an abstract representation, and because it is not based on a bitmap format, the clipping area produced is resolution-independent. Content that is clipped by a complex path-based clipping area, including text characters, is rendered with high quality. The edges of the clipped content are smooth, even when using scaling to magnify the content or to render the content on a high-resolution output device.

All Quartz graphics contexts have a clipping area associated with them prior to any additional clipping operations you may perform. Recall that in "Using Quartz 2D in Cocoa" (page 45), Cocoa sets up the clipping area in the view CGContextRef so that drawing is clipped to the view bounds. Similarly, in "Using Quartz 2D in Carbon" (page 65), you observed that Quartz clips the CGContext-Ref to the bounds of the view when using HIView.

You can make changes to the clipping area in the context in one of two ways:

1. Explicitly apply a clipping operation to the context. One way to do this is to create a new path and then call one of the Quartz clipping functions. This process intersects the new path with the existing clipping area, producing a new, smaller clipping area. The only points inside the new clipping area are those that are inside both the original clipping area and the new path you supply.

2. Use CGContextRestoreGState to restore to a previously saved snapshot of the context that has a clipping area established that differs from the current clipping area.

It is always possible to apply Method 1. You can always create a smaller clipping area than the current one by intersecting a new path with the current clipping area. Method 2 is possible to apply only if you have previously called CGContext-SaveGState to take a snapshot of the context parameters prior to applying a clipping path using Method 1. Because you have no saved snapshot of the context prior to the clip applied by the Cocoa and Carbon frameworks, you cannot draw outside the area they provide for drawing to a window or view.

There are several ways to modify the clipping area using path-based clipping. To intersect the current clipping area with a new path that corresponds to an arbitrary shape, you can use the Quartz path construction functions to create a path that represents a shape and call the functions CGContextClip or CGContextEOClip. Operations that use the path as a clip implicitly close the path prior to clipping, exactly like the filling operations do. Prior to intersecting the current path with the existing clipping area, Quartz determines the inside of the current path by using the same rules that apply to fills. The function CGContextClip uses the non-zero winding number rule to determine the inside of the current path, and CGContextEOClip uses the even-odd fill rule to determine the inside of the current path. After intersecting the interior of the current path with the existing clipping area to create the new clipping area, both these functions replace the current path in the context with an empty path. Recall that Listing 2.7 in "Clipping a Drawing" (page 36) modifies the clipping area by calling the function CGContextClip.

Quartz offers two convenience functions that clip to a rectangular area. The function CGContextClipToRect intersects a rectangle with the existing clipping area. Quartz intersects the supplied rectangle with the existing clipping area to create the new clipping area on the context. The function CGContextClipToRects constructs a clipping area that consists of the interior of a sequence of rectangles. Quartz intersects the interior of these rectangles with the existing clipping area to create a new clipping area. The function CGContextClipToRects uses the non-zero winding number rule to determine the interior of the rectangles. Both these functions ignore any existing path in the context; after they return, the current path in the context is empty.

CGPath Objects (Jaguar)

10.2 ▶ Filling, stroking, and clipping operations replace the current path in the context with an empty path, which is inconvenient in situations where you want to draw a given shape repeatedly. To make it simpler to repeatedly use a path, in Jaguar and later versions, you can use the Quartz data types CGPathRef and CGMutablePathRef. Each represents a path object. The difference between these types is that a CGPathRef cannot be modified or added to but a CGMutablePathRef can be.

To make it easy to work with CGPath objects, Quartz provides path construction and path convenience functions that parallel those described earlier in this chapter but that, instead of operating on the current path in the context, take a CGMutablePathRef as the path to add to or modify. In addition to functions that allow you to modify a CGMutablePathRef, Quartz provides the function CGContextAddPath to add a CGPathRef or CGMutablePathRef to the current path in the context.

For example, the function CGPathAddArc takes the following parameters:

- The CGMutablePathRef of the CGPath object to add the arc path segment to.

- A pointer to an optional CGAffineTranform to apply to the points of the arc path segment before adding them to the path. If this pointer is NULL, Quartz applies no transformation to the arc path coordinates prior to adding them to the CGPath.

- The x,y coordinates for the center of the circle that defines the arc path segment.

- The radius of the circle that defines the arc path segment.

- The starting and ending arc angle for the arc path segment.

- A Boolean value. If true, the arc segment is added clockwise; otherwise it is added counterclockwise.

These parameters closely parallel the parameters to the function CGContextAddArc, which adds an arc path segment to the current path in the context. Instead of passing the context as the first parameter, you pass the mutable CGPath object you want to add the arc to. The second parameter, a pointer to an optional affine transform, allows you to apply coordinate transformations as the path segment is added to the CGPath object. This parallels the way `CGContextAddArc` uses the CTM to transform path segment coordinates as it adds them to the path on the context. If the pointer is `NULL`, Quartz applies no transformation to the points as it adds them to the CGPath object. (This is equivalent to passing an identity transform but is more efficient.)

To see how you can use a CGPath object, take another look at the code to draw a shape to achieve a blend, which is shown in Listing 5.5 (page 97). That example draws a rotated ellipse a number of times, each separated by a small distance and each colored by a slightly different color. The result appears in Figure 5.5 (page 96).

Listing 6.5 shows how to use a CGPath to perform this drawing in a more compact way than that in the original example. The `doRotatedEllipsesWithCGPath` routine creates an affine transform that represents a rotation by 45 degrees, followed by a scaling transformation of 1 along the x axis and 2 along the y axis. It then creates a new mutable CGPath object by calling the function `CGPathCreate-Mutable`. The function `CGPathAddArc` then adds a new path segment to the CGPath object as described previously. The code uses the affine transform it just created to transform the circular arc as it is added to the CGPath object. After adding the arc to the CGPath object, the function `CGPathCloseSubpath` closes the path, ensuring that the path starting point and ending point are joined. The CGPath object now consists of a closed circle that is rotated by 45 degrees and scaled by 1 along the x axis and 2 along the y axis; this is the rotated ellipse.

After the routine doRotatedEllipsesWithCGPath has a CGPath object that represents the transformed shape, it adds that CGPath object to the current path in the context by calling the function `CGContextAddPath`. Quartz treats the points on the CGPath object as user space coordinates and transforms them through the CTM, as it does with other Quartz path construction functions. The function `CGContextAddPath` does not modify the CGPath object passed to it; that CGPath object can be reused again and again. After the code is done with the CGPath object, it calls `CGPathRelease` to release the memory associated with the `CGMutablePathRef` created earlier.

Listing 6.5 Drawing blended ellipses using a CGPath object

```
void doRotatedEllipsesWithCGPath(CGContextRef context)
{
    int i, totreps = 144.;
    CGMutablePathRef path = NULL;
    float  tint = 1., tintIncrement = 1./totreps;
    // Create a new transform consisting of a 45-degree rotation.
    CGAffineTransform theTransform = CGAffineTransformMakeRotation(M_PI/4);
```

```
// Apply a scaling transformation to the transform just created.
theTransform = CGAffineTransformScale(theTransform, 1, 2);
// Create a mutable CGPath object.
path = CGPathCreateMutable();
if(!path){
  fprintf(stderr, "Couldn't create path!\n");
  return;
}
// Add a circular arc to the CGPath object, transformed
// by an affine transform.
CGPathAddArc(path, &theTransform, 0., 0., 45., 0., 2*M_PI, false);
// Close the CGPath object.
CGPathCloseSubpath(path);

// Place the first ellipse at a good location.
CGContextTranslateCTM(context, 100., 100.);
for (i = 0 ; i < totreps ; i++){
  CGContextBeginPath(context);
  // Add the CGPath object to the current path in the context.
  CGContextAddPath(context, path);
  // Set the fill color for this instance of the ellipse.
  CGContextSetRGBFillColor(context, tint, 0., 0., 1.);
  CGContextFillPath(context);
  // Compute the next tint color.
  tint -= tintIncrement;
  // Move over for the next ellipse.
  CGContextTranslateCTM(context, 1, 0.);
}
// Release the path when done with it.
CGPathRelease(path);
}
```

When using a CGPath object, you can transform the points on the path segments as you add them to the CGPath object just as the code example does. Another approach is to construct the CGPath object without any transformations and then transform the Quartz context coordinate system before adding the CGPath object to the context path. The end result is identical. The most efficient choice depends on the way you use the CGPath object. For this example, creating a pretransformed CGPath object avoids the need to apply the following steps each time through the loop:

1. Save the Quartz coordinate system with CGContextSaveGState.

2. Apply the affine transform to the context using CGContextConcatCTM.

3. Add the untransformed path with `CGContextAddPath`.

4. Restore the Quartz coordinate system with `CGContextRestoreGState`.

The code in Listing 6.5 is simpler and more efficient than the code in Listing 5.5 (page 97), all because of the use of a `CGAffineTransform` and a `CGPath` object.

Anti-aliasing

When drawing line art graphics with Quartz, you specify your drawing as shapes that consist of lines and curves for Quartz to stroke and fill. When drawing to a window or an offscreen bitmap, Quartz renders these curves and shapes into bits that represent the original line art. The path description of the line art is, in a sense, an analytical representation of the graphics, and the rendered version is a digitized version of the same graphics. The resolution of the bitmap that Quartz renders determines the sampling frequency of the digitizing process. A low sampling frequency leads to aliasing effects, producing jagged lines and curves.

Quartz uses anti-aliasing techniques to produce superior results at the low resolutions typical of computer displays. Figure 6.20 is a screen shot of two thin lines drawn with Quartz, together with a magnification of the screen as produced by the Mac OS X developer tool, Pixie. The upper of the two lines is drawn without anti-aliasing; the lower of the two lines is drawn with anti-aliasing turned on. On screen the anti-aliased line has the appearance of being smoother, with a less jagged appearance. The upper line is jagged in the way typical of drawing non–anti-aliased lines at low resolution.

Figure 6.20 Anti-aliasing and thin lines

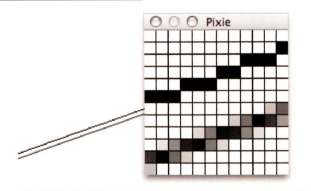

The Pixie magnification of the two lines reveals the difference in how they are rendered. The non–anti-aliased line is exactly what you'd expect. The pixels are either turned on or off. When stroking an anti-aliased line, Quartz paints the pixels along the line by blending the stroke color with the existing color of the pixels along the line. How much of the existing color is blended with the stroke color depends on the amount that a given pixel is covered by the stroke. For pixels that are completely covered by the stroke width, the stroke color is used as the color value for the destination. For pixels that are not touched by the stroke width, the pixel color is unchanged. Pixels that are partially covered by the stroke width are blended in proportion to the amount of the pixel that is covered. When you view this result at a sufficient distance, your eye averages the result so that the line appears to be a solid color but without the jagged appearance it has without anti-aliasing.

Figure 6.21 is another example of Quartz graphics drawn with anti-aliasing. The circle is filled and the boundary is stroked with a 2-unit-wide black stroke. The Pixie magnification shows an edge of the filled circle so that you can see the color blending that Quartz performs. Where pixels are completely covered with the stroke, the pixels are painted with black. Pixels on the inside of the stroke that are covered partially with the fill color and partially with the black stroke have those colors blended together. Pixels on the outside of the stroke that are covered partially with the black stroke and partially by the existing white background are blended with those two colors.

Anti-aliasing depends on pixel coverage. Consider how anti-aliasing affects drawing very thin strokes. When the coverage is less than a single pixel, a black line on top of a white background becomes a shade of gray. As the pixel coverage of a

Figure 6.21 Anti-aliasing and color

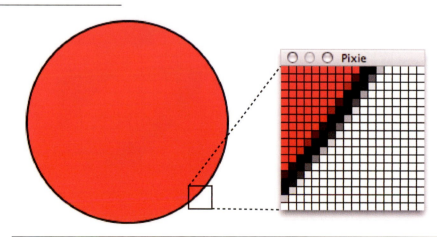

thin line approaches zero, the contribution of the existing color to the final blended result dominates that of the stroke color of the thin line. That is, stroked lines disappear as their thickness approaches zero. Without anti-aliasing, such thin lines are stroked as a single pixel line, even for a very small line width. Thin lines rendered without anti-aliasing do not "disappear."

It's best to avoid anti-aliased drawing that repeatedly paints a graphical shape on top of itself. Because edges of a shape are anti-aliased, when an edge has partial pixel coverage, repeated painting of a shape can affect the edges in an undesirable way. An example of this is shown in the screen shot at the left, in Figure 6.22. The bottom rectangle is painted a single time with a line width of 2 units. The top rectangle is painted several times on top of itself. You can see that the edges of the top graphic are bolder. The Pixie magnification is of the edges of the two rectangles. You can see that both the inner and outer edges of the top rectangle are painted in a darker shade than those of the bottom rectangle, making the top rectangle look thicker. Each time the rectangle is painted, the edges are blended with the underlying shade. The underlying shade starts as white but as the rectangle is repeatedly painted, the underlying shade becomes grayer due to the blending from the previous painting. As the rectangle is repeatedly drawn, the result is a darker and darker blending.

A similar effect of anti-aliasing can occur where portions of drawing abut other portions of drawing. Where a given pixel is partially covered by two different portions of drawing, anti-aliasing can produce color values that do not match the color value of either of the graphical elements being drawn.

Figure 6.22 Repeatedly drawing a shape

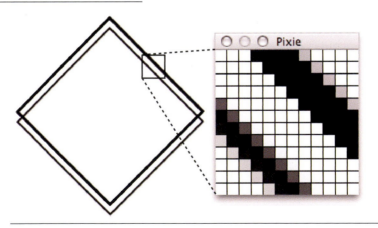

"Aligning User Space Coordinates on Pixel Boundaries (Tiger)" (page 139) discusses techniques for performing adjustments to user space coordinates so that they have specific alignment relative to the device space grid. Using the techniques described in that section is one way to help limit anti-aliasing artifacts.

Whether or not a context allows anti-aliasing depends on the type of context and the purpose of that context. By default, Quartz automatically performs anti-aliasing when it draws to a window context and an offscreen bitmap context. When creating a PDF document with a PDF context, Quartz records into the PDF document whether anti-aliasing is requested. A newly created PDF context turns on the parameter that controls anti-aliasing by default. When printing to raster printers, the printer resolution is large enough that anti-aliasing is not necessary and therefore it is disabled. When printing to PostScript printers, anti-aliasing has no effect because there is no notion of anti-aliasing in the PostScript language and imaging model.

For those contexts that allow and perform anti-aliasing, the function CGContext-SetShouldAntialias lets you turn anti-aliasing on and off. For those contexts that do not support anti-aliasing, this function has no effect.

The function CGContextSetAllowsAntialiasing (available starting in Tiger) allows you to completely disable anti-aliasing for a given context, even if that context supports it. After you call CGContextSetAllowsAntialiasing with the value set to false, all calls to CGContextSetShouldAntialias are ignored and anti-aliasing is disallowed until it is enabled by a later call to CGContextSetAllows-Antialiasing. For example, the Mac OS X printing system uses CGContextSet-AllowsAntialiasing to disable anti-aliasing when rendering the raster for use in raster inkjet printing. This produces better fidelity since printing resolutions are high enough to obviate the need for anti-aliasing. Note that this setting is not part of the graphics state and is unaffected by CGContextSaveGState and CGContextRestoreGState.

Path Utility Functions

Quartz provides several utility functions that obtain information about the current path in the context. Although not typically used, they can be helpful for some situations, such as determining the bounding box for the current path in the context. The bounding box of a path is the smallest rectangle that encloses all the points of the path, including any Bézier curve control points.

The function CGContextGetPathBoundingBox returns a CGRect that corresponds to the bounding box of the current path. The coordinate values in the returned rectangle are expressed in the user space coordinate system in effect at the time you call CGContextGetPathBoundingBox. If the current path in the context is empty, CGContextGetPathBoundingBox returns the special rectangle CGRect-Null. The Quartz utility function CGRectEqualToRect allows comparison of two CGRect structures for equality, making it straightforward to determine if the CGRect returned by CGContextGetPathBoundingBox is CGRectNull.

The function CGContextIsPathEmpty returns a Boolean value indicating whether the current path in the context is empty. An empty path contains no current point or path segments.

The function CGContextGetPathCurrentPoint returns a CGPoint that corresponds to the current point of the path in the context. The coordinate values of the point are expressed in the user space coordinate system in effect at the time you call CGContextGetPathCurrentPoint. If the current path in the context is empty, CGContextGetPathCurrentPoint returns the value CGPointZero. You should not rely on this value to indicate that the path is empty. Instead, you should use CGContextIsPathEmpty to determine whether the path is empty and therefore whether the value returned by CGContextGetPathCurrentPoint is meaningful.

The function CGContextGetClipBoundingBox (available starting in Panther) returns a CGRect that corresponds to the bounding box of the clipping area. The coordinate values of the returned rectangle are expressed in the user space coordinate system in effect at the time you call CGContextGetClipBoundingBox.

The function CGContextReplacePathWithStrokedPath (available starting in Tiger) replaces the current path with a stroked version of that path, using the parameters of the context to determine the new path. The same context parameters that would be used to stroke a path are consulted when creating the stroked version of the path. The new path, if filled, produces the same result as would have been obtained from stroking the original path. One use of this function is to create a clipping path that corresponds to a stroked version of a path. You'd follow a call to CGContextReplacePathWithStrokedPath with a call to CGContextClip.

The function CGContextPathContainsPoint (available starting in Tiger) allows you to perform simple hit detection with Quartz paths. This function takes the following parameters:

- context, the CGContextRef whose path you want to examine.
- point, a CGPoint you want to test with the current path.
- mode, the CGPathDrawingMode of the operation you want to hit test.

The function CGContextPathContainsPoint returns true if point is inside the current path in context. If point is not inside the current path, the function returns false. A point is inside the current path if it would be painted by the drawing operation specified by mode. For purposes of this calculation, the stroke and fill color are treated as an opaque solid color. The function `CGContextPathContains-Point` performs no painting, it only tests whether `point` is inside the context's current path. The function `CGPathContainsPoint` is a CGPath-based version of `CGContextPathContainsPoint` and can be used to determine whether a `CGPoint` is inside a CGPath object.

Aligning User Space Coordinates on Pixel Boundaries (Tiger)

10.4 ▶

In Tiger and later versions, Quartz provides functions that are useful for converting user space coordinates for a context into the device space coordinate system. The functions `CGContextConvertPointToDeviceSpace`, `CGContextConvertSizeTo-DeviceSpace`, and `CGContextConvertRectToDeviceSpace` convert `CGPoint`, `CGSize`, and `CGRect` coordinates from user space to device space, using the current CTM in effect for the context. The functions `CGContextConvertPointToUserSpace`, `CGContextConvertSizeToUserSpace`, and `CGContextConvertRectToUserSpace` perform conversion of `CGPoint`, `CGSize`, or `CGRect` coordinates in device space into the corresponding user space coordinates. These functions are useful for computing user space coordinates that align along device pixel boundaries or intersect the device space grid in other ways that achieve an effect you desire. One typical way they are used is to align a piece of graphics so that it has no partial pixel coverage, avoiding anti-aliasing artifacts.

Listing 6.6 is a simple example of how you might use these functions to perform drawing that is aligned along the device space pixel grid. The routine `doPixel-AlignedFillAndStroke` draws a line and a rectangle, first without performing any pixel alignment, then it draws them a second time after aligning the drawing coordinates so that the results are aligned to the device space pixel grid.

After drawing the unaligned rectangle and line, the code computes the unaligned length in user space of the line it will draw. The code then calculates the starting point of the pixel-aligned line. To align the starting point so that it corresponds to a point in user space that is the corner point of a device pixel, the code calls the routine `alignPointToUserSpace`. Before looking at any additional code in `doPixelAlignedFillAndStroke`, it is useful to see how `alignPointToUserSpace` performs the pixel alignment.

Listing 6.6 Drawing with pixel-aligned coordinates

```
static CGPoint alignPointToUserSpace(CGContextRef context, CGPoint p)
{
    // Compute the coordinates of the point in device space.
    p = CGContextConvertPointToDeviceSpace(context, p);
    // Ensure that coordinates are at exactly the corner
    // of a device pixel.
```

```
      p.x = floor(p.x);
      p.y = floor(p.y);
      // Convert the device-aligned coordinate back to user space.
      return CGContextConvertPointToUserSpace(context, p);
    }

    static CGSize alignSizeToUserSpace(CGContextRef context, CGSize s)
    {
      // Compute the size in device space.
      s = CGContextConvertSizeToDeviceSpace(context, s);
      // Ensure that size is an integer multiple of device pixels.
      s.width = floor(s.width);
      s.height = floor(s.height);
      // Convert back to user space.
      return CGContextConvertSizeToUserSpace(context, s);
    }

    static CGRect alignRectToUserSpace(CGContextRef context, CGRect r)
    {
      // Compute the coordinates of the rectangle in device space.
      r = CGContextConvertRectToDeviceSpace(context, r);
      // Ensure that the x and y coordinates are at a pixel corner.
      r.origin.x = floor(r.origin.x);
      r.origin.y = floor(r.origin.y);
      // Ensure that the width and height are an integer number of
      // device pixels.
      r.size.width = floor(r.size.width);
      r.size.height = floor(r.size.height);

      // Convert back to user space.
      return CGContextConvertRectToUserSpace(context, r);
    }

    void doPixelAlignedFillAndStroke(CGContextRef context)
    {
      CGPoint p1 = CGPointMake(16.7, 17.8);
      CGPoint p2 = CGPointMake(116.7, 17.8);
      CGRect r = CGRectMake(16.7, 20.8, 100.6, 100.6);
      CGSize s;

      CGContextSetLineWidth(context, 2);
      CGContextSetRGBFillColor(context, 1., 0., 0., 1.);
      CGContextSetRGBStrokeColor(context, 1., 0., 0., 1.);
```

```
// ***** Unaligned Drawing *****
CGContextBeginPath(context);
CGContextMoveToPoint(context, p1.x, p1.y);
CGContextAddLineToPoint(context, p2.x, p2.y);
CGContextStrokePath(context);
CGContextFillRect(context, r);

// Translate to the right before drawing along
// aligned coordinates.
CGContextTranslateCTM(context, 115, 0);

// ***** Aligned Drawing *****
// Compute the length of the line in user space.
s = CGSizeMake(p2.x - p1.x, p2.y - p1.y);

CGContextBeginPath(context);
// Align the starting point to a device pixel boundary.
p1 = alignPointToUserSpace(context, p1);
// Establish the starting point of the line.
CGContextMoveToPoint(context, p1.x, p1.y);
// Compute the line length as an integer
// number of device pixels.
s = alignSizeToUserSpace(context, s);
CGContextAddLineToPoint(context,
            p1.x + s.width,
            p1.y + s.height);
CGContextStrokePath(context);
// Compute a rect that is aligned to device space with a width
// that is an integer number of device pixels.
r = alignRectToUserSpace(context, r);
CGContextFillRect(context, r);
}
```

Figure 6.23 illustrates the concept of aligning user space points to the device space grid. A piece of the device space pixel grid is shown as the stroked gray squares in the figure. Notice that y coordinates in the device space coordinate system increase as you traverse down the rows of the pixel grid; this is typical for a raster destination like a display or a bitmap context. A given point in user space, such as the red point in the figure, intersects the device pixel grid at some location in a given pixel in device space. To align that point to the device pixel grid, the code calculates the user space point that is at the top-left corner of that device pixel, which is the point shown in blue in the figure. To calculate the user space coordinates of the blue point from the user space coordinates of the red

Figure 6.23 Aligning user space coordinates to device pixel boundaries

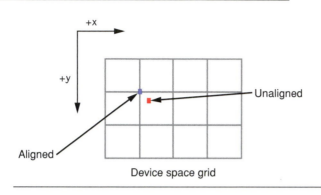

Device space grid

point, alignPointToUserSpace first computes the device space coordinate of the unaligned user space coordinate passed to the function by calling CGContextConvertPointToDeviceSpace. It then uses floor to truncate the x and y coordinates to integer values. The coordinates now correspond to the top-left corner of the pixel in the device space coordinate system. (The point is at the top-left corner of the pixel because smaller y coordinate values are nearer to the top of the pixel because the coordinate system is flipped.) The code then calculates the user space coordinate of that device space coordinate by calling CGContextConvertPointToUserSpace. The value returned from alignPointToUserSpace is the user space coordinate that corresponds to the top-left corner of the device pixel that the unaligned user space coordinate is located in.

Next doPixelAlignedFillAndStroke calls alignSizeToUserSpace to compute a user space line length that corresponds to an integer number of device pixels and uses that length to compute the location of the ending point of the line. The routine alignSizeToUserSpace uses the same technique as alignPointToUserSpace but instead computes a user space size that corresponds to an integer number of device pixels. It transforms the user space size into device space, ensures that the resulting size is an integer number of device pixels, then transforms the resulting size back to a user space size. Once the code has an aligned user space starting point and length, it uses them to compute an aligned endpoint for the line, then strokes the path it creates from these points.

The last portion of doPixelAlignedFillAndStroke uses the alignRectToUserSpace routine to align the rectangle so that it has its top-left corner at a user space point that corresponds to the corner of a device pixel, and the width and height of the rectangle correspond to an integer number of device pixels. Note that the alignRectToUserSpace routine uses floor to compute the rectangle origin as well as the width and height of the rectangle in device space. Using floor produces a rectangle that doesn't necessarily enclose the original one. Another approach would be to calculate the new rectangle so that it encloses the original one.

The results of the drawing appear in Figure 6.24. The rightmost graphic in the figure is the Pixie-magnified view of the portion of the drawing that lies within the rectangular area. As you can see in the figure, the unaligned drawing has faint red portions at its borders because of anti-aliasing at the edges due to the partial pixel coverage. The aligned portion of the drawing is aligned to pixel boundaries and has no partial pixel coverage, as you can see from the absence of anti-aliasing.

One aspect of performing pixel alignment such as that shown in this code is that even if you apply a coordinate transformation such as a scaling transformation prior to performing the drawing, the results of the pixel-aligned drawing continue to be pixel aligned. This is because these calculations use the CTM in effect at the time the code is called, incorporating any scaling and other transformations that have already been applied. If you are performing pixel alignment, it is important to adjust your drawing coordinates after you apply all your coordinate transformations.

This code is an example of doing pixel alignment to the top left of a pixel edge. You may want to align in a different manner, such as by rounding to the closest pixel corner or to a different location in the pixel, such as its center. However, the concept is the same—transform to device space coordinates, adjust the device space coordinates to your desired location within the pixel, and transform the result back to the user space coordinate system.

The routines that convert from user space to device space coordinates and back can be useful for drawing into bit-based contexts but their use should be avoided when drawing into a PDF or printing context. The PDF and printing contexts record drawing for future rendering; the true device space grid associated with these contexts is not defined until the drawing being recorded is actually

Figure 6.24 Drawing with pixel-aligned coordinates

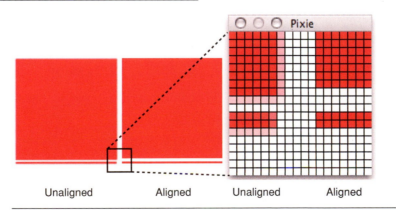

| Unaligned | Aligned | Unaligned | Aligned |

rendered. Making pixel adjustments using these functions makes sense only for contexts that are represented by bits, such as a window context or a bitmap context, where the user space to device space mapping is well known at the time you are making the adjustments.

Summary

This chapter discusses the powerful set of Quartz functions that creates line art graphics containing curves and lines. Path construction functions can describe arbitrary shapes to which you can apply Quartz painting operations. You can also use the path to perform clipping. Quartz has a number of ways to control the way that it applies strokes. Filling a path can be accomplished with one of two different filling rules—the nonzero winding number rule and the even-odd fill rule. In addition to the five versatile primitive path construction functions, Quartz offers a number of convenience functions that are straightforward to use for creating some of the more common shapes, including rectangles and arcs.

You've now learned a great deal of the Quartz drawing model, including most of the context parameters that affect the way Quartz paints paths. The next chapter ties together the context parameters that control the way Quartz renders graphics. You'll learn about the different color models that are available when using Quartz, including those important for producing accurate color reproduction across a wide range of devices. You'll also learn more about alpha compositing.

See Also

Quartz paths and the way they are painted are based on the PostScript and PDF imaging models. These imaging models are described in the books

- *PostScript Language Reference*, 3rd edition, Adobe Systems, Inc.:

  http://partners.adobe.com/public/developer/en/ps/PLRM.pdf

- *PDF Reference: Version 1.6*, 5th edition, Adobe Systems, Inc. and other versions of the PDF specification are available:

  http://partners.adobe.com/public/developer/pdf/index_reference.html

To understand more about the properties and mathematics of Bézier curves, see the following:

- *The METAFONTbook* and *METAFONT: The Program*, Donald E. Knuth, Addison-Wesley, 1986.

- *Principles of Interactive Computer Graphics*, William M. Newman and Robert F. Sproull, McGraw-Hill, 2nd edition, 1979.

- *Computer Graphics, Systems & Concepts*, Rod Salmon and Mel Slater, Addison-Wesley, 1986.

For in-depth information on anti-aliasing techniques, see

- *Digital Image Warping*, George Wolberg, Wiley-IEEE Computer Society Press, 1990.

The header files containing the structures and functions used in this chapter are

- CGContext.h

- CGPath.h

- CGGeometry.h

The relevant reference documentation from the ADC Reference Library is

- *CGContext Reference*

- *CGPath Reference*

- *CGGeometry Reference*

Information about weak linking and Mac OS X is available in the following documents:

- "Technical Note TN2064: Ensuring Backwards Binary Compatibility-Weak Linking and Availability Macros on Mac OS X," available from the ADC Reference Library:

  http://developer.apple.com/technotes/tn2002/tn2064.html

- "Frameworks and Weak Linking," available from the ADC Reference Library:

  http://developer.apple.com/documentation/MacOSX/Conceptual/ BPFrameworks/Concepts/WeakLinking.html

Chapter

Color, Alpha Transparency, and the Quartz Graphics State

A color in Quartz consists of a color space, a set of component values, and an alpha value. The color space determines the number of color components and how the components are interpreted. The alpha value determines the transparency of a color. Alpha transparency is one of the distinguishing features of the Quartz drawing model. Not only does every color have an associated alpha value, but Quartz supports a global alpha, an additional transparency value that can be applied to all drawing.

Quartz offers a wide variety of color models for painting graphics. Because ColorSync color management is integrated into Quartz, it's easy to use calibrated colors and color spaces for drawing, producing consistent color fidelity across a wide range of devices.

The **graphics state** is a set of drawing parameters that affect how Quartz renders graphics. Fill and stroke colors are included in this set along with the current transformation matrix (CTM), the clipping area, the font, and more than a dozen other parameters. Each has a default setting you can override by calling the Quartz function designed to set that parameter value. Some of these parameters—line cap, line join, and miter limit, for example—you've already looked at in detail. This chapter gathers all the graphics state parameters in one place so that you can see exactly what's handled by the graphics state, how to change the parameters, and how to save and restore them.

Color and Color Spaces

Color component values are meaningless without a color space to interpret them. A color space defines the number of color components that make up a color. RGB and CMYK, for example, each use different numbers of color components to describe a color. RGB uses three—red, green, and blue—whereas CMYK uses four—cyan, magenta, yellow, and black. Each achieves a color in a different manner—RGB by adding colors and CMYK by subtracting colors.

Quartz color spaces fall into three basic categories:

- Calibrated color spaces specify color in a well-defined way that is reproducible across a wide range of output devices. The Quartz color spaces in this category are the ICCBased, CalibratedGray, CalibratedRGB, and Lab color spaces.

- Device-dependent color spaces (also referred to as device color spaces) specify color in a way that is tied to a specific output device, and the results obtained when using device color vary from one device to another. The Quartz color spaces in this category are the DeviceGray, DeviceRGB, and DeviceCMYK color spaces.

- Special color spaces build special properties on top of an underlying color space. The Quartz color spaces in this category are the Pattern color space, which allows you to define a pattern to use as paint, and the Indexed color space, which allows you to define color using a color lookup table. "Drawing with Patterns" (page 481) discusses the Pattern color space and how to use it; details about the Indexed color space are given later in this chapter.

Recall that Quartz maintains separate fill and stroke colors. Because a color in Quartz consists of a color space and color components in that color space, the Quartz graphics state maintains a separate color space and color values (interpreted in that color space) for both the fill and stroke colors. When painting strokes, Quartz uses the current stroke color space and stroke color component values in the graphics state for the context. When filling paths, Quartz uses the current fill color space and fill color component values in the graphics state for the context. Quartz also uses the current fill color space and fill color component values when painting images without intrinsic color, such as masked or stencil images. Images with intrinsic color have a color space explicitly associated with them; Quartz does not consult the fill or stroke color in the context when painting images with intrinsic color. "Drawing Images" (page 203) and "Image Masking" (page 263) discuss sampled images and image masks in detail.

There are three different ways to set a fill or stroke color; the appropriate one to use depends on the color spaces you need and how you use color in your application. You've already seen one of the ways to set color. The examples in "Quartz 2D Drawing Basics" (page 15) and other earlier chapters in this book use the functions CGContextSetRGBFillColor and CGContextSetRGBStrokeColor. The function CGContextSetRGBFillColor implicitly uses the DeviceRGB color space. It sets the fill color space to DeviceRGB and sets the fill color component values to those you pass to the function. The function CGContextSetRGBStrokeColor has the same behavior for the stroke color space and stroke color component values. There are similar functions for each of the device color spaces. For example, CGContextSetCMYKFillColor sets the fill color space to DeviceCMYK and the fill color component values to those you pass to the function. As a general rule, it makes sense to use these functions only if you are using just the device color spaces. Otherwise, the best choice is to use techniques that apply to all color spaces because these techniques can be used with device color spaces as well.

Other ways to work with color in Quartz use an explicit color space. Quartz uses the opaque type CGColorSpaceRef to represent a color space. You create or obtain a CGColorSpaceRef and use it to specify color to Quartz. (You'll learn about the details of the different types of color spaces and how to create them in just a moment.) After you have a CGColorSpaceRef, you can work with colors using one of two methods:

1. Set the fill or stroke color space in the graphics state for the context using the functions CGContextSetFillColorSpace or CGContextSetStrokeColorSpace. After you set the fill or stroke color space in the graphics state, use Quartz functions to specify the fill or stroke color component values.

2. In Panther and later versions, create a color object, a CGColorRef, which represents a specific color. A CGColorRef encapsulates a color space, the component values in that color space, and an alpha value. After you have a color object, use it to set the fill or stroke color in the graphics state for the context.

The first method is available in all versions of Mac OS X, and for some applications it may be the best approach for setting color in the context. The second method is a more efficient method for setting color for applications that use a relatively small, fixed set of colors. A combination of the two methods may make sense, depending on the situation. "CGColor Objects (Panther)" (page 152) discusses how to create and use CGColorRefs and when to use them.

The functions CGContextSetFillColorSpace or CGContextSetStrokeColorSpace set the fill or stroke color space separately from setting the color values in the color space. For that, use the function CGContextSetFillColor or CGContextSetStroke-Color. These set the fill or stroke painting color for all except the Pattern color space. There are specialized functions to specify the "pattern color." "Drawing with Patterns" (page 481) discusses how to create and use patterns.

A General Approach to Setting Color

This simple example uses a general approach to setting color by first setting the color space and then setting the painting color. You'll see more detailed examples later. Listing 7.1 draws with the DeviceRGB color space explicitly instead of using the functions CGContextSetRGBFillColor or CGContextSetRGB-StrokeColor. The drawing produced by the code in Listing 7.1 is shown in Figure 7.1.

Listing 7.1 Using Quartz color spaces

```
CGColorSpaceRef getTheRGBColorSpace(void)
{
  static CGColorSpaceRef deviceRGB = NULL;
  // Set once, the first time this function is called.
  if(deviceRGB == NULL)
    deviceRGB = CGColorSpaceCreateDeviceRGB();

  return deviceRGB;
}

void doColorSpaceFillAndStroke(CGContextRef context)
{
  CGColorSpaceRef theColorSpace = getTheRGBColorSpace();
  float opaqueRed[] = {0.663, 0.0, 0.031, 1.0}; // red, green, blue, alpha
  float aBlue[] = {0.482, 0.62, 0.871, 1.0}; // red, green, blue, alpha

  // Set the fill color space to be the device RGB color space.
  CGContextSetFillColorSpace(context, theColorSpace);
  // Set the fill color to opaque red. The number of elements in the
  // array passed to this function must be the number of color
  // components in the current fill color space plus one for alpha.
  CGContextSetFillColor(context, opaqueRed);

  // Set the stroke color space to be the device RGB color space.
  CGContextSetStrokeColorSpace(context, theColorSpace);
  // Set the stroke color to opaque blue. The number of elements
  // in the array passed to this function must be the number of color
  // components in the current stroke color space plus one for alpha.
  CGContextSetStrokeColor(context, aBlue);

  CGContextSetLineWidth(context, 8.);
  // ***** Rectangle 1 *****
  CGContextBeginPath(context);
```

Figure 7.1 The drawing produced by the code in Listing 7.1

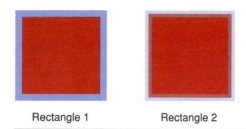

Rectangle 1   Rectangle 2

```
CGContextAddRect(context, CGRectMake(20., 20., 100., 100.));
CGContextDrawPath(context, kCGPathFillStroke);

// Continue to use the stroke color space already set
// but change the stroke alpha value to a semitransparent blue.
aBlue[3] = 0.5;
CGContextSetStrokeColor(context, aBlue);
// ***** Rectangle 2 *****
CGContextBeginPath(context);
CGContextAddRect(context, CGRectMake(140., 20., 100., 100.));
CGContextDrawPath(context, kCGPathFillStroke);

// Don't release the color space since this routine
// didn't create it.
}
```

The code consists of the routine getTheRGBColorSpace, which takes care of the details of obtaining the color space, and the routine doColorSpaceFillAndStroke, which uses the color space and performs the drawing. The routine getTheRGBColorSpace creates a CGColorSpaceRef that corresponds to the DeviceRGB color space by using the function CGColorSpaceCreateDeviceRGB. Because the routine getTheRGBColorSpace is likely to be called repeatedly, the code creates the color space the first time it is called and stores the result in a static variable.

The routine doColorSpaceFillAndStroke first obtains the RGB color space and uses the functions CGContextSetFillColorSpace and CGContextSetStrokeColorSpace to set the current fill and stroke color space in the graphics state. After the color space is set to the desired color space, the color value in that color space can be specified.

The code sets the fill and stroke color by using the functions CGContextSetFillColor and CGContextSetStrokeColor. These functions set the graphics state fill or stroke color for any color space other than the Pattern color space. The number of color components in these color spaces varies, depending on the type of color space; the functions `CGContextSetFillColor` and `CGContextSetStrokeColor` require that the color component data is supplied as an array of floating-point values. When you call the `CGContextSetFillColor` or `CGContextSetStrokeColor` functions, Quartz consults the current fill or stroke color space in the graphics state and uses the corresponding number of entries from the array of floating-point values passed to the function. The number of elements required in the array is the number of components in the current color space plus one for the alpha value. Because the example uses a three-component color space, the DeviceRGB color space, the color array passed to the `CGContextSetFillColor` and `CGContextSetStrokeColor` functions must have four entries.

The code draws Rectangle 1 and then, before calling Quartz to draw Rectangle 2, the code changes the alpha component in the `aBlue` array and calls `CGContextSetStrokeColor`. When the code calls `CGContextSetStrokeColor`, Quartz consults the current stroke color space in the graphics state to determine how to interpret the array of color values passed to it. The stroke color space in the graphics state is the same as that set earlier in the code, the DeviceRGB color space.

The `getTheRGBColorSpace` routine creates the DeviceRGB color space by calling `CGColorSpaceCreateDeviceRGB` so it is responsible for releasing the color space when the routine no longer needs the color space. To release a color space you create, call `CGColorSpaceRelease`. In the case of this example, the intention is to reuse the same color space for the lifetime of the program so there is no call to `CGColorSpaceRelease`. Typically your use of Quartz will require the use of a given color space across a number of your subroutines. The approach taken with the routine `getTheRGBColorSpace` is a good one for such a situation. For situations where you create a color space that you do not need for the duration of your program's execution, you must release it when you are done with it; failing to do so is a source of memory leaks. "Quartz Object and Memory Model" (page 599) discusses releasing Quartz objects in more detail.

Listing 7.1 shows how to use only one color space, DeviceRGB, but it shows the generalized functions that set color using a general color space and color values. With the exception of the Pattern color space, the approach for setting color used in this example can be used for any of the color spaces Quartz provides. "Calibrated Color Spaces" (page 155) and the two sections that follow introduce the different types of color spaces in more detail.

CGColor Objects (Panther)

10.3 ▶

CGColor objects, introduced in Panther, provide an efficient and easy way for applications to manage color. A CGColor object is represented by the opaque type `CGColorRef`. These objects capture a color specification—color space, component values, and alpha value—elminating the need to set these parameters separately, as described previously. Quartz is inherently more efficient at utilizing color specified with a `CGColorRef` than it is at utilizing color specified in the other ways of setting color. This is because a `CGColorRef` is more readily converted into the representation of color that Quartz uses internally. Additionally, a CGColor object is immutable; it can't be changed. This allows Quartz to perform additional optimizations when you reuse a `CGColorRef`. To obtain the best performance, use CGColor objects in your application whenever you use a given color repeatedly.

Using a `CGColorRef` in an application makes sense for applications that use a relatively small set of fixed colors. In that case you can create CGColor objects for each of the colors your application provides and use them as needed. Even if your application has a large set of drawing colors in its drawing palette, almost every application repeatedly uses the colors black and white. For many applications, these are the two most frequently used colors. By creating a `CGColorRef` for each of these colors, application performance can improve.

Typically, you create a `CGColorRef` for a color by using the function `CGColorCreate`, passing the color space and an array of color values plus alpha. You can also create a new CGColor object from an existing `CGColorRef` with the function `CGColorCreateCopyWithAlpha`. This creates a new CGColor object with the same color space and component values as the original CGColor object but with the alpha value that you supply to the function. When you are done with any CGColor object that you create, you call the function `CGColorRelease` to release the memory and other associated resources.

Listing 7.2 draws the same content (shown in Figure 7.1) as that drawn by Listing 7.1, however it does so by using CGColor objects. This example is well suited to using CGColor objects because it draws using a fixed set of drawing colors. The CGColor objects are created once and reused each time the routine is called.

Listing 7.2 Using CGColor objects to represent fixed colors

```
void drawWithColorRefs(CGContextRef context)
{
  static CGColorRef opaqueRedColor = NULL, opaqueBlueColor = NULL,
            transparentBlueColor = NULL;

  // Initialize the CGColorRefs if necessary.
  if(opaqueRedColor == NULL){
    // Initialize the color array to an opaque red
    // in an RGB color space.
    float color[4] = { 0.663, 0.0, 0.031, 1.0 };
```

```
        CGColorSpaceRef theColorSpace = getTheRGBColorSpace();
        // Create a CGColorRef for opaque red.
        opaqueRedColor = CGColorCreate(theColorSpace, color);
        // Make the color array correspond to an opaque blue color.
        color[0] = 0.482; color[1] = 0.62; color[2] = 0.871;
        // Create another CGColorRef for opaque blue.
        opaqueBlueColor = CGColorCreate(theColorSpace, color);
        // Create a new CGColorRef from the opaqueBlue CGColorRef
        // but with a different alpha value.
        transparentBlueColor = CGColorCreateCopyWithAlpha(
                    opaqueBlueColor, 0.5);
        if(!(opaqueRedColor && opaqueBlueColor && transparentBlueColor)){
          fprintf(stderr, "couldn't create one of the CGColorRefs!!!\n");
          return;
        }
    }

    // Set the fill color to the opaque red CGColor object.
    CGContextSetFillColorWithColor(context, opaqueRedColor);
    // Set the stroke color to the opaque blue CGColor object.
    CGContextSetStrokeColorWithColor(context, opaqueBlueColor);

    CGContextSetLineWidth(context, 8.);
    // Draw Rectangle 1.
    CGContextBeginPath(context);
    CGContextAddRect(context, CGRectMake(20., 20., 100., 100.));
    CGContextDrawPath(context, kCGPathFillStroke);

    // Set the stroke color to be that of the transparent blue
    // CGColor object.
    CGContextSetStrokeColorWithColor(context, transparentBlueColor);
    // Draw Rectangle 2 to the right of the first one.
    CGContextBeginPath(context);
    CGContextAddRect(context, CGRectMake(140., 20., 100., 100.));
    CGContextDrawPath(context, kCGPathFillStroke);
}
```

The drawWithColorRefs routine makes use of static references to the CGColor objects it creates so that it needs to create them only the first time the routine is called. It uses the getTheRGBColorSpace routine from Listing 7.1 (page 150) to obtain an RGB color space. The first call to CGColorCreate uses the initial value of the color array and the color space to create a CGColorRef that corresponds to opaque red. It then changes the values of the color array so that the color components correspond to an opaque blue and then creates a new CGColorRef for that color. Notice that changing the values in the color array variable does not affect any previously created CGColorRef; Quartz copies the data it needs from the data you pass to CGColorCreate. After creating the opaque blue CGColor object, the code uses CGColorCreateCopyWithAlpha to make a new CGColor object with the same color space and component color values as the opaque blue CGColor object but with the alpha value of 0.5.

After creating the CGColor objects, the code uses them to set the fill and stroke color space and color by calling the Quartz functions CGContextSetFillColorWithColor and CGContextSetStrokeColorWithColor. Each of these functions simultaneously sets the corresponding color space and color, using the CGColor object passed to it.

When you create a CGColor object, you are responsible for releasing it; however, the routine drawWithColorRefs never releases the CGColorRefs it creates. This routine is intended to be invoked more than once, so it creates the CGColor objects and saves them in static variables. Again, one of the benefits of using CGColor objects is that Quartz reuses color objects efficiently.

After you set the stroke or fill color using a CGColorRef, the corresponding color space in the graphics state is set to that of the CGColorRef you supply. To change the drawing color later with the color-setting functions CGContextSetFillColor or CGContextSetStrokeColor, call CGContextSetFillColorSpace or CGContextSetStrokeColorSpace if the current fill or stroke color space is not already the color space you require.

In addition to the CGColor object creation functions discussed here, Quartz provides the function CGColorCreateWithPattern to create a CGColorRef for a Quartz pattern. Patterns are discussed in detail in "Drawing with Patterns" (page 481).

Calibrated Color Spaces

The goal of color management is to allow accurate reproduction of color across a wide range of output devices. Ideally, the colors specified when drawing appear the same to an observer, regardless of the destination of the drawing. The drawing you see on a display should closely match the output produced when you print. The results you see on one computer display should also match the results you see on another computer display, regardless of the underlying display technology. Obtaining consistent results requires a model for color that is independent of any particular device, a way of modeling color called **device-independent color**. Figure 7.2 illustrates the difference between using device-dependent color and device-independent color. When using device-independent color, the color

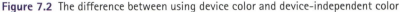

Figure 7.2 The difference between using device color and device-independent color

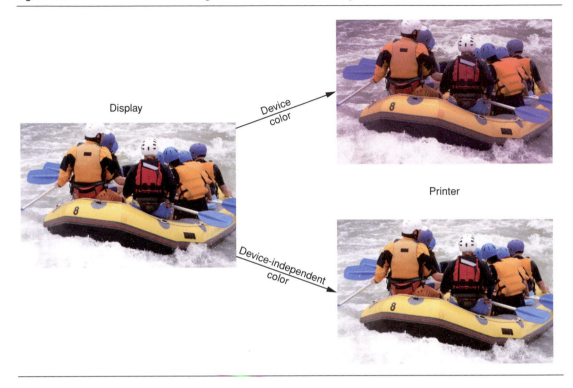

in the image on the display is faithfully reproduced on a printer, whereas when using device color, the resulting colors differ between the display and a printer.

The way device-independent color is characterized has its basis in the study of human visual perception. Color scientists studied the way humans perceive color and have created a color model to describe it. The model used today is one where a standard coordinate system for color has been defined by the Commission Internationale de l'Éclairage (International Commission on Illumination), or CIE. The **CIE XYZ** and **CIE L*a*b*** color spaces are device-independent color spaces; colors in these color spaces have a well-defined meaning.

A color space C is a **calibrated color space** if it provides data, sometimes referred to as a "calibration record," that specifies how to transform a color in that color space (or "color coordinate system") into one of the well-defined, device-independent color spaces; either the CIE XYZ or CIE L*a*b* color space. Some uses of a calibrated color space C also require calibration record data to describe how to transform color values from either the CIE XYZ or CIE L*a*b* color space into the C color space.

Note This discussion of device-independent and calibrated color spaces and the color science behind them is intended solely to provide a basic understanding of the concepts helpful for using calibrated color spaces in Quartz. Readers who want a deeper understanding of CIE color, its history, and the science behind it can explore the references at the end of this chapter.

Color management is tightly integrated into the Quartz imaging model and rendering capabilities. You can take advantage of color management in two ways:

- By using a calibrated color space when you draw with Quartz. When you use a calibrated color space as a fill or stroke color space to paint graphics or when you use a calibrated color space to characterize images you draw with Quartz, the calibrated color space is a **source** color space. By using a calibrated color space, you characterize the component color values of your source drawing as being in a well-defined "color coordinate system," one that has a known mapping to either the CIE XYZ or L*a*b* color space.

- By associating a calibrated color space with a destination, characterizing the "color coordinate system" of that destination. By doing so, color drawn with a calibrated source color space can be transformed (or "matched") accurately into a destination color for that destination, such as a display or printer. Quartz, together with the application frameworks, does this automatically for a context associated with a window. Quartz contexts that represent a specific destination, such as a bitmap context, require a color space to characterize the destination. "Creating Bits" (page 345) discusses this in more detail.

When you use calibrated color spaces for drawing, Quartz transforms the colors you specify into the equivalent color appropriate for the destination device. This allows an application to generate reproducible color, without knowing the destination monitor characteristics or the ultimate destination of printed output or PDF files.

Specifying a calibrated color space when drawing with Quartz is the same as using any other color space. One approach is to create the CGColorSpaceRef for the calibrated color space you want to use, then use the functions CGContextSet-FillColorSpace and CGContextSetStrokeColorSpace to set the appropriate color space in the graphics state for the context. After setting the color space, you use CGContextSetFillColor and CGContextSetStrokeColor to set specific color values in that color space. Another approach is to use a calibrated color space when creating CGColor objects to use for setting color.

The types of calibrated color spaces available in Quartz fall into three broad categories. The first category includes those created by the Quartz functions CGColor-SpaceCreateCalibratedGray and CGColorSpaceCreateCalibratedRGB. These color spaces are specified by parameters that describe monitor phosphors and gamma curves. The second category includes those created by the function CGColor-SpaceCreateLab, which creates a color space corresponding to the device-independent CIE L*a*b* color space. While none of these functions are used by the typical Quartz programmer, developers already familiar with calibrated color in terms of calibrated Gray, RGB, or L*a*b* color spaces may find it useful to create color spaces using these functions.

The third category of calibrated spaces is used by most Quartz programmers and is characterized by **ICC profiles**. ICC profiles are calibration record data based on a specification by the International Color Consortium, the ICC. An ICC profile contains information that allows the transformation of color from the color space characterized by the profile into either the CIE XYZ or L*a*b* color space. An ICC profile can also provide data that allows the transformation of colors from either the CIE XYZ or L*a*b* color space into the color space characterized by the profile. Quartz color spaces based on ICC profiles are called **ICC-Based** color spaces.

The Quartz functions CGColorSpaceCreateWithPlatformColorSpace and CGColor-SpaceCreateICCBased create ICCBased color spaces. The result of using these functions to create the color space is functionally identical; the difference between them is the source of the ICC profile data used to create a color space. The function CGColorSpaceCreateICCBased is a general way to create an ICC-Based color space where the source of the ICC profile data can be arbitrary and is supplied by you to the creation function. While very flexible, most developers do not need to use this method.

The function CGColorSpaceCreateWithPlatformColorSpace is a more typical way to create a Quartz color space that represents an ICC profile. The phrase "platform color space" refers to the fact that the ColorSync framework in Mac OS X creates a representation of the ICC profile that you then pass to Quartz to create the color space. ColorSync is the engine behind the color management that Quartz performs.

Listing 7.3 defines an updated version of the getTheRGBColorSpace routine from Listing 7.1 (page 150). This version creates an ICCBased Quartz color space that corresponds to the generic RGB ICC profile, as provided by Mac OS X. The generic RGB profile is a well-defined calibrated color space that represents a typical display. Using this version of the getTheRGBColorSpace routine with the doColorSpaceFillAndStroke routine from Listing 7.1 produces the same result as before, but with the specification of the drawing colors in a calibrated color space. For those applications that don't have an application-specific calibrated space to draw with, the generic RGB ICC profile is a good choice as the basis for drawing in a calibrated RGB color space.

Listing 7.3 Creating an ICCBased color space for the generic RGB profile

```
// The full path to the generic RGB ICC profile.
#define kGenericRGBProfilePathStr \
  "/System/Library/ColorSync/Profiles/Generic RGB Profile.icc"

CGColorSpaceRef getTheRGBColorSpace(void)
{
  static CGColorSpaceRef genericRGBColorSpace = NULL;
  if (genericRGBColorSpace == NULL)
  {
    CMProfileRef genericRGBProfile = NULL;
    OSStatus err = noErr;
    CMProfileLocation loc;
    // Build up a profile location for ColorSync.
    loc.locType = cmPathBasedProfile;
    strcpy(loc.u.pathLoc.path, kGenericRGBProfilePathStr);
    // Open the profile with ColorSync.
    err = CMOpenProfile(&genericRGBProfile, &loc);
    if(err == noErr){
      genericRGBColorSpace =
        CGColorSpaceCreateWithPlatformColorSpace(
          genericRGBProfile);
      if(genericRGBColorSpace == NULL)
        fprintf(stderr,
          "Couldn't create the generic RGB color space\n");
      // This code opened the profile so it is up to it to close it.
      CMCloseProfile(genericRGBProfile);
    }else{
      // ColorSync could not open the profile so log a message
      // to the console.
      fprintf(stderr,
        "Couldn't open generic profile due to error %d\n",
        (int)err);
    }
  }
  return genericRGBColorSpace;
}
```

This version of the getTheRGBColorSpace routine also uses a static variable to store the CGColorSpaceRef that it creates on the first call to the function. First the code uses the path to the system-supplied generic RGB profile when filling in the CMProfileLocation structure it passes to the ColorSync function CMOpenProfile. The profile reference returned by CMOpenProfile is the input parameter to the Quartz function CGColorSpaceCreateWithPlatformColorSpace. After that color space is created, the code must close the profile it opened by calling the ColorSync function CMCloseProfile.

Mac OS X provides a number of other useful ICC profiles. In addition to the generic RGB profile, there are also system-supplied generic calibrated ICC profiles for the Gray and CMYK color spaces as well as device-independent CIE XYZ and CIE L*a*b* profiles, plus a profile for the sRGB color space. All these profiles are located in the same directory as the generic RGB profile used by the code in Listing 7.3. The code there can easily be modified to use one of these other profiles; just change the path supplied to strcpy in the getTheRGBColorSpace routine. Of course, the number of color components the set-color functions need and the meaning of those color values depends on the color space.

Matching color from a source color space to a destination color space usually has a performance cost associated with it. If the source and the destination are characterized by the same color space, there is no computation required and the destination color is the same as the source color. However, when the source and the destination color space are different, Quartz transforms the source color into a destination color using ColorSync color management.

When drawing text and line art, the cost associated with performing color matching is not usually significant, because the number of colors that need to be matched is relatively small. Because sampled images typically contain a signficant number of color values that must be matched, there is a measurable cost associated with drawing calibrated images to a drawing destination such as a window. This is an important consideration when you draw a given image repeatedly. In some cases, it may make sense to cache drawing so that the color matching takes place only once, allowing significantly better performance for subsequent redrawing of the image. "Caching Drawing Offscreen" (page 379) demonstrates techniques for caching content so that color matching happens only when the content is cached, not each time you draw from the cache to the destination.

Device Color Spaces

Quartz offers three device-dependent color spaces: the DeviceGray, DeviceRGB, and DeviceCMYK color spaces, which correspond to the Gray, RGB, and CMYK color models. For more information on the meaning of color values in these color models, see the references at the end of this chapter. To create a CGColorSpaceRef that corresponds to the DeviceGray, DeviceRGB, and DeviceCMYK color spaces, use the Quartz functions CGColorSpaceCreateDeviceGray, CGColorSpaceCreateDeviceRGB, and CGColorSpaceCreateDeviceCMYK, respectively.

Device color spaces specify color in a way that is tied to a specific device. Consider the color component values needed to reproduce a specific color of red on a specific monitor when using the DeviceRGB color space. The RGB color values that produce that red on that monitor when using the DeviceRGB color space may produce a different red on a different monitor or on a printer. Color component values in the DeviceRGB color space or any device color space are tied to the device and produce different results for different devices. This is the result of using device color.

To ensure the reproducibility of color in the drawing you perform with Quartz, use a calibrated color space instead of a device color space. Quartz makes using them straightforward by having a uniform way of setting a color and color space in the context, regardless of whether it is a calibrated color space or device color space, as you've seen in the code in Listing 7.1 (page 150) and Listing 7.3 (page 159). Device color spaces are legacy color spaces and their usage should be avoided when you care about color fidelity.

The DeviceGray color space does have a special use for certain situations when you want to use a grayscale image as a clipping area or to mask another image. See "Masking an Image (Tiger)" (page 273) and "Clipping to a Mask (Tiger)" (page 282) for information about this use of the DeviceGray color space.

Special Color Spaces

Quartz offers two special color spaces that are not directly based on the Gray, RGB, or CMYK color model: the Pattern color space and the Indexed color space. The Pattern color space allows you to create a piece of Quartz graphics that is itself used as a color when filling or stroking other graphics. "Drawing with Patterns" (page 481) discusses the Pattern color space and shows how to use it.

The Indexed color space is a color space that is based on an underlying color space and a color lookup table, sometimes referred to as a CLUT. Color values are specified in an Indexed color space by an index that is used to look up a set of color component values in the color lookup table. The number of component values for each entry in the lookup table and their meaning depends on the underlying color space that characterizes a given Indexed color space. The Indexed color space is typically used when drawing sampled images that are represented by a color lookup table, such as GIF images, but an Indexed color space can also be used for drawing of text and line art.

To create a CGColorSpaceRef that corresponds to an Indexed color space, use the function CGColorSpaceCreateIndexed, which takes the following parameters:

- baseSpace, the CGColorSpaceRef that characterizes the component values in the color lookup table. This color space can be any color space other than a Pattern color space or an Indexed color space.

- lastIndex, an integer that specifies the maximum valid index value; it must be less than or equal to 255.

- colorTable[], an array of m*(lastIndex+1) bytes, where m is the number of color components in the base color space. Each byte is an unsigned integer in the range 0 to 255 that is scaled to the range of the corresponding color component in the base color space. For a base color space where the component values range from 0.0 to 1.0, the byte value 0 maps to the component value 0.0 and the byte value 255 maps to the component value 1.0. The function CGColorSpaceCreateIndexed copies the contents of the colorTable array when creating the Indexed color space so that the array you pass to this function does not need to be available after the call to create the Indexed color space.

The code in Listing 7.4 performs the same drawing as that in Listing 7.1 (page 150), also producing the results shown in Figure 7.1 (page 151), but instead uses an Indexed color space.

Listing 7.4 Line art graphics drawn with an Indexed color space

```
void doIndexedColorDrawGraphics(CGContextRef context)
{
  CGColorSpaceRef theBaseRGBSpace = getTheRGBColorSpace();
  CGColorSpaceRef theIndexedSpace = NULL;
  unsigned char lookupTable[6];
  float opaqueRed[] = { 0, 1.}; // index, alpha
  float aBlue[] = {1, 1.};      // index, alpha

  // Set the first three values in the lookup table to red = 169/255 = 0.663,
  // no green, and blue = 8/255 = 0.031. This is a shade of red.
  lookupTable[0] = 169; lookupTable[1] = 0; lookupTable[2] = 8;

  // Set the next three values in the lookup table to red = 123/255 = 0.482,
  // green = 158/255 = 0.62, blue = 222/255 = 0.871; a shade of blue.
  lookupTable[3] = 123; lookupTable[4] = 158; lookupTable[5] = 222;

  // Create the Indexed color space with this color lookup table,
  // using the RGB color space as the base color space and a two-element
  // color lookup table to characterize the Indexed color space.
  theIndexedSpace = CGColorSpaceCreateIndexed(theBaseRGBSpace, 1,
                  lookupTable);
  if(theIndexedSpace != NULL){
    CGContextSetStrokeColorSpace(context, theIndexedSpace);
    CGContextSetFillColorSpace(context, theIndexedSpace);
    // Release the color space this code created since it is no
    // longer needed in this routine.
    CGColorSpaceRelease(theIndexedSpace);
```

```
    // Set the stroke color to opaque blue.
    CGContextSetStrokeColor(context, aBlue);
    // Set the fill color to opaque red.
    CGContextSetFillColor(context, opaqueRed);

    CGContextSetLineWidth(context, 8.);
    // Draw Rectangle 1.
    CGContextBeginPath(context);
    CGContextAddRect(context, CGRectMake(20., 20., 100., 100.));
    CGContextDrawPath(context, kCGPathFillStroke);

    // Continue to use the stroke color space already set,
    // but change the stroke alpha value to a semitransparent value
    // while leaving the index value unchanged.
    aBlue[1] = 0.5;
    CGContextSetStrokeColor(context, aBlue);
    // Draw Rectangle 2 to the right of the first one.
    CGContextBeginPath(context);
    CGContextAddRect(context, CGRectMake(140., 20., 100., 100.));
    CGContextDrawPath(context, kCGPathFillStroke);
  }else
    fprintf(stderr, "Couldn't make the indexed color space!\n");
}
```

The doIndexedColorDrawGraphics routine first uses a getTheRGBColorSpace routine to obtain an RGB color space used to characterize the colors in the color lookup table. To characterize the colors in the lookup table with the calibrated generic RGB color space, the example uses the version of the getTheRGBColorSpace routine from Listing 7.3 (page 159). Next the code fills in the values of the color lookup table entries. Because the color lookup table entries are RGB values, the color table has three component values for each index in the color table. The first three array elements are the red, green, and blue component values for the index 0 entry in the color table. The next three elements are the red, green, and blue component values for the index 1 entry in the color lookup table. For this example, the color lookup table has only two entries.

After the color lookup table is filled in, the code creates an Indexed color space by calling the function CGColorSpaceCreateIndexed, passing the base color space that characterizes the entries in the lookup table, the last index value, and the color lookup table array. The code uses the Indexed color space to set the fill and stroke color space, and then calls CGColorSpaceRelease to release the Indexed color space it created. Quartz keeps its own reference to the color space passed to CGContextSetFillColorSpace and CGContextSetStrokeColorSpace. If you no longer need your own reference to a color space that you created, make sure to release it to avoid memory leaks.

The number of components in an Indexed color space is one plus an alpha value. The code creates an opaque red color, the variable opaqueRed, using the index value 0 for the color component in the Indexed color space and an alpha value of 1.0. It uses the function CGContextSetFillColor with this array of floats. The stroke color is constructed similarly, but there the blue color is represented by the index value 1, the first entry in the array of floats passed to CGContextSet-StrokeColor. After drawing the first rectangle, the code changes the stroke color to a semitransparent color of blue by changing the alpha value of the color passed to CGContextSetStrokeColor. Quartz paints the second rectangle with the new stroke color.

The decision whether to create a color space once and keep it around for the duration of the program execution depends on how that color space is used. Typically, Indexed color spaces are created for drawing a particular image, not vector line art, so it is unlikely that a particular Indexed color space is used beyond the drawing of a single image. In a situation that calls for drawing a number of images with the same color table, you could reuse the Indexed color space that represents that color table.

Creating Color Spaces by Name (Jaguar)

10.2 ▶ In Jaguar and later versions, Quartz provides the function CGColorSpaceCreate-WithName to create a Quartz color space for the name supplied. Creating a color space by name is a convenient way to specify a color space without having to write much code or know anything about ColorSync profiles and how to access them. As of Tiger, only a small number of names are supported; other names may be added in the future. In Tiger, for the names kCGColorSpaceGenericGray, kCGColorSpaceGenericRGB, or kCGColorSpaceGenericCMYK, Quartz returns a CGColorSpaceRef that corresponds to the generic color space for the color model requested. For example, passing the name kCGColorSpaceGenericRGB to CGColorSpaceCreateWithName creates the same color space as the code in Listing 7.3 (page 159). When you use CGColorSpaceCreateWithName to create a color space, you should release it with CGColorSpaceRelease after you no longer need it.

If you pass CGColorSpaceCreateWithName the name of a color space that is not supported on a given version of Mac OS X, the color space returned is NULL, so it's important to check the result returned by this function.

Listing 7.5 is an updated version of the getTheRGBColorSpace routine from Listing 7.3. This version uses the function CGColorSpaceCreateWithName together with the external string constant kCGColorSpaceGenericRGB and it does so in a manner that works correctly, even on versions of Mac OS X where the string constant does not exist. First, the code tests whether the symbol kCGColorSpaceGenericRGB exists, and if it does it calls CGColorSpaceCreateWithName. If the symbol does not exist, the updated routine uses the routine getTheRGBColorSpace as defined in Listing 7.3.

This code can only be built correctly in Tiger and later versions because the string `kCGColorSpaceGenericRGB` is not defined in earlier versions of Quartz. In addition, the build environment variable `MACOSX_DEPLOYMENT_TARGET` must be set to 10.2 or later because the weak linking capability this code relies on is only available in Jaguar and later versions. See the references at the end of this chapter for more information about weak linking and Mac OS X.

Listing 7.5 A `getTheRGBColorSpace` routine that uses `CGColorSpaceCreateWithName`

```
CGColorSpaceRef updatedGetTheRGBColorSpace(void)
{
  static CGColorSpaceRef genericRGBColorSpace = NULL;
  if (genericRGBColorSpace == NULL)
  {
    // Test the symbol kCGColorSpaceGenericRGB to see if
    // it is available. If so, use it.
    if(&kCGColorSpaceGenericRGB != NULL)
      genericRGBColorSpace =
        CGColorSpaceCreateWithName(kCGColorSpaceGenericRGB);
    // If genericRGBColorSpace is still NULL, use the technique
    // of using ColorSync to open the disk-based profile from
    // Listing 7.2.
    if(genericRGBColorSpace == NULL){
      genericRGBColorSpace = getTheRGBColorSpace();
    }
  }
  return genericRGBColorSpace;
}
```

Rendering Intents

Color management and color matching of colors across a range of devices cannot produce exact results, because different devices have different inherent abilities to reproduce color. For example, the color **gamut**, or range of colors, that can be reproduced with a device that uses additive color, such as a display device, differs significantly from that of a device that uses subtractive color, such as a printer. In addition to the color gamut, different devices have a different **white point**, which is the whitest white that a given device can render.

Because there are differences in the ability of different physical devices to reproduce color, it is necessary to specify what aspects of color are most important when reproducing the color for a given piece of graphics. The **rendering intent** captures this information. The Quartz imaging model uses the rendering intent as defined in the ICC specification. There are four distinct rendering intents, each of which specifies how in-gamut colors are reproduced on a destination device. The different rendering intents each have a different Quartz constant to represent them:

- `kCGRenderingIntentPerceptual` specifies the "perceptual" rendering intent. This rendering intent produces pleasing visual results and preserves the relationships between colors at the expense of the absolute color reproduction. This intent is typically used for photographic images.

- `kCGRenderingIntentSaturation` specifies the "saturation" rendering intent. This rendering intent attempts to maximize the saturation of colors. This rendering intent is mostly used for business charts or graphics.

- `kCGRenderingIntentRelativeColorimetric` specifies the "relative colorimetric" rendering intent. This rendering intent uses the white point information about the source and destination and adjusts the color information so that the white point of the source maps into the white point of the destination and in-gamut colors are adjusted accordingly. This rendering intent is typically used for line art graphics.

- `kCGRenderingIntentAbsoluteColorimetric` specifies the "absolute colorimetric" rendering intent. This rendering intent performs no white point adjustment to the colors. A color that appears to be white on a screen display may be reproduced on a printed medium as a bluish color because a white color on screen actually has a bluish cast. This rendering intent is useful for simulating one device on another or for rendering logos where exact color reproduction is important.

Quartz also provides the constant `kCGRenderingIntentDefault`; this is the best choice for most situations. When you specify a rendering intent of `kCGRenderingIntentDefault`, Quartz uses the relative colorimetric intent for all drawing except that of sampled images; for sampled images, Quartz uses the perceptual rendering intent.

The rendering intent is a graphics state parameter that affects all drawing except the rendering of images with intrinsic color. (You'll see how rendering intents and images work together in "Drawing Images" (page 203).) To change the rendering intent in the graphics state, use the function `CGContextSetRenderingIntent`, passing either the value `kCGRenderingIntentDefault` or one of the values just summarized. The default value of rendering intent for a context is `kCGRenderingIntentDefault`.

Alpha Transparency

Alpha transparency gives Quartz drawing its layered appearance. By default, Quartz blends drawing that is partially transparent with any drawing underneath using the Porter–Duff blend mode "Source Over Destination." This blending is expressed mathematically as

$$D' = S \times \alpha_s + D \times (1 - \alpha_s)$$

where D' is the new destination color, S is the source color, α_s is the alpha value of the source, and D is the original destination color. For a source alpha value of 1 (completely opaque), the destination is completely replaced by the source color; this is the same as a copy operation. For a source alpha value of 0 (completely transparent), the destination is unchanged. For a source alpha value of 0.5 (50 percent transparent), the new destination is 50 percent of the source color and 50 percent of the original destination color.

As introduced in "Painting with Alpha" (page 30), the fill and stroke colors in the graphics state each have an explicit alpha transparency value. The alpha value in the fill and stroke color is a floating-point value that varies between zero and one, where 0 is fully transparent and 1 is fully opaque. When drawing images with Quartz, the image data has either an explicit alpha value for each image sample or the alpha value is implicitly opaque. (You'll see how to draw images with Quartz in "Drawing Images" (page 203).)

Quartz also has a global alpha value that is part of the graphics state for the context. This global alpha value modifies all drawing to the context by applying additional transparency to the painting color. The global alpha value multiplies the source alpha in the fill or stroke color to produce an effective alpha value that is used for subsequent filling or stroking. The graphics state global alpha value defaults to 1.0; this means that the alpha value of the fill and stroke colors is the effective alpha value of drawing unless you change the global alpha value. To change the graphics state global alpha value you use the function CGContext-SetAlpha. The code in Listing 7.6 changes the context global alpha to modify its drawing.

Listing 7.6 Using the graphics state global alpha to apply an additional alpha value

```
void drawWithGlobalAlpha(CGContextRef context)
{
  int i;
  CGRect rect = CGRectMake(40., 210., 100., 100.);
  float color[4] = { 1., 0., 0., 1. }; // opaque red
  // Set the fill color space to that returned by getTheRGBColorSpace.
  CGContextSetFillColorSpace(context, getTheRGBColorSpace());

  CGContextSetFillColor(context, color);
  for(i = 0; i < 2 ; i++){
    CGContextSaveGState(context);
      // Paint the left rectangle on this row with 100% opaque red.
      CGContextFillRect(context, rect);
```

```
        CGContextTranslateCTM(context, rect.size.width + 70., 0.);
        // Set the alpha value of this rgba color to 0.5.
        color[3] = 0.5;
        // Use the new color as the fill color in the graphics state.
        CGContextSetFillColor(context, color);
        // Paint the center rectangle on this row with 50% opaque red.
        CGContextFillRect(context, rect);

        CGContextTranslateCTM(context, rect.size.width + 70., 0.);
        // Set the alpha value of this rgba color to 0.25.
        color[3] = 0.25;
        // Use the new color as the fill color in the graphics state.
        CGContextSetFillColor(context, color);
        // Paint the right rectangle on this row with 25% opaque red.
        CGContextFillRect(context, rect);
    CGContextRestoreGState(context);
    // After restoring the graphics state, the fill color is set to
    // that prior to calling CGContextSaveGState, that is, opaque
    // red. The coordinate system is also restored.
    // Now set the context global alpha value to 50% opaque.
    CGContextSetAlpha(context, 0.5);
    // Translate down for a second row of rectangles.
    CGContextTranslateCTM(context, 0., -(rect.size.height + 70.));
    // Reset the alpha value of the color array to fully opaque.
    color[3] = 1.;
  }
}
```

The code first sets the fill color space in the graphics state to that returned by the routine getTheRGBColorSpace, the same routine used by the previous examples in this chapter. To set colors in this RGB color space, the code supplies an array of floating-point values consisting of RGB component values and an alpha value. Before entering the for loop the code sets the fill color to a fully opaque red.

The code draws three rectangles each time through the for loop. The first rectangle is the leftmost rectangle, and it is drawn with the fill color that was already set before the beginning of the loop. The second rectangle is the center rectangle; it is drawn with a fill color of 50 percent opaque red. The third rectangle is the rightmost rectangle and is drawn with a fill color of 25 percent opaque red.

The first time through the loop, the graphics state global alpha value is the default, 1.0. Prior to looping a second time, the code translates the CTM in the negative y direction to draw a second row of rectangles and calls CGContextSet-Alpha to change the global alpha value to 0.5. It also sets the alpha component on the color array back to 1.0. When the code executes the loop a second time, the graphics state for the context has the same values as it did during the first time through the loop, except the CTM has translated user space in the negative y direction (down the page) and the global alpha value is now 0.5. The change of the global alpha value between the first and second execution of the loop modifies the drawing that Quartz performs.

Executing the routine drawWithGlobalAlpha produces the result shown in Figure 7.3. As just described, the global alpha value multiplies the fill color alpha. You can see that the top-center rectangle and the bottom-left rectangle are painted with the same color. This is because the top-center rectangle is painted with a context global alpha value of 1.0 and a fill color alpha value of 0.5, resulting in an effective alpha value of 0.5. This is the same result as the bottom-left rectangle that was painted with a fill color alpha value of 1.0 and a global alpha value of 0.5, producing the same effective alpha value of 0.5. For the same reason, the top-right rectangle is painted with the same color as the middle-bottom rectangle; both are painted with the effective alpha value of 0.25.

One particularly important use of the global alpha value occurs when drawing with transparency layers, discussed in "Drawing with Transparency Layers (Panther)" (page 522). A transparency layer groups together a sequence of drawing and then applies an alpha value to the whole sequence, rather than to the individual elements.

Figure 7.3 Applying the graphics state global alpha to Quartz drawing

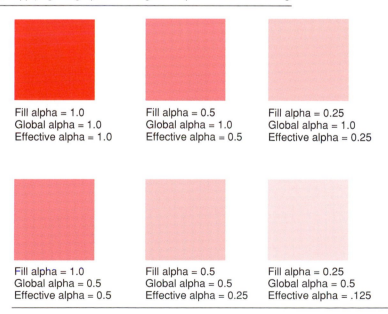

Fill alpha = 1.0
Global alpha = 1.0
Effective alpha = 1.0

Fill alpha = 0.5
Global alpha = 1.0
Effective alpha = 0.5

Fill alpha = 0.25
Global alpha = 1.0
Effective alpha = 0.25

Fill alpha = 1.0
Global alpha = 0.5
Effective alpha = 0.5

Fill alpha = 0.5
Global alpha = 0.5
Effective alpha = 0.25

Fill alpha = 0.25
Global alpha = 0.5
Effective alpha = .125

Blend Modes (Tiger)

10.4 ▶ Added to the Quartz imaging model in Tiger is support for special alpha compositing **blend modes**, modeled after the blend modes available in the PDF imaging model. By default Quartz uses the Normal blend mode; that is the Porter–Duff "Source Over Destination" compositing discussed earlier. The new blend modes available in Tiger and later versions provide additional methods of compositing source graphics to a destination, allowing potentially interesting and useful effects.

Quartz uses the type `CGBlendMode` to represent the available blend modes. The value `kCGBlendModeNormal` represents the Normal blend mode, the Quartz default. To change the blend mode, you use the function `CGContextSetBlendMode`.

Figure 7.4 demonstrates the use of the blend mode `kCGBlendModeColor` to colorize Quartz drawing. The left side of the figure is the drawing of a PDF document without applying any special effects. The top-right portion of the figure is the drawing of the PDF document followed by the drawing of an opaque green rectangle using the default blend mode `kCGBlendModeNormal`. Because the fill color in the graphics state is an opaque color and the blend mode is Normal, the green rectangle obscures the drawing underneath. The bottom-right portion of the figure is the result of drawing the PDF document with the Normal blend mode, then changing the blend mode to `kCGBlendModeColor` and drawing the

Figure 7.4   Using the Quartz blend mode `kCGBlendModeColor` to colorize drawing

rectangle over the PDF document. Quartz blends the rectangle drawing with the background using the kCGBlendModeColor blend mode, producing the effect of colorizing the destination with the source. The blend mode kCGBlendModeColor is useful for colorizing grayscale images and applying a tint to color images, such as the one in the figure.

Listing 7.7 uses the blend mode kCGBlendModeColor to produce the output in Figure 7.4. The code uses the same technique as Listing 2.8 in "Drawing PDF Content" (page 38) to draw a PDF document. It first uses the function CGPDFDocumentCreateWithURL to create a CGPDFDocumentRef from a CFURL object that represents the source PDF document. It obtains the rectangle that describes the size of the document and sets its origin to (0,0). To draw the left side of the figure, the code translates up the drawing canvas to position the drawing and draws the first page of the PDF document with CGContextDrawPDFDocument.

Next the code sets the fill color to an opaque shade of green in an RGB color space and positions to draw the top-right portion of the figure. It draws the PDF document, then draws the rectangle on top. To draw the bottom-right side of the figure, the code positions the origin and draws the PDF document again. This provides the background on which the code again composites the opaque green rectangle. Before drawing the rectangle, the code sets the blend mode in the graphics state by calling CGContextSetBlendMode with the blend mode kCGBlendModeColor. Drawing with this blend mode causes Quartz to composite subsequent drawing by blending the source drawing with the background present in the destination, colorizing the destination with the source color. Finally, the code draws the rectangle over the PDF document it has just drawn. The portion of the background that is covered by the rectangle is colorized with the green fill color with which the rectangle is painted.

Listing 7.7 Colorizing drawing with the kCGBlendModeColor blend mode

```
void drawWithColorBlendMode(CGContextRef context, CFURLRef url)
{
  // A green color.
  float green[4] = { 0.584, 0.871, 0.318, 1. };
  CGRect insetRect, pdfRect;

  // Create a CGPDFDocument object from the URL.
  CGPDFDocumentRef pdfDoc = CGPDFDocumentCreateWithURL(url);
  if(pdfDoc == NULL){
    fprintf(stderr, "Couldn't create CGPDFDocument from URL!\n");
    return;
  }
```

```
// Obtain the media box for page 1 of the PDF document.
pdfRect = CGPDFDocumentGetMediaBox(pdfDoc, 1);
// Set the origin of the rectangle to (0,0).
pdfRect.origin.x = pdfRect.origin.y = 0;

// Graphic 1, the left side of the figure.
CGContextTranslateCTM(context, 20, 10 + CGRectGetHeight(pdfRect)/2);

// Draw the PDF document.
CGContextDrawPDFDocument(context, pdfRect, pdfDoc, 1);

// Set the fill color space to that returned by getTheRGBColorSpace.
CGContextSetFillColorSpace(context, getTheRGBColorSpace());
// Set the fill color to green.
CGContextSetFillColor(context, green);

// Graphic 2, the top-right portion of the figure.
CGContextTranslateCTM(context, CGRectGetWidth(pdfRect) + 10,
            CGRectGetHeight(pdfRect)/2 + 10);

// Draw the PDF document again.
CGContextDrawPDFDocument(context, pdfRect, pdfDoc, 1);

// Make a fill rectangle that is the same size as the PDF document
// but inset each side by 80 units in x and 20 units in y.
insetRect = CGRectInset(pdfRect, 80, 20);
// Fill the rectangle with green. Because the fill color is opaque and
// the blend mode is Normal, this obscures the drawing underneath.
CGContextFillRect(context, insetRect);

// Graphic 3, the bottom-right portion of the figure.
CGContextTranslateCTM(context, 0, -(10 + CGRectGetHeight(pdfRect)));

// Draw the PDF document again.
CGContextDrawPDFDocument(context, pdfRect, pdfDoc, 1);

// Set the blend mode to kCGBlendModeColor, which will
// colorize the destination with subsequent drawing.
CGContextSetBlendMode(context, kCGBlendModeColor);
// Draw the rectangle on top of the PDF document.
CGContextFillRect(context, insetRect);

// Release the CGPDFDocumentRef that the code created.
CGPDFDocumentRelease(pdfDoc);
}
```

The effects available with each blend mode and details about how a blend mode composites the source to a destination are beyond the scope of this book; the references at the end of this chapter provide more information about the blend modes. You are encouraged to explore the available blend modes and use them to achieve effects you find useful.

The compositing operations available in Cocoa, represented by the Cocoa type NSCompositingOperation, allow drawing with compositing operations not available explicitly with Quartz API, including additional Porter–Duff compositing modes beyond the "Source Over Destination" mode that is the Quartz default. However, drawing with these additional Cocoa compositing operations is only supported when drawing to bit-based contexts because they don't correspond to the PDF blend modes that Quartz supports. Using compositing operations other than NSCompositeSourceOver is not supported by the Quartz PDF context or during printing. If support of other compositing operations is important to you for PDF generation or printing, you'll have to render those portions of your content to a bitmap and print the resulting bitmap. Using Cocoa compositing modes overrides any Quartz blend mode you may set in the graphics state.

Caution   The NSCompositingOperation modes other than NSCompositeSourceOver are not supported for drawing to contexts that are not bit-based, such as the PDF and printing contexts.

Graphics State Parameters

Quartz functions that create a path or draw to a graphics context consult various parameters in the graphics state, or **gstate**. Which parameters are consulted depends on the operation that's performed. For example, when you call a path construction function, Quartz uses the current CTM in the graphics state to transform user space coordinates into device space coordinates. When you stroke a path, Quartz uses the current value of the graphics state parameters that affect stroking to determine the style of the stroke, such as the line width. Similarly, Quartz consults the graphics state parameters that affect how it fills paths when you fill a path, such as the fill color.

Important   For every Quartz operation that is affected by a parameter in the graphics state, Quartz consults the current value of that parameter *at the time the operation is performed.*

Table 7.1 describes all the parameters in the Quartz graphics state, includes a cross-reference to the section of this book that discusses that parameter in detail, and lists the default value for each parameter.

Table 7.1 The Quartz Graphics State Parameters

Graphics State Parameter	Discussion	Default Value	Section Reference
CTM	The current transformation matrix. Determines the mapping of coordinates from user space to device space.	Context dependent	"The Current Transformation Matrix" (page 87)
Clipping area	The clipping area is the only portion of the drawing canvas into which Quartz renders.	Context dependent	"Clipping with Paths" (page 129), "Clipping to a Mask (Tiger)" (page 282)
Fill color	The color space and the component values, plus an alpha value, used by Quartz when performing fill operations and the painting of image masks.	DeviceGray opaque black	"Color and Color Spaces" (page 148)
Stroke color	The color space and the component values, plus an alpha value, used by Quartz when performing stroking operations.	DeviceGray opaque black	"Color and Color Spaces" (page 148)
Line width	The thickness, in user space units, that Quartz uses when stroking paths.	1.0	"Line Width" (page 120)
Line cap	The style Quartz uses to paint open endpoints on a subpath when stroking.	kCGLineCapButt	"Line Caps" (page 123)
Line join	The style Quartz uses to paint the join of connected path segments when stroking.	kCGLineJoinMiter	"Line Joins" (page 121)
Miter limit	Determines the angle between connected path segments where Quartz replaces a miter join with a bevel join when stroking.	10.0	"Line Joins" (page 121)
Line dash	The dash pattern Quartz uses when stroking paths.	A solid line	"Line Dash" (page 125)
Alpha	A global alpha value that applies an additional alpha value to all drawing in the context.	1.0	"Alpha Transparency" (page 166)
Rendering intent	The rendering intent applied when painting paths, text, or image masks.	kCGRenderingIntentDefault	"Rendering Intents" (page 165)

continued

Table 7.1   Continued

Graphics State Parameter	Discussion	Default Value	Section Reference
Interpolation quality	The interpolation quality to apply when rendering sampled images.	kCGInterpolationDefault	"Interpolation" (page 217)
Should anti-alias	A Boolean value that determines whether Quartz anti-aliases when rendering.	true, for those contexts that support anti-aliasing	"Anti-aliasing" (page 134)
Shadow	Determines the shadow applied when rendering. Panther and later versions only.	No shadow	"Drawing with Shadows (Panther)" (page 512)
Pattern phase	The offset to the starting point of a pattern.	CGSizeZero	"Drawing with Patterns" (page 481)
Should smooth fonts	A Boolean value that determines whether Quartz should smooth fonts when drawing text. Jaguar and later versions only.	true, for those contexts that support font smoothing	"Font Smoothing (Jaguar)" (page 295)
Text drawing mode	The painting mode Quartz uses when drawing text.	kCGTextFill	"Text Drawing Modes" (page 292)
Font	The font Quartz uses when drawing text.	None	"Font and Font Size" (page 290)
Font size	The point size Quartz uses when drawing text.	0.0	"Font and Font Size" (page 290)
Character spacing	An additional spacing that Quartz adds after each text character when drawing text.	0.0	"Character Spacing" (page 296)
Blend mode	Determines how Quartz composites source drawing to the destination. Available in Tiger and later versions only.	kCGBlendModeNormal	"Blend Modes (Tiger)" (page 170)

If you create a context, it is created with the default context parameters listed in Table 7.1. If you obtain a context from a framework or another source, you should not assume the context parameters are set to the values you need. You need to set the graphics state parameters to those appropriate for your drawing task.

The Quartz functions CGContextSaveGState and CGContextRestoreGState, introduced in "Saving and Restoring a Coordinate System" (page 91), operate on the graphics state as a whole; saving or restoring all the parameters in the graphics state. For each context, Quartz maintains a stack of saved graphics states, the **graphics state stack** or **gstate stack**. This stack is a last-in, first-out stack. The function `CGContextSaveGState` makes a copy of the current graphics state in the context and pushes that copy onto the top of the graphics state stack. The execution of `CGContextSaveGState` does not modify any of the values in the current graphics state. The function `CGContextRestoreGState` pops off (or removes) the topmost graphics state on the graphics state stack and it becomes the current graphics state in the context.

The function `CGContextSaveGState` saves a "snapshot" of the graphics state parameters, pushing the saved graphics state onto the top of the graphics state stack. You can then modify the graphics state parameters such as the CTM, the stroke or fill color, the clipping area, and so on. Functions that modify parameters in the graphics state, such as `CGContextSetLineWidth`, `CGContextScaleCTM`, and `CGContextClip`, affect only the parameters in the current graphics state in the context and do not affect any of the saved graphics states in the graphics state stack. After you are done with the changes you've made to the graphics state, call `CGContextRestoreGState` to pop the topmost entry off the graphics state stack and use that graphics state as the current graphics state.

Important | The current path is not part of the Quartz graphics state. This means that the functions `CGContextSaveGState` and `CGContextRestoreGState` do not affect the current path in the context. This is the same behavior as the PDF imaging model but differs from the PostScript imaging model. In the PostScript imaging model the path is part of the graphics state.

The functions `CGContextSaveGState` and `CGContextRestoreGState` are especially important for managing changes to the clipping area and the CTM. Those Quartz functions that affect these graphics state parameters do so by modifying them rather than replacing them. For example, the function `CGContextClip` intersects the current clipping area in the graphics state with that of the current path in the context; this can only produce a clipping area that is the same as or smaller than the existing clipping area. In order to return to the original clipping area during execution of your code, use `CGContextSaveGState` to save the graphics state that contains the original clipping area prior to modifying the clipping area. When you want to return to the original clipping area, call `CGContextRestoreGState` to return to the saved graphics state that contains the original clipping area. The same is true when changing the CTM; to return to a coordinate system that exists prior to your modifications of the CTM with `CGContextScaleCTM` or the other functions that modify the CTM, call `CGContextSaveGState` prior to changing the CTM and `CGContextRestoreGState` to return to the coordinate system prior to your changes.

By maintaining a stack of graphics states for each context, Quartz allows nested calls to `CGContextSaveGState` and `CGContextRestoreGState`. You can call `CGContextSaveGState` to save a copy of the current graphics state, make changes to the graphics state, and again call `CGContextSaveGState`, prior to calling `CGContextRe-`

storeGState. Listing 7.8 demonstrates the behavior of nested calls to CGContext-
SaveGState and CGContextRestoreGState.

Listing 7.8 The behavior of nested calls to CGContextSaveGState

```
...
CGContextSetLineWidth(context, 2.);
// The line width in the current graphics state is 2.
// Now push a copy of the current graphics state onto the
// graphics state stack. Call that copy "graphics state 1."
CGContextSaveGState(context);
    // "graphics state 1" is now at the top of the graphics state
    // stack; the current graphics state is a copy of
    // "graphics state 1."
    CGContextSetLineWidth(context, 10.);
    // Now the line width in the current graphics state is 10.
    // Now push a copy of the current graphics state onto
    // the graphics state stack. Call that copy "graphics state 2."
    CGContextSaveGState(context);
        // "graphics state 2" is now at the top of
        // the graphics state stack; the current graphics state
        // is a copy of "graphics state 2."
        CGContextSetLineWidth(context, 5.);
        // The line width in the current graphics state is now 5.
    // Now restore to the topmost graphics state on the
    // graphics state stack, that of "graphics state 2." This removes
    // "graphics state 2" from the graphics state stack and
    // "graphics state 1" is now at the top of the graphics
    // state stack.
    CGContextRestoreGState(context);
    // Now the current graphics state is "graphics state 2" and
    // the line width is now 10.

// Now restore to the topmost graphics state on the
// graphics state stack, that of "graphics state 1." This removes
// "graphics state 1" from the top of the graphics state stack.
CGContextRestoreGState(context);
// Now the current graphics state is "graphics state 1" and
// the line width is 2. The top of the graphics state stack has
// whatever it had on it at the time this code fragment started.
```

By making multiple calls to CGContextSaveGState prior to the balancing call to
CGContextRestoreGState, you can isolate changes you make to the graphics state

in one portion of your code from another. Listing 7.9 shows how to take advantage of this behavior. This code produces the output shown in Figure 7.5 (page 180).

Listing 7.9 Typical usage of nested calls to CGContextSaveGState to manage the graphics state

```
static inline float DEGREES_TO_RADIANS(float degrees){
  return degrees * M_PI/180;
}

void createEllipsePath(CGContextRef context, CGPoint center,
               CGSize ellipseSize)
{
  CGContextSaveGState(context);
    // Translate the coordinate origin to the center point.
    CGContextTranslateCTM(context, center.x, center.y);
    // Scale the coordinate system to half the width and height
    // of the ellipse.
    CGContextScaleCTM(context,
               ellipseSize.width/2, ellipseSize.height/2);
    CGContextBeginPath(context);
    // Add a circular arc to the path, centered at the origin and
    // with a radius of 1.0. This radius, together with the
    // scaling above for the width and height, produces an ellipse
    // of the correct size.
    CGContextAddArc(context, 0., 0., 1.0, 0., DEGREES_TO_RADIANS(360), 0);
    // Close the path so that this path is suitable for stroking,
    // should that be desired.
    CGContextClosePath(context);
  CGContextRestoreGState(context);
}

void doClippedEllipse(CGContextRef context)
{
  CGPoint theCenterPoint = { 120., 120. };
  CGSize theEllipseSize = { 100., 200. };
  float dash[1] = { 2 };
  static CGColorRef opaqueBrownColor = NULL, opaqueOrangeColor = NULL;
  // Initialize the CGColorRefs if necessary.
  if(opaqueBrownColor == NULL){
    // The initial value of the color array is an
    // opaque brown in an RGB color space.
    float color[4] = { 0.325, 0.208, 0.157, 1. };
```

```
  CGColorSpaceRef theColorSpace = getTheRGBColorSpace();
  // Create a CGColorRef for opaque brown.
  opaqueBrownColor = CGColorCreate(theColorSpace, color);
  // Make the color array correspond to an opaque orange color.
  color[0] = 0.965 ; color[1] = 0.584; color[2] = 0.059;
  // Create another CGColorRef for opaque orange.
  opaqueOrangeColor = CGColorCreate(theColorSpace, color);
}
// Draw two ellipses centered about the same point, one
// rotated 45 degrees from the other.
CGContextSaveGState(context);
  // ***** Ellipse 1 *****
  createEllipsePath(context, theCenterPoint, theEllipseSize);
  CGContextSetFillColorWithColor(context, opaqueBrownColor);
  CGContextFillPath(context);
  // Translate and rotate about the center point of the ellipse.
  CGContextTranslateCTM(context,
              theCenterPoint.x, theCenterPoint.y);
  // Rotate by 45 degrees.
  CGContextRotateCTM(context, DEGREES_TO_RADIANS(45));
  // CGPointZero is a predefined Quartz point corresponding to
  // the coordinate (0,0).
  // ***** Ellipse 2 *****
  createEllipsePath(context, CGPointZero, theEllipseSize);
  CGContextSetFillColorWithColor(context, opaqueOrangeColor);
  CGContextFillPath(context);
CGContextRestoreGState(context);

CGContextTranslateCTM(context, 170., 0.);
// Now use the first ellipse as a clipping area prior to
// painting the second ellipse.
CGContextSaveGState(context);
  // ***** Ellipse 3 *****
  createEllipsePath(context, theCenterPoint, theEllipseSize);
  CGContextSetStrokeColorWithColor(context, opaqueBrownColor);
  CGContextSetLineDash(context, 0, dash, 1);
  // Stroke the path with a dash.
  CGContextStrokePath(context);
  // ***** Ellipse 4 *****
  createEllipsePath(context, theCenterPoint, theEllipseSize);
  // Clip to the elliptical path.
  CGContextClip(context);
  CGContextTranslateCTM(context,
              theCenterPoint.x, theCenterPoint.y);
```

```
        // Rotate by 45 degrees.
        CGContextRotateCTM(context, DEGREES_TO_RADIANS(45));
        // ***** Ellipse 5 *****
        createEllipsePath(context, CGPointZero, theEllipseSize);
        CGContextSetFillColorWithColor(context, opaqueOrangeColor);
        CGContextFillPath(context);
    CGContextRestoreGState(context);
}
```

The code consists of an inline routine that converts degrees to radians and two routines: createEllipsePath, which creates a closed elliptical path and doClipped-Ellipse, which draws several elliptical shapes, using the createEllipsePath routine to construct the elliptical paths.

The routine createEllipsePath creates a closed elliptical path centered about an x and y location specified by a CGPoint structure. The width and height of the ellipse are passed to the routine as a CGSize structure. To draw the ellipse about the center point passed to the routine, the code translates the Quartz origin to the center point. To draw a circular arc that has the correct width and height of the ellipse, the code scales the coordinate system so that a circle of radius 1.0 units is an elliptical shape of the correct width and height. The code in the createEllipsePath routine uses CGContextSaveGState and CGContextRestoreGState so that after it returns, the only change to the context and the current graphics state is that the path in the context is the closed elliptical shape. By using CGContextSaveGState and CGContextRestoreGState in createEllipsePath, any code that calls this routine is isolated from the temporary changes createEllipsePath needs to make to the graphics state during its execution.

The doClippedEllipse routine first creates CGColor objects for the two drawing colors it uses during its execution. Again the code stores these CGColor objects in static variables since it is written with the expectation that the doClippedEllipse routine is called many times as part of an application's execution.

Figure 7.5 Drawing and clipping with ellipses

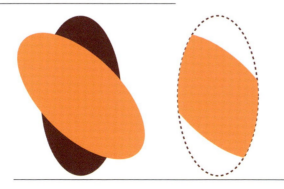

After creating the CGColor objects, doClippedEllipse calls CGContextSaveGState to push the current Quartz graphics state onto the graphics state stack. It then calls createEllipsePath to create Ellipse 1 and fills it with the opaque brown color. It then prepares to draw Ellipse 2, an ellipse that is rotated by 45 degrees relative to Ellipse 1. It translates the coordinate system to the center of the ellipse, then rotates by 45 degrees. The code then creates an elliptical path that is identical to Ellipse 1 but in the transformed coordinate system. The current origin is at the center of the ellipse after translating and rotating the coordinate system; therefore, the code calls createEllipsePath with the point CGPointZero as the origin of the ellipse. Quartz defines the point CGPointZero as the coordinate point (0,0). After creating the path, the code fills that path with the opaque orange color. After it completes the drawing of the first two ellipses, the code calls CGContextRestoreGState to restore the Quartz graphics state to that before it set up the drawing for Ellipse 1.

Note that this code doesn't need to track whether createEllipsePath also uses CGContextSaveGState, because the graphics state save and restore routines use an infinitely deep graphics state stack that is a last-in, first-out stack. As long as the routines that doClippedEllipse calls take care of using CGContextSave-GState and CGContextRestoreGState as a pair, the code in doClippedEllipse can use CGContextSaveGState and CGContextRestoreGState for its own graphics state management.

The routine doClippedEllipse draws the second set of ellipses in a similar fashion but instead of filling Ellipse 3, the code strokes it with a dash pattern. It then creates Ellipse 4 and calls CGContextClip to intersect the elliptical path with the current clipping area, creating a new, smaller clipping area; that inside of Ellipse 4. Finally, it creates Ellipse 5 and paints it; the only portions of Ellipse 5 that are painted are those portions that are inside the clipping area.

Important Every call you make to CGContextSaveGState must be balanced with a subsequent call to CGContextRestoreGState. Failing to do so produces undefined results.

Saving and restoring the graphics state is a relatively cheap operation. You should use CGContextSaveGState and CGContextRestoreGState to manage the graphics state as needed rather than working hard to avoid their use.

Summary

Quartz provides a wide variety of color spaces to choose from when drawing, including calibrated color spaces. Because ColorSync color management is built into Quartz, drawing with a calibrated color space is just as easy as with any other color space and achieves consistent color fidelity across a range of output devices. The fill and stroke colors each consist of a color space, a set of color component values in that color space, and an alpha value. Because alpha compositing is an integral part of Quartz drawing, an alpha value is one of the color components for every painting color. Quartz provides several flexible ways to specify color, including the CGColor object. Using CGColor objects appropriately can improve application performance.

The stroke and fill colors are part of the graphics state—the drawing parameters that affect the way Quartz constructs paths and paints graphics. The functions `CGContextSaveGState` and `CGContextRestoreGState` work together with the graphics state stack that each Quartz context provides to manage graphics states. By using these graphics state save and restore functions, you can effectively manage changes to the graphics state parameters and isolate those changes to the portions of the code that require them.

In this and previous chapters you have seen how to create content using Quartz. The next chapter shows how to get existing content into Quartz using an opaque object, the data provider. You'll also see how to write out the content you create using another opaque object, the data consumer. Data providers and data consumers abstract the data reading and writing process, making it straightforward to perform either task.

See Also

Quartz color spaces are based on those available in the PDF imaging model:

- *PDF Reference: Version 1.6*, 5th edition, Adobe Systems, Inc. and other versions of the PDF specification are available:

  http://partners.adobe.com/public/developer/pdf/index_reference.html

Alpha compositing and the Source Over Destination compositing operation is described in

- "Compositing Digital Images." Thomas Porter and Tom Duff. *Proceedings of the 11th Annual Conference on Computer Graphics and Interactive Techniques*, 1984, pp. 253–259.

The Quartz blend modes are the same as the PDF blend modes described in the PDF specification. Examples and a description of each Quartz blend mode are available in Apple's document *Quartz 2D Programming Guide*, available from the ADC Reference Library:

■ *http://developer.apple.com/documentation/GraphicsImaging/Conceptual/drawingwithquartz2d/index.html*

For more information on color management and the way the eye perceives color, see the following:

■ *Color Appearance Models*, Mark D. Fairchild, John Wiley and Sons, 2nd edition, 2005.

■ *Digital Color Management: Encoding Solutions*, Edward J. Giorgianni and Thomas E. Madden, Prentice Hall PTR, 1998.

Information on ColorSync is available from Apple in the following document:

■ "Color Management Overview", available from the ADC Reference Library:

http://developer.apple.com/documentation/GraphicsImaging/Conceptual/csintro/

The following are useful resources about color on the Web:

■ The website for the International Commission on Illumination (CIE) is at

www.cie.co.at

■ The website for the International Color Consortium is at

www.color.org

Information about weak linking and Mac OS X is available online in the following documents:

■ "Technical Note TN2064: Ensuring Backwards Binary Compatibility-Weak Linking and Availability Macros on Mac OS X," available from the ADC Reference Library:

http://developer.apple.com/technotes/tn2002/tn2064.html

■ "Frameworks and Weak Linking", available from the ADC Reference Library:

http://developer.apple.com/documentation/MacOSX/Conceptual/BPFrameworks/Concepts/WeakLinking.html

The Quartz header files that contain the structures and functions used in this chapter are

- `CGContext.h`
- `CGColor.h`
- `CGColorSpace.h`

The ColorSync header file combining the structures and functions used in this chapter is

- `CMApplication.h`

The ColorSync header files are located in

- `/System/Library/Frameworks/ApplicationServices.framework/Frameworks/ColorSync.framework/Headers`

The relevant reference documentation from the ADC Reference Library is

- *CGContext Reference*
- *CGColor Reference*
- *CGColorSpace Reference*
- *ColorSync Manager Reference*

Chapter **8**

Data Providers and Data Consumers

Just about all the examples in the book so far create content using Quartz line art drawing routines to draw to a graphics context. But what if an application needs to draw from other sources—JPEG, GIF, PDF, and so forth—or write content to such destinations as the hard disk, the Clipboard, a location on the Web, or a block of memory? Quartz provides two opaque data types—CGDataProviderRef and CGDataConsumerRef—that abstract the data access process, making it easy to obtain data from a variety of sources as well as to write data to various destinations. Data providers (CGDataProviderRef) read data from a source, while data consumers (CGDataConsumerRef) write data to a destination, as Figure 8.1 depicts.

Figure 8.1 Data providers and data consumers abstract data access

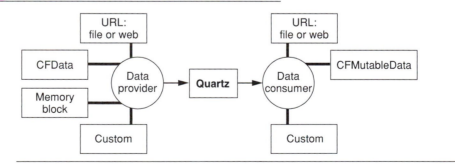

Data providers and data consumers aren't the only data types Quartz provides for reading and writing data, but they are the most versatile. They can access PDF, PostScript, and bitmap image data and they have been part of Quartz since its beginning, making them backward-compatible. The next chapter, "Drawing Images" (page 203), uses data providers to access image data. Later in that chapter, you'll learn additional ways to access data sources and destinations.

Data Providers

Data providers retrieve and package data so that the data can be used by Quartz for such tasks as drawing images and PDF documents and supplying PostScript data to a PostScript-to-PDF converter. Quartz uses the opaque data type `CGDataProviderRef` to represent data providers (CGDataProvider objects). These objects encapsulate the source of data and separate the task of obtaining the data from what the data is used for. The creator of a data provider supplies the data that the provider references. Once created, a CGDataProvider object manages the source of the data, freeing you from that task. The code that uses the data provider may need to know the type of data that the data provider supplies but doesn't need to worry about how the data provider supplies the data.

There are several functions for creating data providers; each function creates a data provider that accesses the underlying data in a different way. The data provider appropriate for your needs depends on the source of the data. After you create a data provider, you can use it without regard to how it supplies the data. If you have code that draws an image or PDF document page from a data provider, it doesn't matter how you create the CGDataProvider object.

You can choose from these functions to create a CGDataProvider object:

- `CGDataProviderCreateWithURL` is the best choice for data whose location can be specified by a Core Foundation URL object (`CFURLRef`). The typical use for this is to access a local file.

- `CGDataProviderCreateWithData` is typically used to obtain data of a specific size from a block of memory.

- `CGDataProviderCreate` is recommended when you can only provide sequential access to data. You supply a series of callbacks to obtain the data.

- `CGDataProviderCreateDirectAccess` provides random access to data through a series of callbacks you supply to obtain the data.

- `CGDataProviderCreateWithCFData` provides data from a Core Foundation data object (`CFDataRef`). One typical use of this data provider is to obtain data from a Macintosh pasteboard, such as the Clipboard.

The next five sections detail how to use each function. Subsequent chapters (see "Drawing Images" (page 203), "Opening and Drawing PDF Documents" (page 397), and "Creating and Examining PDF Documents" (page 435)) use the code described in these sections to create data providers and data consumers. "Guidelines for Using Data Providers" (page 198) discusses coding practices that ensure the integrity of the data referenced by any data providers that you create.

CGDataProviderCreateWithURL

The function CGDataProviderCreateWithURL accesses data at a location that can be specified as a URL, which can be a location on a disk or a location on the Web. The URL must be packaged as a Core Foundation URL (CFURL) object. The createDataProviderFromPathName routine in Listing 8.1 creates a URL-based data provider from a path name. The routine takes a CFString object as a parameter and calls the Core Foundation function CFURLCreateWithFileSystemPath to create a CFURL object that is then passed to CGDataProviderCreateWithURL.

Listing 8.1 Creating a data provider from a path name

```
CGDataProviderRef createDataProviderFromPathName(CFStringRef path)
{
  CFURLRef url;
  // Create a CFURL for the supplied file system path.
  url = CFURLCreateWithFileSystemPath(NULL, path,
                 kCFURLPOSIXPathStyle, false);
  if(url == NULL){
    fprintf(stderr, "Couldn't create url!\n");
    return NULL;
  }
  // Create a Quartz data provider for the URL.
  CGDataProviderRef dataProvider = CGDataProviderCreateWithURL(url);
  // Release the URL when done with it.
  CFRelease(url);
  if(dataProvider == NULL){
    fprintf(stderr, "Couldn't create data provider!\n");
    return NULL;
  }
  return dataProvider;
}
```

CGDataProviderCreateWithData

You can use the function `CGDataProviderCreateWithData` for data that is available in a single contiguous block of memory. You provide the pointer to the memory and its size, together with a release function that Quartz calls when it is done using the memory. After you create such a data provider, you must ensure that the pointer you supply to the function `CGDataProviderCreateWithData` is valid and points to the data until Quartz calls the release function that you supply.

The parameters to this function consist of the following:

- `info`, a pointer to a block of memory that contains any data that your data release function needs in order to clean up when it is called.

- `data`, a pointer to the block of memory that Quartz uses as the source of the data. Quartz uses the first byte of `data` as the beginning of the data stream supplied by the data provider.

- `size`, the number of valid bytes supplied in the `data` parameter.

- `releaseData`, a release function that Quartz calls when it no longer needs access to the memory specified by the `data` parameter. Your function should release any memory or other resources associated with `data`.

Listing 8.2 shows how to create a data provider from a block of memory. This example generates data corresponding to a synthetic image—an 8-bits-per-component RGB image of a red-green color ramp. The example generates the color ramp data, then creates a data provider for that data. The routine `create-RGBRampDataProvider` first allocates a block of memory to contain the generated data and it writes the color ramp data into that memory. The red component color data in the ramp varies linearly from 0 at the left edge of each scanline to 255 at the right edge of the scanline. The green component color data varies linearly from 0 in the first scanline to 255 in the last scanline.

After the data is initialized, the function `CGDataProviderCreateWithData` creates the data provider from the data. The data provider requires no data other than the memory block itself, which is why the `info` parameter for the function `CGDataProviderCreateWithData` is NULL. The function also takes as parameters the data, the data size, and the release routine `rgbRampDataRelease`, which releases the memory needed for the ramp data. Because the data was created with `malloc`, the release routine is simple—it calls `free`.

The data supplied by the data provider must be available until Quartz no longer needs it, which is why you must supply a data release routine when you call the function `CGDataProviderCreateWithData`. Listing 8.2 shows how to create a data provider but does not actually use the data provider to get data. You'll see in

"Drawing Images" (page 203) how to use the data provider with Quartz functions to use image data. After Quartz finishes with the data, it calls your function to release the data associated with the data provider.

Failure to keep the data available until Quartz calls your release function is a source of bugs that may not be immediately apparent. "Guidelines for Using Data Providers" (page 198) and "Checking for Data Provider Integrity" (page 619) discuss this in greater detail.

Listing 8.2 Using CGDataProviderCreateWithData to access an in-memory block of data

```
static void rgbReleaseRampData(void *info,
                const void *data, size_t size)
{
  free((char *)data);
}


CGDataProviderRef createRGBRampDataProvider(void)
{
  CGDataProviderRef dataProvider = NULL;
  size_t width = 256, height = 256;
  size_t imageDataSize = width*height*3;
  unsigned char *p;
  unsigned char *dataP = (unsigned char *)malloc(imageDataSize);
  if(dataP == NULL){
    return NULL;
  }

  p = dataP;
  // Build an image that is RGB 24 bits per sample. This is a ramp
  // where the red component value increases in red from left to
  // right and the green component increases from top to bottom.
  int r, g;
  for(g = 0 ; g < height ; g++){
    for(r = 0 ; r < width ; r++){
      *p++ = r; *p++ = g; *p++ = 0;
    }
  }
  // Once this data provider is created, the data associated
  // with dataP MUST be available until Quartz calls the data
  // release function 'rgbReleaseRampData'.
  dataProvider = CGDataProviderCreateWithData(NULL, dataP,
                imageDataSize, rgbReleaseRampData);
  return dataProvider;
}
```

CGDataProviderCreate

The function `CGDataProviderCreate` creates a data provider that, instead of accessing data from a block of memory, accesses the data through a series of application-supplied callback routines. This function is appropriate for handling large amounts of data that don't fit in memory or for providing data that requires processing prior to supplying it to Quartz. For example, this function provides a way for you to read data that uses a compression scheme that Quartz doesn't support.

The function `CGDataProviderCreate` takes a pointer to a `CGDataProviderCallbacks` structure as a parameter. The structure contains four fields that point to callback functions:

- `getBytes` points to a routine that fills in a Quartz-supplied buffer with the number of bytes that Quartz requests.

- `skipBytes` points to a routine that Quartz calls to skip a specific number of bytes in the data stream.

- `rewind` points to a routine that Quartz calls to reset the current position in the data stream to the beginning of the data.

- `releaseProvider` points to a routine that Quartz calls when it is done with the data provider and signals it's okay to release any resources used to provide the data.

This type of data provider has an implicit location in the data stream you provide to Quartz; initially it is 0. This location in the data stream may be unrelated to the originating data; instead, it refers to the location in the stream of bytes that Quartz expects to be passed back to it. For example, if you use this kind of data provider to provide access to compressed data that you are uncompressing, the location in the data stream is the location in the uncompressed data stream passed to Quartz through the data provider.

Quartz calls your `getBytes` routine with a `count` of the number of bytes you should provide and a `buffer` into which you write that number of bytes. You copy `count` number of bytes, beginning at the current location in the data stream you provide to Quartz, into `buffer`.

Quartz calls the `skipBytes` routine when it needs to move ahead in the data stream of the data provider but does not need to obtain the intermediate bytes. Quartz calls the `rewind` routine to reset the position in the data stream to the beginning.

The code in Listing 8.3 defines the routine `createSequentialAccessDPForURL` and its associated callbacks and data structures. This routine creates a data provider that accesses a file in the file system that is specified with a `CFURLRef`. The code and its callbacks use standard UNIX file system calls (`fread`, `fseek`, `rewind`, fclose) to read uncompressed data from a file and provide that data to Quartz. This code takes advantage of the fact that the current file location maintained by the file system functions keeps track of the location in the data stream provided to Quartz. The rewind routine is equivalent to rewinding to the beginning of the file. The skipBytes routine skips the specified number of bytes by seeking ahead by the requested number of bytes relative to the current location in the file. The getBytes routine reads the requested number of bytes from the current file location into the buffer Quartz provides. The releaseProvider function closes the file and releases the memory allocated for the info parameter that the data provider uses.

The code contains some conditionally compiled debugging code that tracks the total number of bytes read during the lifetime of the data provider, the total number of bytes skipped, and the total number of times the data stream is rewound to its beginning. These statistics are written to stderr when Quartz calls the data provider's release routine.

Note   Listing 8.3 illustrates sequential-access data provider callbacks and their usage. Don't use the code as a model for accessing files on disk—the code does not scale well when a large number of files must be accessed since there is a limit on the number of open files a process can have. Use the Quartz function CGDataProviderCreateWithURL to access files on disk.

Listing 8.3 Using CGDataProviderCreate to access sequential data

```
typedef struct MyImageDataInfo{
  FILE *fp;
#if DEBUG
  size_t totalBytesRead;
  size_t skippedBytes;
  size_t numRewinds;
#endif
}MyImageDataInfo;

static size_t getBytesSequentialAccessDP(void *data,
              void *buffer, size_t count)
{
  size_t readSize = 0;
  FILE *fp = ((MyImageDataInfo *)data)->fp;
  // This reads 'count' 1-byte objects and returns
  // the number of objects (i.e., bytes) read.
  readSize = fread(buffer, 1, count, fp);
#if DEBUG
  ((MyImageDataInfo *)data)->totalBytesRead += readSize;
```

```
#endif
  return readSize;
}


static void skipBytesSequentialAccessDP(void *data, size_t count)
{
  int result = fseek(((MyImageDataInfo *)data)->fp, count, SEEK_CUR);
  if(result != 0)
    fprintf(stderr, "Couldn't seek by %zd bytes because of: %s!\n",
                count, strerror(errno));
#if DEBUG
  ((MyImageDataInfo *)data)->skippedBytes += count;
#endif
}


static void rewindSequentialAccessDP(void *data)
{
  // Rewind the beginning of the data.
  rewind(((MyImageDataInfo *)data)->fp);
#if DEBUG
  ((MyImageDataInfo *)data)->numRewinds++;
#endif
}


static void releaseSequentialAccessDP(void *data)
{
  if(data){
    MyImageDataInfo *imageDataInfoP = (MyImageDataInfo *)data;
#if DEBUG
    fprintf(stderr,
      "read %zd bytes, skipped %zd bytes, rewind called %zd times\n",
      imageDataInfoP->totalBytesRead, imageDataInfoP->skippedBytes,
      imageDataInfoP->numRewinds);
#endif
    if(imageDataInfoP->fp != NULL)
      fclose(imageDataInfoP->fp);
    free(imageDataInfoP);
  }
}


CGDataProviderRef createSequentialAccessDPForURL(CFURLRef url)
{
  MyImageDataInfo *imageDataInfoP = NULL;
  CGDataProviderRef provider = NULL;
```

```
      FILE *fp = NULL;
      CGDataProviderCallbacks callbacks;
      char pathString[PATH_MAX + 1];
      Boolean success = CFURLGetFileSystemRepresentation(url, true,
                  pathString, sizeof(pathString));
      if(!success)
      {
        fprintf(stderr, "Couldn't get the path name C string!\n");
        return NULL;
      }

      fp = fopen(pathString, "r");
      if(fp == NULL){
        fprintf(stderr, "Couldn't open path to file %s!\n", pathString);
        return NULL;
      }
      imageDataInfoP = (MyImageDataInfo *)malloc(sizeof(MyImageDataInfo));
      if(imageDataInfoP == NULL){
        fclose(fp);
        fprintf(stderr, "Couldn't malloc block for info data!\n");
        return NULL;
      }
      imageDataInfoP->fp = fp;

#if DEBUG
      imageDataInfoP->totalBytesRead =
      imageDataInfoP->skippedBytes =
      imageDataInfoP->numRewinds = 0;
#endif

      callbacks.getBytes = getBytesSequentialAccessDP;
      callbacks.skipBytes = skipBytesSequentialAccessDP;
      callbacks.rewind = rewindSequentialAccessDP;
      callbacks.releaseProvider = releaseSequentialAccessDP;
      provider = CGDataProviderCreate(imageDataInfoP, &callbacks);
      if(provider == NULL){
        fprintf(stderr, "Couldn't create data provider!\n");
        // Release the info data and clean up.
        releaseSequentialAccessDP(imageDataInfoP);
        return NULL;
      }
      return provider;
}
```

CGDataProviderCreateDirectAccess

The function `CGDataProviderCreateDirectAccess` creates a data provider that uses a set of callbacks to provide data to Quartz. This type of data provider gives Quartz random access to data that you need to manage.

The function takes a pointer to a `CGDataProviderDirectAccessCallbacks` structure as a parameter. The structure contains four fields, each of which can contain a pointer to callback functions. You either fill in the `getBytes` field or the `getBytePointer` and `releaseBytePointer` fields, depending on whether you want to access data as one block in memory or to access data randomly.

- `getBytes` points to a routine, and if the pointer is not NULL, Quartz calls this routine to obtain a specific number of bytes starting at a specific offset into the data stream supplied by the data provider. If you specify a callback routine for both the `getBytes` and `getBytePointer` fields, Quartz uses the routine specified in the `getBytePointer` and ignores the `getBytes` field.

- `getBytePointer` optionally points to a routine, and if the pointer is not NULL, Quartz calls this routine to obtain a pointer to a block of memory that contains the data that you are providing. The returned pointer must point to all the data provided by the data provider and must be valid until Quartz invokes your routine to release the memory (as specified by the `releaseBytePointer` field).

- `releaseBytePointer` points to a routine, and if the pointer is not NULL, Quartz calls this routine to release the byte pointer it obtained previously by calling the routine pointed to by the `getBytePointer` field.

- `releaseProvider` points to a routine, and if the pointer is not NULL, Quartz calls this routine when it no longer needs the data provider and to signal to release any resources that provide the data.

Fill in the `getBytes` field, and specify NULL for the `getBytePointer` and `releaseBytePointer` fields, when you can supply random access to data that is not completely resident in memory. This is the most typical use of this data provider. Quartz calls your `getBytes` callback requesting count bytes at offset bytes into the data stream you provide to Quartz. The data provider created by the function `CGDataProviderCreateDirectAccess` is similar to the sequential access data provider created with the function `CGDataProviderCreate` except that the `getBytes` routine here receives requests for data at a specific offset rather than at an implied position in the data stream.

Specify routines for the `getBytePointer` and `releaseBytePointer` fields, and NULL for the `getBytes` field, to provide direct access to the data as a single block of memory. Note that the data provider created for `CGDataProviderCreateDirectAccess` is similar to that created by the function `CGDataProviderCreate-`

WithData. Both functions access data as a single block of memory. The difference is that with a data provider created with CGDataProviderCreateWith-Data, you provide access to that memory for the lifetime of the data provider, whereas with the in-memory form of a data provider created with CGDataProviderCreateDirectAccess, the block of data is only required at the actual times Quartz needs to access it.

Regardless of which callback you provide—one for getting a pointer to memory or one to obtain a specific number of bytes—you must provide access to the underlying data until Quartz calls your function (specified by the releaseProvider field) to release the data provider.

Listing 8.4 demonstrates how to create a data provider for random access to data that defines a synthetic 8-bits-per-sample gray ramp image. The routine get-BytesGrayRampDirectAccess generates synthetic image data that is 256 samples wide and 1 scanline high, with each 8-bit sample corresponding to a value of gray between 0 (black) and 255 (white). The *i*th byte in the image is the sample value *i*. The function follows the prototype of the CGDataProviderGetBytesAtOff-setCallback, so it takes four parameters—info, buffer, offset, and count. In this example, the info parameter is not used in the function. The data is computed solely from the three other parameters by computing count bytes of the gray ramp values at offset bytes into the data.

The routine createGrayRampDirectAccessDP provides a pointer to getBytes-GrayRampDirectAccess in the getBytes field and fills the getBytePointer and releaseBytePointer fields of the callbacks structure with NULL. The routine calls the function CGDataProviderCreateDirectAccess passing NULL for the info param-eter, 256 for the number of bytes, and a pointer to the callbacks structure filled out previously. Recall that the info parameter is NULL because the routine get-BytesGrayRampDirectAccess does not require any application-supplied data passed to it. Your use of CGDataProviderCreateDirectAccess might need such data.

Listing 8.4 Using CGDataProviderCreateDirectAccess to provide direct access to synthetic image data

```
static size_t getBytesGrayRampDirectAccess(void *info, void *buffer,
              size_t offset, size_t count)
{
  unsigned char *p = buffer;
  int i;
  // This data provider provides 256 bytes total. If Quartz
  // requests more data than is available, return only
  // the available data.
  if( (offset + count) > 256 )
    count = 256 - offset;
```

```
      for(i = offset; i < (offset + count) ; i++)
        *p++ = i;

    return count;
}


CGDataProviderRef createGrayRampDirectAccessDP(void)
{
  CGDataProviderRef provider = NULL;
  CGDataProviderDirectAccessCallbacks callbacks;
  callbacks.getBytes = getBytesGrayRampDirectAccess;
  callbacks.getBytePointer = NULL;
  callbacks.releaseBytePointer = NULL;
  callbacks.releaseProvider = NULL;
  provider = CGDataProviderCreateDirectAccess(NULL, 256, &callbacks);
  if(provider == NULL){
    fprintf(stderr, "couldn't create data provider!\n");
  }
  return provider;
}
```

CGDataProviderCreateWithCFData (Tiger)

10.4 ▶ The function `CGDataProviderCreateWithCFData` creates a data provider from a Core Foundation data object (`CFDataRef`) that you supply. One typical use of this function is when drawing data obtained from a Macintosh pasteboard, such as the Clipboard. The data provider created by `CGDataProviderCreateWithCFData` operates in a manner identical to any other CGDataProvider object.

This function is available only in Tiger and later versions. If you need a data provider for a CFData object in code that runs on earlier versions of Mac OS X, see Listing 8.5. This code checks to see whether the function `CGDataProviderCreate-WithCFData` is available at runtime. If not, the routine provides the equivalent functionality without using the Quartz function. Successfully using this code requires weak linking; see the information about weak linking described in "Creating Color Spaces by Name (Jaguar)" (page 164).

Both the Quartz function `CGDataProviderCreateWithCFData` and the routine `myCG-DataProviderCreateWithCFData` in Listing 8.5 retain the CFData object supplied to them. Unless you have another reason to retain the CFData object, after you create the data provider, you can safely release any references to it that you own.

Listing 8.5 An implementation of a data provider created from a CFData object

```
static void myCFDataRelease(void *info, const void *data, size_t size)
{
  // Only called on systems where CGDataProviderCreateWithCFData
  // is not available.
  if(info)
    CFRelease(info);
}


CGDataProviderRef myCGDataProviderCreateWithCFData(CFDataRef data)
{
  CGDataProviderRef provider = NULL;
  // If the CFData object passed in is NULL, this code returns
  // a NULL data provider.
  if(data == NULL)
    return NULL;

  // Test to see if the Quartz version is available and if so, use it.
  if(&CGDataProviderCreateWithCFData != NULL){
    return CGDataProviderCreateWithCFData(data);
  }
  if(provider == NULL){
    size_t dataSize = CFDataGetLength(data);
    const UInt8 *dataPtr = CFDataGetBytePtr(data);
    // Retain the data so that this code owns a reference.
    CFRetain(data);
    provider = CGDataProviderCreateWithData((void *)data, dataPtr,
                  dataSize, myCFDataRelease);
    if(provider == NULL){
      // Release the data if for some reason the
      // data provider couldn't be created.
      CFRelease(data);
    }
  }
  return provider;
}
```

Guidelines for Using Data Providers

These guidelines will help you to ensure the integrity of the underlying data referenced by the CGDataProvider objects you create.

1. You are responsible for ensuring that the data underlying the data provider is available until Quartz calls the data release function of the data provider. It is not sufficient to make the data available only until you "think" Quartz is done with it, such as after you draw an image and later release it. The data must be available until Quartz invokes your callback to release the data. "Checking for Data Provider Integrity" (page 619) discusses debugging programming errors caused by failing to follow this guideline.

2. You must release the data provider after you've finished using it to create your Quartz objects. Without doing so, your callback for releasing the data will never be invoked, leading to memory leaks and unreleased resources that, for images or PDF documents, can be very large.

3. Your data provider is required to provide a data stream whose contents do not change during the lifetime of the data provider. If the contents of the data stream that the data provider supplies change over time, the results obtained when using the data provider with Quartz are unpredictable and undefined.

"Best Practices for Working with Images" (page 241) discusses additional memory management issues and "Quartz Object and Memory Model" (page 599) discusses the Quartz memory management model in detail. Working appropriately with the Quartz memory model ensures the best possible memory footprint, performance, and functionality in your application. The application MallocDebug is a Mac OS X developer tool useful for finding memory leaks caused by failure to follow these guidelines. This debugging tool has many sophisticated capabilities, so it's worthwhile for you to spend some time learning to use it.

Data Consumers

Data consumers are useful when you want to write PDF documents and image files. They direct data to a location specified by a URL, to a destination managed by the creator of the data consumer through a callback routine, or to a CFData object. The three functions that create data consumers are `CGDataConsumerCreateWithURL`, `CGDataConsumerCreate`, and `CGDataConsumerCreateWithCFData`.

The function `CGDataConsumerCreateWithURL` requires a CFURL object that specifies a disk- or web-based location. As you can see by looking at Listing 8.6, the code to create a URL-based data consumer is similar to the code that creates a URL-based data provider (compare with Listing 8.1 (page 187)). The function createDataConsumerFromPathName first converts a path name to a CFURL and then calls the function CGDataConsumerCreateWithURL.

Listing 8.6 Creating a data consumer from a path name

```
CGDataConsumerRef createDataConsumerFromPathName(CFStringRef path)
{
  CFURLRef url;

  // Create a CFURL for the supplied file system path.
  url = CFURLCreateWithFileSystemPath(NULL, path,
               kCFURLPOSIXPathStyle, false);
  if(url == NULL){
    fprintf(stderr, "Couldn't create url!\n");
    return NULL;
  }
  // Create a Quartz data provider for the URL.
  CGDataConsumerRef dataConsumer = CGDataConsumerCreateWithURL(url);
  // Release the URL when the code is done with it.
  CFRelease(url);
  if(dataConsumer == NULL){
    fprintf(stderr, "Couldn't create data consumer!\n");
    return NULL;
  }
  return dataConsumer;
}
```

The function CGDataConsumerCreate is similar to CGDataProviderCreate in that it uses a callback routine you supply to consume the data. This function is useful for creating a data consumer for writing to a special location, for example, in memory for use with a pasteboard, such as the Clipboard. The function CGData-ConsumerCreateWithCFData, available in Tiger and later versions, takes a CFData object as a parameter. You can use CGDataConsumerCreateWithCFData when you need to write Quartz-generated data to memory or a pasteboard.

Listing 8.7 shows how to use CGDataConsumerCreateWithCFData but provides a fallback that uses CGDataConsumerCreate when the code runs on a version of Mac OS X that is earlier than Tiger. The routine myCGDataConsumerCreateWith-CFData checks to see if the function CGDataConsumerCreateWithCFData is available and, if it is, calls that function to create a data consumer. If the code is not running on a system that has CGDataConsumerCreateWithCFData, it fills a callbacks structure with two callbacks. One callback—myCFDataConsumerPut-Bytes—writes the Quartz-supplied data buffer to the CFData object. The second callback—myCFDataConsumerRelease—releases the CFData object that the data consumer retained.

Listing 8.7 Creating a data consumer from a CFData object, with a fallback option

```
size_t myCFDataConsumerPutBytes(void *info,
              const void *buffer, size_t count)
{
  CFMutableDataRef data  = (CFMutableDataRef)info;
  // Append 'count' bytes from 'buffer' to the CFData
  // object 'data'.
  CFDataAppendBytes(data, buffer, count);
  return count;
}

void myCFDataConsumerRelease(void *info)
{
  if(info != NULL)
    CFRelease((CFDataRef)info);
}

CGDataConsumerRef myCGDataConsumerCreateWithCFData(
              CFMutableDataRef data)
{
  CGDataConsumerRef consumer = NULL;
  // If the CFData object passed in is NULL, this code returns
  // a NULL data consumer.
  if(data == NULL)
    return NULL;

  // Test to see if the Quartz version is available.
  if(&CGDataConsumerCreateWithCFData != NULL){
    return CGDataConsumerCreateWithCFData(data);
  }

  if(consumer == NULL){
    CGDataConsumerCallbacks callbacks;
    callbacks.putBytes = myCFDataConsumerPutBytes;
    callbacks.releaseConsumer = myCFDataConsumerRelease;

    // Retain the data so that this code owns a reference.
    CFRetain(data);
    consumer = CGDataConsumerCreate(data, &callbacks);
    if(consumer == NULL){
      // Release the data if for some reason the
      // data consumer couldn't be created.
```

```
        CFRelease(data);
    }
  }
  return consumer;
}
```

Data consumers aren't quite as important to Quartz as data providers are, primarily because data consumers aren't used by many functions. And, as you'll see later, there are other Quartz functions, specialized for images, that write data without using a data consumer object. As of Tiger, only three Quartz functions take a CGDataConsumer object as a parameter, as shown in Table 8.1.

The function CGPDFContextCreate creates a destination that creates PDF content. If you need only to write a PDF document in a location that can be specified by a URL, you can use CGPDFContextCreateWithURL. It's a more direct route to creating a PDF on disk because it does not require a data consumer object. See "Creating and Examining PDF Documents" (page 435) for more information about creating PDF content. The function CGPSConverterConvert is specialized for converting PostScript data to a PDF document. It's the only Quartz function that performs this task. See "Overview of the Conversion Process" (page 566) for more information about converting PostScript data to PDF.

The function CGImageDestinationCreateWithDataConsumer creates a destination for bitmap image data. There are other image destination functions that don't require a data consumer as a parameter and that you might find easier to use. The function CGImageDestinationCreateWithURL creates a destination for bitmap image data corresponding to a location specified by a URL, and the function CGImageDestinationCreateWithData creates a destination for bitmap image data from a CFData object. You'll see how to use these functions in "Writing Image Data Using CGImageDestination (Tiger)" (page 255). However, image destination functions aren't available prior to Tiger.

Table 8.1 Functions That Take a CGDataConsumer Object as a Parameter

Function	Can also use
CGPDFContextCreate	CGPDFContextCreateWithURL to render to a location specified by a URL
CGPSConverterConvert	Nothing else available
CGImageDestinationCreateWithDataConsumer	Any CGImageDestination creation function

Summary

Data provider and data consumer objects, and the functions that operate on them, allow applications to access data without the need to manage a raw data buffer. Data providers abstract the data reading process for URL-based data, whether the data is on a hard disk or located on the Web. When you need to provide access to data, either through direct or sequential access, you supply callback routines.

Data consumer objects have a functionality that parallels that of the data provider object. Consumers manage writing data instead of reading data, and can write to URL-based locations and to a CFData object. You can also provide custom callbacks to handle writing data in a specialized way or to a custom location.

See Also

The Quartz header files containing the structures and functions used in this chapter are

- CGDataProvider.h
- CGDataConsumer.h

The relevant reference documentation from the ADC Reference Library is

- *CGDataProvider Reference*
- *CGDataConsumer Reference*

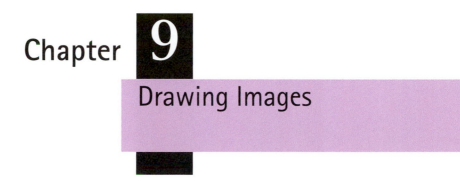

Chapter 9

Drawing Images

A **bitmap image** is a rectangular array of image **samples** (also called pixels), with each sample representing a single color value at a particular location in the image. There are a wide variety of sources of images. Digital cameras produce bitmap photographic images directly. Digital scanners can produce images from a wide variety of source material. Quartz produces bitmap image data when it renders to a bitmap context. Pixel painting programs produce images through human interaction. Images can be produced synthetically, such as with special-purpose rendering software to algorithmically produce a rendered scene. Figure 9.1 illustrates a few different image sources.

Quartz uses the opaque data type CGImageRef to represent an image, regardless of the format of the image data, the type of image, or how you supply the image data to Quartz. Quartz provides a number of different functions that can create a CGImage object (CGImageRef) from bitmap images. The data itself can be in one of a wide variety of image pixel formats and data layouts, including image samples that are represented by floating-point values. Image samples can contain per-sample alpha data in one of several different formats.

Quartz supports images that have intrinsic color as well as images that are used as a mask or stencil. An **image with intrinsic color** contains pixel values in a specific color space and an optional alpha value for each pixel; that is, the image sample data contains color values. Quartz uses the supplied color space to interpret these values when it paints pixels to the destination. The rest of this chapter focuses on images with intrinsic color that, for simplicity, are referred to as images.

Figure 9.1 Images come from many sources, such as photographs, fractal algorithms, and Quartz drawing

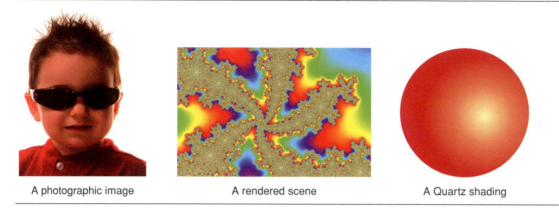

| A photographic image | A rendered scene | A Quartz shading |

Masking (or stencil) images are images whose sample values indicate an alpha coverage of paint to apply but not the painting color itself. You'll find out more about how to create and use these images in Chapter 10, "Image Masking" (page 263).

Creating CGImage Objects

The functions listed in Table 9.1 create CGImage objects. Which one you choose depends on the format of the input data and the versions of Mac OS X your code needs to work on. After you create a CGImage object the hard work is done, since drawing it with Quartz is straightforward, as you'll see throughout this chapter. The function `CGContextDrawImage` draws an image regardless of the image format or image type used to create the CGImage object. Images can be transformed just as line art graphics can, by transforming the coordinate system.

You'll learn to use each of the image creation functions in the order they are listed in the table. "Guidelines for Image Creation" (page 240) provides a discussion to help you decide which function suits the needs of your application.

Specialized Functions for JPEG and PNG

Quartz provides two specialized functions for creating images from data compressed in the JPEG or portable network graphics (PNG) format. The function `CGImageCreateWithJPEGDataProvider` creates a CGImage object from compressed JPEG data that you supply together with parameters that specify how to draw with the data. Quartz automatically determines the image width and height, the

Table 9.1 Functions That Create CGImage Objects

Function	Comments
CGImageCreateWithJPEGDataProvider	Allows easy creation of a CGImage object from JPEG data. Available in 10.1 and later.
CGImageCreateWithPNGDataProvider	Allows easy creation of a CGImage object from PNG data. Available in 10.2 and later.
CGImageCreate	Versatile; useful for raw data or custom data formats. Available in 10.0 and later.
CGImageSourceCreateWithDataProvider	Allows easy creation of CGImage objects from a large number of image formats. Best choice when running in 10.4 and later.
CGImageSourceCreateWithData	Allows easy creation of CGImage objects from a large number of image formats. Best choice when running in 10.4 and later.
CGImageSourceCreateWithURL	Allows easy creation of CGImage objects from a large number of image formats. Best choice when running in 10.4 and later.
GraphicsImportCreateCGImage	A QuickTime function that can be used to create a CGImage object from any format QuickTime supports (TIFF, GIF, Photoshop, and so on). Available in QuickTime 6.4 and later.

pixel format, and so on from the JPEG data. The function `CGImageCreateWith-PNGDataProvider` provides the equivalent capability for working with PNG format data. For working with other standard data formats such as TIFF or GIF on Panther systems and later, see "Generalized Functions for Compressed Image Data (Tiger)" (page 226) and "Importing Image Data with QuickTime" (page 238).

Each of these functions takes the following parameters:

- `source`, a data provider that supplies JPEG-encoded data or PNG-encoded data, depending on the function. "Data Providers" (page 186) describes how to create data providers.

- `decode`, an optional array of color component values that determines how image sample values are mapped into color component values in the image color space. You'll learn more about decode arrays in "A General Function for Uncompressed Data" (page 211). For now, assume this parameter should be `NULL`, which is the value you'll typically use.

- shouldInterpolate, a bool parameter that is a hint as to whether Quartz should interpolate image sample values when rendering. You'll learn more about interpolation in "A General Function for Uncompressed Data" (page 211). For now, assume this parameter should be true.

- intent, the rendering intent to use when drawing the image, as described in "Rendering Intents" (page 165). For now, assume this parameter should be kCGRenderingIntentDefault.

The drawJPEGImage routine shown in Listing 9.1 creates a CGImage object from a JPEG file that is stored on disk and then draws the four images shown in Figure 9.2.

Listing 9.1 Drawing a JPEG image with Quartz

```
void drawJPEGImage(CGContextRef context, CFURLRef url)
{
  CGRect   jpgRect;
  CGImageRef jpgImage = NULL;
  // Create a Quartz data provider for the supplied URL.
  CGDataProviderRef jpgProvider = CGDataProviderCreateWithURL(url);
  if(jpgProvider == NULL){
    fprintf(stderr, "Couldn't create JPEG Data provider!\n");
    return;
  }

  // Create the CGImageRef for the JPEG image from the data provider.
  jpgImage = CGImageCreateWithJPEGDataProvider(jpgProvider, NULL,
              true, kCGRenderingIntentDefault);

  // CGImageCreateWithJPEGDataProvider retains the data provider.
  // Since this code created the data provider and this code no
  // longer needs it, this code must release it.
  CGDataProviderRelease(jpgProvider);
  if(jpgImage == NULL){
    fprintf(stderr, "Couldn't create CGImageRef for JPEG data!\n");
    return;
  }

  // Make a rectangle that has its origin at (0,0) and
  // has a width and height that is 1/4 the native width
  // and height of the image.
  jpgRect = CGRectMake(0., 0.,
              CGImageGetWidth(jpgImage)/4, CGImageGetHeight(jpgImage)/4);
```

```
  // Draw the image into the rectangle.
  // This is Image 1.
  CGContextDrawImage(context, jpgRect, jpgImage);
  CGContextSaveGState(context);
    // Translate to the top-right corner of the image just drawn.
    CGContextTranslateCTM(context, jpgRect.size.width,
                jpgRect.size.height);
    // Rotate by -90 degrees.
    CGContextRotateCTM(context, DEGREES_TO_RADIANS(-90));
    // Translate in -x by the width of the drawing.
    CGContextTranslateCTM(context, -jpgRect.size.width, 0);
    // Draw the image into the same rectangle as before.
    // This is Image 2.
    CGContextDrawImage(context, jpgRect, jpgImage);
  CGContextRestoreGState(context);
  CGContextSaveGState(context);
    // Translate so that the next drawing of the image appears
    // below and to the right of the image just drawn.
    CGContextTranslateCTM(context,
                jpgRect.size.width+jpgRect.size.height,
                jpgRect.size.height);
    // Scale the y axis by a negative value to flip the image.
    CGContextScaleCTM(context, 0.75, -1.0);
    // This is Image 3.
    CGContextDrawImage(context, jpgRect, jpgImage);
  CGContextRestoreGState(context);

  // Adjust the position of the rectangle so that its origin is
  // to the right and above where Image 3 was drawn. Adjust the
  // size of the rectangle so that it is 1/4 the image width
  // and 1/6 the image height.
  jpgRect = CGRectMake(1.75*jpgRect.size.width + jpgRect.size.height,
                jpgRect.size.height,
                CGImageGetWidth(jpgImage)/4,
                CGImageGetHeight(jpgImage)/6);
  // This is Image 4.
  CGContextDrawImage(context, jpgRect, jpgImage);

  // Release the CGImageRef when it is no longer needed.
  CGImageRelease(jpgImage);
}
```

Figure 9.2 Drawing the same CGImage object four times, from a JPEG source file

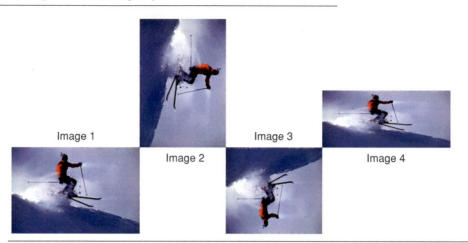

The code first creates a data provider using the URL for the JPEG file. Next, the function `CGImageCreateWithJPEGDataProvider` creates a CGImage object from the data provider, using the typical values for the three other parameters. When you use `CGImageCreateWithJPEGDataProvider`, Quartz understands that the image data supplied by the data provider you supply is compressed JPEG data. Quartz reads the file format, determines the width and height of the image, creates the correct color space for the image, and uncompresses the image data when the image is drawn.

The function `CGDataProviderRelease` releases the reference your code has to the data provider; Quartz retains its own reference to the data provider when you create the image. By retaining its own reference, Quartz can access the data supplied by the data provider at any time it needs to do so. Failing to release a data provider creates a memory leak; it is important to release references to Quartz objects you no longer need. "Quartz Object and Memory Model" (page 599) discusses releasing objects in more detail.

The CGImage object is ready to draw. The functions `CGImageGetWidth` and `CGImageGetHeight` return the size of the image. The call to the function `CGRectMake` uses those dimensions to construct a `CGRect` data structure whose origin is (0,0) and that has dimensions that are one-fourth the size of the image. The function `CGContextDrawImage` draws the image into the supplied rectangle, translating and scaling as necessary to fill the rectangle. The image completely fills the rectangle with the lower-left corner of the image at the lower-left corner of the rectangle and the top-left corner of the image at the top-left corner of the rectangle. The rectangle coordinates are in Quartz user space units. You can see the first drawing of the image in the lower left of Figure 9.2.

The next chunk of code in Listing 9.1 uses the coordinate transformation functions introduced in "Quartz 2D Drawing Basics" (page 15) to draw Image 2 and Image 3 of Figure 9.2. Notice that the code that performs the transformation and drawing for each image is bracketed by the functions `CGContextSaveGState` and `CGContextRestoreGState`.

The last piece of code in Listing 9.1 draws Image 4 in Figure 9.2. Notice that this code does not save or restore the graphics state, and it does not operate on the Quartz coordinate system directly. Instead, the function `CGRectMake` creates a modified version of the drawing rectangle that it then passes to the function `CGContextDrawImage`. You can perform the most typical operations needed when drawing images—translating and scaling—by modifying the drawing rectangle rather than by calling the coordinate transformation functions. When all drawing is complete, the function `CGImageRelease` releases the reference to the image.

Listing 9.1 demonstrates an important coding practice when using a CGImage object—the code uses the same CGImage object for each drawing instead of creating and releasing the CGImage object each time it draws the image. When you use the same CGImage object, Quartz caches the object to improve performance. Depending on the version of Mac OS X and the hardware on which your code runs, this caching can dramatically improve performance. If you draw into a graphics context (`CGContextRef`) that represents a PDF document, the image data appears only once in the resulting document, regardless of the number of times you draw the image, even if the same image appears on multiple pages. As a result, Quartz can substantially reduce the size of PDF documents it creates.

In some cases JPEG data files have an optional embedded ICC profile that characterizes the source color data. For JPEG files that contain embedded ICC profiles, the CGImage object created with `CGImageCreateWithJPEGDataProvider` has a source color space created from the embedded ICC data. CGImage objects created from JPEG files that do not have embedded ICC data are characterized by the device color space of the color model appropriate to the JPEG data itself. You can change the color space characterizing the data if you want. Quartz offers a utility function that allows you to replace the color space associated with a given CGImage object. See "Image Utility Functions" (page 244) for more detail.

Quartz CGImage objects created using the JPEG data provider have special behavior when drawn to a PDF context. The PDF data format directly supports JPEG data, allowing Quartz to optimize its handling of JPEG images when it creates PDF documents. Drawing images created using `CGImageCreateWithJPEG-DataProvider` to a PDF context captures the original JPEG compressed data into the PDF output rather than as uncompressed image data. The first benefit of this is that Quartz does not have to decompress the JPEG data in order to write it out to the PDF destination. The second is that JPEG compression of photographic images produces much smaller images compared to the lossless compression methods Quartz normally uses when it generates PDF data. Additionally, because the source data itself is JPEG data, there is no data loss incurred by writing the image data out as JPEG data.

A further advantage occurs when using the JPEG data provider when printing to a PostScript printer. When Quartz generates PostScript data from a Quartz drawing, image data provided by the JPEG data provider can in some cases be sent directly to the printer as compressed JPEG data. This again avoids a decompression step and results in far less data transmitted to the printer. The use of the CGImageSource functionality for using JPEG data, described in "Generalized Functions for Compressed Image Data (Tiger)" (page 226), is also optimized in this manner. For these reasons, when reading JPEG data, you are urged to use either a JPEG data provider or the equivalent CGImageSource functionality to take advantage of these optimizations.

The function `CGImageCreateWithPNGDataProvider` is available in Jaguar and later versions. This is an equivalent function to `CGImageCreateWithJPEGDataProvider` except that it expects the data supplied by the data provider to be PNG format data. After you create a CGImage object using `CGImageCreateWithPNGDataProvider`, you can draw it with `CGContextDrawImage` or otherwise use it as you can any other CGImage object.

Both the functions `CGImageCreateWithPNGDataProvider` and `CGImageCreateWithJPEGDataProvider` determine the width, height, and other characteristics of the image directly from the image data supplied by the data provider. For this reason, the image utility functions described in "Image Utility Functions" (page 244), such as `CGImageGetWidth` and `CGImageGetHeight`, are quite useful.

Drawing Images into a Flipped Coordinate System

The examples in this book so far assume a coordinate system where the origin is in the lower-left corner of the drawing canvas, with positive y values increasing as you go up the drawing canvas. Most applications, and in some cases the application frameworks themselves, prefer to draw into a **flipped coordinate system** where the origin is at the top-left corner, with positive y values increasing as you go down the drawing canvas.

Working in a flipped coordinate system requires some extra care when drawing images, otherwise the image will be flipped along with the coordinate system. The NSImage class, available for drawing images with the Cocoa framework, handles drawing images into a flipped view automatically. In Jaguar and later versions, the Carbon framework provides the function `HIViewDrawCGImage` that is a wrapper around `CGContextDrawImage` and allows you to draw a CGImage object into a Quartz context that has a flipped coordinate system. "Drawing PDF Documents in a Flipped Coordinate System" (page 408) discusses the issues involved with drawing PDF documents into a flipped view. The same techniques demonstrated there can be used when using `CGContextDrawImage` directly.

A General Function for Uncompressed Data

The function `CGImageCreate` provides the most flexible way to create a CGImage object. When using this function you must fully describe the image data to Quartz, which requires a lot more information than the functions described in "Specialized Functions for JPEG and PNG" (page 204). The trade-off for this complexity is that the function can create a CGImage object from just about any type of image data, and it is available in all versions of Mac OS X.

You'll want to understand each of the input parameters to the function `CGImageCreate` before you use it. A brief explanation for each parameter follows. Those that require more in-depth information have a cross-reference. You'll see how to use `CGImageCreate` to create CGImage objects from image data in "Drawing Uncompressed, Raw Image Data" (page 219), "Drawing a Synthetic Image from Data in Memory" (page 222), and "Drawing a Synthetic Image by Accessing Data Directly" (page 223).

These are the input parameters for the function `CGImageCreate`:

- `width`, the number of image samples in a row (or **scanline**) of the image.

- `height`, the number of rows in the image. The parameters `width` and `height` together describe the dimensions of the array of samples comprising the image.

- `bitsPerComponent`, the number of bits for each component of each image sample. The number is the same for each component, including alpha, and for images with integer sample values, the number of bits per component can range from 1 to 32. (Prior to Jaguar, the only allowable values were 1, 2, 4, 5, and 8 bits per component.) Tiger and later versions also support floating-point pixel values of 32 bits per component.

- `bitsPerPixel`, the total number of bits comprising each image pixel. Pixels can be padded with bits that are not to be interpreted as component data. This means the total number of bits per pixel can exceed the total number of bits of component data for each sample. For example, Quartz supports 32-bit RGB images with no alpha in the format XRGB, where the leading bits in the data stream are ignored for each pixel.

- bytesPerRow, the total number of bytes in each row, including any padding data that may be at the end of each row of image data. Each scanline of data must be an integer multiple of 8 bits wide, padded with extra bits as needed. This parameter must be greater than zero.

- colorSpace, a CGColorSpace object for the color space the image sample values are interpreted in. The colorSpace parameter specifies the source color space for the image and, by doing so, implicitly specifies the number of components of color data for each pixel. For example, using an RGB color space as the color space for an image means that there are three color component values for each sample (ignoring alpha) in the image.

- bitmapInfo, a value that describes the layout and format of each pixel. It specifies whether or not there is alpha data in the image. If the image contains alpha data then this value indicates the type and location of the alpha data within each image pixel. If there is no alpha data, then this value specifies the location of any unused bits in the pixel. This value also contains a flag bit used to indicate whether the pixel data is supplied as floating-point values. (The bitmapInfo parameter was called alphaInfo in the Quartz header files prior to Tiger.) See "Alpha Information" below.

- dataProvider, the data provider for Quartz to use to read the image pixel data.

- decode, an optional array of color component values that determines a mapping from image sample values to color component values in the image color space. Pass NULL for this parameter to indicate that image sample values map into the default range of color values. See "Decode Array" (page 215).

- shouldInterpolate, a bool parameter that is a hint to Quartz as to whether it should interpolate image sample values when rendering. See "Interpolation" (page 217).

- intent, the rendering intent. When Quartz paints graphics, including images, in addition to the source and destination color spaces, it uses the rendering intent to determine how to map colors from a source into a destination, as described in "Rendering Intents" (page 165). Typically, you use the value kCGRenderingIntentDefault. When drawing images, this default value is the same as kCGRenderingIntentPerceptual.

Alpha Information

Quartz supports images that contain per-pixel alpha data as well as images with no alpha data. Recall from "Alpha Transparency" (page 166) that when Quartz renders using alpha data in a source, it uses the following formula to calculate destination color values:

$$D' = S \times \alpha_S + D \times (1 - \alpha_S)$$

where D' is the new destination color, S is the source color, α_S is the alpha value of the source, and D is the original destination color.

Notice that the first term in the calculation is a multiplication of the source color by the alpha value of the source. Because the contribution of the source color to the updated destination color is always multiplied by the source alpha, for large amounts of source data such as sampled images, processing may be more efficient when color values are supplied as component color values already multiplied by the source alpha value.

Premultiplied colors are those whose source colors are already multiplied by the source alpha value. **Nonpremultiplied colors** are those whose source component values have not already been multiplied by the source alpha. The stroke and fill colors in the graphics state are always set using nonpremultiplied colors. When drawing sampled images that contain alpha data, the `bitmapInfo` parameter specifies whether the image data is provided as premultiplied or nonpremultiplied color values.

Quartz supports the full range of values of the `CGImageAlphaInfo` enumeration with the exception of a few specific formats. These constants in Table 9.2 are what you supply for the `bitmapInfo` parameter to the function `CGImageCreate`. The values `kCGImageAlphaPremultipliedLast` and `kCGImageAlphaPremultiplied-First` cannot be used with images whose color space is CIE L*a*b*, an Indexed color space, and some ICC color spaces such as CIE XYZ. These color spaces do not use premultiplied alpha values. The value `kCGImageAlphaOnly` is not supported for image creation. To draw with an alpha-only image, you instead create a masking image as described in "Creating an Image Mask" (page 264).

For images without alpha, the total number of bits per pixel must be greater than or equal to the number of bits per component times the number of color components. When an image has alpha, the total number of bits per pixel must be greater than or equal to the number of bits per component times one plus the number of color components. For pixel formats where the number of bits per component, multiplied by the number of components (plus one for alpha if the image contains alpha) is less than the number of bits per pixel, the location of the unused bits within the pixel depends on the `bitmapInfo` parameter, as follows:

- If the value of `bitmapInfo` specifies that alpha data is last (`kCGImageAlphaPremultipliedLast` or `kCGImageAlphaLast`) or there is no alpha and the format is `kCGImageAlphaNoneSkipLast`, then Quartz considers the bits for a given pixel to be packed so that the last bits in the bit stream for a pixel value are ignored.

Table 9.2 Constants Defined by the CGAlphaInfo Enumeration

Constant	Specifies
kCGImageAlphaNone	There is no alpha data.
kCGImageAlphaPremultipliedLast	The alpha data is in the least significant bits of each pixel. The color components are already multiplied by this value.
kCGImageAlphaPremultipliedFirst	The alpha data is in the most significant bits of each pixel. The color components are already multiplied by this value.
kCGImageAlphaLast	The alpha data is in the least significant bits of each pixel.
kCGImageAlphaFirst	The alpha data is in the most significant bits of each pixel.
kCGImageAlphaNoneSkipLast	There is no alpha data. Ignore the least significant bits of each pixel.
kCGImageAlphaNoneSkipFirst	There is no alpha data. Ignore the most significant bits of each pixel.
kCGImageAlphaOnly	Contains only alpha data. Not supported for image creation.

- If the value of bitmapInfo is one where the alpha data is first (kCGImageAlpha-PremultipliedFirst or kCGImageAlphaFirst) or there is no alpha and the format is kCGImageAlphaNoneSkipFirst, then Quartz considers the bits for a given pixel to be packed so that the first bits in the bit stream for a pixel value are ignored.

Quartz expects that the data provider you use to create the image using CGImageCreate supplies data that is interleaved on a per-pixel basis. Quartz does not directly support planar component image data or formats where the component data is interleaved on a scanline basis. However, the data provider mechanism offers great flexibility in how you supply the data to Quartz. With this mechanism it is possible to read data that uses formats that are not directly supported in Quartz and then for your application to convert the data into a format that Quartz can use directly. (See "Data Providers" (page 186) for more information.)

Pixel Formats

The bitsPerComponent, bitsPerPixel, and bitmapInfo parameters together specify a variety of pixel formats and the layout of pixel data, including the typical 1,

2, 4, and 8 bits of data per component, with or without alpha data, as well as deeper image formats. Table 9.3 lists some typical pixel formats and the combinations of these parameters that you use to indicate a given format when calling the function `CGImageCreate`.

Starting with Tiger, Quartz supports drawing with floating-point image data where each image sample consists of 32-bit, floating-point data per color component (plus alpha if the image contains alpha). To distinguish 32-bit, floating-point image sample data from 32-bit integer image samples, you use the constant `kCGBitmapFloatComponents` when computing the appropriate `bitmapInfo` value to pass to `CGImageCreate`. For floating-point images, you calculate the `bitmapInfo` parameter by applying a bitwise `OR` operation to the appropriate `CGAlphaInfo` value from Table 9.2 and the `kCGBitmapFloatComponents` constant.

Note When drawing images consisting of floating-point pixel values, Quartz clips the input data range to the range [0–1]. Pixel values less than zero are clipped to zero and pixel values greater than 1 are clipped to 1.

Decode Array

The decode array controls how Quartz maps image sample values into color component values. Quartz linearly maps image sample values into color component values by mapping the minimum image sample component value (0) into the first element of the decode array for that color component and the maximum image sample component value into the second element of the decode array for that color component. The decode parameter passed to `CGImageCreate` is either `NULL` or a 2*m-element array of floating-point component color values, where m is the number of components in the source image color space. Passing a `NULL` decode array specifies to use the default decode array, which is one that maps a sample value of 0 into the minimum value (typically 0) of a color component in the source color space and the maximum value of an image sample into the maximum value of a color component (typically 1) in the source color space.

Although `NULL` is the typical value to supply for the decode parameter, other values can be used to change the mapping of image sample values into component values. For example, with QuickDraw, 1-bit images use a 1 bit for black and a 0 bit for white. Using the same image data with Quartz and supplying a `NULL` decode array with a Gray color space draws the image with black and white inverted. To achieve the same meaning of the sample values as QuickDraw, you supply a decode array that maps 0 values to 1 and 1 values to 0. "Creating an Image Mask" (page 264) demonstrates how to use a decode array to invert the sense of the sample data.

Table 9.3   Typical Pixel Formats and the Associated Quartz Parameters

Pixel Format	Bits per Component	Bits per Pixel	Bitmap Info Constant	Color Space
One-component, 8-bit data, no alpha, e.g., GGGG...	8	8	`kCGImageAlphaNone`	One-component color space, e.g., Gray
One-component, 1-bit data, no alpha, e.g., GGGG...	1	1	`kCGImageAlphaNone`	One-component color space, e.g., Gray
Three-component, 24-bit data, no alpha, no padding bytes, e.g., RGBRGB...	8	24	`kCGImageAlphaNone`	Three-component color space, e.g., RGB
Three-component, 16-bit data, no alpha, 1 leading padding bit, e.g., XRGBXRGB...	5	16	`kCGImageAlphaNoneSkipFirst`	Three-component color space, e.g., RGB
Three-component, 32-bit data, no alpha, 1 leading padding byte, e.g., XRGBXRGB...	8	32	`kCGImageAlphaNoneSkipFirst`	Three-component color space, e.g., RGB
Three-component, 32-bit data with leading alpha byte, nonpremultiplied data, e.g., ARGBARGB...	8	32	`kCGImageAlphaFirst`	Three-component color space, e.g., RGB
Three-component, 32-bit data with leading alpha byte, premultiplied data, e.g., ARGBARGB...	8	32	`kCGImageAlphaPremultipliedFirst`	Three-component color space, e.g., RGB
Three-component, 32-bit data with trailing alpha byte, premultiplied data, e.g., RGBARGBA...	8	32	`kCGImageAlphaPremultipliedLast`	Three-component color space, e.g., RGB
Four-component, 32-bit data with no alpha, no padding bytes, e.g., CMYKCMYK...	8	32	`kCGImageAlphaNone`	Four-component color space, e.g., CMYK
Three-component, 32-bit floating-point data per component, with no alpha, no padding bytes, e.g., RGBRGB...	32	96	`kCGImageAlphaNone | kCGBitmapFloatComponents` (Tiger and later versions)	Three-component color space, e.g., RGB

Interpolation

Rendering sampled images typically requires scaling image samples up or down, depending on the resolution of the output device and the size of the destination image. When an image is scaled up, additional image samples must be computed from the source image data. When an image is scaled down, the image data can't be simply replicated; some processing of the image data must occur. In both cases, Quartz has the ability to use image interpolation algorithms to compute the image samples it paints to the destination. Image interpolation is device dependent; not all devices support interpolation. For those that do, not all have the same ability to control it.

Quartz has several different algorithms it can use to rescale the images it draws to a window or a bitmap context. You have some control over the quality of image interpolation. Figure 9.3 demonstrates the different types of interpolation that are currently available. Keep in mind that Quartz image interpolation algorithms are subject to change so the results you see in future versions of Mac OS X may be different. This information is presented here to help you become familiar with the concept of image interpolation and how it works in Tiger.

The images in the leftmost column in the figure are drawn with no interpolation. Those in the center column are drawn with low-quality interpolation. The images in the rightmost column are drawn with high-quality interpolation. The top row of images is drawn with no scaling. Quartz does not consult the interpolation quality when drawing an image to a destination that requires no scaling. Consequently, the images are all identical. The images in the middle row are each scaled to 80 percent of the original image size. When there is no interpolation, the results are chunky. Pixels are replicated to fill in intermediate locations instead of being calculated in intermediate locations. Low-quality interpolation produces a smoother result. High-quality interpolation produces the smoothest result but also with what appears to be some blurring of the image. The images in the last row are each scaled to 120 percent of the original image. Again, no interpolation results in a chunky look. In the case of this particular example, increasing the scale factor in Tiger and earlier versions, low-quality interpolation and high-quality interpolation produce identical results.

There are several parameters that interact to determine how Quartz performs image interpolation. Some of these parameters are internal to a given graphics context, but two of them are specified when you create and draw a CGImage object. When you call the `CGImageCreate` function, you pass a `shouldInterpolate` parameter to the function. If you pass `true` for the `shouldInterpolate` parameter, then you have the ability to control image interpolation. If you pass `false` for `shouldInterpolate`, Quartz does not necessarily disable image interpolation; instead, it consults its internal parameters to determine what type of image interpolation to perform. If you want to exercise any control over image interpolation, pass `true` for the `shouldInterpolate` parameter.

Figure 9.3 Interpolation quality and scaling with Quartz

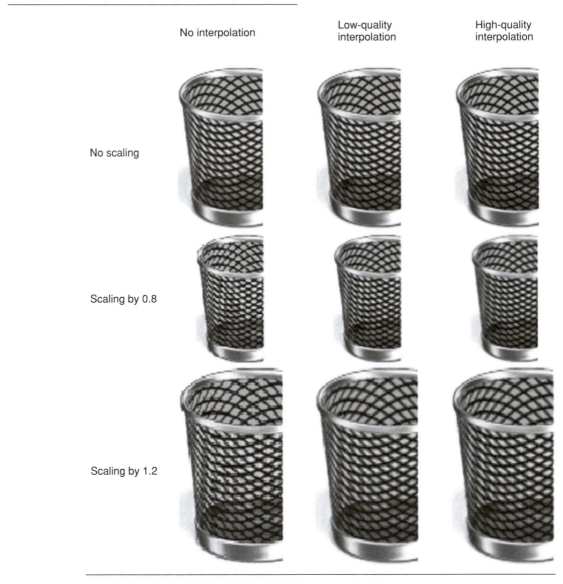

When drawing an image with the shouldInterpolate value set to true, Quartz consults the **interpolation quality** parameter in the Quartz graphics state. You use the function CGContextSetInterpolationQuality to set the interpolation quality parameter in the graphics state; the set of possible values is kCGInterpolationDefault, kCGInterpolationNone, kCGInterpolationLow, and kCGInterpolationHigh. The latter three values correspond to the settings demonstrated in Figure 9.3.

Typically, you do not call the function CGContextSetInterpolationQuality, you simply pass a value of true for the shouldInterpolate value when you create a CGImage object and allow Quartz to perform the default image interpolation. There may, however, be unusual situations where it is important for you to exercise additional control. Note that because the interpolation quality is a graphics state parameter, calls to CGContextSaveGState and CGContextRestoreGState save and restore the interpolation quality.

The Quartz interpolation quality and anti-aliasing parameters affect different aspects of image rendering. The interpolation quality determines how Quartz reproduces image samples when an image is scaled; it affects destination pixels throughout the area covered by the image. Anti-aliasing only affects destination pixels at the edge of an image and does so only when the edge pixels of the image cover destination pixels with less than 100 percent coverage.

Drawing Uncompressed, Raw Image Data

Now that you are familiar with the function CGImageCreate and its parameters, you can see how to use it to create a CGImage object and then draw the object. The routine drawImageFromURL in Listing 9.2 draws images from Gray or RGB data files that contain uncompressed, raw image data that has no alpha component and is packed as GGGGG… pixels or RGBRGBRGB… pixels. The caller specifies whether the data file is RGB or Gray by supplying a Boolean value in the isRGB parameter passed to the routine; true for RGB or false for Gray.

The caller also supplies the width and height of the image sample array of the image data as well as the number of bits per component for each image sample. The routine draws the image at the Quartz coordinate origin with a width and height that matches the image width and height—one image sample in each Quartz coordinate unit square. The routine drawImageFromURL in Listing 9.2 draws the color image shown in Figure 9.4.

Listing 9.2 A routine that draws Gray or RGB images from raw image files on disk

```
void drawImageFromURL(CGContextRef context, CFURLRef url,
            size_t width, size_t height,
            size_t bitsPerComponent, Boolean isRGB)
{
  CGImageRef image = NULL;
  CGRect imageRect;
  size_t bitsPerPixel =
            isRGB ? (bitsPerComponent * 3) : bitsPerComponent;
  size_t bytesPerRow = (width * bitsPerPixel + 7)/8;
```

```
    bool shouldInterpolate = true;
    CGColorSpaceRef colorspace = NULL;
    // Create a Quartz data provider from the supplied URL.
    CGDataProviderRef dataProvider = CGDataProviderCreateWithURL(url);
    if(dataProvider == NULL){
      fprintf(stderr, "Couldn't create Image data provider!\n");
      return;
    }
    // Get a Quartz color space object appropriate for the image type.
    colorspace = isRGB ?
                    getTheCalibratedRGBColorSpace() :
                    getTheCalibratedGrayColorSpace();
    // Create an image of the width, height, and bitsPerComponent with
    // no alpha data, the default decode array, with interpolation,
    // and the default rendering intent for images.
    image = CGImageCreate(width, height, bitsPerComponent,
                    bitsPerPixel, bytesPerRow, colorspace,
                    kCGImageAlphaNone, dataProvider, NULL,
                    shouldInterpolate, kCGRenderingIntentDefault);
    // Quartz retains the data provider with the image and since this
    // code does not create any more images with the data provider, it
    // releases it.
    CGDataProviderRelease(dataProvider);
    if(image == NULL){
      fprintf(stderr, "Couldn't create CGImageRef for this data!\n");
      return;
    }
    // Create a rectangle into which the code will draw the image.
    imageRect = CGRectMake(0., 0., width, height);

    // Draw the image into the rectangle.
    CGContextDrawImage(context, imageRect, image);
    // Release the CGImage object when it is no longer needed.
    CGImageRelease(image);
}
```

The value of bytesPerRow is computed based on the assumption that the input data format is packed with no extra bytes at the end of each scanline but that for pixel depths of less than 8 bits per pixel, each scanline is packed with just enough extra bits to ensure that the number of bits per scanline is an integer multiple of 8.

The function CGDataProviderCreateWithURL creates a data provider from the specified URL. This function is the preferred method for reading data from a file

Figure 9.4 The result of drawing a raw image from disk

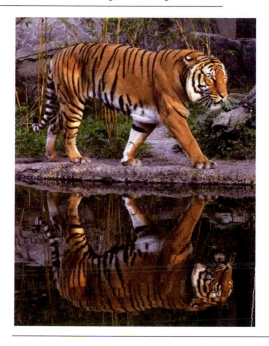

in the file system. Although this data provider is most often used to access a file-based URL, you can also provide a valid web-based location.

The routines `getTheCalibratedRGBColorSpace` and `getTheCalibratedGrayColorSpace` are routines you would write to obtain a `CGColorSpaceRef` for a Gray or RGB color space of your choosing. These routines have *Get* semantics—the code should not release the color space after using it in this code. An example of an equivalent routine that obtains a color space for the generic RGB ICC profile is shown in Listing 7.3 (page 159). The equivalent version for the generic calibrated Gray color space would simply use the full path to the `Generic Gray Profile.icc` file instead of that for the RGB profile.

Next, the function `CGImageCreate` creates a CGImage object that corresponds to the source image, using `kCGImageAlphaNone` for the `bitmapInfo` parameter, which specifies that the image data has no alpha information and there are no padding bits in each pixel value. The `decode` parameter is `NULL` so that image sample values of 0 map into the component color value 0 and image sample values of $(2^{bitsPerComponent} - 1)$ map to the component color value 1.0. For an 8-bits-per-component image, this mapping ensures that sample values of 255 have the color value 1.0. The `shouldInterpolate` parameter is `true`, allowing the interpolation quality parameter in the graphics state for the context to control image interpolation. The rendering intent parameter is `kCGRenderingIntentDefault`, specifying to use the Quartz default rendering intent, which is `kCGRenderingIntentPerceptual` when drawing images.

Drawing a Synthetic Image from Data in Memory

"Data Providers and Data Consumers" (page 185) demonstrates how to create a data provider from a block of memory that contains data for a synthetic image—a green-to-red color ramp. The code in Listing 9.3 calls the `createRGBRampData-Provider` routine that is described in that chapter (see Listing 8.2 (page 189)), creates a CGImage object for that data provider, and then draws the image. Figure 9.5 shows the resulting image.

Listing 9.3 Code that creates a CGImage object from an in-memory block of data

```
void doColorRampImage(CGContextRef context)
{
  CGImageRef image = NULL;
  CGRect imageRect;
  size_t width = 256, height = 256;
  size_t bitsPerComponent = 8, bitsPerPixel = 24;
  size_t bytesPerRow = width * 3;
  bool shouldInterpolate = true;
  CGColorSpaceRef colorspace = NULL;

  CGDataProviderRef imageDataProvider = createRGBRampDataProvider();
  if(imageDataProvider == NULL){
    fprintf(stderr, "Couldn't create Image Data provider!\n");
    return;
  }

  colorspace = getTheCalibratedRGBColorSpace();
  image = CGImageCreate(width, height, bitsPerComponent,
                bitsPerPixel, bytesPerRow, colorspace, kCGImageAlphaNone,
                imageDataProvider, NULL, shouldInterpolate,
                kCGRenderingIntentDefault);
  // No longer need the data provider.
  CGDataProviderRelease(imageDataProvider);
  if(image == NULL){
    fprintf(stderr, "Couldn't create CGImageRef for this data!\n");
    return;
  }
  imageRect = CGRectMake(0., 0, width, height);
  // Draw the image.
  CGContextDrawImage(context, imageRect, image);
```

Figure 9.5 A synthetic image (green-to-red ramp) drawn using `CGContextDrawImage`

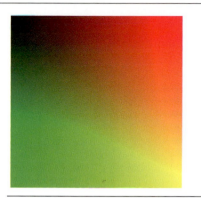

```
  // Release the image.
  CGImageRelease(image);
}
```

Drawing a Synthetic Image by Accessing Data Directly

"Data Providers and Data Consumers" (page 185) demonstrates how to create a data provider by calling the function `CGDataProviderCreateDirectAccess`, which uses a set of callbacks to provide the data. The `createGrayRampDirectAccessDP` routine (see Listing 8.4 (page 195)) returns a data provider for synthetic image data that describes a gray ramp that is 256 samples wide.

The code in Listing 9.3 calls the `createGrayRampDirectAccessDP` routine, creates a CGImage object for that data provider, and then draws the image. Figure 9.6 shows the resulting image. Note that since the image is 256 samples wide and 1 scanline high, drawing the image to a square destination rectangle causes the image to be stretched vertically.

Listing 9.4 Code that creates a CGImage object by accessing synthetic data directly

```
void doGrayRamp(CGContextRef context)
{
  CGImageRef image = NULL;
  CGRect imageRect;
  size_t width = 256, height = 1;
  size_t bitsPerComponent = 8, bitsPerPixel = 8;
  size_t bytesPerRow = width;
```

```
        bool shouldInterpolate = true;
        CGDataProviderRef dataProvider = NULL;
        CGColorSpaceRef colorspace = NULL;

        dataProvider = createGrayRampDirectAccessDP();
        if(dataProvider == NULL){
          fprintf(stderr, "Couldn't create Gray Ramp provider!\n");
          return;
        }
        colorspace = getTheCalibratedGrayColorSpace();
        image = CGImageCreate(width, height, bitsPerComponent, bitsPerPixel,
                    bytesPerRow, colorspace, kCGImageAlphaNone, dataProvider,
                    NULL, shouldInterpolate,
                    kCGRenderingIntentDefault);
        CGDataProviderRelease(dataProvider);
        if(image == NULL){
          fprintf(stderr, "Couldn't create CGImageRef for image data!\n");
          return;
        }
        imageRect = CGRectMake(0., 0., 256, 256);
        // Drawing the image that is 256 samples wide and
        // 1 scanline high into a rectangle that is 256 x 256 units
        // on a side causes Quartz to stretch the image to fill
        // the destination rectangle.
        CGContextDrawImage(context, imageRect, image);
        CGImageRelease(image);
}
```

Figure 9.6 A synthetic image (gray ramp) drawn using `CGContextDrawImage`

Bitmap Images and Universal Binaries (Tiger)

10.4 ▶ Universal binaries run natively on both PowerPC- and Intel-based Macintosh computers. The differences in the architectures of these processors is, for the most part, transparent to code that uses the Quartz API. Most applications can use Quartz without concern about which processor is executing the code.

One potential exception to this is when creating Quartz images using `CGImageCreate`. By default, Quartz treats image data supplied by a data provider as a sequence of bits with the high-order bit in the first byte in the data stream as the first bit of image data. The following bit in that byte is the next bit in the data stream, and so on. Once the bits in the first byte are consumed, the high-order bit in the next byte in the data stream is the next bit in the sequence of image bits supplied by the data provider. For data produced as a sequence of bytes to be consumed, this is the natural order in which the data is stored. For data produced as a sequence of 16-bit or 32-bit quantities, this is known as **big-endian data** format. That is, the byte in the 16- or 32-bit quantum with the lowest memory address is the most significant byte in the sequence, the next byte in memory is the next most significant byte in the sequence, and so on. For most sources of image data, this is the typical ordering of the data.

However, your image data may be stored in an order different than big-endian byte order. (If you only have data that is in big-endian byte order, the remainder of this section is not relevant for your application.) Quartz provides the Bitmap Info flag values `kCGBitmapByteOrder32Little` and `kCGBitmapByteOrder16Little` so that you can specify to Quartz that your data provider supplies its image data in a byte sequence that is characterized by a 16- or 32-bit little-endian order. To calculate a Bitmap Info value that specifies a little-endian order, you perform a bitwise `OR` operation using one of these values, together with the Bitmap Info value from Table 9.3 (page 216) that describes your data. As of Mac OS X version 10.4.3, the constants `kCGBitmapByteOrder32Little` and `kCGBitmapByteOrder16Little` are supported only for versions of Mac OS X that run on Intel-based Macintosh computers.

The value `kCGBitmapByteOrder32Little` specifies that each 32-bit chunk of data supplied by your data provider should be treated by Quartz as data in little-endian order. Prior to treating the data as a sequence of bits, Quartz must first swap the data appropriately. For example, when using a value of `kCGBitmapByteOrder32Little` for an image that specifies an ARGB format with 8 bits per component and 32 bits per pixel, your data provider supplies BGRA data for each pixel and Quartz properly treats it as ARGB data.

The value `kCGBitmapByteOrder16Little` specifies to Quartz that each 16-bit chunk of data supplied by your data provider should be treated as data in little-endian order and that prior to treating the data as a sequence of bits, Quartz must swap the data appropriately. For example, when using a value of `kCGBitmapByteOrder16Little` for an image that specifies an RGB format with 16 bits per component and 48 bits per pixel, your data provider supplies the data for each pixel where the components are ordered R, G, B, but each color component value is in little-endian order and Quartz properly interprets the data.

For best performance when using `kCGBitmapByteOrder32Little`, either the pixel size or the component size of the image must be 32 bits. For best performance when using `kCGBitmapByteOrder16Little`, either the pixel size or the component size of the image must be 16 bits.

See the references at the end of this chapter for more information about creating universal binaries.

Generalized Functions for Compressed Image Data (Tiger)

10.4 ▶

Up to this point you've seen how to create CGImage objects for both compressed and uncompressed data and then draw those images. CGImageSource functions, available starting in Tiger, provide a straightforward way to access a wide variety of image data formats and create CGImage objects from the data. The general idea is that you create an image source object that gets the data. Then you create an image from that image source object.

Table 9.4 lists five of the CGImageSource functions—three that create image source objects and two that extract image data from an image source object and return a CGImage object. You can then pass the CGImage object as a parameter to other Quartz functions, including the function `CGContextDrawImage`. Quartz provides a number of other functions beyond those listed in the table that operate on CGImageSource objects or obtain useful data from them.

If you are writing an application that will run only in Tiger or later versions, the CGImageSource functions provide the best way to access image data and create CGImage objects. (Alternatively, you might write your application so that it can take advantage of the functionality available in Tiger, while still having the capability to run on older versions of Mac OS X.) CGImageSource functions have many advantages. These functions

■ Don't require the need to know anything about the format of the image source data to use them. Quartz takes care of figuring out what the type of data is from the data itself and creates a `CGImageRef` that corresponds to the image.

Table 9.4 Functions That Create CGImageSource Objects or CGImage Objects

Function	Use to
CGImageSourceCreateWithDataProvider	Create an image source object using data from a data provider.
CGImageSourceCreateWithData	Create an image source object using data from a CFData object.
CGImageSourceCreateWithURL	Create an image source object using data from a file-based or web-based URL.
CGImageSourceCreateImageAtIndex	Returns the CGImage object located at the specified index in an image source. You can use the function CGContextDrawImage to draw the image.
CGImageSourceCreateThumbnailAtIndex	Returns the thumbnail image (which is a CGImage object) located at the specified index in an image source. You can use the function CGContextDrawImage to draw the thumbnail image.

- Support a wide variety of image formats, including JPEG, JPEG2000, GIF, OpenEXR, TIFF, TIFF files that contain multiple images, image files that contain thumbnails, many raw camera formats, and many of the formats that QuickTime supports. (The function CGImageSourceCopyTypeIdentifiers returns a CFArray object that describes the import image formats supported by Quartz on a given version of Mac OS X.)

- Can inspect the metadata associated with an image and retrieve certain image properties for some formats.

- Allow you to use a specific image from a multiple-image file.

- Can use and create thumbnail images.

- Allow you to incrementally load an image, which is useful when you need to load large images over the Web.

Listing 9.5 shows how to create an image from a CGImageSource object that reads image data from a URL. The routine myCreateImageFromImageSource first calls CGImageSourceCreateWithURL to create a CGImageSource object. Next, it gets the property dictionary for the first image in the image source. Recall that an image source can contain more than one image, but it doesn't have to. The first image is referenced by index 0. The routine uses the dictionary to retrieve the x and y resolution of the image if those properties are available. Next the routine calls the function CGImageSourceCreateImageAtIndex to create a CGImage object from the first image (index 0) located in the image source. Since it is then finished with the image source, it releases it. There is no specialized Quartz release function for a CGImageSource; you release it by calling the Core Foundation function CFRelease since a CGImageSource object is implemented as a Core Foundation object. Note that the caller of myCreateImageFromImageSource is responsible for releasing the CGImageRef that the function returns.

Listing 9.5 Creating an image with a CGImageSource function

```
CGImageRef myCreateImageUsingImageSource(CFURLRef url,
              float* xdpiP, float* ydpiP)
{
  CGImageRef image = NULL;
  CGImageSourceRef imageSource = NULL;
  CFDictionaryRef properties = NULL;
  CFNumberRef val;

  // Set to zero, indicating the property was unavailable.
  *xdpiP = *ydpiP = 0;

  // Create the image source from the URL.
  imageSource = CGImageSourceCreateWithURL(url, NULL);
  if(imageSource == NULL){
    fprintf(stderr,
    "Couldn't create image source from URL!\n");
    return NULL;
  }

  // Obtain the properties dictionary for the first image
  // in the image source. This is a copy function so this
  // code owns the reference returned.
  properties = CGImageSourceCopyPropertiesAtIndex(
                imageSource, 0, NULL);
  if(properties != NULL){
    // Check for the x and y resolution of the image.
    val = CFDictionaryGetValue(properties, kCGImagePropertyDPIWidth);
    if (val != NULL)
      CFNumberGetValue(val, kCFNumberFloatType, xdpiP);
    val = CFDictionaryGetValue(properties, kCGImagePropertyDPIHeight);
    if (val != NULL)
      CFNumberGetValue(val, kCFNumberFloatType, ydpiP);
    CFRelease(properties);
  }
```

```
  // Create a CGImageRef from the first image in the CGImageSource.
  image = CGImageSourceCreateImageAtIndex(imageSource, 0, NULL);
  // Release the CGImageSource object since it is no longer needed
  // and this code created it. This code uses CFRelease since a
  // CGImageSource object is a Core Foundation object.
  CFRelease(imageSource);

  if(image == NULL){
    fprintf(stderr,
      "Couldn't create image from image source!\n");
    return NULL;
  }

  return image;
}
```

There are situations where you might want to use a thumbnail representation of an image rather than the full image. Some data formats contain thumbnail images as part of the stored image data. You can use the CGImageSource function `CGImageSourceCreateThumbnailAtIndex` to create a CGImage object from the thumbnail image data in an image source. By default, Quartz only creates a thumbnail image if there is thumbnail data in the file. However, you can have Quartz create a thumbnail from the full image by adding the key `kCGImageSourceCreateThumbnailFromImageIfAbsent` with a value of `kCFBooleanTrue` to the options dictionary you pass to `CGImageSourceCreateThumbnailAtIndex`. In this case, Quartz will use the thumbnail data from the image source if it exists but create one if it does not.

You can also have Quartz always create a thumbnail representation from the full image data, even if thumbnail data is present in the image source. You do this by adding the key `kCGImageSourceCreateThumbnailFromImageAlways` with a value of `kCFBooleanTrue` to the options dictionary you pass to `CGImageSourceCreateThumbnailAtIndex`. In this case, Quartz never uses thumbnail data from the image source.

As a general rule, you probably want to limit the size of thumbnail images Quartz creates from a full-size image, otherwise you could end up with a thumbnail image that is the same size as the original image. When you use the `kCGImageSourceCreateThumbnailFromImageIfAbsent` or `kCGImageSourceCreateThumbnailFromImageAlways` key to request that Quartz create a thumbnail image, you can also add the key `kCGImageSourceThumbnailMaxPixelSize` to limit the maximum size of the thumbnail image that Quartz will create. You add this key with a `CFNumberRef` value that contains an integer specifying the maximum width and height (in pixels) for the thumbnail image.

Listing 9.6 contains the routine myCreateThumbnailFromImageSource that creates a thumbnail from an image source. It first creates a CGImageSource object by supplying a URL. Next, it sets up key-value pairs to specify that Quartz should create a thumbnail if one is not already present in the image source and that the maximum size of the thumbnail created should be 160 pixels in the largest dimension. The key-value pairs instantiate a dictionary that can be passed as a parameter to the function CGImageSourceCreateThumbnailAtIndex. Quartz either returns a preexisting thumbnail or creates one.

Listing 9.6 Creating a thumbnail image

```
CGImageRef myCreateThumbnailFromImageSource(CFURLRef url)
{
  CGImageRef thumb = NULL;
  CGImageSourceRef imageSource = NULL;
  int maxThumbSize = 160;
  CFNumberRef maxThumbSizeRef;
  CFStringRef keys[2];
  CFTypeRef values[2];
  CFDictionaryRef options = NULL;

  // Create the image source from the URL.
  imageSource = CGImageSourceCreateWithURL(url, NULL);
  if(imageSource == NULL){
    fprintf(stderr,
      "Couldn't create image source from URL!\n");
    return NULL;
  }

  // Specify the maximum size of the thumbnail for
  // Quartz to create as 160 pixels in width and height.
  maxThumbSizeRef = CFNumberCreate(NULL, kCFNumberIntType,
               &maxThumbSize);

  // Request that Quartz create a thumbnail image if
  // thumbnail data isn't present in the file.
  keys[0] = kCGImageSourceCreateThumbnailFromImageIfAbsent;
  values[0] = (CFTypeRef)kCFBooleanTrue;

  // Request that the maximum size of the thumbnail is
  // that specified by maxThumbSizeRef, 160 pixels.
  keys[1] = kCGImageSourceThumbnailMaxPixelSize;
  values[1] = (CFTypeRef)maxThumbSizeRef;
```

```
// Create an options dictionary with these keys.
options = CFDictionaryCreate(NULL,
    (const void **)keys,
    (const void **)values,
    2,
    &kCFTypeDictionaryKeyCallBacks,
    &kCFTypeDictionaryValueCallBacks);
// Release the CFNumber this code created.
CFRelease(maxThumbSizeRef);

// Create the thumbnail image for the first image in the
// image source, that at index 0, using the options
// dictionary that the code just created.
thumb = CGImageSourceCreateThumbnailAtIndex(imageSource, 0, options);

// Release the options dictionary.
CFRelease(options);
// Release the image source the code created.
CFRelease(imageSource);

if(thumb == NULL){
  fprintf(stderr,
    "Couldn't create thumbnail from image source!\n");
  return NULL;
}

return thumb;
}
```

Large images delivered over the Internet can be a challenge to display. Web browsers often display parts of the image as the data accumulates, thus providing the user with feedback about the image-loading process. Listing 9.7 shows pseudocode for how to use a CGImageSource object to load and draw an image incrementally.

Listing 9.7 Pseudocode for loading and drawing an image incrementally

```
Step 1: Create a CGImageSource with CGImageSourceCreateIncremental.
Step 2: Accumulate the next portion of data for the image.
Step 3: Call CGImageSourceUpdateData with the image data accumulated
        so far.
Step 4: If necessary, determine the full height of the image. If
        successful, there has been enough data accumulated to continue
        to Step 5; otherwise return to Step 2.
```

Step 5: Use CGImageSourceCreateImageAtIndex to create a CGImage object.
        If successful, there has been enough data accumulated to
        continue to Step 6; otherwise return to Step 2.
Step 6: Draw the partial image, using the height of the CGImage object and
        the full height obtained in Step 4 to correctly position the image.
Step 7: Check whether all the image data has been loaded. If not, return to
        Step 2; otherwise, the complete image has been loaded and drawn.
Step 8: Release the CGImageSource created in Step 1.

Listing 9.8 contains code that implements the approach described in the pseudo-code. The routine myDrawFirstImageIncrementally creates an incrementally loaded CGImageSource object by calling the function CGImageSourceCreateIncremental, passing NULL as the options dictionary. The routine then calls an application-supplied function (myCreateAccumulatedDataSoFar—you have to supply this routine) to fetch the data that has been accumulated so far. This data is passed to the function CGImageSourceUpdateData, passing the image source, the data, and a Boolean value that specifies whether or not the data passed to the function is all the data for the data source. You must pass the function CGImageSourceUpdateData all the data accumulated so far, not just the data loaded since the last call to the function.

Before drawing the image, the routine myDrawFirstImageIncrementally first uses CGImageSourceCopyPropertiesAtIndex to obtain the pixel height of the full image so that it can locate the partially loaded image correctly. For most image formats, Quartz can determine this before all the image data is available. The code loops, adding more image data each time through the loop until the height can be determined.

Once the image height is determined, the code calls CGImageSourceCreateImageAtIndex to create a CGImageRef for the first image in the data source. If CGImageSourceCreateImageAtIndex returns a CGImage object, the routine calls MyDrawIncrementalImage to draw the image, then it releases the image. It is important to release each partial image. The routine repeats this process until all the image data for the first image is loaded and the full image is drawn.

The routine MyDrawIncrementalImage uses the CGImage object passed to it and the full image height to draw the image. The functions CGImageGetWidth and CGImageGetHeight return the number of samples per row and the number of rows in the partial image passed to them. This routine then adjusts the location of the image so that when a partial image is drawn, its origin is such that the top-left corner of the image does not change its location as each subsequent partial image is drawn.

Note that if you are drawing the image into a flipped view, there is no need to obtain the full image height or perform the adjustment of the image rectangle origin that this code performs. The image height of the partial image is sufficient for drawing the image in the correct location in a flipped view.

Listing 9.8 Loading an image incrementally

```
static void MyDrawIncrementalImage(CGContextRef context,
                CGImageRef image, float fullHeight)
{
  // Obtain the width and height of the image that has been
  // accumulated so far.
  float width = CGImageGetWidth(image);
  float height = CGImageGetHeight(image);
  // Adjust the location of the imageRect so that the origin is
  // such that the full image would be located at (0,0) and the partial
  // image top-left corner does not move as the image is filled in.
  CGRect imageRect = CGRectMake(0, fullHeight-height, width, height);
  CGContextDrawImage(context, imageRect, image);
}

static void myDrawFirstImageIncrementally(CGContextRef context,
                MyIncrementalData *myDataP)
{
  bool done;
  float height = -1;
  CGRect imageRect;
  CGImageSourceStatus status;
  // Create an incremental image source.
  CGImageSourceRef imageSource =
                CGImageSourceCreateIncremental(NULL);
  if(imageSource == NULL){
    fprintf(stderr,
      "Couldn't create incremental imagesource!\n");
    return;
  }

  // Loop, gathering the necessary data to find the true
  // height of the image and draw it.
  do
  {
    // Accumulate the data.
    CFDataRef data = myCreateAccumulatedDataSoFar(myDataP, &done);
    CGImageSourceUpdateData(imageSource, data, done);
    // Release the data since Quartz retains it and this code
    // no longer needs it.
    CFRelease(data);

    if(height < 0){
      // Determine the height of the full image at index 0.
```

```
            CFDictionaryRef properties =
                    CGImageSourceCopyPropertiesAtIndex(
                    imageSource, 0, NULL);
        if(properties){
          CFTypeRef val = CFDictionaryGetValue(properties,
                    kCGImagePropertyPixelHeight);
          if (val != NULL)
                    CFNumberGetValue(val, kCFNumberFloatType, &height);

          CFRelease(properties);
        }
      }
      // Once the height is obtained, go ahead and see if Quartz
      // has enough data to create a CGImage object.
      if(height > 0){
        // Now create the CGImageRef from the image source for the
        // first image.
        CGImageRef image = CGImageSourceCreateImageAtIndex(
                    imageSource, 0, NULL);
        if(image){
          // Draw the image using the height of the full image
          // to adjust the location where the partial image is drawn.
          MyDrawIncrementalImage(context, image, height);
          CGImageRelease(image);
          // Potentially you would want to flush the context so
          // that drawing to a window would appear, even inside this loop.
          // See Chapter 17 for more information about flushing.
          CGContextFlush(context);
        }
      }
      // Obtain the status for the image source for the first image.
      status = CGImageSourceGetStatusAtIndex(imageSource, 0);

      // Continue the loop until either all the data has loaded
      // or the status of the first image is complete.
    } while (!done && status != kCGImageStatusComplete);
  CFRelease(imageSource);
}
```

The functions CGImageSourceCopyPropertiesAtIndex and CGImageSourceCreate-ImageAtIndex each have an optional options dictionary parameter that you can supply. The examples so far use NULL to specify that Quartz should perform its default handling of the source data. However, there may be cases for which you want to override this default handling. In those cases, you pass an options dictionary containing keys that specify custom behavior. Some of the keys that these functions support are listed in Table 9.5. Each key in the table has an associated CFBoolean value.

Many of the data formats supported by the CGImageSource functions have some type of compression applied to the image data. Depending on how you use the CGImage objects you create from a `CGImageSourceRef`, it may be beneficial to have Quartz cache a decompressed representation of the image data if you are using an image repeatedly. There is of course a trade-off between using more memory to cache the uncompressed data compared to more processor bandwidth to repeatedly decompress an image when using it. By default, a CGImage-Source object does not cache a decompressed representation, but for your usage you may find it appropriate to do so. Adding the key `kCGImageSourceShouldCache` with the value `kCFBooleanTrue` to the options dictionary is a hint to Quartz about how it should treat the image data.

Data formats such as OpenEXR support floating-point pixel values. When you use a CGImageSource object to create a `CGImageRef` from data sources that have floating-point data, by default Quartz creates a CGImage object that uses integer image component values of 8 or 16 bits per component; the size depends on the input format. This default is chosen because most applications have no need to work directly with the underlying floating-point data, nor to incur the extra memory overhead that 32-bit floating-point component data imposes. When creating integer image component data from floating-point formats such as OpenEXR, Quartz applies a special mapping algorithm to the data so that the decoded component values range from 0–1. This mapping algorithm creates a CGImage object that produces pleasing visual results when drawn with Quartz.

Table 9.5 Some of the Keys for Use with CGImageSource Functions

Key	Usage	Default
kCGImageSourceShouldCache	Specifies that Quartz should cache an uncompressed representation of the image data to improve performance at the likely expense of memory footprint.	False. No caching.
kCGImageSourceShouldAllowFloat	Specifies that Quartz should return a floating-point format image when appropriate for the source data format.	False. Produce integer data from images that have floating-point sample values.

Some applications want to work with floating-point data rather than have Quartz map floating-point images into integer sample values. To override this default mapping, you pass an options dictionary to the functions CGImageSource-CopyPropertiesAtIndex and CGImageSourceCreateImageAtIndex with a key that specifies that you want Quartz to disable this mapping. The routine create-FloatingPointImageOptions in Listing 9.9 adds the key kCGImageSourceShouldAllowFloat to the options dictionary it creates to check whether the first image in a CGImageSource object is available in a floating-point format.

After instantiating a dictionary with the appropriate key-value pair, create-FloatingPointImageOptions calls CGImageSourceCopyPropertiesAtIndex with this options dictionary to examine the properties of the first image in the CGImage-Source object. The floating-point property is returned as the value of the kCGImagePropertyIsFloat key. The code checks whether the image is available in a floating-point format, and if so, it returns the options dictionary so that the dictionary can be used with CGImageSourceCreateImageAtIndex to create such an image. If the image is not a floating-point image, the code releases the options dictionary it creates and returns NULL.

Listing 9.9 Creating an options dictionary appropriate for obtaining full dynamic range floating-point data

```
CFDictionaryRef createFloatingPointImageOptions(
            CGImageSourceRef imageSource)
{
  CFDictionaryRef properties, options = NULL;
  Boolean isFloat = false;
  CFTypeRef keys[1];
  CFTypeRef values[1];
  // Allow the image to be a floating-point image. Without this,
  // Quartz returns integer pixel data, even for floating-point images.
  keys[0] = kCGImageSourceShouldAllowFloat;
  values[0] = kCFBooleanTrue;

  options = CFDictionaryCreate(NULL, keys, values, 1,
            &kCFTypeDictionaryKeyCallBacks,
            &kCFTypeDictionaryValueCallBacks);
  // Obtain the properties for the first image
  // in the image source. This is a 'Copy' function
  // so the code owns a reference to the dictionary returned.
  properties = CGImageSourceCopyPropertiesAtIndex(imageSource,
            0, options);
  if(properties != NULL){
    CFTypeRef value;
    // Get the value for the kCGImagePropertyIsFloat if it exists
    // and if the value is a CFBoolean, then get the corresponding
```

```
      // Boolean result.
      if( CFDictionaryGetValueIfPresent(properties,
                 kCGImagePropertyIsFloat, &value)
        && CFGetTypeID(value) == CFBooleanGetTypeID()
      ){
        isFloat = CFBooleanGetValue(value);
      }
      CFRelease(properties);
  }

  if(!isFloat){
    // Release the options dictionary if the image isn't
    // a floating-point image; otherwise return it.
    CFRelease(options);
    options = NULL;
  }

  return options;
}
```

The options dictionary you pass to CGImageSourceCopyPropertiesAtIndex speci-fies the way you want Quartz to process the image. The properties returned reflect the options dictionary you supply. In the case of floating-point images, if you don't specify that you want floating-point data, the properties returned by CGImageSourceCopyPropertiesAtIndex reflect the way Quartz would handle the image by default, that is, integer values instead of floating-point data, regardless of the input image format.

Important   Obtaining the image properties for some image formats requires that Quartz performs a significant amount of work, including creating the CGImage object in some cases. It is strongly recommended that you use the same CGImageSource object to inspect the properties of an image in the source and that you use to create a CGImage object from that source. To produce the most consistent results and obtain the best performance, use the same key-value pairs in the dictionary you pass to both CGImageSourceCopyPropertiesAtIndex and CGImageSourceCreate-ImageAtIndex. The simplest approach is to use the same dictionary.

When you request floating-point image data, Quartz returns the raw floating-point data without any special processing. This is useful when using Core Image filters to process high-dynamic-range images that you want to then export as OpenEXR data. However, drawing floating-point images directly with the Quartz function CGContextDrawImage clips all image data that is outside the range of allowable color values in the source color space (typically 0–1) into the allowed range. In most cases, the raw floating-point data needs additional processing to be drawn in a pleasing manner with Quartz. This is because the data in high-dynamic-range, floating-point image formats such as OpenEXR is outside the range 0–1 that Quartz color spaces are typically restricted to. Most applications don't want to work with floating-point data at all, so the Quartz default of converting floating-point data into integer data is usually the best choice.

Importing Image Data with QuickTime

The QuickTime framework that's installed with Panther and later versions has functions that can create a CGImage object from a wide variety of input image data formats, including TIFF, Photoshop, GIF, BMP, PICT, MacPaint, JPEG, and PNG file formats. Users of Mac OS X version 10.2.5 and later can also get this functionality by installing QuickTime version 6.4 (or later), which is available as a software update.

By appropriately using these new capabilities of QuickTime with Quartz, you can expand the image drawing and export capabilities of your application to include these additional formats. There are caveats to using QuickTime to create a CGImage object. Before you decide to use QuickTime for this purpose, read the discussion in "Guidelines for Image Creation" (page 240).

Listing 9.10 demonstrates how to use QuickTime to create a CGImage object that can be used just like those you create using the functions described previously. The routine createCGImageWithQuickTimeFromURL in the listing takes a CFURL object and returns a CGImage object that corresponds to the image in the file, if the file contains an image format that QuickTime supports. The result of drawing a CGImage object created from a TIFF file by using the routine createCGImageWithQuickTimeFromURL is shown in Figure 9.7.

Listing 9.10 Creating a CGImageRef from an arbitrary file

```
// This code requires the QuickTime framework.
#include <QuickTime/QuickTime.h>
static CGImageRef createCGImageWithQuickTimeFromURL(CFURLRef url)
{
  OSStatus err = noErr;
  CGImageRef    imageRef = NULL;
  Handle        dataRef = NULL;
  OSType        dataRefType;
  GraphicsImportComponent gi;
  ComponentResult result;
  result = QTNewDataReferenceFromCFURL(url,
              0, &dataRef, &dataRefType);
  if (NULL != dataRef) {
```

```
        err = GetGraphicsImporterForDataRefWithFlags(dataRef,
                    dataRefType, &gi, 0);
    if(!err && gi){
      // Tell the graphics importer that it shouldn't perform
      // gamma correction and it should create an image in
      // the original source color space rather than matching it to
      // a generic calibrated color space.
      result = GraphicsImportSetFlags(gi,
                    (kGraphicsImporterDontDoGammaCorrection +
                    kGraphicsImporterDontUseColorMatching)
              );
      if(!result)
        result = GraphicsImportCreateCGImage(gi, &imageRef, 0);
      if(result)
        fprintf(stderr,"Got a bad result = %d!\n", (int)result);
      DisposeHandle(dataRef);
      CloseComponent(gi);
    }
  }
  return imageRef;
}
```

Figure 9.7 An image from a TIFF file using a QuickTime-created CGImage object

Apple provides sample code to demonstrate the concepts involved in using Quartz to draw images from compressed files in versions of Mac OS X that do not support the QuickTime function `GraphicsImportCreateCGImage`. That sample code (see references at the end of this chapter) uses QuickTime routines to render the image contained in the file into a piece of memory that you then use as the source image data to create a CGImage object.

Guidelines for Image Creation

You've seen four approaches to creating Quartz images. The approach you decide to take depends on the versions of Mac OS X you need your software to run on, the image file formats your application works with, and the level of performance you want to achieve. Here are a few guidelines:

- CGImageSource functions provide the highest performance on the platform and are the best choice for creating CGImage objects for use with Quartz.

- If your application runs only in Tiger or later versions, use CGImageSource functions to support compressed data.

- When using JPEG or PNG source data with versions of Mac OS X prior to Tiger, use the native Quartz JPEG and PNG data providers rather than using the QuickTime functions. See "Specialized Functions for JPEG and PNG" (page 204) for the benefits of the JPEG data provider.

- If your application runs in versions of Mac OS X from 10.2.5 and later, and you must support compressed image formats in addition to JPEG and PNG, use the QuickTime functions. This gives your application the ability to read (and write) compressed formats that are available in these earlier software versions.

- When running in Tiger and later versions, instead of using the QuickTime functions, use the CGImageSource functions.

- Although QuickTime and CGImageSource support the creation of a CGImage object from PICT data, the result of using a `CGImageRef` to represent PICT data produces rendered bits, not the original line art, text, and graphics that make up the original PICT. For this reason, it is recommended that you use other available means to draw PICT data to a Quartz context, such as the QDPict family of functions available in QuickDraw. See the references in "Opening and Drawing PDF Documents" (page 397) for more details.

Best Practices for Working with Images

You can make your image code fast and efficient by following a few guidelines. The guidelines make the most sense if you understand how Quartz represents and processes images.

A CGImage object is immutable. It represents a specific image that does not change over the lifetime of the object. Each time you use a specific CGImage object, Quartz accesses the same underlying image data. Quartz leverages image immutability

- For any internal image caching it provides.

- To improve image rendering performance.

- To efficiently represent any image that is painted multiple times in a PDF document.

In some cases, Quartz may use caching to improve performance. If a CGImage object is used repeatedly, Quartz may keep the image in its cache. If the cache gets full, CGImage objects that are not reused, or that have been used least recently, are moved out of the cache to make room for new images.

Best Practice   Reuse CGImage objects instead of creating and releasing the object each time you want to access the same image data. If you want to draw a given image multiple times, use the same CGImage object to represent the image, rather than repeatedly creating, drawing, and releasing it each time you want to draw the image.

Reusing CGImage objects does more than speed up performance; it can decrease the size of PDF documents you create with Quartz that use the same image repeatedly. How? Quartz notices when you reuse a CGImage object in a PDF document, and it streams the image data only once into the PDF document it produces, regardless of the number of times you draw the image on a given PDF page or throughout the document. This is true even when you change the current transformation matrix (CTM) or other graphics state parameters between the times you draw your image. The difference in size can be dramatic when the same image is used many times.

The fact that CGImage objects are immutable places some restrictions on how you handle image data. In particular, you must ensure that you do not change the underlying data associated with an image during its lifetime. The Quartz data provider mechanism assists you in this manner, provided you use it correctly by following the rules described in "Guidelines for Using Data Providers" (page 198). Most important is that you do not change the underlying data associated with your data provider and that you ensure that the data is available until Quartz calls your data provider release function.

Best Practice   Do not attempt to change the underlying data associated with a CGImage object during the lifetime of the object.

But what if you want to draw into an offscreen piece of memory and then want to use those bits as an image to draw into an onscreen window? This is a common technique for many programmers, particularly those most familiar with working with systems for which the onscreen windows have no window backing store. There is far less need for using this technique with Mac OS X than on most computer platforms, so you may not need to perform this style of drawing. "Performance and Debugging" (page 593) discusses in detail why you might not need to perform offscreen drawing. "Creating Bits" (page 345) discusses different methods for performing offscreen drawing with Quartz, should you find that you need to do so in your application.

If you encounter a situation for which you need to render to an offscreen buffer, you may want to use a bitmap context to create the bits and then create a CGImage object from those bits. The most common technique is to create a bitmap context using a given block of memory for the raster and then draw to that bitmap context. After you are done drawing, call the function `CGDataProvider-CreateWithData` to create a data provider for the memory block used for the bitmap context raster. "Creating Bits" shows more details on how to accomplish this.

Best Practice   Draw to a bitmap context if you need to render to an offscreen buffer. But be careful not to violate the immutability of a CGImage object by drawing to the same bitmap context more than once if you are using that bitmap context as a source of data for a CGImage object that is in use. Quartz also provides CGLayer objects that can be used for offscreen drawing. In many cases, for offscreen drawing, CGLayer objects are preferable to bitmap contexts. You'll learn more about CGLayer objects, including when to use them, in "Creating Bits."

If you want to render to an offscreen buffer a second time, you can't simply draw again to the same bitmap context and use the same CGImage object to draw the image. Doing so violates the immutability of a CGImage object. It's reasonable to think that you could simply draw again to the same bitmap context and then create a new CGImage object from the new bits. However, this operation violates the rule of not modifying data that underlies an existing data provider. As long as a data provider for a specific CGImage object exists, none of the underlying data can change. That means that none of the bitmap context data can change and that the CGImage object cannot change. The data provider hangs on to its data until its data release function is called. If you change the data or pull the data out from under the data provider, your application is likely to experience problems. For example, it could render the wrong data or crash due to attempts by Quartz to access data that no longer exists.

Best Practice   Don't pull the image data out from under a data provider.

The best way to handle rendering to an offscreen buffer a second time is to create a new bitmap context for drawing that uses a different block of memory than that being used by the data provider. Then use that new context as the basis for the CGImage object you need for the new rendering.

Quartz provides several new mechanisms in Tiger and later versions that make it easier to manage offscreen drawing. "Creating Bits" (page 345) provides detailed information.

When you are sure you no longer need a CGImage object, call the function `CGImageRelease` to signal to Quartz that you no longer need the image. If you don't release an unneeded object, Quartz has no way of knowing that you don't need it. Unless all references to a given CGImage object are released, Quartz will never release the resources and memory associated with the image, and the release function for the data provider that you used to create the CGImage object is never called.

Best Practice   Release a CGImage object when you are certain you no longer need it.

What if you are not sure that your code follows best coding practice for Quartz? You can use a PDF context to debug your image drawing code. Create a PDF context, draw to that context, and view the resulting PDF document. If what you see is not what you expect, look for places in your code where you tried to change the underlying data. For example, if you incorrectly make changes to the underlying data for a CGImage object during the lifetime of its data provider, the results recorded into the PDF document are likely to contain the wrong image data for some of your image drawing. You may still see the results you expect when drawing to a window onscreen, but the PDF drawing will not be correct.

If your PDF drawing produces garbage image data or your code crashes due to a bad memory access, it's likely you released the underlying data associated with a data provider before Quartz called your data provider release routine. For more information about creating and using a PDF context, see "Creating and Examining PDF Documents" (page 435).

Image Utility Functions

Quartz offers a number of additional functions that fall into one of two categories. The first category contains functions that allow inspection of a CGImage object to determine various attributes. Functions in the second category are those that create a new CGImage object from either an existing CGImage object or similar data.

Getting Image Dimensions

The functions CGImageGetWidth and CGImageGetHeight are useful when you create a CGImage object using any of the functions where you don't explicitly supply the width and height of the image. For example, when you use the JPEG data provider, as you saw in Listing 9.1 (page 206), or the CGImageSource functionality described in "Generalized Functions for Compressed Image Data (Tiger)" (page 226), you don't supply the width and height of the image.

Getting the Pixel Format

Quartz provides the function CGImageGetAlphaInfo that returns the CGAlphaInfo value for an image, which can be one of the values listed in Table 9.2 (page 214). The function CGImageGetBitmapInfo, available in Tiger and later versions, returns the CGBitmapInfo for an image. The CGAlphaInfo and CGBitmapInfo values returned from these functions are identical for images that do not contain floating-point sample data and do not use the endian flags discussed in "Bitmap Images and Universal Binaries (Tiger)" (page 225).

If you have a CGImage object, you can determine whether it is a floating-point image with the code in Listing 9.11. This code first tests whether the symbol for the function CGImageGetBitmapInfo exists and, if so, calls the function to obtain the CGBitmapInfo for the image. It then computes a bitwise AND with the constant kCGBitmapFloatComponents. If the result is nonzero, the image is a floating-point image, otherwise it has integer sample values. When the code executes on a version of Mac OS X prior to Tiger, the function CGImageGetBitmapInfo doesn't exist. The routine imageHasFloatingPointSamples then returns false because floating-point images aren't supported by Quartz on systems where CGImageGet-BitmapInfo is not present.

Listing 9.11 Using CGImageGetBitmapInfo to determine if an image has floating-point image samples

```
bool imageHasFloatingPointSamples(CGImageRef image)
{
  if(&CGImageGetBitmapInfo != NULL){
    return
      (kCGBitmapFloatComponents & CGImageGetBitmapInfo(image));
  }
  return false;
}
```

Creating an Image from a Bitmap Context

One way to create CGImage objects that correspond to drawing you perform with Quartz is to use the utility function CGBitmapContextCreateImage. This function, available in Tiger and later versions, creates a CGImage object from the pixel data contained in a bitmap context. "Creating Bits" (page 345) discusses how to use this function in detail, including guidelines as to when you might use it.

Creating CGImage objects from Quartz drawing is useful if you want to write an image data file from Quartz drawing by using Quartz or QuickTime, as described in "Writing Image Data Using CGImageDestination (Tiger)" (page 255). It's also useful for creating a CGImage object from Quartz drawing that you want to process using Core Image image processing filters. See the references at the end of this chapter for more on Core Image.

Working with Color Spaces

The function CGImageGetColorSpace returns the color space that characterizes the image sample data. For masking images, which are discussed in Chapter 10, "Image Masking" (page 263), it returns NULL. This function can be combined with some of the utility functions that work with CGColorSpace objects, as you'll see in a moment. The function CGImageGetBitmapInfo (or CGImageGetAlphaInfo for the equivalent data prior to Tiger) allows you to determine whether an image has intrinsic alpha. Quartz has other image introspection functions that are more rarely used, such as CGImageGetBitsPerComponent and CGImageGetDecode.

The function CGImageCreateCopyWithColorSpace, available in Panther and later versions, creates a new image from an existing image with intrinsic color and a color space. This allows you to assign a different color space to the image data associated with an existing CGImage object. You can use this function for a number of interesting situations. For example, this function allows you to use a calibrated color space when drawing an image that is characterized by a device color space.

Another situation is for processing pictures from a digital camera. Many digital cameras currently embed an ICC profile, such as an sRGB profile, into the JPEG data they create. The embedded profile data may not accurately characterize the data from the camera, therefore it might be beneficial to users to use a custom profile when drawing the data from a camera. By replacing the color space of a CGImage created from that JPEG data with an updated one created from a different profile, you can potentially produce colors that better match the original scene.

The routine drawJPEGDocumentWithMultipleProfiles in Listing 9.12 demonstrates how to read a color space from an image, create different color spaces for the image, and draw the image using each color space. Each image drawing uses the same underlying image sample data but tagged with a different color space. The result in Figure 9.8 demonstrates how different color spaces affect the interpretation of color data used with them.

Listing 9.12 Assigning color spaces to images

```
void drawJPEGDocumentWithMultipleProfiles(CGContextRef context,
                CFURLRef url){
  CGImageRef jpgImage = NULL, updatedImage1 = NULL, updatedImage2 = NULL;
  Boolean isDeviceRGBImage = false;
  CGColorSpaceRef originalColorSpace = NULL;
  CGColorSpaceRef comparisonColorSpace = NULL;
  CGRect imageRect;
  // Create a Quartz data provider for the supplied URL.
  CGDataProviderRef jpgProvider = CGDataProviderCreateWithURL(url);
  if(jpgProvider == NULL){
    fprintf(stderr, "Couldn't create JPEG Data provider!\n");
    return;
  }

  // Create the CGImageRef for the JPEG image from the data provider.
  jpgImage = CGImageCreateWithJPEGDataProvider(jpgProvider, NULL,
                true, kCGRenderingIntentDefault);
  CGDataProviderRelease(jpgProvider);
  if(jpgImage == NULL){
    fprintf(stderr, "Couldn't create CGImageRef for JPEG data!\n");
    return;
  }
```

```
// Get the color space characterizing the image. This is a
// 'Get' function so the code doesn't own a reference
// to the color space returned and must not release it.
originalColorSpace = CGImageGetColorSpace(jpgImage);
if(originalColorSpace == NULL){
  fprintf(stderr,
    "Image is a masking image, not an image with intrinsic color!\n");
  return;
}

if(CGColorSpaceGetNumberOfComponents(originalColorSpace) != 3){
  fprintf(stderr,
    "This example only works with three-component JPEG images\n!");
  return;
}
// Determine if the original color space is DeviceRGB. If that is
// not the case, then return.
comparisonColorSpace = CGColorSpaceCreateDeviceRGB();

// Note that this comparison of color spaces works only on
// Jaguar and later versions where a CGColorSpaceRef is a
// Core Foundation object. Otherwise this will crash!
isDeviceRGBImage = CFEqual(comparisonColorSpace, originalColorSpace);
// This code created 'comparisonColorSpace' so it must release it.
CGColorSpaceRelease(comparisonColorSpace);
if(!isDeviceRGBImage){
  fprintf(stderr,
    "The color space for the JPEG image is not DeviceRGB!\n");
  return;
}

imageRect = CGRectMake(0., CGImageGetHeight(jpgImage)/2,
            CGImageGetWidth(jpgImage), CGImageGetHeight(jpgImage));
// Draw the original image to the left of the other two.
CGContextDrawImage(context, imageRect, jpgImage);
// Recharacterize the original image with the generic Calibrated RGB
// color space.
updatedImage1 = CGImageCreateCopyWithColorSpace(jpgImage,
            getTheCalibratedRGBColorSpace());
// Release the original image since this code is done with it.
CGImageRelease(jpgImage);
if(updatedImage1 == NULL){
  fprintf(stderr, "There is no updated image to draw!\n");
  return;
}
```

```
// Draw the image characterized by the Generic profile
// to the right of the other image.
imageRect = CGRectOffset(imageRect, CGRectGetWidth(imageRect) + 10, 0);
CGContextDrawImage(context, imageRect, updatedImage1);

// Recharacterize the image but now with a color space
// created with the sRGB profile.
updatedImage2 = CGImageCreateCopyWithColorSpace(updatedImage1,
            getTheSRGBColorSpace());
// Release updatedImage1 since this code is done with it.
CGImageRelease(updatedImage1);
if(updatedImage2 == NULL){
  fprintf(stderr, "There is no second updated image to draw!\n");
  return;
}
// Draw the image characterized by the sRGB profile to the right of
// the image characterized by the generic RGB profile.
imageRect = CGRectOffset(imageRect, CGRectGetWidth(imageRect) + 10, 0);
CGContextDrawImage(context, imageRect, updatedImage2);
CGImageRelease(updatedImage2);
}
```

The routine first creates a data provider for a JPEG image format and then creates a CGImage object that corresponds to the JPEG image. The function CGImageGetColorSpace obtains the color space from the original JPEG data, and the function CGColorSpaceGetNumberOfComponents obtains the number of components in that color space. (The routine is written so that it only handles three-component JPEG images; you could easily update it to handle Gray and CMYK JPEG files.) After ensuring the color space has only three components, the routine calls the function CFEqual to compare the original color space of

Figure 9.8 An image characterized by DeviceRGB (left), GenericRGB (center), and sRGB (right)

the JPEG data with a DeviceRGB color space. If CFEqual returns false, the JPEG data has an embedded profile; otherwise, it is characterized by the DeviceRGB color space.

There are two interesting aspects of using a Core Foundation function to compare Quartz objects like a CGColorSpaceRef. In Jaguar and later versions, Quartz objects such as a CGColorSpaceRef are implemented as Core Foundation (CF) objects with a unique type. This means that generalized operations you might use with other CF objects, such as adding them to arrays or dictionaries or comparing them, as in this example, can be performed. The second interesting aspect of using CFEqual to compare two CGColorSpace objects is that Quartz implements the CF comparison function for color spaces in a way that determines if the color spaces are equivalent and therefore equal, not simply that the two objects are identical. "Quartz Object and Memory Model" (page 599) discusses Quartz objects as CF objects in more detail.

After the routine determines that the original image is characterized by the DeviceRGB color space, the function CGContextDrawImage draws the image. See the left side of Figure 9.8. The function CGImageCreateCopyWithColorSpace creates a new image from the original image, passing the calibrated generic RGB color space obtained by the routine getTheCalibratedRGBColorSpace, described in "A General Function for Uncompressed Data" (page 211). The function CGContextDrawImage draws the image to the right of the original image. The routine then calls the function CGImageCreateCopyWithColorSpace to create a third CGImage object for the same image, but this time characterized with the sRGB color space. This color space can be created using the same code as Listing 7.3 (page 159), but with the full path to the sRGB ICC profile rather than the calibrated generic RGB profile. The function CGContextDrawImage draws the image a third time, but using the sRGB color space. See the image located in the far right of Figure 9.8.

Creating Subimages

The function CGImageCreateWithImageInRect, available in Tiger and later versions, creates a new CGImage object from an existing one that's specified by a subrectangle inside the image. This is useful if you need to draw a small portion of a larger image. Developers familiar with QuickDraw may be accustomed to using the QuickDraw CopyBits function to draw a portion of a larger image. The srcRect passed to CopyBits can be a rectangle that is smaller than that enclosing all the bits in the image.

To use CGImageCreateWithImageInRect, you supply the source image you want to create the subimage from and a CGRect that encloses the image samples of the subimage to create. Quartz interprets the rectangle in a coordinate system based on the original image. In this coordinate system, each image sample is 1 unit and the first pixel in the image, that of the top-left corner of the image sample data, is the origin of coordinates. The x coordinate increases along the width of the image such that the last pixel on the first image scanline has the coordinate (0,width − 1) for an original image that is width samples wide. The y coordinate increases as the scanline number increases such that the first pixel on the last scanline has the coordinate (0,height − 1) for an original image that is height samples high. The subrectangle passed to the function describes the image samples that it encloses; for example, the smallest rectangle that completely encloses the first scanline has its origin at (0,0) and a size of (width,1).

When it is available, the function CGImageCreateWithImageInRect is the best way to create a subimage from a larger image, but for those versions of Mac OS X where it isn't available, you can use other means to draw a smaller portion of a given image. One way to do so is to use a clipping path tailored to mask off those portions of the original image you don't want to draw. However, there are two disadvantages of using clipping to mask off pixels on the boundary of an image. The first is that it is difficult to clip individual source pixels in an image when using a clipping path. This is especially true when the ultimate destination of the drawing is unknown, such as when you create a PDF document from your drawing. A second disadvantage to using clipping is that creating PDF documents from this data records all the bitmap data into the PDF document, including data that will be clipped out. In most situations, it is preferable to record only the data for the subimage.

Another strategy for drawing a subimage from a larger image is to create the subimage directly by adjusting the data provider that provides the data so that it only supplies the data needed to draw the subimage. This can be straightforward for images that have bitsPerPixel that are multiples of 8 bits in size. You might use this strategy to draw a subimage similar to that shown in Figure 9.9. The red rectangle in the figure encloses the image samples that make up the subimage.

Listing 9.13 shows how to use the function CGImageCreateWithImageInRect and the data provider strategy to draw a subimage of a 24-bit RGB image. To draw the subimage, the code first calculates the subrectangle that encloses the image samples to draw. This example draws the subimage that is inset from the full image by 16 samples from the left side and 4 scanlines from the top, and inset by 64 samples on the right and 40 scanlines from the bottom.

The routine doColorRampSubImage takes advantage of the Quartz function CGImageCreateWithImageInRect available in Tiger and later versions, if it can. The code tests for the symbol and if it is available, creates a full-size image of the color ramp by using the data provider created with the routine createRGBRampDataProvider. Recall that this routine (from Listing 8.2 (page 189)) provides the image data for the complete image, using the width and height of the full image. The code then creates the subimage by calling CGImageCreateWithImageInRect

Figure 9.9 Subimage data as part of a larger image

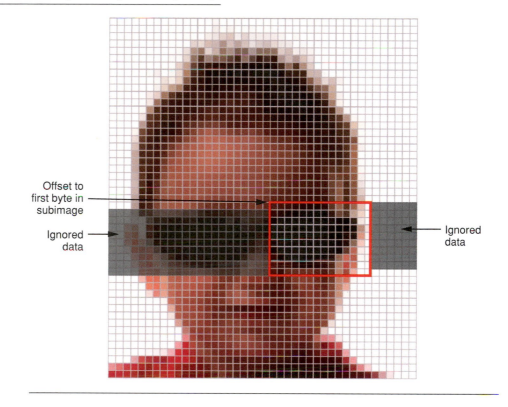

Offset to first byte in subimage

Ignored data

Ignored data

with the full-size image and the subrectangle that represents the portion of the image to draw.

When the function `CGImageCreateWithImageInRect` isn't available, the code instead creates a specialized data provider that obtains the data needed for the subimage, using the routine `createRGBRampSubDataProvider`. This routine creates the color ramp data for the full image by calling `createRedGreenRampImageData`. It then uses that data to create a data provider that returns only the data corresponding to the subimage. It calculates the offset to the first byte of data in the subimage and uses that offset to calculate the pointer to the first byte of the subimage data. The block of data passed to the data provider contains extra data at the end of each scanline and the beginning of the next. These bytes are the extra sample data outside the subimage. By supplying the appropriate parameters when creating the image, Quartz skips this extra data, as you'll see in a moment.

After the data provider for the subimage is created, the function `CGImageCreate` creates the CGImage object. The `width` and `height` supplied to `CGImageCreate` are the size of the subimage rectangle. Those values correspond to the number of samples in each row of the subimage and the number of rows in the subimage. The value of bytesPerRow is the same bytesPerRow as you would use for the larger image. This is because the data provider is providing the same data (offset from the beginning, that is) as you would provide for the larger image, as shown in Figure 9.9. The extra data at the end of each scanline and the beginning of the next scanline of the larger image is ignored, as shown by the gray rectangles in the figure. Quartz uses the number of row bytes (bytesPerRow) and the image width to determine which bytes, if any, to skip after it obtains the data for a given scanline in the subimage.

Listing 9.13 Drawing a subrectangle of an image

```
static void rgbRampSubDataRelease(void *info, const void *data,
                  size_t size)
{
  free((char *)info);
}
static unsigned char *createRedGreenRampImageData(size_t width,
                  size_t height, size_t size)
{
  unsigned char *p;
  unsigned char *dataP = (unsigned char *)malloc(size);

  if(dataP == NULL)
     return NULL;

  p = dataP;
  // Build an image that is RGB 24 bits per sample. This is a ramp
  // where the red component value increases in red from left to
  // right and the green component increases from top to bottom.
  int r, g;
  for(g = 0 ; g < height ; g++){
    for(r = 0 ; r < width ; r++){
       *p++ = r; *p++ = g; *p++ = 0;
    }
  }
  return dataP;
}

static CGDataProviderRef createRGBRampSubDataProvider(CGRect subRect)
{
  CGDataProviderRef dataProvider = NULL;
  size_t bytesPerSample = 3;
  size_t width = 256, height = 256;
  size_t bytesPerRow = width*bytesPerSample;
  size_t startOffsetX = subRect.origin.x;
```

```
        size_t startOffsetY = subRect.origin.y;
        size_t imageDataSize = bytesPerRow*height;
        // The first image sample is at
        // (startOffsetY*bytesPerRow + startOffsetX*bytesPerSample)
        // bytes into the RGB ramp data.
        size_t firstByteOffset = startOffsetY*bytesPerRow +
                    startOffsetX*bytesPerSample;
        // The actual size of the image data provided is the full image size
        // minus the amount skipped at the beginning. This is more than the
        // total amount of data that is needed for the subimage, but it is
        // valid and easy to calculate.
        size_t totalBytesProvided = imageDataSize - firstByteOffset;
        // Create the full color ramp.
        unsigned char *dataP = createRedGreenRampImageData(width, height,
                    imageDataSize);
        if(dataP == NULL){
          fprintf(stderr, "Couldn't create image data\n!");
          return NULL;
        }

        // Use the pointer to the first byte as the info parameter since
        // that is the pointer to the block to free when done.
        dataProvider = CGDataProviderCreateWithData(dataP,
                    dataP + firstByteOffset,
                    totalBytesProvided, rgbRampSubDataRelease);

      if(dataProvider == NULL){
        free(dataP);
        return NULL;
      }
      return dataProvider;
}

void doColorRampSubImage(CGContextRef context)
{
  CGImageRef image = NULL;
  CGRect imageSubRect, rect;
  // Start 4 scanlines from the top and 16 pixels from the left edge;
  // skip the last 40 scanlines of the image and the rightmost
  // 64 pixels.
  size_t insetLeft = 16,insetTop = 4,insetRight = 64,insetBottom = 40;

  size_t fullImageWidth = 256, fullImageHeight = 256;
  size_t subImageWidth = fullImageWidth-insetLeft-insetRight;
```

```
size_t subImageHeight = fullImageHeight-insetTop-insetBottom;
size_t bitsPerComponent = 8, bitsPerPixel = 24;
size_t bytesPerRow = fullImageWidth * 3;
bool shouldInterpolate = true;
CGColorSpaceRef colorspace = NULL;
CGDataProviderRef imageDataProvider = NULL;
imageSubRect = CGRectMake(insetLeft, insetTop,
                subImageWidth, subImageHeight);
colorspace = getTheCalibratedRGBColorSpace();
if(&CGImageCreateWithImageInRect != NULL){
  CGImageRef fullImage = NULL;
  imageDataProvider = createRGBRampDataProvider();
  if(imageDataProvider == NULL){
    fprintf(stderr, "Couldn't create Image Data provider!\n");
    return;
  }
  fullImage = CGImageCreate(fullImageWidth, fullImageHeight,
                bitsPerComponent,
                bitsPerPixel,
                bytesPerRow, colorspace, kCGImageAlphaNone,
                imageDataProvider, NULL, shouldInterpolate,
                kCGRenderingIntentDefault);
  if(fullImage){
    image = CGImageCreateWithImageInRect(fullImage,
                imageSubRect);
    // Release the full image since it is no longer required.
    CGImageRelease(fullImage);
  }
}
// If the image hasn't been created yet, this code uses the
// customized data provider to do so.
if(image == NULL){
  imageDataProvider = createRGBRampSubDataProvider(imageSubRect);
  if(imageDataProvider == NULL){
    fprintf(stderr, "Couldn't create Image Data provider!\n");
    return;
  }

  // By supplying bytesPerRow, the extra data at the end of
  // each scanline and the beginning of the next is properly skipped.
  image = CGImageCreate(subImageWidth, subImageHeight,
                bitsPerComponent,
                bitsPerPixel,
```

Figure 9.10 An image (left) and a subimage (right) from the image

```
                 bytesPerRow, colorspace, kCGImageAlphaNone,
                 imageDataProvider, NULL, shouldInterpolate,
                 kCGRenderingIntentDefault);
   }
   // This code no longer needs the data provider.
   CGDataProviderRelease(imageDataProvider);
   if(image == NULL){
     fprintf(stderr, "Couldn't create CGImageRef for this data!\n");
     return;
   }
   // Draw the subimage.
   rect = CGRectMake(0, 0, subImageWidth, subImageHeight);
   CGContextDrawImage(context, rect, image);
   CGImageRelease(image);
}
```

After the image is created, regardless of the method used, it can be drawn just like any other Quartz image. Figure 9.10 shows the drawing of an image and a subimage of that image.

Writing Image Data Using CGImageDestination (Tiger)

10.4 ▶ Most of the time CGImage objects are used to draw images in Quartz. In Tiger and later versions, however, there are functions available to export CGImage objects into various standard data file formats, such as JPEG, PNG, TIFF, Open-EXR, and Photoshop formats. These functions allow you to create image data files. (The function CGImageDestinationCopyTypeIdentifiers creates a CFArray object that describes the export image formats supported by Quartz on a given version of Mac OS X.)

You've seen how easy it is to use CGImageSource functions. Their complements—CGImageDestination functions—provide a straightforward and easy way to write a wide variety of image data files from CGImage objects. Just as you can read an image file that contains multiple images, you can write these same kinds of files. First, you create a destination object, specifying one of three destinations—a data consumer, a CFData object, or a CFURL object. Then you add one or more images to the destination object. (Not all image file formats support more than one image.) You can also specify metadata properties for the data. When you are finished adding images, call the function `CGImageDestination-Finalize` to complete the process and finish writing the contents of the destination object to the specified destination. Table 9.6 lists the CGImageDestination functions you are most likely to use.

Listing 9.14 is a routine `exportCGImageToPNGFileWithDestination` that creates a PNG format file from a CGImage object using a `CGImageDestinationRef`. The code first creates a CGImageDestination object from the supplied URL with the type `kUTTypePNG` and specifies 1 for the number of images that it will add to the file. Not all image formats support more than one image per file and the PNG format only supports one image per file.

Next the code creates a CFDictionary object to use as the options dictionary that describes the image. (The options dictionary is optional and you can pass NULL if you have no optional information to add.) The code adds keys to the options dictionary specifying that the x and y resolution are both 144 dpi for the image. It then calls `CGImageDestinationAddImage` to add the image to the destination. It completes the writing of the destination file by calling `CGImageDestinationFinalize` and releases the CGImageDestination object.

Table 9.6 CGImageDestination Functions Most Typically Used by Applications

Function	Use to
CGImageDestinationCreateWithDataConsumer	Create a destination object with a data consumer.
CGImageDestinationCreateWithData	Create a destination object with CFData.
CGImageDestinationCreateWithURL	Create a destination object with a CFURL.
CGImageDestinationAddImage	Add a CGImage object to a destination object.
CGImageDestinationAddImageFromSource	Add an image from an image source object to a destination object.
CGImageDestinationFinalize	Write out the contents of the destination object.

Important Creating a CGImageDestination object for a destination that corresponds to a file scheme URL replaces any existing file that may exist. If you want to add multiple images to a file, you create the destination and add all the images to the file prior to calling `CGImageDestinationFinalize`.

Listing 9.14 Creating a PNG file from a CGImage object

```
void exportCGImageToPNGFileWithDestination(CGImageRef image,
                CFURLRef url)
{
  float resolution = 144.;
  CFTypeRef keys[2];
  CFTypeRef values[2];
  CFDictionaryRef options = NULL;

  // Create an image destination at the supplied URL that
  // corresponds to the PNG image format.
  CGImageDestinationRef imageDestination =
    CGImageDestinationCreateWithURL(url, kUTTypePNG, 1, NULL);

  if(imageDestination == NULL){
    fprintf(stderr, "Couldn't create image destination!\n");
    return;
  }

  // Set the keys to be the x and y resolution of the image.
  keys[0] = kCGImagePropertyDPIWidth;
  keys[1] = kCGImagePropertyDPIHeight;

  // Create a CFNumber for the resolution and use it as the
  // x and y resolution.
  values[0] = CFNumberCreate(NULL, kCFNumberFloatType, &resolution);
  values[1] = values[0];

  // Create an options dictionary with these keys.
  options = CFDictionaryCreate(NULL,
          (const void **)keys,
          (const void **)values,
          2,
          &kCFTypeDictionaryKeyCallBacks,
          &kCFTypeDictionaryValueCallBacks);

  // Release the CFNumber the code created.
  CFRelease(values[0]);
```

```
    // Add the image with the options dictionary to the destination.
    CGImageDestinationAddImage(imageDestination, image, options);

    // Release the options dictionary this code created.
    CFRelease(options);

    // When all the images are added to the destination, finalize it.
    CGImageDestinationFinalize(imageDestination);

    // Release the destination when done with it.
    CFRelease(imageDestination);
}
```

You might want to use CGImageDestination functions to save the results of Quartz drawing in a compressed image format such as PNG. You'll see an example of how to use Quartz drawing to create an image in the PNG format in "Creating Bits" (page 345).

Exporting to JPEG Using a QuickTime Exporter

Just as QuickTime supports importing images to create a CGImage object, the QuickTime API also supports exporting a CGImage object to a number of file formats, including TIFF, PNG, and JPEG. As is the case with importing CGImage objects, exporting CGImage objects is a feature of QuickTime version 6.4 and later, which is automatically installed with Panther and is also available as a software update for users of Mac OS X version 10.2.5 and later 10.2.x releases.

Note   For output formats that are supported by Quartz, it is recommended that you use the CGImageDestination functionality instead of QuickTime when your application executes on Tiger and later versions.

Writing a CGImage to a compressed file using QuickTime is similarly straightforward. The code in Listing 9.15 demonstrates how to export an arbitrary CGImage object to a JPEG file. The routine exportCGImageToJPEGFile takes a CGImage object and creates a JPEG file at the location on disk as specified by a CFURL object that represents the full path to a disk location.

Listing 9.15 Exporting a CGImage object to a JPEG file

```
// This code requires the QuickTime framework.
#include <QuickTime/QuickTime.h>
void exportCGImageToJPEGFile(CGImageRef imageRef, CFURLRef url)
{
  Handle                    dataRef = NULL;
  OSType                    dataRefType;
  GraphicsExportComponent   graphicsExporter;
  unsigned long             sizeWritten;
  ComponentResult           result;
  result = QTNewDataReferenceFromCFURL(url, 0,
              &dataRef, &dataRefType);
  if(!result)
  {
    result = OpenADefaultComponent(GraphicsExporterComponentType,
                kQTFileTypeJPEG, &graphicsExporter);
    if(!result){
      result = GraphicsExportSetInputCGImage(graphicsExporter, imageRef);
      if(!result)
        result = GraphicsExportSetOutputDataReference(
                graphicsExporter, dataRef, dataRefType);
      if(!result)
        result = GraphicsExportDoExport(
                graphicsExporter, &sizeWritten);
      CloseComponent(graphicsExporter);
    }
  }
  if(dataRef)
    DisposeHandle(dataRef);
  if(result)
    fprintf(stderr, "Bad result = %d!\n", (int)result);
  return;
}
```

Summary

Quartz supports a variety of pixel formats and data layouts for bitmap images. Image samples can be integer or floating-point values and can contain per-sample alpha data in several different formats. You can create Quartz images—CGImage objects—using data from any of a number of different sources including URL-based files, data in memory, and the Clipboard.

Image utility functions support such tasks as obtaining image dimensions, working with color spaces, and creating a subimage from an image. You can also use Quartz functions to write image data to a number of standard image data formats using Quartz functionality in Tiger or in earlier versions of Mac OS X by using a QuickTime exporter.

This chapter focused exclusively on images with intrinsic color. The next chapter shows how to perform image masking using "traditional" masks as well as using an image as a mask.

See Also

The Core Image framework, available in Tiger and later versions, is an image processing API that can operate on CGImage objects. You can use the Core Image framework to apply image processing filters to a CGImage object. Compositing, color adjustment, distortion, and geometry filters are just a few of the categories of filters that are available. You can also use Core Image to create your own image processing filters. You can find more information in these documents available from the ADC Reference Library:

- *Core Image Programming Guide* provides conceptual information about Core Image and how to use it:

  http://developer.apple.com/documentation/GraphicsImaging/Conceptual/ CoreImaging/index.html

- *Core Image Reference* is the API reference for Core Image:

  http://developer.apple.com/documentation/GraphicsImaging/Reference/ CoreImagingRef/index.html

Many of the properties and capabilities of Quartz images are the same as those of the PDF imaging model, described in *PDF Reference: Version 1.6*, 5th edition, Adobe Systems, Inc.

Information about the QuickTime functions in QuickTime v6.4 and later that create CGImage objects or export them to file are available from the ADC Reference Library:

  http://developer.apple.com/documentation/QuickTime/WhatsNewQT6_4/ Chap1/chapter_1_section_20.html

Apple provides sample code that may be useful for using earlier QuickTime versions to create CGImage objects from data formats that QuickTime supports. This code is available from the ADC Reference Library:

http://developer.apple.com/samplecode/QTtoCG/QTtoCG.html

Universal Binary Programming Guidelines discusses how to create a universal binary that executes properly on Mac OS X running on both PowerPC- and Intel-based Macintosh computers and is available at

http://developer.apple.com/documentation/MacOSX/Conceptual/ universal_binary/

The Quartz header files containing the structures and functions used in this chapter are

- `CGContext.h`
- `CGImage.h`
- `CGColorSpace.h`

The CGImageSource and CGImageDestination functionality, while part of Quartz 2D, is implemented in the ImageIO framework, which is a subframework of the ApplicationServices framework. The header files for this functionality are located in

`/System/Library/Frameworks/ApplicationServices.framework/Frameworks/ ImageIO.framework/Headers`

The header files containing the prototypes and constants for CGImageSource and CGImageDestination are

- `CGImageSource.h`
- `CGImageDestination.h`
- `CGImageProperties.h`

The relevant reference documentation from the ADC Reference Library is

- *CGContext Reference*
- *CGImage Reference*
- *CGColorSpace Reference*
- *CGImageSource Reference*
- *CGImageDestination Reference*

Chapter 10

Image Masking

Broadly speaking, image masking is a process that controls the coverage of paint to apply when painting an image. Image masking is typically performed using an **image mask**. The terms **image mask**, **masking image**, and **mask** are interchangeable terms to describe an image whose sample values indicate a percentage of paint to apply but not the color of the paint itself. Such an image is sometimes called a **stencil mask** because the mask does not itself have any intrinsic color; instead, color "pours" through the stencil. An image mask has only one component value, the coverage value.

An image mask is not the only way in Quartz to accomplish image masking. Colors and images can also serve as masking devices. Each masking device—image masks, colors, and images—produces its own unique and interesting effect in Quartz.

An image mask can be 1, 2, 4, or 8 bits per sample. A sample value that decodes to 0 allows paint to go through it—it's the "hole" in the stencil. A sample value that decodes to 1 doesn't allow paint through—it's the solid part of the stencil. A 1-bit mask, by definition, has only "on/off" options—0 or 1. Deeper masks, such as an 8-bit mask, can contain intermediate values ($0 < x < 1$) that specify gradations of paint that get through the mask, with lower values allowing more paint than higher values.

An image, when used as a masking device, produces an effect opposite to that of an image mask. A sample value of 0 doesn't allow paint through, while a sample value of 1 does allow paint through. Intermediate values specify gradations of paint, with lower values allowing less paint than higher values.

Figure 10.1 Masking devices: image masks (1 bit and 8 bit), an image for use as a mask, and using color as a mask

Color, when used as a masking device, has an effect different from the other two devices. The masking color components define the transparent portions of an image. Any paint underneath the transparent portions shows through the parts of the image that contain the masking color. The rightmost image in Figure 10.1 has the green masked out to reveal a red background underneath.

Quartz provides four functions that perform various aspects of image masking, as shown in Table 10.1. The function `CGImageMaskCreate` creates a mask that you can draw to a graphics context or apply to an image using the function `CGImageCreateWithMask`. The function `CGImageCreateWithMask` applies either an image or an image mask to an image, returning the masked image. The function `CGImageCreateWithMaskingColors` masks a range of colors, returning the color-masked image. The function `CGContextClipToMask` clips a graphics context with either an image mask or an image; all content painted to the context is masked accordingly, with an image having the inverse effect of using an image mask. The sections that follow provide detailed information on how to use each function.

Table 10.1 Image Masking Functions

Function	Use to
`CGImageMaskCreate`	Create an image mask.
`CGImageCreateWithMask`	Mask an image with an image mask or an image.
`CGImageCreateWithMaskingColors`	Mask one or more colors in an image.
`CGContextClipToMask`	Clip a graphics context with an image mask or an image.

Creating an Image Mask

The function `CGImageMaskCreate` creates an image mask that can be drawn directly to a graphics context or that can be passed as a parameter to the functions CGImageCreateWithMask or CGContextClipToMask. In this section, you'll create 1-bit and 8-bit image masks and draw each to a graphics context. Used in this way, the image mask gets its color from the current fill color in the graphics state. The amount of paint is determined by the values of the image samples.

There are many similarities between the information you supply to create an image mask and those you supply to create an image. If you've mastered creating images, you'll find creating image masks easier. You use the function CGImage-MaskCreate instead of CGImageCreate. The two functions are similar, except that CGImageMaskCreate requires fewer parameters, because masks don't have intrinsic color. As Table 10.2 shows, the three parameters related to color—colorspace, bitmapInfo, and intent—are not needed to create an image mask.

Unlike CGImageCreate, the function CGImageMaskCreate has no CGBitmapInfo parameter that specifies the data format. Unlike images with intrinsic color, image masks are limited to 1, 2, 4, and 8 bits per component. If you supply a bitsPerPixel value that is greater than bitsPerComponent, then the padding bits must be the last bits in the bit stream for each pixel; this is equivalent to kCGImageAlphaNoneSkipLast for images with color. There is also no rendering intent parameter associated with an image mask. When you draw an image mask with CGContextDrawImage, Quartz consults the rendering intent in the graphics state, just as it does for the painting color.

For 1-bit-deep masks, a sample value of 0 means that paint should be applied for that sample and a sample value of 1 means that the sample should not be painted. One way to think about painting with masks is that values in a mask act as an inverse of the alpha value. A value of 1 is opaque; for a mask this means

Table 10.2 Comparison of the Parameters to Create an Image and Image Mask

CGImageCreate	CGImageMaskCreate
Width	Width
Height	Height
BitsPerComponent	BitsPerComponent
BitsPerPixel	BitsPerPixel
BytesPerRow	BytesPerRow
Colorspace	—
BitmapInfo	—
Provider	Provider
Decode	Decode
ShouldInterpolate	ShouldInterpolate
Intent	—

that paint does not pass through the mask. A value of 0 is transparent; for a mask this means that paint passes through the mask to the destination. If this sense of a mask is inverted from the data you need to draw, you can use the decode parameter you pass to CGImageMaskCreate to invert the effect of the mask.

Drawing and Inverting a 1–Bit Image Mask

The code in Listing 10.1 draws two simple 1-bit image masks a number of different ways to illustrate the way masks behave. The data itself is small enough that it is included as static data inline, and a portion is shown in the listing. The code creates a data provider with CGDataProviderCreateWithData, using the static image data. Because the data is static, there is no need to have a data release function for the data provider; the data lives for the life of the program. Nothing about the data provider is specific to image masks. It is a data provider just like any of those you've seen previously; the contents of the data itself are what make it unique.

Because the image data is 1 bit per sample with no padding bits, the number of bits per component and the number of bits per pixel are both 1. The code creates two image masks, the first with a decode value of NULL, the second with a decode array that inverts the sense of the mask.

When you supply a decode array for a mask, you supply an array that contains two float values. Quartz maps mask values of 0 into the first entry in the decode array and mask values of 1 into the second entry in the decode array. Mask values between 0 and 1 are linearly interpolated between the minimum and maximum entries in the decode array.

In this example, the first entry (the minimum value) in the decode array is 1.0, meaning that mask sample values of 0 are decoded into the value 1.0. The second entry (the maximum value) in the decode array is 0.0, meaning that the maximum mask sample value (1 for a 1-bit mask), is decoded into the value 0.0. This inverts the sense of the mask data.

After creating a mask and its corresponding inverted mask from the first mask data, the code does the same for the second mask.

Listing 10.1 Drawing image masks created with CGImageMaskCreate

```
static const unsigned char *getMaskData1()
{
  static const unsigned char data[] = {
    0xFF, 0xFF, 0xFF, 0xFF, 0xFF, 0x7F, 0xFF,
    ...
    0x7F, 0xC0, 0x00, 0x00, 0x00, 0x07, 0xFF, 0xFF
```

```
    };
    return data;
}

static const unsigned char *getMaskData2()
{
    static const unsigned char data[] = {
        0xFF, 0xFF, 0xFF, 0xFF, 0xFF, 0xFF, 0xFF,
        ...
        0xFF, 0xFF, 0xBF, 0xFF
    };
    return data;
}

void doOneBitMaskImages(CGContextRef context)
{
    static const size_t bitsPerComponent = 1, bitsPerPixel = 1;
    static const size_t width = 96, height = 96;
    static const size_t bytesPerRow = 12;
    CGImageRef mask1, invertedmask1, mask2, invertedmask2;
    CGRect imageRect, backRect;
    size_t imageDataSize = bytesPerRow*height;
    Boolean shouldInterpolate = true;
    static const float lightBlue[] = { 0.482, 0.62, 0.871, 1. };
    static const float black[] = { 0., 0., 0., 1. };
    static const float darkRed[] = { 0.663, 0., 0.031, 1. };
    static const float darkGreen[] = { 0.404, 0.808, 0.239, 1. };
    static const float darkBlue[] = { 0.11, 0.208, 0.451, 1. };
    float purple[] = { 0.69, 0.486, 0.722, 1. };
    float darkOrange[] = { 0.965, 0.584, 0.059, 1. };

    CGColorSpaceRef colorSpace = NULL;
    float decode[2] = {1 , 0};

    // Create a Quartz data provider for the image data. Because this
    // data is static data, there is no need to release it, so the data
    // release function is NULL.
    unsigned const char *data = getMaskData1();
    CGDataProviderRef dataProvider = CGDataProviderCreateWithData(NULL,
                data, imageDataSize, NULL);
    if(dataProvider == NULL){
        fprintf(stderr, "Couldn't create Mask1 Data provider!\n");
        return;
    }
```

```
// Create a mask from the data.
mask1 = CGImageMaskCreate(width, height, bitsPerComponent,
              bitsPerPixel, bytesPerRow, dataProvider,
              NULL, shouldInterpolate);
// Create the same mask but with a decode array that
// inverts the sense of the mask.
invertedmask1 = CGImageMaskCreate(width, height,
              bitsPerComponent, bitsPerPixel, bytesPerRow,
              dataProvider, decode, shouldInterpolate);
// Release the data provider now that this code no longer needs it.
CGDataProviderRelease(dataProvider);
if(mask1 == NULL || invertedmask1 == NULL){
  if(mask1 == NULL)
    fprintf(stderr,
      "Couldn't create CGImageRef for the mask data 1!\n");
  else
    CGImageRelease(mask1);

  if(invertedmask1 == NULL)
    fprintf(stderr,
      "Couldn't create CGImageRef for the inverted mask data 1!\n");
  else
    CGImageRelease(invertedmask1);

  return;
}

// Get the pointer to the data for the second mask.
data = getMaskData2();
dataProvider = CGDataProviderCreateWithData(NULL,
              data, imageDataSize, NULL);
if(dataProvider == NULL){
  CGImageRelease(mask1);
  CGImageRelease(invertedmask1);
  fprintf(stderr, "Couldn't create Mask2 Data provider!\n");
  return;
}

mask2 = CGImageMaskCreate(width, height, bitsPerComponent,
              bitsPerPixel, bytesPerRow, dataProvider,
              NULL, shouldInterpolate);
// Create the same mask but with a decode array that
// inverts the sense of the mask.
```

```
invertedmask2 = CGImageMaskCreate(width, height,
                bitsPerComponent, bitsPerPixel, bytesPerRow,
                dataProvider, decode, shouldInterpolate);
// Release the data provider now that this code no longer needs it.
CGDataProviderRelease(dataProvider);
if(mask2 == NULL || invertedmask2 == NULL){
  if(mask2 == NULL)
    fprintf(stderr,
      "Couldn't create CGImageRef for the mask data 2!\n");
  else
    CGImageRelease(mask2);

  if(invertedmask2 == NULL)
    fprintf(stderr,
      "Couldn't create CGImageRef for the inverted mask data 2!\n");
  else
    CGImageRelease(invertedmask2);

  CGImageRelease(mask1);
  CGImageRelease(invertedmask1);
  return;
}

CGContextScaleCTM(context, 1.5, 1.5);
colorSpace = getTheCalibratedRGBColorSpace();
CGContextSetFillColorSpace(context, colorSpace);

// Set the fill color to a light blue.
CGContextSetFillColor(context, lightBlue);
// Paint part of the background.
backRect = CGRectMake(width/2, height/2, width*3, height);
CGContextFillRect(context, backRect);

imageRect = CGRectMake(0., height, width, height);
CGContextSaveGState(context);
  // Set the fill color to opaque black.
  CGContextSetFillColor(context, black);
  // ***** Mask 1 *****
  CGContextDrawImage(context, imageRect, mask1);

  CGContextTranslateCTM(context, width, 0);
  // Set the fill color to opaque red.
  CGContextSetFillColor(context, darkRed);
```

```
                    // ***** Mask 2 *****
                    CGContextDrawImage(context, imageRect, mask2);
                    CGContextTranslateCTM(context, width, 0);
                    // Set the fill color to dark orange.
                    CGContextSetFillColor(context, darkOrange);
                    // ***** Mask 3 *****
                    CGContextDrawImage(context, imageRect, mask1);

                    CGContextTranslateCTM(context, width, 0);
                    // Make the orange 50% transparent.
                    darkOrange[3] = 0.5;
                    CGContextSetFillColor(context, darkOrange);
                    // ***** Mask 4 *****
                    CGContextDrawImage(context, imageRect, mask2);
                CGContextRestoreGState(context);

                // Translate down the page. The cast is necessary
                // since height is typed as size_t which is unsigned.
                CGContextTranslateCTM(context, 0, -(signed)height);
                // Set the fill color to an opaque green.
                CGContextSetFillColor(context, darkGreen);
                // ***** Mask 5 *****
                CGContextDrawImage(context, imageRect, invertedmask2);

                CGContextTranslateCTM(context, width, 0);
                // Set the fill color to a dark blue.
                CGContextSetFillColor(context, darkBlue);
                // ***** Mask 6 *****
                CGContextDrawImage(context, imageRect, invertedmask1);
                CGContextTranslateCTM(context, width, 0);
                // Set the fill color to purple.
                CGContextSetFillColor(context, purple);
                // ***** Mask 7 *****
                CGContextDrawImage(context, imageRect, invertedmask2);
                CGContextTranslateCTM(context, width, 0);

                // Make the purple 50% transparent.
                purple[3] = 0.5;
                CGContextSetFillColor(context, purple);
                // ***** Mask 8 *****
                CGContextDrawImage(context, imageRect, invertedmask1);
                // Release the CGImageRefs when they are no longer needed.
                CGImageRelease(mask1);
                CGImageRelease(invertedmask1);
```

```
    CGImageRelease(mask2);
    CGImageRelease(invertedmask2);
}
```

After the routine doOneBitMaskImages creates the four image masks—mask1, invertedmask1, mask2, and invertedmask2, the application-supplied function getTheCalibratedRGBColorSpace gets an RGB color space and CGContextSetFill-ColorSpace makes it the fill color space. The next few lines of code create a rectangle and paint it with a light blue color so that the drawing canvas has some color associated with it prior to repeatedly painting the image masks. You can see the background rectangle in Figure 10.2.

The next block of code paints the two different masks two times each across the top of Figure 10.2. The sample values are painted with the current fill color so that the first rendering of the image paints the 0 samples opaque black and leaves the other samples unpainted so that the background shows through. The next three calls to CGContextDrawImage with mask1 and mask2 each use the current fill color to paint the 0 samples in the mask and leave the 1 samples unpainted. Notice that when the fill color has an alpha value that is partially transparent, the mask is painted with that partially transparent color.

Figure 10.2 Drawing an image mask with different context fill colors

The next block of code paints the inverted masks four times across the bottom of Figure 10.2. The painting of these image masks inverts the sense of the mask so that now mask sample values of 0 are unpainted and values of 1 are painted with the fill color.

Drawing an 8-Bit-Deep Mask

Masks that are 1 bit deep can specify only whether a fill color is or is not painted. Masks that are 8 bits deep behave the same way for sample values that decode to 0 or 1. The sample values act as inverse alpha values. Sample values that decode to 0 paint the fill color as if it were blended with an additional alpha value of 1. Sample values that decode to 1 paint the fill color as if it were blended with an additional alpha value of 0; that is, such samples are fully transparent and are not painted. But 8-bit masks can also have sample values that decode to values between 0 and 1. For these values, the fill color is blended with an additional alpha value of $(1 - S)$, where S is the decoded sample value of the 8-bit mask.

Figure 10.3 is an example of painting an 8-bit image mask that contains image samples that span from the minimum to the maximum values. The code that produced the graphic in the figure created an 8-bit mask from 8-bit, one-component image data. Prior to painting the left image mask, it set the context fill color to an opaque black and prior to painting the right image in the figure it used the same mask and set the fill color to a blue color. The mask is painted on a white background.

Figure 10.3 An 8-bit mask painted with black (left) and blue (right)

The left image in the figure shows the image as it would have been painted had it been used as an 8-bit grayscale image. The right image in the figure shows the mask used as an inverse alpha mask. The opacity of the fill color varies depending on the mask sample values. The result is that locations in the image that are closer to black (0.0) are painted with blue component values that are more opaque and locations in the image that are closer to white (1.0) are painted with blue component values that are more transparent. Because the background is white, the result is a colorized image.

Quartz fully supports deep masks (>1 bit) when drawing to window contexts and bitmap contexts. Prior to Tiger, drawing an image mask with more than 1 bit per component is not correctly drawn into a PDF context; the resulting PDF document does not correctly capture the mask. Because printing in Mac OS X captures application drawing into a PDF document, this means that deep masks don't print correctly prior to Tiger.

Masking an Image (Tiger)

10.4 ▶ The function `CGImageCreateWithMask` allows you to mask one image with another. The resulting image is called a **masked image**—an image that is masked with another. It is important to distinguish between a masked image (an image that is masked by another) and an image mask (an image you use as a mask).

When you call `CGImageCreateWithMask`, you pass the following parameters:

- `image`, a CGImage object that represents an image with intrinsic color to which you want a mask applied. This image may or may not already have an alpha component.

- `mask`, a CGImage object that represents either an image mask or a one-component image without alpha and that is characterized by the DeviceGray color space.

Quartz applies the `mask` to the image in one of two ways, depending on whether the `mask` parameter is an image mask or an image. Recall that you create an image mask using the function `CGImageMaskCreate`. As described in "Creating an Image Mask" (page 264), the image mask sample values act as an inverse alpha; that is, a decoded sample value of S acts as an alpha value of $(1 - S)$. Masking an image with an image mask behaves the same way as painting a mask with the context fill color, but instead of using the context fill color as the source color you are painting through the mask, Quartz uses the sample values of the image with intrinsic color as the source color. The image sample values on the image being masked by the `mask` parameter may contain alpha data. The alpha of the mask is blended with the image alpha value just like it is when painting any other mask.

A mask parameter that is an image must be a one-component image in the DeviceGray color space that has no alpha component. If the mask parameter is an image, Quartz applies the mask parameter as an alpha mask—a decoded sample value of S acts as an alpha value of S.

Masking an Image with an Image Mask

The routine doMaskImageWithMaskFromURL in Listing 10.2 shows how to mask an image with an image mask. The output from the listing is shown in Figure 10.4. The code creates an image with intrinsic color and paints it and then creates an image mask and paints it. Next, the code calls the function CGImageCreateWith-Mask with the image and image mask as parameters. (Note that the routine doMaskImageWithMaskFromURL combines code from Listing 9.2 (page 219) and Listing 10.1 (page 266).) This creates a new CGImage object that corresponds to the masked image. After the masked image is created, the CGImage objects corresponding to the original source image and the image mask can be released because the code no longer uses them. Finally the masked image is painted and drawn to the right of the other images shown in the figure.

Listing 10.2 Masking an image with an image mask using CGImageCreateWithMask

```
void doMaskImageWithMaskFromURL(CGContextRef context,
              CFURLRef imageURL, size_t imagewidth,
              size_t imageheight, size_t bitsPerComponent,
              CFURLRef theMaskingImageURL, size_t maskwidth,
              size_t maskheight)
{
  CGImageRef image = NULL, mask = NULL, imageMaskedWithImage = NULL;
  CGRect imageRect, maskRect;
  size_t imageBitsPerPixel = bitsPerComponent * 3;
  size_t bytesPerRow = ( (imagewidth * imageBitsPerPixel) + 7)/8;
  Boolean shouldInterpolate = true;
  CGColorSpaceRef colorspace = NULL;
  CGDataProviderRef maskDataProvider = NULL;
  CGDataProviderRef imageDataProvider =
              CGDataProviderCreateWithURL(imageURL);
  if(imageDataProvider == NULL){
    fprintf(stderr, "Couldn't create Image Data provider!\n");
    return;
  }
  colorspace = getTheCalibratedRGBColorSpace();
```

```
image = CGImageCreate(imagewidth, imageheight, bitsPerComponent,
                imageBitsPerPixel, bytesPerRow, colorspace,
                kCGImageAlphaNone, imageDataProvider,
                NULL, shouldInterpolate,
                kCGRenderingIntentDefault);
CGDataProviderRelease(imageDataProvider);
if(image == NULL){
  fprintf(stderr, "Couldn't create CGImageRef for this data!\n");
  return;
}
imageRect = CGRectMake(0.,imageheight/2, imagewidth/2, imageheight/2);
// Draw the image.
CGContextDrawImage(context, imageRect, image);

// Now the mask.
maskDataProvider = CGDataProviderCreateWithURL(theMaskingImageURL);
if(maskDataProvider == NULL){
  fprintf(stderr, "Couldn't create Mask Data provider!\n");
  return;
}

mask = CGImageMaskCreate(maskwidth, maskheight, bitsPerComponent,
                bitsPerComponent, maskwidth,
                maskDataProvider, NULL, shouldInterpolate);
CGDataProviderRelease(maskDataProvider);
if(mask == NULL){
  fprintf(stderr, "Couldn't create CGImageRef for mask data!\n");
  return;
}

// Draw the mask below the image. The current fill color (black)
// is painted through the mask.
maskRect = CGRectMake(0., 0., maskwidth/2, maskheight/2);
CGContextDrawImage(context, maskRect, mask);

// Create a new CGImage object, the image, masked with mask.
imageMaskedWithImage = CGImageCreateWithMask(image, mask);
// Once the new image is created, the code can release the image
// and the mask that make it up. Quartz retains what it needs
// for the new masked image 'imageMaskedWithImage'.
CGImageRelease(image);
CGImageRelease(mask);
if(imageMaskedWithImage == NULL){
  fprintf(stderr, "Couldn't create image masked with mask!\n");
```

```
    return;
}
imageRect = CGRectMake(imagewidth/2 + 10.0, imageheight/4,
            imagewidth/2, imageheight/2);
// Draw the masked image to the right of the image and its mask.
CGContextDrawImage(context, imageRect, imageMaskedWithImage);
// Be sure to release the masked image.
CGImageRelease(imageMaskedWithImage);
}
```

For purposes of generating Figure 10.4, an image of a police officer is the image mask. The top-left image in the figure is the image with intrinsic color; the image mask is the image in the bottom-left corner of the figure. All the painting is done on top of a white background and the fill color in the context is black. When Quartz paints the masked image, pixels with decoded sample values of 0 in the image mask (the "black" pixels) pass through 100 percent of the image painted through them. Pixels with decoded sample values of 1 in the image mask (the "white" pixels) pass through none of the image painted through them. Intermediate pixel values in the image mask pass through a percentage of the image painted through them.

Figure 10.4 Image (top), image mask (bottom), and resulting masked image (right)

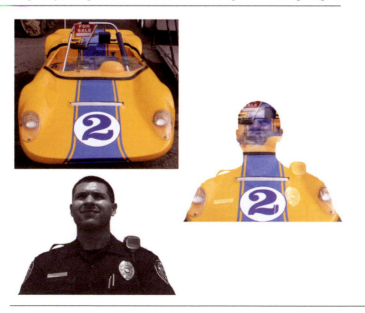

Figure 10.5 An 8-bit image mask (bottom) masks the top image; the result is on the right

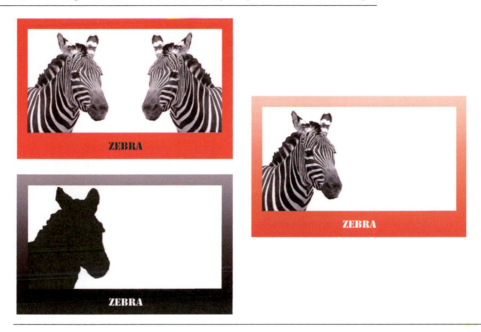

Figure 10.5 is drawn with the same code, but using a mask constructed from the image it is masking. The result is the same alpha blending effect of the image painted through the mask. In this case, the result appears visually to be a blending of the images and the use of the mask eliminates the painting of one of the zebras.

Masking an Image with an Image

Quartz also allows you to use a one-component nonalpha image in the Device-Gray color space as a mask used to create a masked image. The code fragment in Listing 10.3 is a replacement for the mask creation code in Listing 10.2. Instead of using the 8-bit image as a mask, Listing 10.3 creates a DeviceGray color space and uses `CGImageCreate` to create an image in that color space. After it creates the image, it releases the color space.

Listing 10.3 Creating an image in the DeviceGray color space

```
// The color space for the image MUST be DeviceGray to be
// used as an image mask with CGImageCreateWithMask.
colorspace = CGColorSpaceCreateDeviceGray();
```

```
mask = CGImageCreate(maskwidth, maskheight, bitsPerComponent,
            bitsPerComponent, maskwidth,
            colorspace,
            kCGImageAlphaNone, maskDataProvider,
            NULL, shouldInterpolate,
            kCGRenderingIntentDefault);
CGColorSpaceRelease(colorspace);
```

Figure 10.6 is the result of using the same input data as that used to create Figure 10.5. By comparing the two figures, you can see how passing an image as the `mask` parameter to the function `CGImageCreateWithMask` produces an inverse effect to passing the same image after it's been converted to an image mask by the function `CGImageMaskCreate`.

The grayscale image is drawn in the lower-left portion of Figure 10.6. It is then used to create a new masked image, which is the result of masking the image at the top left with the image at the bottom left. The image samples in the image shown at the bottom of Figure 10.6 are used as alpha values applied to the source image data painted through the mask, producing the image on the right side of the figure. In this case, the sense of the masking data is inverted from that when using a true image mask. Pixels in the mask that have decoded sample values of 1 pass 100 percent of the source color; portions of the mask that have decoded sample values of 0 pass none of the source color. Intermediate values within that range pass a percentage of the source color.

Figure 10.6 A grayscale image (bottom) applied to the top image; the result is on the right.

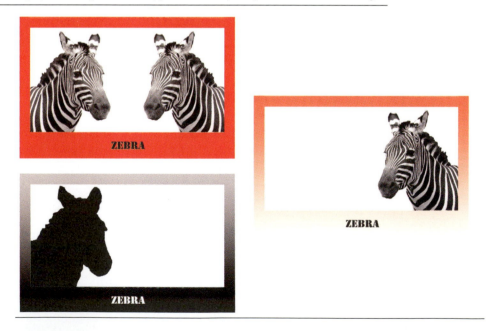

Masking Guidelines

When masking an image with another image or with an image mask, the pixel arrays of the two sources do not need to be the same width and height. Quartz compensates for any differences. However, the image parameter must be an image with intrinsic color, not an image mask, and the image may not already be masked with another image or already masked with a color. Passing such an image to CGImageCreateWithMask returns NULL. You can, however, obtain the equivalent result of masking an image mask with another mask by applying the mask to the clipping area for the context and then painting the image with CGContextDrawImage. "Clipping to a Mask (Tiger)" (page 282) describes how to apply an image mask to the context clipping area.

As long as image conforms to these restrictions, it does not matter how you create the image. For example, you could create image using the Quartz functions CGImageCreate, CGImageCreateWithJPEGDataProvider (or the PNG equivalent), or any of the methods described in "Creating CGImage Objects" (page 204) or "Image Utility Functions" (page 244).

The mask parameter must be either an image mask or a one-component image with intrinsic color that does not contain alpha, characterized with the Device-Gray color space.

Using Color as a Mask (Tiger)

10.4 ▶ Chroma key masking is a technique used in television and film to place an actor in a virtual scene. It's also used by photographers to place an object in a scene. An object is placed in front of a solid-color backdrop, such as a blue screen. The object is photographed. Then the solid color is removed digitally, leaving the object free to be copied and pasted into any other scene.

The function CGImageCreateWithMaskingColors allows the creation of effects similar to chroma key masking by using a range of image sample values (**masking colors**) to determine what's not painted in an image. When painting an image created with CGImageCreateWithMaskingColors, any image sample value that falls in the range of the masking colors is not painted. Quartz compares the masking colors and the image sample values *before* it remaps values using the decode array specified for the image.

The function CGImageCreateWithMaskingColors takes two parameters:

- image, an image with intrinsic color that is not already masked and does not contain alpha.

- maskingColors, a 2*N element array of image sample values, where N is the number of components in the source color space characterizing the image.

The values in the array are floating point because Quartz supports floating-point format image sample data.

The `maskingColors` array requires two entries for each color component in the source color space—a minimum and maximum sample value. The entry `2*i` in the array is the minimum image sample value for the *i*th component. The entry (`2*i + 1`) is the maximum image sample value for the *i*th component. For example, for an image characterized by an RGB color space, the zeroth entry in the array is the minimum value of the red sample values; the next entry is the maximum value of red sample values; the next entry is the minimum value of green samples; and so on. For an image sample value where all components fall within the ranges in the `maskingColors` array, that image sample is masked and therefore Quartz does not paint it. If you want to mask only one specific sample value, for each component, set the minimum and maximum values for each entry in the `maskingColors` array to the sample value you want to mask.

The routine `doMaskImageWithColorFromURL` in Listing 10.4 uses `CGImageCreateWithMaskingColors` to mask a range of color values in the source image. Figure 10.7 is the result of executing the code with a specific image. This code paints two images, each on top of a red background. The left image is the source image unmasked by any colors. Because the image contains no alpha, it is opaque and none of the red background shows through. Any red you see in this image is part of the image. The right image is the source image masked by the `maskingColors` array. The entries in this array are image sample values, a minimum and maximum for each color component in the image. The component values range from 0–255 because the source image is an 8-bit image in an RGB or Gray color space. Using a `maskingColors` array with entries from 0x00–0x1F masks a range of gray-scale colors, from a very dark gray to black. The code first paints the area behind the image with red, so red shows in places where image sample values are masked.

Listing 10.4   Masking an image with colors using `CGImageCreateWithMaskingColors`

```
void doMaskImageWithColorFromURL(CGContextRef context, CFURLRef url,
                size_t width, size_t height,
                Boolean isColor)
{
    CGImageRef image = NULL, imageMaskedWithColor = NULL;
    // This routine treats color images as RGB.
    size_t bitsPerComponent = 8;
    size_t bitsPerPixel =
                isColor ? (bitsPerComponent * 3) : bitsPerComponent;
    size_t bytesPerRow = ( (width * bitsPerPixel) + 7)/8;
    Boolean shouldInterpolate = true;
```

```
CGRect imageRect;
// This is a range of black colors for an 8-bits-per-component
// image in a gray or RGB color space.
// The entries are image sample values of 0-0x1F for the first
// color component, 0-0x1F for the second color component, and
// so on. For image sample values where all components fall
// within the ranges in maskingColors, the sample value is
// masked and therefore unpainted.
float maskingColors[6] = { 0x00, 0x1F, 0x00, 0x1F, 0x00, 0x1F };
float backColor[] = {1., 0., 0., 1.}; // Opaque red.
CGColorSpaceRef colorspace = NULL;
// Create a Quartz data provider from the supplied URL.
CGDataProviderRef dataProvider = CGDataProviderCreateWithURL(url);
if(dataProvider == NULL){
  fprintf(stderr, "Couldn't create Image data provider!\n");
  return;
}
// Create an image of the specified width, height, and bits per pixel
// from the URL.
colorspace =  isColor ?
  getTheCalibratedRGBColorSpace() :
  getTheCalibratedGrayColorSpace();
image = CGImageCreate(width, height, bitsPerComponent, bitsPerPixel,
              bytesPerRow, colorspace, kCGImageAlphaNone,
              dataProvider, NULL, shouldInterpolate,
              kCGRenderingIntentDefault);
CGDataProviderRelease(dataProvider);
if(image == NULL){
  fprintf(stderr, "Couldn't create CGImageRef for this data!\n");
  return;
}
imageRect = CGRectMake(10, 10, width, height);
CGContextScaleCTM(context, 0.33, 0.33);
// Set the color space and the color, then
// paint a red rectangle behind the image.
CGContextSetFillColorSpace(context, colorspace);
CGContextSetFillColor(context, backColor);
CGContextFillRect(context, imageRect);
// Draw the image into the rectangle.
CGContextDrawImage(context, imageRect, image);
// Create a new image from the original one, masking out a range
// of the blackest sample values.
imageMaskedWithColor = CGImageCreateWithMaskingColors(image,
              maskingColors);
// Release the original image; it is no longer needed.
```

Figure 10.7 Original image (left); image with black masked out, painted on top of red background (right)

```
    CGImageRelease(image);
    if(imageMaskedWithColor == NULL){
      fprintf(stderr, "Couldn't create CGImageRef for masking color!\n");
      return;
    }

    // Paint the rectangle behind the next image with red.
    imageRect = CGRectMake(30 + width, 10, width, height);
    CGContextFillRect(context, imageRect);
    // Draw the image. Image sample values in the range of
    // the masking color are unpainted, allowing the background
    // to show through.
    CGContextDrawImage(context, imageRect, imageMaskedWithColor);

    // Release the image masked with color.
    CGImageRelease(imageMaskedWithColor);
}
```

The source image you pass to `CGImageCreateWithMaskingColors` can be an image in any color space, without alpha. The source image cannot itself already be masked, either with another image or mask, or with a masking color.

Clipping to a Mask (Tiger)

10.4 ▶   The ability to clip the drawing area using paths is available in Quartz since its initial release (see "Clipping with Paths" (page 129)). If you are writing an application that runs in Tiger and later versions, you can also apply an image mask to the clipping area. The mask can be either of the types of images described in "Masking an Image (Tiger)" (page 273), that is, either an image mask created with `CGImageMaskCreate` or a nonalpha, one-component image in the DeviceGray color space. Applying an image mask to the clipping area is similar to applying an image mask to an image. The mask serves as an alpha mask through which additional painting can be performed. If the function `CGImageMaskCreate` creates the image mask, the sample values are treated as inverse alpha, where a decoded sample value of S produces a clipping alpha value of $(1 - S)$. If the mask is a one-component image without alpha in the DeviceGray color space, the decoded sample values are treated as alpha values through which Quartz paints.

The function `CGContextClipToMask` takes the following parameters:

- `context`, the context to clip.

- `rect`, the rectangle in user space coordinates into which Quartz maps the image for purposes of clipping.

- `mask`, the CGImage object to use as the clipping mask.

The function `CGContextClipToMask` intersects the supplied rectangle with the current clipping area. Subsequent drawing outside the intersection of the rectangle and the existing clipping area is not painted. Drawing inside the new clipping area is painted through the alpha mask specified by `mask`. You can think of clipping to a mask as an extension of clipping with a path. The difference is that path-based clipping is fully opaque whereas clipping to a mask allows an additional opacity provided by the clipping mask.

Listing 10.5 uses a one-component DeviceGray image to clip the drawing of a 3x3 grid of rectangles. Figure 10.8 is the result of executing the code in Listing 10.5.

Figure 10.8 Using a grayscale image for clipping

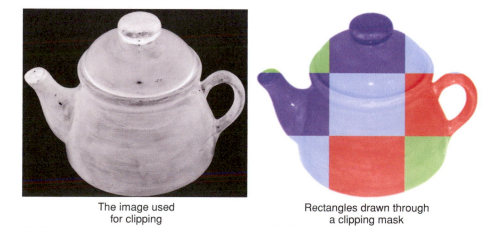

The image used
for clipping

Rectangles drawn through
a clipping mask

Listing 10.5 Clipping with a grayscale image

```
CGColorRef getRGBOpaqueDarkGreenColor(void)
{
  static CGColorRef rgbGreen = NULL;
  if(rgbGreen == NULL){
    // This is an opaque green.
    float opaqueGreen[4] = { 0.404, 0.808, 0.239, 1.0 };
    rgbGreen = CGColorCreate(getTheRGBColorSpace(), opaqueGreen);
  }
  return rgbGreen;
}
// getRGBOpaqueDarkBlueColor, getRGBOpaqueBlueColor, and
// getRGBOpaqueRedColor are defined similarly.

void drawWithClippingMask(CGContextRef context,
                CFURLRef theMaskingImageURL,
                size_t imagewidth, size_t imageheight)
{
  // An array of CGColor objects.
  CGColorRef colors[4] = { getRGBOpaqueDarkGreenColor(),
    getRGBOpaqueDarkBlueColor(), getRGBOpaqueBlueColor(),
    getRGBOpaqueRedColor() };
  size_t imageBitsPerComponent = 8;
  size_t bytesPerRow = imagewidth;
  CGImageRef image;
  CGDataProviderRef dataProvider;
  CGRect imageRect, rect;
  float decode[] = { 1, 0 };
  int i,j;
  CGColorSpaceRef cs;

  // Create the data provider.
  dataProvider = CGDataProviderCreateWithURL(theMaskingImageURL);
  if(dataProvider == NULL){
    fprintf(stderr, "Couldn't create Image data provider!\n");
    return;
  }
  cs = CGColorSpaceCreateDeviceGray();
  image = CGImageCreate(imagewidth, imageheight,
                imageBitsPerComponent, imageBitsPerComponent,
                bytesPerRow, cs, kCGImageAlphaNone, dataProvider, decode,
                true, kCGRenderingIntentDefault);
  CGColorSpaceRelease(cs);
  CGDataProviderRelease(dataProvider);
```

```
    if(image == NULL){
      fprintf(stderr, "Couldn't create Image!\n");
      return;
    }
    imageRect = CGRectMake(0, 0, imagewidth/3, imageheight/3);

    // Position for drawing the image at the left side of the figure.
    CGContextTranslateCTM(context, 50, 50 );
    // Draw the image.
    CGContextDrawImage(context, imageRect, image);

    // Position to the right of the image just painted.
    CGContextTranslateCTM(context, CGRectGetWidth(imageRect) + 25,  0);

    // Clip to the image.
    CGContextClipToMask(context, imageRect, image);
    // Release the image since this code no longer needs it.
    CGImageRelease(image);

    // Make a rect that has a width and height 1/3 that of the image.
    rect = CGRectMake(0, 0, CGRectGetWidth(imageRect)/3,
                  CGRectGetHeight(imageRect)/3);

    CGContextTranslateCTM(context, 0, 2*CGRectGetHeight(rect));

    // Draw a 3x3 grid of rectangles, setting the color for each rectangle
    // by cycling through the array of CGColor objects in the 'colors' array.
    for(j = 0 ; j < 3 ; j++){
      CGContextSaveGState(context);
      for(i = 0 ; i < 3 ; i++){
        // Draw a row of rectangles. Set the fill color using
        // one of the CGColor objects in the colors array.
        CGContextSetFillColorWithColor(context, colors[(i+j) % 4]);
        CGContextFillRect(context, rect);
        CGContextTranslateCTM(context, CGRectGetWidth(rect), 0);
      }
      CGContextRestoreGState(context);
      // Position to draw the next row.
      CGContextTranslateCTM(context, 0, -CGRectGetHeight(rect));
    }
}
```

The code first creates an array `colors` containing CGColor objects, using the routines `getRGBOpaqueDarkGreenColor`, `getRGBOpaqueDarkBlueColor`, `getRGBOpaqueBlueColor`, and `getRGBOpaqueRedColor` to populate the array. Only the routine `getRGBOpaqueDarkGreenColor` is shown in the listing, but the other routines can be written in a similar fashion using different color values. Recall that CGColor objects encapsulate the color space and a set of color values in that color space into a single object that represents a given color. See "CGColor Objects (Panther)" (page 152) for details about CGColor objects.

The code next creates an image from 8-bit grayscale image data, characterizing the data with the DeviceGray color space. The code then paints this image, producing the graphic on the left side of Figure 10.8. Recall that when drawing in the DeviceGray color space, image sample values that decode to 0 are painted black and image sample values that decode to 1 are painted white.

Next the code positions to draw the right side of the figure and calls the routine `CGContextClipToMask` with the image. This produces no painting but instead intersects the image with the current clipping area, producing a new clipping area that incorporates the image. Subsequent drawing outside the `imageRect` rectangle passed to `CGContextClipToMask` is obscured by the clipping area because that is the extent of the image. Drawing inside the rectangle specified by `imageRect` is clipped by the image. Because the image is an 8-bit image, the clipping mask that results is an alpha mask, not just an on/off mask value for each pixel in the image. Drawing inside the clipping area applies an additional alpha value corresponding to the image value at that location.

The code that follows the call to `CGContextClipToMask` draws a 3x3 grid of rectangles. Before painting each rectangle, it sets the fill color to a CGColor object from the `colors` array created earlier in the code. When a given rectangle is painted, the color of each point inside the rectangle is blended using the alpha value in the clipping mask at that point. The result is the right side of the figure, where the color inside each rectangle varies with the alpha values from the clipping mask.

Recall that when clipping with a DeviceGray image rather than a mask, image sample values that decode to 0 produce an alpha value of 0 and image sample values that decode to 1 produce an alpha value of 1. This means that locations in the image painted on the left that are a light shade of gray correspond to alpha values in the clipping mask that are close to 1 (fully opaque), and locations in the image on the left that are a dark shade of gray correspond to alpha values in the clipping mask that are close to 0 (fully transparent).

You can use a DeviceGray image as a clipping mask as Listing 10.5 demonstrates or you can use an image mask produced by `CGImageMaskCreate`. Both work correctly when drawing to a window or other bit-based context; however, prior to Mac OS X version 10.4.3, Quartz had a bug such that when drawing to a PDF or printing context, clipping with a mask created with `CGImageMaskCreate` produces drawing that appears completely clipped out. To work around this bug, use a one-component DeviceGray image without alpha, as shown in Listing 10.5.

Summary

Quartz provides three masking devices that can control how pixels are painted—image masks, images that are used for the purpose of masking another image, and masking colors. Image masks painted to a graphics context determine how and where the context fill color is painted. Image masks applied to a source image determine which pixels in the source image are painted and also add additional alpha blending to the source image. In each case, the image mask acts as an inverse alpha value. The value `1.0` specifies that the source pixel is fully transparent (does not show through the mask) and `0.0` specifies that the source pixel is fully opaque (shows through the mask).

When images are used to mask a source image, the sample values in the image mask act as an alpha component for the source image. The value `1.0` specifies that the source pixel is fully opaque and `0.0` specifies that the source pixel is fully transparent.

Image masks and images can be applied to a graphics context as a clip. Quartz maps the mask, which may be either an image mask or an image, to the specified rectangle and intersects it with the current clipping area of the context.

Masking colors, when applied to an image, make transparent any pixels in the image that fall within the range of the masking colors. Anything behind the image, such as a fill color or another image, shows through the transparent portion of the masked image.

See Also

The Quartz header files containing the structures and functions used in this chapter are

- `CGContext.h`
- `CGImage.h`
- `CGColorSpace.h`

The relevant reference documentation from the ADC Reference Library is

- *CGContext Reference*
- *CGImage Reference*
- *CGColorSpace Reference*

Chapter 11

Text

Quartz provides high-quality text rendering in Mac OS X, including the drawing of high-quality anti-aliased text using several different user-selectable anti-aliasing algorithms. The Mac OS X user interface is built on top of Quartz text drawing. This is one of the reasons that the user interface in Mac OS X looks so good.

The Quartz API provides low-level text drawing functions and a drawing model that, for the most part, is intended as building blocks for other system services to use. Quartz performs no text layout, only text rendering. As a general rule, most applications are better served by the higher-level framework text facilities that are built on top of Quartz. These frameworks provide higher-level text support including full Unicode text support and text layout. Most Cocoa applications are best served by using the Cocoa text classes and methods. "Drawing Text Using Cocoa" (page 306) discusses many of the options available to Cocoa applications. Some of the different text APIs available to Carbon applications are discussed in "Drawing Text Using Carbon" (page 324).

The text drawing services available in the different application frameworks are built on top of Quartz. By reading this chapter, you'll learn about the low-level Quartz text drawing functions and the graphics state and context parameters that affect how Quartz renders text when you use the Quartz APIs directly. The text drawing parameters are important to understand if you use the Quartz API rather than the framework text APIs built on top of Quartz. In many cases, some or all of the Quartz text drawing parameters affect the drawing of framework text. This chapter describes how framework text drawing interacts with the Quartz text drawing parameters in the context.

Text Drawing Parameters

The graphics state parameters that affect image and line art drawing also affect the drawing of text with Quartz. In addition, Quartz has several text drawing parameters that only affect the way it performs text drawing. These include the font face, font size, extra character spacing, text position and text transformation matrix, text drawing mode, and control of font smoothing. All of these parameters are part of the Quartz graphics state except for the text position and text transformation matrix. Quartz provides functions for setting each parameter, as you'll see in each of the following sections. You'll want to understand these parameters if you plan to use the Quartz text drawing APIs to draw text.

The text drawing functions available in the higher-level frameworks built on top of Quartz modify some of the text drawing parameters to perform their drawing. However, even when you use the higher-level frameworks for drawing text, knowledge of Quartz text parameters and how the Quartz graphics state affects the appearance of text can be useful. In some cases, Quartz text parameters that you set affect framework text drawing, as you'll see in the Cocoa and Carbon sections later in this chapter.

Font and Font Size

The **font** and the **font size** graphics state parameters control the appearance and size of the text drawn. A font is a collection of glyphs in a given typeface that can be rendered. By default, there is no font set in the Quartz graphics state. This means that if you don't set the font before drawing text using the Quartz text drawing APIs, nothing is rendered. The font size parameter specifies the size that the glyphs in the font will be rendered in. The default font size in the Quartz graphics state is 0—if the current font size in the graphics state is 0 when you call Quartz to draw text, no text is rendered.

Quartz provides two functions for setting the font—CGContextSetFont and CGContextSelectFont. The function CGContextSelectFont sets both the font and the font size, while CGContextSetFont sets only the font. Which way you set the font depends on whether you want to draw using characters in the MacRoman encoding or using font glyph identifiers. A **glyph identifier** is a unique number that, for a given font, identifies a specific glyph. Unfortunately, there is no simple explanation for which function to use. "Drawing Text Using Quartz" (page 296) provides an in-depth discussion.

The function CGContextSetFontSize sets the font size parameter in the graphics state. If you use CGContextSetFont to set the font parameter, you should use CGContextSetFontSize to set the size. If you use CGContextSelectFont to set the font and size together, you can use `CGContextSetFontSize` afterwards to set the size parameter independently.

Text Matrix and Text Position

Quartz text is drawn in a special coordinate system called **text space**. The **text matrix** is an affine transform that maps text space coordinates into user space coordinates. If the text matrix is the identity transform, text space coincides directly with the origin, scale, and orientation of Quartz user space. Having an additional affine transform that applies only to text drawing adds a lot of flexibility and can be quite useful, as you'll see in "Using the Text Matrix" (page 300).

Quartz always positions text drawing at the text space origin. The **text position** defines the translation of the text space origin to the starting location in user space when drawing text. Quartz has two flavors of text drawing calls—those that start drawing text at the text position currently set in the context and those that explicitly set the text position prior to drawing the text. The text position, while a useful concept in its own right, is defined by the tx, ty components of the text matrix. The other portions of the text matrix provide an additional coordinate transformation, such as scaling, flipping, skewing, or rotation, that only applies to text. Quartz concatenates the text matrix with the current transformation matrix (CTM) to produce the transformation matrix that maps from text space to device space. This is the matrix actually used to draw the text to a destination.

Important The text matrix and, therefore, the text position are not part of the Quartz graphics state and are not affected by `CGContextSaveGState` and `CGContextRestoreGState`.

After you draw text, the text position portion of the text matrix is updated to reflect the width of the text just drawn. This is where the next text drawing begins, assuming you don't perform any operations that change the text matrix. (The text position is not affected by saving and restoring the graphics state.) As a convenience, you can set the text position with the function `CGContextSetTextPosition` and you can retrieve the current text position with `CGContextGetTextPosition`.

The text matrix applies an affine transformation to text drawing. You can use it to transform text independently from the CTM. One typical use is to draw text upright in a coordinate system that has its y axis oriented with positive y values going down the drawing canvas (a "flipped" coordinate system). Using a text matrix that is scaled by -1 in the y coordinate allows you to flip the text you draw without modifying the CTM prior to text drawing. Another common use of the text matrix is to produce artificially italicized (or oblique) text.

Keep in mind that most framework text drawing sets the text matrix. When that's the case, you can't modify the Quartz text matrix to affect the higher-level framework text drawing. (The details are discussed in "Drawing Text Using Cocoa" (page 306) and "Drawing Text Using Carbon" (page 324)).

You explicitly set the text matrix in its entirety (including the text position) by using CGContextSetTextMatrix. You can obtain the current text matrix in the context by using CGContextGetTextMatrix. Because the text matrix is not part of the graphics state, you cannot use CGContextSaveGState and CGContextRestore-GState to save and restore it. If you do need to save and restore the text matrix, you call the function CGContextGetTextMatrix to obtain the current text matrix and later restore to that matrix by calling CGContextSetTextMatrix. These functions come in handy if you use a framework that might change the text matrix and you want to mix the framework text drawing with direct use of the Quartz text drawing API.

Note that the current point in a Quartz path has no connection to where text drawing begins. This is different than the PostScript graphics model, where the current point in the PostScript graphics state specifies where text drawing begins. In Quartz drawing, the current point and the current text position are completely distinct from one another. The current path in the graphics context has no effect on text drawing, and drawing text has no effect on the current path in the graphics context.

Text Drawing Modes

The **text drawing mode** parameter in the graphics state determines the painting mode that Quartz uses to paint text characters. The values available for the text drawing mode are defined by the CGTextDrawingMode enumeration. You set the text drawing mode by calling the function CGContextSetTextDrawingMode, supplying one of the text modes discussed next.

The default mode kCGTextFill draws text characters as you expect—it fills the outlines of the paths that make up the glyphs, using the current fill color. (Note that the fill algorithms for painting text characters are significantly different than those for line art graphics. To achieve good results, Quartz uses different rendering techniques for painting text characters than it does for painting line art.)

The kCGTextStroke mode strokes the outlines of the characters, using the current line width in the graphics state. The glyphs are painted with the current stroke color. The other parameters of the graphics state that affect stroking, such as the line dash, line cap, and line join, also affect the stroking of text.

The kCGTextFillStroke mode both fills and strokes the text. The effect is that of first filling, then stroking the text. Note that if you want to draw shadowed text that is both stroked and filled, you may need to use transparency layers to achieve the effect you most likely will want. See "Drawing with Transparency Layers (Panther)" (page 522) for a discussion of transparency layers and shadows.

The kCGTextInvisible mode performs no painting of the characters, but it updates the text matrix as if it had painted them. This is potentially useful for measuring text before drawing it or positioning pieces of text as if other text were drawn first.

The kCGTextClip mode intersects the current clipping area with the area described by the interior of the paths making up the text characters. Note that this is an atomic operation; that is, when making a single Quartz drawing call, the interiors of the glyphs being drawn are treated as a single object when clipping. Subsequent calls to text drawing functions with the text drawing mode kCGTextClip most likely will produce an empty clipping area unless the additional text drawing is placed so that it intersects the previous clipping area.

The text drawing modes kCGTextFillClip, kCGTextStrokeClip, and kCGTextFill-StrokeClip each perform multiple operations. The kCGTextFillClip mode first paints the text as if the drawing mode is kCGTextFill; then it intersects the outlines with the current clipping area. The adjustment of the text position is done only after the text is painted and the clip is applied.

The kCGTextStrokeClip mode first paints the text as if the drawing mode is kCG-TextStroke; then it intersects the outlines with the current clipping area. The adjustment of the text position is done only after the text is painted and the clip is applied.

The kCGTextFillStrokeClip mode first paints the text as if the drawing mode is kCGTextFillStroke; then it intersects the outlines with the current clipping area. The adjustment of the text position is done only after the text is painted and the clip is applied.

Figure 11.1 has examples of most of the Quartz text drawing modes. The first line in the figure is drawn with the mode kCGTextFill, first with a black fill color, then with a red fill color. The second line is drawn with the mode kCGTextStroke, initially with no dash and a thin line width and then a second time with a dash and slightly thicker line width. The third text line is drawn with the text mode kCGTextFillStroke, varying the thickness on the stroke to achieve a slightly different effect each time. The next "line" of text is invisible because it is drawn with the text mode kCGTextInvisible. The last line of text is drawn first with the text mode kCGTextClip, applying a clip that corresponds to the characters "Clip-Text." Then a grid of lines is drawn through the clip, revealing the outline of the text characters. The last piece of text drawn on the last line is drawn with the text mode kCGTextFillStrokeClip, again followed by the drawing of a grid of lines through the clip. The result is text that is filled and stroked, followed by the drawing of the grid lines through the filled and stroked shapes of the glyphs.

Figure 11.1 Examples of the Quartz text drawing modes

Using the Quartz text modes that include a clip associated with them can produce interesting effects, such as those shown in the figure; however, they must be used carefully in order to produce the intended result. Multiple runs of text, when used to create a single clipping area, typically produce an empty clipping area. This happens because applying a clip to the existing clipping area intersects the two areas to produce the new clipping area. When drawing text characters to apply as a clip, subsequent drawing of additional characters you want to clip with will most likely fail to intersect the newly created clipping area. To achieve the effect of clipping to all the text characters in a sequence of multiple runs, each containing a different font and/or size, the best approach is to (1) clip to a single run at a time, (2) draw the graphics you want clipped to the multiple run of text, (3) restore to a saved graphics state without the clip, and (4) repeat the process for the next run of characters.

During PDF generation, Quartz may break a single run of text drawing into multiple runs. Drawing the generated PDF document works fine to the screen, but using the generated PDF drawing to create a new PDF document may produce an empty clip if the text is broken into multiple runs. For example, this can cause the subsequent drawing of graphics clipped through the text to be completely clipped out during printing. For this situation, the safest approach is to yourself break your text runs into runs of a single character each, using the strategy just described for providing the appearance of clipping graphics by the complete run of text.

Quartz has no notions of synthetic bold, italic, or outline styles as available in some graphics systems such as QuickDraw. Many fonts themselves have the intrinsic styles corresponding to the bold, italic, and bold-italic styles and you should use the intrinsic font faces to obtain these text styles.

Font Smoothing (Jaguar)

10.2 ▶ The appearance of text is controlled by two parameters: anti-aliasing and (starting in Jaguar) **font smoothing**. The font smoothing parameter provides limited control over the style of text anti-aliasing that Quartz performs. The default value of the font smoothing parameter is `true`.

Quartz has provided anti-aliased text since its inception. Starting with Jaguar, when drawing anti-aliasing text, Quartz has the ability to apply special font smoothing algorithms that produce superior results on flat panel displays such as LCD monitors. The font smoothing algorithm that Quartz uses is influenced by the font smoothing style setting that the user chooses in the Appearance pane of System Preferences. There are four settings: Standard–best for CRT, Light, Medium–best for Flat Panel, or Strong. If the user chooses Standard–best for CRT, Quartz uses its standard (font smoothing equals `false`) algorithm. For any other setting, Quartz uses a special font smoothing algorithm.

If the current anti-aliasing mode for a graphics context is set to `false`, Quartz doesn't draw anti-aliased text and the value of the font smoothing parameter is irrelevant. If the current anti-aliasing mode is `true`, and the context supports anti-aliasing, Quartz consults the font smoothing parameter to determine whether to apply the user setting for font smoothing. If the context font smoothing parameter is `true`, Quartz applies the user setting. If the context font smoothing parameter is `false`, Quartz uses the Standard–best for CRT setting, regardless of what the user chose. Note that there is no programmatic control over which font smoothing algorithm to use, only whether or not to use the type chosen by the user or the Standard–best for CRT setting. Table 11.1 summarizes the interaction between the context anti-aliasing and font smoothing settings and their effect on how Quartz performs anti-aliasing of text.

Table 11.1 Font Smoothing Setting and Its Effect on the Anti-aliasing Style

Context Anti-aliasing	Context Font Smoothing	Text Anti-aliasing Style
true	true	Style selected in Appearance panel
true	false	Standard–best for CRT
false	true	No anti-aliasing
false	false	No anti-aliasing

Font smoothing works well for text drawn on LCD displays but may not work as well for other kinds of drawing. The algorithms Quartz uses when drawing text with font smoothing enabled work best when drawn to a destination that is completely opaque, as is typical for onscreen drawing. If your drawing destination is partially or completely transparent, it's a good idea to turn off font smoothing. For example, if you are drawing text offscreen for caching purposes and when caching the text it is drawn on top of a clear background, it is a good idea to turn off font smoothing prior to drawing your text.

When font smoothing is not appropriate, you can call the function `CGContextSetShouldSmoothFonts`, passing `false` and the graphics context for which you want to disable smoothing. Note that some contexts (such as a PDF or printing context) do not support font smoothing and ignore the current setting of the font smoothing parameter.

"Creating Bits" (page 345) is an example of how to set the font smoothing parameter based on the drawing destination. You may want to set this parameter to `false`, for example, when creating bits to export as a portable network graphics (PNG) image because the text rendering appropriate for the current display is not appropriate for a PNG image.

Character Spacing

The **character spacing** parameter actually specifies extra character spacing, not the normal character spacing that's specified by the font designer. The character spacing specifies a text space advance to add to the width of any glyph and is independent of the font point size. This parameter is interpreted in text space and is affected by text matrix transformations. To set it, call the function `CGContextSetCharacterSpacing`. The character spacing parameter affects all low-level Quartz text drawing calls except calls to the function `CGContextShowGlyphsWithAdvances`, where you've calculated advances yourself.

Drawing Text Using Quartz

Quartz functions provide two methods to draw text: using characters in a specific encoding or using glyph identifiers. The first method limits text drawing to only those glyphs in the encoding, which when using Quartz is essentially MacRoman encoding. The second method, using glyph identifiers, allows you to draw any glyph in that font but requires detailed knowledge about the internals of a given font. A font glyph identifier is an identifier that identifies a given glyph in a specific font. A given glyph identifier produces one glyph in one font and often a completely different glyph (or no glyph) in another font. Translating the character codes in a specific font encoding and font into glyph identifiers for that font is a difficult task and one well beyond how most applications want to work with text.

If you want to use Quartz functions to draw text, you need to choose between the two ways to draw text. The next two sections show how to draw text using each method. After you read these sections, make sure you go on to read "Drawing Text Using Cocoa" (page 306) and "Drawing Text Using Carbon" (page 324). You will find that the Carbon and Cocoa frameworks provide far better support for drawing text and are more appropriate for the needs of most developers. Remember that because these frameworks call into Quartz, your application gets all the benefits of the Quartz "look" without needing to deal with the low-level details.

Drawing with Characters

Before you can use Quartz functions to draw text using characters, you need to call the function `CGContextSelectFont` to set the font face, font size, and text encoding. The font selected becomes the new font in the graphics state and the size becomes the new font size. This function takes four parameters:

- `context`, the graphics context in which to set the font.

- `name`, the PostScript name of the font.

- `size`, the size of the font in text space units.

- `textEncoding`, a value of type `CGTextEncoding`. The possible values are `kCGEncodingMacRoman` or `kCGEncodingFontSpecific`.

The value `kCGEncodingMacRoman` corresponds to the MacRoman font encoding. This is an 8-bit encoding of the standard Roman character set defined for the Macintosh since its inception. Depending on the font, using `kCGEncodingMacRoman` may produce no glyphs since not all fonts contain characters in MacRoman encoding. This is true of symbolic fonts such as ZapfDingbats and Carta. The `CGTextEncoding` value `kCGEncodingFontSpecific` simply produces a mapping between 8-bit character codes and the first 256 glyph identifiers for the font. Use of `kCGEncodingFontSpecific` is not recommended. If you want to perform Quartz drawing using glyph identifiers, you should use the functions tailored to do so, discussed in "Drawing with Glyphs" (page 305). After you set the font with `CGContextSelectFont`, you can change the font size in the graphics state without changing the face by calling `CGContextSetFontSize`.

The two functions that you can use to draw text when you've chosen the font with the function CGContextSelectFont are CGContextShowText and CGContext-ShowTextAtPoint. These functions draw the glyphs that correspond to the character codes in the string either at the current text position or at the point passed to CGContextShowTextAtPoint. The character advances that these routines use are the natural advances of the glyphs (scaled by the font size and text matrix), plus any extra character spacing for each glyph. The extra character spacing is a text space value added to each glyph width.

Drawing Text in MacRoman Encoding. Listing 11.1 shows how to perform simple text drawing using characters in MacRoman encoding. By using the Quartz text position carefully, the code produces the results shown in Figure 11.2.

Listing 11.1 A routine that draws Roman text using CGContextShowText and CGContextShowTextAtPoint

```
void drawQuartzRomanText(CGContextRef context)
{
  int i;
  static const char *text = "Quartz";
  size_t textlen = strlen(text);
  float fontSize = 60;

  float opaqueBlack[] = { 0., 0., 0., 1. };
  float opaqueRed[] = { 0.663, 0., 0.031, 1. };

  // Set the fill color space. This sets the
  // fill painting color to opaque black.
  CGContextSetFillColorSpace(context, getTheRGBColorSpace());

  // Set the text matrix this code requires.
  CGContextSetTextMatrix(context, CGAffineTransformIdentity);

  // Choose the font with the PostScript name "Times-Roman", at
  // fontSize points, with the MacRoman encoding.
  CGContextSelectFont(context, "Times-Roman", fontSize,
            kCGEncodingMacRoman);

  // The default text drawing mode is fill. Draw the text at (70, 400).
  CGContextShowTextAtPoint(context, 70, 400, text, textlen);

  // Set the fill color to red.
  CGContextSetFillColor(context, opaqueRed);
```

```
// Draw the next piece of text where the previous one left off.
CGContextShowText(context, text, textlen);

for(i = 0 ; i < 3 ; i++){
    // Get the current text pen position.
    CGPoint p = CGContextGetTextPosition(context);
    // Translate to the current text pen position.
    CGContextTranslateCTM(context, p.x, p.y);

    // Rotate clockwise by 90 degrees for the next
    // piece of text.
    CGContextRotateCTM(context, DEGREES_TO_RADIANS(-90));
    // Draw the next piece of text at the origin in black.
    CGContextSetFillColor(context, opaqueBlack);
    CGContextShowTextAtPoint(context, 0, 0, text, textlen);
    // Draw the next piece of text where the previous piece
    // left off and paint it with red.
    CGContextSetFillColor(context, opaqueRed);
    CGContextShowText(context, text, textlen);
}
}
```

Figure 11.2 Drawing rotated text using MacRoman encoding

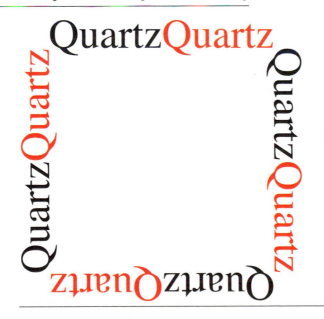

The code first sets the fill color space to the generic calibrated RGB color space returned by getTheRGBColorSpace. Setting the color space sets the color to the default color in that color space, in this case opaque black. Next the code sets the text matrix to the identity transform; this makes text space initially the same as current user space; the text scaling and orientation is the same as user space and the text position is the Quartz origin. This code explicitly sets the text matrix. Because the text matrix in effect at the time your drawing code is called by the application frameworks is not well defined, it's a good idea to set it to the value you require. Next the code sets the font and font size in the Quartz graphics state by calling CGContextSelectFont, selecting the font with the PostScript name Times-Roman, at a size of 60 points, with the MacRoman encoding. Once the graphics state and text matrix are set correctly, the code calls CGContextShow-TextAtPoint, drawing the text at the starting point of (70,400). This is the black text "Quartz" in the top line of text in Figure 11.2.

After painting the text, Quartz updates the text position entry in the text matrix so that the updated text position is located immediately after the text just drawn. The code sets the fill color to an opaque red and again draws the same text, this time calling CGContextShowText, which uses the current text position in the context. Because the current text position was updated to reflect the drawing of the first piece of text, the red text "Quartz" follows the black text as if it were all part of the same text string.

The remaining pieces of text in the figure are drawn in a for loop by first adjusting the CTM appropriately. The code in the loop begins by first obtaining the current text position using CGContextGetTextPosition—this is the point in user space where the text drawing pen is located after the last piece of text that was drawn. The code translates to this point, then rotates by –90 degrees in preparation for drawing the next text segments. The code calls CGContextShowTextAt-Point to draw the text at the current user space origin. Because of the coordinate transformations just performed, this draws the text at the ending point of the previously drawn text, but rotated by –90 degrees. By drawing the text in black, then drawing it again in red, the first time through the loop produces the text that goes down the right side of the figure.

The next time the code loop executes, the code draws the text at the bottom of the figure, continuing from the point where the text along the right side ended. The last time through the loop, the code draws the black and red text on the left side of the figure.

Using the Text Matrix. The text matrix is a matrix that you can use with Quartz text drawing to apply additional transformations in addition to those of the CTM. The text matrix can be used to apply scaling or other coordinate transformations to text, in addition to those that the CTM applies to all graphics.

The code in Listing 11.2 demonstrates how the text matrix affects Quartz text drawing by using the text matrix to apply text scaling, flipping, and positioning of text. The code consists of the routine drawQuartzTextWithTextMatrix and the supporting routine showFlippedTextAtPoint. Executing the code produces the output shown in Figure 11.3.

Listing 11.2 Code that uses the Quartz text matrix to apply text scaling and positioning

```
void showFlippedTextAtPoint(CGContextRef c, float x, float y,
                const char *text, const size_t textLen)
{
  CGAffineTransform s;
  CGAffineTransform t = {1., 0., 0., -1., 0., 0.};
  CGPoint p;
  // Get the existing text matrix.
  s = CGContextGetTextMatrix(c);
  // Set the text matrix to the one that flips in y.
  CGContextSetTextMatrix(c, t);
  // Draw the text at the point.
  CGContextShowTextAtPoint(c, x, y, text, textLen);
  // Get the updated text position.
  p = CGContextGetTextPosition(c);
  // Update the saved text matrix to reflect the updated
  // text position.
  s.tx = p.x ; s.ty = p.y;
  // Reset to the text matrix in effect when this
  // routine was called but with the text position updated.
  CGContextSetTextMatrix(c, s);
}

void drawQuartzTextWithTextMatrix(CGContextRef context)
{
  float fontSize = 60, extraLeading = 10;
  static const char *text = "Quartz ";
  size_t textlen = strlen(text);
  CGPoint textPosition;
  CGAffineTransform t;

  // Set the initial text matrix to the identity transform.
  CGContextSetTextMatrix(context, CGAffineTransformIdentity);

  // Use the Times-Roman font at 60 points.
  CGContextSelectFont(context, "Times-Roman", fontSize,
                kCGEncodingMacRoman);
  // ***** Text Line 1 *****
  // Draw the text at (10, 600).
  CGContextShowTextAtPoint(context, 10, 600, text, textlen);
```

```
    // Get the current text position. The text pen is at the trailing
    // point from the text just drawn.
    textPosition = CGContextGetTextPosition(context);

    // Set the text matrix to one that flips text in y and sets
    // the text position to the user space coordinate (0,0).
    t = CGAffineTransformMake(1, 0, 0, -1, 0, 0);
    CGContextSetTextMatrix(context, t);

    // Set the text position to the point where the previous text ended.
    CGContextSetTextPosition(context, textPosition.x, textPosition.y);

    // Draw the text at the current text position. It will be drawn
    // flipped in y, relative to the text drawn previously.
    CGContextShowText(context, text, textlen);

    // ***** Text Line 2 *****
    // Translate down for the next piece of text.
    CGContextTranslateCTM(context, 0, -(3*fontSize + extraLeading));

    CGContextSaveGState(context);
      // Make a transform that scales by a factor of 1 in x and 3 in y.
      t = CGAffineTransformMake(1, 0, 0, 3, 0, 0);
      CGContextSetTextMatrix(context, t);

      // This text is scaled relative to the previous text
      // because of the text matrix scaling.
      CGContextShowTextAtPoint(context, 10, 600, text, textlen);

    // Restore the graphics state to what it was at the time
    // of the last CGContextSaveGState.
    CGContextRestoreGState(context);

    // The text matrix isn't affected by CGContextSaveGState and
    // CGContextRestoreGState.
    CGContextShowText(context, text, textlen);

    // ***** Text Line 3 *****
    // Translate down for the next piece of text.
    CGContextTranslateCTM(context, 0, -(fontSize + extraLeading));

    // Reset the text matrix to the identity matrix.
    CGContextSetTextMatrix(context, CGAffineTransformIdentity);
```

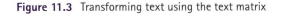

Figure 11.3 Transforming text using the text matrix

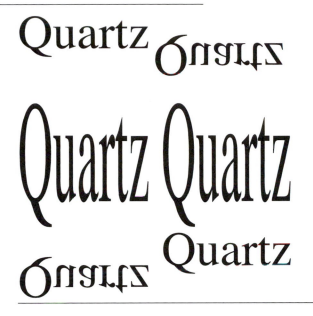

```
// Now draw text in a flipped coordinate system.
CGContextSaveGState(context);
    // Scale the coordinate system to mimic text drawing into
    // a flipped coordinate system.
    CGContextConcatCTM(context,
                CGAffineTransformMake(1, 0, 0, -1, 0, 600));
    // This text will be flipped along with the CTM.
    CGContextShowTextAtPoint(context, 10, 10, text, textlen);
    // Obtain the user space coordinates of the current
    // text position.
    textPosition = CGContextGetTextPosition(context);
    // Draw the text at that point but flipped in y.
    showFlippedTextAtPoint(context, textPosition.x,
                textPosition.y, text, textlen);
CGContextRestoreGState(context);
}
```

The drawQuartzTextWithTextMatrix routine begins by setting the text matrix to the identity matrix and setting the font to Times-Roman at 60 points with the MacRoman encoding. It then draws the first piece of text on the first line of text in the figure by drawing the text at (10,600). So that it can draw the next piece of text where the previous one left off, it obtains the current text position using

CGContextGetTextPosition. To draw the next piece of text so that it is flipped in the y coordinate, it makes an affine transform that is a scaling transform of 1 in x and -1 in y and sets the text matrix to that affine transform. Because setting the text matrix also affects the text position, after setting the text matrix, the code sets the text position so that it corresponds to the previous text position. Calling CGContextShowText draws the text at the current text position, but since the text matrix is flipped relative to current Quartz user space, the resulting text is flipped. As you see, the text matrix can be used to flip text.

Next the code prepares for drawing the second line of text. First, it uses CGContextSaveGState to take a snapshot of the Quartz graphics state. To achieve the nonuniform scaling of the text, it makes an affine transform that scales by a scaling factor of 1 in x and 3 in y and uses that transform as the text matrix. It draws the text, then uses CGContextRestoreGState to restore to the previously saved graphics state. It then draws the text at the current text position by calling CGContextShowText. This draws the same text immediately after the first piece of text on the second line.

You can see that indeed the text matrix is not part of the Quartz graphics state and is unaffected by CGContextSaveGState and CGContextRestoreGState. Even though the text matrix was changed after the code saved the graphics state, the call to CGContextRestoreGState did not change either the text scaling factor or the text position in the text matrix. If it had, the second piece of text in the second line of text in the figure would have been drawn with different scaling factors than the first piece of text. The text position portion of the text matrix was also unaffected, as you can see by observing that the second piece of text is drawn just after the first piece, as if it were part of the same text drawing call.

The last portion of the code in Listing 11.2 draws the last line of text in Figure 11.3 and demonstrates Quartz text drawing in a "flipped" coordinate system. First the code resets the text matrix to the identity transform, making Quartz text space coincide with current user space in scale and orientation. To draw Text Line 3, the code first transforms Quartz user space so that the origin is at the point (0,600) and the y axis points down the drawing canvas. This mimics a coordinate system where the origin is in the top-left corner of a window and the y axis is flipped relative to default Quartz user space. When the code draws text at the point (10,10) in this coordinate system, the text is flipped in the y coordinate because the CTM scales text just like any other graphics.

The code next obtains the current text position and calls the routine showFlippedTextAtPoint in Listing 11.2 to draw the text at that point. This routine is a simple cover routine for the Quartz function CGContextShowTextAtPoint; however, prior to drawing the text, it sets a text matrix that flips text in the y coordinate in order to compensate for the fact that the coordinate system is flipped. The result is the second piece of text on the third line in the figure—the text is upright and is drawn starting at the point where the previous text ended.

The routine `showFlippedTextAtPoint` is one way of drawing upright text with Quartz in a flipped coordinate system. It preserves the existing text matrix across calls to `showFlippedTextAtPoint` but updates the text position to reflect the text drawing. Note that this code ignores any existing text matrix and establishes a new one. As such, this routine is not appropriate for use when you are also using the text matrix to achieve other effects. If all the text you draw is flipped, it isn't necessary to use a routine like `showFlippedTextAtPoint` that sets the text matrix each time you call it. Instead you could simply call `CGContextSetTextMatrix` once to set up the text flipping each time your drawing code is called.

As noted previously, virtually all the application framework text drawing routines that sit on top of Quartz ignore any text matrix currently in effect; instead, they establish their own text matrix as part of their drawing. This means that if you want to flip text when you draw with framework text drawing routines and they don't provide a way to do it, you'll need to use the CTM to produce the correct result. See "Drawing Text in a Flipped Coordinate System" (page 338) for an example of how to achieve text flipping with framework text drawing.

Drawing with Glyphs

To draw with glyphs, you supply Quartz with the glyph identifiers that are specific to the font you are drawing with. Prior to drawing any text, you first create or obtain a CGFont object that represents the font you want to draw with. Quartz uses the `CGFontRef` opaque type to represent a CGFont object. You create a CGFont object by calling the function `CGFontCreateWithPlatformFont`, passing a pointer to an `ATSFontRef`. You obtain an `ATSFontRef` from the Apple Type Services (ATS) framework. ATS provides a number of ways to obtain an `ATSFontRef`. (See the references at the end of the chapter for information about ATS documentation.)

Once you have the CGFont object for the font you want to draw with, you use the function `CGContextSetFont` to set the font in the graphics state. Recall that the default font size is zero in a graphics context; a font size of zero produces no text rendering. To set the font size to a nonzero size, you call `CGContextSetFontSize`.

To draw glyphs from the font you've set, you use `CGContextShowGlyphs` and `CGContextShowGlyphsAtPoint`, passing in an array of glyph identifiers specifying the glyphs to draw. The first glyph in the array of glyphs is drawn at the current text position if you call `CGContextShowGlyphs` or at the point passed to `CGContextShowGlyphsAtPoint`. The character advances are the natural advances of the glyphs (scaled by the font size and transformed by the text matrix), plus any extra character spacing for each glyph. The extra character spacing graphics state parameter is a text space value that is added to each glyph width in text space.

In Panther and later versions, the function CGContextShowGlyphsWithAdvances is also available. You pass in the same data, plus an array of advances that specifies the advance to use for each glyph in the array of glyphs. (Advances are specified as an array of CGSize structures, therefore they have an x and y value.) These advances are the absolute advance for each glyph in user space.

As a general rule, Apple recommends the Unicode text drawing APIs that are part of the application frameworks built on top of Quartz. One example of when you might work directly with glyph identifiers is if you perform custom Cocoa text drawing, such as that discussed in "Subclassing to Get Additional Control" (page 315). General drawing with glyph identifiers and determining the correct glyph identifier to use for a given glyph in the font you are using is beyond the scope of this book.

Drawing Text Using Cocoa

Cocoa provides a number of ways to draw text, each with a different degree of complexity, set of capabilities, and performance. Cocoa has a rich set of classes that make it easy to work with large amounts of text as well as rich text documents (both RTF and RTFD). The NSTextView and NSText classes are intended for working with text documents and the TextEdit application is built on top of these classes. The discussion in this section focuses on the Cocoa methods for drawing individual pieces of text.

There are three basic ways to draw strings of text programmatically in Cocoa:

- The NSString or NSAttributedString classes provide the simplest way of drawing small pieces of text. Prior to Panther, this was the slowest way to draw the same string repeatedly in most cases because Cocoa performed no caching of intermediate data used to draw the string.

- The NSCell class provides primitives for displaying (and editing) text. Prior to Panther, using NSCell was more efficient than NSString but less efficient than using NSLayoutManager.

- The NSLayoutManager class, together with other supporting classes, is the most efficient and flexible means of drawing strings of text with Cocoa.

Prior to Panther, Apple recommended that to obtain the best performance when drawing a piece of text multiple times, you should use the NSLayoutManager methods for drawing text. Because of performance improvements Apple has made to the NSString and NSAttributedString methods in Panther and later versions, the current recommendation is that you start by using the NSString and NSAttributedString classes to draw text strings and determine whether their performance characteristics are suitable for your needs.

These different ways of drawing text can all draw text encoded in the Unicode text encoding, and each performs layout of the text it draws. They position the text in typographically correct ways, utilize text kerning attributes, automatically perform ligature substitution, and take advantage of other font features. This produces high-quality text layout beyond what most applications would otherwise produce.

Generally speaking, the Cocoa text system sets the Quartz text drawing parameters necessary to implement its APIs and overrides any existing context parameters. For example, Cocoa sets the text matrix and those parameters in the Quartz graphics state that affect text drawing. The font and font size are set based on the attributes of the text or, if there is no font attribute, are set to the Cocoa text default value of 12-point Helvetica. The context's existing font and font size are always ignored. The text painting color either is specified as an attribute of the text or is set to the default text painting color, black. While it may be possible to have the Quartz context drawing parameters affect text drawing on various versions of Mac OS X, the best approach is to set the Cocoa text attributes to achieve the effect you intend. It is possible to override the context drawing state that Cocoa imposes with appropriate subclassing; you'll see an example of this shortly.

Cocoa text drawing does respect the CTM and the context clipping area. This allows you to apply coordinate transformations and clipping to Cocoa text in the same ways you can apply them to any Quartz drawing.

The Cocoa text system ignores any existing setting of the text matrix and instead imposes its own settings as part of drawing text. In order to obtain text that is properly oriented in a view that is flipped, the view should implement an `isFlipped` method that returns `YES`. Cocoa uses this to determine whether to flip text you draw to a view. You can use the CTM to apply other coordinate transformation effects, but the Cocoa text system doesn't require you to do so in order to get properly oriented text in a flipped view.

If you mix Quartz text drawing with Cocoa text drawing, you should isolate changes you make to the text matrix so they don't interfere with Cocoa text drawing. The best approach is to use `CGContextGetTextMatrix` to save Cocoa's text matrix before you set the text matrix for use with Quartz text drawing APIs, and restore the saved text matrix with `CGContextSetTextMatrix` after you are done drawing text with Quartz. This is only necessary if you mix Quartz and Cocoa text drawing. If you only draw with one or the other, this is not necessary.

Cocoa sets most other graphics state parameters for drawing text based on the attributes of the text. A given piece of text can have font, foreground color, stroke width, stroke color, shadow, and other attributes that Cocoa uses to set the proper Quartz graphics state prior to drawing that piece of text.

Using NSString

The NSString class is the simplest way to draw small pieces of static text. Listing 11.3 draws an NSString object with various attributes, producing the output in Figure 11.4. The code consists of the routine drawNSStringWithAttributes and the supporting routine getTextString.

The routine drawNSStringWithAttributes first calls getTextString to obtain a reference to an NSString object that contains the Unicode characters to draw. The routine getTextString is implemented so that it creates the text string once the first time it is called and retains that string; future calls to it return the same string. The string it creates consists of the Unicode characters corresponding to the letters in the word *Quartz* plus a few additional Unicode characters that are outside the character set contained in most fonts.

The code draws several lines of text, each with different text attributes. The code draws the first line of text by calling the drawAtPoint:withAttributes: method of the NSString class using a withAttributes value that is nil. This causes the string to be drawn with the default attributes. The font face, font size, and text color are all set by Cocoa to the default values 12-point Helvetica, black text color. The existing context text matrix is ignored and the font, font size, and fill color are set to the Cocoa default values prior to drawing the text.

There are a few important aspects of Cocoa text drawing that drawing the text in Line 1 reveals. First, Cocoa can draw Unicode text without a lot of effort on your part; you simply provide your text as a string of Unicode characters and Cocoa takes care of mapping the Unicode characters into the glyph identifiers that Quartz needs to draw the text. (See the references at the end of this chapter for information about Unicode character charts.) As you see in Figure 11.4, Cocoa draws all the glyphs, including the extra glyphs eighth-note, floral heart, black chess queen, and the two Japanese glyphs. These glyphs aren't necessarily in the font that was used for drawing, but Cocoa performs font fallback; that is, if the current font it is drawing with doesn't contain the glyphs it needs to draw the requested string, it temporarily switches to a font that does. This is much more powerful than the low-level Quartz API that performs no automatic glyph substitution.

Another aspect worth noting is how the drawAtPoint:withAttributes: method of the NSString class positions the text it draws. In Figure 11.4, the point drawn near the start of each text line is the point passed to the routine to draw the text. As you can see from Line 1, the text is drawn so that the lower-left corner of the text box coincides with that point. The drawAtPoint:withAttributes: method does not draw the text with the baseline at the point supplied but instead positions the text box so that its corner is at that point. (If you were to draw in a flipped view, the point passed to the method would be the top-left corner of the text box, not the lower-left corner.)

After drawing Line 1 with the Cocoa default text attributes, the code creates an attributes dictionary `stringAttributes` so that it can specify some of the text attributes rather than using the default values. It first obtains an NSFont object that corresponds to the font with the PostScript name Times-Roman at a size of 40 points. It adds this font to the `stringAttributes` dictionary using the key `NSFontAttributeName`. Selecting the font based on the PostScript name is merely a convenience for this example and is consistent with the previous examples that draw directly with Quartz. Typically you'd use a symbolically named font using the `NSFont` class methods `systemFontOfSize:` or `userFontOfSize:` or a font selected from the font panel, rather than a hard-coded PostScript name.

The code next creates an NSColor object that corresponds to an opaque red in a calibrated RGB color space and adds that color to the `stringAttributes` dictionary using the key `NSForegroundColorAttributeName`. This specifies that the text will be painted in that color. Now the attributes dictionary contains the keys needed to draw the next line of text in the Times-Roman font in an opaque red color. The code calls the `drawAtPoint:withAttributes:` method, this time passing in the attributes dictionary. The result is the text in Line 2 in the figure.

In Panther, Cocoa text added support for attributes that cause the text to be stroked rather than filled. The code takes advantage of this by adding a key `NSStrokeWidthAttributeName` with a value that is an `NSNumber` corresponding to a stroke width of +3.0 units. It then draws the text in Line 3 by using the updated attributes dictionary. This time the text is stroked instead of filled and is again painted red.

Listing 11.3 Code that uses NSString methods to draw text

```
static NSString *getTextString()
{
  static NSString *textString = nil;
  if(textString == nil){
    // These Unicode values are the glyphs: Q, u, a, r, t, z,
    // eighth-note, floral heart, chess queen, and 2 CJK glyphs.
    const unichar chars[] = {0x0051, 0x0075, 0x0061, 0x0072, 0x0074,
      0x007A, 0x266A, 0x2766, 0x265B, 0x3042, 0x304E };
    textString = [NSString stringWithCharacters:chars
      length: sizeof(chars)/sizeof(unichar)];
    [textString retain];
  }
  return textString;
}
```

```
void drawNSStringWithAttributes(void)
{
  NSString *textString = getTextString();
  NSPoint p;
  NSFont *font;
  NSColor *redColor;
  NSMutableDictionary *stringAttributes;

  p = NSMakePoint(20., 400.);
  // ***** Text Line 1 *****
  // Draw the text with the default text attributes.
  [ textString drawAtPoint:p withAttributes:nil];

  // ***** Text Line 2 *****
  // Draw with a specific font and color.

  // Position the text 50 units below the previous text.
  p.y -= 50;
  // Set attributes to use when drawing the string.
  stringAttributes = [NSMutableDictionary dictionaryWithCapacity:4];

  // Use the font with the PostScript name "Times-Roman" at 40 point.
  font = [ NSFont fontWithName:@"Times-Roman" size: 40];
  [stringAttributes setObject:font forKey:NSFontAttributeName];

  // Set the color attribute to an opaque red.
  redColor = [NSColor colorWithCalibratedRed:1
                green:0 blue:0 alpha:1.0];

  [stringAttributes setObject:redColor
    forKey:NSForegroundColorAttributeName];

  [textString drawAtPoint:p withAttributes:stringAttributes];

  // ***** Text Line 3 *****
  // Draw stroked text.

  // Position the text 50 units below the previous text.
  p.y -= 50;

  // Set the stroke text mode by using a positive stroke value.
  [ stringAttributes setObject:[NSNumber numberWithFloat:3.0]
                forKey:NSStrokeWidthAttributeName];
```

```
    [ textString drawAtPoint:p withAttributes:stringAttributes];

    // ***** Text Line 4 *****
    // Draw with fill and stroke.

    // Position the text 50 units below the previous text.
    p.y -= 50;

    // Set the fill-stroke text mode by using a negative stroke value.
    [stringAttributes setObject:
        [NSNumber numberWithFloat:-3.0]
        forKey:NSStrokeWidthAttributeName];
    // Set the stroke color attribute to black.
    [stringAttributes setObject:
        [NSColor colorWithCalibratedRed:0 green:0 blue:0 alpha:1.0]
        forKey:NSStrokeColorAttributeName];

    [ textString drawAtPoint:p withAttributes:stringAttributes];

    // ***** Text Line 5 *****
    // Draw at the text baseline.
    NSRect rect;

    p.y -= 50;
    rect.origin = p;
    rect.size = NSMakeSize(0,0);
    [ textString drawWithRect:rect
                    options:NSStringDrawingDisableScreenFontSubstitution
                    attributes:stringAttributes ];
}
```

In addition to stroking text, in Panther and later versions, Cocoa can paint text with a fill and stroke together. The code replaces the attributes dictionary entry with the key NSStrokeWidthAttributeName with an NSNumber that is a stroke width of –3.0. Negative values for the NSStrokeWidthAttributeName key are a signal to Cocoa to fill and stroke the text. Next the code adds the key NSStroke-ColorAttributeName with an NSColor that corresponds to black. It then paints the text by calling the drawAtPoint:withAttributes: with the string and the attributes dictionary it has built up. This produces the text in Line 4 in the figure—text that is filled with the red text color specified by the NSForeground-ColorAttributeName key and stroked with a line width of 3.0 units in the black

Figure 11.4 Drawing text using methods provided by the NSString class

Line 1 ——

Line 2 ——

Line 3 ——

Line 4 ——

Line 5 ——

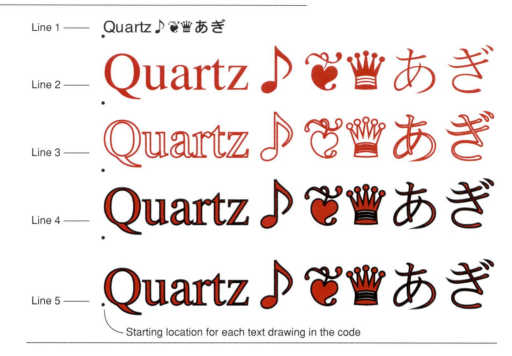

Starting location for each text drawing in the code

color specified by the `NSStrokeColorAttributeName` key. Note that when you use negative numbers in the `NSStrokeWidthAttributeName` key, if you don't specify an `NSStrokeColorAttributeName` key, Cocoa will use the same color as that specified in the `NSForegroundColorAttributeName` key.

With the mechanisms just discussed, Cocoa supports the Quartz text drawing modes `kCGTextFill`, `kCGTextStroke`, and `kCGTextFillStroke`. There is no high-level support for the text modes that clip with text; however, you can achieve clipping with appropriate subclassing, as demonstrated in "Subclassing to Get Additional Control" (page 315), or by obtaining the character outlines for your text and using them to create a clipping area.

The first four lines of text in Figure 11.4 are each drawn with the NSString drawing method `drawAtPoint:withAttributes:`. As mentioned earlier, this method positions the text so that the corner of the text box coincides with the point you pass to the method. In Tiger and later versions, Cocoa provides the NSString method `drawWithRect:options:attribute:`, which allows you to directly position the text baseline at a point of your choosing. The code draws the text in Line 5 in the figure by supplying a rectangle with an origin at the y coordinate where the text baseline should be located and a size that has zero width and height. Cocoa draws the text on a single line without any wrapping and with the baseline starting at the origin of the supplied rectangle.

Using NSLayoutManager

One of the most efficient ways of drawing text repeatedly with Cocoa is to use the NSLayoutManager class together with the companion classes NSTextStorage and NSTextContainer. Listing 11.4 is a simple example of drawing the same string with similar attributes as that of the previous example but instead uses an NSLayoutManager text drawing method. Since the same text with the same attributes is drawn each time the drawWithNSLayout routine is called, the layout and associated objects are created the first time the routine is called and are reused each subsequent time.

One of the purposes of using an NSLayoutManager object for drawing text is so that the layout of the text can be cached, providing for improved performance upon subsequent redrawing of the text. Therefore, the code in the listing creates the NSLayoutManager object it will draw the first time the drawWithNSLayout routine is called and reuses that object when drawWithNSLayout is called again. To create a layout, the code first creates an NSTextStorage object, initialized with the NSString object returned by the getTextString routine from Listing 11.3. It next creates an NSLayoutManager object and an NSTextContainer object. It adds the text container to the layout object and adds the layout to the text storage. The layout now contains the text with the default attributes. The code creates an attributes dictionary that specifies to draw the text in the font with the PostScript name Times-Roman at 40 points in the color red. It then applies that attributes dictionary to the full range of text in the text storage. Now the layout contains a single run of text drawn with the same attributes and is ready for drawing. To draw the text, the code calls the NSLayoutManager instance method drawGlyphsForGlyphRange:atPoint:. The point passed to drawGlyphsForGlyphRange:atPoint: specifies the user space point where the origin of the text container in the layout should be located.

Listing 11.4 A routine that draws text using methods provided by the NSLayoutManager class

```
void drawWithNSLayout(void)
{
  static NSLayoutManager *myLayout = nil;
  static NSTextStorage *textStorage = nil;
  static NSRange myTextRange;
  NSPoint p;
  if(myLayout == nil){
    NSTextContainer *textContainer;
    NSMutableDictionary *stringAttributes;
    NSFont *font;
    NSColor *redColor;
```

```
    // Initialize the text storage with the string to draw.
    textStorage = [ [NSTextStorage alloc]
              initWithString: getTextString()];
    // Initialize the layout manager to use with the text storage.
    myLayout = [[NSLayoutManager alloc] init];
    // Allocate and initialize a text container object.
    textContainer = [[NSTextContainer alloc] init];
    // Add the text container to the layout.
    [myLayout addTextContainer:textContainer];
    // The layout retains the text container; now release it.
    [textContainer release];
    // Add the layout to the text storage.
    [textStorage addLayoutManager:myLayout];
    // The text storage retains the layout so this code can release it.
    [myLayout release];

    // Set attributes to use when drawing the string.
    stringAttributes = [NSMutableDictionary dictionaryWithCapacity:2];

    // Use the font with the PostScript name "Times-Roman" at 40 point.
    font = [ NSFont fontWithName:@"Times-Roman" size: 40];
    [stringAttributes setObject:font forKey:NSFontAttributeName];

    // Set the text color attribute to an opaque red.
    redColor = [NSColor colorWithCalibratedRed:0.663
              green:0 blue:0.031 alpha:1.0];
    [stringAttributes setObject:redColor
      forKey:NSForegroundColorAttributeName];

    // Create the range of text for the entire length of text
    // in the textStorage object.
    myTextRange = NSMakeRange(0, [textStorage length]);
    // Set the attributes on the entire range of text.
    [textStorage setAttributes:stringAttributes range:myTextRange];
}

// Set the point for drawing the layout.
p = NSMakePoint(20., 400.);

// Draw the text range at the point.
[myLayout drawGlyphsForGlyphRange:myTextRange atPoint:p];

}
```

Figure 11.5 Drawing with NSLayoutManager methods to a flipped and unflipped view

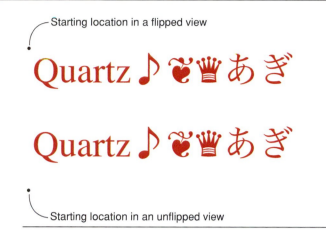

Starting location in a flipped view

Starting location in an unflipped view

The NSLayoutManager class works best when drawing into a flipped view, that is, a view where y coordinate values increase as you move down the drawing canvas. The positioning that NSLayoutManager performs to lay out text that requires special positioning (such as underlines, superscripts, or subscripts) only works correctly when the view is flipped. In addition, the location of the text container origin that you pass to drawGlyphsForGlyphRange:atPoint: compared to where the text is drawn is quite different when drawing to a flipped view as compared to drawing to a view that is unflipped. Figure 11.5 illustrates the location of the starting point when drawing in both a flipped and unflipped view. For a flipped view, the starting point is at the top-left corner of the text container of the text drawn. For an unflipped view, the starting point is at the lower-left corner of the text container of the text drawn, which is well below the text baseline.

Subclassing to Get Additional Control

One interesting aspect of using the NSLayoutManager class for text drawing is the ability to subclass it to achieve custom handling of text drawing. Most Cocoa developers don't need to perform this kind of custom drawing and can safely skip this section—it is provided for those developers who want to achieve an extra degree of control over their Cocoa text drawing or perhaps obtain some special effect.

Listing 11.5 (page 318) is an example of subclassing NSLayoutManager to achieve some special effects that would otherwise be difficult to obtain from

Cocoa text drawing. This example draws with text drawing modes other than kCGTextFill in versions prior to Panther, which is the first time Cocoa text drawing supported them directly. It also draws using the clipping text mode that Cocoa text drawing doesn't directly support. In addition, it draws the text with the text baseline at the y coordinate of the point passed to drawGlyphsForGlyph-Range. The result of executing the code appears in Figure 11.6 (page 323). In the figure, the point at the beginning of each text line is the starting point used to draw the text.

The NSLayoutManager class performs all its drawing by calling the showPacked-Glyphs:length:glyphRange:atPoint:font:color:printingAdjustment method that it implements. (This method will be referred to as showPackedGlyphs for the remainder of this section.) You can perform custom drawing by subclassing NSLayoutManager and overriding this method. The code in Listing 11.5 uses this approach for drawing with the different text drawing modes. To achieve the effect of drawing the text baseline at the point passed to its drawGlyphsForGlyph-Range:atPoint: method, the code also overrides this method in addition to show-PackedGlyphs.

The code in the listing first defines a typedef for a function ClippingDrawProc that is the function that the code uses to draw through the clipped text. You'll see how this function is used in a moment.

Next the code defines the public interface to the MyNSLayoutManager class it creates by subclassing the NSLayoutManager class. This subclass adds methods for setting the text mode that will be used to draw the layout, the layout fill color, the layout stroke color, the layout stroke line width, and the ClippingDraw-Proc that will be executed when the text drawing mode for the layout is one that performs clipping.

After defining the interface to the MyNSLayoutManager class, the code defines its implementation. The methods added to the class are relatively straightforward; each simply records the attribute being assigned in a private instance variable. The setFillColor: and setStrokeColor: methods are each careful to retain the CGColorRef passed to them so that they can be assured the reference they store is valid when it is used at a later time. Because these instance variables retain the CGColor objects passed to them, the MyNSLayoutManager class implements a dealloc method so that when an instance of MyNSLayoutManager is deallocated, it releases any CGColor objects it retains. Note that by using CGColor objects in the implementation of MyNSLayoutManager, this code will only run on Panther and later versions.

The implementation of MyNSLayoutManager contains only two other methods, each overriding a method in the superclass. First, the code implements a drawGlyphsForGlyphRange:atPoint: method that records the value of the y coordinate in the point passed to the method, then calls the drawGlyphsForGlyphRange:

`atPoint:` method in its superclass. Finally, it defines the `showPackedGlyphs` method that implements its drawing.

The custom `showPackedGlyphs` method begins by obtaining the Quartz context corresponding to the current Cocoa `NSGraphicsContext`. This is the Quartz context into which the code must perform its drawing. The location that `showPackedGlyphs` must draw to is given by the `point` argument passed to the method. Because the MyNSLayoutManager wants to draw the text baseline at the y coordinate passed to `drawGlyphsForGlyphRange:atPoint:`, it adjusts the y coordinate of the point passed in to that recorded at the time `drawGlyphsForGlyphRange:atPoint:` is called. The resulting point is the point that `showPackedGlyphs` will draw its text. Note that this technique won't work correctly for text that has a superscript, subscript, or underline, but for this example it is just fine.

It is important that `showPackedGlyphs` isolate any changes it needs to make during its execution so that the graphics state in effect when it returns is that which was in effect when it was called. The custom `showPackedGlyphs` method saves and restores the graphics state to ensure that this is the case.

Next the code sets the Quartz text drawing mode using that set on the layout and checks whether the text drawing mode is one of the fill drawing modes. If it is and the layout's fill color instance variable contains a CGColor object, it uses that color as the current fill color. It then checks if the text mode is one of the stroke text modes and, if so, it sets the stroke line width and the stroke color as needed.

The last thing the `showPackedGlyphs` method needs to do prior to drawing the text is to adjust for any character width adjustment that is required. If the width of the `printingAdjustment` argument passed to `showPackedGlyphs` is nonzero, that extra width must be added to the total width of each glyph drawn. To achieve this, the code sets the character spacing parameter in the graphics state. Recall from "Character Spacing" (page 296) that the extra character spacing parameter is interpreted in text space; that is, it is transformed by the text matrix. Prior to calling `showPackedGlyphs`, Cocoa sets the text matrix x and y scaling to the point size of the font being drawn. By dividing (or "unscaling") the `printingAdjustment` width by the font point size and using that result as the extra character spacing to apply to each character in text space, the total amount of user space adjustment per character is the `printingAdjustment` width, as desired.

Now that the Quartz context is properly set up to draw the text, the code calls the Quartz function `CGContextShowGlyphsAtPoint`, passing the `CGPoint` updated to correspond to the point where the baseline should be drawn. The `glyphs` array passed to `showPackedGlyphs` is an array of Quartz glyph identifiers and can be passed directly to `CGContextShowGlyphsAtPoint`. The length of the array is the number of bytes in the `glyphsArray` and, because each `CGGlyph` is 2 bytes, the total number of glyphs in the array is `glyphLen/2`.

Once the text had been drawn with the proper text drawing mode, the code checks if the drawing mode is one that specifies a clip text mode. If it does and the layout contains a clippingDrawProc, showPackedGlyphs calls it. This is important to do as part of showPackedGlyphs because prior to returning, showPacked-Glyphs must restore the graphics state to that in effect when it was called. The only time that the clipping with the glyphs is in effect is after the call to CGContextShowGlyphsAtPoint but before the graphics state is restored.

Listing 11.5 Code that creates and uses an NSLayoutManager subclass to customize drawing

```
// A clipping procedure that will be used by the
// subclass of NSLayoutManager defined by this code.
typedef void (ClippingDrawProc)(CGContextRef c, float x,
                float y, void *info);

// The interface to the NSLayoutManager subclass.
@interface MyNSLayoutManager : NSLayoutManager
{
  // The extra instance variables for this subclass.
  CGTextDrawingMode _textMode;
  CGColorRef _fColor;
  CGColorRef _sColor;
  float _yStartPosition;
  float _lineWidth;
  ClippingDrawProc *_clippingDrawProc;
  void *_clippingInfo;
}
- (void)setTextMode:(CGTextDrawingMode)textMode;
- (void)setFillColor:(CGColorRef)color;
- (void)setStrokeColor:(CGColorRef)color;
- (void)setTextLineWidth:(float)width;
- (void)setClippingDrawProc:(ClippingDrawProc *)clippingDrawProc
                withInfo:(void *)info;
@end

// The implementation of the MyNSLayoutManager custom subclass.
@implementation MyNSLayoutManager

// Public methods to set the special attributes
// of the MyNSLayoutManager instance.
- (void)setTextMode:(CGTextDrawingMode)textMode{ _textMode = textMode;}
- (void)setFillColor:(CGColorRef)color{
     CGColorRetain(color);
```

```
        CGColorRelease(_fColor);
        _fColor = color;
    }
- (void)setStrokeColor:(CGColorRef)color{
        CGColorRetain(color);
        CGColorRelease(_sColor);
        _sColor = color;
    }
- (void)setTextLineWidth:(float)width{ _lineWidth = width;}
- (void)setClippingDrawProc: (ClippingDrawProc *)clippingDrawProc
                withInfo:(void *)info
    { _clippingDrawProc = clippingDrawProc; _clippingInfo = info; }

// The init method initializes the custom instance variables.
- (id)init
{
    if (self = [super init]) {
        // Initialize the custom instance variables.
        _textMode = kCGTextFill;
        _fColor = nil; _sColor = nil;
        _yStartPosition = 0;
        _lineWidth = 1;
        _clippingDrawProc = NULL; _clippingInfo = NULL;
    }
    return self;
}


// This class needs a dealloc method to ensure that
// the retained fill and stroke colors are released.
- (void)dealloc {
    CGColorRelease(_sColor);
    CGColorRelease(_fColor);
    [super dealloc];
}


// This code overrides this method to record the y coordinate
// to use as the true baseline for the text drawing.
- (void)drawGlyphsForGlyphRange:(NSRange)glyphsToShow
                atPoint:(NSPoint)origin
{
    _yStartPosition = origin.y;
    [ super drawGlyphsForGlyphRange:glyphsToShow atPoint:origin];
}
```

```
    // This is the rendering method of NSLayoutManager that the
    // code overrides to perform its custom rendering.
- (void)showPackedGlyphs:(char *)glyphs
        length:(unsigned)glyphLen
        glyphRange:(NSRange)glyphRange
        atPoint:(NSPoint)point
        font:(NSFont *)font
        color:(NSColor *)color
        printingAdjustment:(NSSize)printingAdjustment
{
  // Obtain the destination drawing context.
  CGContextRef context = (CGContextRef)[
    [NSGraphicsContext currentContext] graphicsPort];

  // Adjust the start position y based on the adjusted y coordinate.
  point.y = _yStartPosition;

  // The Quartz graphics state should be preserved by showPackedGlyphs.
  CGContextSaveGState(context);

  // Set the desired text drawing mode.
  CGContextSetTextDrawingMode(context, _textMode);
  // Set the fill color if needed.
  if( _textMode == kCGTextFill || _textMode == kCGTextFillStroke ||
    _textMode == kCGTextFillClip ||
    _textMode == kCGTextFillStrokeClip){
    if(_fColor) CGContextSetFillColorWithColor(context, _fColor);
  }
  // Set the line width and stroke color if needed.
  if( _textMode == kCGTextStroke || _textMode == kCGTextFillStroke ||
    _textMode == kCGTextStrokeClip ||
    _textMode == kCGTextFillStrokeClip){
    CGContextSetLineWidth(context, _lineWidth);
    if(_sColor) CGContextSetStrokeColorWithColor(context, _sColor);
  }

  // Check whether to adjust for printing widths
  // and if needed, adjust extra character spacing accordingly.
  if(printingAdjustment.width != 0.0){
    // Adjust the character spacing to produce the desired
    // extra adjustment width.
    float charAdjust = printingAdjustment.width / [ font pointSize ];
    CGContextSetCharacterSpacing(context, charAdjust);
  } else {
```

```
      CGContextSetCharacterSpacing(context, 0.0);
  }

  // Draw the glyphs.
  CGContextShowGlyphsAtPoint(context, point.x, point.y,
                (CGGlyph *)glyphs, glyphLen/2);

  // If the text drawing mode requires clipping, call the custom
  // clipping proc. This allows drawing through clipped text before
  // the graphics state is restored.
  if( (_textMode == kCGTextClip || _textMode == kCGTextFillClip ||
    _textMode == kCGTextStrokeClip ||
    _textMode == kCGTextFillStrokeClip)
    && _clippingDrawProc != NULL)
    _clippingDrawProc(context, point.x, point.y, _clippingInfo);

  CGContextRestoreGState(context);
}
@end

void MyClipProc(CGContextRef c, float x, float y, void *info)
{
  CGContextTranslateCTM(c, x, y);
  CGContextSetStrokeColorWithColor(c, getRGBOpaqueBlackColor());
  drawGridLines(c); // Draw a grid of lines through the clip.
}

void drawWithCustomNSLayout(void)
{
  static MyNSLayoutManager *myLayout = nil;
  static NSTextStorage *textStorage = nil;
  static NSRange myTextRange;
  NSPoint p;
  if(myLayout == nil){
    NSTextContainer *textContainer = [[NSTextContainer alloc] init];
    NSMutableDictionary *stringAttributes;

    textStorage = [[NSTextStorage alloc]
                initWithString:getTextString()];
    // Create an instance of the MyNSLayoutManager class.
    myLayout = [[MyNSLayoutManager alloc] init];
    [myLayout addTextContainer:textContainer];
    [textContainer release];
    [textStorage addLayoutManager:myLayout];
```

```
    // The text storage retains the layout so this code can release it.
    [myLayout release];
    // Set attributes to use when drawing the string.
    stringAttributes = [NSMutableDictionary dictionaryWithCapacity:2];

    // Use the font with the PostScript name "Times-Roman" at 40 point.
    [stringAttributes setObject: [ NSFont fontWithName:@"Times-Roman"
                size: 40] forKey:NSFontAttributeName];
    // Create the range.
    myTextRange = NSMakeRange(0, [textStorage length]);
    // Set the attributes on the entire range of text.
    [textStorage setAttributes:stringAttributes range:myTextRange];
}

p = NSMakePoint(20., 400.);

// Set the custom attributes of the layout subclass so that
// the text will be filled with black.
[myLayout setTextMode:kCGTextFill];
[myLayout setFillColor: getRGBOpaqueBlackColor()];

// Draw text line 1.
[myLayout drawGlyphsForGlyphRange:myTextRange atPoint:p];

// Draw text line 2.
// Set the custom attributes of the layout subclass so that
// the text will be stroked with black and a line width of 2.
[myLayout setTextMode:kCGTextStroke];
[myLayout setStrokeColor: getRGBOpaqueBlackColor()];
[myLayout setTextLineWidth:2];
p.y -= 50;
[myLayout drawGlyphsForGlyphRange:myTextRange atPoint:p];

// Draw text line 3.
// Set the custom attributes to fill the text with red and
// stroke the text with black.
[myLayout setTextMode:kCGTextFillStroke];
[myLayout setFillColor: getRGBOpaqueRedColor()];
p.y -= 50;
[myLayout drawGlyphsForGlyphRange:myTextRange atPoint:p];

// Draw text line 4.
// Set the custom attributes of the layout subclass so that
// the text will be filled, stroked, then clipped.
[myLayout setTextMode:kCGTextFillStrokeClip];
```

```
// Set the clipping proc to the MyClipProc that requires
// no info data.
[myLayout setClippingDrawProc:&MyClipProc withInfo:NULL];
p.y -= 50;
[myLayout drawGlyphsForGlyphRange:myTextRange atPoint:p];

// Set the clipping proc to NULL for future drawing.
[myLayout setClippingDrawProc:NULL withInfo:NULL];

}
```

Note that a single call to drawGlyphsForGlyphRange can result in multiple calls to showPackedGlyphs as the Cocoa text system does text layout and font fall-back. The implementation of showPackedGlyphs in Listing 11.5 works just fine in this circumstance. It draws with the current font at the correct x coordinate. As mentioned before, if the text layout requires changes to the y coordinate value, such as for drawing superscripts or subscripts, this code will not work correctly.

In addition to performing custom drawing, another reason you might want to have a custom showPackedGlyphs method is to obtain character outlines. The

Figure 11.6 The result of drawing text using a custom subclass of NSLayoutManager

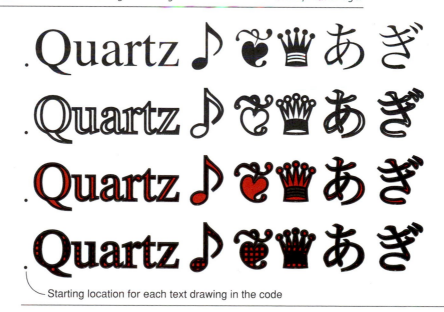

Starting location for each text drawing in the code

NSBezierPath method `appendBezierPathWithGlyphs:count:inFont:` is one way of adding the glyphs from a layout to a path. One approach to creating a path containing the glyph outlines is to subclass NSLayoutManager in a manner similar to the previous example, but instead of imaging the text in the `showPackedGlyphs` method, you call `appendBezierPathWithGlyphs:count:inFont:` to add the glyphs to the path you are creating.

Drawing Text Using Carbon

Carbon has a number of technologies to provide higher-level text support than that available directly in Quartz. Each can draw text encoded as Unicode and performs layout of the text it draws. Just like Cocoa text drawing, they position the text in typographically correct ways, utilize text kerning attributes, automatically perform ligature substitution, and take advantage of other font features. Drawing with the high-level text drawing routines in Carbon produces high-quality text layout beyond what most applications would otherwise produce.

The different ways of drawing text in Carbon are listed here starting with the least complex and flexible. As you go down this list, the flexibility and corresponding complexity increase.

- The Carbon HIToolbox provides theme text drawing using `HIThemeDrawText-Box` and `DrawThemeTextBox`. These functions are useful for drawing text using a limited set of fonts and sizes. One typical use of these functions is to draw user interface elements.

- Multilingual Text Engine (MLTE) is an API that provides Unicode-compliant text editing fields and allows your application to draw static text. You can also use MLTE to provide text editing within a full-size window. MLTE is built as a replacement for Apple's legacy TextEdit API (not to be confused with the Mac OS X application TextEdit.app).

- Apple Type Services for Unicode Imaging (ATSUI) provides fine-grained control of text drawing.

The function `DrawThemeTextBox` is available on all versions of Mac OS X, but it isn't as well suited to drawing to a Quartz context. You can use it, but it has a number of problems when drawing to a Quartz context that limit its utility. Some of the limitations of `DrawThemeTextBox` are as follows:

- It resets the coordinate system prior to drawing so that all scaling, translation, and rotation is removed prior to drawing.

- It always interprets the coordinates you pass for the rectangle to draw into as QuickDraw coordinates with the origin at the top-left corner of the window or view, regardless of the current CTM in effect.

- It resets the clip to a default value.

- For contexts that are not associated with a window, it produces undefined results.

Using DrawThemeTextBox for onscreen text drawing works correctly as long as you don't need to apply coordinate transformations to the text or apply a clipping area to the text drawing, and you can work with a flipped coordinate system. Don't expect correct results when printing or drawing to any other kind of Quartz context.

Using HIThemeDrawTextBox (Panther)

10.3 ▶ In Panther and later versions, the Carbon HIToolbox provides the theme text drawing function HIThemeDrawTextBox, which is well matched to drawing with Quartz. The arguments to HIThemeDrawTextBox are

- drawString, a CFString object that contains the Unicode characters to draw.

- bounds, a pointer to an HIRect structure that specifies the box to draw the text into. Text is wrapped to this box and clipped if the box is not large enough to hold the text.

- textInfo, a pointer to an HIThemeTextInfo structure that specifies the font to use and controls how the text is laid out.

- context, the CGContextRef into which the text will be drawn.

- orientation, an HIThemeOrientation value that specifies whether to flip the y axis of the coordinate system prior to drawing the text.

Listing 11.6 is a simple example of using HIThemeDrawTextBox to draw a small piece of text into a Quartz context. It changes the Quartz graphics state to affect the text drawing color and text drawing mode. The output from this code is shown in Figure 11.7. While not demonstrated in this example, text drawing with the theme text APIs performs font fallback substitution similar to that performed when drawing Cocoa text. If the specified theme font doesn't contain the needed text characters, a substitute font will be used for those characters.

The example constructs a text box that is large enough so that the text does not need to wrap to fit into the text box; for simplicity the origin of the text box is the Quartz origin. In the HIThemeTextInfo structure the code fills in, the font is specified as the application theme font; the other values it uses are typical defaults. Theme text drawing is limited to the fonts specified by a ThemeFontID. A ThemeFontID uniquely identifies a font face, style, and size. There are about 20 unique ThemeFontID values available for drawing using theme text drawing.

The code first sets the context fill color to an opaque red in the generic calibrated RGB color space before drawing any text. Theme text drawing respects many of the parameters in the Quartz graphics state, as you'll see in a moment. To draw the first line of text, the code translates the Quartz origin so that it coincides with the location where the lower-left corner of the text box should be drawn; then it calls HIThemeDrawTextBox to draw the text. The function HIThemeDraw-TextBox is prepared to draw upright, unflipped text in both flipped and unflipped coordinate systems. Because the code in Listing 11.6 is written to draw into a coordinate system that has the same orientation as the default Quartz coordinate system, it passes the value kHIThemeOrientationInverted for the HIThemeOrientation to use when drawing the text. The HIToolbox notion of an inverted coordinate system is one that is flipped relative to the default orientation of an HIView. Because HIView coordinates are by default in the top-left corner of the view with the y coordinate values increasing as you go down the view, you use the value kHIThemeOrientationInverted when drawing to a coordinate system that corresponds to the default Quartz orientation. If you were using the default HIView coordinate system orientation, you would pass kHIThemeOrientationNormal.

Prior to drawing the second text line, the code translates down the page and scales the CTM with a uniform scaling factor of 2 in x and y. It sets the fill color to an opaque blue and draws the text. As you can see, the text is scaled by a factor of 2 when it is drawn. Drawing with a given theme font specifies the font face, style, and point size of the text drawing. While you can't explicitly change the font size, you can affect the actual size of the text drawing by scaling the CTM prior to drawing.

Theme text drawing also respects the Quartz text drawing mode. Prior to drawing the third line of text, the code sets the stroke color space to the generic calibrated RGB color space. This sets the stroke color to opaque black in that color space. It then sets the fill color to green, positions the text, and scales the coordinate system again with a uniform scaling factor of 2 in x and y. Combined with the previous scaling factor of 2, this produces a total scaling of 4. The code uses a line width value of 0.5 to produce a stroke that is not excessively thick when drawn in the scaled coordinate system. Finally, it sets the text drawing mode to kCGTextFillStroke so that the text drawing painted by the last call to HITheme-DrawTextBox is filled with green and is stroked with black.

Figure 11.7 Drawing text using the function HIThemeDrawTextBox

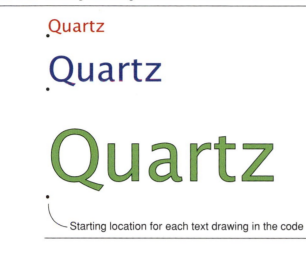

Starting location for each text drawing in the code

Listing 11.6 Code that draws text using the function HIThemeDrawTextBox

```
void drawTextWithThemeText(CGContextRef context)
{
    CFStringRef    textString = CFSTR("Quartz");
    float opaqueRed[] = { 0.663, 0., 0.031, 1. };
    float opaqueBlue[] = { 0.11, 0.208, 0.451, 1. };
    float opaqueGreen[] = { 0.404, 0.808, 0.239, 1. };
    // Use a text box that will contain the text on a single line.
    static const CGRect textBox = {0., 0., 1000., 1000.};
    // Use the application theme font together with other
    // typical values for the HIThemeTextInfo.
    HIThemeTextInfo textInfo = { 0, kThemeStateActive,
        kThemeApplicationFont,
        kHIThemeTextHorizontalFlushLeft,
        kHIThemeTextVerticalFlushBottom,
        kHIThemeTextBoxOptionNone,
        kHIThemeTextTruncationNone,
        0,
        false
    };

    // Theme text drawing respects the context fill color.
    CGContextSetFillColorSpace(context, getTheRGBColorSpace());
    // Set the fill color to opaque red.
    CGContextSetFillColor(context, opaqueRed);
```

```
        // Use HIThemeDrawTextBox (Panther and later versions) to draw the text.
        CGContextTranslateCTM(context, 10, 300);
        // ***** Text Line 1 *****
        // Draw the text using kHIThemeOrientationInverted since the
        // CTM is flipped relative to the HIToolbox default.
        (void)HIThemeDrawTextBox(textString, &textBox, &textInfo,
                    context, kHIThemeOrientationInverted);

    CGContextSaveGState(context);
        // HIThemeDrawTextBox works with the CTM as you would expect.

        // ***** Text Line 2 *****
        CGContextTranslateCTM(context, 0, -40);
        CGContextScaleCTM(context, 2, 2);
        CGContextSetFillColor(context, opaqueBlue);

        (void)HIThemeDrawTextBox(textString, &textBox, &textInfo,
                    context, kHIThemeOrientationInverted);

        // ***** Text Line 3 *****
        CGContextSetStrokeColorSpace(context, getTheRGBColorSpace());
        CGContextSetFillColor(context, opaqueGreen);
        CGContextTranslateCTM(context, 0, -40);
        CGContextScaleCTM(context, 2, 2);

        CGContextSetLineWidth(context, 0.5);
        // Theme text drawing respects the text drawing mode.
        CGContextSetTextDrawingMode(context, kCGTextFillStroke);

        (void)HIThemeDrawTextBox(textString, &textBox, &textInfo,
                    context, kHIThemeOrientationInverted);
    CGContextRestoreGState(context);

}
```

The point at the beginning of each line of text in Figure 11.7 indicates the lower-left corner of the text box passed to HIThemeDrawTextBox. As you can see, this corner is not at the baseline of the text but is at the corner of the box that contains the text, similar to many of the Cocoa text drawing methods. If you were instead drawing into a flipped coordinate system, such as the default orientation of an HIView, the origin of the HIRect passed to HIThemeDrawTextBox would be the top-left corner of the text box.

As you've seen, unlike Cocoa text drawing, when drawing text using the theme text drawing, most of the graphics state and context parameters that affect the low-level Quartz text drawing primitives also affect the Carbon theme text drawing functions. However, there are a few exceptions that you should be aware of. Theme text drawing ignores the font face and size in the Quartz graphics state—instead HIThemeDrawTextBox sets the font face and size specified by the ThemeFontID you pass to the function. Theme text drawing also ignores the current text matrix set in the context. Instead, the text position is determined by the HIRect passed in. Any text transformations that might be present in the text matrix prior to calling HIThemeDrawTextBox are ignored. Because HIThemeDraw-TextBox performs text layout, the extra character spacing parameter in the context graphics state is also ignored.

Theme text drawing does respect the anti-aliasing and smoothing parameters in the graphics state, although the setting in the Appearance system preference is respected. Theme text drawing respects the user's font smoothing style preference when the font smoothing parameter is true in the graphics state and anti-aliasing is turned on. However, for point sizes at or below the threshold set by the user in the Appearance system preference, text is not anti-aliased, even if the context parameters request anti-aliasing.

The Quartz shadow parameter is respected, although some theme fonts are themselves shadowed, overriding the shadow settings you may set in the context. (Shadows are discussed in "Drawing with Shadows (Panther)" (page 512).)

Theme text drawing encapsulates its use of the low-level Quartz text drawing functions with CGContextSaveGState and CGContextRestoreGState. This means that theme text drawing doesn't leave any residual changes to the Quartz graphics state—all the graphics state parameters are the same as before you call HIThemeDrawTextBox. As you've seen in the example, you can use the Quartz text drawing mode and the fill and stroke color to affect theme text drawing. Theme text's use of CGContextSaveGState and CGContextRestoreGState prevents use of the clipping text modes to achieve clipping effects because its use of CGContext-RestoreGState resets the clip after the text is drawn but before control is returned to the caller.

The CTM and context clipping area are respected by HIThemeDrawTextBox but, as mentioned previously, not by DrawThemeTextBox.

Using Multilingual Text Engine

A potentially more flexible way of drawing text in Carbon applications and that also supports text editing is provided by Multilingual Text Engine (MLTE). This is a modern replacement for the venerable TextEdit API introduced with the original Macintosh in 1984. MLTE provides the ability to display and edit large amounts of text and is integrated into the HITextView functionality available in Panther and later versions.

The MLTE API also provides two functions for drawing static text—TXNDrawUnicodeTextBox and TXNDrawCFStringTextBox. When calling each of these functions, you pass an ATSU style object that describes the text style and a QuickDraw Rect structure specifying the location of the text box. To draw to a Quartz context, you use the kTXNUseCGContextRefMask bit in the optionTags field of the TXNTextBoxOptionsData you pass to these functions and pass the destination context in the options field.

The TXNDrawUnicodeTextBox and TXNDrawCFStringTextBox functions are suitable for drawing to a Quartz context obtained from a Carbon window, but because of their dependence on QuickDraw, they do not work well with any other type of Quartz context. The rectangle passed to the functions is interpreted in a QuickDraw coordinate system. Modifications to the Quartz coordinate system can produce unexpected results. Rather than using these functions for drawing pieces of text to an arbitrary Quartz context, a better choice is to use Apple Type Services for Unicode Imaging (ATSUI).

Using Apple Type Services for Unicode Imaging

Apple Type Services for Unicode Imaging (ATSUI) provides a powerful and flexible way to draw text, but using it is more involved than the theme text drawing routines. With the added complexity comes significantly greater control. For example, you can specify the starting text position at the baseline of the text, rather than specifying a rectangle that encloses the text. ATSUI text drawing is part of the umbrella framework ApplicationServices and as such can be used independently from the Carbon framework. ATSUI text drawing can be used in a Cocoa application if desired and can also be used in code that has no user interface, including command line tools.

Listing 11.7 is an example of drawing a piece of text in one font at a specific point size using ATSUI. The code creates an ATSU style that describes the font and size requested and an ATSU text layout that specifies the style and glyphs to be drawn. The drawing that the code performs is shown in Figure 11.8. The point at the beginning of each line of text in the figure indicates the starting point for the text drawing on that line. As you can see from the figure, ATSUI text drawing uses the y coordinate of the starting point for positioning the text baseline when drawing text.

The code in the example consists of the routine drawTextWithATSUI and several supporting routines. The first time drawTextWithATSUI is called, it calls createTheATSUIStyle to create an ATSUStyle object that corresponds to the PostScript

Figure 11.8 Drawing text using the function ATSUDrawText

Starting location for each text drawing in the code

font Times-Roman at a size of 60 points. It then creates an ATSUTextLayout object for the text string to draw with the style. It keeps the layout in a static variable so that it keeps the layout object across calls to drawTextWithATSUI. By doing so, it caches the results of laying out the text so that subsequent redraws take advantage of the cached results. Note that as with several of the earlier text drawing examples, for convenience this example selects the font by its PostScript font name. Most applications will choose the font based on a user selection in the font panel or some other method.

Once the layout is constructed, the code calls the routine setContextForLayout to specify the drawing destination. The ATSUI text drawing functions don't explicitly have the destination context as a function argument but instead the context is specified as an attribute of the layout. (This is a result of the fact that the ATSUI programming interface is originally based on the QuickDraw graphics API where the drawing destination is an application global variable.) The routine setContextForLayout sets the kATSUCGContextTag attribute on the layout, using the destination CGContextRef as the value. ATSUI does *not* retain the context (such as by using `CGContextRetain` or `CFRetain`); instead, the context is simply associated with the layout for a subsequent drawing call. Typically, you set the context in the layout just before drawing it.

The code draws each of the lines of text, first setting the appropriate fill and stroke color, then calling the routine `myATSUDrawTextAtPoint`. This routine is an inline routine that is a simple cover routine for the ATSUI function `ATSUDraw-Text`. Instead of taking a fixed-point number for the x and y coordinates of the initial starting point, it takes a floating-point number that it converts to a fixed-point value prior to calling `ATSUDrawText`. This means that coordinate values passed to `myATSUDrawTextAtPoint` must be limited to the range that can be represented by a fixed-point number (approximately that of an `SInt16`). While unlikely to be an issue for most developers, you can work around this limitation by using Quartz coordinate translations if necessary.

While not demonstrated in this example, ATSUI text drawing supports font fallback substitution. Font fallback substitution is not on by default, but you can turn it on by setting the font matching attribute on the layout using function `ATSUSetTransientFontMatching` to obtain equivalent behavior to that in Cocoa text drawing and Carbon theme text drawing.

Listing 11.7　Drawing text with ATSUI

```
static OSStatus createTheATSUIStyle(
            const unsigned char *postScriptFontName,
            float fontSize, ATSUStyle *theStyle)
{
  OSStatus err = noErr;;
  ATSUStyle style;
  ATSUFontID atsuFont;
  Fixed atsuSize;

  // Create three parallel arrays for setting up attributes.
  ATSUAttributeTag theTags[2];
  ByteCount theSizes[2];
  ATSUAttributeValuePtr theValues[2];

  // Set up to return a NULL style to the caller if there is
  // any error before the correct style is created.
  *theStyle = NULL;

  style = NULL;
  atsuFont = 0;
  atsuSize = FloatToFixed(fontSize);
```

```
    // Obtain the ATSUFontID for the PostScript name.
    err = ATSUFindFontFromName(postScriptFontName,
                strlen(postScriptFontName),
                kFontPostscriptName, kFontNoPlatformCode,
                kFontNoScriptCode,  kFontNoLanguageCode,
                &atsuFont);
    if(err){
      fprintf(stderr, "Couldn't get ATSU font!\n");
      return err;
    }

    // The 0 element of these three arrays is the ATSU font.
    theTags[0] = kATSUFontTag;
    theSizes[0] = sizeof(ATSUFontID);
    theValues[0] = &atsuFont;

    // The 1 element of these three arrays is the font size.
    theTags[1] = kATSUSizeTag;
    theSizes[1] = sizeof(Fixed);
    theValues[1] = &atsuSize;

    // Create an ATSU style.
    err = ATSUCreateStyle(&style);
    if(err){
      if(style)ATSUDisposeStyle(style);
      return err;
    }

    // Set the attributes on the style.
    err = ATSUSetAttributes(style,
      sizeof(theTags)/sizeof(theTags[0]),
      theTags, theSizes, theValues);
    if(err){
      if(style)ATSUDisposeStyle(style);
      return err;
    }

    // Pass the style created back to the caller.
    *theStyle = style;
    return noErr;
}
static OSStatus createLayoutForString(CFStringRef theString,
                ATSUStyle style, ATSUTextLayout *layoutP)
{
```

```
            ATSUTextLayout theLayout = NULL;
            CFIndex textLength;
            OSStatus err = noErr;
            UniChar *uniBuffer;
            CFRange uniRange;

            // Set up to return a NULL layout to the caller if there is an
            // error creating the desired layout.
            *layoutP = NULL;

            textLength = CFStringGetLength(theString);
            if (textLength == 0) return noErr;

            // Get the Unicode data from the CFString.
            uniRange = CFRangeMake(0, textLength);
            uniBuffer = (UniChar *) malloc(textLength * sizeof(UniChar) );
            if (uniBuffer == NULL){
              return memFullErr;
            }
            CFStringGetCharacters(theString, uniRange, uniBuffer);

            // Create the ATSUI layout as a single run with the
            // requested style.
            err = ATSUCreateTextLayoutWithTextPtr(uniBuffer, 0,
                        textLength, textLength, 1,
                        (unsigned long *) &textLength, &style,
                        &theLayout);
            if(err){
              free(uniBuffer);
              return err;
            }

            *layoutP = theLayout;

            return err;
        }

        static OSStatus setContextForLayout(CGContextRef context,
                    ATSUTextLayout theLayout)
        {
          ByteCount iSize = sizeof(CGContextRef);
          ATSUAttributeTag iTag = kATSUCGContextTag;
          ATSUAttributeValuePtr iValuePtr = &context;
          // Setting this tag on the layout causes ATSUI to draw to
```

```
    // this context.
    return ATSUSetLayoutControls(theLayout, 1, &iTag,
                &iSize, &iValuePtr );
}


static inline OSStatus myATSUDrawTextAtPoint(ATSUTextLayout theLayout,
                UniCharCount numUnicodeChars,
                float x, float y)
{
    return ATSUDrawText(theLayout, 0, numUnicodeChars,
                FloatToFixed(x), FloatToFixed(y));
}


void drawTextWithATSUI(CGContextRef context)
{
    OSStatus err = noErr;
    static ATSUTextLayout theLayout = NULL;
    CFStringRef    textString = CFSTR("Quartz");
    UniCharCount numTextChars = CFStringGetLength(textString);

    float opaqueRed[] = { 0.663, 0., 0.031, 1. };
    float fontSize = 60;

    // For this drawing routine, the layout will be created the first time
    // it is called and that layout will be used upon subsequent redraws.
    if(theLayout == NULL){
        ATSUStyle theTextStyle = NULL;
        // Create the style to use for the text to draw.
        err = createTheATSUIStyle("Times-Roman", fontSize,
                &theTextStyle);
        if(err){
            fprintf(stderr,
                "Got error %d creating ATSU style!\n", err);
            return;
        }
        // Create the layout with the text and style.
        err = createLayoutForString(textString, theTextStyle,
                &theLayout);
        if(err){
            ATSUDisposeStyle(theTextStyle);
            fprintf(stderr,
                "Got error %d creating the layout!\n", err);
            return;
        }
    }
```

```
// To have ATSUI draw to a specific context, the context is added
// to the layout. This must be done each time the destination
// context changes.
err = setContextForLayout(context, theLayout);
if(err){
  fprintf(stderr,
    "Got error %d setting the context on the layout!\n", err);
  return;
}

// Set the fill and stroke color space. This sets the
// fill and stroke painting color to opaque black.
CGContextSetFillColorSpace(context, getTheRGBColorSpace());
CGContextSetStrokeColorSpace(context, getTheRGBColorSpace());

// ***** Text Line 1: filled text *****

// ATSUI text drawing respects the fill color as long as it
// isn't a style attribute. Set the fill color to red.
CGContextSetFillColor(context, opaqueRed);

CGContextTranslateCTM(context, 20, 220);

err = myATSUDrawTextAtPoint(theLayout, numTextChars, 0, 0);
if(err)fprintf(stderr, "Got error %d showing ATSUI text\n", err);

// ***** Text Line 2: stroked text *****

CGContextTranslateCTM(context, 0, -65);

// Set the text drawing mode to stroke.
CGContextSetTextDrawingMode(context, kCGTextStroke);

err = myATSUDrawTextAtPoint(theLayout, numTextChars, 0, 0);
if(err)fprintf(stderr, "Got error %d showing ATSUI text\n", err);

// ***** Text Line 3: filled and stroked text *****
CGContextTranslateCTM(context, 0, -65);

// Set the text drawing mode to fill+stroke.
CGContextSetTextDrawingMode(context, kCGTextFillStroke);

err = myATSUDrawTextAtPoint(theLayout, numTextChars, 0, 0);
if(err)fprintf(stderr, "Got error %d showing ATSUI text\n", err);
```

```
// ***** Text Line 4: filled and stroked text, then clipped *****
CGContextTranslateCTM(context, 0, -65);

CGContextSaveGState(context);
   // Set the text drawing mode to fill+stroke, then clip.
   CGContextSetTextDrawingMode(context, kCGTextFillStrokeClip);

   err = myATSUDrawTextAtPoint(theLayout, numTextChars, 0, 0);
   if(err)fprintf(stderr, "Got error %d showing ATSUI text\n", err);

   // Draw a set of grid lines, clipped by the text characters.
   drawGridLines(context);
CGContextRestoreGState(context);

}
```

ATSUI text drawing respects most of the Quartz graphics state and context parameters (such as the CTM and the current clipping area) with a few notable exceptions. ATSUI text drawing ignores the font and font styles in the graphics state; these parameters are specified by the style in the layout being drawn. The current text matrix in the context at the time you call ATSUI text drawing routines is ignored; instead, ATSUI sets the text matrix for its text drawing. ATSUI performs layout of the text, positions the text characters, and ignores the extra character space parameter of the graphics state. After it performs text rendering, ATSUI restores the text matrix to the one in effect prior to calling ATSUI and updates the tx, ty components of the text matrix to reflect the width of the text just drawn.

As long as the ATSUStyle object characterizing the layout doesn't contain attributes that override the context values, the current graphics state parameters are used when drawing text with ATSUI. If you don't specify the text color in the style characterizing the layout, the context fill or stroke color is used appropriately. Note that since ATSUI draws underlines as filled rectangles, the context fill color is used to paint underlines unless you specify an underline color attribute in the style. The anti-alias parameter in the graphics state is respected as long as you don't use the ATSUI-defined anti-aliasing tags. (Text is not anti-aliased for point sizes at or below the threshold set by the user in the Appearance system preference, even if the context parameters request anti-aliasing.) The graphics state shadow parameter is respected as long as you don't use the kATSUStyleDropShadowTag on the style; doing so overrides the shadow in the context. ATSUI text drawing is affected by the current font smoothing setting in the graphics state.

As just seen in the example, the Quartz text drawing mode is respected by ATSUI text drawing. (The exception to this is where you set the style attribute kATSUQDBoldfaceTag and the font does not contain an intrinsic bold style—in this case, ATSUI synthesizes a bold face by using the kCGTextFillStroke mode to artificially embolden the text.) You can use the clip text drawing modes; however, if there is a style run that requires multiple calls to the low-level Quartz text drawing API to render, the resulting clipping area is most likely empty. You can work around this by drawing one character at a time if need be—see the discussion about the clip text modes in "Text Drawing Modes" (page 292).

Other than modifying the graphics state clipping area when using a text drawing mode that applies a clip, using ATSUI text rendering does not produce any changes to the context graphics state. ATSUI text rendering carefully manages any changes it needs to make to the graphics state so that they behave as if they are encapsulated within CGContextSaveGState and CGContextRestoreGState.

ATSUI performs its text drawing so that drawing into a context that has the default Quartz orientation (y coordinate values increase as you go up the drawing canvas) produces upright reading text. When drawing into a view where the coordinate system is flipped, such as in an HIView with the standard HIView orientation, you can adjust the coordinate system prior to drawing the text so that it is upright, draw the text using ATSUI, then restore the coordinate system. See "Drawing Text in a Flipped Coordinate System" (below) for an example of how you might do this.

ATSUI also provides the ability to obtain the outlines of the glyphs in a layout. This would be useful, for example, if you want to clip to these glyphs without concerns about font changes in a text run. The references at the end of this chapter provide a link to a code example Apple provides to demonstrate this.

Drawing Text in a Flipped Coordinate System

Working in a flipped coordinate system, such as the default HIView coordinate system, where the y axis is inverted relative to the default Quartz coordinate system, requires some extra care when drawing text. Without taking into account the flipped nature of the coordinate system, you may find that your text drawing produces text that is upside down and appears like it would look in a mirror, such as the text on the left side of Figure 11.9. The Cocoa text drawing methods draw correctly in flipped views—in order to obtain text that is properly oriented in a Cocoa view that is flipped, the view should implement an isFlipped method that returns YES. Theme text drawing with

Figure 11.9 Drawing text with ATSUI in a flipped coordinate system (each dot indicates the text starting location)

`HIThemeDrawTextBox` can accommodate drawing into a flipped view by passing `kHIThemeOrientationNormal` for the `orientation` parameter.

As shown earlier, the text matrix can be used to flip text if drawing directly with a text drawing framework that respects the text matrix, such as Quartz. This allows you to flip text without adjusting the CTM prior to drawing the text. The code in Listing 11.2 (page 301) shows one way you might accomplish this. However, all the Cocoa and Carbon framework text drawing facilities discussed in this chapter use the text matrix as part of their drawing, ignoring any setting you may have applied. If you need to flip text when drawing framework text and the framework doesn't supply a way for you to do so, you'll have to apply changes to the CTM prior to drawing your text.

The code in Listing 11.8 draws ATSUI text into a context that has a flipped coordinate system. It defines a routine `myFlippedATSUDrawTextAtPoint` that is equivalent to the `myATSUDrawTextAtPoint` routine in Listing 11.7 (page 332), except that prior to drawing the text with `ATSUDrawText`, the code adjusts for a flipped coordinate system. The code first makes a snapshot of the context graphics state so that it can isolate the caller from any coordinate transformations it performs. Next it translates the origin of coordinates to the point where the starting point of the text is to begin. It then scales the CTM with an x scaling factor of 1 and a y scaling factor of -1 to flip the coordinate system about the x axis so that the orientation matches the default Quartz coordinate system. Now the coordinate origin is located at the starting location of the text and the orientation will produce upright reading text. The code calls `ATSUDrawText` to draw the text, using (0,0) as the starting point for the text since the current Quartz origin now corresponds to the point passed to the function. After drawing the text, the code restores the graphics state to that in effect when the routine was called.

The remaining code fragment in Listing 11.8 demonstrates use of the `myFlipped-ATSUDrawTextAtPoint` to draw text in a flipped context. The output of the code is shown in Figure 11.9. If the coordinate system of the context is flipped prior to the execution of the code fragment in Listing 11.8, the result will be that shown in the figure. The text on the left of the figure is drawn using myATSUDrawTextAt-Point in Listing 11.7 (page 332) and is flipped because it is drawn into a view where the coordinate system is flipped. The text that is drawn on the right using myFlippedATSUDrawTextAtPoint is upright. The point at the beginning of each piece of text is the starting location of the text.

Note that the myFlippedATSUDrawTextAtPoint routine assumes that the context passed to the routine is the destination context and is the same context associated with the layout, as set by setContextForLayout in Listing 11.7 (page 332). Recall that ATSUI requires the destination context to be set as an attribute of the layout in order to draw to that context.

Listing 11.8 Drawing flipped text with ATSUI

```
static OSStatus myFlippedATSUDrawTextAtPoint(
                CGContextRef c,
                ATSUTextLayout theLayout,
                UniCharCount numUnicodeChars,
                float x, float y)
{
  OSStatus err;
  CGContextSaveGState(c);
    // Translate to the point where the text should start.
    CGContextTranslateCTM(c, x, y);
    // Scale by -1 in the y coordinate.
    CGContextScaleCTM(c, 1, -1);
    err = ATSUDrawText(theLayout, 0, numUnicodeChars, 0, 0);
  // Restore to the graphics state in effect when this code was called.
  CGContextRestoreGState(c);

  return err;
}


  ...
  // Now some code to demonstrate using this code in a flipped view.
  // Draw text at (20, 120). In a flipped view this text will be flipped.
  myATSUDrawTextAtPoint(theLayout, numTextChars, 20, 120);
  // Draw flipped text at (220, 120). In a flipped view this text
  // will be upright.
  myFlippedATSUDrawTextAtPoint(context, theLayout,
                numTextChars, 220, 120);
```

Summary

Quartz text drawing produces high-quality anti-aliased text that is part of what gives the Mac OS X user interface its good looks. However, the Quartz text drawing API is a low-level API that is not suitable for most application developers and is better suited as a building block for building the higher-level text drawing frameworks. Knowing the way Quartz text drawing is affected by the graphics state and context parameters can be helpful when using the higher-level text facilities available in Cocoa and Carbon.

The text drawing facilities in both the Cocoa and Carbon frameworks support Unicode text and provide powerful text layout capabilities. This chapter only scratches the surface as to what is available. You are encouraged to explore the sample code and references that Apple makes available on the ADC website.

See Also

For more information on Cocoa text drawing, see the following documents from the ADC Reference Library:

- A large number of documents discussing Cocoa text are available at

  http://developer.apple.com/documentation/Cocoa/TextFonts-date.html

- An overview of drawing strings using Cocoa can be found at

  http://developer.apple.com/documentation/Cocoa/Conceptual/TextLayout/Tasks/DrawingStrings.html

- Documentation on the attributes that Cocoa text strings can have is available at

  http://developer.apple.com/documentation/Cocoa/Reference/ApplicationKit/ObjC_classic/Classes/NSAttributedString.html

  The header file `NSAttributedString.h` in the AppKit framework headers also has information about the attributes you can apply.

For more information on Carbon text drawing, see the following documents from the ADC Reference Library:

- Carbon text and font documentation is available at

  http://developer.apple.com/documentation/Carbon/TextFonts-date.html

  This includes documentation on a variety of text and font related topics.

- DrawThemeTextBox and the associated functions are documented in *Appearance Manager Reference* available at

  http://developer.apple.com/documentation/Carbon/Reference/ Appearance_Manager/index.html

  The prototypes and structures associated with these functions are defined in `Appearance.h` in the HIToolbox subframework that is part of the Carbon framework.

- *ATSUI Reference* is the reference documentation for ATSUI and is available at

  http://developer.apple.com/documentation/Carbon/Reference/ATSUI_Reference/ index.html

- *Rendering Unicode Text with ATSUI* provides conceptual material about ATSUI useful for working with ATSUI and is available at

  http://developer.apple.com/documentation/Carbon/Conceptual/ ATSUI_Concepts/index.html

- Discussion and an example of obtaining the glyph outlines of an ATSUI layout are available at

  http://developer.apple.com/documentation/Carbon/Conceptual/ ATSUI_Concepts/atsui_chap7/chapter_7_section_3.html

- *Multilingual Text Engine Reference* is the reference documentation for MLTE and is available at

  http://developer.apple.com/documentation/Carbon/Reference/ Multilingual_Text_Engine/index.html

- *Handling Unicode Text Editing with MLTE* provides conceptual material about MLTE and is available at

  http://developer.apple.com/documentation/Carbon/Conceptual/ HandlingUnicodeText_MLTE/index.html

  The prototypes and structures associated with these functions are defined in the header file `MacTextEditor.h` in the HIToolbox subframework that is part of the Carbon framework.

- Many examples of using ATSUI are installed as part of the Tiger Developer SDK. See the directory `/Developer/Examples/ATSUI`.

The Unicode website *www.unicode.org* provides extensive information about Unicode, including character charts.

- Unicode character code charts are available at

  www.unicode.org/charts

- The MacRoman character encoding is documented at

  www.unicode.org/Public/MAPPINGS/VENDORS/APPLE/ROMAN.TXT

For more information about Apple Type Services (ATS), see the following documents from the ADC Reference Library:

- *Apple Type Services for Fonts Reference* is the reference documentation for ATS and is available at

  http://developer.apple.com/documentation/Carbon/Reference/ATS/index.html

- *Managing Fonts: ATS* provides conceptual material about ATS and is available at

  http://developer.apple.com/documentation/Carbon/Conceptual/ATS_Concepts/index.html

The header files relevant to drawing text with Quartz are

- `CGFont.h`, which contains the Quartz functions for creating and working with CGFont objects.
- `CGContext.h`, which contains the Quartz functions for text drawing.

The relevant reference documentation from the ADC Reference Library is

- *CGFont Reference*
- *CGContext Reference*

Chapter

12

Creating Bits

There are two ways to capture drawing in Quartz—through drawing commands or by creating bitmap raster data (or bits). A PDF representation of Quartz drawing captures drawing commands in their most abstract form. The commands execute when you view the content, which means you can choose the resolution of a PDF document at viewing time. You can change the resolution of the content as you view it and the content still appears sharp.

Bitmap image formats, in contrast, represent a pre-rendered (or rasterized) form of Quartz drawing. You set the image resolution when you create the image content. Drawing the image at the original size produces good fidelity, but if you zoom in on the image, you'll see artifacts because the clarity is limited by the image resolution.

Despite the limitations of using bits to capture drawing, there are times when bits are a better choice than PDF. Not all applications in Mac OS X support PDF data and most other computing platforms do not have the rich PDF support that Mac OS X has. However, image formats like PNG and JPEG are almost universally supported. If the drawing you want to capture might be used outside your application, you'll want to be able to export your drawing into graphics formats other than PDF.

There are other reasons for creating bits from Quartz drawing. Some applications want to capture drawing so that they can cache content that they later want to draw to the screen. In this case, capturing the drawing as bits rather than as PDF data is typically a better choice.

Quartz provides two drawing destinations for creating bits: the bitmap graphics context and the CGLayer object. A bitmap graphics context allows you to draw to a piece of memory you have access to. Most developers are familiar with this concept from QuickDraw or other graphics systems.

The CGLayer object, when created from a context that represents a window or a bitmap context, works as an optimized offspring of a bitmap graphics context. (A CGLayer object can be used for more than creating bits; see "Advanced Drawing Features" (page 481) for more details.) Introduced in Tiger, CGLayer objects offer a number of benefits over bitmap graphics contexts, as you'll see in "CGLayers (Tiger)" (page 371).

Bitmap Graphics Context

A bitmap graphics context allows you to draw content to a piece of memory that you have access to. Like every other Quartz graphics context, a bitmap context is represented by the `CGContextRef` data type. Bitmap graphics contexts are available that support Gray, RGB, and CMYK destinations. In addition, Quartz provides a bitmap context that records only the alpha coverage of Quartz drawing.

You can use bitmap contexts for a variety of reasons, including to

- Perform offscreen drawing for later copying to a window context so that the drawing is shown onscreen. "Caching Drawing Offscreen" (page 379) discusses the topic in detail.

- Export a CGImage object as PNG or JPEG data to a URL, the Clipboard, or other destination. See "Using the Bitmap Data from a Bitmap Context" (page 357) for details.

- Create a CGImage object from Quartz drawing that you want to process with one or more Core Image filters. ("See Also" (page 393) lists references for the Core Image framework.)

- Create a bitmap representation to use as a texture with OpenGL so that you can mix Quartz drawing with OpenGL drawing.

- Mix Quartz content with content that your application draws using its own custom rendering code.

Supported Pixel Formats

Quartz supports the creation of a bitmap context with any of the pixel formats shown in Table 12.1. The table lists the complete set of bitmap context formats that are available as of Tiger. Not all formats are available in all versions of Mac OS X. The last column of the table indicates the first version of Mac OS X in which a given format is available.

A pixel format consists of the number of components in the color space, the number of bits per component, the number of bits per pixel, and the location of the alpha data (if any). For creation of a bitmap context, Quartz only supports one-, three-, and four-component color spaces (Gray, RGB, and CMYK), plus a special bitmap context that consists only of alpha coverage. (CMYK pixel formats are only available in Panther and later versions.) Most of the supported pixel formats are 8 bits per component, with the exception of the 5-bits-per-component format (16 bits per pixel) available in all versions of Mac OS X and the 32-bits-per-component floating-point formats added in Tiger.

Several bitmap context formats support the capturing of alpha data along with the component color data; these are the ARGB and RGBA formats listed in the table. (Note that alpha is premultiplied when rendering to the ARGB or RGBA formats.) In addition to the ARGB and RGBA bitmap formats that capture alpha, the XRGB and RGBX bitmap formats are available. These formats treat the destination alpha as if it is always 1 (completely opaque). The Gray and CMYK bitmap context formats have no support for recording alpha data; they treat the destination alpha as if it is always 1 (completely opaque). In addition to these formats, Panther introduced a special bitmap context that supports the recording of alpha data only.

You might be wondering why Quartz provides ARGB and RGBA format bitmap contexts in addition to XRGB and RGBX bitmap contexts. Typically, you use RGB format contexts that record alpha when you are drawing content offscreen that you later want to composite onscreen. In that situation you want to be sure that the portions of your drawing that are transparent are treated as such. Another situation where you want to capture alpha in your bitmap context is when you are exporting the bitmap data to a format that can represent alpha, such as PNG or TIFF. If you are instead exporting bitmap data to a format that doesn't support alpha, such as JPEG, you don't want any alpha data component.

In Table 12.1 the Bitmap Info Value column refers to the Quartz constant that specifies the type and location of the alpha data and whether the format is floating point (available in Tiger and later versions). Table 12.1 is exhaustive; it contains the complete set of bitmap contexts available as of the initial release of Tiger. This is different than Table 9.3 (page 216), which describes a subset of source bitmap *image* formats supported by Quartz. Note that "Bitmap Contexts and Universal Binaries (Tiger)" (page 355) discusses issues of the data byte ordering in a bitmap context.

Table 12.1 Complete List of Supported Quartz Bitmap Content Formats as of Tiger

Pixel Format	Bits per Component	Bits per Pixel	Bitmap Info Value	Color Space	Available Starting in Mac OS X
1-component, 8-bit data, no alpha: GGGG...	8	8	kCGImageAlphaNone	Gray	10.0
3-component, 16-bit data, no alpha, 1 leading padding bit: XRGBXRGB...	5	16	kCGImageAlphaNoneSkipFirst	RGB	10.0
3-component, 32-bit data, no alpha, 1 leading padding byte: XRGBXRGB...	8	32	kCGImageAlphaNoneSkipFirst	RGB	10.0
3-component, 32-bit data, no alpha, 1 trailing padding byte: RGBXRGBX...	8	32	kCGImageAlphaNoneSkipLast	RGB	10.0
3-component, 32-bit data with leading premultiplied alpha byte: ARGBARGB...	8	32	kCGImageAlphaPremultipliedFirst	RGB	10.0
3-component, 32-bit data with trailing premultiplied alpha byte: RGBARGBA...	8	32	kCGImageAlphaPremultipliedLast	RGB	10.0
4-component, 32-bit data with no alpha, no padding bits: CMYKCMYK...	8	32	kCGImageAlphaNone	CMYK	10.3
1-component, 8-bit alpha only: AAAA...	8	8	kCGImageAlphaOnly	NULL	10.3
1-component, 32-bit floating-point data per component with no alpha, no padding bits: GGGG...	32	32	kCGImageAlphaNone | kCGBitmapFloatComponents	Gray	10.4
3-component, 32-bit floating-point data per component, with no alpha, 4 trailing padding bytes: RGBXRGBX...	32	128	kCGImageAlphaNoneSkipLast | kCGBitmapFloatComponents	RGB	10.4
3-component, 32-bit floating-point data per component, with trailing premultiplied alpha: RGBARGBA...	32	128	kCGImageAlphaPremultiplied-Last | kCGBitmapFloatComponents	RGB	10.4

continued

Table 12.1 Continued

Pixel Format	Bits per Component	Bits per Pixel	Bitmap Info Value	Color Space	Available Starting in Mac OS X
4-component, 32-bit floating-point data per component, with no alpha, no padding bits: CMYKCMYK...	32	128	kCGImageAlphaNone | kCGBitmapFloatComponents	CMYK	10.4

Creating a Bitmap Graphics Context

You create a bitmap graphics context using the function CGBitmapContextCreate. This function takes the following parameters:

- data, a pointer to the memory buffer you provide for the raster bitmap data. The size must be at least (bytesPerRow*height) bytes.
- width, the number of pixels in each row of the raster.
- height, the number of rows in the raster.
- bitsPerComponent, the number of bits per component in each pixel.
- bytesPerRow, the number of bytes in each row of the raster.
- colorSpace, a Quartz color space characterizing the raster data.
- bitmapInfo (formerly called alphaInfo), which specifies the location of alpha data in each pixel. In Tiger and later versions, bitmapInfo also specifies whether the pixel format is floating point.

The function CGBitmapContextCreate which returns a Quartz bitmap context that you can use to draw to and capture any Quartz drawing as bits. If Quartz can't create a bitmap context using the parameters you specify, it returns NULL. This happens if you supply parameters that specify a format that is not available in the version of Mac OS X that's executing your code.

The new bitmap context is created with an initial CTM that is the identity transform. The initial coordinate system scaling is 1 unit equals 1 pixel and the Quartz origin is at the lower-left corner of the bitmap raster. Whether this coordinate system is appropriate depends on your needs. You may need to scale the coordinate system to produce high-resolution images or transform it for other purposes. The initial clipping area of the context is the rectangle that bounds the raster, that is, (0,0), (width, height).

A bitmap context that you create has the default context parameters listed in Table 7.1 (page 174) in "Graphics State Parameters" (page 173). If you create the bitmap context yourself you know the initial graphics state. As always, you need to set the graphics state and context parameters appropriate for your drawing task.

There are a few issues associated with creating bitmap contexts that are important to understand, and then you'll see how to create a bitmap graphics context that uses an RGB color space.

Memory Allocation and Byte Alignment. The first parameter you pass to CGBitmap-ContextCreate is the memory block you provide to Quartz for rendering the raster. You are responsible for allocating the memory you want to use for your bitmap. As a general rule, it's a good idea to use the UNIX function calloc to allocate the memory, because it initializes the memory to zero. The Mac OS X memory allocation routines ensure that your memory block starts with appropriate byte alignment, helping to ensure you'll get optimum performance with the Quartz rendering engine.

The bytesPerRow parameter that you pass to CGBitmapContextCreate is the number of bytes in each row of your raster. The minimum allowable value is the number of bytes for each pixel, multiplied by the number of pixels in a row of the raster, which is specified in the width parameter. (Specifying a value lower than the minimum allowable value will cause Quartz to return a NULL context.) However, in many cases you can achieve improved Quartz performance by providing additional padding bytes at the end of each row. For example, Quartz optimizes performance on Altivec-enabled systems and can benefit from special byte alignment values. The optimal padding for bytesPerRow is system dependent. A good rule of thumb is to use a value of bytesPerRow that is a multiple of 16. The example code in this chapter shows how to do this.

Note   The guideline to use a bytesPerRow value that is a multiple of 16 is current as of Tiger. It's important to look to the ADC website for updates to these guidelines as Quartz is optimized in the future.

Color Space Considerations. You might notice that none of the arguments to CGBitmapContextCreate explicitly specifies the number of color components in each pixel. Quartz deduces the number of color components for the bitmap context from the colorSpace parameter you supply. The colorSpace is a Quartz CGColorSpace object that characterizes the bitmap data you are creating. The number of components in the color space, together with the bitmapInfo parameter, specifies the pixel format.

The color space associated with the bitmap context does more than determine the type and number of color components, it also determines what destination color space is used for matching color. From earlier chapters you know that when you draw using Quartz, the color values you use in your source graphics are color matched to the destination. For a window-based context, the destination is the screen display; the bits associated with a window are characterized by a color space appropriate for the display. For a bitmap context, the creator of the context determines what color space is appropriate for it. The best choice depends on the ultimate purpose of the bits being created.

Which color space you should use depends on your usage of the bitmap context. If you create content that you later want to draw to a display, you'll want to use a color space characterized by the color profile of the display. If you create content that you want to export as bits, you probably want to use a calibrated profile. Typically, the generic calibrated profiles are good choices. When exporting bits using generic calibrated profiles, which profile you'll want to use depends on the number of color components and how you'll use the data you are exporting.

If you create a bitmap context to capture only alpha data (the alpha-only context), you pass NULL for the colorSpace parameter. An alpha-only context has no color information, only alpha coverage data, as you'll see in "Using an Alpha-Only Bitmap Context (Panther)" (page 366).

Erasing and Clearing a Context. Quartz doesn't initialize or erase the memory you provide—that is up to you. How you intend to use the bitmap context determines how you'll want to prepare it before you begin your drawing. Typical ways of preparing the context are either to fill it with a background color such as white or to clear the pixels.

When you create a bitmap context to use for capturing alpha data, before drawing you usually want to first clear the pixels in the context so that each pixel has a starting color that is completely transparent. When you then draw to the raster, the only pixels that have a pixel value that is not completely transparent are those pixels that are painted by your drawing. Areas that are not touched by your drawing will have an alpha value of zero.

The function CGContextClearRect takes a context and a rectangle that specifies the area in the context to clear. As with all Quartz drawing, the rectangle coordinates are interpreted in the Quartz user space coordinate system. Pixels that are completely inside the rectangle are completely cleared; their alpha value is set to 0. Pixels that are only partially inside the rectangle are only cleared to the extent of their coverage. For example, if the rectangle passed to CGContextClearRect only covers 50% of a given pixel, that pixel has its alpha value set to 0.5.

Be sure to adjust your rectangle to completely enclose those pixels that you want to clear. The simplest way to ensure that all of the pixels in a context are cleared is to clear immediately after you create the context and before applying any coordinate transformations to it. In that case, the complete context raster is covered by a CGRect that has its origin at (0,0) with a size specified by the width and height of the bitmap context.

You should use CGContextClearRect solely with bit-based contexts, such as bitmap contexts that capture alpha or CGLayer objects created from windows. Depending on your use of transparent windows, you may also want to use CGContextClearRect. When used with these types of contexts, CGContextClearRect has the semantics just described. The behavior of CGContextClearRect with other contexts such as nontransparent windows or PDF and printing contexts is undefined. The function CGContextClearRect should not be used with these types of contexts.

Caution   The behavior of CGContextClearRect with contexts that are not bit-based, such as a PDF or printing context, is undefined and you should avoid using it.

For bitmap contexts that don't capture alpha, you probably want to initialize the contents with a background drawing color, typically white. Quartz provides no direct function to do this. Instead, you set the fill color to the background color and use CGContextFillRect to fill a rectangle that encloses the pixels in the bitmap context.

Failing to clear or erase your pixels can be a source of drawing artifacts you might not understand. You can avoid artifacts by properly initializing or clearing the context raster prior to drawing.

Note that if you are mixing Quartz drawing with that of another drawing system, such as a custom drawing system you provide in your code or with another Mac OS X drawing system such as QuickDraw, it is probably best to first create the context and initialize it with Quartz prior to drawing into it at all.

Text Smoothing. In Jaguar and later versions, Quartz and Mac OS X provide special text rendering referred to as text smoothing. Text smoothing does not determine whether text is anti-aliased but instead determines whether special techniques are used when drawing anti-aliased text, some of which depend on the alpha value of the destination in order to produce optimal and visually appealing results.

Depending on the ultimate destination for the data you are creating in your bitmap context, you may want to disable text smoothing using CGContextSetShouldSmoothFonts. For example, the default text smoothing setting may be appropriate for drawing to an LCD display but not for exporting in an image. See "Font Smoothing (Jaguar)" (page 295) for additional discussion of text smoothing.

Creating an RGB Bitmap Context. Now that you've seen some of the issues involved in creating a bitmap context, take a look at Listing 12.1. This code defines a routine `createRGBBitmapContext` that takes four parameters and returns the `CGContextRef` for the RGB bitmap context it creates. You'll see the `createRGB-BitmapContext` routine used a few times later on. You'll use it to export Quartz drawing into several different image formats and also to create an offscreen representation of drawing that will be used to render to an onscreen window.

The parameters to the `createRGBBitmapContext` routine are

- `width`, the number of pixels you want in each row of the bitmap raster context you are creating.

- `height`, the number of rows you want in the bitmap raster context you are creating.

- `wantDisplayColorSpace`, a `Boolean` that if `true`, creates a bitmap context characterized by the display color space; otherwise the context is characterized by the generic calibrated RGB color space.

- `needsTransparentBitmap`, a `Boolean` that if `true`, causes the bitmap context to be created as an ARGB context and cleared by `CGContextClearRect`. If `false`, the context returned is an XRGB context filled with opaque white.

Listing 12.1 Code that creates an RGB bitmap context

```
#define BEST_BYTE_ALIGNMENT 16
#define COMPUTE_BEST_BYTES_PER_ROW(bpr)\
  ( ( (bpr) + (BEST_BYTE_ALIGNMENT-1) ) & ~(BEST_BYTE_ALIGNMENT-1) )

CGContextRef createRGBBitmapContext(size_t width, size_t height,
            Boolean wantDisplayColorSpace,
            Boolean needsTransparentBitmap)
{
  CGContextRef context;
  size_t bytesPerRow;
  unsigned char *rasterData;

  // Minimum bytes per row is 4 bytes per sample * number of samples.
  bytesPerRow = width*4;
  // Round up to nearest multiple of 16.
  bytesPerRow = COMPUTE_BEST_BYTES_PER_ROW(bytesPerRow);
```

```
// Use the function 'calloc' so that the memory is
// initialized to 0.
rasterData = calloc(1, bytesPerRow * height);
if(rasterData == NULL){
  fprintf(stderr,
    "Couldn't allocate the needed amount of memory!\n");
  return NULL;
}

// The wantDisplayColorSpace argument passed to the function
// determines whether or not to use the display color space or
// the generic calibrated RGB color space.
context = CGBitmapContextCreate(rasterData, width, height,
              8, bytesPerRow,
              (wantDisplayColorSpace ? getTheDisplayColorSpace():
                getTheCalibratedRGBColorSpace()),
              (needsTransparentBitmap ? kCGImageAlphaPremultipliedFirst :
                kCGImageAlphaNoneSkipFirst)
  );
if(context == NULL){
  // If the context couldn't be created, release the raster memory.
  free(rasterData);
  fprintf(stderr, "Couldn't create the context!\n");
  return NULL;
}

// Either clear the rect or paint with opaque white, depending on
// the needs of the caller.
if(needsTransparentBitmap){
  // Clear the context bits so they are transparent.
  CGContextClearRect(context, CGRectMake(0, 0, width, height));
}else{
  // Since the drawing destination is opaque, first paint
  // the context bits white.
  CGContextSaveGState(context);
  CGContextSetFillColorWithColor(context, getRGBOpaqueWhiteColor());
  CGContextFillRect(context, CGRectMake(0, 0, width, height));
  CGContextRestoreGState(context);
}

  return context;
}
```

The routine createRGBBitmapContext first calculates the number of bytes to use for each row of the raster. For an XRGB or ARGB context, each pixel in the bitmap uses 4 bytes, 1 byte for alpha (or a skip byte if no alpha is needed) and 3 bytes for the RGB color values. The minimum number of bytes needed for each row of the bitmap is four times the number of pixels in each row of the raster. The actual number of bytesPerRow is computed from the minimum bytesPerRow, using the macro COMPUTE_BEST_BYTES_PER_ROW that rounds up to the nearest multiple of 16 bytes. Recall that 16 bytes is the recommended alignment for each row in a bitmap context.

Next the code uses calloc to allocate and clear the memory for the raster. The size of the block allocated is the number of rows (or scanlines) in the bitmap times the number of bytes in each row. After it allocates the memory for the raster, the code calls CGBitmapContextCreate to create the bitmap context. It passes the pointer to the memory it allocated for the raster, the width and height of the raster, 8 for the number of bits per component, and bytesPerRow.

The color space parameter passed to CGBitmapContextCreate depends on the value of wantDisplayColorSpace supplied to createRGBBitmapContext. When wantDisplayColorSpace is true, the code calls getTheDisplayColorSpace. This is a routine your application would provide (it's not implemented in the listing) that returns a Quartz CGColorSpaceRef that represents the main display of the computer. An implementation of this routine is discussed in detail in "Display Profile Issues" (page 389). In the case where the display color space isn't requested, the routine getTheCalibratedRGBColorSpace obtains a color space for the generic RGB ICC profile, as shown in Listing 7.3 (page 159).

The bitmapInfo parameter passed to CGBitmapContextCreate depends on the value of needsTransparentBitmap passed to the createRGBBitmapContext routine. If the bitmap needs to allow transparent bits, the code uses the bitmapInfo value kCGImageAlphaPremultipliedFirst to specify premultiplied alpha, followed by the pixel color components. If the bitmap needs to be fully opaque, the code uses the bitmapInfo value kCGImageAlphaNoneSkipFirst to specify a skip byte that has no alpha, followed by the pixel color components.

Bitmap Contexts and Universal Binaries (Tiger)

10.4 ▶ As discussed in "Bitmap Images and Universal Binaries (Tiger)" (page 225), universal binaries run natively on both PowerPC- and Intel-based Macintosh computers. The differences in the architectures between these processors is, for the most part, transparent to code that uses the Quartz API. Most applications can use Quartz without concern about which processor is executing the code.

One potential exception is an application that uses a Quartz bitmap context to mix custom rendering with Quartz drawing. Depending on how the application performs its custom rendering, it may be affected by the differences in byte order between processor architectures. Unless otherwise specified, the byte order for a bitmap context is big-endian, also called network byte order, which is the native format for PowerPC processors. If your custom rendering code requires a little-endian ordering of the bitmap data in the context when executing on an Intel-based Macintosh computer, you can use the Bitmap Info value `kCGBitmapByteOrder32Little` or `kCGBitmapByteOrder16Little` to specify a little-endian bitmap data format to Quartz. To calculate a Bitmap Info value that represents a little-endian format, you perform a bitwise `OR` operation using one of these values with the Bitmap Info value from Table 12.1 (page 348) that describes your data. As of Mac OS X version 10.4.3, these constants are only supported on versions of Mac OS X that run on Intel-based Macintosh computers.

The value of `kCGBitmapByteOrder32Little` specifies to Quartz that each 32-bit data word should be treated as little-endian format. For example, using a value of `kCGBitmapByteOrder32Little` when creating a context that specifies an ARGB format with 8 bits per component and 32 bits per pixel produces bitmap data where the ordering of the component data is reversed to BGRA. Using a value of `kCGBitmapByteOrder32Little` to create a context that specifies RGBA floating-point data that is 32 bits per component, produces bitmap data where each color component value is little-endian, but the ordering of the color components in each pixel is unchanged. When using a value of `kCGBitmapByteOrder32Little` when creating a context, either the pixel size or the component size must be 32 bits or else `CGBitmapContextCreate` returns NULL.

See the references at the end of this chapter for more information about creating universal binaries.

Getting Information About a Bitmap Context

After you have a bitmap context, you can use Quartz utility functions (available in Jaguar and later versions) to obtain the parameters used to create a bitmap context. These utility functions are listed in Table 12.2, one to obtain each parameter associated with a bitmap context. These functions are particularly useful when creating an image from a bitmap context.

The function `CGBitmapContextGetBitmapInfo`, available only in Tiger and later versions, returns the same result as `CGBitmapContextGetAlphaInfo` for bitmap contexts that do not have floating-point pixel values or use the endian constants discussed in the preceding section. Calling `CGBitmapContextGetAlphaInfo` in Tiger

Table 12.2 Bitmap Context Utility Functions

Function	Value Returned
CGBitmapContextGetWidth	Width
CGBitmapContextGetHeight	Height
CGBitmapContextGetBitsPerComponent	Bits per component
CGBitmapContextGetBitsPerPixel	Bits per pixel
CGBitmapContextGetBytesPerRow	Bytes per row
CGBitmapContextGetData	A pointer to the bitmap raster data
CGBitmapContextGetColorSpace	Color space
CGBitmapContextGetAlphaInfo	Alpha info (see text)
CGBitmapContextGetBitmapInfo	Bitmap info (see text; Tiger and later versions)

and later versions returns the same data as it did previously. Listing 12.2 includes code that conditionally uses CGBitmapContextGetBitmapInfo to obtain bitmapInfo data when running on systems prior to Tiger.

The bitmap context utility functions each return a nominal default value if the context passed to them is not a bitmap context but is another type of Quartz context. For example, CGBitmapContextGetWidth returns 0 if the context passed to it is a Quartz CGContextRef but is not a bitmap context.

Using the Bitmap Data from a Bitmap Context

There are a number of situations where you might want to create an image from data rendered into a bitmap context. For example, you might want to

- Export offscreen drawing to an external compressed data format using the Quartz CGImageDestination functionality or with QuickTime.
- Move offscreen drawing onscreen by creating an image from your offscreen drawing and drawing that image to a window graphics context. Quartz doesn't provide a direct way to copy or move bitmap data from a bitmap context to another context; instead, you create an image from the bitmap data in the bitmap context and draw that image to the destination context.
- Manipulate the bitmap drawing, either with Quartz or by using Core Image filters.

There are two ways to create an image from a bitmap context. One of them is available only in Tiger and later versions. First you'll see how to create an image in a way that works with all versions of Mac OS X. Later you'll see the Tiger way.

Creating an Image from a Bitmap Context (pre-Tiger). Conceptually, creating an image from the data in a bitmap context is no different from creating any other image. As with any image, you start by creating the image data you want to create the image from. With a bitmap context, this means creating the context and drawing your content to it. After you've rendered your content into the bitmap context, you are ready to create your image.

The code in Listing 12.2 creates a CGImageRef from a bitmap context. The listing consists of the routine createImageFromBitmapContext and two supporting routines. Note that this code uses the bitmap context utility routines shown in Table 12.2 that are available in Jaguar and later versions only. If you need equivalent code to work prior to Jaguar, you'll have to keep track of the bitmap context data in a structure of your own making.

Listing 12.2 Code that creates a CGImage object from bitmap context data

```
static void releaseBitmapContextImageData(void *info,
                const void *data, size_t size)
{
  // Release the image data when Quartz is done with it.
  free((char *)data);
}


CGBitmapInfo myCGContextGetBitmapInfo(CGContextRef c)
{
  // Prior to the availability of CGBitmapContextGetBitmapInfo,
  // the CGAlphaInfo data is equivalent.
  if(&CGBitmapContextGetBitmapInfo != NULL)
    return CGBitmapContextGetBitmapInfo(c);
  else
    return CGBitmapContextGetAlphaInfo(c);
}


// By calling createImageFromBitmapContext, the caller passes
// ownership of the raster memory in the context to this routine.
CGImageRef createImageFromBitmapContext(CGContextRef c)
{
  CGImageRef image;
  // Obtain the raster data from the context.
```

```
      unsigned char *rasterData = CGBitmapContextGetData(c);
      size_t imageDataSize = CGBitmapContextGetBytesPerRow(c)*
                  CGBitmapContextGetHeight(c);
      if(rasterData == NULL){
        fprintf(stderr, "Context is not a bitmap context!\n");
        return NULL;
      }
      // Create the data provider from the raster data, using
      // the release function releaseBitmapContextImageData.
      CGDataProviderRef dataProvider = CGDataProviderCreateWithData(NULL,
                  rasterData,
                  imageDataSize,
                  releaseBitmapContextImageData);

      if(dataProvider == NULL){
        // Since this routine owns the raster memory, it must
        // free it if it can't create the data provider.
        free(rasterData);
        fprintf(stderr, "Couldn't create data provider!\n");
        return NULL;
      }
      // Now create the image. The parameters for the image closely match
      // the parameters of the bitmap context.
      image = CGImageCreate(CGBitmapContextGetWidth(c),
                  CGBitmapContextGetHeight(c),
                  CGBitmapContextGetBitsPerComponent(c),
                  CGBitmapContextGetBitsPerPixel(c),
                  CGBitmapContextGetBytesPerRow(c),
                  CGBitmapContextGetColorSpace(c),
                  myCGContextGetBitmapInfo(c),
                  dataProvider,
                  NULL, // decode
                  true, // shouldInterpolate
                  kCGRenderingIntentDefault);

      // Release the data provider since the image retains it.
      CGDataProviderRelease(dataProvider);

      if(image == NULL){
        fprintf(stderr, "Couldn't create image!\n");
        return NULL;
      }
      return image;
  }
```

One crucial aspect of creating an image from the raster data that is contained in a bitmap context is that once you create the image, you cannot draw to the bitmap context unless you use a copy of the bitmap context raster data when you create the image. Otherwise, drawing to the bitmap context after creating the image modifies the data that makes up the image and violates the immutability of a CGImage object. To conform to this requirement, createImageFromBitmap-Context is structured so that it takes "ownership" of the raster memory from the context passed to it and is responsible for releasing that memory when it is done with it. Callers of createImageFromBitmapContext pass ownership of the raster memory in the context they supply. They must not modify or free that memory after calling createImageFromBitmapContext.

Caution Quartz images are immutable. It is important not to change the data underlying an image after you create the image. This also applies to images created from a bitmap context; see "Best Practices for Working with Images" (page 241). If you need to continue to draw to the context after you create your image, your image creation code should use a copy of the context raster data as the data for the image. "Checking for Data Provider Integrity" (page 619) and "Checking for Immutability Violations" (page 620) discuss what happens if you violate the immutability of images.

The code for createImageFromBitmapContext begins by calling CGBitmapContext-GetData to obtain a pointer to the raster data from the bitmap context. It is careful to check that the pointer it obtains is not NULL before continuing. The function CGBitmapContextGetData returns NULL if the context passed to it is not a bitmap context. The code then creates a data provider from the raster data. Since the bitmap data is in memory, the code creates an in-memory data provider using CGDataProviderCreateWithData. It computes the size of the data by multiplying the bitmap context bytesPerRow value by the number of rows in the bitmap and then creates the data provider, ensuring that the raster memory is freed when the data provider is released. If the data provider cannot be created, the code frees the memory associated with the bitmap context raster data.

After it has created the data provider, the code creates the image by calling the Quartz function CGImageCreate, using the bitmap context utility functions to obtain the parameters it needs. Then it releases the data provider it created, since the image retains the data provider and the code no longer needs the data provider. If for some reason the image can't be created from the bitmap context data, the image returned is NULL.

The routine createImageFromBitmapContext calls myCGContextGetBitmapInfo, which takes advantage of the way Quartz defines the bitmapInfo parameter for bitmap contexts. When the Quartz function CGBitmapContextGetBitmapInfo is not available on a given Mac OS X system, the routine CGBitmapContextGetAlphaInfo returns the alphaInfo value, which is equivalent to the bitmapInfo parameter on pre-Tiger systems.

As you'll soon see, the examples that use the `createImageFromBitmapContext` routine in Listing 12.2 are careful to ensure that the bitmap context is not drawn to after the image is created and that the raster memory is handled properly. They ensure this by releasing the context immediately after the image is created and before performing any drawing of the CGImage.

The routine `createImageFromBitmapContext` can be used with almost any bitmap context format to create a CGImage object from it. Most of the formats Quartz supports as bitmap context formats can be turned into an image that Quartz can draw. The exception is the alpha-only context, which corresponds not to an image but to a mask. See "Using an Alpha-Only Bitmap Context (Panther)" (page 366) for details about the alpha-only context.

10.4 ▶ **Creating an Image from a Bitmap Context in Tiger.** In Tiger and later versions, Quartz provides the convenience function `CGBitmapContextCreateImage` that makes it easy to create a `CGImageRef` from a bitmap context. This function is similar to the code you've just seen; however, it uses copy-on-write semantics on the context raster data that it uses to create the image. This means that you can, if desired, perform additional drawing to the bitmap context that you pass to the function without altering the data associated with the image. Note, however, that if you intend to use a bitmap context as a way of repeatedly rendering offscreen followed by copying onscreen, in most cases you should instead use a CGLayer object in Tiger and later versions. See "CGLayers (Tiger)" (page 371) and "Drawing Repeatedly with CGLayer Caching" (page 386).

For most of the bitmap context formats that you pass to `CGBitmapContextCreateImage`, the `CGImageRef` returned is an image, not a mask. However, if the bitmap context supplied to `CGBitmapContextCreateImage` is an alpha-only context, the `CGImageRef` returned is an image mask. If the context passed to `CGBitmapContextCreateImage` is not a bitmap context, it returns `NULL`.

Exporting Bitmap Drawing to a Graphics File. Now that you can create a bitmap context and create an image from that context, you have all the pieces needed to convert Quartz drawing into an output graphics file in formats such as PNG or JPEG. You convert Quartz drawing by first creating a bitmap context of an appropriate resolution, then drawing to that bitmap context. Next you create a `CGImageRef` using the bits from the bitmap context and export that image. As introduced in "Drawing Images" (page 203), there are several ways you can export a CGImage object to various compressed formats. The CGImageDestination functions introduced in Tiger let you write image data into a variety of data formats. As you've seen, QuickTime also has the ability to allow you to export data to a variety of output formats.

The code in Listing 12.3 uses the previous code examples to export Quartz drawing into a specific output format at a given resolution. The code consists of a routine MakeImageDocument and supporting routines, together with the code already discussed in previous sections. The routine MakeImageDocument takes the following arguments:

- url, a CFURL object that represents the destination location for the image file.

- imageType, a CFString object that describes the destination data format to the CGImageDestination functions. Examples of this string are the strings kUT-TypePNG or kUTTypeJPEG. Many of these strings are defined in UTCoreTypes.h in the Application Services framework.

- dpi, a floating-point number that specifies the resolution (in pixels per inch) to use when exporting the drawing.

Listing 12.3 Code that exports Quartz drawing as an image file

```
static void exportCGImageToFileWithDestination(CGImageRef image,
  CFURLRef url, CFStringRef outputFormat, float dpi)
{
  CFTypeRef keys[2];
  CFTypeRef values[2];
  CFDictionaryRef options = NULL;

  // Create an image destination for 1 image at the supplied URL that
  // corresponds to the output image format.
  CGImageDestinationRef imageDestination =
    CGImageDestinationCreateWithURL(url, outputFormat, 1, NULL);

  if(imageDestination == NULL){
    fprintf(stderr, "Couldn't create image destination!\n");
    return;
  }

  // Set the keys to be the x and y resolution of the image.
  keys[0] = kCGImagePropertyDPIWidth;
  keys[1] = kCGImagePropertyDPIHeight;

  // Create a CFNumber for the resolution and use it as the
  // x and y resolution.
  values[0] = values[1] = CFNumberCreate(NULL, kCFNumberFloatType, &dpi);

  // Create an options dictionary with these keys.
  options = CFDictionaryCreate(NULL,
    (const void **)keys,
    (const void **)values,
```

```
        2,
        &kCFTypeDictionaryKeyCallBacks,
        &kCFTypeDictionaryValueCallBacks);

    // Release the CFNumber the code created.
    CFRelease(values[0]);

    // Add the image with the options dictionary to the destination.
    CGImageDestinationAddImage(imageDestination, image, options);

    // Release the options dictionary this code created.
    CFRelease(options);

    // When all the images are added to the destination, finalize it.
    CGImageDestinationFinalize(imageDestination);

    // Release the destination when done with it.
    CFRelease(imageDestination);
}

void MakeImageDocument(CFURLRef url, CFStringRef imageType,
                    float dpi)
{
    CGContextRef c = NULL;
    CGImageRef image;
    Boolean useDisplayColorSpace;
    // Make a bitmap context for a letter-size raster at the requested
    // resolution. This size should really be limited to the bounding
    // box of the drawing to be performed, multiplied by dpi.
    size_t width = (size_t)(8.5*dpi), height = (size_t)11*dpi;

    // For JPEG output type, the bitmap should not be transparent.
    // imageType is one of the types supported by CGImageSource, such as
    // kUTTypePNG or kUTTypeJPEG.
    Boolean needTransparentBitmap =
        !(CFStringCompare(imageType, kUTTypeJPEG, kCFCompareCaseInsensitive)
                    == kCFCompareEqualTo);

    // Create an RGB bitmap context using the generic calibrated RGB
    // color space instead of the display color space.
    useDisplayColorSpace = false;
    c = createRGBBitmapContext(width, height, useDisplayColorSpace,
                    needTransparentBitmap);
```

```
  if(c == NULL){
    fprintf(stderr,
      "Couldn't make destination bitmap context!\n");
    return;
  }

  // Scale the coordinate system based on the resolution in dots per inch.
  CGContextScaleCTM(c, dpi/72, dpi/72);

  // Set the font smoothing parameter to false since it's better to
  // draw any text without special LCD text rendering when creating
  // rendered data for export.
  if(&CGContextSetShouldSmoothFonts != NULL)
    CGContextSetShouldSmoothFonts(c, false);

  // Draw into the bitmap context.
  DoDrawing(c);

  // Create an image from the raster data. Calling
  // createImageFromBitmapContext transfers ownership of the
  // raster memory to that routine.
  image = createImageFromBitmapContext(c);
  // This code must release the context since it no longer owns
  // the raster data associated with it and shouldn't draw to it.
  CGContextRelease(c);
  if(image == NULL){
    return;
  }

  // Now export the image.
  exportCGImageToFileWithDestination(image, url, imageType, dpi);

  CGImageRelease(image);
  return;
}
```

The MakeImageDocument routine first calculates the number of pixels that should make up the exported graphic. This code exports a graphic the size of a US-letter-size page. It would be preferable to use the width and height of a bounding rectangle of the graphics that you want to export. The MakeImageDocument routine uses the dpi supplied to it to create the number of pixels needed for the desired resolution.

The code then sets up the remaining parameters it uses when it calls the create-RGBBitmapContext routine from Listing 12.1 (page 353). Recall that when you pass a true value for needTransparentBitmap to createRGBBitmapContext, the resulting bitmap context supports alpha transparency and is cleared. Otherwise, a bitmap context that doesn't support alpha is created and initialized to white.

If the export format is JPEG, the bitmap context should be opaque because the JPEG format does not support alpha transparency. For other formats such as PNG or TIFF that do support transparent data, the resulting bitmap context should support transparency. The needTransparentBitmap variable is initialized accordingly. (You need to expand the test for JPEG format if you want to use this code to export to other formats in addition to JPEG that do not support transparency.)

Recall that the useDisplayColorSpace parameter passed to the createRGBBitmap-Context routine determines which color space is used to characterize the bitmap context. A value of true uses the display color space to characterize the context you are creating, while false uses the generic calibrated RGB color space to characterize the context. Because the bits to be exported are not for rendering to the current display, the appropriate color space for the context is the generic calibrated RGB color space, so the code sets useDisplayColorSpace to false.

After the context is created, the next lines of code set up the graphics state so that it is correct for drawing the content to export. Because the initial default coordinate system for a bitmap graphics context is 1 unit equals 1 device pixel, the code scales the coordinate system so that the bitmap context is scaled appropriately for the requested dpi. Prior to scaling, the default Quartz coordinate system is 1 unit equals 1/72 of an inch. After scaling by dpi/72, the Quartz coordinate system maps 72 units into dpi pixels.

Prior to drawing, the code needs to disable font smoothing. First, it needs to test for the existence of the function CGContextSetShouldSmoothFonts before calling it. (Font smoothing and control over font smoothing are available in Jaguar and later versions only.) Because the ultimate destination for the bits produced by the drawing is an external file, not the display, it is important to turn off font smoothing. Failing to do so can produce poorer text quality when exporting Quartz drawing as an image.

The context is finally set up for rendering. The code calls the DoDrawing routine, a routine that you supply to draw the content you want to export as rendered bits. This function can make full use of any Quartz drawing functions or any other code that knows how to render to a Quartz context, such as application framework drawing.

After you draw to the bitmap context raster, you can export the bits. The first step is to create a CGImage object from the rendered bits. For that, the code calls the createImageFromBitmapContext routine from Listing 12.2 (page 358), which takes a bitmap context and creates a `CGImageRef` from the bits contained in it. As indicated in the discussion in "Creating an Image from a Bitmap Context (pre-Tiger)" (page 358), it is important that after you call `createImageFromBitmapContext`, you don't draw to the bitmap context you passed to the function. Otherwise, you violate the immutability of the image that `createImageFromBitmapContext` creates.

After the image is created, the bitmap context is no longer needed and the code releases it. The raster memory for the context is released when the image is released. This is because the data provider for the image created by `createImageFromBitmapContext` has an image release function that releases the raster memory when the data provider associated with the image is released.

Next the code calls the supporting routine `exportCGImageToFileWithDestination`, which uses the CGImageDestination functions to export the image in the requested format. Details about exporting images using CGImageDestination are discussed in "Writing Image Data Using CGImageDestination (Tiger)" (page 255).

The code releases the image after it exports the image. Releasing the image releases the data provider associated with the image and this, in turn, releases the raster memory used to create the image.

10.3 ▶ **Using an Alpha-Only Bitmap Context (Panther).** In addition to the bitmap context formats that capture color and (optionally) alpha information for the pixels that Quartz paints, starting in Panther, Quartz provides a context that you can use to capture the alpha coverage of the rendering Quartz performs. An alpha-only context can be used for many purposes, including to

- Create masks to mask other images such as those described in "Masking an Image (Tiger)" (page 273).

- Capture the alpha channel of an alpha image.

- Create a mask of alpha coverage for hit-testing purposes.

- Create a pre-rendered mask of path drawing for use as a cached version of the path. See "Performance Tips" (page 604) for additional discussion.

- Perform limited colorizing effects. For example, drawing to an alpha-only context produces a mask that you can then paint with your color of choice. (This same approach can be used with an 8-bit Gray context to capture the luminance of graphics. You then create a mask from the context raster data that you colorize.)

Listing 12.4 demonstrates using an alpha channel for colorizing. The routine doAlphaOnlyContext uses an alpha-only context to capture the coverage of the drawing of the doAlphaRects routine from Listing 2.5 (page 31). It then colorizes the result with blue.

The code begins by calling createAlphaOnlyContext with a width and height that corresponds to the width and height of the graphics being captured. The routine createAlphaOnlyContext uses the width, together with the macro COMPUTE_BEST_BYTES_PER_ROW from Listing 12.1 (page 353) to compute the bytesPerRow appropriate for the alpha-only context. It allocates the memory and calls CGBitmapContextCreate to create the context. The code passes NULL for the colorSpace parameter. An alpha-only context has no color space associated with it since it doesn't capture color. The appropriate value to use for the bitmapInfo parameter is kCGImageAlphaOnly. Note that the bitsPerComponent value used in the call is 8; the context captures 8 bits of alpha data per pixel. As of Tiger, this is the only depth supported by Quartz for the alpha-only context. (If you only need 1-bit-deep coverage, you can use the 8-bit alpha-only context and compute your 1-bit coverage values from that.) The alpha-only context is available starting in Panther. Calling the function CGBitmapContextCreate to create an alpha-only context on earlier systems returns NULL.

After the context is created, createAlphaOnlyContext clears the context by calling the Quartz function CGContextClearRect. Clearing an alpha-only context before drawing to it is crucial since otherwise the pixels in the context have an undefined alpha value. When you are capturing alpha, you want to ensure that the initial value of each pixel is completely transparent so that only pixels that later are actually painted have nonzero alpha values.

Listing 12.4 Code that creates and uses an alpha-only context to colorize alpha drawing

```
static CGContextRef createAlphaOnlyContext(size_t width, size_t height)
{
    CGContextRef context;
    size_t bytesPerRow;
    unsigned char *rasterData;

    // Minimum bytes per row is 1 byte per sample * number of samples.
    bytesPerRow = width;
    // Round up to nearest multiple of 16.
    bytesPerRow = COMPUTE_BEST_BYTES_PER_ROW(bytesPerRow);

    // Allocate the data for the raster using calloc.
    rasterData = calloc(1, bytesPerRow * height);
    if(rasterData == NULL){
```

```
      fprintf(stderr,
        "Couldn't allocate the needed amount of memory!\n");
      return NULL;
    }

    // The color space for an alpha-only context is NULL and
    // the BitmapInfo value is kCGImageAlphaOnly.
    context = CGBitmapContextCreate(rasterData, width, height, 8,
                bytesPerRow, NULL, kCGImageAlphaOnly);
    if(context == NULL){
      // If the context couldn't be created, release the raster memory.
      free(rasterData);
      fprintf(stderr, "Couldn't create the context!\n");
      return NULL;
    }

    // Clear the context bits so they are initially transparent.
    CGContextClearRect(context, CGRectMake(0, 0, width, height));

    return context;
}

// The caller of createMaskFromAlphaOnlyContext passes ownership
// of the raster data associated with alphaContext to this routine.
static CGImageRef createMaskFromAlphaOnlyContext(
                CGContextRef alphaContext)
{
  CGImageRef mask;
  unsigned char *rasterData = CGBitmapContextGetData(alphaContext);
  size_t imageDataSize = CGBitmapContextGetBytesPerRow(alphaContext)*
                CGBitmapContextGetHeight(alphaContext);
  float invertDecode[] = { 1. , 0. };

  if(rasterData == NULL){
    fprintf(stderr, "Context is not a bitmap context!\n");
    return NULL;
  }
  // Create the data provider from the image data.
  CGDataProviderRef dataProvider = CGDataProviderCreateWithData(NULL,
                rasterData,
                imageDataSize,
                releaseBitmapContextImageData);

  if(dataProvider == NULL){
    // Must free the memory if the data provider couldn't be created
```

```
    // since this routine now owns it.
    free(rasterData);
    fprintf(stderr, "Couldn't create data provider!\n");
    return NULL;
  }
  mask = CGImageMaskCreate(CGBitmapContextGetWidth(alphaContext),
                CGBitmapContextGetHeight(alphaContext),
                CGBitmapContextGetBitsPerComponent(alphaContext),
                CGBitmapContextGetBitsPerPixel(alphaContext),
                CGBitmapContextGetBytesPerRow(alphaContext),
                dataProvider,
                invertDecode,
                true);
  // Release the data provider since the mask retains it.
  CGDataProviderRelease(dataProvider);
  if(mask == NULL){
    fprintf(stderr, "Couldn't create image mask!\n");
    return NULL;
  }
  return mask;
}

void doAlphaOnlyContext(CGContextRef context)
{
  CGImageRef mask = NULL;
  // This width and height is the size of the bounding rectangle
  // of the drawing done by the doAlphaRects routine.
  size_t width = 520, height = 400;
  CGContextRef alphaContext = createAlphaOnlyContext(width, height);
  if(context == NULL){
    fprintf(stderr, "Couldn't create the alpha-only context!\n");
    return;
  }

  // Draw the content to the alpha-only context, capturing
  // the alpha coverage. The doAlphaRects routine paints
  // a series of translucent red rectangles.
  doAlphaRects(alphaContext);

  // Finished drawing to the context and now the raster contains
  // the alpha data captured from the drawing. Calling
  // createMaskFromAlphaOnlyContext passes ownership of the
  // bitmap data to that routine.
  mask = createMaskFromAlphaOnlyContext(alphaContext);
```

```
  // This code is now finished with the context so it can release it.
  CGContextRelease(alphaContext);

  if(mask == NULL){
    return;
  }

  // Set the fill color space.
  CGContextSetFillColorSpace(context, getTheCalibratedRGBColorSpace());
  float opaqueBlue[] = { 0.11, 0.208, 0.451, 1. };
  // Set the painting color to opaque blue.
  CGContextSetFillColor(context, opaqueBlue);
  // Draw the mask, painting the mask with blue. This colorizes
  // the image to blue and it is as if we painted the
  // alpha rects with blue instead of red.
  CGContextDrawImage(context, CGRectMake(0, 0, width, height), mask);
  // Releasing the mask will cause Quartz to release the data provider
  // and therefore the raster memory used to create the context.
  CGImageRelease(mask);
}
```

The routine doAlphaOnlyContext creates the alpha-only context and then calls the doAlphaRects routine to draw to the context. Afterwards, the context raster contains the alpha coverage of the drawing. Next the code calls createMask-FromAlphaOnlyContext to create a mask from the raster data in the context. The routine createMaskFromAlphaOnlyContext parallels the code in createImageFrom-BitmapContext in Listing 12.2 (page 358). The primary difference between the two routines is that createMaskFromAlphaOnlyContext creates a mask instead of an image. Notice that the decode array that is passed to CGImageMaskCreate inverts the sense of the data—a mask has the opposite sense compared to alpha; that is, 0 in a mask paints 100 percent, but 1 in a mask paints nothing.

Note that the routines createImageFromBitmapContext and createMaskFromAlpha-OnlyContext can be combined into a single routine that takes an arbitrary bitmap context and returns a mask or an image, depending on the bitmap context supplied. To determine whether to create a mask or an image, you can use the function CGBitmapContextGetAlphaInfo. If the return value is kCGImageAlphaOnly, you create a mask; otherwise you create an image. The example code uses separate functions for the sake of clarity.

After creating the mask from the alpha-only context, the code releases the context to ensure that no further drawing is done to it. The code is now ready to draw the mask. It sets the fill color space to a color space that corresponds to the

Figure 12.1 Colorizing (as blue) the drawing produced by the doAlphaRects routine

generic calibrated RGB profile and sets the fill color to an opaque blue. (Recall that Quartz uses the context fill color when it draws masks.) The code then draws the mask and releases it. When Quartz releases the mask, it releases the data provider associated with the mask, thus releasing the raster data. The colorized rectangles shown in Figure 12.1 are the result of executing the code in Listing 12.4.

CGLayers (Tiger)

10.4 ▶ Quartz added a new drawing abstraction, the CGLayer, in Tiger. CGLayer objects are specifically intended to capture drawing that you want to redraw multiple times. A CGLayer provides a way to capture, and cache, Quartz drawing and then later draw (and redraw) the captured drawing to a Quartz context such as a window or a PDF document. Quartz uses the abstract type `CGLayerRef` to represent a CGLayer object. Unlike a bitmap context or PDF context, you can't access the results of drawing to a CGLayer object. You can only draw the layer to a destination context. "Caching Drawing Offscreen" (page 379) discusses when you would use a bitmap context instead of a CGLayer object for caching drawing offscreen.

While the typical usage for CGLayer objects is to cache offscreen drawing for later drawing onscreen, CGLayer objects are not limited to this use. CGLayer objects can be used to capture Quartz drawing for image processing with one or more Core Image filters. ("See Also," on page 393, lists references for the Core Image framework.) CGLayer objects can also be used to capture a cached high-level representation of graphics for drawing to contexts like a PDF or printing context. Because developers typically use CGLayer objects to record a bit-based representation for later drawing onscreen, CGLayers are introduced side by side with creating bitmap graphics contexts.

Using CGLayer objects to cache graphics and draw them later is straightforward. First, you create a CGLayer object by calling the Quartz function `CGLayerCreate-WithContext`. Next you call `CGLayerGetContext` to obtain a Quartz context that represents the layer, and then you draw content into that context. At that point

Figure 12.2 Creating and using a CGLayer object for drawing to a destination

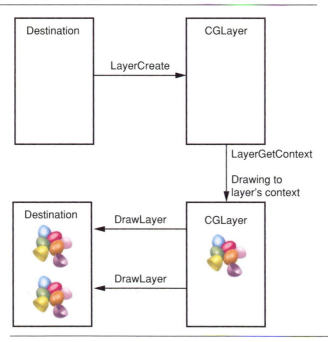

your layer contains the cached content. When you want to transfer the drawing from the layer to a destination Quartz context, you call one of the layer-drawing functions—CGContextDrawLayerAtPoint or CGContextDrawLayerInRect. Figure 12.2 shows the process of creating a layer from a destination, drawing to the layer, then drawing the contents of the layer multiple times to the destination.

Note   Don't confuse CGLayer objects with transparency layers, discussed in "Drawing with Transparency Layers (Panther)" (page 522). Transparency layers have much more restrictive semantics and are not useful for capturing graphics that you want to draw multiple times. CGLayer objects do share some of the properties of transparency layers with respect to how the content in a CGLayer object is composited to a destination when you draw the layer. See "Transparency Layers Compared to CGLayers" (page 531) for more information.

Creating a CGLayer Object

You create a CGLayer object using CGLayerCreateWithContext. The parameters you pass are

- context, the CGContextRef that specifies the context to relate the layer to. Quartz uses context to optimize the layer it creates.

- size, a CGSize structure that describes the width and height of the layer to create.

- auxiliaryInfo, a CFDictionaryRef. This parameter is for future capabilities. In Tiger, pass NULL.

Quartz optimizes how drawing to the layer is captured based on the type of context that you use to create the layer. A CGLayer object created from a bitmap context or window context is matched to the source context in terms of destination color space, pixel format, and so on. This makes a layer created from a window context appropriate for offscreen drawing that you want to later draw (and redraw) to that window. For example, if the context that you use to create the layer is a window, Quartz most likely stores the rendering of graphics to the layer as bits, possibly storing the result on the graphics card for that machine. The layer contents are represented in an optimal way for later redrawing to the window context that the layer is created from.

You should always create a CGLayer object from a Quartz context (or a context of the same type) that you want to later draw the layer to. In the preceding example, a layer created from a window does not have contents that are appropriate for drawing to a PDF or printing context since the layer drawing is pre-rasterized rather than stored as text, line art, and images without rendering.

Important   A CGLayer object should always be created from a context that is of the same type as the context that you are planning to draw the layer contents to. Doing otherwise may produce pre-rasterized drawing to a context that is not bit-based or lower performance when drawing to a bit-based context.

The size parameter passed to CGLayerCreateWithContext is the size of the layer that is created and should be chosen with care. Typically, the size is the size of the bounding rectangle of the graphics that you cache in the layer. For layers derived from bit-based contexts, the size parameter may determine the amount of memory that is used to represent the layer. Because large sizes may correspond to a large amount of memory, you should ensure that your layer size is the smallest size necessary to capture the cached graphics.

When you are finished with a layer, make sure you release it, since the resources associated with a CGLayer object may be significant. If you don't, the memory and resources associated with the CGLayerRef are not released. You can release a CGLayerRef using either CGLayerRelease or the Core Foundation function CFRelease.

Drawing to a CGLayer

After you create a CGLayer object, you use CGLayerGetContext to obtain a CGContextRef that represents the layer. Drawing to the graphics context returned by CGLayerGetContext is the equivalent of "drawing to the layer." Quartz captures the drawing performed to that context in the associated layer.

When you create a layer, the initial graphics state for the context associated with the layer is the default graphics state described in Table 7.1 (page 174). The default CTM for the context is the same as the default CTM of the context you use to create the layer. When you make changes to the graphics state returned by CGLayerGetContext, you are responsible for managing the context and graphics state parameters. If you change the context parameters or graphics state and again call CGLayerGetContext, the context returned is the same context with the same context and graphics state changes as those you made previously.

A newly created CGLayer object is initially completely transparent and contains no drawing. For CGLayer objects created from bit-based contexts, you can return them to their initially transparent state by calling CGContextClearRect. For CGLayer objects derived from contexts that are not bit-based, such as a PDF or printing context, to create a clear layer you should instead create a new layer as opposed to clearing an existing layer. Calling the function CGContextClearRect with a layer that is not created from a bit-based context produces undefined results.

Drawing the Contents of a CGLayer

Quartz provides the functions CGContextDrawLayerAtPoint and CGContextDraw-LayerInRect to draw the contents of a layer to a destination context. Both these functions composite the content of the layer to a new context. The difference between these functions is how Quartz scales the layer content when drawing it to the destination.

The function CGContextDrawLayerInRect takes the following parameters:

- context, the CGContextRef to draw the contents of the layer to.
- rect, the destination CGRect to draw the layer to. The coordinates of rect are in the current user space coordinate system of context.
- layer, the CGLayerRef of the layer whose contents you want to draw to the context.

When you call CGContextDrawLayerInRect, the layer contents are translated and scaled so that they are mapped into rect. The scaling is such that the width and height of the layer are scaled to the width and height of rect. This scaling is similar to the scaling performed by the functions CGContextDrawImage and CGContextDrawPDFDocument.

The function CGContextDrawLayerAtPoint takes the following parameters:

- context, the CGContextRef to draw the contents of the layer to.
- point, a CGPoint that contains the user space coordinates of the lower-left corner of where you want to place the layer contents.
- layer, the CGLayerRef of the layer whose contents you want to draw to the context.

The function CGContextDrawLayerAtPoint is equivalent to calling CGContextDrawLayerInRect with a destination rectangle whose size is the same size as the layer itself. This routine performs no explicit scaling. That is, the origin of the layer contents is placed at point and the only scaling performed is that due to the CTM at the time you call CGContextDrawLayerAtPoint.

When Quartz draws the contents of the layer to the destination context, the graphics state of the destination context at the time that you draw the layer affects the way Quartz draws the layer to the destination. The context CTM affects the origin, scale, and orientation of the drawing, just as it does any other drawing. The clipping area affects the drawing just as it would for any other drawing.

The layer contents are composited to the destination as a single object, rather than as a list of objects that are composited individually. As such, the destination context global alpha value and blend mode at the time that you draw the layer determine how the layer contents are blended to the destination. If the destination context shadow style specifies a shadow, the layer contents are shadowed as a single object. Quartz CGLayer objects and transparency layers are composited to their destination in the same way. See "Drawing with Transparency Layers (Panther)" (page 522) for illustrations and discussion of how transparency layers are composited. Note that drawing a layer to a context obtained from that layer produces undefined results.

Important When a layer is drawn to a destination, the graphics state parameters of the destination context affect the way the layer is drawn to the destination. The graphics state of the context associated with the layer, that is, the graphics state of the context returned by CGLayerGetContext, has no effect on the drawing of the layer to a destination.

Using a CGLayer to Draw a Checkerboard

Now that you've seen how to create and use CGLayer objects, take a look at a concrete example—one that draws the checkerboard grid shown in Figure 12.3. The drawing performed in this example is not typically what you'd use a CGLayer object for, but it illustrates the overall concepts involved in an easy-to-understand manner. (A more optimal way to draw a checkerboard is to create an array of rectangles that represent the drawing and call the function CGContextFillRects.) Later, you'll see how to cache complex drawing in a CGLayer object. The basic procedure is the same whether the drawing is simple or complex.

Figure 12.3 A checkerboard drawn using a CGLayer object

Listing 12.5 takes the approach of caching the drawing of a filled black rectangle into a layer that is the size of that rectangle. The code then draws the grid of rectangles by using the cached content in the layer to draw each black square in the checkerboard. The listing consists of the doSimpleCGLayer routine and the createCGLayerForDrawing supporting routine.

Listing 12.5 Code that uses a CGLayer object to draw a checkerboard

```
static CGLayerRef createCGLayerForDrawing(CGContextRef c)
{
  CGRect rect = { 0, 0, 50, 50 };
  CGSize layerSize;
  CGLayerRef layer;

  // Make the layer the size of the rectangle that
  // this code draws into the layer.
  layerSize.width = rect.size.width;
  layerSize.height = rect.size.height;

  // Create the layer to draw into.
  layer = CGLayerCreateWithContext(c, layerSize, NULL);
  if(layer == NULL)
    return NULL;

  // Get the context corresponding to the layer.
  CGContextRef layerContext = CGLayerGetContext(layer);
  if(layerContext == NULL){
    CGLayerRelease(layer);
    return NULL;
  }

  // Set the fill color to opaque black.
  CGContextSetFillColorWithColor(layerContext,
            getRGBOpaqueBlackColor());

  // Draw the content into the layer.
  CGContextFillRect(layerContext, rect);

  // Now the layer has the contents needed.
  return layer;
}

void doSimpleCGLayer(CGContextRef context)
{
```

```
int i,j;
CGSize s;
// Create the layer.
CGLayerRef layer = createCGLayerForDrawing(context);
if(layer == NULL){
  fprintf(stderr, "Couldn't create layer!\n");
  return;
}

// Get the size of the layer created.
s = CGLayerGetSize(layer);

// Clip to a rectangle that corresponds to
// a grid of 8x8 layer objects.
CGContextClipToRect(context,
  CGRectMake(0, 0, 8*s.width, 8*s.height));

// Paint eight rows of layer objects.
for(j = 0 ; j < 8 ; j++){
  CGContextSaveGState(context);
  // Paint four columns of layer objects, moving
  // across the drawing canvas by skipping a
  // square on the grid each time across.
  for(i = 0 ; i < 4 ; i++){
    // Draw the layer at the current origin.
    CGContextDrawLayerAtPoint(context,
      CGPointZero,
      layer);
    // Translate across two layer widths.
    CGContextTranslateCTM(context, 2*s.width, 0);
  }
  CGContextRestoreGState(context);
  // Translate to the left one layer width on
  // even loop counts and to the right one
  // layer width on odd loop counts. Each
  // time through the outer loop, translate up
  // one layer height.
  CGContextTranslateCTM(context,
    (j % 2) ? s.width: -s.width,
    s.height);
}
// Release the layer when finished drawing with it.
CGLayerRelease(layer);
}
```

The routine doSimpleCGLayer begins by calling createCGLayerForDrawing to create the layer object from the destination context and draw the desired content to the layer. The routine createCGLayerForDrawing creates a layer that corresponds to one black cell of the checkerboard. It computes the size of the layer to correspond to the size of the content the layer will contain, which is the black rectangle. The context passed to CGLayerCreateWithContext is the context the layer contents will later be repeatedly drawn to—the destination context for checkerboard drawing.

If the code successfully creates the layer, it calls CGLayerGetContext to obtain the drawing context for the layer. This is the context to use for your cached drawing (that is, the filled opaque black rectangle). Because CGLayerGetContext is a function with *Get* semantics, you should not release the context that it returns.

After doSimpleCGLayer calls createCGLayerForDrawing to create the layer and its contents, it can use the cached content in the layer. The routine doSimpleCGLayer calls the Quartz utility function CGLayerGetSize to obtain the intrinsic size of the layer and uses the size of the layer to determine the placement of each square it draws. The code draws a 4x4 grid of black squares, offset so that between each square is an empty square. The total size of the square grid is eight rectangles wide and tall.

The remainder of the code loops to draw the grid. To draw a given black square on the grid, the code uses the function CGContextDrawLayerAtPoint to draw the layer at the current Quartz origin. There is no scaling of the CTM in the destination context so the layer contents are drawn without any resizing. By using CGContextTranslateCTM between each drawing of the layer, the layer is drawn at different locations on the drawing canvas each time through the loop. After the code has completed its usage of the layer, it calls CGLayerRelease to release the layer.

This example is an artificial one because the cached content is not expensive to draw without layers. Typically, you use layers to cache content that is expensive to draw, such as a large image that you down-sample or some other complex scene that you redraw multiple times. However, the usage pattern is the same. Create a layer and draw your content to it, then draw the layer when you need to draw its contents to a new destination context of the same type as that you used to create the layer. Layers are only useful if you intend to use their contents more than once; otherwise, you simply perform the drawing to the true destination rather than first caching it in a layer.

Caching Drawing Offscreen

Historically, many applications used offscreen drawing to obtain smooth visual updates of their drawing and to avoid tearing while drawing onscreen. In Mac

OS X you don't need to use offscreen drawing for this purpose because the window system performs this buffering for you. (See "Performance and Debugging" (page 593) for information on window buffering in Mac OS X.) However, there are other reasons you might want to capture drawing offscreen. For example, caching your drawing offscreen can improve performance when you need to draw complex objects repeatedly. Another reason you might want to draw content offscreen is if you need to use custom application drawing routines that render bits. Whether it's best to draw onscreen or cache offscreen depends on the version of the operating system your program runs on and how your application performs drawing. This discussion assumes you've decided that offscreen drawing is necessary, so the discussion focuses on whether to use a bitmap context or a CGLayer object for offscreen drawing.

When an application needs to draw offscreen, then render the results onscreen, the generally recommended approach is to use CGLayer objects. When you create a CGLayer object from a window context, the CGLayer is optimized for drawing to a window of that bit depth and with the monitor profile associated with the display. You don't need to worry about creating a bitmap context for your offscreen drawing and copying the results onscreen. Even better, Quartz can potentially obtain significantly better performance when you use a CGLayer object because its content may be cached on the graphics card. When cached content is on the graphics card, transferring the contents of a CGLayer to the screen is much faster than copying bits from a bitmap context because when you create a bitmap context, the associated raster data is always in main memory.

There are situations for which using a layer isn't suitable. You would instead render into a bitmap context and create an image from those bits to render to the destination context by calling the function `CGContextDrawImage`. Some situations where a CGLayer isn't appropriate or possible include the following:

- Code that executes on pre-Tiger systems. CGLayer objects aren't available prior to Tiger.

- Your drawing includes content that isn't rendered solely by Quartz or another Mac OS X framework that renders to a Quartz context (for example, custom rendering or rendering by other graphics systems like QuickDraw).

- You need a CGImage object of your drawing for export or other usage besides simply drawing that image to a window context.

The next several sections contain code that draws a complex PDF page repeatedly to achieve the result shown in Figure 12.4. You'll see how to draw complex graphics repeatedly, first without any caching of the content, then by using a bitmap context to cache the content, and finally by using a CGLayer object. All of the code samples produce the graphic in Figure 12.4; the differences are in how that drawing is achieved. The focus of the discussion here is on cached content,

Figure 12.4 Tiling a PDF document

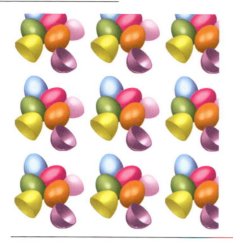

not on how to draw PDF documents. See "Opening and Drawing PDF Documents" (page 397) for detailed information about drawing PDF documents with Quartz.

Drawing Repeatedly Without Caching

The drawing in Figure 12.4 is created by drawing a complex PDF document many times by tiling it across the drawing canvas. Because the document being drawn is complex, drawing it multiple times to a window without any caching takes an amount of time that is approximately N times the amount of time it takes to draw the PDF once, where N is the number of times you draw the document. By caching the drawing of the document, you can potentially reduce the amount of time it takes to redraw the document.

Listing 12.6 tiles the PDF document without performing any caching. Take note of this code, which provides a baseline metric for drawing performance so that you can measure performance with no caching involved. Without the ability to draw without caching, you can't accurately measure whether your caching code actually improves performance. The routine `TilePDFNoBuffer` contains the drawing code. This routine calls `getThePDFDoc`, which creates a `CGPDFDocumentRef` from a supplied URL and returns it, along with the width and height of the media box of the PDF document. The routine returns a CGPDFDocument object that should not be released by the caller.

The code then uses the width and height of the document media box to compute the size of each tile. So as to have many tiles in a smaller area, the code reduces the width and height to 1/3 their original size. Next the tile spacing is calculated to add two units between tiles in each dimension. Finally the code loops to draw the tiles, calling the Quartz function CGContextDrawPDFDocument to render each tile. Content is not cached; the first page of the PDF document is rendered from the CGPDFDocumentRef each time a tile is drawn.

The getThePDFDoc routine performs some caching. It has a 1-document-deep cache of CGPDFDocument objects that it keeps around. This means that each time TilePDFNoBuffer is called with a CFURL object for a PDF document, the getThePDFDoc routine doesn't necessarily need to open the document from scratch. This scheme is just for demonstration purposes; in your own code, you would release the PDF document reference during the course of managing your application resources.

Listing 12.6 Code that repeatedly draws a PDF document without caching

```
CGPDFDocumentRef getThePDFDoc(CFURLRef url, float *w, float *h)
{
  static CGPDFDocumentRef pdfDoc = NULL;
  static CFURLRef pdfURL = NULL;
  static float width = 0, height = 0;

  if(url == NULL)
    return;

  // See whether to update the cached PDF document.
  if(pdfDoc == NULL || url != pdfURL){
    // Release any cached document or URL.
    if (pdfDoc) CGPDFDocumentRelease(pdfDoc);
    if (pdfURL) CFRelease(pdfURL);

    pdfDoc = CGPDFDocumentCreateWithURL(url);
    if(pdfDoc != NULL){
      CGRect pdfMediaRect = CGPDFDocumentGetMediaBox(pdfDoc, 1);
      width = pdfMediaRect.size.width;
      height = pdfMediaRect.size.height;
      // Retain the URL of the PDF file being cached.
      pdfURL = CFRetain(url);
    }else{
      pdfURL = NULL;
    }
  }
```

```
    if(pdfDoc){
      // Let the caller know the width and height of the document.
      *w = width;
      *h = height;
    }

    return pdfDoc;
}

void TilePDFNoBuffer(CGContextRef context, CFURLRef url)
{
    float fillwidth = 612., fillheight = 792.;
    float tileX, tileY, tileOffsetX, tileOffsetY;
    float w, h;
    CGPDFDocumentRef pdfDoc = getThePDFDoc(url, &tileX, &tileY);
    if(pdfDoc == NULL){
      fprintf(stderr, "Couldn't get the PDF document!\n");
      return;
    }
    // Make the tiles 1/3 the size of the PDF document.
    tileX /= 3;
    tileY /= 3;

    // Space the tiles by the tile width and height
    // plus an extra 2 units in each dimension.
    tileOffsetX = 2. + tileX;
    tileOffsetY = 2. + tileY;

    // Tile the PDF document.
    for(h = 0; h < fillheight ; h += tileOffsetY)
      for(w = 0; w < fillwidth ; w += tileOffsetX){
        CGContextDrawPDFDocument(context,
          CGRectMake(w, h, tileX, tileY),
          pdfDoc, 1);
      }
}
```

In this example, the code tiles a fixed area. You could improve the drawing code by tiling only the area that actually needs to be tiled, rather than a fixed grid. Still better would be to use Quartz pattern drawing, which is a superior way to achieve this kind of repeated drawing (see Listing 15.5 (page 506)).

Drawing Repeatedly with Bitmap Context Caching

Now that you've drawn the content without caching, take a look at code that caches the PDF page to a Quartz bitmap context. This code creates a bitmap context big enough to hold a single tile and then renders the PDF document to that context. The code uses the bits that correspond to one tile to construct a CGImage object that it then uses to draw repeatedly. Listing 12.7 implements this strategy.

As before, the code obtains the CGPDFDocumentRef of the PDF document to draw and computes the tile size and offset between tiles. It then calls the createRGB-BitmapContext routine from Listing 12.1 (page 353) to construct a 32-bit RGB bitmap context. Since the purpose of the bitmap context is to cache drawing that is later drawn to a window context, the call to createRGBBitmapContext requests that the context be characterized by the display color space and that the bitmap context supports transparency. Recall that for these parameters, create-RGBBitmapContext clears the context so that portions of the bitmap that are not painted are transparent when you later draw the image to a new destination.

After the bitmap context is created and cleared, the code draws the PDF document so that the origin coincides with the bitmap context origin and the width and height are the same as the bitmap context. This scales the document to the tile that is later drawn repeatedly. At this point, the bits in the bitmap context are a rendered version of the PDF document. The content is cached.

Now it's time to draw the cached data to the destination. The code calls the routine createImageFromBitmapContext from Listing 12.2 (page 358) to create an image from the raster data in the context. At that point the bitmap context is no longer needed and is released. Recall from "Creating an Image from a Bitmap Context (pre-Tiger)" (page 358) that the routine createImageFromBitmapContext creates an image whose data provider uses the bitmap context raster as its data source and releases that data when the image is released.

After creating the cached image, the code tiles the image similarly to how the PDF document is tiled in Listing 12.6. Instead of using CGContextDrawPDFDocument, the code calls the Quartz function CGContextDrawImage, using the image as a pre-rendered version of the document. The code releases the image after it tiles the drawing area with it.

Listing 12.7 Code that repeatedly draws a PDF document using a bitmap as a cached representation

```
void TilePDFWithOffscreenBitmap(CGContextRef context, CFURLRef url)
{
    float fillwidth = 612., fillheight = 792.;
    float tileX, tileY, tileOffsetX, tileOffsetY;
```

```
float w, h;
CGContextRef bitmapContext;
Boolean useDisplayColorSpace;
Boolean needTransparentBitmap;

CGPDFDocumentRef pdfDoc = getThePDFDoc(url,
                &tileX,
                &tileY);
if(pdfDoc == NULL){
  fprintf(stderr, "Couldn't get the PDF document!\n");
  return;
}

tileX /= 3;
tileY /= 3;

tileOffsetX = 2. + tileX;
tileOffsetY = 2. + tileY;

useDisplayColorSpace = true;
needTransparentBitmap = true;
bitmapContext = createRGBBitmapContext(tileX, tileY,
                useDisplayColorSpace,
                needTransparentBitmap);
if(bitmapContext == NULL){
  fprintf(stderr, "Couldn't create bitmap context!\n");
  return;
}

// Draw the PDF document one time into the bitmap.
CGContextDrawPDFDocument(bitmapContext,
                CGRectMake(0, 0, tileX, tileY),
                pdfDoc, 1);

// Create an image from the bitmap raster data. Calling
// createImageFromBitmapContext passes ownership of the
// raster memory in the context to that routine.
CGImageRef image = createImageFromBitmapContext(bitmapContext);
// Need to release the context.
CGContextRelease(bitmapContext);
if(image == NULL){
  return;
}
```

```
      // Now tile the image.
      for(h = 0; h < fillheight ; h += tileOffsetY)
        for(w = 0; w < fillwidth ; w += tileOffsetX){
          CGContextDrawImage(context,
            CGRectMake(w, h, tileX, tileY), image);
        }

      // Release the image once this code is finished drawing it.
      CGImageRelease(image);
}
```

Note that this code works best for a drawing destination that is a 32-bits-per-pixel destination, as chosen by "Millions" of colors in the Displays preference in the Preferences application. Quartz does not provide a 16-bits-per-pixel bitmap context that captures alpha. If you need alpha to correctly represent your drawing, such as drawing that contains holes or other transparent areas, you can either cache to a 32-bit cache, use a CGLayer object (when available), or choose some other strategy.

Be aware that the strategy of creating a bitmap representation of this drawing is not appropriate to use when drawing to a context other than a bit-based context since the content is pre-rasterized. For printing or generating PDF data, you want to avoid using content cached in this fashion. Instead, use the code that does not cache the content.

Caution   Don't use pre-rendered cached content when the drawing destination is not a bit-based context, such as a PDF or printing context.

As with many examples in this book, Listing 12.7 is designed for clarity and not because it is the optimal way to accomplish a task. A more optimal version of the code would cache the image itself across calls TilePDFWithOffscreenBitmap instead of re-creating the image each time that TilePDFWithOffscreenBitmap is called.

Drawing Repeatedly with CGLayer Caching

CGLayer objects are easier to work with than bitmap contexts and offer a potential performance benefit over them as well. Whenever it is appropriate, you'll want to use a CGLayer instead of a bitmap context to capture cached content; they are the preferred way to draw offscreen when you want to draw that content onscreen later.

The code in Listing 12.8 is functionally equivalent to the code in Listing 12.7 except the new code uses a CGLayer instead of a bitmap context to create a cached representation. After the code has cached the content into a CGLayer, it tiles the drawing using code similar to that in Listing 12.7, but instead of calling CGContextDrawImage, it calls CGContextDrawLayerAtPoint, using the CGLayer as a cached version of the document. The code releases the CGLayer object after tiling the drawing area with the layer contents.

Listing 12.8 Code that repeatedly draws a PDF document using a CGLayer as a cached representation

```
static CGLayerRef createLayerWithImageForContext(CGContextRef c,
                CFURLRef url)
{
  CGSize layerSize;
  CGLayerRef layer;
  CGPDFDocumentRef pdfDoc = getThePDFDoc(url,
                &layerSize.width,
                &layerSize.height);
  if(pdfDoc == NULL){
    return NULL;
  }
  // Make the layer 1/3 the size of the PDF document.
  layerSize.width /= 3;
  layerSize.height /= 3;
  // Create the layer to draw into.
  layer = CGLayerCreateWithContext(c, layerSize, NULL);
  if(layer == NULL)
    return NULL;

  // Get the context corresponding to the layer.
  CGContextRef layerContext = CGLayerGetContext(layer);
  if(layerContext == NULL){
    CGLayerRelease(layer);
    return NULL;
  }

  // Draw the PDF document into the layer.
  CGContextDrawPDFDocument(layerContext,
                CGRectMake(0, 0, layerSize.width, layerSize.height),
                pdfDoc, 1);

  // Now the layer has the contents needed.
  return layer;
}
```

```
void TilePDFWithCGLayer(CGContextRef context, CFURLRef url)
{
  float fillwidth = 612., fillheight = 792.;
  CGSize s;
  float tileX, tileY, tileOffsetX, tileOffsetY;
  float w, h;
  CGLayerRef layer = createLayerWithImageForContext(context, url);
  if(layer == NULL){
    fprintf(stderr, "Couldn't create the layer!\n");
    return;
  }

  // Compute the tile size and offset.
  s = CGLayerGetSize(layer);
  tileX = s.width;
  tileY = s.height;

  tileOffsetX = 2. + tileX;
  tileOffsetY = 2. + tileY;

  // Now draw the contents of the layer to the context. The layer is drawn
  // at its true size (the size of the tile) with its origin located at
  // the lower-left corner of each tile.
  for(h = 0; h < fillheight ; h += tileOffsetY)
    for(w = 0; w < fillwidth ; w += tileOffsetX){
      CGContextDrawLayerAtPoint(context,
        CGPointMake(w, h), layer);
  }

  // Release the layer when finished drawing with it.
  CGLayerRelease(layer);
}
```

As with other examples, the code is designed for clarity. You could make it more optimal by caching the layer across calls to TilePDFWithCGLayer instead of re-creating the layer each time TilePDFWithCGLayer is called.

Note   One difference between using a bitmap context and a CGLayer object is that a CGLayer object doesn't necessarily pre-rasterize content that you draw to it. A CGLayer object that is created by passing a context that is not bit-based to CGLayerCreateWith-Context captures a representation suitable for drawing to a context such as a PDF or printing context. In these cases the content is recorded in the layer so that it preserves the object nature of the drawing rather than rendering to bits.

Display Profile Issues

Up to now, you've been encouraged to use calibrated color spaces that are not tied to a specific device. An exception to this guideline is the case of drawing content to create an offscreen representation that later is drawn onscreen. For this special case, it is important to use a color space that corresponds to the display color space so that you achieve the correct colors and optimal performance. You want to ensure that any required color matching is performed only when you create your cached content, not when you draw that content to the onscreen window. Since the cached content is used repeatedly, you want color matching to happen when you first create the cached content, not each time you draw from the cache.

To ensure that colors are correctly matched to the display and that there is no color matching performed when you draw your offscreen content onscreen, use the ICC color profile for the display when creating a bitmap context for this purpose. Recall that the routine createRGBBitmapContext in Listing 12.1 (page 353) called an application-defined function—getTheDisplayColorSpace—based on the value of the wantDisplayColorSpace parameter passed to createRGBBitmapContext. A value of true caused createRGBBitmapContext to call the routine getTheDisplay-ColorSpace. Listing 12.9 shows an implementation for getTheDisplayColorSpace that should satisfy the needs of most applications.

Most applications are only concerned with the color profile of the main display. Indeed, most users only have one display, so using the profile of the main display to create a color space for offscreen content that is later drawn to that display is a reasonable approach.

Listing 12.9 A routine that creates a color space for the main display

```
CGColorSpaceRef getTheDisplayColorSpace(void)
{
  static CGColorSpaceRef displayCS = NULL;
  if(displayCS == NULL){
    CMProfileRef systemProfile = NULL;
    OSStatus err = CMGetSystemProfile(&systemProfile);
    if (!err){
      displayCS =
        CGColorSpaceCreateWithPlatformColorSpace(systemProfile);
      CMCloseProfile(systemProfile);
    }else{
      fprintf(stderr,
        "Got error %d when getting system profile!\n", err);
```

```
            return NULL;
        }
    }
    return displayCS;
}
```

The getTheDisplayColorSpace routine uses the ColorSync framework function CMGetSystemProfile to obtain the system ColorSync profile. This is the profile associated with the main display. The routine then calls the Quartz function CGColorSpaceCreateWithPlatformColorSpace to create a Quartz color space that corresponds to the profile. The function closes the profile reference it obtained with CMGetSystemProfile after it creates the color space. The function getThe-DisplayColorSpace uses the static variable displayCS to hold the color space it creates so that future calls to getTheDisplayColorSpace return the color space already created, minimizing the overhead associated with obtaining the display color space. The routine getTheDisplayColorSpace is written as a routine with *Get* semantics, so the code that calls the routine should not release the color space that getTheDisplayColorSpace returns.

Important　Use of a display profile for offscreen content that isn't targeted for a display is a poor choice. A better choice for offscreen content that is exported or used for purposes other than onscreen display is the Generic calibrated RGB profile or another profile better suited for the purpose of the content.

Some high-end applications may want to have specialized support for multiple monitors. For example, a user may have one display connected (such as a CRT) that is used for content when he or she is especially concerned about the color fidelity and another display (such as a large LCD display) that is used as the main display. If your application wants to handle multiple displays or target a display other than the main display, you need to create a color space appropriate for the target display. Listing 12.10 is equivalent to Listing 12.9 but is a good starting point if you want to have special support for multiple displays, such as using different display color spaces for each display a user has. The code uses the Quartz Services API (also called the CGDirectDisplay API) to obtain the CGDirectDisplayID for the main display, then calls ColorSync to open the profile for that display for use with CGColorSpaceCreateWithPlatformColorspace.

Listing 12.10　A routine that creates a display color space using CGDirectDisplay and ColorSync functions

```
CGColorSpaceRef getTheDisplayColorSpace(void)
{
    static CGColorSpaceRef displayCS = NULL;
```

```
    if(displayCS == NULL){
      CMProfileRef displayProfile = NULL;
      // Get the display ID of the main display.

      // For displays other than the main display, use
      // the functions CGGetDisplaysWithPoint,
      // CGGetDisplaysWithRect, etc. in CGDirectDisplay.h.
      CGDirectDisplayID displayID = CGMainDisplayID();
      // The CGDirectDisplayID is the same as the
      // CMDisplayIDType passed to CMGetProfileByAVID.
      CMError err = CMGetProfileByAVID((CMDisplayIDType)displayID,
                &displayProfile);
      if(err || displayProfile == NULL){
        fprintf(stderr,
          "Got error %d when getting profile for main display!\n",err);
        return NULL;
      }

      displayCS =
        CGColorSpaceCreateWithPlatformColorSpace(displayProfile);
      CMCloseProfile(displayProfile);
    }
    return displayCS;
}
```

Important

When these routines aren't able to obtain a color space for the display, they return NULL. This can happen for two reasons: (1) the system doesn't have an attached display (so there isn't a display profile) or (2) the code is executed by a user who cannot access the display, such as by a daemon process or a user who is remotely logged in. You need to concern yourself with a NULL result only if you write a tool or other code that doesn't have a graphical user interface (GUI). It does not affect your usage of this code for a GUI application.

Replacing CopyBits

QuickDraw programmers new to Quartz frequently ask the question, Where is the replacement for CopyBits? CopyBits is a general-purpose QuickDraw function that developers historically have used for everything from drawing images to copying content from a QuickDraw offscreen GWorld to an onscreen window.

You've already seen how to perform these types of tasks with Quartz. "Drawing Images" (page 203) and "Image Masking" (page 263) discuss in detail how to draw images and masks with Quartz where the source of the data is arbitrary. The way you supply the source data of the image or mask is quite flexible when using Quartz and can of course be from a memory buffer as with QuickDraw. You've just seen how to use a bitmap context and a CGLayer object to draw with Quartz offscreen and copy the result onscreen in "Caching Drawing Offscreen" (page 379).

There may be some situations where a Carbon developer might want to use QuickDraw or QuickTime to render content to an offscreen GWorld and then use that content to create a CGImage object they can then draw to a Quartz context. This is straightforward for a 16- or 32-bit GWorld. Once the content has been rendered to the GWorld, you use LockPixels to lock the pixels in the GWorld, then call GetPixBaseAddr to get the in-memory address of the pixel data. This is the data to use with CGDataProviderCreateWithData to create a data provider from the GWorld data. It is important that you not unlock or dispose of the GWorld until Quartz releases the data provider you create. The data provider release function you pass to CGDataProviderCreateWithData should dispose of the GWorld if you no longer need it.

Once you have a data provider, you can use CGImageCreate to create a CGImageRef from the data, as shown in Listing 12.11.

Listing 12.11 Code to create a CGImage object from a QuickDraw GWorld

```
image = CGImageCreate(
  width,                          // The width, in pixels, of the GWorld.
  height,                         // The height, in pixels, of the GWorld.
  bitsPerComponent,               // 8 for a 32-bit GWorld,
                                  // 5 for a 16-bit GWorld.
  bitsPerPixel,                   // 32 for a 32-bit GWorld,
                                  // 16 for a 16-bit GWorld.
  bytesPerRow,                    // The value of GetPixRowBytes
                                  // for the PixMap of the GWorld.
  colorspace,                     // Typically the display color space.
  kCGImageAlphaNoneSkipFirst,     // QuickDraw drawing has no
                                  // alpha data and the padding data
                                  // is at the beginning of each pixel.
  imageDataProvider,              // The data provider that provides
                                  // the GWorld's data.
  NULL, shouldInterpolate, kCGRenderingIntentDefault
  );
```

Once you create a `CGImageRef` from the GWorld data, you shouldn't draw to the GWorld or otherwise modify the content drawn in the GWorld until Quartz releases the data provider you supplied to create the image. This advice about handling the data provider with a GWorld conforms to the guidelines described in "Guidelines for Using Data Providers" (page 198).

See the references at the end of this chapter for more information regarding replacing your usage of CopyBits with the functionality available in Quartz.

Summary

Although Quartz is not a pixel-based graphics model, it is quite capable of drawing bits. Bitmap image formats, unlike object-based Quartz drawing, represent a pre-rendered form of Quartz drawing. This chapter discusses situations for which you might want to use bitmap graphics contexts and shows how to create and use them. As an alternative, and a preferable one in most cases, Quartz introduced CGLayer objects in Tiger. You saw how to create and use CGLayers to cache and then repeatedly draw the contents of the cached layer. You also saw how to accomplish the same tiled drawing using a bitmap graphics context as a cache and using no caching at all. Offscreen drawing that's later used to draw onscreen can be optimized by using a color space for the display profile when you create the cache.

See Also

For more information on the topics discussed in this chapter, see the following documents from the ADC Reference Library:

- *Quartz 2D Programming Guide* contains a list of supported pixel formats for bitmap contexts:

  http://developer.apple.com/documentation/GraphicsImaging/Conceptual/drawingwithquartz2d/index.html

- *Quartz 2D Programming Guide for QuickDraw Developers* has information on CopyBits replacement strategies and has a chapter on performance that provides coding guidelines and information on analyzing performance:

  http://developer.apple.com/documentation/Carbon/Conceptual/QuickDrawToQuartz2D/index.html

- *Universal Binary Programming Guidelines* discusses how to create a universal binary that executes properly on Mac OS X running on both PowerPC- and Intel-based Macintosh computers:

  http://developer.apple.com/documentation/MacOSX/Conceptual/ universal_binary/

- *Core Image Programming Guide* provides conceptual information about Core Image and how to use it:

  http://developer.apple.com/documentation/GraphicsImaging/Conceptual/ CoreImaging/index.html

- *Core Image Reference* is the API reference for Core Image:

  http://developer.apple.com/documentation/GraphicsImaging/Reference/ CoreImagingRef/index.html

- *Quartz Services Reference* describes the CGDirectDisplay API:

  http://developer.apple.com/documentation/GraphicsImaging/Reference/ Quartz_Services_Ref/index.html

- *ColorSync Manager Reference:*

  http://developer.apple.com/documentation/GraphicsImaging/Reference/ ColorSync_Manager/index.html

The header files relevant to creating bits and working with layers are

- `CGBitmapContext.h`, which contains the routines that create and operate on bitmap contexts.

- `CGLayer.h`, which contains the Quartz routines that create and operate on CGLayer objects.

- `CGContext.h`, which contains the functions that draw layers to a context.

- `CGDirectDisplay.h`, which contains the functions available in the Core Graphics framework that allow you to enumerate displays and manipulate them in various ways.

- `CMApplication.h`, which contains the prototype and definitions of the function `CMGetProfileByAVID`. This header file is part of the ColorSync framework and is located in

  `/System/Library/Frameworks/ApplicationServices.framework/Frameworks/ ColorSync.framework/Headers`

The relevant Quartz 2D reference documentation from the ADC Reference Library is

- *CGBitmapContext Reference*
- *CGLayer Reference*
- *CGContext Reference*

Chapter 13

Opening and Drawing PDF Documents

Adobe Systems introduced Portable Document Format (PDF) and the corresponding PDF imaging model in 1993. Since its introduction, PDF has grown in both popularity and capabilities. The power of the PDF imaging model and the fact that PDF has evolved into a de facto standard are some of the reasons why Apple adopted PDF as the native graphics format for Quartz.

Because of the close relationship between Quartz and the PDF imaging model, Quartz natively supports the drawing of PDF documents into any Quartz context. This support includes PDF documents created with Quartz itself, as well as those created by other PDF creation tools. The ability to treat a page from an arbitrary PDF document just like any other graphic element is an important aspect of Quartz drawing.

The purpose of this chapter is to show how to open existing PDF documents and use them as source graphics. First, you'll take a look at the properties of a PDF document and learn PDF document terminology. Then you'll see how to use Quartz PDF functions to open a PDF document, use PDF as a graphical interchange format, draw pages, rotate pages, handle protected documents, and get information about a PDF document. In "Creating and Examining PDF Documents" (page 435), you'll learn about creating PDF documents with Quartz as well as how to use Quartz to look deeper into the contents of a PDF document.

Mac OS X provides other ways to open and view PDF documents in Tiger. If you only need to work with PDF documents in Tiger and later versions, you may want to consider using PDF Kit, which is a high-level toolkit that provides Objective-C classes for drawing, inspecting, adding annotations, and searching through PDF documents. This chapter doesn't discuss PDF Kit, but you can find more information about it in the ADC Reference Library (*http://developer .apple.com*).

PDF Document Properties

A PDF document is a container for a sequence of pages and the data that describes those pages. The document itself has properties that apply to it. For example, the document can be password protected and encrypted. Each page in a PDF document is independent from each other page and has attributes that apply to the page as a whole. In addition to the attributes that apply to that page, each page in a PDF document has a **page content stream**—an ordered list of drawing operations that describes how to render the page content when it is drawn.

When the page content stream describes the drawing of line art such as rectangles and Bézier curves, the data describing those rectangles and curves is directly inline in the content stream. When the page content stream describes the drawing of images, the selection of a font, or the setting of a color space, that data is described by references to resources that are not inline in the content stream. Because PDF files use indirect references to describe large resources such as images, fonts, and color spaces, these objects can be shared within a given page or by several pages. This use of references allows a PDF document to have a much more compact representation of drawing than it would without this resource sharing. This also means that Quartz can store a single copy of a given resource, such as an image, in the PDF documents that it produces, even when that resource is used multiple times.

Each page in a PDF document has one or more rectangles that describe the page dimensions. All pages in a PDF document have a **media box**, a rectangle that defines the boundaries of the physical medium the page is to be printed on. All the visual content of a given page falls inside its media box; however, some of the page content may include additional content such as printing registration marks or printing instructions that are not part of the finished page. For most PDF documents, the media box is the only rectangle that describes the page dimensions.

There are four optional additional rectangles that specify boundary information about a given PDF page, although most PDF documents do not explicitly define them. The **crop box** defines a rectangle to which the page contents should be clipped when drawing. If the crop box is not explicitly present, the media box defines the crop box.

The **art box** defines the boundary of the meaningful content of the page as expressed by the designer. This area may include white space intended as part of the design and is not necessarily a tight bounding box around the graphical content. Some graphics applications use the art box when importing a PDF graphic. If the art box is not explicitly present, the crop box defines the art box.

The **bleed box** and **trim box** are boundaries used in a printing prepress environment or page imposition environment and include portions of the drawing content physically removed (by cutting, folding, or trimming). If either of these boxes is not explicitly present, the crop box defines the missing box.

Each page of a PDF document can have an optional rotation angle associated with it. When present, the rotation angle is an integer multiple of 90 degrees and specifies the number of degrees that the page must be rotated *clockwise* prior to drawing. (Note that this rotation direction is the PDF convention and is in the opposite direction of the default direction of positive angles in Quartz user space.) Some PDF processing applications, such as Adobe Acrobat, rotate a page by modifying the rotation angle of the page, leaving the page content stream unaffected. When drawing PDF pages that have a rotation angle, you typically want to rotate the page clockwise by the rotation angle. Most PDF documents do not have a rotation angle associated with any of the pages. When there is no rotation angle explicitly specified in the document, the default value is zero degrees.

A page in a PDF document can also have ancillary data that is not part of the page content, such as **annotations**. One example of an annotation is a **link**, which is data that indicates a rectangle on the page, together with a reference to another portion of the document that a PDF viewer should navigate to or a URL to be opened when the link is clicked. Pages can have other types of annotations as well, including **text annotations**. Text annotations are essentially sticky notes that provide visual comments about the page content. These are typically used by people who review a finished PDF document.

Some PDF documents contain additional data (sometimes called PDF metadata) in addition to the data associated with a given page. For example, a PDF document can contain a table-of-contents-style outline with navigation links to allow you to go from an outline topic to the portion of the document that corresponds to that topic. Another type of document metadata consists of a thumbnail image that is a small representation of a given page.

PDF documents can be encrypted with password protection using encryption keys that range from 40 to 128 bits in length. Protected documents have two distinct passwords: an owner password that allows access to the document with no restrictions and a user password that allows access to the document with restricted permissions. The most typical restrictions imposed on a protected PDF document are to disallow printing and to disallow copying or extracting the content. PDF protection and permissions apply to the PDF document as a whole.

Opening a PDF Document

Applications that support working with existing PDF documents typically obtain the PDF data in one of two ways:

- From a disk file or other source that can be represented with a CFURLRef.

- From the Macintosh Clipboard. PDF data is the format that Mac OS X uses for the interchange of Quartz graphics between applications.

Regardless of which source you use, the first step to accessing PDF content is to create a CGPDFDocument object (CGPDFDocumentRef data type). After you create the object, you use it to obtain information about a PDF document, such as the total number of pages in the document and the properties of a given page, including the media box and other boundary rectangles. You also use a CGPDFDocument object to draw pages in a PDF document and to perform other operations on a PDF document such as examining the metadata content of the document (see "Examining PDF Document Content (Panther, Tiger)" (page 467)).

The function that you use to create a CGPDFDocumentRef depends on the source of the PDF data:

- The function CGPDFDocumentCreateWithURL creates a CGPDFDocumentRef that represents an existing PDF document at the location described by the CFURL-Ref supplied to the function. Typically, you use this function to access file-based PDF documents, but you can also use it to access PDF data from a URL that obtains data from a web-based location, such as a URL beginning with http://.

- The function CGPDFDocumentCreateWithProvider creates a CGPDFDocumentRef from a CGDataProviderRef that you supply, allowing you to work with PDF data from any data source, as represented by a Quartz data provider. The data provider can be any of the forms described in "Data Providers" (page 186). Your data provider must be prepared to supply the complete contents of the PDF document it refers to and must obey all the restrictions of data providers described in "Guidelines for Using Data Providers" (page 198). Typically, you use this function to get data from a pasteboard such as the Clipboard.

After you have a CGPDFDocumentRef, you can use it to determine the total number of pages contained in the PDF document by calling CGPDFDocumentGetNumber-OfPages. Quartz provides the functions CGPDFDocumentGetMediaBox, CGPDFDocumentGetCropBox, CGPDFDocumentGetArtBox, CGPDFDocumentGetBleedBox, and CGPDF-DocumentGetTrimBox to obtain the corresponding boundary rectangles for a given page. If the requested box is not explicitly present for a given page, Quartz supplies the correct default based on the boxes that are present. You can also obtain the rotation angle for a given page by calling the function `CGPDFDocumentGetRotationAngle`. Each of these functions takes a `CGPDFDocumentRef` that specifies the PDF of interest and the page number whose information you want to obtain.

The CGPDFDocument functions all work directly with a PDF document. The CGPDFPage functions, available in Panther and later versions, are the preferred functions to use when working with PDF documents on systems where they are available. See "Using CGPDFPage Objects (Panther)" (page 412) for more information about these functions.

Using PDF as a Graphical Interchange

Prior to Mac OS X, the QuickDraw PICT data format was the data type that most applications used to import graphical data from another application or to export its data in graphical form. This was a natural fit because the PICT format was a data format that captured QuickDraw graphics. But the PICT format is not capable of capturing the graphics generated with the Quartz drawing model. As a result, PDF data is the preferred format for interchanging graphics between applications in Mac OS X. An additional bonus of adopting PDF as a graphical interchange format for your applications is that PDF is an industry standard that is used across multiple computing platforms.

For legacy reasons, many applications need to draw QuickDraw pictures to a Quartz context. The Cocoa NSImage class provides this capability directly. For Carbon applications, QuickDraw provides the QDPict family of functions for drawing QuickDraw picture data to a `CGContextRef`. See the references at the end of this chapter for information about drawing PICT data to a Quartz context.

Whether you are using the Cocoa or Carbon frameworks for building your graphical applications, the data that a Mac OS X pasteboard returns is a CFData object (or the equivalent NSData in Cocoa). You create a CGPDFDocument object from pasteboard data using the function `CGPDFDocumentCreateWithProvider` together with a data provider that provides the data from a CFData object. You've already seen how this is done in Listing 8.5 (page 197) in "CGDataProviderCreateWithCFData (Tiger)" (page 196). Now you'll see how to define a routine that creates a `CGPDFDocumentRef` from PDF data on a pasteboard such as the Clipboard. Take a look at `createNewPDFRefFromPasteBoard` in Listing 13.1.

The code calls the routine `myCreatePDFDataFromPasteBoard`, which returns a `CFDataRef` that contains the PDF data. The implementation of `myCreatePDFDataFromPasteBoard` depends on which application framework you use, Carbon or Cocoa. You'll see how to implement this routine for each framework in the sections that follow. The reference returned by `myCreatePDFDataFromPasteBoard` is owned by the calling application.

After the code creates a reference to the PDF data, it creates a data provider from the CFDataRef using myCGDataProviderCreateWithCFData. (This routine is in Listing 8.5 (page 197) in "Data Providers and Data Consumers" (page 185).) Once it creates the data provider, it then releases the reference to the pasteboard data since the application owns the reference and no longer needs it. The data provider, however, retains the reference to the pasteboard data. The code calls CGPDFDocumentCreateWithProvider to create a CGPDFDocument object using the data provider. The code releases the data provider after the CGPDFDocument object is created because the function CGPDFDocumentCreateWithProvider retains its own reference to the data provider.

Listing 13.1 Code that creates a CGPDFDocumentRef from a CFData-based Quartz data provider

```
CGPDFDocumentRef createNewPDFRefFromPasteBoard(void)
{
  CGDataProviderRef dataProvider = NULL;
  CGPDFDocumentRef pasteBoardPDFDocument = NULL;

  // Create a reference to the PDF data on the pasteboard.
  CFDataRef pasteBoardData = myCreatePDFDataFromPasteBoard();

  if(pasteBoardData == NULL){
    fprintf(stderr, "There is no PDF data on pasteboard!\n");
    return NULL;
  }

  // Create a data provider from the pasteboard data.
  dataProvider = myCGDataProviderCreateWithCFData(pasteBoardData);
  CFRelease(pasteBoardData);

  if(dataProvider == NULL){
    fprintf(stderr, "Couldn't create data provider.\n");
    return NULL;
  }
  pasteBoardPDFDocument = CGPDFDocumentCreateWithProvider(dataProvider);
  CGDataProviderRelease(dataProvider);
  if(pasteBoardPDFDocument == NULL){
    fprintf(stderr,
      "Couldn't create PDF document from pasteboard data provider.\n");
    return NULL;
  }
  return pasteBoardPDFDocument;
}
```

Creating PDF Data from a Pasteboard: Cocoa

Listing 13.2 is an implementation of the routine myCreatePDFDataFromPasteBoard for use with the Cocoa framework. This code uses the pasteboard associated with cut, copy, and paste operations but could be easily modified to use another pasteboard, such as the drag pasteboard. The first interesting portion of the code is the creation of an array with a list of relevant pasteboard types and the use of that array in the availableTypeFromArray: message to the pasteboard object. In this code, the only item in that array is the NSPDFPBoardType. The NSString object returned is the data type of the first item on the pasteboard that matches one of the types in the array. If no data of any of the requested types is available, the method returns a nil object. If data of type NSPDFPBoardType is available, the code obtains it using the method dataForType:, which returns an NSData object. The code retains the data obtained since the myCreatePDFDataFromPasteBoard routine has *Create* semantics and dataForType: does not. The last important feature of this code is that an NSData object is the same as a CFDataRef so the function only needs to cast the NSData object as a CFDataRef in order to return data of the expected type.

Listing 13.2 A Cocoa implementation of myCreatePDFDataFromPasteBoard

```
static CFDataRef myCreatePDFDataFromPasteBoard(void)
{
  CFDataRef pdfCFData = NULL;
  // Obtain the pasteboard to examine.
  NSPasteboard *pboard = [NSPasteboard generalPasteboard];
  // Here the array of requested types contains only one type,
  // that of PDF data. If your application could handle more types,
  // you would list them in the creation of this array.
  NSString *type = [ pboard availableTypeFromArray:
              [NSArray arrayWithObjects:NSPDFPboardType, nil] ];
  // If the NSString is not NULL, there was PDF data on the pasteboard that
  // can be obtained.
  if(type) {
    // Test that the type is the PDF data type. This code is not
    // strictly necessary for this example but is appropriate if you can
    // handle more types than just PDF.
    if([type isEqualToString:NSPDFPboardType]) {
      // Get the PDF data from the pasteboard.
      NSData *pdfData = [pboard dataForType:type];
      if(pdfData){
        // Retain the data since this is a "Create" function.
        [pdfData retain];
```

```
            // An NSData object is a CFDataRef so only a
            // cast is required.
            pdfCFData = (CFDataRef)pdfData;
          }else
            NSLog(@"Couldn't get PDF data from pasteboard!\n");
      }
    }else
      NSLog(@"Pasteboard doesn't contain PDF data!\n");

    return pdfCFData;
}
```

Creating PDF from a Pasteboard: Carbon

Listing 13.3 is an implementation of myCreatePDFDataFromPasteBoard for use with the Carbon framework. The routine uses the Pasteboard Manager functionality available in Carbon starting in Panther. (If you need your application to work with Mac OS X Jaguar and earlier versions, you need to use the Carbon Scrap Manager on those systems.) The code in the listing consists of the routines getThePasteBoard and myCreatePDFDataFromPasteBoard. The routine getThePasteBoard creates a single instance of the global pasteboard object corresponding to the system Clipboard and makes it available any time the application requires it. The function myCreatePDFDataFromPasteBoard loops over the items on the pasteboard and, for each item, it examines the flavor information of the item. If that item has a flavor of PDF data, the function copies that flavor data and returns it. The flavor type that corresponds to PDF data is the type kUTTypePDF (defined in UTCoreTypes.h in Mac OS X Tiger). Because this constant is actually an extern string rather than a #define, it isn't available to applications that execute in Panther and it is therefore simpler to define it yourself if you want to execute on those systems.

Listing 13.3 A Carbon implementation of myCreatePDFDataFromPasteBoard

```
PasteboardRef getThePasteBoard(void)
{
  static PasteboardRef pasteBoard = NULL;
  if(pasteBoard == NULL){
    OSStatus err = PasteboardCreate(kPasteboardClipboard, &pasteBoard);
    if(err || pasteBoard == NULL){
      fprintf(stderr,
        "Got error %d trying to get pasteboard!\n", (int)err);
    }
```

```
    }
    return pasteBoard;
}

CFDataRef myCreatePDFDataFromPasteBoard(void)
{
    OSStatus err = noErr;
    // This is the extern string kUTTypePDF in UTCoreTypes.h in
    // Tiger and later.
    static CFStringRef kPasteBoardTypePDF = CFSTR("com.adobe.pdf");
    CFDataRef pasteBoardData = NULL;
    PasteboardRef pasteBoard = getThePasteBoard();
    ItemCount    numPasteBoardItems;
    UInt32       i;
    (void)PasteboardSynchronize(pasteBoard);
    err = PasteboardGetItemCount(pasteBoard, &numPasteBoardItems);
    if(err || numPasteBoardItems == 0){
        fprintf(stderr, "There is NO data on pasteboard!\n");
        return NULL;
    }
    // Iterate over the items on the pasteboard.
    for(i = 1; i <= numPasteBoardItems && pasteBoardData == NULL; i++ )
    {
        PasteboardItemID      id;
        CFArrayRef            flavorTypeArray;
        CFIndex               flavorCount;
        CFIndex               flavorIndex;

        // Every item on the pasteboard has a unique identifier.
        err = PasteboardGetItemIdentifier(pasteBoard, i, &id);
        if(err)
            return NULL;


        // Each pasteboard item has a flavor array associated with it.
        err = PasteboardCopyItemFlavors(pasteBoard, id, &flavorTypeArray);
        if(err || flavorTypeArray == NULL)
            return NULL;

        flavorCount = CFArrayGetCount( flavorTypeArray );
        // Iterate over the flavors for this pasteboard item and see
        // if one of them is type PDF.
        for(flavorIndex = 0; flavorIndex < flavorCount; flavorIndex++)
        {
```

```
            CFStringRef flavorType = (CFStringRef)CFArrayGetValueAtIndex(
                    flavorTypeArray, flavorIndex );
            if(flavorType &&
              (CFStringCompare(flavorType, kPasteBoardTypePDF, 0)
                == kCFCompareEqualTo)
            ){
              err = PasteboardCopyItemFlavorData(pasteBoard, id,
                    flavorType, &pasteBoardData);
              if(err || pasteBoardData == NULL){
                fprintf(stderr,
                  "Couldn't get PDF data from pasteboard!\n");
              }
              // Got the PDF data so break out of the loop.
              break;
            }
          }
          // Release each flavor type array this code creates or copies.
          CFRelease(flavorTypeArray);
        }
        return pasteBoardData;
      }
```

Drawing PDF Pages

Quartz makes it easy to draw existing PDF content without knowing anything about the details of the PDF document format and structure. By using a few Quartz functions to extract the document properties, you'll have all the information you need to compute the correct location and orientation of any page of the PDF document that you want to draw. Quartz provides two primary functions for drawing PDF content—CGContextDrawPDFDocument, which is available in all versions of Mac OS X, and CGContextDrawPDFPage, which is available starting in Panther. You'll see how to use CGContextDrawPDFDocument, the more available function, first. Then you'll learn how to work with CGPDFPage objects using the function CGContextDrawPDFPage, which is the preferred approach for applications that run in Panther and later versions.

Drawing with CGContextDrawPDFDocument

The function CGContextDrawPDFDocument takes the following parameters:

- context, the CGContextRef into which to draw the page of the PDF document.

- rect, a rectangle in user space into which Quartz draws the page.

- document, the CGPDFDocumentRef of the document you want to draw.

- page, the page number of the page you want to draw. Pages are numbered starting with 1.

Recall that Listing 2.8 (page 39) in "Drawing PDF Content" (page 38) is a simple example that shows how to draw the first page of a complex PDF document using Quartz. It uses CGPDFDocumentCreateWithURL to create a CGPDFDocumentRef and uses CGPDFDocumentGetMediaBox to obtain the media box for the supplied PDF document. It then uses CGContextDrawPDFDocument to draw the PDF document to a supplied destination rectangle. The discussion for that example glosses over some details that you'll learn now and that are important for a better understanding of how to use Quartz to draw PDF documents.

When you call CGContextDrawPDFDocument, Quartz maps the media box of the PDF document into the rectangle you supply, performing any scaling necessary to fit the media box into the rectangle. Quartz draws only the intrinsic content of the page. That is, Quartz draws only the page content stream of the PDF document page; it does not draw any annotations such as text annotations or link annotations. (The PDF Kit framework, which is available starting in Tiger, is built on top of Quartz 2D and can draw a PDF page with various annotations.)

Note   If you look for the PDF Kit and Quartz 2D headers in Mac OS X, make sure you look in the correct framework for each. Quartz 2D is part of CoreGraphics.framework. PDF Kit is in Quartz.framework. Why isn't Quartz 2D in the Quartz framework? The answer is mostly historical. Quartz 2D was originally called Core Graphics. When Apple decided to use Quartz 2D as the public name for Core Graphics, the Core Graphics framework was already established.

Prior to rendering a PDF document, CGContextDrawPDFDocument first resets most of the graphics state parameters to their default values. The CTM and the clipping area are not reset, but the fill and stroke colors, the line dash, and other graphics state parameters are set to the default values required to render the PDF document correctly. Quartz does not reset the CTM or the clipping area prior to rendering the PDF document in order to allow you to apply coordinate transformations or clipping effects to the drawing of a PDF document.

The exceptions to the resetting of the graphics state parameters are the global alpha value, the CGBlendMode value, and the Quartz shadow parameter (see "Drawing with Shadows (Panther)" (page 512) for information about shadows). The current value of these parameters applies to the drawing of the PDF document as a whole, as if it were a single graphical element. If the global alpha value is not 1 (completely opaque), the PDF graphic is composited to the destination with the global alpha value used as the opacity of the graphic. The current value of the Quartz blend mode determines the type of compositing performed. If there is a shadow setting in the graphics state, the shadow applies to the graphic as a whole, instead of to the individual elements in the graphic. "Drawing with Transparency Layers (Panther)" (page 522) discusses the notion of applying shadows and transparency to objects that are made up of individual objects. Note that the function CGContextDrawPDFPage discussed later in this chapter treats the global alpha, blend mode, and shadow in this same manner.

Important Prior to Tiger, Quartz ignores the global alpha and shadow values in the graphics state when drawing PDF documents. In previous versions of Mac OS X, the PDF document drawing routines would treat global alpha as always opaque and behave as if there were no shadow. In Panther, you can carefully use transparency layers to work around this problem; see "Drawing with Transparency Layers (Panther)" (page 522). In Jaguar and earlier versions, the only work-around is to render the graphic to an image and apply global alpha when drawing the resulting image.

Quartz clips its drawing to the clipping area on the context but otherwise CGContextDrawPDFDocument performs no additional clipping. In addition, CGContextDrawPDFDocument ignores any rotation angle information that applies to the page you are drawing. This allows you to draw any portion of the content of a given PDF page, including content that is outside the crop box or other boundary rectangles specified for a given page. However, if you want to clip to the crop box of the PDF document, draw the content of a boundary rectangle (such as the art box) into a specified rectangle, or use the rotation angle when you perform your drawing, there is additional work required. In Panther and later versions, Quartz provides convenience functions that make it simple to perform these operations. You'll soon see how to use these convenience functions as well as how to obtain equivalent results on earlier versions of Mac OS X.

Note Nothing prevents you from passing a nonexistent page number to any of the Quartz functions that return data about a page in a PDF document or that draw a page. For example, if you call CGContextDrawPDFDocument with a page number that does not exist, Quartz draws nothing.

Drawing PDF Documents in a Flipped Coordinate System

The examples in this book so far assume a coordinate system where the origin is in the lower-left corner of the drawing canvas, with positive y values increasing as you go up the drawing canvas. Most applications, and in some cases the application frameworks themselves, prefer to draw into a flipped coordinate system where the origin is at the top-left corner, with positive y values increasing as you go down the drawing canvas.

Quartz is well suited to working with different coordinate systems. In general, the only difference between a coordinate system with a top-left origin and bottom-right origin is a coordinate transformation. This is demonstrated in Listing 4.3 (page 77), which shows how to transform from the default Carbon HIView coordinate system with a top-left origin to the default Quartz coordinate system.

Working in a flipped coordinate system does require some extra care when drawing PDF documents. For example, the left portion of Figure 13.1 is the result of drawing a PDF document directly with Quartz into a flipped view. (Of course you most likely want the result on the right side of the figure.) Without adjusting for the difference between the framework coordinate system and the coordinate system Quartz uses by default, the graphics you draw will be flipped. The Cocoa framework drawing API handles the details of drawing into a flipped view; it's when you use Quartz drawing directly that you need to account for the flipped nature of the context.

Drawing a PDF document so that it is upright in a flipped coordinate system is straightforward. The basic approach is to temporarily set up a coordinate system where the origin is in the lower-left corner of the object to draw and the coordinate axes are in a standard Quartz coordinate system with y increasing as you go up. You do this by first translating the origin so that it is located at the lower-left corner of the PDF document you want to draw, then you flip the coordinate system in y and adjust the coordinate origin appropriately.

The code in Listing 13.4 produces the results in Figure 13.1 when drawn into a flipped view. The routine `doPDFDocumentInFlippedView` first draws the PDF document without adjusting for the fact that the view is flipped. This produces the graphic on the left of the figure. Next it translates to the right, leaving space between the two renderings of the PDF document. It then calls `myDrawPDFDocumentToFlippedContext`, which draws a PDF document into the `CGRect` passed to the routine. The rectangle is interpreted in the flipped coordinate system; its origin is at the top-left corner of the PDF graphic being drawn.

The routine `myDrawPDFDocumentToFlippedContext` draws the PDF document upright into the flipped view. By using `CGContextSaveGState` and `CGContextRestoreGState`, the routine `myDrawPDFDocumentToFlippedContext` limits any coordinate transformations it performs so that they do not affect the calling routine. After saving the graphics state, the code translates the coordinate origin so that the new coordinate origin is at the lower-left corner of the destination rectangle for the graphic. Because the rectangle passed to `myDrawPDFDocumentToFlippedContext` describes the rectangle in the flipped view, the lower-left corner of the destination rectangle is at the minimum x coordinate of the rectangle and the maximum y coordinate.

Figure 13.1 Drawing a PDF document into a flipped coordinate system

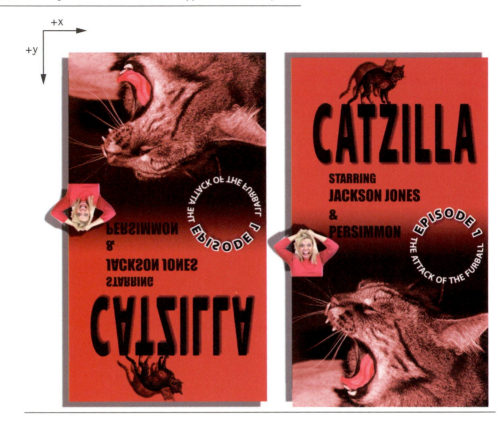

The code then flips the coordinate system to produce a y-coordinate axis that points up, rather than down. Now the coordinate system is in the upright coordinate system with its origin at the lower-left corner of the PDF page origin. The last step it takes before drawing the document is to translate the coordinate origin so that drawing the PDF document using the destination rectangle places the PDF page origin at the lower-left corner of rect. This is equivalent to changing the destination rectangle origin to (0,0). After the code calls CGContextDrawPDFDocument to draw the PDF document into the unflipped Quartz coordinate system, it restores the graphics state to that prior to the call to myDrawPDFDocumentToFlippedContext.

This strategy of drawing PDF documents into a flipped coordinate system applies also to drawing images into a flipped coordinate system. The code you use to set up the coordinate system before and restore to the previous coordinate system after your drawing is the same as this example; the only difference is that for images, you'd perform your drawing with CGContextDrawImage instead of CGContextDrawPDFDocument or other PDF drawing routines.

Listing 13.4 Code that draws a PDF document into a flipped view

```
void myDrawPDFDocumentToFlippedContext(CGContextRef context,
    CGRect rect, CGPDFDocumentRef doc, int page)
{
  // Save the graphics state so all coordinate transformations are
  // confined to this routine.
  CGContextSaveGState(context);
    // Because rect is that for drawing in a flipped coordinate
    // system, this translates to the lower-left corner of rect
    // in an upright coordinate system.
    CGContextTranslateCTM(context, CGRectGetMinX(rect),
              CGRectGetMaxY(rect));
    // Scale to flip the coordinate system so that the y axis
    // goes up the drawing canvas.
    CGContextScaleCTM(context, 1, -1);
    // Translate so the origin is offset by exactly the
    // rect origin.
    CGContextTranslateCTM(context, -rect.origin.x, -rect.origin.y);
    // Now draw the document, producing a rendering that is upright.
    CGContextDrawPDFDocument(context, rect, doc, page);
    // Restore the previous coordinate system.
  CGContextRestoreGState(context);
}

void doPDFDocumentInFlippedView(CGContextRef context, CFURLRef url)
{
  CGRect pdfRect;
  CGPDFDocumentRef pdfDoc = CGPDFDocumentCreateWithURL(url);
  if(pdfDoc != NULL){
    // First draw the PDF into the flipped view.
    pdfRect = CGPDFDocumentGetMediaBox(pdfDoc, 1);
    // Set the rect origin to be at the top-left corner
    // of where the graphic should go.
    pdfRect.origin.x = 20;
    pdfRect.origin.y = 200.;
    CGContextSaveGState(context);
    // Clip to the PDF document media rect.
    CGContextClipToRect(context, pdfRect);
    CGContextDrawPDFDocument(context, pdfRect, pdfDoc, 1); // page 1
    // Translate to the right to prepare for drawing again.
    CGContextTranslateCTM(context, pdfRect.size.width*1.2, 0);
    // Now call the routine that takes into account the
    // fact that the view is flipped.
```

```
            myDrawPDFDocumentToFlippedContext(context, pdfRect, pdfDoc, 1);
            CGContextRestoreGState(pdfDoc);
            CGPDFDocumentRelease(pdfDoc);
        }else
            fprintf(stderr, "Can't create PDF document for URL\n");
    }
```

Using CGPDFPage Objects (Panther)

10.3 ▶
In Panther, Quartz introduced a way to represent an individual page in a PDF document with an opaque data type—CGPDFPageRef. This data type, together with the Quartz functions that use it, allows you to work with PDF pages as individual entities. The CGPDFPage object and the associated functions provide a somewhat more streamlined interface for working with pages in a PDF document.

You obtain a CGPDFPage object by calling the function CGPDFDocumentGetPage, passing the CGPDFDocumentRef for the PDF document of interest and the page number of the page that you want to examine or draw. If the page does not exist, the function returns a NULL reference. Note that this function has *Get* semantics; you do not own the reference that is returned. If you need a reference that you own, call CGPDFPageRetain on the CGPDFPageRef that is returned from CGPDFDocumentGetPage.

After you have a CGPDFPage object, you can obtain any of the boundary rectangles for the page using the function CGPDFPageGetBoxRect. This function uses the enumerated type CGPDFBox to specify which boundary rectangle you want to obtain. The function CGPDFPageGetRotationAngle returns the rotation angle for the page.

To draw a CGPDFPage object, use the function CGContextDrawPDFPage, passing the following parameters:

- context, the CGContextRef into which to draw the PDF page.
- page, a CGPDFPageRef of the PDF page you want to draw.

This function is similar to CGContextDrawPDFDocument described in "Drawing with CGContextDrawPDFDocument" (page 406) with two important differences. The most obvious difference is that you pass in the CGPDFPage object to draw, rather than a CGPDFDocument object and the page number. The second difference is that CGContextDrawPDFPage doesn't use a mapping rectangle and as a result doesn't provide any scaling or translating as CGContextDrawPDFDocument does.

Typically, when drawing a page you have a destination rectangle you want to draw the page into and you want to map one of the PDF boundary rectangles into that destination, taking into account the rotation angle of the page. Quartz provides the function `CGPDFPageGetDrawingTransform`, making it straightforward to do this. This function allows you to obtain the affine transform appropriate for centering the drawing of a page into a specified rectangle, while rotating the page when necessary. The transform returned by this function incorporates any scaling that's necessary to fit the boundary rectangle inside the destination rectangle. The resulting transform only scales down, it does not scale up to force the boundary rectangle to the size of the destination rectangle if the boundary rectangle is smaller than the destination. To avoid any scaling at all, specify a destination rectangle that has the same width and height as the PDF boundary rectangle you specify.

The function `CGPDFPageGetDrawingTransform` takes the following parameters:

- `page`, the `CGPDFPageRef` of the page you want to draw.

- `boxType`, one of the enumerated values of type `CGPDFBox`. This value specifies which of the PDF boundary rectangles of `page` you want to center in the destination rectangle.

- `rect`, the `CGRect` of the user space destination rectangle you want to center in. If the boundary rectangle does not fit inside of `rect`, Quartz returns a transform that properly scales the boundary rectangle so that it does fit. If the boundary rectangle fits inside of `rect`, it is centered inside `rect`, but not scaled to the size of `rect`.

- `rotate`, an integer multiple of 90 degrees, corresponding to the number of degrees of *additional* rotation you want to incorporate into the coordinate mapping. The `rotate` value uses the same sense of rotation as the `rotate` value of the PDF document; positive values are clockwise. The function `CGPDFPageGetDrawingTransform` automatically takes into account the rotation value of `page`; however, you can apply an additional rotation in increments of 90 degrees. Typically, you pass 0 for this value to obtain the correct transformation based on the intrinsic rotation of the page, but if you want to apply an *additional* rotation of 90 degrees to the page, you pass 90 for the `rotate` parameter.

- `preserveAspectRatio`, a `bool`, indicating whether you want to preserve the aspect ratio as part of the coordinate mapping. If `true`, and the boundary rectangle is scaled down to fit in the destination rectangle, the transformation always represents a uniform scaling of the page into `rect`, with the page centered in `rect`. If `false`, and the boundary rectangle is scaled down to fit in the destination rectangle, the transform returned fits the boundary rectangle represented by `boxType` inside of `rect` without regard for whether the scaling is uniform.

Listing 13.5 demonstrates a typical usage of the CGPDFPage functions to draw a PDF page at its natural size (using the boundary rectangle you specify), adjusted for the rotation angle of the page plus any additional rotation you want. It defines three routines: `getRotatedPDFPageDimensions`, `drawPDFPageInRect`, and `drawWithPDFPage`.

The routine `getRotatedPDFPageDimensions` takes a CGPDFPage object and the CGPDFBox of the boundary rectangle of interest and obtains the width and height, after accounting for any rotation intrinsic to the page plus any additional rotation you want. To compute the dimensions, it first intersects the boundary rectangle of interest with the media box. Intersecting the two rectangles ensures that the boundary rectangle is constrained by the media box, conforming to the meaning of a given boundary rectangle in the PDF specification.

The routine `drawPDFPageInRect` draws a PDF page by centering the specified CGPDFBox boundary rectangle into the supplied CGRect, scaling down if necessary and preserving the aspect ratio. It uses the Quartz function `CGPDFPageGetDraw-ingTransform` to obtain the required coordinate transformation with the specified additional rotation and applies that transformation prior to drawing the page. To ensure that Quartz draws only the content inside the requested boundary rectangle, the code clips its drawing to the intersection of the media box and the CGPDFBox requested. It then uses `CGContextDrawPDFPage` to draw the page. The function `CGContextDrawPDFPage` performs no coordinate transformations, it simply draws the PDF document. Since the code has already transformed the coordinate system using the transformation returned by `CGPDFPageGetDraw-ingTransform`, the drawing appears centered in the destination rectangle.

The routine `drawWithPDFPage` draws a specified page of a PDF document into a rectangle with the width and height of the CGPDFBox requested, transformed by the intrinsic page rotation plus any additional page rotation requested by the `extraRotation` parameter. A typical value for the `boxType` is `kCGPDFCropBox` to draw the PDF crop box for the page. The typical value for the `extraRotation` parameter is 0; this causes the page to be rotated only by the intrinsic rotation. The routine calls the Quartz function `CGPDFDocumentGetPage` to obtain the CGPDFPage object for the page number supplied and uses `getRotatedPDFPage-Dimensions` to obtain the width and height of the rectangle to draw into. It then uses `drawPDFPageInRect` to draw the page.

The routine `drawWithPDFPage` draws the page in an orientation adjusted by the page rotation plus the requested additional rotation but otherwise performs no additional scaling, translation, or rotations. It simply draws the PDF page into a rectangle located at the origin of coordinates with a width and height of the requested CGPDFBox. If you want to scale the drawing (either up or down) or locate the page other than at the origin, simply transform user space prior to calling `drawWithPDFPage`. There are situations for which you may need the natural dimensions of the PDF page to determine what transformations to apply prior to calling the routine `drawWithPDFPage`. For that reason, the routine `getRotatedPDF-PageDimensions` is designed to obtain these dimensions.

Listing 13.5 Code that draws a PDF page inside of a rectangle using CGPDFPageGetDrawingTransform

```
void getRotatedPDFPageDimensions(CGPDFPageRef page, CGPDFBox boxType,
                int rotation,
                float *widthP, float *heightP)
{
  float width, height;
  CGRect boxRect = CGPDFPageGetBoxRect(page, boxType);
  // Intersect the boundary rect with the media box if necessary.
  if(boxType != kCGPDFMediaBox){
    CGRect mediaBox = CGPDFPageGetBoxRect(page, kCGPDFMediaBox);
    boxRect = CGRectIntersection(boxRect, mediaBox);
  }
  width = CGRectGetWidth(boxRect);
  height = CGRectGetHeight(boxRect);
  // Obtain the page rotation angle, add it to the
  // requested additional rotation and ensure
  // that the result is within the range of 0-360 degrees.
  rotation += CGPDFPageGetRotationAngle(page);
  rotation %= 360;
  if(rotation < 0)
    rotation += 360;

  if(rotation == 90 || rotation == 270){
    // Interchange the width and height if rotation angle
    // is 90 or 270 degrees.
    float tmp = width;
    width = height;
    height = tmp;
  }

  *widthP = width;
  *heightP = height;
  return;
}

void drawPDFPageInRect(CGContextRef context, CGPDFPageRef pdfPage,
                CGPDFBox boxType, CGRect destRect,
                int additionalPageRotation)
{
  bool preserveAspectRatio = true;
  CGRect clipRect;
  // Calculate the drawing transform to center the specified box
  // into the destRect.
  CGAffineTransform t = CGPDFPageGetDrawingTransform(pdfPage,
                boxType, destRect,
                additionalPageRotation, preserveAspectRatio);
```

```
    CGContextSaveGState(context);
      CGContextConcatCTM(context, t);
      clipRect = CGPDFPageGetBoxRect(pdfPage, boxType);
      // Intersect this rect with the media box if necessary.
      if(boxType != kCGPDFMediaBox){
        CGRect mediaBox = CGPDFPageGetBoxRect(pdfPage,
                  kCGPDFMediaBox);
        clipRect = CGRectIntersection(clipRect, mediaBox);
      }
      CGContextClipToRect(context, clipRect);
      CGContextDrawPDFPage(context, pdfPage);
    CGContextRestoreGState(context);
}

void drawWithPDFPage(CGContextRef context, CGPDFDocumentRef pdfDoc,
            size_t pageNumber, CGPDFBox boxType, int extraRotation)
{
  float width, height;
  CGRect destRect;
  CGPDFPageRef pdfPage = CGPDFDocumentGetPage(pdfDoc, pageNumber);
  if(!pdfPage){
    fprintf(stderr, "Couldn't get page number %zd !\n", pageNumber);
    return;
  }
  getRotatedPDFPageDimensions(pdfPage, boxType,
            extraRotation, &width, &height);
  destRect = CGRectMake(0, 0, width, height);
  // The rect that is supplied preserves the aspect ratio since the
  // width and height are that of the PDF box being drawn.
  drawPDFPageInRect(context, pdfPage, boxType, destRect, extraRotation);
}
```

Drawing with PDF Rotation on Jaguar and Earlier Versions

Listing 13.5 demonstrates the preferred way to draw a given PDF page, handling the rotation angle intrinsic to the page. However, this code uses the CGPDFPage object and associated Quartz functions that are not available in Mac OS X versions prior to Panther. However, it's possible to achieve the same result without using CGPDFPage objects and functions. Emulating CGPDFPageGetDrawingTransform involves some interesting coordinate transformation calculations. This next section discusses these coordinate transformations and the concepts behind them. If you aren't interested in these concepts, feel free to skip over it and go straight to the emulation routine.

Transforming from Object Space to Quartz User Space. The calculation that the function `CGPDFPageGetDrawingTransform` performs is equivalent to determining the proper transformation matrix to apply to map an object in one coordinate system, referred to here as **object space**, into another coordinate system (current Quartz user space). In the example here, the object space is that of the PDF document page to draw. (Recall that `CGPDFPageGetDrawingTransform` takes the boundary rectangle specified by a `CGPDFBox`, an optional additional rotation, and a destination rectangle to map into and computes the `CGAffineTransform`, which if applied prior to drawing the page, fits that page into the destination rectangle.)

Affine transforms map coordinates from one coordinate system to another. As discussed in "The Mathematics of Affine Transforms" (page 88), affine transforms can be mathematically described as follows:

$$Point' = Point \times M_{transform}$$

where *Point* is the coordinate in the coordinate system you are transforming from, $M_{transform}$ is the transformation being applied, and *Point'* is the transformed coordinate. For the calculation in this section, the object space is the starting coordinate system and the destination coordinate system is that of the user space destination rectangle to map to.

The mapping from the PDF page space to the Quartz user space destination rectangle is essentially a sequence of four transformations, as you can see by looking at Figure 13.2. The first transformation translates the PDF page so that its center is at the origin of object space. The second transformation rotates the PDF page about its origin as needed. The third transformation scales the PDF page so that its dimensions fit inside of the destination rectangle. The fourth and final transformation translates the PDF page so that its center coincides with the center of the destination rectangle.

Using this sequence of transformations, you can construct the affine transform. These transformations of the points in object space can be mathematically represented as the following:

$$Point_{userspace} = Point \times M_{translate_1} \times M_{rotate} \times M_{scale} \times M_{translate_2}$$

Quartz provides the `CGAffineTransformConcat` function for multiplying two matrices together to compute the resultant matrix. The first parameter you pass to `CGAffineTransformConcat` is the matrix on the left side of the multiplication and the second parameter is the matrix on the right. To compute the entire transformation, you need to multiply these four matrices together.

The details of this particular transformation are specific to the goal of mapping a PDF page rectangle into Quartz user space, but the general concept described

Figure 13.2 Transforming from PDF page space to a destination rectangle in user space

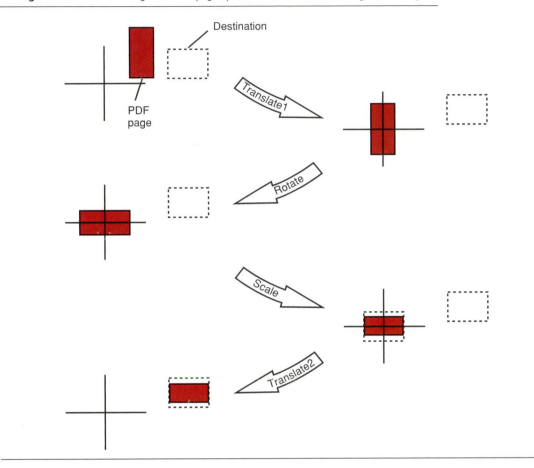

here applies to transforming from any object coordinate system to another coordinate system.

Emulating the CGPDFPage Drawing. The code in Listing 13.6 produces an equivalent result to the code in Listing 13.5, but the current code can execute on versions of Mac OS X that don't have the CGPDFPage functions available. It contains the routines getRotatedPageDimensions, drawPageInRect, and drawPage, which parallel the functionality in the previous code, and adds the routines myCG-PDFDocumentPageGetBoxRect and myPageGetDrawingTransform, which take the place of the CGPDFPage functions CGPDFPageGetBoxRect and CGPDFPageGetDrawingTransform.

The routine myCGPDFDocumentPageGetBoxRect simply uses the CGPDFDocument routines to obtain the boundary rectangle for the specified CGPDFBox for the document and page number supplied. The implementation of `myPageGetDrawingTransform` emulates the functionality of `CGPDFPageGetDrawingTransform` and deserves a closer examination.

The first portion of `myPageGetDrawingTransform` obtains the boundary rectangle associated with the requested `CGPDFBox` and intersects it with the media box of the document, constructing `boxRect`. It then creates the sequence of transformations described in Figure . It begins by constructing the first transformation, a translation of the center of `boxRect` to the coordinate origin.

Next the code obtains the rotation angle of the PDF page, adds in the additional rotation factor, and adjusts the rotation to fall in the range 0–360 degrees. The code then creates a matrix corresponding to a rotation by this angle. Because the PDF specification and the routine `drawPage` in the listing treat positive angles as clockwise rotations, the code negates the rotation angle when constructing a rotation matrix using `CGAffineTransformMakeRotation`, since this function considers a clockwise rotation to be a negative angle.

For rotations that correspond to 90 or 270 degrees, the width of the PDF box becomes the height of the box and the height of the box becomes the width for the purpose of determining the scaling of the page into the destination rectangle. To compute the correct scale factor to fit the resulting width and height into the destination rectangle, the ratio of the destination width to the source width and the destination height to the source height computes the scaling. Because the functionality implemented here is only to scale down the page to fit into the destination rectangle and never to scale up, the code performs a minimum operation to ensure that the scale factor is never greater than 1. (If you want to allow both scaling up and scaling down, there is no need to limit the scaling values to a maximum scaling factor of 1.) If the request is to preserve the aspect ratio of the page, then the minimum of the x and y scale factors is used. This ensures that neither of the two dimensions protrudes outside the destination rectangle. After computing the scaling factors, the code creates a scaling matrix using the function `CGAffineTransformMakeScale`.

The last affine transform computed is the transform from the origin of coordinates to the center of the destination rectangle. Now the code has created each of the transformations from Figure , and it can compute the affine transform that corresponds to applying all the transformations in the correct order. This is computed by multiplying the affine transforms together in the order shown in the final equation in "Transforming from Object Space to Quartz User Space" (page 417).

The code uses `CGAffineTransformConcat` to perform the matrix multiplications. It concatenates the matrix `t1Transform` with `rTransform`, the transformation that corresponds to the rotation. It then concatenates the result with `sTransform`, the transformation that corresponds to the scaling. Finally, it concatenates that result with t2Transform, the final translation. In each case, the correct order of concatenation is to multiply each subsequent transformation to the right of the previously calculated result. The resulting affine transform captures the four transformations in left-to-right order, just as described by "Transforming from Object Space to Quartz User Space" (page 417). The affine transformation matrix fullTransform returned from myPageGetDrawingTransform is functionally identical to that returned from the Quartz drawing function CGPDFPageGetDrawingTransform.

The routine drawPageInRect parallels that of the drawPDFPageInRect routine in Listing 13.5 (page 415); however, this routine uses the Quartz function CGContextDrawPDFDocument, which scales the media box to fit into the destination rectangle. Because the coordinate system is already transformed to draw the PDF document in the correct location without any additional transformations, the code calls CGContextDrawPDFDocument with the media box as the destination rectangle. This ensures that Quartz performs no additional coordinate transformations when it draws the document.

Listing 13.6 Code that draws a PDF page inside of a rectangle (Jaguar and earlier versions)

```
CGRect myCGPDFDocumentPageGetBoxRect(CGPDFDocumentRef pdfDoc,
                size_t pageNumber, CGPDFBox boxType)
{
  switch(boxType){
    default:
    case kCGPDFMediaBox:
      return CGPDFDocumentGetMediaBox(pdfDoc, pageNumber);

    case kCGPDFCropBox:
      return CGPDFDocumentGetCropBox(pdfDoc, pageNumber);

    case kCGPDFBleedBox:
      return CGPDFDocumentGetBleedBox(pdfDoc, pageNumber);

    case kCGPDFTrimBox:
      return CGPDFDocumentGetTrimBox(pdfDoc, pageNumber);

    case kCGPDFArtBox:
      return CGPDFDocumentGetArtBox(pdfDoc, pageNumber);
  }
}
```

```
void getRotatedPageDimensions(CGPDFDocumentRef pdfDoc, size_t pageNumber,
                CGPDFBox boxType, int rotationAngle,
                float *widthP, float *heightP)
{
  float width, height;
  CGRect rect = myCGPDFDocumentPageGetBoxRect(pdfDoc, pageNumber, boxType);
  if(boxType != kCGPDFMediaBox){
    CGRect mediaBox = CGPDFDocumentGetMediaBox(pdfDoc, pageNumber);
    rect = CGRectIntersection(rect, mediaBox);
  }
  width = CGRectGetWidth(rect);
  height = CGRectGetHeight(rect);
  // Obtain the page rotation angle and ensure that it is
  // within the range of 0-360 degrees.
  rotationAngle += CGPDFDocumentGetRotationAngle(pdfDoc, pageNumber);
  rotationAngle %= 360;
  if(rotationAngle < 0)
    rotationAngle += 360;

  if(rotationAngle == 90 || rotationAngle == 270){
    // Interchange the width and height if rotation angle
    // is 90 or 270 degrees.
    float tmp = width;
    width = height;
    height = tmp;
  }

  *widthP = width;
  *heightP = height;
  return;
}


CGAffineTransform myPageGetDrawingTransform(CGPDFDocumentRef pdfDoc,
                size_t pageNumber, CGPDFBox boxType,
                CGRect destRect,
                int rotate, bool preserveAspectRatio)
{
  CGAffineTransform fullTransform, rTransform, sTransform,
                t1Transform, t2Transform;
  float boxOriginX, boxOriginY, boxWidth, boxHeight;
  float destOriginX, destOriginY, destWidth, destHeight;
  float scaleX, scaleY;
```

```
    // First intersect the boundary rectangle of boxType with the
    // media box. This is to conform with the meaning of a given
    // boundary rectangle in the PDF spec.
    CGRect boxRect = myCGPDFDocumentPageGetBoxRect(pdfDoc,
                pageNumber, boxType);
    if(boxType != kCGPDFMediaBox){
      CGRect mediaBox = CGPDFDocumentGetMediaBox(pdfDoc, pageNumber);
      boxRect = CGRectIntersection(boxRect, mediaBox);
    }

    // Obtain the origin, width, and height of the PDF box to transform.
    boxOriginX = CGRectGetMinX(boxRect);
    boxOriginY = CGRectGetMinY(boxRect);
    boxWidth = CGRectGetWidth(boxRect);
    boxHeight = CGRectGetHeight(boxRect);

    // Construct a transformation that translates the center of the box
    // to the origin.
    t1Transform = CGAffineTransformMakeTranslation(
                -(boxOriginX + boxWidth/2),
                -(boxOriginY + boxHeight/2) );

    // Add the intrinsic page rotation to the rotation requested.
    rotate += CGPDFDocumentGetRotationAngle(pdfDoc, pageNumber);
    // Adjust the page rotation angle to between 0-360 degrees.
    rotate %= 360;
    if (rotate < 0)
      rotate += 360;

    // Construct a transformation that rotates by the rotation angle.
    rTransform = CGAffineTransformMakeRotation(
                DEGREES_TO_RADIANS(-rotate) );

    // If the rotation is 90 or 270 degrees, then the rotation
    // interchanges the width and height.
    if(rotate == 90 || rotate == 270){
      float tmp = boxWidth;
      boxWidth = boxHeight;
      boxHeight = tmp;
    }

    // Obtain the origin, width, and height of the destination rectangle.
    destOriginX = CGRectGetMinX(destRect);
    destOriginY = CGRectGetMinY(destRect);
```

```
    destWidth = CGRectGetWidth(destRect);
    destHeight = CGRectGetHeight(destRect);

    // Compute x and y scaling factors to scale the box dimensions
    // into the destination dimensions. Don't scale up, only down.
    scaleX = MIN(1, destWidth/boxWidth);
    scaleY = MIN(1, destHeight/boxHeight);

    // If necessary, ensure scale factors are the same.
    if(preserveAspectRatio)
      scaleX = scaleY = MIN(scaleX, scaleY);

    // Construct an affine transform that represents this scaling.
    sTransform = CGAffineTransformMakeScale(scaleX, scaleY);

    // Construct a transform from the origin to the center of destRect.
    t2Transform = CGAffineTransformMakeTranslation(
                destOriginX + destWidth/2,
                destOriginY + destHeight/2);

    // Concatenate the first translation with the rotation.
    fullTransform = CGAffineTransformConcat(t1Transform, rTransform);

    // Concatenate the previous result with the scaling.
    fullTransform = CGAffineTransformConcat(fullTransform, sTransform);

    // Concatenate the previous result with translation 2.
    fullTransform = CGAffineTransformConcat(fullTransform, t2Transform);

    return fullTransform;
}


void drawPageInRect(CGContextRef context, CGPDFDocumentRef pdfDoc,
                size_t pageNumber,
                CGPDFBox boxType, CGRect destRect,
                int additionalPageRotation)
{
    bool preserveAspectRatio = true;
    CGRect clipRect;
    // Calculate the drawing transform to center the specified box into the
    // destRect.
    CGAffineTransform t = myPageGetDrawingTransform(pdfDoc, pageNumber,
                boxType, destRect,
                additionalPageRotation, preserveAspectRatio);
```

```
        CGContextSaveGState(context);
          CGContextConcatCTM(context, t);
          // Clip to the rectangle that is being drawn.
          clipRect = myCGPDFDocumentPageGetBoxRect(pdfDoc,
                      pageNumber, boxType);
          // Intersect this rectangle with the media box if necessary.
          if(boxType != kCGPDFMediaBox){
            CGRect mediaBox = CGPDFDocumentGetMediaBox(pdfDoc, pageNumber);
            clipRect = CGRectIntersection(clipRect, mediaBox);
          }
          CGContextClipToRect(context, clipRect);
          // Draw the PDF document into the media box to ensure no further
          // translation or scaling.
          CGContextDrawPDFDocument(context,
                      CGPDFDocumentGetMediaBox(pdfDoc, pageNumber),
                      pdfDoc, pageNumber);
        CGContextRestoreGState(context);
}


void drawPage(CGContextRef context, CGPDFDocumentRef pdfDoc,
              size_t pageNumber,
              CGPDFBox boxType, int extraRotation)
{
  float width, height;
  CGRect destRect;
  // Obtain the page dimensions of the page of interest.
  getRotatedPageDimensions(pdfDoc, pageNumber, boxType,
              extraRotation, &width, &height);

  destRect = CGRectMake(0, 0, width, height);
  // The rectangle that is supplied preserves the aspect ratio
  // since the width and height are that of the PDF box being drawn.
  drawPageInRect(context, pdfDoc, pageNumber, boxType,
              destRect, extraRotation);
}
```

Handling Protected PDF Documents (Jaguar)

10.2 ▶ The PDF specification describes a document model for the treatment of encrypted PDF documents. Starting with the Jaguar release of Mac OS X,

Quartz provides the ability to handle encrypted PDF documents. There are two passwords that can be used to decrypt an encrypted PDF document, the **owner** password and the **user** password. Supplying either password allows Quartz to decrypt a document and provide access to it through Quartz programming interfaces.

Quartz provides the tools to allow the software that accesses an encrypted PDF document to decrypt and use the document when an access password is supplied (or is empty) and has functions that allow you to determine what permissions the supplied password allows. Once an encrypted PDF document is unlocked with an access password, it is up to the application software that uses Quartz to enforce the access permissions that follow the encrypted document model that the PDF specification describes.

The PDF encrypted document model consists of the following:

1. When using a PDF document by unlocking it with the **owner** password, there are no permissions restrictions and the owner is allowed to use the document freely, including potentially changing the permissions of the document.

2. When unlocking the document with the **user** password, those permission attributes stored in the document apply and the user is restricted from any operations those permissions forbid.

Important   Software developers who want to handle encrypted PDF documents are urged to consult the PDF specification to understand the details of the document model for handling encrypted PDF documents.

In addition to requiring a password to decrypt the document (thereby unlocking it and enabling the viewing of its contents), encrypted PDF documents support a set of permissions attributes that indicate which operations are considered restricted. Examples of the permissions restrictions that can be assigned to a PDF document include disallowing the printing of the document and disallowing copying of the content.

Nothing contained in the PDF document inherently prevents access to the data in a PDF document other than encryption. That is, once a document is decrypted (using either the owner or user password), full access to the document is available. Nothing in the document forces the access permissions attributes to be respected; there is simply data that says what the intended permissions restrictions are. Additionally, nothing in the document forces a distinction between the capabilities that are allowed if you unlock the document with the owner password or user password. The distinction between the permissions available when unlocking with an owner password or a user password is enforced solely by the software application that presents the PDF document and allows user manipulation.

Some applications do not need to be concerned with encrypted documents. For example, if your application does not support opening PDF documents but does support importing PDF data from other applications via the Clipboard, you probably don't need to be concerned with encryption.

When you create a CGPDFDocumentRef from an existing PDF document that is encrypted, Quartz treats the document specially. If the document can be decrypted with an empty password string, Quartz automatically unlocks the document and makes it available for drawing. If the document requires a password other than the empty string, Quartz cannot automatically unlock the document and you must supply a password in order for Quartz to decrypt the document and allow you to use it.

After a document is unlocked, Quartz keeps track of the access permissions that apply to the unlocked document. If you unlock the document with the user password, Quartz considers the access permissions to be those specified in the PDF document. If you unlock the document with the owner password, Quartz considers the access permissions to be unrestricted. You use the functions CGPDF-DocumentAllowsPrinting and CGPDFDocumentAllowsCopying to find out the permissions that are available with the current level of access.

In all versions of Mac OS X, Quartz can draw an encrypted PDF document to most types of Quartz contexts, including window contexts and bitmap contexts. The PDF context is used to create new PDF documents from Quartz drawing and is also used by the printing system during printing. Starting in Panther, the Quartz functions that draw PDF document pages don't draw content to a PDF context if the permissions of the unlocked document do not allow printing. This restriction prevents you from creating unprotected PDF documents from those that are locked for printing and also prevents you from printing PDF documents that are locked for printing. Note that if you unlock a PDF document with the owner password, Quartz allows you to draw it to any context, including a PDF context.

The code in Listing 13.7 uses the Quartz CGPDFDocument functions to determine whether a document can be unlocked without a special password and if it can be, whether printing or copying is allowed. The code defines a structure of type MyPDFDocumentInfo that holds the PDF document reference being created plus permissions information about the document. In addition, Listing 13.7 contains two routines: checkPDFDocumentPermissions and createMy-PDFDocumentWithURL.

Listing 13.7 Code that detects an encrypted PDF document and determines its permissions

```
typedef struct MyPDFDocumentInfo
{
  CGPDFDocumentRef pdfDoc;
  bool documentIsUnlocked;
  bool documentForbidsNewDocument;
  bool documentForbidsPrinting;
  bool documentForbidsCopying;
}MyPDFDocumentInfo;

// This code handles a document that either is not encrypted or
// is encrypted but has an empty password.
void checkPDFDocumentPermissions(MyPDFDocumentInfo *infoP)
{
  CGPDFDocumentRef pdfDoc = infoP->pdfDoc;
  infoP->documentIsUnlocked = false;
  infoP->documentForbidsNewDocument = true;
  infoP->documentForbidsPrinting = true;
  infoP->documentForbidsCopying = true;
  if(CGPDFDocumentIsUnlocked(pdfDoc)){
    // Mark that the document is unlocked.
    infoP->documentIsUnlocked = true;
    // Check the permissions that are allowed.
    infoP->documentForbidsPrinting =
                !CGPDFDocumentAllowsPrinting(pdfDoc);
    infoP->documentForbidsCopying =
                !CGPDFDocumentAllowsCopying(pdfDoc);
    // Keep track of whether the document is encrypted
    // to ensure that permissions are respected.
    infoP->documentForbidsNewDocument =
                CGPDFDocumentIsEncrypted(pdfDoc);
  }
  return;
}

void createMyPDFDocumentWithURL(CFURLRef url,
                MyPDFDocumentInfo *pdfDocInfoP)
{
  pdfDocInfoP->pdfDoc = CGPDFDocumentCreateWithURL(url);
  if(pdfDocInfoP->pdfDoc){
    // Check whether the document is encrypted and obtain
    // the appropriate permissions if so.
    checkPDFDocumentPermissions(pdfDocInfoP);
```

```
        // If it can't be unlocked with an empty password, warn the user.
        if(!pdfDocInfoP->documentIsUnlocked){
          WarnAboutEncryptedPDFDocument();
          CGPDFDocumentRelease(pdfDocInfoP->pdfDoc);
          pdfDocInfoP->pdfDoc = NULL;
        }else{
          if( pdfDocInfoP->documentForbidsPrinting ||
            pdfDocInfoP->documentForbidsCopying
          ){
            // Warn user about restrictions.
            WarnAboutNoPrintingOrCopying(
              pdfDocInfoP->documentForbidsCopying,
              pdfDocInfoP->documentForbidsPrinting
            );
          }else{
            // Respect restrictions at print time or new PDF document.
            if(pdfDocInfoP->documentForbidsNewDocument){
              WarnAboutNoNewPDFDocument();
            }
          }
        }
      }
    }
}
```

The routine createMyPDFDocumentWithURL uses CGPDFDocumentIsUnlocked to determine if a PDF document is unlocked. When you first create a CGPDFDocumentRef with Quartz, it is unlocked either if the document it represents is not encrypted or if it is encrypted but can be decrypted with an empty password string. If the document is encrypted and requires a nonempty password to decrypt it, the function CGPDFDocumentIsUnlocked returns false. For PDF documents that are unlocked, the code checks the permissions for printing and copying and fills in the relevant fields in the MyPDFDocumentInfo structure. The MyPDFDocumentInfo structure defined by the code contains a field named documentForbidsNewDocument, which is set to true if the PDF document is encrypted. This will be discussed in a moment.

The routine createMyPDFDocumentWithURL creates a CGPDFDocumentRef from a supplied CFURLRef and then calls checkPDFDocumentPermissions to fill in the permissions information in the MyPDFDocumentInfo it uses to track the document information. If the documentIsUnlocked field in the structure is false, the document requires a user-supplied password to access it. In that case, the code calls a WarnAboutEncryptedPDFDocument routine that you would write or, if you were supporting user-supplied password entry to unlock documents, you'd obtain a password from the user to unlock the document.

To unlock a document with a password, you use the Quartz function `CGPDFDocumentUnlockWithPassword`, passing the CGPDFDocument object and the password string, and it returns a `bool` result that, if `true`, indicates the password unlocked the document. Password strings are passed to `CGPDFDocumentUnlockWithPassword` as a C string.

You need to respect the copying and printing permissions on a PDF document in order to follow the encrypted PDF document model. If the document does not support copying, you should not allow the user to copy content from the document to a pasteboard. If the document doesn't allow printing and the user chooses the print command, you should alert the user that printing isn't allowed or, if your application allows the user to enter a password, you can prompt the user for the owner password for the document. If you unlock a document with the owner password, the Quartz function `CGPDFDocumentAllowsPrinting` returns `true`.

There is one more aspect of working with encrypted PDF documents that requires care. Your application should not allow a user to inadvertently convert a PDF document that is encrypted into a PDF document that is not encrypted. This can happen in several ways. For example, if your application allows users to export content by creating a new PDF document from an existing encrypted document, you might want to alert the user that they are creating an unprotected version of a protected document. In addition, users can create PDF documents when printing; you should also restrict your application's printing so that you prevent the user from creating new PDF documents when printing without warning them. You can detect whether the user is saving to a file as PDF, using print preview (from which they can save the resulting PDF document as a new document), or printing using a PDF Services workflow item. The printing system represents these destinations as `kPMDestinationFile` (with the format `kPMDocumentFormatPDF`), `kPMDestinationPreview`, and `kPMDestinationProcessPDF`. See the references at the end of the chapter for more information.

In Tiger and later versions, Quartz has the ability to create encrypted PDF documents. This allows you to potentially preserve the password and permissions bits of PDF documents that are encrypted and that you want to modify. See "Creating Encrypted PDF Output (Tiger)" (page 462) for information about creating encrypted PDF documents.

PDF Document Utility Functions

Quartz has several general-purpose routines that are useful for obtaining information about a PDF document. Note that if the PDF document is encrypted and has not been unlocked with Quartz, the data returned by many of these functions is encrypted and is not meaningful.

PDF documents contain a document information dictionary that contains optional information such as the author, title, creator, creation date, and other information about the document. The Quartz function CGPDFDocumentGetInfo, available starting in Tiger, returns a CFDictionary object that contains the entries in the PDF document information dictionary. The entries are the keys in the PDF document information dictionary with their corresponding values.

PDF documents store dates as strings in a specialized format. For example, the document creation date in the document information dictionary that is returned by CGPDFDocumentGetInfo can contain a CreationDate key. The value associated with this key is a CFStringRef with string data in this specialized form. In Tiger and later versions, Quartz provides the CGPDFStringCopyDate function to convert a string in this format into a Core Foundation CFDate object.

PDF documents contain an optional file identifier that uniquely identifies a document. The file identifier is an array of two strings. The function CGPDFDocumentGetID is available starting in Tiger and returns a CFArray object containing the file identifier for the specified PDF document. Because the file identifier is not present in all documents, the array returned may be NULL.

The function CGPDFDocumentGetVersion is available in Panther and later versions and returns the major and minor versions of a given PDF document.

There are several utility functions that you can use with CGPDFPage objects. As with the CGPDFPage objects themselves, these functions are only available in Panther and later versions. The function CGPDFPageGetDocument allows you to obtain the CGPDFDocumentRef that contains a given CGPDFPageRef. The function CGPDFPageGetPageNumber returns the page number from the CGPDFPage object. These functions allow you to use a CGPDFPage as a self-describing representation of a given page of a PDF document.

Quartz also offers two additional functions in Panther and later: CGPDFDocumentGetCatalog and CGPDFPageGetDictionary. The document catalog returned by CGPDFDocumentGetCatalog is the top-level structure in the document and allows access to virtually all the structures of a PDF document, such as individual pages, link information, and outline data for the document. The function CGPDFPageGetDictionary returns a dictionary that contains information about the page such as

■ The stream of data that makes up the drawing commands of the page.

■ The thumbnail for the page if it exists.

■ The annotations that are associated with the page.

The document catalog and the page dictionary for a given page are the first items to retrieve if you want to examine PDF documents and extract content from the document, beyond that needed for drawing the contents of individual pages. "Examining PDF Document Content (Panther, Tiger)" (page 467) discusses the capabilities Quartz has for extracting this information.

Summary

It's easy to use Quartz to open an existing PDF document and then treat it as source graphics. Using Quartz you can draw PDF pages, rotate them, examine the properties of a PDF document, and retrieve the information dictionaries associated with a document and each page in a document. You can also handle documents that are protected by passwords and restricted as to what the user can do with the document. PDF is the graphical interchange format in Mac OS X. It's what you use to transfer data to and from a pasteboard and maintain the high quality of Quartz drawing.

This chapter focused on opening and drawing existing PDF documents. The next chapter shows how to create new PDF documents. It also shows how to examine PDF content, including PDF metadata and the PDF content stream that includes drawing commands.

See Also

For more information on opening and using PDF documents, see

- *PDF Reference: Version 1.6*, 5th edition, Adobe Systems, Inc. and other versions of the PDF specification are available:

  http://partners.adobe.com/public/developer/pdf/index_reference.html

- The CGPDFViewer Xcode project is a sample Cocoa project that uses Quartz for viewing PDF documents onscreen:

  `/Developer/Examples/Quartz/PDF/CGPDFViewer`

- *PDF Kit Programming Guide* shows how to program using the PDF Kit API introduced in Tiger and is available from the ADC Reference Library at

  http://developer.apple.com/documentation/GraphicsImaging/Conceptual/PDFKitGuide/index.html

- *PDF Kit Reference* provides a complete reference to the PDF Kit API and is available from the ADC Reference Library at

  http://developer.apple.com/documentation/GraphicsImaging/Reference/ PDFKit_Ref/index.html

- The PDFKitViewer Xcode project contains sample code that shows how to use PDF Kit to open and view PDF documents:

  `/Developer/Examples/Quartz/PDFKit`

For information about printing and PDF documents, see the following documents from the ADC Reference Library:

- *Carbon Printing Manager Reference* describes the functions used to determine the destination of a print job.

  http://developer.apple.com/documentation/Carbon/Reference/ CarbonPrintingManager_Ref/

- *Providing PDF Workflow Options in the Print Dialog* describes the PDF workflow in printing and how to create workflows.

  http://developer.apple.com/documentation/Printing/Conceptual/PDF_Workflow/ index.html

The header files relevant to drawing PDF documents are

- `CGPDFDocument.h`, which contains the functions related to working with CG-PDFDocument objects.

- `CGPDFPage.h`, available starting in Panther, which contains the functions related to working with CGPDFPage objects.

The relevant Quartz 2D reference documentation from the ADC Reference Library is

- *CGPDFDocument Reference*
- *CGPDFPage Reference*

For information about drawing QuickDraw pictures into a Quartz context, see the following from the ADC Reference Library:

- *QuickDraw Reference* describes the QDPict family of functions.

  http://developer.apple.com/documentation/Carbon/Reference/QuickDraw_Ref/ index.html

- Apple provides source code to the CGDrawPicture sample application that uses the QDPict functions to draw PICT data files to a Quartz context.

  http://developer.apple.com/samplecode/CGDrawPicture/CGDrawPicture.html

- *Quartz 2D Programming Guide for QuickDraw Developers* contains additional discussion about moving from PICT to PDF.

  http://developer.apple.com/documentation/Carbon/Conceptual/ QuickDrawToQuartz2D/index.html

Chapter 14

Creating and Examining PDF Documents

The last chapter discussed how to open and draw existing PDF documents. The PDF discussion continues in this chapter by showing how to use Quartz to create new PDF documents. Working with PDF in this way is straightforward because Quartz uses the PDF file format as its graphics metafile format. Creating a PDF document from Quartz drawing captures virtually all of the original drawing without lossy data compression and without down-sampling (unless required to conform with the PDF specification). Line art graphics, images, text drawing, drawing of existing PDF pages, and path- and image-based clipping can all be represented with their full fidelity in PDF documents created by Quartz.

The ability to examine the structure of an existing PDF document and access the data that corresponds to the content stream of a PDF document is important to many developers. Beginning with Panther, Quartz provides functions that allow you to extract virtually any information you want from a PDF document, including the raw data that makes up the page content stream of any page. Starting in Tiger, Quartz provides the ability to parse the content stream data. Through parsing, you can examine the drawing content of any page in a PDF document.

Creating New PDF Documents

A special type of Quartz graphics context called a **PDF context** is what captures Quartz drawing as a PDF document. Like all Quartz graphics contexts, a PDF context is an opaque object of type `CGContextRef`. You create a PDF context and draw into it using Quartz, then release the context when you are done with it. The result is a PDF document that contains your Quartz drawing.

Quartz provides two functions to create a PDF document—CGPDFContextCreate-WithURL and CGPDFContextCreate. The function CGPDFContextCreateWithURL creates a new PDF document at a location you specify with a URL. You'll see how to use this function in "Using CGPDFContextCreateWithURL" (below). The function CGPDFContextCreate creates a new PDF document and writes the contents of the document to a Quartz data consumer. You'll see how to use this function in "Copying PDF Content to a Pasteboard" (page 443).

These two functions are similar; each takes three parameters:

- A place for the PDF output data. One function requires a Core Foundation URL that specifies where to place the resulting PDF file and the other requires a data consumer.

- A rectangle (CGRect) to use as the media box for the document. This is the media box to use for each page of the new PDF document when the page media box is not explicitly specified. Typically, you supply a media box whose origin is (0,0).

- An auxiliary information dictionary (CFDictionaryRef) that contains optional information about the PDF document that you are creating. If you don't have optional information to specify, pass NULL. "Using the Auxiliary Information Dictionary" (page 439) discusses the auxiliaryInfo dictionary in detail.

Either function returns NULL if for any reason the PDF context can't be created.

A Quartz-created PDF document is compact because Quartz uses a number of techniques to reduce the size of the files it produces. The data streams that Quartz generates into the PDF document are compressed using Flate compression—a lossless compression technique. To reduce the size of the font data it puts into PDF documents it creates, Quartz includes only the glyphs in the fonts that are used in the document. When you follow the guidelines in "Best Practices for Working with Images" (page 241), a given image is captured as a single resource, regardless of how many times it is rendered. This is also true for other resources such as Quartz patterns and color spaces.

Using CGPDFContextCreateWithURL

PDF documents are page oriented; that is, they contain one or more pages and the graphics within them are drawn on a given page. To delineate pages, use the Quartz functions CGContextBeginPage and CGContextEndPage to bracket the drawing code for a given page. Each call to CGContextBeginPage must be followed with a matching call to CGContextEndPage. You can't nest begin- and end-page functions. You must also make sure that all drawing calls, as well as all changes to graphics state parameters, occur between calls to CGContextBeginPage and CGContextEndPage.

Listing 14.1 creates a new PDF document from some very simple Quartz drawing. The purpose of this example is to show how to create a PDF document, not how to draw graphics to the PDF—you already know how to do that because you draw to a PDF context just like any other Quartz context. The routine myCreatePDFDocumentAtURL creates a new PDF document at the disk location specified by a supplied URL. The PDF document that's created is a single page with a media box that is the bounding box of the content of the graphics drawn, a single filled rectangle.

The code creates a PDF context by calling the function CGPDFContextCreateWithURL. The choice of the media box depends on the purpose of the PDF document. For generating a PDF document that is intended as a clip-art-style graphic, the media box is typically the bounding box of the graphics contained in the file. For generating a PDF document that represents the pages of a document, the media box is typically the size of the media that will be used to print the document. For this example, the code uses the bounding box of the graphic as the media box when it creates the context.

When you create a PDF context, Quartz sets default values for the context parameters and the graphics state. The CTM is initially set so that 1 unit in the Quartz coordinate system is 1 unit in the default coordinate system of a PDF document: 1 unit is 1/72 of an inch. The media box data is supplied in this same coordinate system. As with any Quartz context, you can modify the coordinate system using the CTM functions.

After creating the PDF context, the code calls CGContextBeginPage to mark the beginning of the content of the first page. This function takes two parameters, the CGContextRef and a pointer to a CGRect that corresponds to the media box for that page. The pointer to the CGRect that you pass to the function CGContextBeginPage can be NULL. If it is NULL, the page media box is inherited from the document media box that you pass to the PDF context creation function, which in this example is CGPDFContextCreateWithURL.

The code uses CGContextSaveGState and CGContextRestoreGState to save and restore the graphics state around each page that it draws. The function CGContextBeginPage resets the graphics state to the default values so this is not strictly required, but saving and restoring the graphics state for each page enforces the notion that the graphics state for each page is independent from that of every other page. After the code saves the graphics state, it calls CGContextClipToRect to clip to the media box of the page. This ensures that no content on the page is drawn outside the media rectangle.

After the graphics state is set up on the page, the code does some simple drawing; it fills a rectangle the size of the media box with red. This code uses a function getTheCalibratedRGBColorSpace borrowed from earlier chapters to draw using the generic calibrated RGB color space.

When the content for the page is created, the code ends the page and calls CGContextRelease to release the PDF graphics context it created. You must release a PDF graphics context that you create, otherwise the PDF document you are creating will not be properly finalized. Releasing the context also reclaims the memory and resources associated with the context, thereby avoiding possible memory leaks.

Tip   If the PDF document you create with Quartz is damaged and cannot be read by PDF reading applications, the most likely reason is that you did not release the PDF context that you used to create the document.

Listing 14.1 Code that creates a one-page PDF document using Quartz

```
void myCreatePDFDocumentAtURL(CFURLRef url)
{
  float red[] = { 1., 0., 0., 1. };
  // Make the media box the same size as the graphics this code draws.
  CGRect mediaBox = CGRectMake(0, 0, 200, 200);

  CGContextRef pdfContext = CGPDFContextCreateWithURL(url,
               &mediaBox, NULL);
  if(!pdfContext){
    fprintf(stderr, "Couldn't create PDF context!\n");
    return;
  }


  // Calling CGContextBeginPage indicates the following content is
  // to appear on the first page. The rectangle passed to this function
  // specifies the media box for this page.
  CGContextBeginPage(pdfContext, &mediaBox);
  // It is good programming practice to bracket the drawing you
  // perform on a page with calls to save and restore the graphics state.
  CGContextSaveGState(pdfContext);
    // Clip to the media box.
    CGContextClipToRect(pdfContext, mediaBox);
    // Set the fill color and color space.
```

```
      CGContextSetFillColorSpace(pdfContext,
                  getTheCalibratedRGBColorSpace());
      CGContextSetFillColor(pdfContext, red);
      // Fill the rectangle of the media box with red.
      CGContextFillRect(pdfContext, mediaBox);

    CGContextRestoreGState(pdfContext);
    // Calling CGContextEndPage denotes the end of the first page.
    CGContextEndPage(pdfContext);

    // You MUST release the PDF context when finished with it.
    CGContextRelease(pdfContext);
}
```

Using the Auxiliary Information Dictionary

The functions that allow you to create a PDF context—CGPDFContextCreateWith-URL and CGPDFContextCreate—have an optional auxiliaryInfo parameter that you can use to pass additional information to the PDF context that you create. Since the PDF context represents the PDF document you want to create, the auxiliary information dictionary is what you use to specify document-level information for Quartz to add. You provide this additional information in the form of key-value pairs in a CFDictionary object that you pass as the auxiliaryInfo parameter.

Quartz defines the set of supported auxiliaryInfo dictionary keys and the meaning of those keys. None of the keys is required; omission of a key produces either a default value or no value, depending on the key. As Quartz evolves, so does the set of supported keys. Table 14.1 lists the most interesting keys, together with the version of Mac OS X that each key is first available in. Quartz also defines keys that relate to generating encrypted PDF documents; those keys aren't in this table. They are discussed in detail in "Creating Encrypted PDF Output (Tiger)" (page 462).

The Quartz header file CGPDFContext.h defines additional keys that allow developers to add keys relevant to generating PDF/X-3 compliant documents. PDF/X-3 is a set of standards developed to aid the ability of professional printing systems to handle PDF content reliably. Discussion of PDF/X-3 and these additional keys is beyond the scope of this book. See the references at the end of this chapter for more information.

Table 14.1 Some of the Auxilliary Information Dictionary Keys That Quartz Supports

Key	Data Type	Mac OS X Version
kCGPDFContextTitle	CFStringRef	10.2
kCGPDFContextAuthor	CFStringRef	10.2
kCGPDFContextCreator	CFStringRef	10.2
kCGPDFContextMediaBox	CFDataRef	10.4
kCGPDFContextCropBox	CFDataRef	10.4
kCGPDFContextBleedBox	CFDataRef	10.4
kCGPDFContextTrimBox	CFDataRef	10.4
kCGPDFContextArtBox	CFDataRef	10.4

The document information dictionary for a PDF file contains information about the PDF document as a whole. For example, Quartz adds Producer and CreationDate entries to this dictionary for all PDF documents that it produces. The Producer entry indicates that the document was created by the Quartz PDF context; the producer string also includes the major version number of Mac OS X used. The CreationDate entry is the PDF style date string of the date and time that the document was created. Most other entries in the document information dictionary are specific to the content or creator of the document. Quartz can only add these entries if you provide the corresponding information.

If the key kCGPDFContextTitle is present in the auxiliaryInfo dictionary and its value is a CFString object, Quartz uses the CFString data to generate the Title entry in the document information dictionary for the PDF document. If there is no kCGPDFContextTitle entry in the auxiliaryInfo dictionary, Quartz does not generate a Title entry in the PDF document represented by the PDF context.

Quartz uses the keys kCGPDFContextAuthor and kCGPDFContextCreator to generate the Author and Creator keys in a similar fashion. (Note that versions of Mac OS X prior to Jaguar pay no attention to entries in the auxiliaryInfo dictionary with these keys.) Again, if one of these keys is not present, the PDF document produced won't have an entry for that key. The Author key is intended to be the name of the person that created the document. The Creator key typically specifies the name of the application that created the document.

Recall that when you create a PDF context you pass a CGRect that corresponds to the media box of the PDF document you want to generate. Additionally, for each page of the PDF document you create, you call CGContextBeginPage, passing in an optional pointer to a CGRect, which, if it is not NULL, overrides the document media box for that page. Starting in Tiger, Quartz supports keys that allow you to add other boundary rectangle information to the PDF document in addition to that of the media box. Adding the kCGPDFContextCropBox, kCGPDFContext-

BleedBox, kCGPDFContextTrimBox, or kCGPDFContextArtBox entries to the auxiliaryInfo dictionary adds the corresponding entries for the crop box, bleed box, trim box, or art box to the document. The values for the boundary rectangle keys are CFData objects that correspond to the CGRect data for that rectangle. You can choose to add any mix of the boundary rectangles to the document. However, you must ensure that the media box rectangle encloses the other rectangles you add.

Listing 14.2 demonstrates how to use the auxiliaryInfo dictionary to pass data to the PDF context during its creation. The code adds title, author, and creator entries to the dictionary. It then checks for the availability of the symbol kCGPDF-ContextCropBox. This key and the other keys defined starting in Tiger appear in the CGPDFContext.h header file as extern CFStringRef values rather than values using #define. This means that when you use such CFStringRef values in your code, you first need to check for the availability of the symbol, if you want your code to run on a Mac OS X system prior to the definition of the constant string. In Listing 14.2, the code performs the check and adds the entry for the crop box only if the symbol is defined. To add a value for the kCGPDFContextCropBox key, the code creates a CFDataRef that corresponds to the CGRect of the crop box. After the code creates the CFData object, it adds the entry to the dictionary and then releases the CFData object it created.

The code passes the prepared auxiliaryInfo dictionary to the function CGPDF-ContextCreateWithURL to create the PDF context. The PDF document that Quartz creates reflects the data in the auxiliaryInfo dictionary, in this case, the title, author, creator, and crop box information, as well as the media box that is used to create the context or passed to the function CGContextBeginPage for a given page. After the code creates the context, it releases the auxiliaryInfo dictionary. Now the code is ready to draw to the context to create the PDF document page content. Drawing to the PDF context adds content to the PDF document that Quartz creates at the location specified by the URL.

Listing 14.2 Code that uses the auxiliaryInfo dictionary to add metadata when creating a PDF context

```
// Create an auxiliaryInfo dictionary of unlimited size.
CFMutableDictionaryRef info =
   CFDictionaryCreateMutable(NULL, 0,
             &kCFTypeDictionaryKeyCallBacks,
             &kCFTypeDictionaryValueCallBacks);
// Use this rectangle as the media box for the document.
const CGRect mediaRect = { {0, 0}, {612, 792} };
if(info){
  // Add the title information for this document.
  CFDictionarySetValue(info, kCGPDFContextTitle,
             CFSTR("BasicDrawing Sample Graphics"));
  // Add the author information for this document.
```

```
CFDictionarySetValue(info, kCGPDFContextAuthor,
            CFSTR("David Gelphman and Bunny Laden"));
// The creator is the application creating the document.
CFDictionarySetValue(info, kCGPDFContextCreator,
            CFSTR("BasicDrawing Application"));
// Before using the kCGPDFContextCropBox key, check to ensure
// that the key is available in this version of Mac OS X.
if(&kCGPDFContextCropBox != NULL){
  // Use this rectangle as the crop box for this example.
  CGRect cropBox = CGRectMake(100, 100, 200, 200);
  // Create a CFData object from the crop box rectangle.
  CFDataRef cropBoxData = CFDataCreate(NULL,
            (UInt8 *)&cropBox, sizeof(cropBox));
  if(cropBoxData){
    // Add the crop box entry to the auxiliaryInfo dictionary.
    CFDictionarySetValue(info, kCGPDFContextCropBox,
            cropBoxData);
    // Release the CFData created to add the crop box entry.
    CFRelease(cropBoxData);
  }
}
}else{
  fprintf(stderr, "Couldn't create info dictionary!\n");
}

// Create the PDF context with the info dictionary.
pdfContext = CGPDFContextCreateWithURL(url, &mediaRect, info);
// Release the info dictionary used to create the context.
if(info)CFRelease(info);
// Use the PDF context just created.
// ...
```

As you've just seen, Quartz introduces in Tiger the ability to add the crop box and other boundary rectangle information on a document-wide basis to the PDF documents that you create using a PDF context. Also, starting in Tiger, Quartz provides the ability to specify any of these boundary rectangles for a given page. To allow for this, Quartz provides the function CGPDFContextBeginPage as a substitute for CGContextBeginPage and the function CGPDFContextEndPage as a substitute for CGContextEndPage. When you use the function CGPDFContextBeginPage, you need to pair it with CGPDFContextEndPage. If you don't have any reason to override any of the boundary rectangles other than the media box for a given page, you can instead use CGContextBeginPage together with CGContextEndPage.

These new functions have the same semantics as their pre-Tiger counterparts, but instead of passing the media box CGRect to CGPDFContextBeginPage, pass a pageInfo dictionary that contains the keys corresponding to the boundary rectangles that you want to customize for the specific page. For example, if you want to specify a crop box entry for a given page that overrides any crop box entry that you supply when creating the context, you add the kCGPDFContextCropBox key with the value of the crop box rectangle to the pageInfo dictionary that you pass to the function CGPDFContextBeginPage. Note that the function CGPDFContextBeginPage has no media box parameter. If you want to override the media box for a given page when you use this function, add the key kCGPDFContextMediaBox to the pageInfo dictionary that you pass to CGPDFContextBeginPage.

Copying PDF Content to a Pasteboard

You've now seen how to use CGPDFContextCreateWithURL to create a PDF document on disk. It's also possible to write PDF data to a destination other than a URL. The Quartz function CGPDFContextCreate creates a PDF context that writes PDF data to a CGDataConsumer object that you supply. Your data consumer can do whatever it wants with the data. Data consumers are discussed in detail in "Data Consumers" (page 198).

A typical situation where you might want to generate PDF content to a data consumer is when you want to support copying Quartz drawing to a pasteboard, such as the Clipboard. For that, you typically write the PDF data to a memory-based data consumer that creates a CFData object from the PDF content you create. Then you add the CFData object to a pasteboard. The routine cfDataCreatePDFDocumentFromDrawing (see Listing 14.3) returns a CFDataRef that contains the PDF data for arbitrary Quartz drawing.

Listing 14.3 A routine that creates PDF data for writing to a pasteboard

```
CFDataRef cfDataCreatePDFDocumentFromDrawing(void)
{
    // The media rectangle for the drawing is the bounding
    // rectangle for the graphics being drawn. This example
    // uses a US-letter-size page for simplicity.
    const CGRect mediaRect = { {0, 0}, {612, 792} };
    CFMutableDictionaryRef dict = NULL;
    CGContextRef pdfContext = NULL;
    CGDataConsumerRef consumer = NULL;
    CFMutableDataRef data = NULL;
```

```
// Create a dictionary to hold the optional PDF metadata.
dict = CFDictionaryCreateMutable(NULL, 0,
               &kCFTypeDictionaryKeyCallBacks,
               &kCFTypeDictionaryValueCallBacks);
if(dict == NULL){
  fprintf(stderr, "Couldn't make auxiliaryInfo dictionary.\n");
  return NULL;
}

// Add the creator information to the info dictionary.
CFDictionarySetValue(dict, kCGPDFContextCreator,
   CFSTR("Sample Quartz Application"));

// Create a mutable CFData object with unlimited capacity.
data = CFDataCreateMutable(NULL, 0);
if(data == NULL){
  CFRelease(dict);
  fprintf(stderr, "Couldn't make CFData!\n");
  return NULL;
}

// Create the data consumer to capture the PDF data.
consumer = myCGDataConsumerCreateWithCFData(data);
if(consumer == NULL){
  CFRelease(data);
  CFRelease(dict);
  fprintf(stderr, "Couldn't create data consumer!\n");
  return NULL;
}

pdfContext = CGPDFContextCreate(consumer, &mediaRect, dict);
CGDataConsumerRelease(consumer);
CFRelease(dict);

if(pdfContext == NULL){
  CFRelease(data);
  fprintf(stderr, "Couldn't create PDF context!\n");
  return NULL;
}

CGContextBeginPage(pdfContext, &mediaRect);
CGContextSaveGState(pdfContext);
  CGContextClipToRect(pdfContext, mediaRect);
  //... Your Quartz code to draw the content goes here.
```

```
    CGContextRestoreGState(pdfContext);
    CGContextEndPage(pdfContext);
    CGContextRelease(pdfContext);

    return data;
}
```

This code creates a data consumer that writes to a CFData object by using the routine myCGDataConsumerCreateWithCFData defined in Listing 8.7 (page 200) in "Data Consumers" (page 198). It calls CGPDFContextCreate, passing the data consumer that the function myCGDataConsumerCreateWithCFData returns, together with an auxiliaryInfo dictionary, and a CGRect the size of the media box for the PDF data. The example here uses a media box appropriate for a US-letter-size page since the code doesn't perform specific drawing. In your code you need to use a media box that is a tight bounding box around the graphics you are adding to a pasteboard. A tight bounding box produces the best results for applications that read PDF data from a pasteboard.

After the code creates the PDF context, it releases the data consumer, indicates the start of the page, and draws the content. After indicating the end of the page, the code releases the context, which causes Quartz to finalize the PDF data written to the data consumer. After the context is released, the CFData object used by the data consumer contains all the PDF data. It's ready to add to a pasteboard or to do whatever the caller of cfDataCreatePDFDocumentFromDrawing wants to do with the data. The caller of cfDataCreatePDFDocumentFromDrawing owns the returned reference; the caller is responsible for releasing the returned CFDataRef.

Listing 14.4 shows how to use Cocoa to write PDF data to a pasteboard. The writePDFDataToPasteBoard routine adds a single representation of type PDF to the general pasteboard that supports cut, copy, and paste. (You may want to add other data representations of your graphics in addition to the PDF data.) Note that writePDFDataToPasteBoard calls the cfDataCreatePDFDocumentFromDrawing routine from Listing 14.3.

Listing 14.4 A Cocoa routine that writes PDF data to a pasteboard

```
void writePDFDataToPasteBoard(void)
{
    // Create the PDF data to add.
    CFDataRef pdfData = cfDataCreatePDFDocumentFromDrawing();
    if(pdfData){
        // Get the pasteboard to add to.
        NSPasteboard *pboard = [NSPasteboard generalPasteboard];
        // Declare the types being added. In this case there
        // is only one type: PDF.
```

```
    [pboard declareTypes:
      [NSArray arrayWithObjects:NSPDFPboardType, nil] owner:nil];
    // Add the data for the type PDF. This code takes advantage
    // of toll-free bridging between CFDataRef and (NSData *).
    [pboard setData:(NSData *)pdfData forType:NSPDFPboardType];
    // Release the CFDataRef after it is added to the pasteboard.
    CFRelease(pdfData);
  }
}
```

Listing 14.5 shows how to use Carbon to write PDF data to a pasteboard. The writePDFDataToPasteBoard routine adds a single representation of type PDF to the pasteboard that is the system Clipboard. (You may want to add other representations of your graphics in addition to the PDF data.) Like the Cocoa implementation, the Carbon version also uses the cfDataCreatePDFDocumentFromDrawing routine from Listing 14.3. In addition, the Carbon implementation uses the getThePasteBoard routine defined in Listing 13.3 (page 404).

As with Listing 13.3, which creates a CGPDFDocumentRef from a pasteboard in Carbon, Listing 14.5 uses the Pasteboard Manager API that is available in Carbon starting in Panther. (If you need your application to work with Jaguar and earlier versions, you must use the Carbon Scrap Manager on those systems.)

Listing 14.5 simply writes the data to the pasteboard. Another approach is to take advantage of the "promise data" feature supported by the Pasteboard Manager. For that, you add a promise for the data to the pasteboard instead of the data itself. You then create the data only if someone attempts to read it from the pasteboard.

Listing 14.5 A Carbon routine that writes PDF data to a pasteboard

```
void writePDFDataToPasteBoard(void)
{
  OSStatus err = noErr;
  PasteboardRef pasteBoard;
  // Create the content to add to the pasteboard.
  CFDataRef pdfData = cfDataCreatePDFDocumentFromDrawing();
  if(pdfData == NULL){
    fprintf(stderr, "Couldn't create data to put on pasteboard!\n");
    return;
  }
```

```
pasteBoard = getThePasteBoard();

// First clear the pasteboard of its current contents.
err = PasteboardClear(pasteBoard);
if(err){
  CFRelease(pdfData);
  fprintf(stderr,
    "Couldn't clear the pasteboard due to err = %d!\n",
    (int)err);
  return;
}

// Put the PDF data on the pasteboard.
err = PasteboardPutItemFlavor( pasteBoard, (PasteboardItemID)1,
            CFSTR("com.adobe.pdf"),
            pdfData,
            kPasteboardFlavorNoFlags);
// Release the data since the code is done with it.
CFRelease(pdfData);
if(err){
  fprintf(stderr,
    "Got err = %d putting data on pasteboard.\n",
    (int)err);
}
}
```

Adding Content to Existing PDF Documents

The fact that Quartz can both draw existing PDF documents and create new PDF documents from any Quartz drawing opens up a world of possibilities for processing PDF documents. For example, you can

- Rearrange the pages of an existing PDF document. For example, you can reverse the pages of an existing PDF document by creating a PDF context for the new destination document and then creating a CGPDFDocumentRef for the document whose pages you want to rearrange. You then draw each page of the CGPDFDocumentRef starting with the last page in reverse order to the PDF context. The resulting PDF document would have its pages in the reverse order compared to the original.

- Reformat the pages of an existing PDF document, such as generating a two-up representation of the original pages in a new document or creating other arbitrary page impositions.

- Extract or remove a page or set of pages from a PDF document.
- Add a logo, time stamp, or other content to an existing document.

This section shows how to add a PDF graphic to each page of an existing PDF document. You'll see how to add the PDF graphic of the "Confidential" text that's shown at the bottom of Figure 14.1 to each page of a document, which is similar to the page shown at the top of the figure. Figure 14.2 shows the result. The PDF graphic that contains the text "Confidential" is stamped on each page of the PDF document. Note that the "Confidential" graphic is placed so that it is centered on an imaginary diagonal line from the lower-left corner to the upper-right corner of the page being created.

Figure 14.1   A page from a PDF document and a small PDF graphic to be added to the page

Figure 14.2 Stamping a PDF graphic on top of a page of another PDF document

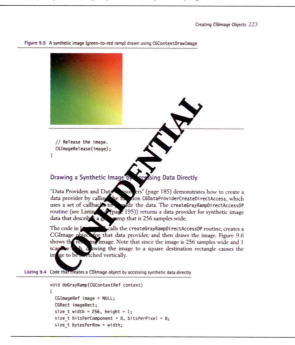

To achieve the effect shown in Figure 14.2, you need to take this general approach:

- Open an existing multipage PDF document, as described in "Opening and Drawing PDF Documents" (page 397).

- Open the existing document that contains the PDF graphic to stamp on each page.

- Create a PDF context to draw to.

- Call the function `CGContextBeginPage` to indicate the start of a page.

- Draw a page from the source document to the newly created PDF context.

- Draw the "Confidential" graphic to that same PDF context.

- Call the function `CGContextEndPage` to indicate the end of a page.

- Repeat the process, starting with `CGContextBeginPage` and ending with `CGContextEndPage`, for each page of the original document.

Of course, there are many specific tasks to do, such as locating the "Confidential" graphic so that it's angled on the page. But you'll see how to accomplish them as you look at the example in Listing 14.6. The listing contains the routines myCreatePDFContext, myCreatePDFSourceDocument, myStampWithPDFDocument, and createStampedFileWithFile. The top-level routine is createStampedFileWithFile; it calls the other routines as part of its execution. You'll look at that first.

Listing 14.6 Code that stamps each page of a PDF document with graphics from another one

```
// A data type used to pass around a PDF document and its media box.
typedef struct MyPDFData
{
  CGPDFDocumentRef pdfDoc;
  CGRect          mediaRect;
}MyPDFData;

CGContextRef myCreatePDFContext(CFURLRef url, CGRect mediaBox)
{
  CGContextRef pdfContext = NULL;
  CFMutableDictionaryRef dict = CFDictionaryCreateMutable(
                NULL, 0,
                &kCFTypeDictionaryKeyCallBacks,
                &kCFTypeDictionaryValueCallBacks);
  // Add some creator information to the generated PDF file.
  if(dict){
    CFDictionarySetValue(dict, kCGPDFContextCreator,
                CFSTR("PDF Stamper Application"));
    pdfContext = CGPDFContextCreateWithURL(url, &mediaBox, dict);
    CFRelease(dict);
  }
  return pdfContext;
}

MyPDFData myCreatePDFSourceDocument(CFURLRef url)
{
  MyPDFData myPDFData;
  myPDFData.pdfDoc = CGPDFDocumentCreateWithURL(url);
  if(myPDFData.pdfDoc){
    myPDFData.mediaRect = CGPDFDocumentGetMediaBox(
                myPDFData.pdfDoc, 1);
```

```
      // Make the media rectangle origin at (0,0).
      myPDFData.mediaRect.origin.x =
      myPDFData.mediaRect.origin.y = 0.;
    }
    return myPDFData;
}


void myStampWithPDFDocument(CGContextRef context,
        CGPDFDocumentRef sourcePDFDoc,
        CGPDFDocumentRef stampFileDoc, CGRect stampMediaRect)
{
    CGRect pageRect;
    float angle;
    size_t i, numPages = CGPDFDocumentGetNumberOfPages(sourcePDFDoc);

    // Loop over document pages and stamp each one appropriately.
    for(i = 1 ; i <= numPages ; i++)
    {
      // Use the page rectangle of each page from the source to compute
      // the destination media box for each page and the location of
      // the stamp.
      CGRect pageRect = CGPDFDocumentGetMediaBox(sourcePDFDoc, i);
      CGContextBeginPage(context, &pageRect);
      CGContextSaveGState(context);
        // Clip to the media box of the page.
        CGContextClipToRect(pdfContext, pageRect);
        // First draw the content of the source document.
        CGContextDrawPDFDocument(context, pageRect, sourcePDFDoc, i);
        // Translate to center of destination rectangle; that is the
        // center of the media box of the content to draw on top of.
        CGContextTranslateCTM(context,
                  pageRect.size.width/2, pageRect.size.height/2);
        // Compute the angle of the diagonal across the destination page.
        angle = atan(pageRect.size.height/pageRect.size.width);
        // Rotate by an amount so that drawn content goes along
        // a diagonal axis across the page.
        CGContextRotateCTM(context, angle);
        // Move the origin so that the media box of the PDF to stamp
        // is centered around center point of destination.
        CGContextTranslateCTM(context,
                  -stampMediaRect.size.width/2,
                  -stampMediaRect.size.height/2);
        // Draw the document to stamp with on top.
```

```
            CGContextDrawPDFDocument(context, stampMediaRect,
                    stampFileDoc, 1);
        CGContextRestoreGState(context);
        CGContextEndPage(context);
    }
}


// The top-level routine.
void createStampedFileWithFile(CFURLRef inURL,
                CFURLRef stampURL, CFURLRef outURL)
{
    CGContextRef pdfContext = NULL;
    MyPDFData stampFileData, sourceFileData;
    sourceFileData = myCreatePDFSourceDocument(inURL);
    if(!sourceFileData.pdfDoc){
        fprintf(stderr,
            "Can't create PDFDocumentRef for source input file!\n");
        return;
    }

    stampFileData = myCreatePDFSourceDocument(stampURL);
    if(!stampFileData.pdfDoc){
        CGPDFDocumentRelease(sourceFileData.pdfDoc);
        fprintf(stderr,
            "Can't create PDFDocumentRef for file to stamp with!\n");
        return;
    }

    pdfContext = myCreatePDFContext(outURL, sourceFileData.mediaRect);
    if(!pdfContext){
        CGPDFDocumentRelease(sourceFileData.pdfDoc);
        CGPDFDocumentRelease(stampFileData.pdfDoc);
        fprintf(stderr,
            "Can't create PDFContext for output file!\n");
        return;
    }

    myStampWithPDFDocument(pdfContext, sourceFileData.pdfDoc,
                    stampFileData.pdfDoc, stampFileData.mediaRect);

    CGContextRelease(pdfContext);
    CGPDFDocumentRelease(sourceFileData.pdfDoc);
    CGPDFDocumentRelease(stampFileData.pdfDoc);
}
```

The routine `createStampedFileWithFile` takes three parameters, each of which is a URL.

- `inURL`, the `CFURLRef` of the source PDF document whose pages will be stamped with the PDF document containing the "Confidential" graphic.

- `stampURL`, the `CFURLRef` of the PDF document to stamp on top of the source document's pages; in this case, the PDF document containing the "Confidential" graphic.

- `outURL`, the `CFURLRef` of the output PDF document that Quartz will create.

The routine creates a new PDF document that contains all the pages of the source document with the first page of the stamping document overlaid on each page.

The routine `createStampedFileWithFile` first calls the `myCreatePDFSourceDocument` routine, which returns a `MyPDFData` structure that contains a `CGPDFDocumentRef` for an existing PDF document on disk, and the media box for the first page of this document. In this example, `createStampedFileWithFile` passes `inURL` to create a `CGPDFDocumentRef` for the source PDF document whose pages the code will stamp onto. It then calls `myCreatePDFSourceDocument` again with `stampURL` to create a `CGPDFDocumentRef` for the PDF document to be used as a stamp.

Next the `createStampedFileWithFile` routine calls the `myCreatePDFContext` routine, which creates a PDF file at the specified URL (`outURL`) using the supplied rectangle as the document media box. In this case, `createStampedFileWithFile` passes `outURL` as the destination for the new PDF document to create and it passes the media box of the PDF document represented by `inURL`.

With the source CGPDFDocument objects in hand and the PDF context ready, `createStampedFileWithFile` calls `myStampWithPDFDocument` to perform the drawing. This is where the real action occurs. The routine `myStampWithPDFDocument` draws the source PDF document into the PDF context and then draws the stamp PDF document on top of it. When the routine draws the stamp, it places it along the diagonal from the lower-left corner to the upper-right corner, centering its media rectangle to the center of that diagonal. Now take a closer look at how this routine works.

The `myStampWithPDFDocument` routine first determines the total number of pages in the source PDF document, then loops once for each page. Note that the loop starts at 1, the first page of the document. For each page of the source document, the code first obtains the media box of that page and calls `CGContextBeginPage` with that rectangle. This starts a new PDF page in the destination document and ensures that the media rectangle for that page is the same as the media rectangle for the corresponding page in the source PDF document.

The code uses CGContextSaveGState and CGContextRestoreGState to isolate the drawing of each page from each subsequent page. After saving the graphics state for the page, the code clips to the media box for that page, ensuring that no drawing occurs outside the page media box. It then draws the page from the source PDF document by calling the Quartz function CGContextDrawPDFDocument, using the media box from the source page as the destination rectangle, ensuring there is no scaling to the destination.

After the source page is drawn, it's time to stamp the PDF graphic onto the page. The myStampWithPDFDocument routine starts the stamping process by translating the origin of coordinates so that the origin is located at the center of the destination PDF document. The routine then computes the angle of the diagonal between the lower-left corner and the top-right corner of the page and rotates by that angle. Finally, the routine translates the origin so that the center of the media box of the PDF document to stamp coincides with the center of the destination page. It then draws the PDF document to stamp and ends the page. By repeating this process for each page of the source PDF document, the resulting output contains all the pages of the source document with the graphic stamped on top.

After all the stamping is complete, the createStampedFileWithFile routine cleans up by releasing the PDF context and the CGPDFDocument objects. Recall that Quartz finalizes the PDF output data only after the code releases the PDF context.

You can apply the technique described in this section to add any PDF graphic to any existing PDF document. While this example draws a PDF graphic on top of every page of another document, you could easily modify the code to draw any Quartz content underneath or on top of the page of another document.

The code presented here is a bit simpler than what you might use, but it was intentionally simplified to make it easier to see how to add content to an existing PDF document. It's worth noting a few places where you might want to improve the code. This code ignores any crop box that might be present in the source PDF document. It also ignores any rotation angle that might be present on a given page of the source PDF document; it always treats the rotation angle for a page as 0. You could improve the code by using the crop box of the source PDF document to clip the destination content and take into account the rotation angle when drawing. Additionally, if the media box of the source PDF document is so small that the media box of the PDF document used as the stamp does not fit, it would be a good idea to scale down the stamp so that it fits over the content.

You might achieve a more aesthetic visual result if, instead of stamping the PDF document on top of the underlying content in a completely opaque fashion, you applied an alpha value of 50 percent or less to the stamped content. This allows the underlying content to show through, even if the stamped graphics are completely opaque.

In Tiger and later versions, you can achieve this effect by setting the Quartz global alpha value to 0.5 prior to rendering the PDF stamp. The entire PDF document is treated as a single object and is composited with the global alpha. In Panther and earlier versions, Quartz ignores the global alpha in effect when you draw a PDF document—global alpha is treated as if it is 1.0, regardless of the actual setting. However, in Panther you can use Quartz transparency layers to achieve this effect. "Transparency Layers and PDF Documents" (page 528) discusses how to do this.

Adding Links to PDF Documents (Tiger)

10.4 ▶ The PDF file format supports special annotations, called **link annotations**, that provide navigation features in a PDF document. A link in a PDF document consists of a rectangle on a specific page and data that specifies what should happen if the user clicks on that rectangle. There are two types of PDF links that Quartz supports (starting in Tiger):

- A link that specifies the navigation to a specific web page. You use the Quartz function `CGPDFContextSetURLForRect` to create this kind of link (see "Creating a Link to a URL" (page 456)).

- A link that specifies the navigation from one location in a PDF document to another location. You use the Quartz functions `CGPDFContextAddDestination-AtPoint` and `CGPDFContextSetDestinationForRect` together to specify this kind of link (see "Creating a Link to Another Page in the Document" (page 458)).

Adding navigation features to PDF documents can make the PDF documents you create more useful. This is especially true if your application already maintains document navigation information in its native document format and you want to produce PDF documents that users can navigate in a similar manner. For example, when web browsers create PDF documents from a web page, the PDF documents they create can have live links.

When drawing a PDF page that contains a link annotation, Quartz itself does not draw anything related to the link. Programs such as the Apple Preview application perform the drawing of the link as a separate piece of drawing from the page itself and the program is responsible for providing the navigation features implicit in the link. The PDF Kit framework provides the ability to draw and navigate link annotations; these capabilities are not built into Quartz 2D.

Creating a Link to a URL

Adding a link annotation that points to a URL is simple; you use the function CGPDFContextSetURLForRect. This function has the following arguments:

- context, the PDF context that represents the PDF document you are creating. Using this function with any other type of graphics context, such as a window or bitmap context, does nothing.

- url, a CFURL object that contains the destination URL for the link.

- rect, the CGRect that the link is associated with. Programs that allow navigation through links use this rectangle as the hot rectangle that the user clicks to navigate to the link destination.

A URL link annotation is associated with a specific page. The page that the link appears on depends on which PDF page you are creating when you call CGPDFContextSetURLForRect. The coordinate system used for the link rectangle rect is always the default Quartz coordinate system and is unaffected by any Quartz coordinate system changes you make prior to calling CGPDFContextSetURLForRect.

Important   Most Quartz functions treat coordinates passed to them as user space coordinates. However, the rectangle passed to CGPDFContextSetURLForRect is interpreted in default Quartz user space, not current user space.

The addURLAnnotationToPDFPage routine in Listing 14.7 creates a CFURL object for a URL that points to the ADC Reference Library Graphics and Imaging Documentation page. This routine calls the Quartz function CGPDFContextSetURLForRect to create a URL link annotation on a given page of a PDF document. The listing also contains a code fragment copied from Listing 14.1 (page 438) that creates a one-page PDF document that consists of a red rectangle. In this version, the code images the content of the page (the red rectangle), then calls addURLAnnotationToPDFPage to add a link annotation that points to the Graphics and Imaging documentation. When you use Preview to look at the resulting PDF document, the cursor changes to a hand pointer when you hover over the red rectangle; clicking in the rectangle opens the corresponding link in your default web browser.

Listing 14.7   Code that adds a URL link annotation to a PDF page

```
void addURLAnnotationToPDFPage(CGContextRef pdfContext, CGRect rect)
{
  char *link =
```

```
      "http://developer.apple.com/documentation/GraphicsImaging/";
    CFURLRef linkURL = CFURLCreateWithBytes(NULL, link, strlen(link),
                kCFStringEncodingUTF8, NULL);
    if(!linkURL){
      fprintf(stderr, "Couldn't create url for link!\n");
      return;
    }
    CGPDFContextSetURLForRect(pdfContext, linkURL, rect);
    CFRelease(linkURL);
}


...
    // This starts the page the link appears on.
    CGContextBeginPage(pdfContext, &mediaBox);
    CGContextSaveGState(pdfContext);
      // Clip to the media box.
      CGContextClipToRect(pdfContext, mediaBox);
      // Set the fill color and color space.
      CGContextSetFillColorSpace(pdfContext,
                  getTheCalibratedRGBColorSpace());
      CGContextSetFillColor(pdfContext, red);
      // Fill the rectangle of the media box with red.
      CGContextFillRect(pdfContext, mediaBox);

      // Add a link to a URL so that if you click
      // on the rectangle you will go to that URL.
      addURLAnnotationToPDFPage(pdfContext, mediaBox);
    CGContextRestoreGState(pdfContext);
    CGContextEndPage(pdfContext);
...
```

This example is simple because the graphical element associated with the link is drawn in the default Quartz coordinate system. Associating a rectangle in Quartz user space with that graphical element is straightforward.

If you instead work in a coordinate system other than that of the default Quartz coordinate system and want to compute a rectangle in default Quartz coordinates from a rectangle in your custom coordinate system, you need to compute the equivalent rectangle in Quartz default user space. This is the same as computing the default user space bounding rectangle of any graphic you draw. The usual way to accomplish this is to compute the affine transformation that maps from your object's coordinate system to default Quartz user space and then apply that transform to the coordinates of the bounding rectangle of the graphic.

In Tiger, Quartz introduces the function CGRectApplyAffineTransform, which transforms a rectangle with an affine transform that you supply.

Creating a Link to Another Page in the Document

Creating a link from one page in a PDF document to another page in that same document is also straightforward but involves slightly more work than creating a link to a URL because such links have two components: the location of the link on the page and the destination that the link navigates to.

Defining this kind of link is a two-step process. You create the link with the function CGPDFContextSetDestinationForRect and you create the destination that the link navigates to by calling the function CGPDFContextAddDestinationAtPoint. The order in which you perform these operations depends on the drawing order of the link and destination pages. If the link and the destination are on the same page, it does not matter in which order you define the link and its destination. Note that more than one link can point to a given destination.

You create a named destination on the current page by calling the Quartz function CGPDFContextAddDestinationAtPoint, passing the following arguments:

- context, the PDF context that represents the PDF document you are creating and to which you want to add the destination. Using this function with any other type of graphics context does nothing.

- name, a CFString object that contains the name to use for this destination. This name must be unique for each destination in the PDF document.

- point, the CGPoint that specifies the location of this destination on the page. The coordinates of this point are in default user space.

Calling the function CGPDFContextAddDestinationAtPoint associates the destination name with the location of the destination specified by point. The destination is defined on the current page; the current page is defined by the most recent CGContextBeginPage (or CGPDFContextBeginPage) call. PDF document viewers that support destinations generally navigate to a destination by ensuring that point is visible within the current document view. For a given PDF context, you can only call CGPDFContextAddDestinationAtPoint once with a given name. Defining multiple destinations with the same name in a PDF document has no meaning and produces undefined results.

To create a link annotation that links to the destination defined by name, you use the function CGPDFContextSetDestinationForRect. This function takes the following arguments:

- context, the PDF context that represents the PDF document you are creating and that you want to add the link to. As with other PDF link functions, using this function with any other type of graphics context does nothing.

- name, a CFString object that contains the name of the destination to link to.

- rect, the CGRect that the link is associated with. Programs that allow navigation through links use this rectangle as the hot rectangle that the user clicks to navigate to the link destination. As with CGPDFContextSetURLForRect, the coordinates of this rectangle are in default user space.

Calling CGPDFContextSetDestinationForRect adds a link annotation to the document on the current page, which is the page represented by the most recent CGContextBeginPage (or CGPDFContextBeginPage) call. The link annotation links to the destination name. PDF viewing applications that support link annotations navigate to the page and location defined by name when you click in the rectangle defined by rect.

Note that the destination referred to by name does not need to be defined prior to calling the function CGPDFContextSetDestinationForRect. This means that you can create links to destinations on pages that are not yet drawn.

Take a look at how this works for a new PDF document that has a link from page 2 to a location on page 1 of that same document. You first create a named destination by calling the function CGPDFContextAddDestinationAtPoint after the first CGContextBeginPage and before the corresponding call to CGContextEndPage. This ensures that the destination is defined on the first page.

On page two of the document, you call CGPDFContextSetDestinationForRect, using the same destination name you used to create the destination on page 1. Again, as long as you call CGPDFContextSetDestinationForRect after the second CGContextBeginPage and before the second call to CGContextEndPage, the destination is defined on the second page. When the PDF document is complete, it contains a link from the second page to the first page.

Listing 14.8 shows how to create two pages that contain links to each other. Figure 14.3 demonstrates the links and their destinations. Page 1 consists of a red rectangle drawn on a US-letter-size page and page 2 consists of a blue rectangle also drawn on a US-letter-size page. When you open the document in Preview, clicking the red rectangle on page 1 opens page 2 of the document with the blue rectangle visible. Clicking on the blue rectangle returns to page 1.

The myCreate2PagePDFDocumentAtURL in Listing 14.8 creates a two-page document similar to what's shown in Figure 14.3. The routine first creates a PDF context with a media box the size of a sheet of US-letter paper. It calls CGContextBeginPage to begin the first page and draws a red square whose origin is at (55,55) and that is 500 units wide and 680 units high. Next the routine calls the function CGPDFContextAddDestinationAtPoint to create a named destination

Figure 14.3 Links between pages of a PDF document

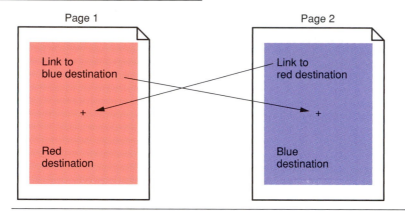

for the point at the center of the painted rectangle. The routine uses redPageName to define a named destination on page 1 that can be used by links on this page or any other page of the document.

Next the routine creates a link on page 1 by calling the Quartz function CGPDF-ContextSetDestinationForRect. It uses bluePageName to name the destination of the link and rectBox as the link rectangle. It's all right that there is not yet a destination with this name; forward references must be used if the page containing the destination comes later in the document than the one on which you create the link.

After the drawing, destination creation, and link creation for page 1 are complete, the code indicates the end of the page by calling CGContextEndPage and starts the second page by calling CGContextBeginPage. After drawing the blue rectangle on page 2, the code calls CGPDFContextAddDestinationAtPoint to define the destination bluePageName on page 2 at the point at the center of the blue rectangle. Now the destination referred to by the link on page 1 is defined. Then the code creates a link to the destination redPageName, ends the page, and ends the document. Finally, the code releases the PDF context because it is no longer needed. When the retain count of the PDF context reaches zero, Quartz flushes the drawing content to the PDF file and closes it.

The resulting PDF document has a link from page 1 to page 2 and a similar link from page 2 to page 1.

Listing 14.8 A routine that creates link annotations between pages of a PDF document

```
void myCreate2PagePDFDocumentAtURL(CFURLRef url)
{
```

```
float red[] = { 1., 0., 0., 1. };
float blue[] = { 0., 0., 1., 1. };
CGRect annotRect;
CFStringRef redPageName = CFSTR("com.mycompany.links.dg.redpage");
CFStringRef bluePageName = CFSTR("com.mycompany.links.dg.bluepage");
// Make the media box the same size as US letter paper.
CGRect mediaBox = CGRectMake(0, 0, 612, 792);
CGRect rectBox = CGRectMake(55, 55, 500, 680);
// Create a point whose center is the center of rectBox.
CGPoint centerPoint = { rectBox.origin.x + rectBox.size.width/2,
                rectBox.origin.y + rectBox.size.height/2 };
CGContextRef pdfContext = CGPDFContextCreateWithURL(url,
                &mediaBox, NULL);
if(!pdfContext){
  fprintf(stderr, "Couldn't create PDF context!\n");
  return;
}

// Start the first page.
CGContextBeginPage(pdfContext, &mediaBox);
CGContextSaveGState(pdfContext);
  // Clip to the media box.
  CGContextClipToRect(pdfContext, mediaBox);
  // Set the fill color and color space.
  CGContextSetFillColorSpace(pdfContext,
                getTheCalibratedRGBColorSpace());
  CGContextSetFillColor(pdfContext, red);
  // Fill the rectangle of the media box with red.
  CGContextFillRect(pdfContext, rectBox);
  // Make a named destination at the center of the painted rectangle.
  CGPDFContextAddDestinationAtPoint(pdfContext,
                redPageName, centerPoint);
  // Make a link to the "blue page."
  CGPDFContextSetDestinationForRect(pdfContext, bluePageName,
                rectBox);
CGContextRestoreGState(pdfContext);
CGContextEndPage(pdfContext);

// Start the second page.
CGContextBeginPage(pdfContext, &mediaBox);
CGContextSaveGState(pdfContext);
  // Clip to the media box.
  CGContextClipToRect(pdfContext, mediaBox);
  // Set the fill color and color space.
```

```
                    CGContextSetFillColorSpace(pdfContext,
                            getTheCalibratedRGBColorSpace());
                    CGContextSetFillColor(pdfContext, blue);
                    // Fill the rectangle of the media box with blue.
                    CGContextFillRect(pdfContext, rectBox);
                    // Make a named destination at the center of the painted rectangle.
                    CGPDFContextAddDestinationAtPoint(pdfContext,
                            bluePageName, centerPoint);
                    // Make a link to the already created red page destination.
                    CGPDFContextSetDestinationForRect(pdfContext, redPageName,
                            rectBox);
                CGContextRestoreGState(pdfContext);
                CGContextEndPage(pdfContext);

                // You MUST release the PDF context when done with it.
                CGContextRelease(pdfContext);
            }
```

The destinations in the examples are CFString objects as required by Quartz, but the names themselves are more complex than is strictly necessary. Quartz requires that named destinations in PDF documents are unique within a given document. This makes sense since the way a given link refers to its destination is by name. If two destinations have the same name, a link using that name does not have a unique destination.

The effort required for your code to generate destinations that are unique to a given PDF document depends on how your code obtains and uses the PDF context. If your code creates the context and is the sole software entity to use it, it is straightforward to create destination names that are unique. If instead your code obtains the context (such as during printing) or the context your code creates is passed to other code that may define named destinations, you should take care to use techniques that ensure your destination names are unique. The code in the example uses a technique borrowed from Java class naming to generate a prefix to the destination name. If each software entity that defines a named destination uses such a technique, the possibility of name space collisions when creating PDF documents is negligible.

Creating Encrypted PDF Output (Tiger)

10.4 ▶ Beginning with Tiger, Quartz provides the ability to generate encrypted PDF documents and to set the printing and copying permissions of those documents. By default, the PDF documents that Quartz creates are not encrypted. If you want to produce encrypted output, you must request encryption by adding the necessary keys and values to the auxiliaryInfo dictionary that you pass to the Quartz functions CGPDFContextCreateWithURL and CGPDFContextCreate. Table 14.2 lists the auxiliaryInfo keys related to encryption.

To create an encrypted document with Quartz, you must add an entry to the auxiliaryInfo dictionary that you pass to the context creation function. You supply the key kCGPDFContextOwnerPassword along with a value that's a CFString object represented by a pure ASCII string. (This restriction stems from the definition of passwords in the PDF specification.) If you don't pass the context creation function an auxiliaryInfo dictionary or if the dictionary does not contain a kCGPDFContextOwnerPassword key, the PDF document created by the context is not encrypted.

If the auxiliaryInfo dictionary contains a kCGPDFContextOwnerPassword key, Quartz examines the value of the key and if it is not a CFString object or the CFString object does not represent a pure ASCII string, the context creation function returns a NULL context. This prevents you from unintentionally creating an unencrypted document when an encrypted document is the intent of the request. It is important to check that the context returned by the context creation functions is not NULL. Note that only the first 32 bytes of the string are used as the password; additional bytes are ignored.

The remaining keys in Table 14.2 are optional; if you do not supply them, Quartz uses the default values listed in the table. If the kCGPDFContextUserPassword key is not present and a valid kCGPDFContextOwnerPassword entry is provided, Quartz uses the empty string as the user password when encrypting the document. If a kCGPDFContextUserPassword key is present, it must represent a pure ASCII string. If the user password is supplied but is not a valid ASCII encoded string, the context creation function returns NULL. As with the owner password, only the first 32 bytes of the string are used as the password; additional bytes are ignored. Quartz imposes a 32-byte limit to reflect the limit in the PDF specification.

Table 14.2 Auxiliary Information Dictionary Keys Relating to PDF Encryption

Key	Data Type	Default Value
kCGPDFContextOwnerPassword	CFStringRef	None
kCGPDFContextUserPassword	CFStringRef	Empty string
kCGPDFContextAllowsPrinting	CFBooleanRef	kCFBooleanTrue
kCGPDFContextAllowsCopying	CFBooleanRef	kCFBooleanTrue

When creating encrypted PDF documents, by default Quartz marks the document as allowing printing and copying. If you want to disallow printing, add the key kCGPDFContextAllowsPrinting with the value kCFBooleanFalse to the auxiliaryInfo dictionary when you create the context. If you want to disallow copying, add the key kCGPDFContextAllowsCopying with the value kCFBooleanFalse to the auxiliaryInfo dictionary when you create the context. Note that Quartz ignores these keys if you don't request encryption by using the owner password key kCGPDFContextOwnerPassword.

Listing 14.9 shows how to specify an owner password and restricted printing permissions when creating a PDF context. The routine createPasswordString takes a C string and checks to make sure that it is 32 bytes or less in length and that it contains only characters in the printable ASCII character set. This routine returns a NULL result if the password string passed to it doesn't comply with the requirements that Quartz and the PDF specification impose on the password. The code uses the string only for the owner password since this example uses the default user password. You can modify this code to screen for both owner and user passwords.

Listing 14.9 Code that creates an encrypted PDF document

```
// This function returns a NULL CFStringRef if the password
// is greater than 32 bytes long or isn't pure ASCII.
CFStringRef createPasswordString(const unsigned char *password)
{
  int i, len = strlen(password);
  // Check the length.
  if(len > 32){
    return NULL;
  }
  // Check that the byte codes are in the printable ASCII range.
  for(i = 0; i < len ; i++){
    if(password[i] < 32 || password[i] > 127)
    return NULL;
  }

  return CFStringCreateWithCString(NULL, password,
            kCFStringEncodingASCII);
}

void addEncryptionKeys(CFMutableDictionaryRef dict)
{
  const unsigned char *ownerPassword = "test";
  CFStringRef ownerPasswordRef = NULL;
  if(dict == NULL){
```

```
    return;
  }

  ownerPasswordRef = createPasswordString(ownerPassword);
  if(!ownerPasswordRef){
    fprintf(stderr, "Invalid owner password %s!\n", ownerPassword);
    return;
  }

  // Check whether owner password CFString is available.
  if(&kCGPDFContextOwnerPassword != NULL){
    // Add the owner password.
    CFDictionarySetValue(dict, kCGPDFContextOwnerPassword,
                ownerPasswordRef);
    CFRelease(ownerPasswordRef);
    // No user password is supplied so Quartz uses the empty string.

    // Mark that printing is disallowed.
    CFDictionarySetValue(dict, kCGPDFContextAllowsPrinting,
                kCFBooleanFalse);
  }else{
    CFRelease(ownerPasswordRef);
    fprintf(stderr,
      "Encrypted PDF not available in this version of Mac OS X!\n");
  }
}

  // ... Context creation code and usage...
  CGContextRef pdfContext = NULL;
  CFMutableDictionaryRef auxiliaryInfo =
                CFDictionaryCreateMutable(NULL, 0,
                &kCFTypeDictionaryKeyCallBacks,
                &kCFTypeDictionaryValueCallBacks);
  // Add the needed encryption keys with a hard-coded owner password.
  addEncryptionKeys(auxiliaryInfo);
  // Use the auxiliaryInfo dictionary to create the context.
  pdfContext = CGPDFContextCreateWithURL(url, &mediaBox,
                auxiliaryInfo);
  if(auxiliaryInfo)
    CFRelease(auxiliaryInfo);
  if(!pdfContext){
    fprintf(stderr, "Couldn't create the PDF context!\n");
    return;
  }
  // ... Usage of PDF context ...
```

PDF Document Generation Issues

There are several aspects to the PDF documents that Quartz creates and the process of creating them that merit additional discussion.

When generating PDF documents, Quartz replaces use of the `DeviceGray` and `DeviceRGB` color spaces with the calibrated generic Gray and RGB color spaces, respectively, producing calibrated output in the PDF files it produces. Quartz drawing with `DeviceCMYK` is recorded as `DeviceCMYK` when producing PDF documents. This substitution of device color spaces with calibrated color spaces is performed to improve the reproducibility of color in PDF documents produced on Mac OS X.

Creating a PDF document from Quartz drawing captures virtually all of the original drawing without lossy data compression and without down-sampling unless required to conform with the PDF specification. One exception is that images may need to be resampled when captured into a PDF document. (More on this in a moment.) There are two other areas where Quartz graphics cannot be captured at full resolution in a PDF document without taking advantage of Quartz-specific extensions to the PDF document format. The first of these is when drawing Quartz graphics with shadows, discussed in "Shadows and Grouped Objects" (page 520). The second is when drawing images that have EPS data associated with them, discussed in "Printing Source EPS Data" (page 582).

Prior to PDF version 1.5, sampled images in PDF documents were limited to 1, 2, 4, or 8 bits per component. In Panther and earlier versions, during PDF document generation, Quartz converts an image of any other depth to the nearest larger depth that is allowed. Images that are deeper than 8 bits per component are converted to 8-bit images. In Tiger, Quartz takes advantage of the fact that PDF version 1.5 adds support for images with 16 bits per component. When writing a PDF document on Tiger, Quartz converts a floating-point image or an image that has more than 8 bits per component to an image that has 16 bits per component in an integer format.

When generating PDF documents, Quartz marks the document with the lowest PDF version number that reflects the document content. The base version number it uses is PDF 1.3; however, certain features require a higher version number. Use of alpha transparency requires PDF version 1.4 features. If the drawing captured into a PDF document contains any content with an alpha value that is not fully opaque, that drawing requires PDF version 1.4 or higher to be generated. When Quartz writes sampled image data utilizing the 16-bits-per-component feature that is only available in PDF version 1.5 and later, it marks the document as PDF version 1.5.

When executing on systems prior to Panther, there is a bug that occurs when drawing a PDF document to a PDF context. (This bug only occurs when drawing to a PDF context or during printing, not when drawing to a bitmap or window context.) In this situation, Quartz does not respect the clipping area in the context when it draws a PDF document. In addition, the drawing of a PDF document resets the clipping area of a PDF context to the context default, even if you save and restore the graphics state around the drawing of the PDF document. There is no known work-around to this bug that allows you to apply the clipping area to the PDF document drawing; however, you can force Quartz to properly reset the clipping area after it draws the PDF document by adding the code in Listing 14.10 immediately *after* you draw a PDF document. This bug only occurs on Jaguar and earlier systems; you should not execute this work-around on Panther and later versions.

Listing 14.10 Code that works around the PDF context clipping bug present in Jaguar and earlier versions

```
// ... drawing PDF document to PDF context, followed by:
if(beforePanther){
  CGContextSaveGState(pdfContext);
    CGRect r = CGRectMake(0, 0, 1, 1);
    CGContextClipToRect(pdfContext, r);
    CGContextFillRect(pdfContext, CGRectOffset(r, 5, 5));
  CGContextRestoreGState(pdfContext);
}
```

Examining PDF Document Content (Panther, Tiger)

10.3 ▶

10.4 ▶

For most developers who want to support PDF content in their applications, the PDF drawing and creation features are the only Quartz PDF processing features of interest. The discussion in this section is for the developer who wants to go beyond the basic PDF drawing and creation capabilities and use Quartz to examine PDF documents and potentially extract, process, or render some of the PDF features that are not directly supported by the Quartz drawing functions.

Starting in Panther, Apple added the ability to programmatically examine the detailed features of a PDF document. These features include PDF annotations, metadata, and other items that have nothing to do with rendering the page content stream. These items contain useful information that certain kinds of applications will want to examine and possibly act upon. For example, a PDF viewing application can locate PDF annotations (which are not rendered by Quartz) and display them as it deems appropriate. That same application might also locate the outline data that some PDF documents contain and then display the PDF outline in its own view.

Note   The PDF Kit framework available in Tiger and later versions directly supports some of the more interesting features in PDF documents, such as link annotations and outline data, so you may not need to use Quartz directly for the PDF processing you want to perform.

PDF documents have a well-defined structure that is described by the Adobe PDF specification. Using the functions that Quartz provides for introspecting or examining PDF documents requires detailed knowledge of the PDF document structure. These details aren't covered in this book. Developers interested in using these capabilities in Quartz will want to read the relevant portions of the PDF document specification to learn the structure and features of PDF documents.

The next sections briefly discuss Quartz PDF introspection and provide an example that shows how to use Quartz to scan the PDF page content stream.

Quartz PDF Introspection

As you learn about the structure of PDF documents, you'll see that Quartz handles many of the details involved with obtaining the data that PDF documents contain. For example, Quartz handles the process of finding the objects in a PDF document through the document's xref table; you don't need to know anything about how individual objects in a PDF document are accessed. Quartz also handles the decompression and decoding of the data associated with any streams in the PDF document, making it much easier for you to use that data.

Apple developer tools include two useful code examples that demonstrate the use of the Quartz introspection capabilities provided in Panther and later versions. Voyeur is a Cocoa project that presents a browser that allows you to visually explore the hierarchy of objects in a PDF document in detail. Using Voyeur as an application is useful as part of the process of learning about the structure of PDF documents. Reading the code that comprises the Voyeur project is a great way to get started learning the Quartz introspection programming functions. The Voyeur sample project is installed in /Developer/Examples/Quartz/PDF/Voyeur.

Apple also provides sample code for the Outline command line tool. This tool extracts Outline data, if it exists in a PDF document, and writes the outline text to stdout. If you want to obtain the outline information from a PDF document, this code example is a good starting point. The Outline sample project is installed in /Developer/Examples/Quartz/PDF/Outline.

The details of the functions that make up the generalized PDF introspection functions are not discussed in this book. Apple reference documentation and these example programs, together with the PDF specification, are more than enough to get you started. The next section presents one specific aspect of document introspection—examining the page content of a PDF document.

Scanning the PDF Content Stream (Tiger)

10.4 ▶

Tiger adds the interesting ability to parse the drawing content stream of a PDF page and examine it in a structured way. Examining the page content stream requires detailed knowledge of the PDF operators that are part of the drawing you want to examine. This information appears in the PDF specification and is beyond the scope of this book, but a discussion of the concepts involved in using Quartz to parse the content stream and an example of doing so will help you get started.

When you scan the content stream of a PDF document, you use the following Quartz objects:

- A `CGPDFContentStreamRef`, which is an opaque type that represents the content stream on a given PDF page. You create a `CGPDFContentStreamRef` from a CGPDFPage object that represents the page of the document whose content stream you want to scan.

- A `CGPDFOperatorTableRef`, which is an opaque type that contains callbacks for each of the PDF operators that might make up the content stream in a PDF document. You add your customized callbacks to a CGPDFOperatorTable object, enabling Quartz to invoke your code when the corresponding operator is encountered in the PDF page content stream.

- A `CGPDFScannerRef`, which is an opaque type that you use to tell Quartz to scan the content stream of a page. You create a CGPDFScanner object with the `CGPDFContentStreamRef` of a given page and a `CGPDFOperatorTableRef`.

Listing 14.11 (page 472) gives you a taste for how you examine the PDF content stream using the Quartz functions available in Tiger. The code uses this capability to count the images on each page in a PDF document, categorizing the images in one of these four categories:

- Image mask.

- Image masked by another image.

- Image masked by a color.

- Image with intrinsic color with no mask.

Listing 14.11 contains the routines `checkImageType`, `myOperator_Do`, `myOperator_EI`, `createMyOperatorTable`, and `dumpPageStreams`. The entry point for the code is the routine `dumpPageStreams`, which takes a CFURL object of a PDF file and a UNIX file object to write its output. It examines each page of the PDF document for images and counts the number of images of the various flavors on that page, calling a `printPageResults` routine that you might write to generate the results to an output file. After it has processed each page, the routine `dumpPageStreams` calls a `printDocResults` routine that you might write to generate the results to an output file.

To scan each page, the code creates a `CGPDFDocumentRef` from the URL of the input PDF document to scan. It then calls `createMyOperatorTable` to create a `CGPDFOperatorTableRef` that contains the callbacks for the operators it is interested in examining. This will be discussed in a moment; for now, consider that the `CGPDFOperatorTableRef` returned by the routine `createMyOperatorTable` contains the actions that this example takes as Quartz scans a given page of the document. Because the code takes the same actions for each page of the PDF document, the code calls `createMyOperatorTable` outside the for loop that handles each page.

Inside the loop for each page, the code obtains the CGPDFPage object for that page and creates a new CGPDFContentStream object from that page. From that content stream and the operator table object, the code creates a CGPDFScanner object for the page. The code passes a pointer to the `myData` structure when it calls `CGPDFScannerCreate` to create the scanner object; this is the `info` parameter that Quartz passes to each of the callbacks that the scanner calls while scanning the page content stream. Creating the CGPDFScanner object merely creates the object; it doesn't cause the scanner object to do anything.

After initializing the counters for each of the types of images for the page, the code calls `CGPDFScannerScan` to scan the page. This is the function that causes Quartz to scan the content stream of the page. As Quartz scans the page, it invokes the custom callback functions registered in the `CGPDFOperatorTableRef` that was used to create the scanner object. Each callback processes only the data appropriate for that callback; you'll see this in a moment. After the page content is scanned, the call to `CGPDFScannerScan` returns a `bool` value that indicates whether the page scan completed without error. The remainder of the loop prints the results for the page using `printPageResults`, updates the total count of images, and releases the scanner and page content stream objects that it created for that page. After the code finishes looping through all the pages, it prints the results for the total document using `printDocResults` and releases the CGPDFOperatorTable and CGPDFDocument objects.

So far in this example, you've seen how to set up and scan the page content stream for a page, but you still don't know anything about what happened when the content stream was scanned. The key to this aspect of the code is the callbacks in the CGPDFOperatorTable object used to create the scanner object. The operator table for the example is created by the `createMyOperatorTable` routine in Listing 14.11. This code is pretty simple: It creates a new CGPDFOperator-Table object, then calls CGPDFOperatorTableSetCallback twice to register callbacks for the Do and EI PDF operators. For the Do operator, the code registers the callback routine myOperator_Do, and for the EI operator, the code registers the callback routine myOperator_EI. These callback routines are the portion of the code that controls what happens when Quartz scans the page contents.

Taking advantage of the Quartz ability to parse the PDF page content stream requires detailed knowledge of the different PDF operators. This discussion presents the high-level concepts involved for this example, not the details.

Remember that the intent of this example is to examine each PDF page of the document for the images it contains and to count each type of image that is drawn. Images can be drawn as part of the content stream in a number of different ways. Images can appear at the top level of the content stream either inline (typically for small images of ~4k of data or less) or as image resources. Images can also appear inside of other resources, such as forms or patterns. Listing 14.11 looks only at images that are either inline to the PDF stream or referenced as image resources; it does not examine images used inside of forms, patterns, or any other resources.

Images that are not inline are referenced in a PDF page content stream as resources and are drawn using the PDF operator Do. To process these kinds of images during the scanning of the content stream of a page, the code registers the routine myOperator_Do as a callback for the Do operator. When Quartz encounters the Do operator during the page scan, it invokes the myOperator_Do callback. Now take a look at how myOperator_Do performs its processing.

Each callback routine handles the specific operator for which it is registered. PDF operators receive their data on the PDF operand stack and each operator is responsible for removing its operands from that stack as part of its processing. The Do operator has one operand, which is the name of the XObject resource that is the object to be drawn. As such, the myOperator_Do routine obtains its argument by calling CGPDFScannerPopName, which fetches the name of the XObject passed to the Do operator. This pops the name from the operand stack. The code then obtains the object with the name popped from the operand stack in the resource category "XObject" by calling CGPDFContentStreamGetResource. This looks up the name in the resource hierarchy appropriate for the PDF page, returning the object with that name in the XObject category. A PDF XObject is a stream object, as defined in the PDF specification. To obtain the CGPDFStream object from the XObject, the code calls CGPDFObjectGetValue, requesting the type kCGPDFObjectTypeStream. Note that this call returns false if the object is not a stream.

PDF streams consist of two parts, a dictionary and the data that makes up the stream. Image streams consist of a dictionary that describes the data, such as the width, height, color space, bits per sample, a masking image or colors, and so on. The stream data associated with an image is the image sample data itself. After the code has the CGPDFStream object associated with the XObject, it obtains the dictionary from the stream and looks for the Subtype entry in that dictionary. The Subtype entry is "Image" for an image stream. If "Image" is not the Subtype of this XObject, the code skips any further processing of this XObject. If it is indeed an Image XObject, the code calls checkImageType with the image dictionary so it can categorize the image. For more details of the image XObject, see the comments in the implementation of checkImageType in Listing 14.11 and consult the PDF specification.

The code registers the myOperator_EI callback to handle the EI operator. Inline images are relatively rare, but this code demonstrates a straightforward way to handle them. Inline images in a content stream end with an EI operator. By registering for the EI operator, you can process inline images in a manner similar to handling them as resources. When Quartz calls an EI operator callback, the operand stack has a stream object on it that corresponds to the inline image.

The myOperator_EI routine in Listing 14.11 calls the function CGPDFScannerPopStream to pop the stream object off the operand stack. After the routine has the stream object, it can obtain the image dictionary from the stream and pass the image dictionary to checkImageType for processing.

As you can see from this example, Quartz provides powerful capabilities with the CGPDFScanner functions and the other types that you use with them. Using them requires quite a bit of knowledge about the PDF operators themselves, but Quartz provides a way of working that allows you to examine and use the PDF content stream data without worrying about most of the messy details of finding and decoding PDF objects in a PDF document.

Listing 14.11 Code that counts and categorizes the images used on each page of a PDF document

```
typedef struct MyDataScan
{
  size_t numImagesWithColorThisPage;
  size_t numImageMasksThisPage;
  size_t numImagesMaskedWithMaskThisPage;
  size_t numImagesMaskedWithColorsThisPage;
}MyDataScan;

void checkImageType(CGPDFDictionaryRef imageDict,
             MyDataScan *myScanDataP)
{
  CGPDFBoolean isMask;
  CGPDFObjectRef object;
```

```
  bool hasMaskKey;
  // If it is an image mask, the dictionary has a key
  // ImageMask with a boolean true or it has
  // a key IM with a boolean true.
  hasMaskKey = CGPDFDictionaryGetBoolean(imageDict, "ImageMask",
                    &isMask);
  if(!hasMaskKey)
    hasMaskKey = CGPDFDictionaryGetBoolean(imageDict, "IM", &isMask);

  if(hasMaskKey && isMask){
    myScanDataP->numImageMasksThisPage++;
    return;
  }
  // If image is masked with an alpha image, it has an SMask entry.
  if(CGPDFDictionaryGetObject(imageDict, "SMask", &object)){
    // This object must be an XObject that is an image.
    // This code assumes the PDF is well formed in this regard.
    myScanDataP->numImagesMaskedWithMaskThisPage++;
    return;
  }


  // If this image is masked with an image or with colors, it has
  // a Mask entry.
  if(CGPDFDictionaryGetObject(imageDict, "Mask", &object)){
    // If the object is an XObject, then the mask is an image.
    // If it is an array, then the mask is an array of colors.
    CGPDFObjectType type = CGPDFObjectGetType(object);
    // Check if it is a stream type (which it must be to be an XObject).
    if(type == kCGPDFObjectTypeStream)
      myScanDataP->numImagesMaskedWithMaskThisPage++;
    else if(type == kCGPDFObjectTypeArray)
      myScanDataP->numImagesMaskedWithColorsThisPage++;
    else
      fprintf(stderr,
        "Mask entry in Image object is not well formed!\n");

    return;
  }
  // This image is not a mask and it is not masked with another image or
  // color, so it must be an image with intrinsic color with no mask.
  myScanDataP->numImagesWithColorThisPage++;
}
```

```
void myOperator_Do(CGPDFScannerRef s, void *info)
{
  // Check to see if this is an image or not.
  const char *name;
  CGPDFObjectRef xobject;
  CGPDFDictionaryRef dict;
  CGPDFStreamRef stream;
  CGPDFContentStreamRef cs = CGPDFScannerGetContentStream(s);

  // The Do operator takes a name. Pop the name off the
  // stack. If this fails, then the argument to the
  // Do operator is not a name and is therefore invalid!
  if(!CGPDFScannerPopName(s, &name)){
    fprintf(stderr, "Couldn't pop name off stack!\n");
    return;
  }
  // Get the resource with type "XObject" and the name
  // obtained from the stack.
  xobject = CGPDFContentStreamGetResource(cs, "XObject", name);
  if(!xobject){
    fprintf(stderr, "Couldn't get XObject with name %s\n", name);
    return;
  }

  // An XObject must be a stream so obtain the value from the XObject
  // as if it were a stream. If this fails, the PDF is malformed.
  if (!CGPDFObjectGetValue(xobject, kCGPDFObjectTypeStream, &stream)){
    fprintf(stderr, "XObject '%s' is not a stream!\n", name);
    return;
  }
  // Streams consist of a dictionary and the data associated
  // with the stream. This code only cares about the dictionary.
  dict = CGPDFStreamGetDictionary(stream);
  if(!dict){
    fprintf(stderr,
      "Couldn't obtain dictionary from stream %s!\n", name);
    return;
  }
  // An XObject dictionary has a Subtype that indicates what kind it is.
  if(!CGPDFDictionaryGetName(dict, "Subtype", &name)){
    fprintf(stderr, "Couldn't get SubType of dictionary object!\n");
    return;
  }
```

```
  // This code is interested in the "Image" Subtype of an XObject.
  // Check whether this object has the Subtype of "Image".
  if(strcmp(name, "Image") != 0){
    // The Subtype is not "Image" so this must be a form
    // or other type of XObject.
    return;
  }

  // This is an Image so figure out what variety of image it is.
  checkImageType(dict, (MyDataScan *)info);

}

// This callback handles inline images. Inline images end with the
// "EI" operator.
void myOperator_EI(CGPDFScannerRef s, void *info)
{
  CGPDFStreamRef stream;
  CGPDFDictionaryRef dict;
  // When the scanner encounters the EI operator, it has a
  // stream corresponding to the image on the operand stack.
  // This code pops the stream off the stack in order to
  // examine it.
  if(!CGPDFScannerPopStream(s, &stream)){
    fprintf(stderr, "Couldn't create stream from inline image!\n");
    return;
  }
  // Get the image dictionary from the stream.
  dict = CGPDFStreamGetDictionary(stream);
  if(!dict){
    fprintf(stderr,
      "Couldn't get dict from inline image stream!\n");
    return;
  }
  // By definition, the stream passed to EI is an image so
  // pass it to the code to check the type of image.
  checkImageType(dict, (MyDataScan *)info);
}

static CGPDFOperatorTableRef createMyOperatorTable(void)
{
  // Create a new operator table.
  CGPDFOperatorTableRef myTable = CGPDFOperatorTableCreate();
```

```
    // Add a callback for the "Do" operator.
    CGPDFOperatorTableSetCallback(myTable, "Do", myOperator_Do);
    // Add a callback for the "EI" operator.
    CGPDFOperatorTableSetCallback(myTable, "EI", myOperator_EI);
    return myTable;
}

void dumpPageStreams(CFURLRef url, FILE *outFile)
{
    CGPDFDocumentRef pdfDoc = NULL;
    CGPDFOperatorTableRef table = NULL;
    MyDataScan myData;
    size_t totalImages, totPages, i;

    // Create a CGPDFDocumentRef from the input PDF file.
    pdfDoc = CGPDFDocumentCreateWithURL(url);
    if(!pdfDoc){
        fprintf(stderr, "Couldn't open PDF document!\n");
        return;
    }
    // Create the operator table with the needed callbacks.
    table = createMyOperatorTable();
    if(!table){
        CGPDFDocumentRelease(pdfDoc);
        fprintf(stderr, "Couldn't create operator table\n!");
        return;
    }
    // Initialize the count of the images in the document.
    totalImages = 0;

    // Obtain the total number of pages for the document.
    totPages = CGPDFDocumentGetNumberOfPages(pdfDoc);

    // Loop over all the pages in the document, scanning the
    // content stream of each one.
    for(i = 1; i <= totPages; i++){
        CGPDFScannerRef scanner = NULL;
        // Get the PDF page for this page in the document.
        CGPDFPageRef p = CGPDFDocumentGetPage(pdfDoc, i);
        // Create a reference to the content stream for this page.
        CGPDFContentStreamRef cs = CGPDFContentStreamCreateWithPage(p);
        if(!cs){
            CGPDFOperatorTableRelease(table);
            CGPDFDocumentRelease(pdfDoc);
```

```
      fprintf(stderr,
        "Couldn't create content stream for page #%zd!\n", i);
      return;
  }
  // Create a scanner for this PDF document page.
  scanner = CGPDFScannerCreate(cs, table, &myData);
  if(!scanner){
    CGPDFContentStreamRelease(cs);
    CGPDFOperatorTableRelease(table);
    CGPDFDocumentRelease(pdfDoc);
    fprintf(stderr,
      "Couldn't create scanner for page #%zd!\n", i);
    return;
  }
  // Initialize the counters of images for this page.
  myData.numImagesWithColorThisPage = 0;
  myData.numImageMasksThisPage = 0;
  myData.numImagesMaskedWithMaskThisPage = 0;
  myData.numImagesMaskedWithColorsThisPage = 0;

  // CGPDFScannerScan causes Quartz to scan the content stream,
  // calling the callbacks in the table when the corresponding
  // operator is encountered.
  if(!CGPDFScannerScan(scanner)){
    fprintf(stderr,
      "Scanner couldn't scan all of page #%zd!\n", i);
  }
  // Print the results for this page.
  printPageResults(outFile, myData, i);

  // Update the total count of images with the count of the
  // images on this page.
  totalImages +=
    myData.numImagesWithColorThisPage +
    myData.numImageMasksThisPage +
    myData.numImagesMaskedWithMaskThisPage +
    myData.numImagesMaskedWithColorsThisPage;

  // Once the page has been scanned, release the
  // scanner for this page.
  CGPDFScannerRelease(scanner);
  // Release the content stream for this page.
  CGPDFContentStreamRelease(cs);
```

```
        // Done with this page; loop to next page.
    }
    printDocResults(outFile, totPages, totalImages);

    // Release the operator table this code created.
    CGPDFOperatorTableRelease(table);
    // Release the input PDF CGPDFDocumentRef.
    CGPDFDocumentRelease(pdfDoc);
}
```

Summary

Creating new PDF documents in Quartz is straightforward, primarily because the PDF file format is the graphics metafile format used by the Quartz imaging model. All drawing you perform using Quartz is captured with high fidelity when you capture the content as a PDF document. Further, PDF is the graphics data format used on the Clipboard, so to support cutting and pasting data between applications, you'll want to create PDF content. (The previous chapter showed how to obtain PDF data from a pasteboard.)

Quartz provides numerous functions that let you examine PDF content, including PDF metadata and the PDF content stream that includes drawing commands. This chapter gives a brief introduction to these capabilities. Developers who want to support PDF introspection need to read those portions of the PDF specification that discuss the file format itself and consult the Apple reference documentation for the pertinent Quartz functions.

See Also

In addition to the resources listed at the end of Chapter 13, "Opening and Drawing PDF Documents" (page 397), the following header files contain the Quartz constants, definitions, and functions for creating a PDF context and for examining existing PDF documents:

- CGPDFContext.h contains the functions and keys used to create and use a PDF context.

- CGPDFObject.h, CGPDFStream.h, CGPDFDictionary.h, CGPDFString.h, and CGPDF-Array.h contain the functions related to Quartz PDF document introspection, introduced in Panther.

- `CGPDFOperatorTable.h`, `CGPDFContentStream.h`, and `CGPDFScanner.h` contain the functions in Tiger and later for examining the PDF page content stream.

The relevant Quartz reference documentation from the ADC Reference Library is

- *CGPDFContext Reference*
- *CGPDFObject Reference*
- *CGPDFStream Reference*
- *CGPDFDictionary Reference*
- *CGPDFString Reference*
- *CGPDFArray Reference*
- *CGPDFOperatorTable Reference*
- *CGPDFContentStream Reference*
- *CGPDFScanner Reference*

PDF/X encompasses a set of International Standards Organization (ISO) standards. The ISO number for the PDF/X specification is 15930; the specification is broken into several parts. The ISO website makes these specifications available for a fee. One way to find these documents is to search the ISO website (*www.iso.org*) for "15930." In addition, the website *www.pdfx3.org* contains useful information about PDF/X-3, including a FAQ, links to tools, and mailing lists about PDF/X.

Chapter **15**

Advanced Drawing Features

Quartz offers a number of advanced drawing capabilities that build on top of the basic graphic primitives and features you've already learned about—patterns, shadows, transparency layers, and shadings. Patterns provide a way for you to create a repeating tile that contains arbitrary Quartz drawing and use that tile as a fill or stroke color. You've probably noticed the drop shadow that is present in the Aqua user interface in Mac OS X. Using Quartz, you can get that same look in your own drawing. Transparency layers allow you to group drawing elements together and treat them as a single unit for purposes of applying shadows or alpha transparency. Shadings, sometimes called gradients or blends, provide a way to smoothly vary color across a shape, giving the appearance of a continuous blending of colors.

The purpose of this chapter is to provide an in-depth discussion of these four advanced drawing features. You'll learn the concepts associated with each one and take a look at simple as well as complex examples of how to incorporate each feature in your drawing code.

Drawing with Patterns

A **pattern** is a graphic that is iteratively tiled across an object. You see patterns used every day in clothing, furniture, wallpaper, and many other objects, including virtual objects such as screen savers. Quartz provides the ability to define a pattern that you can then use as paint to fill or stroke any graphics. You can apply a pattern to any graphics that use stroke and fill colors—text, image masks, and objects created with paths. See Figure 15.1 for some examples.

Before you can draw with a pattern, you define the graphic, called the **pattern cell**, that you want to use to tile the shape you want to paint. The pattern cell that defines the pattern can contain virtually any type of drawing available in Quartz. After you create a pattern, you can use it just like you use any color. You set the fill or stroke color using the pattern and then draw—Quartz uses your description of the pattern cell and tiles it to paint the shape that you are drawing. If the fill color is a pattern, filling line art or text or painting image masks uses the pattern as a repeating tile to fill the shape. If the stroke color is a pattern, stroking line art or text paints the stroke using the pattern.

There are two distinct types of patterns available with Quartz. The first type is a pattern that itself has intrinsic color. For example, if you were to use the flag of a country as a pattern, the pattern would have intrinsic color because every time a given country's flag appears, it has the same color. Apple's original multicolored logo also has intrinsic color. Patterns that have intrinsic color are called **colored patterns**. A colored pattern can contain any Quartz drawing, including images

Figure 15.1 Patterns can fill and stroke shapes and paint text

with intrinsic color. Like all graphics, colored patterns can contain partially transparent content.

The second type of pattern is a **stencil pattern**. Stencil patterns have no intrinsic color; they instead define a shape that you pour paint through. (Sometimes stencil patterns are called **masking patterns** because they act like a mask, similar to an image mask.) For example, Apple frequently uses the Apple logo as a shape that it paints with different colors. If you get a business card from an Apple employee, the apple is painted in one of several different colors; which color depends on which batch that card came from. When you create a stencil pattern, you can only define your pattern with drawing that has no intrinsic color. You can't set the painting color in your code that draws the pattern cell, nor can you draw objects that contain color, such as images with intrinsic color or PDF documents.

Creating Patterns

A Quartz pattern is represented by the CGPatternRef opaque data type. You create a CGPattern object with the function CGPatternCreate. You need to define the pattern cell size and coordinate system, the desired spacing between pattern cells, whether the pattern is colored or a stencil pattern, and how to draw the pattern cell. You pass the following parameters to CGPatternCreate:

- info, a pointer to data that you want Quartz to pass to your pattern callback functions.

- bounds, a CGRect that defines the size of the pattern cell you want to create.

- patternMatrix, a CGAffineTransform that defines the mapping of pattern space to Quartz base space. (Pattern space is not the same as user space, as you'll see in a moment.)

- xStep, the horizontal distance in pattern space between each pattern cell; this value must be nonzero.

- yStep, the vertical distance in pattern space between each pattern cell; this value must be nonzero.

- tilingType, a value of type CGPatternTiling that describes how Quartz should tile the pattern.

- isColored, a value that indicates whether the pattern has intrinsic color. A true value indicates that the pattern has intrinsic color; a value of false indicates that the pattern is a stencil pattern.

- callbacks, a pointer to a CGPatternCallbacks structure that contains the callback functions for your pattern. You use these callbacks to draw your pattern cell and manage any resources associated with it.

The bounds rectangle that you pass to CGPatternCreate is the boundary rectangle of the content contained in your pattern cell. Quartz uses this rectangle to determine the size of your pattern cell and clips the content of your pattern cell to this rectangle. The bounds rectangle is typically a tight bounding box describing your pattern cell content that doesn't clip any content you want visible.

The bounds of a pattern cell is not sufficient to describe how a pattern cell is spaced when Quartz tiles the pattern. You independently choose the spacing between pattern cells with the xStep and yStep parameters. These parameters determine how far apart the pattern cells are placed when Quartz tiles the pattern. As Quartz tiles along the x direction, it moves xStep units in the pattern coordinate system before painting the next tile. As Quartz tiles in the y direction, it moves yStep units in the pattern coordinate system before drawing the next tile. You can choose to have your pattern cells tiled consecutively so that there is no additional space between pattern cells or you can have extra space between the pattern cells. To have no extra space between pattern cells, choose xStep to be the width of the pattern (bounds.size.width) and yStep to be the height of the pattern (bounds.size.height). Obviously, xStep and yStep must both be nonzero.

The size of a pattern cell in the coordinate system in which Quartz paints the pattern tiles might not be an integer number of device pixels. Depending on the size of the pattern cell and the destination into which it is replicated, Quartz might need to make small adjustments to the pattern cell size and the spacing between cells. With the tilingType parameter, you can specify how Quartz performs any adjustments to the spacing between tiles. The tilingType parameter is discussed in more detail in "Pattern Issues" (page 510).

The callbacks parameter that you pass to CGPatternCreate is a structure of type CGPatternCallbacks, defined as follows:

- version, the version number of the CGPatternCallbacks structure. As of Tiger, the only version defined is 0.

- drawPattern, a pointer to a callback of type CGPatternDrawPatternCallback that you supply. Quartz calls your drawPattern callback when it needs to draw your pattern cell. This routine must not be NULL. There are more details about this callback later in this section.

- releaseInfo, a pointer to a callback of type CGPatternReleaseInfoCallback. If it is not NULL, Quartz calls your releaseInfo routine when it releases your pattern. Your releaseInfo routine should release any memory and other resources associated with the info parameter that you supply to CGPatternCreate.

The drawPattern callback that you supply is critical to defining a pattern. This callback is the routine that you use to draw the contents of a single pattern cell. Quartz invokes it when it needs to draw a pattern cell; the results of this drawing are what Quartz tiles to fill or stroke with your pattern. For performance reasons, Quartz might cache the results of the drawing that your drawPattern callback performs.

Your drawPattern callback is a function of type CGPatternReleaseInfoCallback. The parameters passed to a function of this type are

- info, the same value of info that you supply when you define the pattern with CGPatternCreate.

- context, the CGContextRef into which drawPattern draws the pattern cell.

You should not make any assumptions about the state of the context passed to your drawPattern routine; set the context graphics state that's needed to draw your pattern cell. If your pattern is a colored pattern, you must set the painting color appropriate for your drawing. If your pattern is a stencil pattern, you must not perform any color setting operations in your drawPattern routine or draw content that has intrinsic color, such as images or PDF documents.

For a given pattern, your drawPattern callback must draw the exact same content each time it is invoked. You must ensure that any resources you need to draw your pattern cell are available when your drawPattern routine is called. Quartz could invoke your drawPattern callback at unpredictable times; it could call it anytime after you create the pattern until your releaseInfo callback is called. Any resources associated with your pattern must be available to your drawPattern callback until your pattern releaseInfo callback is called.

A pattern cell has its own coordinate system called **pattern space**. This is the coordinate system that you draw in to create your pattern cell content and that the bounds, xStep, and yStep parameters that you pass to CGPatternCreate are interpreted in. The patternMatrix parameter that you supply to CGPatternCreate defines how Quartz maps the pattern space coordinate system into Quartz **base space**. In general, Quartz base space is the default Quartz coordinate system for a given context. That is, base space is the Quartz coordinate system before any coordinate transforms are applied. You'll learn more about base space in "Base Space, the Pattern Matrix, and Transforming Patterns" (page 493).

Creating and Drawing Colored Patterns

Take a look at Figure 15.2 to see what it looks like to draw with a simple colored pattern. This figure, which is the result of executing the code in Listing 15.1, demonstrates some of the features of drawing with patterns. On the left

Figure 15.2 A pattern that fills rectangles, strokes an ellipse, and paints text

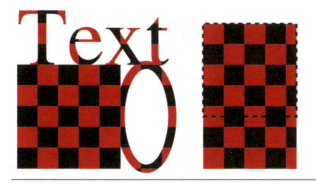

side of the figure is a filled rectangle, a stroked ellipse, and some text that is painted with a pattern. On the right side of the figure are two rectangles drawn with a pattern. These rectangles overlap; one of the rectangles is stroked with a dashed line so that you can see its boundary.

The pattern cell in this example consists of two red and two black rectangles, arranged in a 2x2 grid. Each rectangle is 1 unit on a side, the overall size of the grid is 2 units on a side. The grid is that of a small piece of a red and black checkerboard like you might see in a checkers game.

Listing 15.1 consists of the routine doRedBlackCheckerboard and two supporting routines: createRedBlackCheckerBoardPattern, which creates the CGPatternRef corresponding to the checkerboard pattern, and myDrawRedBlackCheckerBoard-Pattern, which draws the checkerboard pattern cell. The routine doRedBlack-Checkerboard first calls the routine createRedBlackCheckerBoardPattern to make a CGPattern object that corresponds to the checkerboard pattern. It passes an affine transform that createRedBlackCheckerBoardPattern uses as the patternMa-trix for the pattern it creates. By structuring the code in this fashion, the code that uses the pattern can create a new pattern that is transformed in any fashion it wants, without the pattern creation code needing to know the details of the pattern matrix.

Listing 15.1 Code that draws with a colored pattern

```
static void myDrawRedBlackCheckerBoardPattern(void *info,
                CGContextRef patternCellContext)
{
  // Paint black checkerboard boxes.
  CGContextSetFillColorWithColor(patternCellContext,
              getRGBOpaqueBlackColor());
```

```
  // This is a 1x1 unit rectangle whose origin is at (0,0) in pattern space.
  CGContextFillRect(patternCellContext, CGRectMake(0., 0., 1., 1.));
  // This is a 1x1 unit rectangle whose origin is at (1,1) in pattern space.
  CGContextFillRect(patternCellContext, CGRectMake(1., 1., 1., 1.));

  // Paint red checkerboard boxes.
  CGContextSetFillColorWithColor(patternCellContext,
               getRGBOpaqueRedColor());
  // This is a 1x1 unit rectangle whose origin is at (1,0) in pattern space,
  // that is, immediately to the right of the first black checkerboard box.
  CGContextFillRect(patternCellContext, CGRectMake(1., 0., 1., 1.));
  // This is a 1x1 unit rectangle whose origin is at (0,1) in pattern space,
  // that is, immediately above the first black checkerboard box.
  CGContextFillRect(patternCellContext, CGRectMake(0., 1., 1., 1.));
}

static CGPatternRef createRedBlackCheckerBoardPattern(
             CGAffineTransform patternTransform)
{
  CGPatternCallbacks myPatternCallbacks;
  CGPatternRef pattern;
  bool patternIsColored = true;
  // Only version 0 of the pattern callbacks is defined as of Tiger.
  myPatternCallbacks.version = 0;
  // The pattern's drawPattern proc is the routine Quartz calls
  // to draw a pattern cell when it needs to draw one.
  myPatternCallbacks.drawPattern = myDrawRedBlackCheckerBoardPattern;
  // This code has no data associated with it to release, so the
  // releaseInfo callback is NULL.
  myPatternCallbacks.releaseInfo = NULL;

  pattern = CGPatternCreate(NULL,
    // The pattern cell origin is at (0,0) with a
    // width of 2 units and a height of 2 units.
    CGRectMake(0, 0, 2, 2),
    // Use the pattern transform supplied to this routine.
    patternTransform,
    // In pattern space the xStep is 2 units to the next cell in x
    // and the yStep is 2 units to the next row of cells in y.
    2, 2,
    // This value is a good choice for this type of pattern and it
    // avoids seams between tiles.
```

```
        kCGPatternTilingConstantSpacingMinimalDistortion,
        // This pattern has intrinsic color.
        patternIsColored,
        &myPatternCallbacks);
    return pattern;
}

void doRedBlackCheckerboard(CGContextRef context)
{
    CGColorSpaceRef patternColorSpace;
    float color[1];
    float dash[1] = { 4 } ;
    CGPatternRef pattern = createRedBlackCheckerBoardPattern(
                CGAffineTransformMakeScale(20, 20)
                );
    if(pattern == NULL){
        fprintf(stderr, "Couldn't create pattern!\n");
        return;
    }
    // Create the pattern color space. Since the pattern
    // itself has intrinsic color, the 'baseColorSpace' parameter
    // passed to CGColorSpaceCreatePattern must be NULL.
    patternColorSpace = CGColorSpaceCreatePattern(NULL);
    CGContextSetFillColorSpace(context, patternColorSpace);

    // The pattern has intrinsic color so the color components array
    // passed to CGContextSetFillPattern is just the alpha value used
    // to composite the pattern cell.

    // Paint the pattern with alpha = 1.
    color[0] = 1.;
    // Set the fill color to the checkerboard pattern.
    CGContextSetFillPattern(context, pattern, color);

    // Fill a 100x100 unit rectangle at (20,20).
    CGContextFillRect(context, CGRectMake(20, 20, 100, 100));
    // Save the graphics state before changing the stroke color.
    CGContextSaveGState(context);
        // Set the stroke color space and color to the pattern.
        CGContextSetStrokeColorSpace(context, patternColorSpace);
        CGContextSetStrokePattern(context, pattern, color);
        // Stroke an ellipse with the pattern.
        CGContextSetLineWidth(context, 8);
        CGContextBeginPath(context);
```

```
    myCGContextAddEllipseInRect(context,
                CGRectMake(120, 20, 50, 100));
    CGContextStrokePath(context);

  // Restore to the graphics state without the
  // pattern stroke color.
  CGContextRestoreGState(context);

  // Now draw text.
  CGContextSetTextMatrix(context, CGAffineTransformIdentity);
  // Choose the font with the PostScript name "Times-Roman",
  // size 80 points, with the encoding MacRoman encoding.
  CGContextSelectFont(context, "Times-Roman", 80,
                kCGEncodingMacRoman);
  // Use the fill text drawing mode.
  CGContextSetTextDrawingMode(context, kCGTextFill);
  // Draw text with the pattern.
  CGContextShowTextAtPoint(context, 20, 120, "Text", 4);

  // Rectangle 1, filled.
  CGContextFillRect(context, CGRectMake(200, 20, 90, 90));

  // Rectangle 2, filled and stroked with a dash.
  CGContextSetLineWidth(context, 2);
  CGContextSetLineDash(context, 0, dash, 1);
  CGContextBeginPath(context);
  CGContextAddRect(context, CGRectMake(200, 70, 90, 90));
  CGContextDrawPath(context, kCGPathFillStroke);
  // This code won't set the pattern again so it
  // can release it.
  CGPatternRelease(pattern);
  // This code doesn't need the pattern color space
  // any longer so release it.
  CGColorSpaceRelease(patternColorSpace);
}
```

Take a look at the myDrawRedBlackCheckerBoardPattern pattern drawing callback, which is what Quartz invokes to draw a single cell of the pattern. The pattern cell drawing in this example is intentionally simple so that you can focus on the important aspects of how patterns work. The context passed to the routine is the one that Quartz records the pattern cell drawing into. The routine fills two black and two red rectangles, each of which is 1 unit on a side. The code first sets up the graphics state needed to draw the black rectangles and then draws them. The routine getRGBOpaqueBlackColor returns a CGColor object that corresponds to an opaque black color in the generic calibrated RGB color space. It next sets the fill color to red and draws the red rectangles. The routine getRGBOpaqueRedColor returns a CGColor object corresponding to opaque red in the same RGB color space.

Tip CGColor objects (available starting in Panther) are convenient and efficient for setting color.

The createRedBlackCheckerBoardPattern fills in the fields of a CGPatternCall-backs structure and creates a CGPattern object that corresponds to the checker-board pattern. It assigns myDrawRedBlackCheckerBoardPattern as the pattern drawing callback but does not need to assign a releaseInfo callback to the CGPatternCallbacks structure since the pattern is self-contained. The self-contained nature of the pattern is also reflected in the fact the info parameter supplied to the function CGPatternCreate is NULL. The bounding rectangle for this drawing has its origin at (0,0) and the width and height are each 2 units. To ensure that the pattern tiles without extra space between the pattern cells, the pattern xStep and yStep are each 2 units, the same size as the width and height of the pattern cell. Note that the code passes true to CGPatternCreate for the isColored parameter because the pattern has intrinsic color—the black and red of the checkerboard. The myDrawRedBlackCheckerBoardPattern pattern drawing routine and the bounds parameter defines a pattern cell that is relatively small, 2 units on a side.

The relationship between pattern space and the coordinate system that Quartz uses to tile the pattern is an important one to understand. It's defined by the patternMatrix affine transform you supply to CGPatternCreate. Figure 15.3 shows the relationship between the checkerboard pattern space and the coordinate system in which the checkerboard pattern is tiled. A single pattern cell, as created by the code, is on the left side of the figure. The pattern cell is 2 units on a side.

To transform the pattern cell to a size that is appropriate for the drawing, the patternMatrix used in Listing 15.1 scales by a factor of 20 in both x and y. The resulting pattern tile is 40 units on a side, as shown in the center of Figure 15.3. Because the xStep and yStep values are the same as the width and height of the pattern cell, when Quartz tiles the pattern to fill a shape, it replicates the pattern tile without any gaps between tiles, as you see on the right of the figure.

This example is somewhat artificial because it would be easy to define the pattern drawing at the larger size and use a matrix that is the identity transform. However, understanding how to manipulate the patternMatrix is important if you want to scale or otherwise transform your pattern relative to Quartz base

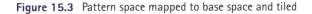

Figure 15.3 Pattern space mapped to base space and tiled

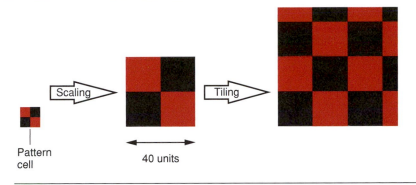

space, as you'll see in "Base Space, the Pattern Matrix, and Transforming Patterns" (page 493).

Now that you've looked at the code that creates the pattern and draws a pattern cell, take a look at the remainder of doRedBlackCheckerboard, the code that uses the checkerboard pattern. After the code creates the CGPattern object that corresponds to the checkerboard pattern, it next sets the pattern as the current fill color.

A pattern is a painting color in a special color space, the pattern color space, introduced in "Color, Alpha Transparency, and the Quartz Graphics State" (page 147). To create a pattern color space, you call the function CGColorSpaceCreate-Pattern with a single parameter, baseColorSpace. Colored patterns (such as this example) have no base color space associated with them; the pattern describes the painting colors (it is *colored*, after all). When creating a pattern color space for use with colored patterns, you must pass NULL.

Important The base color space for a pattern color space used for drawing colored patterns must be NULL. "Checking Pattern Color Space Usage" (page 622) discusses the problems you may encounter if you do not properly create a color space for use with a colored pattern.

The code sets the fill color space to the pattern color space, then sets the fill color to the pattern by calling the Quartz function CGContextSetFillPattern. This function requires both the CGPatternRef for the pattern that you want to set and an array of color values. For colored patterns, there is a single value in the array, the alpha value to composite the pattern with. Even though the pattern contains intrinsic color, you can also apply an additional alpha value when you draw the pattern; this alpha value applies to the pattern cell as if it were a single object. In this example, the code sets the alpha value to fully opaque. Failure to set the pattern color after you set the pattern color space produces a pattern that draws nothing.

Setting the color space and setting the pattern are separate operations in the code. Starting in Panther, you can create a CGColor object for a pattern that encapsulates both the pattern color space and the pattern together by using `CGColor-CreateWithPattern`. You then set that pattern as the painting color using `CGContextSetFillColorWithColor` or `CGContextSetStrokeColorWithColor`.

| Tip | CGColor objects offer a performance advantage when you reuse patterns. |

After setting the fill color space, the code fills a single rectangle with the pattern. To actually paint the object with the pattern, Quartz constructs the pattern cell by invoking the `drawPattern` callback for the pattern—`myDrawRedBlackCheckerBoardPattern`. It then uses the pattern cell to fill the rectangle with pattern tiles.

The code next calls `CGContextSaveGState` to save a snapshot of the graphics state. Then it sets the stroke color space to the pattern color space and the stroke color to the pattern. It calls the routine `myCGContextAddEllipseInRect` (from Listing 6.3 (page 118)) to add an elliptical path to the current path, and then strokes the path with the stroke color, which is the checkerboard pattern. Then the code restores the graphics state so that the stroke color is set to what it was prior to using the pattern.

Quartz can also paint text with a pattern. The code ensures that the text matrix is set properly, then sets the font face and size and the fill text drawing mode. It draws the word "Text" in the Times-Roman font. Because the text is painted with the text drawing mode `kCGTextFill`, Quartz uses the current fill color and fills the character outlines with the checkerboard pattern.

The last piece of drawing performed by the code fills two overlapping rectangles, the second of which is stroked with a dashed line so that you can see its boundary. After the code is done using the pattern and the pattern color space, it releases them.

Take a look again at Figure 15.2 (page 486). All the graphical elements in the figure are drawn with the same pattern. In some places these elements overlap; where they overlap, the pattern tiles match exactly. This is a feature of drawing with patterns. A given pattern is locked to pattern base space so that patterns seamlessly match, regardless of the graphics you draw. "Base Space, the Pattern Matrix, and Transforming Patterns" (page 493) and "Pattern Phase" (page 497) discuss ways you can adjust patterns to achieve different behavior.

The pattern in this example is such that the pattern cell is completely covered with paint and the values it uses for the `xStep` and `yStep` cause the tiled area to be completely covered. A pattern cell can contain unpainted areas. Any unpainted areas in the pattern cell are reflected in the tiling Quartz performs, leaving content underneath visible in those areas of the tiling that are unpainted or only partially covered with paint.

Base Space, the Pattern Matrix, and Transforming Patterns

Quartz uses the pattern matrix that you pass to CGPatternCreate to transform from pattern space to base space. Pattern space is the coordinate system in effect at the time that you draw the pattern with your drawPattern callback. Base space is the coordinate system that Quartz uses for tiling the pattern cell to fill or stroke the shape that you paint. In most circumstances, base space is the default Quartz coordinate system—the initial coordinate system in effect when the context is created.

Base space is unchanged by coordinate transformations, which means that a given pattern is unaffected by changes to the CTM. The scaling, rotation, and translations you perform when you create the shapes you want to paint with patterns do not affect the patterns themselves. Using a pattern when filling a rectangle that is 100 units on a side produces the same filled pattern as scaling by a factor of 2 and then filling a rectangle that is 50 units on a side. The result is a 100x100 unit rectangle that has the pattern tiled the same way, independent of user space scaling. In other words, a given pattern is locked to the base space coordinate system.

The pattern matrix that you pass to CGPatternCreate allows you to specify, and therefore modify, the transformation from pattern space to base space. The checkerboard example in Listing 15.1 (page 486) uses a pattern matrix that applies a uniform scaling factor of 20 to map from pattern space to base space. If you want a different mapping from pattern space to base space, such as a rotation or a different scaling, you can achieve this by changing the pattern matrix.

You can use the pattern matrix to apply transformations to the patterns you create in interesting ways, as shown in Figure 15.4. The red and black checkerboard pattern on the left is also shown rotated and scaled. Listing 15.2, which produced the graphics shown in the figure, uses the createRedBlackCheckerBoard-Pattern routine from Listing 15.1; however, instead of always using a pattern matrix that applies a uniform scaling factor of 20, the code also creates patterns that use other pattern transformations.

The doPatternMatrix routine in the listing fills four rectangles with a pattern. Rectangle 1 is drawn with the same pattern as that created in Listing 15.1. For the basePatternMatrix, it uses an affine transform that specifies a uniform scaling factor of 20.

Before drawing Rectangle 2, the code first changes the current pattern fill color so that it uses the same pattern but with the alpha value set at 65 percent opaque. It then rotates user space by 45 degrees about the center point of the rectangle that it then fills. Note in the figure that even though the rectangle shape is rotated, the pattern is not. The pattern is locked to the same coordinate system as the pattern used to fill Rectangle 1. After the code finishes drawing the first two rectangles, it releases the CGPattern object since it is no longer needed.

Listing 15.2 A routine that rotates and scales patterns using the pattern matrix

```
void doPatternMatrix(CGContextRef context)
{
  CGColorSpaceRef patternColorSpace;
  float color[1];
  CGAffineTransform patTransform;
  CGAffineTransform t, basePatternMatrix =
              CGAffineTransformMakeScale(20, 20);
  CGPatternRef pattern =
              createRedBlackCheckerBoardPattern(basePatternMatrix);
  if(pattern == NULL){
    fprintf(stderr, "Couldn't create pattern!\n");
    return;
  }
  // For colored patterns the 'baseColorSpace' parameter passed
  // to CGColorSpaceCreatePattern must be NULL.
  patternColorSpace = CGColorSpaceCreatePattern(NULL);
```

```
CGContextSetFillColorSpace(context, patternColorSpace);
// Finished with the color space so release it.
CGColorSpaceRelease(patternColorSpace);

// Paint the pattern first with alpha = 1.
color[0] = 1.;
CGContextSetFillPattern(context, pattern, color);

// ***** Rectangle 1 *****
CGContextFillRect(context, CGRectMake(0, 0, 100, 100));

CGContextSaveGState(context);
    // ***** Rectangle 2 *****
    // Paint the pattern with 65% alpha.
    color[0] = 0.65;
    CGContextSetFillPattern(context, pattern, color);
    // Rotate 45 degrees about the point (150,50).
    CGContextTranslateCTM(context, 150, 50);
    CGContextRotateCTM(context, DEGREES_TO_RADIANS(45));
    CGContextTranslateCTM(context, -50, -50);
    // You can see that the pattern tile of this
    // filled rectangle is that of Rectangle 1.
    CGContextFillRect(context, CGRectMake(0, 0, 100, 100));
    // Release the pattern.
    CGPatternRelease(pattern);
CGContextRestoreGState(context);

CGContextSaveGState(context);
    // ***** Rectangle 3 *****
    // The pattern is translated and rotated with the object.
    // Rotate 45 degrees about the point (250,50).
    t = CGAffineTransformMakeTranslation(250, 50);
    t = CGAffineTransformRotate(t, DEGREES_TO_RADIANS(45));
    // Translate back to (-50,-50).
    t = CGAffineTransformTranslate(t, -50, -50);
    CGContextConcatCTM(context, t);
    // Make a new pattern that is equivalent to the old pattern
    // but transformed to current user space.
    patTransform = CGAffineTransformConcat(basePatternMatrix, t);
    pattern = createRedBlackCheckerBoardPattern(patTransform);
    color[0] = 1;
    CGContextSetFillPattern(context, pattern, color);
    // Release the pattern.
    CGPatternRelease(pattern);
```

```
        CGContextFillRect(context, CGRectMake(0, 0, 100, 100));
    CGContextRestoreGState(context);

    CGContextSaveGState(context);
      // ***** Rectangle 4 *****
      // The pattern is translated and scaled with the object.
      // Translate and scale.
      t = CGAffineTransformMakeTranslation(320, 0);
      t = CGAffineTransformScale(t, 2, 2);
      CGContextConcatCTM(context, t);
      // Make a new pattern that is equivalent to the old pattern
      // but transformed to current user space.
      patTransform = CGAffineTransformConcat(basePatternMatrix, t);
      pattern = createRedBlackCheckerBoardPattern(patTransform);
      color[0] = 1;
      CGContextSetFillPattern(context, pattern, color);
      // Release the pattern.
      CGPatternRelease(pattern);
      CGContextFillRect(context, CGRectMake(0, 0, 100, 100));
    CGContextRestoreGState(context);
}
```

Rectangle 3 is painted so that the pattern is rotated along with the shape. To achieve this sort of effect, you need to create a new CGPattern object that has a pattern matrix equivalent to the original pattern but transformed by the same transformation as that applied to the shape. The code creates an affine transform t to transform the coordinate system into which it draws the shape. It applies this transformation to the current CTM by calling the Quartz function CGContextConcatCTM. The code computes the pattern matrix patTransform by concatenating that same transformation t to the pattern matrix basePatternMatrix used to create the previous pattern. The concatenation is equivalent to applying the transformation t to the pattern used earlier; it is also equivalent to applying a transformation t to base space prior to drawing a pattern that uses basePatternMatrix as its pattern matrix.

The order of matrix multiplication is crucial. When transforming patterns, the additional transform you want to apply must be on the right side of the matrix multiplication, as it is in this example. "Transforming from Object Space to Quartz User Space" (page 417) discusses how to transform from object space (such as pattern space) to another coordinate system such as user space or base space.

Rectangle 4 is filled with a pattern that is scaled in the same manner as the rectangle is scaled. You achieve this effect by using the same technique used to draw Rectangle 3. First, you need to compute the transform to apply to the shape, then compute a new pattern matrix patTransform that is the equivalent of the original pattern matrix basePatternMatrix, transformed by the translation and scaling applied to the rectangular shape you want to fill. The resulting drawing is as if you'd zoomed in on Rectangle 1.

Base space is typically the default coordinate system for the context. However, when you draw a PDF document using any Quartz PDF drawing routine, Quartz temporarily adjusts base space to be the coordinate system in effect at the time the PDF is drawn. When drawing PDF documents, this produces the behavior you would expect; that is, translating, scaling, and rotating prior to drawing a PDF document causes a pattern painting any shape contained within the PDF to translate, scale, and rotate along with the shape itself.

Pattern Phase

Although patterns are locked to Quartz base space, typically the default Quartz coordinate system, you can adjust the location of the base space origin used when painting patterns by adjusting the pattern phase. The **pattern phase** is a distance that describes the offset of the pattern origin from the origin of Quartz base space. The initial value of the pattern phase in the graphics state is CGSizeZero; that is, the distance from the Quartz base space origin to the pattern origin is 0 in both x and y.

A typical reason for adjusting the phase is to accommodate scrolling content in a window. If you don't modify the pattern phase, the way a pattern intersects the shape of an object changes when the position of the object changes. You might also want to adjust the origin of a pattern so that it coincides with the origin of a graphic, without changing the pattern itself, as shown in Figure 15.5. Rectangle 1 and Rectangle 2 are each filled with the same pattern but without modifying the pattern phase in any way. Because there has been no special care taken to align the starting point of the pattern with the shapes painted with it, the shapes intersect the pattern tile at arbitrary locations. Compare this with the drawing of Rectangle 3 and Rectangle 4. In each case, the pattern phase is adjusted so that the origin of the pattern coincides with the origin of the rectangle. This produces a pattern that tiles the object as if it were aligned with the object.

The function CGContextSetPatternPhase changes the pattern phase in the context graphics state. The function takes two parameters: the context whose pattern phase you want to modify and a CGSize structure whose values are the new pattern phase. Setting the pattern phase is not cumulative—the new value of the pattern phase is the CGSize you pass to CGContextSetPatternPhase. Because the pattern phase is part of the graphics state, the functions CGContextSaveGState and CGContextRestoreGState save and restore the pattern phase parameter, along with all the other parameters in the graphics state.

Figure 15.5 Changing the pattern phase

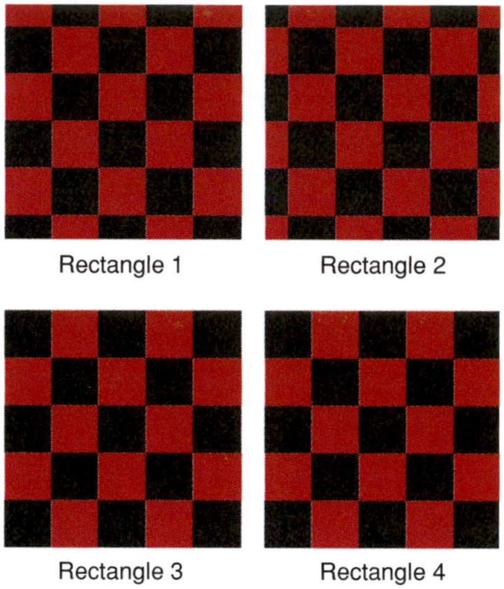

Rectangle 1   Rectangle 2

Rectangle 3   Rectangle 4

The drawing in Figure 15.5 is the graphics created by Listing 15.3. The doPatternPhase routine in the listing creates and uses the same pattern as the previous examples. It draws Rectangle 1 and Rectangle 2 without regard for the pattern phase. Prior to drawing Rectangle 3, the code adjusts the pattern phase so that it coincides with the origin of the rectangle. This produces a pattern origin that begins at the lower-left corner of the rectangle. As part of its setup for drawing Rectangle 4, the code translates the Quartz origin and sets the pattern phase so that the new pattern phase origin is the same as the Quartz origin. When it then draws Rectangle 4 at the origin, the pattern cell begins at the origin of the rectangle. Because the code takes care to set the pattern phase to coincide with the origin of Rectangles 3 and 4, they each are tiled in an identical manner. This kind of adjustment is similar to the kind of adjustment you might apply when translating your graphics to accommodate scrolling.

Listing 15.3 Code that uses the Quartz pattern phase to adjust the pattern origin

```
void doPatternPhase(CGContextRef context)
{
  CGColorSpaceRef patternColorSpace;
  float color[1];
  CGPatternRef pattern = createRedBlackCheckerBoardPattern(
              CGAffineTransformMakeScale(20, 20)
              );
  if(pattern == NULL){
    fprintf(stderr, "Couldn't create pattern!\n");
```

```
    return;
}

// Create the pattern color space for a colored pattern.
patternColorSpace = CGColorSpaceCreatePattern(NULL);
CGContextSetFillColorSpace(context, patternColorSpace);

// Paint the pattern with alpha = 1.
color[0] = 1.;
CGContextSetFillPattern(context, pattern, color);

// ***** Rectangle 1 *****
CGContextFillRect(context, CGRectMake(20, 150, 100, 100));

// ***** Rectangle 2 *****
CGContextFillRect(context, CGRectMake(130, 150, 100, 100));

// ***** Rectangle 3 *****
CGContextSetPatternPhase(context, CGSizeMake(20, 20));
CGContextFillRect(context, CGRectMake(20, 20, 100, 100));

// ***** Rectangle 4 *****
// Set the pattern phase so that the pattern origin
// is at the lower-left corner of the shape.
CGContextTranslateCTM(context, 130, 20);
CGContextSetPatternPhase(context, CGSizeMake(130, 20));
CGContextFillRect(context, CGRectMake(0, 0, 100, 100));

// Set the pattern phase back to (0,0).
CGContextSetPatternPhase(context, CGSizeZero);

CGPatternRelease(pattern);
CGColorSpaceRelease(patternColorSpace);

}
```

Creating and Drawing Stencil Patterns

In addition to patterns that have intrinsic color, Quartz supports patterns that have no intrinsic color. These patterns are called **stencil patterns**. A stencil pattern cell describes where to apply paint, similarly to an image mask. The color used for painting a stencil pattern is specified as part of setting the pattern color space and pattern color. A stencil pattern cell is shown in Figure 15.6. The black portion of the figure indicates the coverage of paint the pattern cell defines; the colored dashed line at the border indicates the bounding box used for this pattern cell.

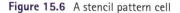
Figure 15.6 A stencil pattern cell

Figure 15.7 Rectangles filled with a stencil pattern

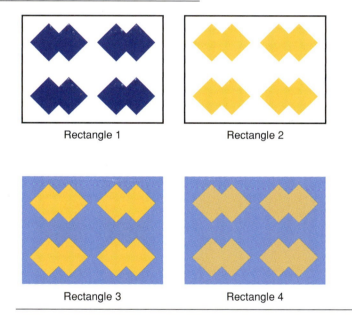

When the pattern cell of a stencil pattern is tiled, Quartz uses the painting color to paint the areas of the stencil where the coverage is nonzero. When painted, the stencil pattern shown in Figure 15.6 can take on any color, including the yellow and blue colors shown in Figure 15.7. You'll take a look at the code that produced this figure next.

The code in Listing 15.4 consists of the primary routine `doStencilPattern` and the supporting routines `createStencilPattern`, `myStencilPatternProc`, and `drawRotatedRect`. This code is structured in the same manner as Listing 15.1 (page 486): `createStencilPattern` creates a stencil pattern that uses `myStencilPatternProc` to draw a pattern cell.

Creating a stencil pattern is similar to creating a colored pattern but with two important differences. First, the isColored parameter passed to CGPatternCreate must be false for a stencil pattern. Second, since stencil patterns are masks, a painting color is not set as part of drawing the pattern cell. It makes no sense to do so.

The routine myStencilPatternProc calls drawRotatedRect twice to draw two rotated rectangles that make up the pattern cell drawing. The code does not set the painting color, it simply paints with whatever painting color is in effect. The drawPattern callback of a stencil pattern inherits the color that is in effect when it is called.

Caution   The drawPattern callback of a stencil pattern must not set the fill or stroke color or draw content with intrinsic color such as images with intrinsic color or PDF documents. Doing so produces undefined results.

Listing 15.4 Code that draws stencil patterns

```
static void drawRotatedRect(CGContextRef c, CGPoint p)
{
  CGRect r = CGRectMake(0, 0, 1, 1);
  CGContextSaveGState(c);
    CGContextTranslateCTM(c, p.x, p.y);
    CGContextRotateCTM(c, DEGREES_TO_RADIANS(45));
    CGContextTranslateCTM(c, -r.size.width/2, -r.size.height/2);
    CGContextFillRect(c, r);
  CGContextRestoreGState(c);
}

static void myStencilPatternProc(void *info,
              CGContextRef patternCellContext)
{
  drawRotatedRect(patternCellContext, CGPointMake(1, 1));
  drawRotatedRect(patternCellContext, CGPointMake(1.75, 1));
}

static CGPatternRef createStencilPattern(
              CGAffineTransform patternTransform)
{
  CGPatternCallbacks myPatternCallbacks;
  CGPatternRef pattern;
  bool patternIsColored.
  // Only version 0 of the pattern callbacks is defined as of Tiger.
  myPatternCallbacks.version = 0;
```

```
        // The pattern's drawPattern proc is the routine Quartz calls
        // to draw a pattern cell when it needs to draw one.
        myPatternCallbacks.drawPattern = myStencilPatternProc;
        // This code has no data to release, so the releaseInfo
        // proc is NULL.
        myPatternCallbacks.releaseInfo = NULL;

        // A stencil pattern.
        patternIsColored = false;
        pattern = CGPatternCreate(NULL,
          // The pattern cell origin is at (0,0) with a
          // width of 2.5 units and a height of 2 units.
          CGRectMake(0, 0, 2.5, 2),
          // Use the pattern transform supplied to this routine.
          patternTransform,
          // Use the width and height of the pattern cell as the
          // xStep and yStep.
          2.5, 2,
          // This value is a good choice for this type of pattern and it
          // avoids seams between tiles.
          kCGPatternTilingConstantSpacingMinimalDistortion,
          // This pattern does not have intrinsic color.
          patternIsColored, // Must be false for a stencil pattern.
          &myPatternCallbacks);
        return pattern;
}

void doStencilPattern(CGContextRef context)
{
    CGColorSpaceRef patternColorSpace, baseColorSpace;
    float color[4];
    CGPatternRef pattern = createStencilPattern(
                    CGAffineTransformMakeScale(20, 20));
    if(pattern == NULL){
      fprintf(stderr, "Couldn't create pattern!\n");
      return;
    }
    // Create the pattern color space using the generic calibrated
    // RGB color space as the color space for painting the pattern.
    baseColorSpace = getTheCalibratedRGBColorSpace();
    patternColorSpace = CGColorSpaceCreatePattern(baseColorSpace);

    CGContextSetFillColorSpace(context, patternColorSpace);
    // This code is finished with the pattern color space and can release
    // it because Quartz retains it while it is the current color space.
    CGColorSpaceRelease(patternColorSpace);
```

```
// First paint the pattern with opaque blue.
color[0] = 0.11; color[1] = 0.208 ; color[2] = 0.451 ; color[3] = 1.;
CGContextSetFillPattern(context, pattern, color);

// ***** Rectangle 1 *****
CGContextSetPatternPhase(context, CGSizeMake(20, 160));
CGContextBeginPath(context);
CGContextAddRect(context, CGRectMake(20, 160, 105, 80));
CGContextDrawPath(context, kCGPathFillStroke);

// ***** Rectangle 2 *****
// Set the pattern color so that the stencil pattern
// is painted in yellow.
color[0] = 1.; color[1] = 0.816 ; color[2] = 0. ; color[3] = 1.;
CGContextSetFillPattern(context, pattern, color);
// Set the pattern phase to the origin of the next object.
CGContextSetPatternPhase(context, CGSizeMake(140, 160));
CGContextBeginPath(context);
CGContextAddRect(context, CGRectMake(140, 160, 105, 80));
CGContextDrawPath(context, kCGPathFillStroke);

CGContextSaveGState(context);
  CGContextSetFillColorWithColor(context, getRGBOpaqueBlueColor());
  // Fill color is now blue. Paint two blue rectangles
  // that will be underneath the drawing that follows.
  CGContextFillRect(context, CGRectMake(20, 40, 105, 80));
  CGContextFillRect(context, CGRectMake(140, 40, 105, 80));
CGContextRestoreGState(context);

// The fill color is again the stencil pattern with
// the underlying opaque yellow fill color.

// ***** Rectangle 3 *****
// This paints over the blue rectangle just painted at (20,40)
// and the blue underneath is visible where the pattern has
// transparent areas.
CGContextSetPatternPhase(context, CGSizeMake(20, 40));
CGContextFillRect(context, CGRectMake(20, 40, 105, 80));

// ***** Rectangle 4 *****
// Change the alpha value of the underlying color used
// to paint the stencil pattern.
color[3] = 0.75;
```

```
    CGContextSetPatternPhase(context, CGSizeMake(140, 40));
    CGContextSetFillPattern(context, pattern, color);
    CGContextFillRect(context, CGRectMake(140, 40, 105, 80));

    CGPatternRelease(pattern);
}
```

Setting a stencil pattern as the current fill or stroke color has two crucial differences compared to using a colored pattern. When you paint with a stencil pattern, there is an underlying color that is used to paint the mask that corresponds to the pattern cell. Part of setting a stencil pattern as a painting color is to specify this underlying color, the color that is poured through the mask.

The first step in using a stencil pattern is to set an appropriate pattern color space. Recall that you create a pattern color space by calling the function CGColorSpaceCreatePattern with a single parameter, baseColorSpace. When drawing with stencil patterns, baseColorSpace is the color space of the color you want to use to paint the pattern cell. Stencil patterns have no intrinsic color; you must specify the color to paint them with when you use them.

Important The baseColorSpace parameter passed to CGColorSpaceCreatePattern must not be NULL if the pattern you want to draw with is a stencil pattern. "Checking Pattern Color Space Usage" (page 622) discusses the problems you may encounter if you do not properly create a pattern color space for use with a stencil pattern.

The doStencilPattern routine uses a stencil pattern to draw several shapes. It uses the generic calibrated RGB color space as the underlying color space to paint the stencil pattern; this is the baseColorSpace parameter passed to CGColorSpaceCreatePattern. It then sets the fill color space to this pattern color space.

The second step in using a stencil pattern is to set the pattern as the painting color. When painting with a stencil pattern, you specify the pattern to use as the stencil pattern, together with the color component values you want to use as the painting color with which to color the pattern. The color component values are characterized by baseColorSpace, the underlying color space of the pattern color space. Failure to set the pattern color after you set the pattern color space produces a pattern cell that draws nothing.

The code in the listing first uses CGContextSetFillPattern to set the fill painting color to the stencil pattern, colored with the color components in the color array it supplies. The number of components in color must be the number of components in baseColorSpace, plus 1 for alpha. Before painting Rectangle 1, the color array corresponds to an opaque blue in an RGB color space.

To draw Rectangle 1 in Figure 15.7 (page 500), the code sets the pattern phase to the origin of the rectangle. This ensures that the pattern cell tiling begins at the lower-left corner of the rectangle, rather than at the origin of Quartz base space. The code then fills and strokes the rectangle. The fill color is the stencil pattern painted with opaque blue; the stroke color is the default stroke color, black.

Next the code changes the fill color to the same stencil pattern but with an underlying color that is opaque yellow. It paints Rectangle 2, to the right of Rectangle 1. The fill pattern is painted yellow, and the rectangle is stroked with black.

As mentioned previously, a pattern cell for a colored or stencil pattern can have areas within it that have no paint. Those portions are transparent when the pattern cell is tiled; content underneath shows through. The code takes advantage of this by first painting two opaque blue rectangles prior to again painting with the yellow colored pattern. When drawing Rectangle 3 over the blue rectangle it already painted, the blue shows through those portions of the pattern where there is no coverage, that is, the portion not colored yellow by the stencil pattern tile. Prior to drawing Rectangle 4, the code changes the pattern drawing color so that the stencil pattern is painted with a yellow that is 75 percent opaque. This allows a portion of the blue rectangle already painted to show through, even in areas where the pattern has coverage.

Drawing Complex Patterns

The pattern examples up to this point use relatively simple patterns. However, patterns can be arbitrarily complex and can include any drawing that you can perform with Quartz, including line art, text, images, and PDF document drawing. Figure 15.8 shows a pattern that uses a PDF document. The pattern is tiled across a page as a result of executing the code in Listing 15.5.

Listing 15.5 reproduces the same drawing done in "Caching Drawing Offscreen" (page 379); however, instead of manually tiling a PDF document across the page, it uses a Quartz pattern as the fill color. The code consists of the main routine `drawWithPDFPattern` and the supporting routines `createPDFPatternPattern`, `myDrawPDFPattern`, and `myPDFPatternRelease`. It also defines the `MyPDFPatternInfo` structure needed to pass data to the `myDrawPDFPattern` routine that draws the pattern cell.

These routines parallel those from the earlier examples in this chapter, except that the earlier examples of pattern drawing are self-contained patterns. Those patterns have no resources or other external data associated with them and therefore use `NULL` values for the `info` parameter and `releaseInfo` callback when calling the Quartz function `CGPatternCreate`. Listing 15.5 uses a PDF document and other data to perform its drawing, so you'll see how to use the

Figure 15.8 A PDF page can be used as a pattern

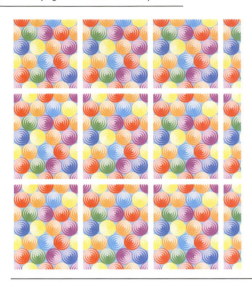

info parameter as well as how to release resources (like the PDF document) appropriately.

The routine `myDrawPDFPattern` is simple; it draws the CGPDFDocument object from the `MyPDFPatternInfo` data passed to the callback into the destination rectangle appropriate for this pattern.

To create this pattern, the code uses the routine `createPDFPatternPattern`, passing a pointer to a `CGAffineTransform` that describes any special transform to apply to the pattern cell when mapping the pattern cell to Quartz base space, together with a CFURL that represents the PDF document to use when drawing the pattern cell. This example uses a pointer to a `CGAffineTransform` that scales the pattern cell down by 1/3. (See the drawing done in "Caching Drawing Off-screen" (page 379).)

Listing 15.5 Code that uses a PDF page as a pattern

```
typedef struct MyPDFPatternInfo{
    CGRect              rect;
    CGPDFDocumentRef    pdfDoc;
}MyPDFPatternInfo;

static void myDrawPDFPattern(void *info, CGContextRef patternCellContext)
{
```

```
    // This pattern proc draws the first page of a PDF document to
    // a destination rectangle.
    MyPDFPatternInfo *patternInfoP = (MyPDFPatternInfo *)info;
    CGContextSaveGState(patternCellContext);
    CGContextClipToRect(patternCellContext, patternInfoP->rect);
    CGContextDrawPDFDocument(patternCellContext, patternInfoP->rect,
                patternInfoP->pdfDoc, 1);
    CGContextRestoreGState(patternCellContext);
}

static void myPDFPatternRelease(void *info)
{
  if(info){
    MyPDFPatternInfo *patternInfoP = (MyPDFPatternInfo *)info;
    CGPDFDocumentRelease(patternInfoP->pdfDoc);
    free(info);
  }
}

static CGPatternRef createPDFPatternPattern(CGAffineTransform
                *additionalTransformP,
                CFURLRef url)
{
  CGPatternCallbacks myPatternCallbacks;
  MyPDFPatternInfo *patternInfoP;
  CGPatternRef pattern;
  CGAffineTransform patternTransform;
  float tileOffsetX, tileOffsetY;

  // Only version 0 of the pattern callbacks is defined as of Tiger.
  myPatternCallbacks.version = 0;
  // The pattern's drawPattern proc is the routine Quartz calls to draw
  // a pattern cell when it needs to draw one.
  myPatternCallbacks.drawPattern = myDrawPDFPattern;
  // Since the pattern has the PDF document as a resource, it should
  // be released when Quartz no longer needs the pattern.
  myPatternCallbacks.releaseInfo = myPDFPatternRelease;

  patternInfoP = (MyPDFPatternInfo *)malloc(sizeof(MyPDFPatternInfo));
  if(patternInfoP == NULL){
    fprintf(stderr, "Couldn't allocate pattern info data!\n");
    return NULL;
  }
```

```
patternInfoP->pdfDoc = CGPDFDocumentCreateWithURL(url);
if(patternInfoP->pdfDoc == NULL){
  fprintf(stderr, "Couldn't create PDF document reference!\n");
  free(patternInfoP);
  return;
}

patternInfoP->rect = CGPDFDocumentGetMediaBox(
            patternInfoP->pdfDoc, 1);
// Set the origin of the media rectangle for the PDF
// document to (0,0).
patternInfoP->rect.origin = CGPointZero;

if(additionalTransformP)
  patternTransform = *additionalTransformP;
else
  patternTransform = CGAffineTransformIdentity;

// To emulate the example from the bitmap context drawing chapter,
// the tile offset in each dimension is the tile size in that
// dimension, plus 6 units.
tileOffsetX = 6. + patternInfoP->rect.size.width;
tileOffsetY = 6. + patternInfoP->rect.size.height;

pattern = CGPatternCreate(patternInfoP,
  // The pattern cell size is the size
  // of the media rectangle of the PDF document.
  patternInfoP->rect,
  patternTransform,
  tileOffsetX, tileOffsetY,
  // This value is a good choice for this type of pattern and
  // it avoids seams between tiles.
  kCGPatternTilingConstantSpacingMinimalDistortion,
  // This pattern has intrinsic color.
  true,
  &myPatternCallbacks);
// If the pattern can't be created, then release the
// pattern resources and info parameter.
if(pattern == NULL){
  myPatternCallbacks.releaseInfo(patternInfoP);
  patternInfoP = NULL;
}
  return pattern;
}
```

```
void drawWithPDFPattern(CGContextRef context, CFURLRef url)
{
  CGColorSpaceRef patternColorSpace;
  float color[1];
  // Scale the PDF pattern down to 1/3 its original size.
  CGAffineTransform patternMatrix =
                CGAffineTransformMakeScale(1./3, 1./3);
  CGPatternRef pdfPattern = createPDFPatternPattern(
                &patternMatrix, url);
  if(pdfPattern == NULL){
    fprintf(stderr, "Couldn't create pattern!\n");
    return;
  }
  // Since the pattern itself has intrinsic color, the 'baseColorSpace'
  // parameter passed to CGColorSpaceCreatePattern must be NULL.
  patternColorSpace = CGColorSpaceCreatePattern(NULL);
  CGContextSetFillColorSpace(context, patternColorSpace);
  // Quartz retains the color space so this code
  // can now release it since it no longer needs it.
  CGColorSpaceRelease(patternColorSpace);

  // Paint the pattern with an alpha of 1.
  color[0] = 1;
  CGContextSetFillPattern(context, pdfPattern, color);
  // Quartz retains the pattern so this code
  // can now release it since it no longer needs it.
  CGPatternRelease(pdfPattern);

  // Fill a US-letter-size rectangle with the pattern.
  CGContextFillRect(context, CGRectMake(0, 0, 612, 792));

}
```

The routine createPDFPatternPattern fills in the CGPatternCallbacks with its drawPattern callback myDrawPDFPattern and its releaseInfo callback myPDF-PatternRelease. Recall that the releaseInfo callback is invoked when Quartz releases the pattern; this is when any resources associated with the pattern need to be released. For this pattern, the routine myPDFPatternRelease releases the CGPDFDocument object associated with the pattern and frees the MyPDFPatternInfo pointer that the code uses as the info parameter to CGPatternCreate.

To set up the data it needs to draw the pattern, createPDFPatternPattern creates the CGPDFDocument object that corresponds to the URL of the PDF document. It uses the media box of the PDF document as the bounding box of the pattern. The code computes the offset from one pattern cell to the next by adding 6 units to the PDF document width and height. This adds space between the pattern tiles that Quartz uses when tiling the pattern. The code passes true for the isColored parameter; PDF documents contain color so the pattern has intrinsic color.

The routine drawWithPDFPattern creates the pattern, creates a pattern color space for use with colored patterns (passing NULL for baseColorSpace), and sets the fill color space. It sets the pattern as the fill color with CGContextSetFillPattern. Recall that the color array passed to CGContextSetFillPattern for a colored pattern has a single component, the alpha value to use to composite the pattern to the destination. This code uses an alpha value that is 100 percent opaque. To draw the pattern, the code simply fills the shape it paints, a rectangle. Quartz tiles the destination with the pattern cell, tiling the filled shape with the first page of the PDF document.

PDF documents and images with intrinsic color cannot be directly used in stencil patterns, because a stencil pattern describes where to apply paint but not the color of the paint to apply. One way to use such data in a stencil pattern is to extract the luminance of a PDF document or image with intrinsic color by first rendering it to a bitmap context that is characterized by a Gray color space. You can then use the resulting bitmap data as the mask data for an image mask that you draw in the pattern drawing callback of a stencil pattern. Of course, this produces device-dependent results because you choose the resolution of the PDF rendering when you draw it to a bitmap context to create the mask data.

Pattern Issues

Mapping a pattern tile into the device space coordinate system and tiling that pattern may require that Quartz perform adjustments to the pattern tile or spacing of the pattern tiles. You specify which method Quartz uses to make these adjustments by supplying a value from the enumeration CGPatternTiling when you create a pattern with CGPatternCreate.

The tiling type kCGPatternTilingNoDistortion specifies that Quartz should not distort the pattern cell or adjust the xStep or yStep values when tiling the pattern. Use of this type of tiling may produce gaps between pattern cells or cause seams at cell boundaries due to anti-aliasing artifacts, because more than one pattern cell may touch an individual device pixel.

The tiling type kCGPatternTilingConstantSpacingMinimalDistortion specifies that Quartz round the pattern step size to the nearest device pixel. To maintain this spacing, Quartz may distort the pattern tile by slightly adjusting the pattern cell size in device space. This distortion is never larger than a device pixel. On average the xStep and yStep values are achieved, but not necessarily for individual pattern cells.

The tiling type kCGPatternTilingConstantSpacing produces results that are similar to kCGPatternTilingConstantSpacingMinimalDistortion but allows Quartz to perform additional distortion to the pattern cell, allowing for better performance with a more distorted pattern cell. Using this tiling type can produce significantly better performance, particularly when the xStep and yStep values match the width and height of the bounds of the pattern. For patterns where the xStep and yStep values are larger than the width and height of the bounds of your pattern, you can achieve improved performance when drawing to a bit-based context by using a bounds rectangle whose width and height are equal to xStep and yStep.

In some cases Quartz caches a pattern cell, which increases drawing efficiency for a given pattern. When drawing patterns to a PDF context, each CGPattern object used in the content appears as a PDF document resource. If you use a given pattern more than once, you should reuse the CGPattern object for that pattern rather than create duplicate pattern objects that represent the same pattern. Reusing CGPattern objects has potential performance benefits for drawing onscreen and produces smaller PDF files. A given pattern resource only appears in the PDF file once, regardless of the number of objects or pages that use that pattern.

Patterns that use resources such as images and PDF documents need to take care to handle those resources appropriately. Quartz calls pattern drawing functions at unpredictable times; any data you need for drawing your pattern needs to be available whenever your drawing callback is invoked. In addition, a CGPattern object is immutable; it must draw the same pattern cell each time it is called. Any resources needed to perform the drawing of a pattern must also be immutable. For example, an image you use to draw your pattern cell must be immutable, and the image must be retained by the pattern and not released until the pattern is released. The image data associated with any image used to draw a pattern cell must be available until the data provider associated with the image is released. See "Guidelines for Using Data Providers" (page 198) and "Best Practices for Working with Images" (page 241) for more details. Many of the guidelines in those sections apply to patterns as well. Failure to follow these guidelines can produce unpredictable results and in some cases cause your program to crash.

Patterns that require large amounts of data, such as images, have a large memory footprint, particularly when printing to PostScript printers. Because printing to PostScript printers requires the resources associated with a pattern to be resident in PostScript memory, memory-intensive patterns may cause printer-out-of-memory errors. For these reasons you might consider handling memory-intensive patterns by manually tiling the pattern tile yourself. This produces larger PDF documents but avoids the memory usage that large patterns require.

As stated many times previously, stencil patterns must not set color or draw objects with intrinsic color in their drawPattern callback. Unfortunately, Quartz doesn't provide any warning or console message if you do this. This caution is repeated here because it has been a source of difficulty for developers. Failure to observe this requirement can produce a number of problems: Drawing with color in a stencil pattern drawPattern callback produces PostScript errors when printing to PostScript printers. Performing this incorrect drawing to a Quartz PDF context produces a malformed PDF document that causes Adobe Acrobat to generate warnings; Acrobat fails to draw a page that contains this incorrect drawing.

Prior to Jaguar, drawing to a PDF context and printing didn't respect the pattern phase. In these versions of Mac OS X, all pattern drawing is treated as if the pattern phase is CGSizeZero.

Drawing with Shadows (Panther)

10.3 ▶

You've probably already noticed the ability Quartz has for adding shadows to the drawing it performs. The use of shadows in the Aqua user interface in Mac OS X, although subtle, gives it a feeling of depth and creates part of Aqua's distinctive look. Starting in Panther, you can use Quartz to add shadows to virtually any drawing content.

Shadow Attributes

A Quartz shadow has three attributes that determine its appearance: offset, blur, and color. The offset is a distance, expressed as a CGSize, that specifies how far and in what direction the shadow is offset from the graphic. The shadow offset parameter is interpreted in Quartz base space and is unaffected by coordinate transformations.

The blur controls the diffuseness of the shadow. Values for blur must be greater than or equal to zero. A blur value of zero is a hard edge, that is, no diffuseness to the shadow. Increasing values soften the blur and make it more diffuse. As a general rule, blur values in the range of 1–3 produce a pleasing effect. You are encouraged to experiment and find values that achieve an effect you like.

The color attribute of a shadow, like any Quartz color, consists of a color space, a set of color component values in that color space, and an alpha value. The color of the shadow cast by an object need not be the same as the object itself. Note that pattern colors cannot be used as the shadow color.

The shadow parameter is part of the Quartz graphics state, just like the fill and stroke colors, the line width, the line dash, and so on. Quartz provides two functions to set the shadow, CGContextSetShadow and CGContextSetShadowWith-Color. The function CGContextSetShadowWithColor allows you to set the color of the shadow you want to use. The function CGContextSetShadow does not; it's equivalent to calling CGContextSetShadowWithColor with a shadow color that is black with an alpha value of 1/3. Because the shadow parameter is part of the graphics state, the functions CGContextSaveGState and CGContextRestoreGState save and restore the shadow parameter, along with all the other parameters in the graphics state.

The function CGContextSetShadowWithColor takes the following parameters:

- context, the CGContextRef in which you want to set the shadow.

- offset, a CGSize that specifies the location of the shadow relative to the object being painted.

- blur, a nonnegative floating-point value that specifies the diffuseness of the shadow.

- color, a CGColor object that specifies the color of the shadow. Passing NULL sets the shadow parameter in the graphics state to "no shadow," effectively turning off the shadow.

The function CGContextSetShadow takes three parameters, context, offset, and blur, each with the same meaning as for CGContextSetShadowWithColor.

Creating and Drawing with Shadows

It's straightforward to create and draw the gray and red shadows shown in Figure 15.9. You'll see how to draw these basic shapes and varieties of shadow effects by taking a look at Listing 15.6, which produced the figure. The listing contains two routines—createTrianglePath and doSimpleShadow. The createTriangle-Path routine is simply a path creation routine that doSimpleShadow calls to create the triangle shape. The routine doSimpleShadow is where all the shadow action happens.

Before painting Object 1 in the figure, the doSimpleShadow routine sets a shadow with an offset of (-7,-7) and a blur of zero. Filling a rectangle then produces a shadow, offset by -7 units in both x and y—the resulting shadow is down and to the left of the rectangle being shadowed. The shadow has a hard edge because the blur value is zero. The code uses CGContextSetShadow, which implicitly sets the shadow color to black with an alpha value of 1/3.

Figure 15.9 Shadow offset, color, and blur affect the drawing of shadows

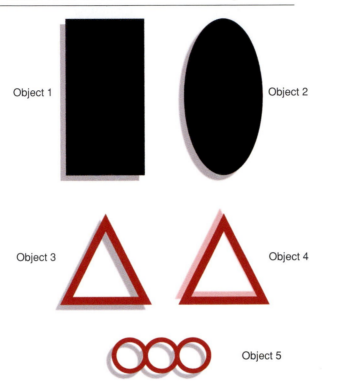

The code next prepares for drawing Object 2 in the figure. It uses the same offset value but changes the blur to 3, producing a soft, diffuse edge to the shadow. The doSimpleShadow calls the myCGContextAddEllipseInRect routine (from Listing 6.3 (page 118)) to create an elliptical path based on a supplied CGRect. Recall that this routine uses the Quartz function CGContextAddEllipseInRect on systems where it is available and emulates the function otherwise.

Before drawing Object 3, the code scales the coordinate system by a uniform scaling factor of 2. It creates a path that is an equilateral triangle, sets the stroke color to an opaque red, and strokes it. The result is a triangle with a red stroke, shadowed by the current shadow. Note that the shadow color is black, even though the stroke is red, because the current shadow in the graphics state is set to black.

Notice that the shadow for Object 3 is offset from the graphic by the same amount as Objects 1 and 2, even though the code scales the CTM prior to drawing the graphic. Quartz interprets the offset in base space, which is typically the default Quartz coordinate system. This means that the offset to the shadow doesn't change as an object is scaled or rotated. Typically, the drawing looks best if the shapes have a uniform shadow offset, regardless of how the shapes are created, scaled, rotated, or otherwise transformed. (See "Base Space, the Pattern Matrix, and Transforming Patterns" (page 493) for more about Quartz base space.)

Listing 15.6 Code that draws simple objects with shadows

```
void createTrianglePath(CGContextRef context)
{
  CGContextBeginPath(context);
  CGContextMoveToPoint(context, 0, 0);
  CGContextAddLineToPoint(context, 50, 0);
  CGContextAddLineToPoint(context, 25, 50);
  CGContextClosePath(context);
}

void drawSimpleShadow(CGContextRef context)
{
  CGSize offset;
  CGRect r = CGRectMake(20, 20, 100, 200);
  float blur;
  CGColorRef shadowColor;

  CGContextTranslateCTM(context, 20, 300);

  // A blur of 0 is a hard edge blur.
  blur = 0;
  // An offset where both components are negative casts
  // a shadow to the left and down from the object.
  offset.width = -7;
  offset.height = -7;
  // Set the shadow in the context.
  CGContextSetShadow(context, offset, blur);

  // ***** Object 1 *****
  // Paint a rectangle.
  CGContextFillRect(context, r);

  // ***** Object 2 *****
  CGContextTranslateCTM(context, 150, 0);
  // A blur of 3 is a soft blur more
  // appropriate for a shadow effect.
  blur = 3;
  CGContextSetShadow(context, offset, blur);
```

```
// Fill an ellipse.
CGContextBeginPath(context);
myCGContextAddEllipseInRect(context, r);
CGContextFillPath(context);

// ***** Object 3 *****
CGContextTranslateCTM(context, -130, -140);
// Scale the coordinate system but the
// shadow offset is not affected.
CGContextScaleCTM(context, 2, 2);
createTrianglePath(context);
CGContextSetStrokeColorWithColor(context,
            getRGBOpaqueRedColor());

CGContextSetLineWidth(context, 5);
// Stroking produces a shadow as well.
CGContextStrokePath(context);

// ***** Object 4 *****
CGContextTranslateCTM(context, 75, 0);
createTrianglePath(context);
// Cast the shadow to the left and up from
// the shape painted.
offset.width = -5;
offset.height = +7;

// The shadow can be colored. Create a CGColorRef
// that represents a red color with opacity of 0.3333....
shadowColor = CGColorCreateCopyWithAlpha(getRGBOpaqueRedColor(),
            1./3.);

CGContextSetShadowWithColor(context, offset, blur, shadowColor);
// Release the color now that the shadow color is set.
CGColorRelease(shadowColor);
CGContextStrokePath(context);

// ***** Object 5 *****
CGContextTranslateCTM(context, -75, -65);
// Set a black shadow offset at (-7,-7).
offset.width = -7;
offset.height = -7;
CGContextSetShadow(context, offset, blur);
// Draw a set of three circles side by side.
CGContextBeginPath(context);
```

```
    CGContextSetLineWidth(context, 3);
    r = CGRectMake(30, 20, 20, 20);
    myCGContextAddEllipseInRect(context, r);
    r = CGRectOffset(r, 20, 0);
    myCGContextAddEllipseInRect(context, r);
    r = CGRectOffset(r, 20, 0);
    myCGContextAddEllipseInRect(context, r);
    CGContextStrokePath(context);
}
```

The doSimpleShadow routine draws Object 4 with a different shadow offset and color by setting the shadow color with CGContextSetShadowWithColor. The code creates the CGColor object by first calling a routine getRGBOpaqueRedColor that returns an opaque red color in the generic calibrated RGB color space. This routine is constructed with *Get* semantics, meaning the caller does not own the reference returned. The code then uses the Quartz function CGColorCreateCopy-WithAlpha that creates a new CGColor object from the CGColor object that you pass to the function—in this case, the alpha value of the new CGColor object is 1/3.

After the code has the CGColor object that corresponds to the shadow color, it calls CGContextSetShadowWithColor with a new offset, a blur of 3, and the partially transparent red color. The offset value has a width of -5 and a height of +7. This produces a shadow that is left of the graphic but up the drawing canvas. After the code sets the shadow, it releases the CGColor object that it created since the object isn't needed any longer.

Before drawing Object 5, the code sets the shadow parameter to a partially transparent black shadow, offset in x and y by -7 units. It then draws the last object, the set of three circles side by side. Because the three circles are painted as a single stroked path, the shadow is painted as if it shadows the object as a whole.

There are two approaches to setting the shadow in the context to "no shadow." One is to call CGContextSetShadowWithColor, passing NULL for the CGColor object that specifies the shadow color. Another is to save the graphics state by calling CGContextSaveGState before you create and use a shadow and then, after using the shadow, to restore to that graphics state by calling CGContext-RestoreGState.

Shadow Offset and Quartz Base Space

As you've just seen, for a given shadow offset, the shadow location is locked to Quartz base space. Changes to the CTM don't change the offset to the shadow.

Typically, you don't want to adjust the shadow based on the coordinate system transformations you perform. However, there may be circumstances where you *do* want the shadow to be scaled or rotated along with your graphics. For example, you might want to scale the offset of a shadow when the user zooms in on a graphical element, similar to the way the shadow looks for Object 3 in Figure 15.10.

You can scale the shadow by applying the necessary coordinate transformation to the offset you want to transform. Quartz provides the function `CGSizeApply-AffineTransform`, which makes it straightforward to apply a coordinate transform represented by a `CGAffineTransform` to a `CGSize`. Listing 15.7 shows how to apply a transform to produce the output shown in Figure 15.10.

The `doShadowScaling` routine in Listing 15.7 draws the objects in the figure from left to right. It sets the shadow and draws Object 1 without any scaling. Next it creates an affine transform that corresponds to a uniform scaling factor of 2 and uses `CGContextConcatCTM` to concatenate that transform to the current CTM. This is equivalent to using `CGContextScaleCTM` with a uniform scaling factor of 2. It then uses the same code to draw Object 2 as it did for Object 1. This produces a scaled triangle, as expected. Quartz scales the shadow along with the object; however, the shadow offset is unaffected, because the offset value is in Quartz base space and base space is unaffected by coordinate transformations.

Next the code computes a new offset value from the offset it used when drawing Objects 1 and 2. The new offset value is the result of applying the same transform t that it used to scale the CTM prior to drawing Object 2. This effectively scales the offset by a scaling factor of 2, producing a shadow offset that is scaled in the same manner as the current Quartz coordinate system relative to Quartz base space. By using this offset value as the `offset` parameter that is passed to `CGContextSetShadow`, when Object 3 is drawn, the result is that the shadow offset

Figure 15.10 Scaling of shadows

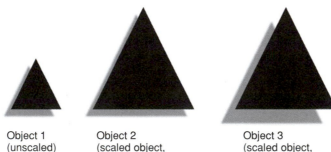

Object 1
(unscaled)

Object 2
(scaled object,
unscaled shadow
offset)

Object 3
(scaled object,
scaled shadow
offset)

is scaled in the same fashion as the graphic is scaled by the CTM. This produces an effect as if you were zooming in on the graphic.

This technique of using CGSizeApplyAffineTransform to transform the shadow offset works equally well for applying other transformations to the shadow when you draw transformed graphics. To have a shadow rotate along with an object you are rotating, transform the shadow offset with the same affine transform that you apply to the object you want to draw.

Listing 15.7 Code that scales the shadow offset

```
void doShadowScaling(CGContextRef context)
{
  CGSize offset = { -7, -7 };
  float blur = 3;
  CGAffineTransform t;

  CGContextTranslateCTM(context, 20, 220);

  CGContextSetShadow(context, offset, blur);

  // ***** Object 1 *****
  // Draw a triangle filled and shadowed with black.
  createTrianglePath(context);
  CGContextFillPath(context);

  // ***** Object 2 *****
  // Scaling without changing the shadow doesn't impact
  // the shadow offset or blur.
  t = CGAffineTransformMakeScale(2, 2);
  CGContextConcatCTM(context, t);
  CGContextTranslateCTM(context, 40, 0);
  createTrianglePath(context);
  CGContextFillPath(context);

  // ***** Object 3 *****
  // By transforming the offset, you can transform the shadow.
  // This may be desirable if you are drawing a zoomed view.
  offset = CGSizeApplyAffineTransform(offset, t);

  CGContextSetShadow(context, offset, blur);
  CGContextTranslateCTM(context, 70, 0);
  createTrianglePath(context);
  CGContextFillPath(context);
}
```

Shadows and Grouped Objects

When you set the shadow parameter in the graphics state, Quartz draws a shadow each time it paints an object. If you draw multiple objects, each object has its own shadow. Take a look at Figure 15.11, produced by the code in Listing 15.8. Each rectangle is painted with its own shadow. Each shape casts a shadow over the shapes underneath.

If you don't want each of the objects in the figure to cast a shadow, you need to take another approach. If instead you want to group drawing together so that it behaves as a single object that Quartz shadows, you need to use transparency layers. See "Drawing with Transparency Layers (Panther)" (page 522) for more on this topic.

Listing 15.8 Code that draws shadows without grouping

```
static void drawColoredLogo(CGContextRef context)
{
  CGRect r = CGRectMake(0, 0, 100, 100);
  CGContextSaveGState(context);
    // Position the center of the rectangle on the left.
    CGContextTranslateCTM(context, 140, 140);
    // Rotate so that the rectangles are rotated 45 degrees
    // about the current coordinate origin.
    CGContextRotateCTM(context, DEGREES_TO_RADIANS(45));
    // Translate so that the center of the rectangle is the previous origin.
    CGContextTranslateCTM(context, -r.size.width/2, -r.size.height/2);
    // Set the fill color to a purple color.
    CGContextSetFillColorWithColor(context,
            getRGBOpaquePurpleColor());
    // Fill the leftmost rectangle.
    CGContextFillRect(context, r);
    // Position to draw the rightmost rectangle.
    CGContextTranslateCTM(context, 60, -60);
    // Set the fill color to a yellow color.
    CGContextSetFillColorWithColor(context,
            getRGBOpaqueYellowColor());
    CGContextFillRect(context, r);

    // Position for the center rectangle.
    CGContextTranslateCTM(context, -30, +30);
    // Set the stroke color to an orange color.
    CGContextSetStrokeColorWithColor(context,
            getRGBOpaqueOrangeColor());
```

Figure 15.11 Shadows on objects without grouping

```
    // Stroke the rectangle with a line width of 12.
    CGContextStrokeRectWithWidth(context, r, 12);
  CGContextRestoreGState(context);
}

void showComplexShadowIssues(CGContextRef context)
{
  CGSize offset = { -6, -6 };
  float blur = 3;

  // Set the shadow.
  CGContextSetShadow(context, offset, blur);
  // Draw the colored logo.
  drawColoredLogo(context);
}
```

Shadows and PDF Documents

The PDF imaging model as defined by version 1.6 of the PDF specification doesn't have native support for shadows, and therefore the PDF specification doesn't have a direct way to specify them. Quartz works around this by creating two representations of the drawing of a shadowed object when it creates a PDF document. One representation is recognized by Quartz when it draws such a PDF document but is ignored by Adobe Acrobat and PDF processing tools that are not based on Quartz. The second representation is a rasterized representation of shadowed object drawing that is used by Adobe Acrobat and PDF processing tools that are not based on Quartz.

In versions of Mac OS X prior to version 10.4.4, Quartz shadows are recorded into a PDF document using an extension to the PDF specification that is recognized only by Quartz. On these systems, copying PDF data to a pasteboard and using that data with other Mac OS X applications that draw PDF data using Quartz will display and print the shadow. However, for the PDF documents produced by these earlier versions of Mac OS X, Adobe Acrobat does not display any Quartz shadows—graphical elements are drawn as if there were no shadow specified.

Drawing with Transparency Layers (Panther)

10.3 ▶ Quartz capabilities such as alpha compositing and shadows allow for interesting results without a lot of effort. So far you've seen these effects applied to the drawing of individual graphic objects. But what if you want to apply a shadow or perform alpha compositing to a group of objects as if it were a single graphic primitive? Quartz makes this possible through the use of **transparency layers**. Transparency layers group a set of drawing operations and then operate on that group as a whole. Sometimes transparency layers are referred to as **transparency groups**.

You can see one effect possible with transparency layers by comparing Figure 15.11 with Figure 15.12. Note that in Figure 15.11, each individual graphic primitive has its own shadow. But the graphic in Figure 15.12 is shadowed as a single object. The rectangles don't cast a shadow over those underneath, but instead the entire graphic has a single shadow. The shadow cast is a complex shape and is only drawn at the border of the graphic as a whole.

Figure 15.12 Shadows on objects as if they are a group

Using Transparency Layers

You use the functions CGContextBeginTransparencyLayer and CGContextEnd-TransparencyLayer to delineate a transparency layer. You first call CGContext-BeginTransparencyLayer to indicate the start of the transparency layer—this records the current value of the clipping area, the global alpha, the current shadow, and the blend mode present in the graphics state and resets them to their default values. (By resetting these parameters to their default values, Quartz helps prevent you from unintentionally drawing a shadow, applying a special blend mode or global alpha to the graphics you are recording for compositing as a group.) You then perform the drawing you want to treat as a single object. Drawing to the context is deferred until you call the function CGContextEndTransparencyLayer, at which time the deferred drawing is rendered to the context. The function CGContextEndTransparencyLayer composites the deferred drawing to the context as a single object, using the clipping area, the global alpha, shadow, and blend mode in effect when you called CGContextBeginTransparencyLayer.

Figure 15.12 is the result of executing the code in Listing 15.9. The code draws the graphics in the figure as if all the rectangles were drawn as a single graphic object when Quartz paints the shadow. It is essentially the same code as that in Listing 15.8, but the current code uses transparency layers to group the graphics.

Listing 15.9 A routine that uses transparency layers with shadow effects

```
void showComplexShadow(CGContextRef context, CFURLRef url)
{
  CGSize offset = { -6, -6 };
  float blur = 3;

  // Set the shadow.
  CGContextSetShadow(context, offset, blur);

  // Begin collecting drawing into a transparency layer.
  // This resets the graphics state shadow parameter to no shadow.
  CGContextBeginTransparencyLayer(context, NULL);
    // Now draw to the transparency layer.
    drawColoredLogo(context);

  // Ending the transparency layer causes all drawing in the
  // transparency layer to be composited to the destination with the
  // shadow in effect when CGContextBeginTransparencyLayer was called.
  CGContextEndTransparencyLayer(context);
}
```

The code first sets the shadow that it wants to apply to the transparency layer as a whole and calls `CGContextBeginTransparencyLayer` to begin a transparency layer. This sets the clipping area to its default value, the global alpha to 1.0, resets the shadow to no shadow, and sets the compositing blend mode to normal. The code then calls the routine `drawColoredLogo` from Listing 15.8 (page 520) to paint the set of colored rectangles. This drawing is deferred and is not painted to the context. Instead, Quartz records the drawing so that it can later composite it as a group. The code then calls `CGContextEndTransparencyLayer` to end the transparency layer. Quartz composites the recorded drawing to the context, using the shadow value that was in effect when the code called `CGContextBeginTransparencyLayer`.

The functions `CGContextBeginTransparencyLayer` and `CGContextEndTransparencyLayer` perform an implicit save/restore to the graphics state so that after you call `CGContextEndTransparencyLayer`, the graphics state is restored to that in effect at the time you called `CGContextBeginTransparencyLayer`. Any changes you've made to the graphics state after you call `CGContextBeginTransparencyLayer` are discarded when you call `CGContextEndTransparencyLayer`. Note that for every call to `CGContextSaveGState` that you make after you call `CGContextBeginTransparencyLayer`, you should have a matching call to `CGContextRestoreGState` before you call `CGContextEndTransparencyLayer` so that you avoid conflicts with the graphics state handling that Quartz performs in these routines.

Transparency layers can be nested to obtain the effect of grouping together several groups. The nesting can be to any depth. To nest transparency layers, you set the clipping area, global alpha, shadow, and blend mode to that which you want for the compositing of the complete group, then call `CGContextBeginTransparencyLayer` to start the outermost group. For each subsequent group you want inside the outer group, you set the clipping area, global alpha, shadow, and blend mode for that group and call `CGContextBeginTransparencyLayer` to begin that group. To end each inner group, you call `CGContextEndTransparencyLayer`. You continue this nesting until you've drawn all the graphics you want in the outer group and then call `CGContextEndTransparencyLayer`, ending the outer transparency layer. Quartz then composites the collected result as a whole.

Important   Every call to `CGContextBeginTransparencyLayer` must be matched by a subsequent call to `CGContextEndTransparencyLayer`.

The objects inside of a transparency layer can themselves contain shadows, be drawn with any blend mode, or be partially transparent by drawing them with a transparent color or by using the context global alpha parameter. The transparency layer simply controls how the group as a whole is composited to the context when you end the layer.

Figure 15.13 Filling and stroking an object with shadows

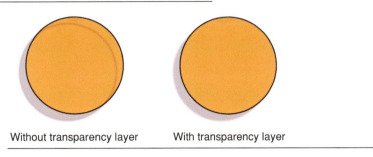

Without transparency layer   With transparency layer

You might expect that painting a path with the kCGPathFillStroke painting mode is an atomic painting operation. However, as of this writing (corresponding to Tiger and earlier versions), Quartz treats this as two separate painting operations, first a fill, then a stroke. This behavior is a bug; it is not part of the Quartz imaging model. Unfortunately, the fact that using kCGPathFillStroke results in two painting operations affects shadows and alpha compositing.

By using transparency layers, you can work around this problem, as shown in Figure 15.13. The graphic on the left is a circular path painted using the kCG-PathFillStroke painting mode on Tiger without using a transparency layer. The graphic on the right is the same painting but drawn inside a transparency layer so that the shadow applies to the transparency layer as a whole rather than to each individual painting operation inside the layer. The code that draws Figure 15.13 is shown in Listing 15.10. Note that when Apple fixes this bug, the work-around of using transparency layers, while no longer necessary, will continue to work correctly.

Listing 15.10 A routine that draws shadows on filled and stroked objects

```
void drawFillAndStrokeWithShadow(CGContextRef context, CFURLRef url)
{
  CGRect r = CGRectMake(60, 60, 100, 100);
  CGSize offset = { -7, -7 };
  float blur = 3;

  // Set the shadow.
  CGContextSetShadow(context, offset, blur);
  // Set the color to an opaque orange.
  CGContextSetFillColorWithColor(context,
                getRGBOpaqueOrangeColor());
```

```
    // Draw the graphic on the left without a transparency layer.
    CGContextBeginPath(context);
    myCGContextAddEllipseInRect(context, r);
    CGContextDrawPath(context, kCGPathFillStroke);

    // Draw the graphic on the right.
    r = CGRectOffset(r, 125, 0);
    // Begin the transparency layer.
    CGContextBeginTransparencyLayer(context, NULL);
      myCGContextAddEllipseInRect(context, r);
      CGContextDrawPath(context, kCGPathFillStroke);
    // End the transparency layer.
    CGContextEndTransparencyLayer(context);
}
```

Alpha Compositing and Transparency Layers

Besides applying shadows to a group of objects, you can use transparency layers to apply alpha compositing effects to a grouped object, rather than to the individual objects within that group. Take a look at Figure 15.14 to see how you can use alpha compositing in this way. An opaque green rectangle is drawn underneath the left half of each object in the figure. Object 1 in the figure is a "complex shape" painted with fully opaque alpha on top of the background. The complex shape is the same set of colored rectangles as Figure 15.11 (page 521) and Figure 15.12 (page 522). Because the colored rectangles are fully opaque, they completely obscure the portions of the background they cover. Object 2 is the same shape drawn with a global alpha value of 75 percent on top of the same background. In Object 2, the individual components of the shape are each visible, since they are not composited as a single object but rather one at a time. Object 3 in the figure is the shape composited as a single object on top of the background. This last result is achieved by using transparency layers to group the drawing of the colored rectangles.

Figure 15.14 is the result of executing the code in Listing 15.11. The doLayerCompositing routine starts by drawing a green background for Object 1 and draws the colored rectangles using the drawColoredLogo routine from Listing 15.8 (page 520). Because the colored rectangles are painted with a fully opaque painting color, the shape appears as a single object.

The doLayerCompositing routine next draws Object 2 in the same basic fashion. The difference is that this time, before calling drawColoredLogo to paint the colored rectangles, it sets the global alpha value to 0.75 to paint the shape with 75 percent opacity. Because the colored rectangles drawn by drawColoredLogo

Figure 15.14 Compositing per object versus group

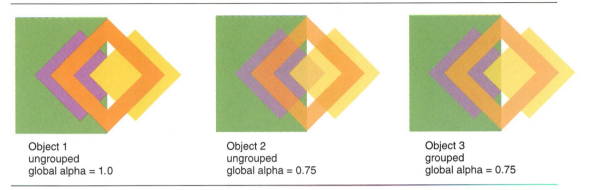

Object 1
ungrouped
global alpha = 1.0

Object 2
ungrouped
global alpha = 0.75

Object 3
grouped
global alpha = 0.75

are not drawn as an atomic operation but instead consist of three distinct Quartz graphic elements, each of those elements is composited to the destination individually. The first rectangle is painted purple with 75 percent alpha on top of the background. The next rectangle is painted yellow with 75 percent alpha on top of the first rectangle and the background. The third rectangle is painted orange with 75 percent alpha. The result is that portions of the second rectangle that overlap with the first are a different color than the portions that are composited only with the background. Similarly, the portions of the third rectangle that overlap the previous two are composited with a different color than those portions drawn directly on top of the background.

Listing 15.11   Code that uses a transparency layer to composite a complex shape

```
void doLayerCompositing(CGContextRef context)
{
  CGRect r = CGRectMake(40, 50, 142, 180);
  // ***** Object 1 *****
  CGContextTranslateCTM(context, 20, 20);
  CGContextSetFillColorWithColor(context,
                getRGBOpaqueGreenColor());
  // Draw a green background.
  CGContextFillRect(context, r);
  // Draw the colored logo.
  drawColoredLogo(context);

  // ***** Object 2 *****
  CGContextTranslateCTM(context, 300, 0);
  CGContextSetFillColorWithColor(context,
                getRGBOpaqueGreenColor());
  // Draw a green background.
  CGContextFillRect(context, r);
```

```
    // Draw the rectangles with opacity 0.75.
    CGContextSetAlpha(context, 0.75);

    drawColoredLogo(context);

    // ***** Object 3 *****
    CGContextTranslateCTM(context, 300, 0);
    // Set the alpha to 1.0 for drawing the background.
    CGContextSetAlpha(context, 1.0);
    CGContextSetFillColorWithColor(context,
                getRGBOpaqueGreenColor());
    CGContextFillRect(context, r);
    // Draw the rectangles with opacity 0.75.
    CGContextSetAlpha(context, 0.75);
    // Begin a transparency layer. Drawing collected in
    // this transparency layer will be composited with an
    // alpha value of 0.75 when the transparency layer is ended.
    CGContextBeginTransparencyLayer(context, NULL);

      // Draw the colored logo into the transparency layer.
      drawColoredLogo(context);

    // Ending the transparency layer causes the drawing
    // to then be composited with the global alpha value
    // in effect when CGContextBeginTransparencyLayer was called.
    CGContextEndTransparencyLayer(context);
}
```

The last portion of the code draws Object 3 in the same manner as Object 2 but with one crucial difference. Before calling drawColoredLogo to draw the colored rectangles, it calls CGContextBeginTransparencyLayer, beginning a transparency layer. Because the global alpha is 0.75 when CGContextBeginTransparencyLayer is called, when the code calls CGContextEndTransparencyLayer, Quartz composites the contents of the transparency layer with an alpha of 0.75. The colored rectangles are treated as a single object and composited with the background as such.

Transparency Layers and PDF Documents

Although the content of a page in a PDF document is a sequence of drawing commands, Quartz treats the drawing of a PDF document as if it were a single object. Quartz composites PDF drawing to the destination as if the PDF page is a single drawing command. If the global alpha is not fully opaque, the whole PDF document is treated as a translucent object. Similarly, if the context shadow parameter has a shadow value other than "no shadow," the PDF page has a shadow as a whole, rather than treating the individual drawing elements as if they each have their own distinct shadows. Figure 15.15 shows a page from a PDF document drawn with and without a shadow.

Prior to Tiger, Quartz ignores the global alpha and shadow values in the graphics state when drawing PDF documents; the PDF document drawing routines treat global alpha as always fully opaque and behave as if there were no shadow. In Panther, you can carefully use transparency layers to work around this problem. In Jaguar and earlier versions, the only work-around is to render the graphic to an image and apply global alpha when drawing the resulting image.

As a general rule, drawing PDF document pages in a transparency layer is no different than drawing any other graphic. However, due to a bug in Panther, special care must be taken when drawing a PDF document inside a transparency layer whose drawing destination is a PDF context or a printing context. A work-around for this Panther bug is to ensure that the CGPDFDocument object that represents the PDF document is not released until the PDF context or printing context into which you draw is released.

Figure 15.15 PDF page drawn without a shadow (left) and with a shadow (right)

Listing 15.12 shows how to apply a shadow to a PDF document in Panther. (This code could also be used to apply a global alpha to a PDF document.) The code creates a CGPDFDocument object from the supplied URL and draws the first page inside a transparency layer. The shadow in effect at the time the code calls CGContextBeginTransparencyLayer is applied when the code calls CGContextEndTransparencyLayer, and Quartz renders the transparency layer to the context. This routine does not release the CGPDFDocument object but instead returns it to the caller so the caller can release the document after it releases the PDF context or ends the printing session. The need to hang on to the CGPDFDocument object until the context is released is a Panther restriction only.

Listing 15.12 Code that applies a shadow to a PDF document in Panther

```
CGPDFDocumentRef shadowPDFDocument(CGContextRef context, CFURLRef url)
{
    CGRect r;
    CGPDFDocumentRef pdfDoc = CGPDFDocumentCreateWithURL(url);
    if(pdfDoc == NULL){
        fprintf(stderr, "Couldn't create PDF document reference!\n");
        return;
    }

    r = CGPDFDocumentGetMediaBox(pdfDoc, 1);
    r.origin.x = 20;
    r.origin.y = 20;

    // Set the shadow.
    CGContextSetShadow(context, CGSizeMake(-7, -7), 3);

    // Drawing collected in this transparency layer is drawn
    // with the shadow when the layer is ended.
    CGContextBeginTransparencyLayer(context, NULL);

        CGContextDrawPDFDocument(context, r, pdfDoc, 1);

    CGContextEndTransparencyLayer(context);

    // On Panther, the PDF document must not be released before the
    // context is released if the context is a PDF or printing context.
    // You should release the document after you release the PDF context.
    //CGPDFDocumentRelease(pdfDoc);
    return pdfDoc;
}
```

Transparency Layers Compared to CGLayers

You may now be wondering why Quartz has both transparency layers and CGLayer objects, described in "CGLayers (Tiger)" (page 371). Transparency layers indeed have some similarities to CGLayers; however, as a general rule you use them in quite different ways.

In a sense, the relationship between a transparency layer and a CGLayer object is similar to the relationship between the current path in a context and a CGPath object. In the case of a transparency layer and the current path, both are tied to a context and can be drawn only once to that context. Both a CGLayer object and a CGPath object are reusable objects that aren't tied to a specific context. (Note that CGLayer objects are tied to a particular type of context—see "CGLayers (Tiger)" for more details.) Both CGLayer objects and CGPath objects are typically used only if you plan to reuse them.

The primary similarity between a transparency layer and a CGLayer object is in how each is composited to the destination. In each case, they are composited as a single object with the global alpha, blend mode, and shadow applied to the drawing as a group. When drawing a transparency layer, Quartz uses the clipping area, global alpha, blend mode, and shadow values in the context at the time you call `CGContextBeginTransparencyLayer`, that is, at the time you begin recording content to treat as a group. When drawing a CGLayer object, Quartz uses the clipping area, global alpha, blend mode, and shadow values in the context at the time you draw the layer using `CGContextDrawLayerAtPoint` or `CGContextDrawLayerInRect`.

Drawing with Shadings (Jaguar)

10.2 ▶ Quartz **shadings**, sometimes also called **gradients** or **blends**, provide a way to paint with color that varies smoothly across the painted area. You've already seen two approaches to drawing shadings. The rotated ellipses shown in Figure 5.5 (page 96) are produced by manually painting a sequence of shapes, smoothly varying the color of the shapes as they are drawn. The green-to-red ramp shown in Figure 9.5 (page 223) is a synthetic image generated by code.

Each of the approaches has disadvantages. The sequence-of-shapes approach relies on the code to decide how many shapes to draw and how far apart to space each shape. The synthetic image approach uses a blend that is pre-rendered as an image. In each approach, the decisions about the resolution and color steps needed for good fidelity are already "baked" into the drawing. Scaling the output produced by these techniques may produce substandard results when drawn at another size or resolution.

A better approach is to use Quartz shadings. Quartz shadings allow you to describe the shading at a high level and postpone the details of how the shading is actually rendered until the rendering actually occurs. Shadings are also captured into PDF documents at a high level, allowing the rendering engine to decide how to render the shading based on the device resolution, bit depth, and CTM at the time the drawing of the PDF document actually occurs.

Quartz provides two different kinds of shadings, **axial** and **radial**. Axial shadings allow you to specify two points that define an axis in space. When you specify the shading, you also supply a **CGFunction** object that describes how the color values vary along that axis. Radial shadings allow you to specify two circles and a CGFunction object that describes how the color values vary as Quartz interpolates between the circles. Figure 15.16 shows several axial and radial shadings.

Figure 15.16 Examples of axial shadings (left) and radial shadings (right)

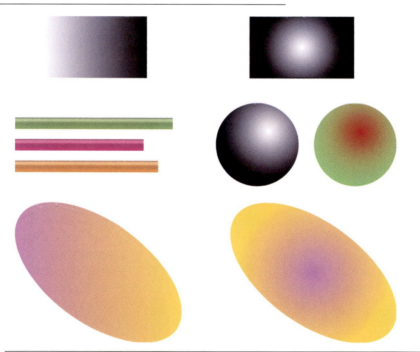

Shading Concepts and the CGFunction

Quartz represents a shading as an opaque object of type `CGShadingRef`. Unlike patterns, shadings are not used to set a color in the graphics state but are an object that you draw. Once you create a shading, you paint it using `CGContext-DrawShading`. Shadings describe their own geometry and Quartz paints that geometry, clipped by the clipping area, when you draw the shading. If you want to fill a shape with a shading, you use that shape to modify the clipping area to that shape and paint the shading. Because shadings have their own geometry, you may need to scale the shading to fill the area you want to paint. You can't directly use a shading to stroke a shape, but you can achieve the equivalent effect in Tiger and later versions by using the function `CGContextReplacePathWith-StrokedPath` to create a path whose interior is the area that would have been painted by stroking the current path. Clipping to the resulting path and then drawing the shading produces the same result as stroking with the shading.

A shading has two aspects to it: the geometry that defines the shading and a function that describes how color varies across the shading geometry. The axial and radial shadings each describe their geometry differently; you'll see those definitions in "Axial Shadings" (page 537) and "Radial Shadings" (page 545), respectively. Both shading types use a CGFunction object to describe how color varies over the area of the shading.

A CGFunction object is represented by the opaque type `CGFunctionRef`. A `CGFunctionRef` used for shadings represents a callback function that parameterizes the color in the shading. A generalized CGFunction has a domain—the set of input points that the function can evaluate, and a range—the set of output values the function produces. As of Tiger, Quartz defines only one type of CGFunction object, that appropriate for shadings. The remainder of this section describes the shading type of CGFunction object.

A CGFunction object used for shadings is an application-defined 1-in, N-out function that specifies the color from the starting point through the ending point of the shading. The function is closely tied to the color space that characterizes the shading. The number N, the number of output values for a given input, depends on the shading color space; N is the number of components in that color space, plus 1 for alpha.

The input value 0 passed to a shading CGFunction represents the starting point of the shading and the input value 1 represents the ending point of the shading. Input values between 0 and 1 represent points along the shading. The output values for a given input consist of the color component values, plus alpha, that correspond to that point on the shading.

You create a CGFunction object by calling the Quartz function CGFunctionCreate, passing the following parameters:

- info, a pointer to data that you need for evaluating the function.

- domainDimension, the number of input values to the function. For a CGFunction object for use with shadings, this is always 1.

- domain, a pointer to an array of floating-point values that defines the set of valid input values that the function can evaluate. The number of elements in this array must be 2*domainDimension. For a CGFunction object for use with shadings this is typically the array {0., 1.}, which corresponds to the set of input values used for shadings (that is, 0–1). The use of a NULL domain is deprecated and you should pass a value for domain that is not NULL.

- rangeDimension, the number of output values for the function. For a CGFunction object used for shadings, rangeDimension is 1 plus the number of color components in the color space that characterizes the shading.

- range, a pointer to an array of floating-point values that defines the set of valid output values from the function. Quartz clips the output from the function to the range. The number of elements in this array must be 2*rangeDimension. For a CGFunction object for use with shadings, this is typically the array {0., 1.,..., 0., 1.}, where the number of elements in the array varies depending on the color space of the shading. The values are the minimum and maximum values of the color component values in the color space that characterizes the shading.

- callbacks, a pointer to a structure of type CGFunctionCallbacks. The callbacks structure contains the callback function that Quartz uses to evaluate the CGFunction object.

The CGFunctionCallbacks structure that you provide to CGFunctionCreate contains the callbacks Quartz uses to evaluate the function and to release any info data that you provide when you create the function. The CGFunctionCallbacks structure is defined as follows:

- version, an unsigned int that defines the version of this CGFunctionCallbacks structure. As of Tiger, only version 0 is defined.

- evaluate, a function of type CGFunctionEvaluateCallback. This is the routine Quartz calls to evaluate the function.

- releaseInfo, a function of type CGFunctionReleaseInfoCallback that Quartz calls when it releases the CGFunction object. You should use the releaseInfo callback to release any memory or other resources associated with the info parameter you pass to CGFunctionCreate. Pass NULL if you do not need to release any data when Quartz releases the CGFunction object.

The heart of a CGFunction object is the evaluate callback that you pass in the CGFunctionCallbacks structure. Quartz calls this function to evaluate the CGFunction object for a given input value. This function takes the following values:

- info, the value of the info parameter that you pass to CGFunctionCreate.

- in, a pointer to an array of floating-point values that correspond to the input data that the function should evaluate. The number of elements in this array is specified by the domainDimension argument supplied when creating the function with CGFunctionCreate. For a CGFunction object used for shadings, this array has one element—the location (parameterized from 0–1) along the shading that evaluate should use to evaluate the color of the shading.

- out, a pointer to an array of floating-point values that your function fills in with the results of evaluating the function for the input in. For a shading, these are the color component values, plus alpha, of the color at the location specified by in[0].

Listing 15.13 creates a CGFunction object appropriate for creating a CGShading-Ref that uses the function for evaluating the shading. The listing contains the routines createFunctionForRGB and RedBlackRedRampEvaluate. The routine createFunctionForRGB takes a CGFunctionEvaluateCallback function (such as Red-BlackRedRampEvaluate) as a parameter and returns the CGFunctionRef that corresponds to that function. The routine createFunctionForRGB is tailored to create a function that is appropriate for use as a function that describes a Quartz shading characterized by an RGB color space. As such, the domain of the function has one dimension with valid input values from 0–1. Colors in an RGB color space have three components, plus 1 for alpha (R,G,B,A). All color values in an RGB color space must be in the range 0–1. Therefore, the range for this function has four dimensions, and the range values are between 0–1.

The routine RedBlackRedRampEvaluate is a function of type CGFunctionEvaluate-Callback, appropriate for use with the routine createFunctionForRGB. This routine takes a single input value, the value of in[0], and uses it to generate a color in an RGB color space. The output values returned by a CGFunctionEvaluate-Callback are stored in the out array passed to the function. Since the output values are the R,G,B,A colors the function evaluates to, these correspond to out[0], out[1], out[2], and out[3], respectively. The routine RedBlackRedRampEvaluate produces relatively simple output. The green and blue components of the colors returned by the function are always zero. The alpha value for each point along the shading is always 1. This evaluate function varies the red value along the shading so that it begins at 1 at the start of the shading (input value 0), varies smoothly to 0 in the middle of the shading (input value 0.5), and then increases smoothly back to 1 at the end of the shading (input value 1). This produces a function result that varies from red at the start, to black in the center, and back to red at the end of the shading.

It's a good idea to use continuous functions for your shadings, otherwise shading transitions can be abrupt and may not look good at different resolutions and scale factors.

Listing 15.13 Routines that create a CGFunction object for use with a shading

```
static void RedBlackRedRampEvaluate(void *info, const float *in,
            float *out)
{
    // The red component evaluates to 1 for an input value of 0,
    // smoothly reduces to 0 at the midpoint (input 0.5), and
    // increases back to 1 at the end.
    out[0] = fabs(1. - in[0]*2);
    // The green and blue components are always 0.
    out[1] = out[2] = 0;
    // The alpha component is 1 for the entire shading.
    out[3] = 1;
}

static CGFunctionRef createFunctionForRGB(CGFunctionEvaluateCallback
            evaluationFunction)
{
  CGFunctionRef function;
  float domain[2];       // 1 input
  float range[8];        // 4 outputs
  CGFunctionCallbacks shadingCallbacks;
  // Shadings parameterize the input between 0 (the starting point
  // of the shading) and 1 (the ending point of the shading).
  domain[0] = 0; domain[1] = 1;

  // The range is the range for the output colors. For an RGB color
  // space the values range from 0-1 for the R,G,B,A components.
  // The red component, min and max.
  range[0] = 0; range[1] = 1;
  // The green component, min and max.
  range[2] = 0; range[3] = 1;
  // The blue component, min and max.
  range[4] = 0; range[5] = 1;
  // The alpha component, min and max.
  range[6] = 0; range[7] = 1;

  // The callbacks structure version is
  // 0, the only defined version as of Tiger.
```

```
    shadingCallbacks.version = 0;
    // The routine Quartz should call to evaluate the function.
    shadingCallbacks.evaluate = evaluationFunction;
    // releaseInfo is NULL since there are no resources that need to
    // be released when the function is released.
    shadingCallbacks.releaseInfo = NULL;

    // Dimension of domain is 1 and dimension of range is 4.
    function = CGFunctionCreate(NULL, 1, domain, 4, range,
                &shadingCallbacks);
    if(function == NULL){
      fprintf(stderr, "Couldn't create the CGFunction!\n");
      return NULL;
    }
    return function;
}
```

Now that you've seen how to create a CGFunction object for use with a shading, you are ready to see how you define the shading geometry to create and use shadings.

Note   As of Tiger, Quartz ignores the alpha value of colors in the shading when capturing a shading to a PDF document and instead treats all colors as if they are completely opaque. In addition, Quartz ignores the global alpha value in the context when it records shadings into a PDF document. One possible work-around is to capture a shading as bits using a bitmap context and use the resulting bits to create a CGImage that you draw through the clipping area. This produces pre-rendered shadings but does capture the alpha content into a PDF document. You should not perform this pre-rendering for shadings that don't contain alpha. In Jaguar, Quartz ignores the alpha value of colors in a shading when drawing to any type of context.

Axial Shadings

An axial shading has a geometry that is defined by the line connecting two points in space. This line is the **axis** of the shading. The first point defining the axis is the **starting point** of the shading and the second point is the **ending point** of the shading. The CGFunction object associated with a shading defines the color at each point along the line between the two points defining the shading geometry. Points along any line orthogonal to the shading axis all have the same color as the point they intersect on the shading axis.

An axial shading can be extended at the starting point or the ending point (or both). Extending a shading means that the line defining the shading is extended past the starting and/or ending points defining the shading. For a shading extended beyond the starting point of the shading, the portion of the shading that is extended is colored with the same color as the starting point. For a shading extended beyond the ending point of the shading, the portion of the shading that is extended is colored with the same color as the ending point.

You create an axial shading by calling the function `CGShadingCreateAxial`, passing the following parameters:

- `colorSpace`, the Quartz color space that characterizes the shading. Color values returned by the `evaluate` callback of `function` are interpreted in this color space.

- `start`, a `CGPoint` in user space that defines the starting point of the shading.

- `end`, a `CGPoint` in user space that defines the ending point of the shading.

- `function`, a `CGFunctionRef` of the function that Quartz uses to evaluate the color of each point along the shading. The color values returned by the `evaluate` callback of `function` are interpreted in the color space specified by the `colorSpace` parameter.

- `extendStart`, a `bool` that indicates whether to extend the shading beyond the starting point.

- `extendEnd`, a `bool` that indicates whether to extend the shading beyond the ending point.

Listing 15.14 draws a simple axial shading, shown in Figure 15.17. It creates a CGFunction object for defining the colors in the shading by calling the routine `createFunctionForRGB`, passing the routine `RedBlackRedRampEvaluate` as the function to use as the `CGFunctionEvaluateCallback` for the CGFunction object. (These routines are defined in Listing 15.13.) The code then specifies the starting and ending points of the line defining the shading geometry, but does not extend the shading beyond the starting and ending points. Quartz retains the CGFunction object passed to the call to `CGShadingCreateAxial`; the code releases it with `CGFunctionRelease` since the code no longer needs it. After it has created the CGShading object, the code draws it by calling `CGContextDrawShading`, and then releases it by calling `CGShadingRelease`.

As mentioned earlier, the CGFunction object used in a shading is closely tied to the color space used to create the shading. The color space used to create the shading determines what the output values of the function mean, that is, what colors they represent. In the case of the function created in this example, as the

Figure 15.17 A simple axial shading

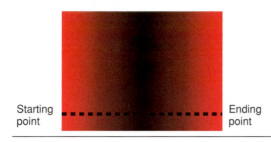

Starting point ⸱⸱⸱⸱⸱⸱⸱⸱⸱⸱ Ending point

function input varies from 0–1, the output varies from red at the starting point of the shading to black at the center point and back to red at the ending point.

Look again at Figure 15.17 to see all the elements involved with creating a shading. The shading color varies along the axis between the starting point and the ending point—the color values along the shading axis vary as the function used to create the shading specifies. The shading begins at the starting point and ends at the ending point. This is because the `extendStart` and `extendEnd` parameters used to create the axial shading are `false`.

Notice that the shading extends out perpendicular to the axis of the shading, up to the edge of the figure. This is because when the code draws the shading, there is no adjustment of the clipping area prior to painting the shading—the shading extends out perpendicular to the shading axis toward "infinity." To bound the shading in the direction perpendicular to the axis of the shading, prior to drawing the shading, establish a clipping area that corresponds to the shape you want to paint.

If `extendStart` were set to `true`, the shading would extend beyond the starting point with the same color as the starting point. If `extendEnd` were set to `true`, the shading would extend beyond the ending point with the same color as the ending point. For axial shadings, any extension of the shading is only bounded by the clipping area.

Listing 15.14 Code that draws a simple axial shading

```
void doSimpleAxialShading(CGContextRef context)
{
  CGFunctionRef axialFunction;
  CGShadingRef shading;
  CGPoint startPoint, endPoint;
  bool extendStart, extendEnd;
```

```
// This shading paints colors in the calibrated Generic RGB
// color space so it needs a function that evaluates 1 in to 4 out.
axialFunction = createFunctionForRGB(RedBlackRedRampEvaluate);
if(axialFunction == NULL){
  return;
}

// Start the shading at the point (20,20) and end it at (420,20).
// The axis of the shading is a line from (20,20) to (420,20).
startPoint.x = 20;
startPoint.y = 20;
endPoint.x = 420;
endPoint.y = 20;

// Don't extend this shading.
extendStart = extendEnd = false;

shading = CGShadingCreateAxial(getTheCalibratedRGBColorSpace(),
            startPoint, endPoint,
            axialFunction,
            extendStart, extendEnd);
// The shading retains the function and this code
// is finished with the function so it should release it.
CGFunctionRelease(axialFunction);
if(shading == NULL){
  fprintf(stderr, "Couldn't create the shading!\n");
  return;
}
// Draw the shading. This paints the shading to the destination
// context, clipped by the current clipping area.
CGContextDrawShading(context, shading);
// Release the shading once the code is finished with it.
CGShadingRelease(shading);
}
```

Listing 15.15 draws some additional shadings, producing the results in Figure 15.18. The routine doExampleAxialShading creates axial shadings using the routine createFunctionForRGB from Listing 15.13 (page 536), but using the routine RedGreenRampEvaluate as the CGFunctionEvaluateCallback to specify the color values along the shading axis. The callback RedGreenRampEvaluate evaluates to a color ramp that starts with pure red and ends with pure green, smoothly varying in between.

Listing 15.15 Code that extends an axial shading and paints text with a shading

```
void RedGreenRampEvaluate(void *info, const float *in, float *out)
{
  // The red component starts at 1 and reduces to zero as the input
  // goes from 0 (the start point of the shading) and increases
  // to 1 (the end point of the shading).
  out[0] = 1. - in[0];
  // The green component starts at 0 for an input of 0 (the start point
  // of the shading) and increases to 1 for an input value of 1
  // (the end point of the shading).
  out[1] = in[0];
  // The blue component is always 0.
  out[2] = 0;
  // The alpha component is always 1, the shading is always opaque.
  out[3] = 1;
}

void doExampleAxialShading(CGContextRef context)
{
  CGFunctionRef redGreenFunction;
  CGShadingRef shading;
  CGPoint startPoint, endPoint;
  bool extendStart, extendEnd;
  CGRect rect = CGRectMake(0, 0, 240, 240);

  // This shading paints colors in the Generic RGB color space
  // so it needs a function that evaluates appropriately.
  redGreenFunction = createFunctionForRGB(RedGreenRampEvaluate);
  if(redGreenFunction == NULL){
    return;
  }

  // The axis of the shading is a diagonal line from
  // (20,20) to (220,220).
  startPoint.x = 20;
  startPoint.y = 20;
  endPoint.x = 220;
  endPoint.y = 220;

  // Don't extend this shading.
  extendStart = extendEnd = false;
  shading = CGShadingCreateAxial(getTheCalibratedRGBColorSpace(),
              startPoint, endPoint,
```

```
                    redGreenFunction,
                    extendStart, extendEnd);

    if(shading == NULL){
      CGFunctionRelease(redGreenFunction);
      fprintf(stderr, "Couldn't create the shading!\n");
      return;
    }

    // Position for the first portion of the drawing.
    CGContextTranslateCTM(context, 40, 260);

    // Stroke a black rectangle that will frame the shading.
    CGContextSetLineWidth(context, 2);
    CGContextSetStrokeColorWithColor(context, getRGBOpaqueBlackColor());
    CGContextStrokeRect(context, rect);

    CGContextSaveGState(context);
        // Clip to the rectangle that was just stroked.
        CGContextClipToRect(context, rect);
        // Draw the shading. This paints the shading to
        // the destination context, clipped to rect.
        CGContextDrawShading(context, shading);
        // Release the shading once the code is finished with it.
        CGShadingRelease(shading);
    // Restore the graphics state so that the rectangular
    // clip is no longer present.
    CGContextRestoreGState(context);

    // Prepare for the next shading.
    CGContextTranslateCTM(context, 0, -250);

    // Extend this shading.
    extendStart = extendEnd = true;
    shading = CGShadingCreateAxial(getTheCalibratedRGBColorSpace(),
                    startPoint, endPoint,
                    redGreenFunction,
                    extendStart, extendEnd);
    // The shading retains the function and this code
    // is finished with the function so it should release it.
    CGFunctionRelease(redGreenFunction);
    if(shading == NULL){
      fprintf(stderr, "Couldn't create the shading!\n");
      return;
    }
```

```
    // Stroke with the current stroke color.
    CGContextStrokeRect(context, rect);

    CGContextSaveGState(context);
      CGContextClipToRect(context, rect);
      // Draw the shading. This paints the shading to
      // the destination context, clipped to rect.
      CGContextDrawShading(context, shading);
    CGContextRestoreGState(context);

    // Now paint some text with a shading.
    CGContextSaveGState(context);
      CGContextTranslateCTM(context, 260, 0);
      CGContextSetTextMatrix(context, CGAffineTransformIdentity);

      // Choose the font with the PostScript name "Times-Roman", at
      // 80 points, with the MacRoman encoding.
      CGContextSelectFont(context, "Times-Roman", 80,
                  kCGEncodingMacRoman);

      // Rotate so that the text characters are rotated
      // relative to the page.
      CGContextRotateCTM(context, DEGREES_TO_RADIANS(45));
      // Set the text drawing mode to clip so that
      // the characters in the string are intersected with
      // the clipping area.
      CGContextSetTextDrawingMode(context, kCGTextClip);
      CGContextShowTextAtPoint(context, 30, 0, "Shading", 7);

      // At this point nothing has been painted; the
      // glyphs in the word "Shading" have been intersected
      // with the previous clipping area to create a new
      // clipping area.

      // Rotate the coordinate system back so that the
      // shading is not rotated relative to the page.
      CGContextRotateCTM(context, DEGREES_TO_RADIANS(-45));

      // Draw the shading, painting the shading
      // to the destination context, clipped by the glyphs.
      CGContextDrawShading(context, shading);

    CGContextRestoreGState(context);
    // Release the shading once the code is finished with it.
    CGShadingRelease(shading);
}
```

Figure 15.18 Axial shadings drawn by Listing 15.15

The code paints three shadings, each with the same user space points defining the axis of the shading. The first shading is shown in the top of Figure 15.18 and the axis of the shading is a diagonal line starting near the lower-left corner of the rectangle and extending to a point near the top-left corner of the rectangle. Prior to painting the shading, the code strokes the rectangle and uses the rectangle as a clipping area. The result is that the shading varies along the diagonal, is bounded by the rectangle, and because neither the starting or ending points are extended, the painting of the shading begins at the starting point and ends at the ending point.

The second shading drawn by the code is identical, except this time the shading is extended at both the starting point and ending point. The red color (the starting color) is extended beyond the starting point to the lower-left corner of the clipping rectangle and the green color (the ending color) is extended to the upper-right corner of the clipping rectangle. Note that the user space coordinates of the starting and ending points that define the second shading are located at the same position relative to the second rectangle as those of the first shading are located relative to the first rectangle. Shadings are defined in Quartz user space coordinates; translating both the shading and the shape it is clipped to produces the same position of the shading relative to the shape used for clipping.

The last shading (drawn at the lower right of the figure) draws shaded text. The code sets the Quartz text drawing mode to kCGTextClip prior to drawing the text characters—this establishes the interior of the path making up the characters in the text "Shading" as the current clipping area. Before drawing the text characters, the code rotates the coordinate system so that the character outlines are rotated, but prior to drawing the shading, the code rotates back to the coordinate system previously in effect. This ensures that the shading is not rotated along with the text but instead intersects the text just like the shading intersects the clipping rectangles it was previously drawn through.

Radial Shadings

Radial shadings are frequently used to give the appearance of three-dimensional spheres and cones. This type of shading is defined by two circles, a starting circle and an ending circle, between which the shading color varies. These two circles define a sequence of circles that are computed by interpolating between the coordinates of the circles that define the shading. The first circle in the sequence is the starting circle, corresponding to location 0 of the shading. The last circle in the sequence is the ending circle, corresponding to location 1 in the shading. The remaining circles in the interpolated sequence lie between the starting circle and ending circle and are at locations in the range 0–1. The color of the circle at location s in the sequence of circles is specified by the color component values obtained by evaluating the CGFunction object describing the shading with the input value s.

Figure 15.19 is an example of a simple radial shading. The starting circle has its origin at the start point in the figure and its radius is r1. The ending circle has its origin at the same point as the starting circle and its radius is r2. The function associated with the shading starts with an opaque orange color and blends smoothly into an opaque yellow color. The sequence of circles that make up the shading vary smoothly between the starting circle and the ending circle. As the radius of a circle in the sequence varies between r1 and r2, the color of that circle varies between the starting color of the blend (orange) and the ending color of the blend (yellow).

The code in Listing 15.16 draws the shading shown in Figure 15.19. The code consists of a routine doSimpleRadialShading that creates and draws the shading and the supporting routines it uses to create the CGFunction object that specifies the colors in the shading. Don't be fooled by the amount of code in the listing. The doSimpleRadialShading that creates and draws the shading is quite simple. The bulk of the code in the listing is useful for creating any number of

Figure 15.19 A simple radial shading

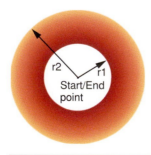

CGFunction objects that describe shading colors that vary linearly between a starting color and an ending color.

You create a radial shading with the function CGShadingCreateRadial, passing the following parameters:

- colorSpace, the Quartz color space that characterizes the shading. Color values returned by the evaluate callback of function are interpreted in this color space.
- start, a CGPoint that specifies the origin of the starting circle.
- startRadius, the radius of the starting circle.
- end, a CGPoint that specifies the origin of the ending circle.
- endRadius, the radius of the ending circle.
- function, a CGFunctionRef of the function that Quartz uses to evaluate the color of each point along the shading. The color values returned by the evaluate callback of function are interpreted in the color space specified by the colorSpace parameter.
- extendStart, a bool that indicates whether to extend the shading beyond the starting circle.
- extendEnd, a bool that indicates whether to extend the shading beyond the ending circle.

The routine doSimpleRadialShading first calls the supporting routine createFunctionWithStartEndColorRamp, passing in two arrays of three floating-point values. The routine createFunctionWithStartEndColorRamp creates a CGFunction object that corresponds to a color ramp between the two colors passed to it. The first color array passed to the function is the starting color and the second is the ending color.

Listing 15.16 Code that draws a simple radial shading

```
typedef struct MyStartEndColor{
   float startColor[3];
   float endColor[3];
}MyStartEndColor;

static void StartColorEndColorEvaluate(void *info,
                const float *in, float *out)
{
   // This function evaluates to produce a blend from
   // a startColor to an endColor.
```

```
    MyStartEndColor *startEndColorP = (MyStartEndColor *)info;
    float *startColor = startEndColorP->startColor;
    float *endColor = startEndColorP->endColor;
    float input = in[0];
    // Weight the starting and ending color components depending
    // on what position in the blend the input value specifies.
    out[0] = (startColor[0]*(1-input) + endColor[0]*input);
    out[1] = (startColor[1]*(1-input) + endColor[1]*input);
    out[2] = (startColor[2]*(1-input) + endColor[2]*input);
    // The alpha component is always 1, the shading is always opaque.
    out[3] = 1;
}

static void releaseStartEndColorInfo(void *info)
{
  if(info)
    free(info);
}

static CGFunctionRef createFunctionWithStartEndColorRamp(
                const float startColor[3],
                const float endColor[3])
{
  CGFunctionRef function;
  float domain[2];      // 1 input
  float range[8];       // 4 outputs
  CGFunctionCallbacks shadingCallbacks;
  MyStartEndColor *startEndColorP;

  // Use a pointer to a MyStartEndColor as a way of
  // parameterizing the color ramp this function produces.
  startEndColorP =
    (MyStartEndColor *)malloc(sizeof(MyStartEndColor));

  if(startEndColorP == NULL){
    fprintf(stderr, "Couldn't malloc memory for startEndColor!\n");
    return NULL;
  }

  // Set up start and end colors in the MyStartEndColor structure.
  startEndColorP->startColor[0] = startColor[0];
  startEndColorP->startColor[1] = startColor[1];
  startEndColorP->startColor[2] = startColor[2];
```

```
        startEndColorP->endColor[0] = endColor[0];
        startEndColorP->endColor[1] = endColor[1];
        startEndColorP->endColor[2] = endColor[2];

        // This is the domain of a shading.
        domain[0] = 0; domain[1] = 1;

        // For an RGB color space the values range from 0-1 for
        // the R,G,B,A components.

        // The red component, min and max.
        range[0] = 0;
        range[1] = 1;
        // The green component, min and max.
        range[2] = 0;
        range[3] = 1;
        // The blue component, min and max.
        range[4] = 0;
        range[5] = 1;
        // The alpha component, min and max.
        range[6] = 0; range[7] = 1;

        // The callbacks structure version is
        // 0, the only defined version as of Tiger.
        shadingCallbacks.version = 0;
        // StartColorEndColorEvaluate is the function to evaluate.
        shadingCallbacks.evaluate = StartColorEndColorEvaluate;
        // releaseStartEndColorInfo releases the pointer to
        // the MyStartEndColor used as the info parameter.
        shadingCallbacks.releaseInfo = releaseStartEndColorInfo;

        // Pass startEndColorP as the info parameter.
        function = CGFunctionCreate(startEndColorP, 1, domain, 4,
                        range, &shadingCallbacks);
        if(function == NULL){
            // Couldn't create the function so this code must free the data.
            free(startEndColorP);
            fprintf(stderr, "Couldn't create the CGFunction!\n");
            return NULL;
        }
        return function;
}


void doSimpleRadialShading(CGContextRef context)
{
```

```
    CGFunctionRef redYellowFunction;
    CGShadingRef shading;
    CGPoint circleACenter, circleBCenter;
    float circleARadius, circleBRadius;
    bool extendStart, extendEnd;
    float startColor[3] = { 0.663, 0., 0.031 };  // Orange.
    float endColor[3] = { 1., 0.8, 0.4 };        // Light Yellow.

    // This function describes a color ramp where the start color
    // is red-orange and the end color is yellow.
    redYellowFunction = createFunctionWithStartEndColorRamp(
                startColor, endColor);
    if(redYellowFunction == NULL){
      return;
    }

    CGContextTranslateCTM(context, 120, 120);

    // Circles whose origin is the same.
    circleACenter.x = 0;
    circleACenter.y = 0;
    circleBCenter = circleACenter;

    // The starting circle is inside the ending circle.
    circleARadius = 50;
    circleBRadius = 100;

    //  Don't extend the shading.
    extendStart = extendEnd = false;
    shading = CGShadingCreateRadial(
      getTheCalibratedRGBColorSpace(),
      circleACenter, circleARadius,
      circleBCenter, circleBRadius,
      redYellowFunction,
      extendStart, extendEnd);

    CGFunctionRelease(redYellowFunction);
    if(shading == NULL){
      fprintf(stderr, "Couldn't create the shading!\n");
      return;
    }
    CGContextDrawShading(context, shading);
    CGShadingRelease(shading);
}
```

The routine doSimpleRadialShading next defines the coordinates of the two circles that define the shading. The circles both have their origin at (0,0). The radius of the first circle is 50 units and the second is 100 units. This defines a geometry where the circles are concentric. The code creates the shading by calling CGShadingCreateRadial, passing the generic calibrated RGB color space, the circle coordinates, and bool values indicating that the shading should not be extended at the start or end. After it successfully creates the shading, the code draws the shading, producing the output in Figure 15.19 (page 545).

The routine doSimpleRadialShading uses the routine createFunctionWithStart-EndColorRamp defined in the listing to create a smooth color ramp between two colors. This routine is similar to the routine createFunctionForRGB in Listing 15.13 (page 536) but instead it parameterizes the function with the data passed to it. To do this, createFunctionWithStartEndColorRamp uses the info parameter it passes to CGFunctionCreate to parameterize its evaluate callback function StartColorEndColorEvaluate. The StartColorEndColorEvaluate callback in the listing obtains the starting and ending colors in the color ramp from the info parameter passed to it and interpolates between them. Quartz clips the values that are output by the function to the range specified when you create the CGFunction object. For this reason, this callback doesn't account for rounding errors that might generate values outside the range 0–1.

The code uses a pointer to the MyStartEndColor structure that it defines so it can pass the data to its evaluate callback. This pointer is created with a malloc call, rather than allocated on the stack, because the data must be available until Quartz releases the CGFunction object. To free the memory associated with the MyStartEndColor structure, the routine createFunctionWithStartEndColor-Ramp uses releaseStartEndColorInfo as the releaseInfo callback in the callback structure it passes to CGFunctionCreate. When Quartz releases the CGFunction object, it calls the releaseInfo callback releaseStartEndColorInfo, which frees the memory associated with the info parameter.

Radial Shading Geometries

Radial shadings can describe a large number of geometries, including many far more complex than that in Figure 15.19. The range of geometries available with radial shadings is significantly greater than that of axial shadings. Another aspect of radial shadings that differs from axial shadings is that radial shadings that are not extended at the start or end are bounded by the shading geometry, as in the case of the shading in Figure 15.19. There is no need (as there is in an axial shading) to limit the clipping area prior to drawing radial shadings that are not extended in order to bound the shaded area. Of course you can use a clipping area to create the effect of filling a shape with a shading.

Radial shading geometries fall into three general categories, each of which produces dramatically different visual results—smaller circle contained in larger circle, non-overlapping circles, and partially overlapping circles. Figure 15.20 shows shadings in each of these three categories. The first row of shadings in the figure, Shadings 1 and 2, are shadings produced where the smaller of the two circles defining the shading is wholly contained inside the larger circle. This produces shadings that appear to look like the surface of a sphere. The geometry of Shading 1 defines that portion of the figure. The graphic for Shading 2 is a shading that is clipped by a clipping area that is the outer boundary of the shape.

The second category is that for which the two circles that define the shading do not overlap. This produces a cylindrical effect if the shading is not extended at either end. Shadings 3 and 4 in the figure are constructed from this category of geometries. Shading 4 utilizes the extend feature of radial shadings to extend the ends of the shading; the shading area in the figure is bounded by clipping to an elliptical shape prior to drawing the shading.

Shadings 5 and 6 in the figure illustrate the partially overlapping radial shading geometry that is created when the two circles defining the shading overlap and neither circle completely contains the other. For shadings that are not extended, this kind of geometry produces the effect of looking down a tube and seeing the light at the other end of the tube. Some of these types of shadings provide the illusion of a perspective view.

The radial shadings shown in Figure 15.20 are produced by the `doExampleRadialShadings` routine in Listing 15.17. This routine uses the `createFunctionWithStartEndColorRamp` from Listing 15.16 (page 546) to create CGFunction objects that produce the color ramps used to draw the different shadings.

The code starts by drawing Shading 1, a shading defined by a geometry where the ending circle completely contains the starting circle and the starting circle has a radius of 0. This produces an effect as if the color at the starting circle originates from a point light source. Shading 2 is similar, except the starting circle has a nonzero radius, producing a hole in the shading at the center of the starting circle. Shading 2 is extended at the ending circle. Extending the larger circle of a radial shading extends the circle, painting the ending color out to the boundary of the clipping area.

Before drawing Shading 2, the code creates a clipping area that is a circle with a wedge removed. Although the shading is extended at the end, the clipping area bounds the shading. In addition, because the radius of the outer circle that defines the shading is larger than that of the arc defining the clipping area, the color at the edge of the clipping area is not the color at the ending circle but rather the color at an intermediate point in the shading.

Figure 15.20 Radial shading geometries

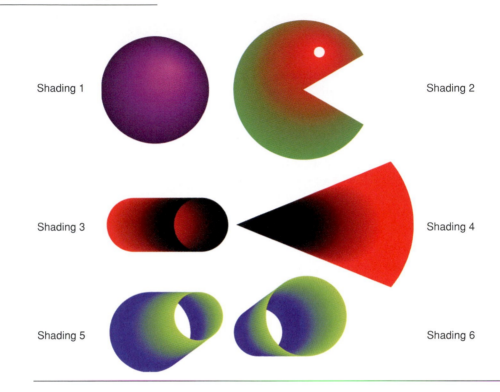

Shading 1

Shading 2

Shading 3

Shading 4

Shading 5

Shading 6

Shading 3 consists of two circles of the same radii where each circle is completely outside the other. The extend parameter is `false` for both ends of the shading. This produces a cylinderlike effect. Shading 4 is another that's defined by two circles completely outside of one another but with one circle smaller than the other. The extend parameter is `true` for both ends of this shading so that the end of each circle is extended. Extending the end of the smaller circle extends the shading down to a point. Extending the end of the larger circle extends the shading out to the boundary of the clipping area. To limit the shading, the code first establishes a clipping area that is an ellipse, using the routine `myCGContextAddEllipseInRect` from Listing 6.3 (page 118).

Shadings 5 and 6 are geometries for which the two circles overlap but neither completely encloses the other. The difference between the two geometries is that Shading 5 is constructed by defining the starting circle radius so that it is larger than the ending circle radius. Shading 6 is defined similarly to Shading 5, but instead the starting circle radius is smaller than the ending circle radius.

Listing 15.17 Code that draws a variety of radial shading geometries

```
void doExampleRadialShadings(CGContextRef context)
{
  CGFunctionRef magentaFunction, redGreenFunction,
                redBlackFunction, blueGreenFunction;
  CGShadingRef shading;
  CGPoint circleACenter, circleBCenter;
  float circleARadius, circleBRadius;
  bool extendStart, extendEnd;
  const float magenta[3] = { 1, 0, 1 };          // Pure magenta.
  const float magenta30[3] = { 0.3, 0, 0.3 };    // 30% magenta.
  const float black[3] = { 0, 0, 0 };
  const float red[3] = { 1, 0, 0 };
  const float green[3] = { 0, 1, 0 };
  const float blue[3] = { 0, 0, 1 };
  const float redgreen[3] = { 0.66, 1, 0.04 };   // A green shade.

  CGContextTranslateCTM(context, 120, 550);

  // This function describes a color ramp where the starting color
  // is a full magenta, the ending color is 30% magenta.
  magentaFunction = createFunctionWithStartEndColorRamp(
                magenta, magenta30);
  if(magentaFunction == NULL){
    return;
  }

  // ***** Shading 1 *****
  // Circle A is completely inside circle B but with different origins.
  // Circle A has radius 0, which produces a point source.

  // The center of circle A is offset from the origin.
  circleACenter.x = 30;
  circleACenter.y = 40;
  // The center of circle B is at the origin.
  circleBCenter = CGPointZero;

  // A radius of zero produces a point source.
  circleARadius = 0;
  circleBRadius = 100;
```

```
  // Don't extend the shading.
  extendStart = extendEnd = false;
  shading = CGShadingCreateRadial(
    getTheCalibratedRGBColorSpace(),
    circleACenter, circleARadius,
    circleBCenter, circleBRadius,
    magentaFunction,
    extendStart, extendEnd);
  // Finished with the magenta function so release it.
  CGFunctionRelease(magentaFunction);
  if(shading == NULL){
    fprintf(stderr, "Couldn't create the shading!\n");
    return;
  }
  CGContextDrawShading(context, shading);
  // Finished with the shading so release it.
  CGShadingRelease(shading);

  // ***** Shading 2 *****
  // Circle A is completely inside circle B but with different origins.

  // The start color is red, the end color is green.
  redGreenFunction = createFunctionWithStartEndColorRamp(
              red, green);
  if(redGreenFunction == NULL){
    return;
  }

  circleACenter.x = 55;
  circleACenter.y = 70;
  circleBCenter.x = 20;
  circleBCenter.y = 0;
  circleARadius = 10;
  circleBRadius = 200;
  // Extend the end of this shading.
  extendStart = false;
  extendEnd = true;
  shading = CGShadingCreateRadial(
    getTheCalibratedRGBColorSpace(),
    circleACenter, circleARadius,
    circleBCenter, circleBRadius,
    redGreenFunction,
    extendStart, extendEnd);
  // Finished with this function so release it.
```

```
CGFunctionRelease(redGreenFunction);
if(shading == NULL){
  fprintf(stderr, "Couldn't create the shading!\n");
  return;
}

// Set a clipping area to bound the extend with the starting circle
// inside the clipping area and the ending circle outside.
CGContextSaveGState(context);
  CGContextTranslateCTM(context, 250, 0);
  CGContextBeginPath(context);
  CGContextMoveToPoint(context, 25, 0);
  CGContextAddArc(context,
    25, 0, 130,
    DEGREES_TO_RADIANS(30),
    DEGREES_TO_RADIANS(-30),
    0);
  CGContextClip(context);
  // Paint the shading.
  CGContextDrawShading(context, shading);
  // Finished with the shading so release it.
  CGShadingRelease(shading);
CGContextRestoreGState(context);

CGContextTranslateCTM(context, -40, -250);

// ***** Shading 3 *****
//The starting circle is completely outside the ending circle,
// no extension. The circles have the same radii.
circleACenter.x = 0;
circleACenter.y = 0;
circleBCenter.x = 125;
circleBCenter.y = 0;

circleARadius = 50;
circleBRadius = 50;

extendStart = extendEnd = false;

// Create a function that paints a red-to-black ramp.
redBlackFunction = createFunctionWithStartEndColorRamp(
            red, black);
if(redBlackFunction == NULL){
  return;
}
```

```
shading = CGShadingCreateRadial(
  getTheCalibratedRGBColorSpace(),
  circleACenter, circleARadius,
  circleBCenter, circleBRadius,
  redBlackFunction,
  extendStart, extendEnd);
if(shading == NULL){
  // Couldn't create the shading so release
  // the function before returning.
  CGFunctionRelease(redBlackFunction);
  fprintf(stderr, "Couldn't create the shading!\n");
  return;
}
CGContextDrawShading(context, shading);
// Finished with the shading so release it.
CGShadingRelease(shading);

// ***** Shading 4 *****
// The starting circle is completely outside the ending circle.
// The circles have different radii.
circleACenter.x = 120;
circleACenter.y = 0;
circleBCenter.x = 0;
circleBCenter.y = 0;

circleARadius = 75;
circleBRadius = 30;

// Extend at the start and end.
extendStart = extendEnd = true;
shading = CGShadingCreateRadial(
  getTheCalibratedRGBColorSpace(),
  circleACenter, circleARadius,
  circleBCenter, circleBRadius,
  redBlackFunction,
  extendStart, extendEnd);
// Finished with this function so release it.
CGFunctionRelease(redBlackFunction);
if(shading == NULL){
  fprintf(stderr, "Couldn't create the shading!\n");
  return;
}
CGContextSaveGState(context);
```

```
        CGContextTranslateCTM(context, 270, 0);
        // Clip to an elliptical path so the shading
        // does not extend to infinity at the larger end.
        CGContextBeginPath(context);
        myCGContextAddEllipseInRect(context,
                    CGRectMake(-200, -200, 450, 400));
        CGContextClip(context);
        CGContextDrawShading(context, shading);
        // Finished with the shading so release it.
        CGShadingRelease(shading);
    CGContextRestoreGState(context);

    CGContextTranslateCTM(context, 30, -200);

    // The starting color is blue, the ending color is a shade of green.
    blueGreenFunction = createFunctionWithStartEndColorRamp(
                    blue, redgreen);
    if(blueGreenFunction == NULL){
      return;
    }

    // ***** Shading 5 *****
    // The circles partially overlap and have different radii
    // with the larger circle at the start.
    circleACenter.x = 0;
    circleACenter.y = 0;
    circleBCenter.x = 90;
    circleBCenter.y = 30;

    circleARadius = 75;
    circleBRadius = 45;

    extendStart = extendEnd = false;
    shading = CGShadingCreateRadial(
      getTheCalibratedRGBColorSpace(),
      circleACenter, circleARadius,
      circleBCenter, circleBRadius,
      blueGreenFunction,
      extendStart, extendEnd);
    if(shading == NULL){
      // Couldn't create the shading so release
      // the function before returning.
```

```
    CGFunctionRelease(blueGreenFunction);
    fprintf(stderr, "Couldn't create the shading!\n");
    return;
}

CGContextDrawShading(context, shading);
// Finished with the shading so release it.
CGShadingRelease(shading);

CGContextTranslateCTM(context, 200, 0);

// ***** Shading 6 *****
// The circles partially overlap and have different
// radii and the larger circle is at the end.

circleARadius = 45;
circleBRadius = 75;
shading = CGShadingCreateRadial(
  getTheCalibratedRGBColorSpace(),
  circleACenter, circleARadius,
  circleBCenter, circleBRadius,
  blueGreenFunction,
  extendStart, extendEnd);
// Finished with this function so release it.
CGFunctionRelease(blueGreenFunction);
if(shading == NULL){
  fprintf(stderr, "Couldn't create the shading!\n");
  return;
}

CGContextDrawShading(context, shading);
// Finished with the shading so release it.
CGShadingRelease(shading);
}
```

Transforming Shadings

You can achieve interesting results with shadings by applying coordinate transformations to user space prior to drawing the shading. Figure 15.21 is an example of drawing two shadings, each defined by two rotated elliptical shapes. Shading 2 is similar to that drawn by explicit painting of a sequence of ellipses in Listing 5.5 (page 97) in "The Quartz Coordinate System and Coordinate Transformations" (page 83) and shown in Figure 5.5 (page 96).

You can see how these effects can be achieved by taking a look at Listing 15.18, which produces the drawing in Figure 15.21. Shading 1 is similar to that of Shading 3 in Figure 15.20 (page 552). The shading is defined by two circles of the same radius that do not intersect, and neither circle wholly contains the other. To produce a shading that is defined by two rotated ellipses requires drawing the shading in a coordinate system where the two circles defining the shading are transformed into rotated ellipses. You get this effect by applying the same coordinate transformation used in Listing 5.5 (page 97)—first apply a rotation by 45 degrees followed by a scaling of 1 in x and 2 in y.

Shading 1 in the code uses this transformation to transform the circles that define the shading into the rotated, elliptical shape seen at the left of Figure 15.21, but it introduces an interesting effect—not only are the ellipses of the shading rotated but the shading itself is rotated relative to the x axis. This is because the origin of the circles that define the shading are rotated and scaled along with the circles defining the starting and ending circles.

Listing 15.18 Code that draws shadings defined by rotated ellipses

```
void doEllipseShading(CGContextRef context)
{
  CGFunctionRef redBlackFunction;
  CGShadingRef shading;
  CGPoint circleACenter, circleBCenter;
  float circleARadius, circleBRadius;
  bool extendStart, extendEnd;
  const float black[3] = { 0, 0, 0 };
  const float red[3] = { 1, 0, 0 };

  // This function describes a color ramp where the starting color
  // is red and the ending color is black.
  redBlackFunction = createFunctionWithStartEndColorRamp(
              red, black);
  if(redBlackFunction == NULL){
    fprintf(stderr, "Couldn't create the red-black function!\n");
    return;
  }

  CGContextTranslateCTM(context, 100, 300);
  // ***** Shading 1 *****
  // Compute the transform needed to create the rotated ellipses.
  CGAffineTransform t =
              CGAffineTransformMakeRotation(DEGREES_TO_RADIANS(45));
  t = CGAffineTransformScale(t, 1, 2);
```

```
                circleACenter.x = 0;
                circleACenter.y = 0;

                circleBCenter.x = circleACenter.x + 144;
                circleBCenter.y = circleACenter.y;

                circleARadius = 45;
                circleBRadius = 45;

                // Don't extend this shading.
                extendStart = extendEnd = false;

                shading = CGShadingCreateRadial(
                  getTheCalibratedRGBColorSpace(),
                  circleACenter, circleARadius,
                  circleBCenter, circleBRadius,
                  redBlackFunction,
                  extendStart, extendEnd);
                if(shading == NULL){
                  // Couldn't create the shading so release
                  // the function before returning.
                  CGFunctionRelease(redBlackFunction);
                  fprintf(stderr, "Couldn't create the shading!\n");
                  return;
                }

                CGContextSaveGState(context);
                  // Applying the transform t produces the rotated elliptical
                  // shading. Both the ellipse and the shading are rotated
                  // relative to default user space.
                  CGContextConcatCTM(context, t);

                  CGContextDrawShading(context, shading);
                  CGShadingRelease(shading);
                CGContextRestoreGState(context);

                CGContextTranslateCTM(context, 300, 10);

                // ***** Shading 2 *****
                // Invert the transform t so it can be used to calculate
                // the points in object space that, when transformed by t,
                // produce the user space points circleACenter and circleBCenter.
                CGAffineTransform inverseT = CGAffineTransformInvert(t);
                // Compute points that, when transformed by transform t,
```

```
// produce the points circleACenter, circleBCenter.
circleACenter = CGPointApplyAffineTransform(circleACenter, inverseT);
circleBCenter = CGPointApplyAffineTransform(circleBCenter, inverseT);

shading = CGShadingCreateRadial(
  getTheCalibratedRGBColorSpace(),
  circleACenter, circleARadius,
  circleBCenter, circleBRadius,
  redBlackFunction,
  extendStart, extendEnd);
// The code is finished with the function so release it.
CGFunctionRelease(redBlackFunction);
if(shading == NULL){
  fprintf(stderr, "Couldn't create the shading!\n");
  return;
}

// Transform coordinates for the drawing of the shading.
// This transform produces the rotated elliptical shading.
CGContextConcatCTM(context, t);

CGContextDrawShading(context, shading);
CGShadingRelease(shading);
}
```

To achieve the results in the right side of the figure, Shading 2 in the code computes the coordinate origins of the circles so that when they are transformed by the transform t to produce the rotated elliptical shapes of the shading, the origins of the circles lie along a horizontal line in the coordinate system that exists

Figure 15.21 Drawing a rotated elliptical shading

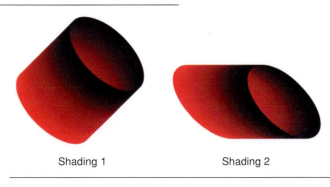

Shading 1   Shading 2

before the transformations. This operation is the same as computing the coordinates in object space that produce a given user space coordinate when transformed by t.

You might want to think about it this way. The code needs to compute the point Point such that transforming Point by the transform M produces Point', the point in untransformed user space that is desired. This coordinate transform is the same as that described in "The Mathematics of Affine Transforms" (page 88):

$$Point' = Point \times M_{transform}$$

However, if you multiply each side of this equation with the inverse of matrix $M_{transform}$, $M_{transform}^{-1}$, (multiplying each side on the right side), the preceding equation becomes

$$(Point' \times M_{transform}^{-1}) = Point \times M_{transform} \times M_{transform}^{-1}$$

Because multiplying a matrix by its inverse produces the identity matrix, this simplifies to

$$(Point' \times M_{transform}^{-1}) = Point$$

This means that the *Point* is equal to the *Point'* transformed by the inverse of the matrix $M_{transform}$.

To compute the coordinates that produce the points circleACenter and circleBCenter after being transformed by t, the code first computes the inverse transform of t and applies that transform to the points circleACenter and circleBCenter using the function CGPointApplyAffineTransform. It uses these new points as the coordinate origins of the two circles defining the shading. It then applies the transform t to user space prior to drawing the shading. This operation transforms the shading so that the circles defining the shading are rotated ellipses but the origins of the circles now lie along a horizontal axis in untransformed user space.

Summary

In addition to the basic drawing operations discussed earlier, Quartz offers a number of advanced drawing features. Advanced drawing features can be used singly or in combination with other features to achieve professional, snazzy-looking graphics.

Patterns can have intrinsic color or be a stencil and are used to stroke and fill. Intrinsic colored patterns use specific colors for the pattern, similar to the way specific colors are used for a flag. Stencil patterns define areas to paint and, in that way, are similar to masks.

Shadows provide a way for you to achieve the "Aqua look" on objects that you draw. Transparency layers allow you to group objects, which in turn lets you apply effects such as shadows and alpha compositing to a group as a whole. Shadings let you paint an area with a color that varies smoothly, and they come in two "flavors"—axial and radial. Axial shadings vary along an axis, whereas radial shadings are defined by two circles. A number of interesting geometries arise depending on how the two circles relate to each other.

See Also

The header files relevant to creating and drawing patterns are

- CGPattern.h, which contains the definitions and prototypes needed for creating CGPattern objects.
- CGColor.h, which contains the functions to create the pattern color space and CGColor objects from patterns.
- CGContext.h, which contains the functions to set a pattern as the stroke or fill color and for setting the pattern phase.

The header files relevant to creating and drawing shadings are

- CGFunction.h, which contains the definitions and prototypes needed for creating CGFunction objects.
- CGShading.h, which contains the definitions and prototypes needed for creating CGShading objects.
- CGContext.h, which contains the functions to draw a shading to a context.

The header file relevant to setting the context shadow parameter and for beginning and ending a transparency layer is

- CGContext.h

The relevant reference information from the ADC Reference Library is

- *CGPattern Reference*
- *CGColor Reference*
- *CGContext Reference*
- *CGFunction Reference*
- *CGShading Reference*

Chapter 16

Supporting PostScript and EPS Data

The PDF imaging model is, for the most part, a superset of the PostScript imaging model. As a result, a conversion from PostScript data to a PDF document is graphically lossless with very few exceptions and does not require rasterization of the data. The Quartz process for converting PostScript and EPS data into PDF data is similar to that performed by Adobe Distiller and other third-party tools: a PostScript interpreter interprets the PostScript data and converts it to an equivalent PDF representation. This interpreter supports PostScript language level 3 and has many capabilities similar to the basic capabilities present in Adobe Distiller, version 5.0.

The PDF data that results from the Quartz conversion process is just like any other PDF data. You can use it just as you would any PDF document. Any of the functions that Quartz supplies for working with PDF data work on the converted data, too. PostScript conversion is not only useful for creating PDF documents, you can also use it as a way to draw Encapsulated PostScript (EPS) or PostScript data with Quartz.

The ability for Quartz to convert PostScript or EPS data into a PDF document was introduced in Panther. Prior to Panther, applications can perform high-quality printing of EPS data to PostScript printers by leveraging the printing framework function `PMCGImageCreateWithEPSDataProvider`.

This chapter provides an overview of the PostScript conversion process, describes the functions you use to perform the conversion, shows how to use these functions to convert PostScript to PDF and then to use that data, describes how to use the printing framework to print PostScript data, and provides guidelines for supporting EPS data in your application.

As of Tiger, Quartz provides no direct mechanism to generate PostScript or EPS data. However, the Mac OS X printing system provides the ability to generate PostScript output from Quartz drawing when printing to a PostScript printer and can programmatically generate PostScript output to a disk file. In addition, the Cocoa NSView class provides the method `dataWithEPSInsideRect:`, which creates an NSData object that contains an EPS data representation of the drawing a view performs. Discussion about using these techniques to generate PostScript or EPS output data is outside the scope of this book. See the references at the end of this chapter for more information on the topic of generating PostScript output data.

Overview of the Conversion Process

The CGPSConverter object is the workhorse of the PostScript-to-PDF conversion process. It encapsulates the callbacks you provide to report progress, obtain status messages, and control the conversion process. To perform the conversion of PostScript data into PDF data, you first create a CGPSConverter object and then you pass the object to the function `CGPSConverterConvert` along with a data provider that supplies PostScript or EPS data and a data consumer that receives the generated PDF data. ("Data Providers and Data Consumers" (page 185) discusses data providers and data consumers in detail.) After you create a CGPSConverter object, you can use it for as many conversions as you'd like. When you are done with the CGPSConverter object you created, you release it with `CFRelease`.

The PostScript-to-PDF conversion process in Quartz handles both multiple-page PostScript data as well as EPS files. For PostScript data and EPS files, it is expected that the data provided by the data provider is valid PostScript and has been stripped of any communications characters and non-PostScript job control data (such as PJL). The conversion process directly handles PC-format EPS files that contain a TIFF or Windows Metafile preview. Such files contain a header that begins with the 4-byte sequence 0xC5D0D3C6, followed by a short table of contents indicating the offset to the PostScript data stream in the file and its size. You don't need to preprocess the data before handing it off to the CGPSConverter routines. The PostScript-to-PDF conversion process finds the PostScript data within the EPS file and converts the resulting PostScript data. See "PSConverter Advanced Issues" (page 580) for more detail about how the CGPSConverter routines process the PostScript data you supply.

In addition to the Quartz routines that are available for converting PostScript to PDF documents (described in the next section), Apple provides the `pstopdf` tool in `/usr/bin`. This tool uses the same underlying PS-to-PDF conversion functionality available in Quartz and is available for use in scripts or executing from your application, if that is more convenient than doing the conversion yourself. The pstopdf always converts PostScript or EPS input data to a PDF file. Input can come from stdin or from a file; its output always goes to a file. See the manual page (man pstopdf) for the tool to get more information about its capabilities.

Beginning with Panther, Cocoa provides support for the NSEPSImageRep class by leveraging this Quartz functionality. Cocoa converts the EPS document into a PDF representation and draws that representation when you draw the corresponding NSImage.

Quartz Conversion Functions and Callbacks (Panther)

10.3 ▶ The two functions you need for PostScript-to-PDF conversion are CGPSConverterCreate and CGPSConverterConvert. The function CGPSConverterCreate creates a CGPSConverter object and the function CGPSConverterConvert performs the conversion. You need to supply a table of callback functions that Quartz invokes during various parts of the conversion process. This section discusses the functions and callbacks. You'll see how to use these functions in "Creating a PDF Data File from PostScript Data" (page 569).

You use the Quartz function CGPSConverterCreate to create the CGPSConverter object by passing the following parameters:

- info, a pointer to data you want passed to your callback functions, if any.
- callbacks, a pointer to a CGPSConverterCallbacks structure that contains the custom callbacks to use for the conversions performed by the CGPSConverter object you create.
- options, a CFDictionaryRef that specifies custom options for the conversions performed by the CGPSConverter object. As of Tiger this parameter is not used, so you should pass NULL. It's there to allow for possible future expansion of the CGPSConverter capabilities.

The CGPSConverterCallbacks structure contains a version field and seven callback functions, any of which can be NULL. The structure has a version field that specifies the version of the callbacks structure. The only version defined as of Tiger is 0. The callbacks that you can supply are described in Table 16.1.

You'll want to take a closer look at a few of these callbacks. Quartz supplies the data that you passed to the CGPSConverterCreate function in the info parameter

Table 16.1 Callbacks Used for the PostScript-to-PDF Conversion Process

Field Name	Callback Function Data Type	When Called
beginDocument	CGPSConverterBeginDocumentCallback	At the beginning of a document conversion.
endDocument	CGPSConverterEndDocumentCallback	At the end of a document conversion.
beginPage	CGPSConverterBeginPageCallback	Not called as of Tiger. Might be used for future expansion.
endPage	CGPSConverterEndPageCallback	At the end of each PostScript page converted.
noteProgress	CGPSConverterProgressCallback	Periodically to update the user on the conversion process.
noteMessage	CGPSConverterMessageCallback	Only if there is a message (status or otherwise) to report during the conversion process.
releaseInfo	CGPSConverterReleaseInfoCallback	When the associated CGPSConverter object is released.

to the CGPSConverterEndPageCallback function, along with the page number of the page that just ended, and a CFDictionary object that contains information about the converted page. The CFDictionary object can be NULL; currently any entries in a dictionary that is not NULL are undocumented.

Quartz also supplies the data that you passed to the CGPSConverterCreate function in the info parameter to the CGPSConverterReleaseInfoCallback function. You can then release any data associated with the info parameter that you supplied when you created the CGPSConverter object.

The CGPSConverterProgressCallback function is what you'd use to provide the user with the opportunity to stop the conversion. For example, you could provide a window with a progress bar and a Cancel button. If, when your callback is invoked, the user has pressed the Cancel button, you could then stop the conversion process.

After you create a CGPSConverter object, you pass it to CGPSConverterConvert, along with these additional parameters:

- provider, a CGDataProvider object that supplies the PostScript or EPS data that you want to convert to PDF data.

- consumer, a CGDataConsumer object that receives the PDF data produced by the conversion process.

- options, a CFDictionary object that provides additional parameters for the conversion. As of Tiger, pass NULL for this parameter. (This parameter allows for possible future expansion of the CGPSConverter capabilities.)

The function CGPSConverterConvert initiates and executes the conversion. Quartz invokes the callbacks you supplied at the times listed in Table 16.1. During the conversion process, Quartz can pass any of the following types of messages to your CGPSConverterMessageCallback function:

- Informational messages. These are normally produced by the back channel of a PostScript interpreter during the execution of a PostScript print job, specifically by the PostScript pstack, print, and == operators. You can use these messages to debug PostScript programs. They do not reflect errors or other problems with the PostScript data.

- Font name messages. These list the font names when a font cache is produced during the first conversion job performed for a given user. The messages consist of font names, such as /Times-Roman and /Helvetica.

- Font substitution messages. These messages are produced when a given font is used but is not available. This situation typically occurs when a font is not embedded in the PostScript data being converted, the corresponding font is not present in the set of fonts available to the user, and the font is not present in the database of fonts built into the Quartz PostScript-to-PDF converter. The message looks similar to MyFont-Bold not found, using Courier.

- PostScript error messages. These messages, generated as part of the conversion process, take the form %%[Error: undefined; OffendingCommand: badluck]%%. The text immediately following the %%[Error: portion of the message is the type of error, which is undefined in this example message. The text immediately following the OffendingCommand: portion of the message is the PostScript command or data that caused the error, which is badluck in this example.

Reporting any of the information supplied to the noteMessage callback is up to you. The messages are not logged automatically and there are no user notifications associated with them.

Creating a PDF Data File from PostScript Data

Now that you know the functions used to perform a conversion, it's time to take a look at some code that creates a PDF data file from PostScript input data. Listing 16.1 contains definitions for two structures, six callback routines, and a conversion routine—convertPStoPDF. Recall that you can provide up to seven callback routines. This example supplies the following callbacks. It doesn't supply a releaseInfo callback because, for this example, there isn't any data to release.

- begin_document_callback, which is invoked when the conversion starts. This sample callback prints "Begin document" to a status file.

- end_document_callback, which is invoked when the conversion terminates. It prints "End document" to a status file and includes text that indicates success or failure.

- begin_page_callback, which is invoked when a page conversion starts. It prints "Beginning page" to a status file, along with the page number. Note that as of Tiger, Quartz does not invoke this callback.

- end_page_callback, which is invoked when a page conversion ends. It prints "Ending page" to a status file, along with the page number.

- progress_callback, which is invoked periodically during the conversion. This example prints a period if the conversion is progressing and "ABORTED" if the conversion is terminated prematurely. Note that there is a call to a myUpdateStatus routine that is commented out. If you want, you can write such a routine to perform status narration and detect a user cancellation action.

- messsage_callback, which extracts an ASCII version of the message and prints it to a status file.

The routine convertPStoPDF takes two parameters: an input URL that refers to PostScript data and an output URL that specifies where to write the resulting PDF data. (Note that any existing file at that URL is overwritten.)

Listing 16.1 Code that creates a PDF data file from PostScript input data

```
typedef struct MyConverterData
{
  bool doProgress;
  bool abortConverter;
  FILE *outStatusFile;
  CGPSConverterRef converter;
} MyConverterData;

// Converter callbacks
```

```c
static void begin_document_callback(void *info)
{
  fprintf( ((MyConverterData *)info)->outStatusFile,
              "\nBegin document\n");
}

static void end_document_callback(void *info, bool success)
{
  fprintf( ((MyConverterData *)info)->outStatusFile,
              "\nEnd document: %s\n",
              success ? "succeeded" : "failed");
}

static void begin_page_callback(void *info, size_t pageno,
              CFDictionaryRef page_info)
{
  fprintf( ((MyConverterData *)info)->outStatusFile,
              "\nBeginning page %zd\n", pageno);
}

static void end_page_callback(void *info, size_t pageno,
              CFDictionaryRef page_info)
{
  fprintf(((MyConverterData *)info)->outStatusFile,
              "\nEnding page %zd\n", pageno);
}

static void progress_callback(void *info)
{
  MyConverterData *converterDataP =
    (MyConverterData *)info;

  if(converterDataP->doProgress)
    fprintf(converterDataP->outStatusFile, ".");

  // Here is where you could include a call to code that would return
  // whether or not to abort the conversion process.

  //myUpdateStatus(converterDataP);

  if(converterDataP->abortConverter){
    CGPSConverterAbort(converterDataP->converter);
```

```
      fprintf(converterDataP->outStatusFile, "ABORTED!\n");
    }
}

static void message_callback(void *info, CFStringRef cfmessage)
{
  char message[256];
  if(CFStringGetCString(cfmessage, message,
                  sizeof(message), kCFStringEncodingASCII)
  ){
    fprintf(((MyConverterData *)info)->outStatusFile,
                  "\nMessage: %s\n", message);
  }
}

static const CGPSConverterCallbacks myCallbacks = {
  // Only callbacks version 0 is defined as of Tiger.
  0,
  begin_document_callback,
  end_document_callback,
  begin_page_callback,
  end_page_callback,
  progress_callback,
  message_callback,
  // There is no releaseInfo callback for this example.
  NULL
};

bool convertPStoPDF(CFURLRef inputPSURL, CFURLRef outPDFURL)
{
  CGDataProviderRef provider = NULL;
  CGDataConsumerRef consumer = NULL;
  bool success = false;
  MyConverterData myConverterData;

  provider = CGDataProviderCreateWithURL(inputPSURL);
  consumer = CGDataConsumerCreateWithURL(outPDFURL);

  if(provider == NULL || consumer == NULL)
  {
    if(provider == NULL)
      fprintf(stderr, "Couldn't create provider\n");
```

```
    if(consumer == NULL)
      fprintf(stderr, "Couldn't create consumer\n");

    CGDataProviderRelease(provider);
    CGDataConsumerRelease(consumer);
    return false;
  }

  // Set up the info data for the callbacks to
  // do progress reporting, set the initial state
  // of the abort flag to false, and use stdout
  // as the file to write status and other information.
  myConverterData.doProgress = true;
  myConverterData.abortConverter = false;
  myConverterData.outStatusFile = stdout;

  // Create a converter object with myConverterData as the
  // info parameter and myCallbacks as the set of callbacks
  // to use for the conversion. There are no converter options
  // defined as of Tiger so the options dictionary passed is NULL.
  myConverterData.converter = CGPSConverterCreate(&myConverterData,
                &myCallbacks, NULL);
  if(myConverterData.converter == NULL){
    CGDataProviderRelease(provider);
    CGDataConsumerRelease(consumer);
    fprintf(stderr, "Couldn't create converter object!\n");
    return false;
  }

  // There are no conversion options so the options
  // dictionary for the conversion is NULL.
  success = CGPSConverterConvert(myConverterData.converter,
                provider, consumer, NULL);
  if(!success)
    fprintf(stderr, "Conversion failed!\n");

  // There is no CGPSConverterRelease function. Because a
  // CGPSConverter object is a CF object, you can use CFRelease.
  CFRelease(myConverterData.converter);
  CGDataProviderRelease(provider);
  CGDataConsumerRelease(consumer);

  return success;
}
```

The routine convertPStoPDF first creates a Quartz data provider for the input URL and a data consumer for the output URL. It then sets up its options for the conversion, stored in the application-defined myConverterData structure. The code calls CGPSConverterCreate, passing a pointer to myConverterData and the myCallbacks callbacks structure that contains the six callbacks defined previously.

The code in Listing 16.1 allocates the myConverterData structure on the stack because it creates, uses, and releases the CGPSConverter object all in one routine. If you need to create a CGPSConverter object that lives beyond your creation routine, allocate your info data using malloc and supply a releaseInfo callback to free the memory and resources associated with the info data.

Important A process in Mac OS X can only perform one conversion at a time. Attempts to perform a second conversion while one is in progress (from a different thread, for example) blocks until the first conversion is complete.

After the code creates the CGPSConverter object, it performs the conversion by calling CGPSConverterConvert, passing the data provider and data consumer. This causes the conversion process to start. During the conversion process Quartz invokes the callback functions associated with the CGPSConverter object when it's appropriate to do so.

The CGPSConverterConvert function does not return until one of three things occurs:

1. The PostScript or EPS input data is exhausted and the conversion process finishes without error.

2. A PostScript error or other error occurs and the conversion process terminates without success.

3. You call CGPSConverterAbort, passing the converter object. Typically, you would do this in your CGPSConverterProgressCallback callback function, indicating that the conversion process should be stopped prematurely. Under most circumstances you would abort the conversion process based on user input, that is, when the user explicitly cancels the conversion.

After the function CGPSConverterConvert returns, the conversion process is complete and the bool result that is returned indicates whether the conversion completed successfully.

The code in the listing releases the CGPSConverter object after it has performed its conversion. Quartz has no release function specific to a CGPSConverter object. But because a CGPSConverter object is a Core Foundation object, you release it with the function CFRelease.

Note   It's possible for the conversion process to report success even though there is no PDF data produced. This can happen when the PostScript input data executes successfully but doesn't produce any pages. For example, a PostScript document (other than an EPS file) that does not use the showpage operator will not produce PDF data.

Using Converted PostScript Data in Your Application

Now that you've seen how to perform conversion of PostScript data into a PDF data file, you're ready to use the PDF data in your application. The lifetime of the converted PostScript data can be permanent or transient. If you plan to reuse the PDF data over time, you may want to store it on disk in a file. If you just need the PDF data for a short time, such as to show the data in a PDF viewer, you might want to create a CGPDFDocument object from temporary storage of the PDF data.

The process of drawing PostScript or EPS data using Quartz involves three steps (Figure 16.1):

1. Create a PDF document from PostScript or EPS data, storing the result in a temporary PDF file on disk. This is exactly what the code in Listing 16.1 does.

2. Create a direct access data provider from the temporary PDF document on disk. You use a custom data provider that accesses the underlying temporary PDF file. The code that creates the custom data provider unlinks the file as part of its creation so that the file is deleted when the data provider closes the file.

3. Create a CGPDFDocument object from the data provider. When the CGPDF-Document object is released, the data provider is released and the temporary PDF file is closed.

Figure 16.1 Creating a CGPDFDocument object from PostScript data

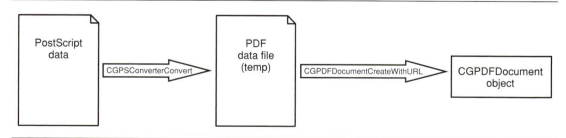

After you have a CGPDFDocument object, you can draw the document or use any of the Quartz PDF document functions to obtain information about the document, such as the number of pages or the bounding boxes of a given page.

Listing 16.2 contains code that creates a CGPDFDocumentRef from a CFURL object that references PostScript or EPS data. The listing contains five routines:

- The createTempFileURL routine uses the UNIX routine tmpnam to obtain the file name to use for the temporary file. You might have another more secure method for naming temporary files; this code is relatively simple. The routine is called by the createCGPDFDocFromPSDoc routine.

- The routine getBytesDirectAccessDP seeks to the offset position in the file and reads the requested number of bytes. This is supplied in the getBytes field of the callbacks structure that is supplied to Quartz when the createTempFile-DirectAccessDP routine sets up the direct access data provider.

- The releaseInfoDP routine closes the temporary file, which in effect deletes the file because the file is unlinked after it is opened. This routine is supplied in the releaseProvider field of the callbacks structure that is supplied to Quartz when the createTempFileDirectAccessDP routine sets up the direct access data provider.

- The createTempFileDirectAccessDP routine gets the pathname of the URL for the temporary file and opens the file for reading. This is called by the create-CGPDFDocFromPSDoc routine. This routine is described in more detail following Listing 16.2.

- The createCGPDFDocFromPSDoc routine, which is the top-level routine, takes a CFURLRef for a PostScript file and returns a CGPDFDocumentRef that you can use to draw the PDF document. This routine is described in more detail following Listing 16.2.

Listing 16.2 Code that creates a CGPDFDocument object from PostScript data

```
static CFURLRef createTempFileURL(void)
{
  char tmpfilepath[PATH_MAX + 1];
  char *filename;
  filename = tmpnam(tmpfilepath);
  // Create the URL from the temp file path.
  return CFURLCreateFromFileSystemRepresentation(NULL,
            filename, strlen(filename), false);
}
```

```
static size_t getBytesDirectAccessDP(void *info, void *buffer,
                size_t offset, size_t count)
{
  FILE *fp = (FILE *)info;
  // Seek to the offset of the bytes requested.
  int result = fseek(fp, offset, SEEK_SET);
  if(result != 0){
    fprintf(stderr,
      "Couldn't seek to offset %zd because of: %s!\n",
      offset, strerror(errno));
    return 0;
  }
  // Reads 'count' 1-byte objects and returns the number of
  // objects (bytes) read.
  return fread(buffer, 1, count, fp);
}

static void releaseInfoDP(void *info)
{
  fclose( (FILE *)info);
}

CGDataProviderRef createTempFileDirectAccessDP(CFURLRef tempURL)
{
  CGDataProviderRef provider = NULL;
  struct stat sb;
  size_t fileSize;
  char path[PATH_MAX + 1];
  FILE *fp;

  // Get the pathname of the URL for the temporary file.
  if(!CFURLGetFileSystemRepresentation(tempURL, true, path,
                sizeof(path))){
    fprintf(stderr, "Couldn't get the path for tempURL!\n");
    return NULL;
  }

  // Stat the file to obtain its size.
  if(stat(path, &sb) != 0){
    fprintf(stderr, "Couldn't stat the file %s!\n", path);
    return NULL;
  }
```

```
      fileSize = sb.st_size;

      // Open the file to provide read-access for the data provider.
      fp = fopen(path, "r");
      if(fp == NULL){
        fprintf(stderr, "Can't open the file!\n");
        return NULL;
      }

      if(unlink(path) != 0){
        // Unlink failed!
        fprintf(stderr, "Couldn't unlink the file!\n");
        fclose(fp);
        return NULL;
      }

      // Set up the callbacks for the direct access data provider.
      CGDataProviderDirectAccessCallbacks callbacks;
      callbacks.getBytes = getBytesDirectAccessDP;
      callbacks.releaseProvider = releaseInfoDP;
      callbacks.getBytePointer = NULL;
      callbacks.releaseBytePointer = NULL;

      // Pass the file pointer as the info parameter.
      provider = CGDataProviderCreateDirectAccess(fp, fileSize,
                    &callbacks);
      if(provider == NULL){
        fprintf(stderr, "Couldn't create data provider!\n");
      }
      return provider;
}

CGPDFDocumentRef createCGPDFDocFromPSDoc(CFURLRef inputPSURL)
{
    CGDataProviderRef provider;
    CGPDFDocumentRef pdfDoc = NULL;
    CFURLRef tempPDFURLRef = NULL;
    bool conversionResult;

    // Create a URL to use for the temporary
    // PDF file on disk.
    tempPDFURLRef = createTempFileURL();
    if(tempPDFURLRef == NULL){
```

```
      fprintf(stderr, "Couldn't create temporary file URL!\n");
      return NULL;
  }

  // ***** Step 1 *****
  conversionResult = convertPStoPDF(inputPSURL, tempPDFURLRef);
  // Test whether the conversion succeeded.
  if(!conversionResult){
    fprintf(stderr, "Conversion to a PDF document failed!\n");
    CFRelease(tempPDFURLRef);
    return NULL;
  }

  // ***** Step 2 *****
  provider = createTempFileDirectAccessDP(tempPDFURLRef);
  // This code is done with the temporary URL object. The
  // data provider still has access to the underlying file.
  CFRelease(tempPDFURLRef);
  if(provider == NULL){
    return NULL;
  }

  // ***** Step 3 *****
  pdfDoc = CGPDFDocumentCreateWithProvider(provider);
  // Release the data provider; this code no longer needs it.
  CGDataProviderRelease(provider);
  if(pdfDoc == NULL){
    fprintf(stderr, "Couldn't create PDFDocument reference!\n");
    return NULL;
  }
  return pdfDoc;
}
```

The createCGPDFDocFromPSDoc routine begins by calling the routine createTemp-FileURL to create a URL that represents a temporary file on disk. This URL is used as the destination URL for the PDF data produced by the conversion process. Next the routine (see Step 1) calls convertPStoPDF (from Listing 16.1 (page 570)) to convert the PostScript data to a temporary PDF document. If the conversion succeeds, the code (see Step 2) calls createTempFileDirectAccessDP to create a direct access data provider that supplies the data from the temporary PDF document.

The routine createTempFileDirectAccessDP in Listing 16.2 is a special-purpose, direct access data provider created specifically for the purpose of accessing the temporary PDF file produced by the conversion process. In principle, the Quartz function `CGDataProviderCreateWithURL` could be used to create a data provider to access the temporary PDF data. However, using `CGDataProvider-CreateWithURL` would not provide a way for the code to know when the temporary PDF file was no longer needed, that is, when the CGPDFDocument object using the file no longer requires the temporary file and the file can be deleted. Instead, the code uses a custom data provider so it can know when the data provider is released and the underlying temporary file data is no longer needed.

Because the underlying data is PDF data, a direct access data provider is the best choice. Quartz typically accesses PDF data in a nonsequential fashion, meaning that a sequential access data provider would be less efficient than a direct access data provider.

The `createTempFileDirectAccessDP` routine first obtains the path corresponding to the supplied `CFURLRef` so it can use UNIX file system routines to access the data. It determines the file size to pass to `CGDataProviderCreateDirectAccess`. It opens the file so that the `getBytes` routine of its data provider callbacks can access the data. After the file is opened, the code uses the UNIX function `unlink` so that the file is not accessible via the file system to any other process. When a file is unlinked, closing the file deletes the file; by unlinking the file, the code only has to close it to delete the temporary file.

After the temporary file is opened and unlinked, the code fills in the `CGDataPro-viderDirectAccessCallbacks` structure so that the `getBytesDirectAccessDP` routine is called to obtain the data for the data provider and `releaseInfoDP` is called when Quartz releases the data provider. The code calls `CGDataProviderCreate-DirectAccess` using the file pointer to the open file as the `info` parameter and the file size as the `size` parameter, then supplies the needed callbacks.

Now look at Step 3 in the `createCGPDFDocFromPSDoc` routine. This portion of the routine creates a `CGPDFDocumentRef` that corresponds to the converted data and is the object that the `createCGPDFDocFromPSDoc` routine returns. If any step of the process fails, including the conversion of the PostScript input data to PDF, `createCGPDFDocFromPSDoc` returns NULL.

PSConverter Advanced Issues

Most developers using the PSConverter routines don't need to know the details about how Quartz converts PostScript data into PDF data and can skip this section. For those developers who are PostScript savvy or who want to understand the characteristics of the conversion process in more detail, this section provides more information about the PostScript conversion process.

One important aspect of converting PostScript to PDF data is the handling of font data. Font data that is contained in the PostScript data stream and is used for drawing by the PostScript data is converted into a font subset and embedded into the output PDF data. (The exception to the automatic embedding of font data contained in the input PostScript stream is with font data that indicates it cannot be embedded; this applies only to special copy-protected fonts and is not typical.)

Fonts that are referenced in the PostScript data but are not available as font programs in the PostScript stream are treated specially. If the referenced font is available as a font to the user in the usual location where fonts are installed, including the user's ~/Library/Fonts folder and Classic System Fonts folder, then that font information and metric data are used during the creation of the PDF document, but the font outline data is not embedded into the PDF document produced during the conversion. This allows the document to draw correctly on a system that has the font and allows for font substitution on those systems that do not have the font.

If a referenced font is not available to the user, as a last resort, the conversion process consults a built-in font metrics database for information about the font. If there is information about that font in the metrics database, that information will be used in the creation of the converted PDF document. Only metric data is included since no glyph data is available.

When converting an EPS file, the resulting PDF output file has a media box that reflects the %%BoundingBox comment obtained from the EPS file. Note that the %%BoundingBox: (atend) comment convention is not supported; the %%Bounding-Box comment in the PostScript header comments must contain the bounding box data for the file or the resulting PDF media box will not reflect the bounding box of the EPS document.

There are features that some PostScript-to-PDF conversion tools, such as Adobe Distiller, support that aren't supported by Quartz in Panther or Tiger. Keep in mind the following:

- When Quartz converts PostScript to PDF, it handles Open Prepress Interface (OPI) images by ignoring any OPI comments and instead embeds the "low resolution" image that is contained in the PostScript data stream.

- Quartz preserves PostScript halftone and transfer functions when it creates the PDF output data, but it ignores this data when drawing a PDF document or creating PostScript output from a PDF document that contains PostScript halftone and transfer functions.

The PostScript interpreter that converts PostScript or EPS data can be memory- and time-intensive. The first conversion performed by a given UNIX process requires the PostScript interpreter to be initialized and requires a significant amount of memory to be allocated for the process. This initialization process needs a nonnegligible amount of time. Subsequent conversions by the same UNIX process (even using different CGPSConverter objects) don't require this initialization, so the conversion time then depends solely on the complexity of the PostScript data that you convert. Note that quitting and relaunching an application produces a new UNIX process that again incurs the startup cost associated should you want to perform a conversion.

The first conversion that each user performs on a given system also incurs a one-time font caching startup cost. Quartz needs to scan the system and user fonts to assess which fonts are available for use during the conversion process. Font scanning takes place only once for a given user because Quartz caches the data for that user.

Printing Source EPS Data

For situations where the CGPSConverter functions aren't available or if you prefer to take a different approach, you can print EPS data when printing to PostScript printers by using a printing framework routine that is specific to this task. The function PMCGImageCreateWithEPSDataProvider creates a CGImageRef that has an EPS preview image that is associated with the EPS data and that produces high-quality results when you print the image to a PostScript printer. (Typically, you construct the EPS preview image from a TIFF or PICT preview supplied as part of the EPS file.) This routine is available in all versions of Mac OS X and may be useful to your application, depending on your needs.

The function PMCGImageCreateWithEPSDataProvider is part of the Print Core framework, which is available along with the Core Graphics framework as part of the Application Services umbrella framework. The function PMCGImageCreate-WithEPSDataProvider takes the following parameters:

- epsDataProvider, a CGDataProvider object that supplies EPS data.

- epsPreview, a CGImage object that is the proxy preview image for the EPS data.

When successful, the function returns a CGImageRef that represents the EPS data. This CGImage object, when drawn to a bit-based context, behaves exactly like the epsPreview image used to create it. When drawn to a PDF or printing context, the image data is recorded in the PDF document. The EPS data is also recorded in the PDF document and is associated with the preview image. When the resulting PDF document is printed to a PostScript printer, the EPS data is sent to the printer instead of the preview image. When the resulting PDF document is printed to a raster printer or drawn to a bit-based context, such as a window, Quartz draws the preview image. Typically, you obtain the best results with `PMCGImageCreateWithEPSDataProvider` when you print to a PostScript printer.

Listing 16.3 demonstrates how to use `PMCGImageCreateWithEPSDataProvider` to create a CGImage object that represents a preview image and EPS data. The listing contains four routines:

- The routine `getEPSBBox` parses the PostScript Document Structuring Conventions (DSC) comments in the EPS data for the value of the `%%BoundingBox` comment, which is needed by the `createEPSPreviewImage` routine. The version of this routine supplied in the listing isn't production-quality code and is provided here for completeness only. The implementation is incomplete, is quite inefficient, and doesn't handle DSC comments correctly. For example, it doesn't ensure that the DSC comments are at the beginning of a line, nor does it handle (atend) style comments at all. The routine simply finds the first occurrence of a `%%BoundingBox` comment, and if it is of the typical form, it obtains the bounding box data. You should instead use the code you already have for DSC parsing instead of this code.

- The routine `createEPSPreviewImage` creates a preview image, which is needed by the `createCGEPSImage` routine. It uses the routines `createRGBBitmapContext` from "Creating a Bitmap Graphics Context" (page 349) and `createImageFromBitmapContext` from "Creating an Image from a Bitmap Context (pre-Tiger)" (page 358). The preview image needs to have the same width and height as the associated EPS data. This routine doesn't attempt to use any preview image associated with the EPS file but instead draws a box of an appropriate size. The routine you write would most likely create an image that reflects a PICT or TIFF preview present in the EPS data.

- The routine `createCGEPSImage` creates a data provider that provides the EPS data and calls the function `PMCGImageCreateWithEPSDataProvider` to create a hybrid CGImage that contains the preview image and the EPS data. The hybrid image is used by the `drawEPSDataImage` routine. This technique of handling EPS data is available starting in Puma. It is an alternative to converting EPS data to PDF data using CGPSConverter, which is available starting in Panther.

- The routine `drawEPSDataImage` creates a CGImage that has data associated with it, and then draws the image two times, first scaled, and then translated, rotated, and scaled. The routine `drawEPSDataImage` draws the CGImage just like any other CGImage object. Viewing the drawing onscreen or viewing a PDF file produced from this drawing displays the preview image. When you print the drawing to a PostScript printer either directly or by using Quartz to print a PDF document produced from this drawing, the EPS data, rather than the preview image, is sent to the printer.

Listing 16.3 Code that uses PMCGImageCreateWithEPSDataProvider to draw EPS data to a Quartz context

```
static CGRect getEPSBBox(char *epspath)
{
  CGRect bbox = CGRectZero;
  FILE *fp = fopen(epspath, "r");
  if(fp){
    int llx, lly, urx, ury, numScanned = 0;
    char ch;
    while(!feof(fp)){
      numScanned = fscanf(fp,
        "%%%%BoundingBox: %d %d %d %d",
        &llx, &lly, &urx, &ury);
      if(numScanned == 4){
        bbox.origin.x = llx;
        bbox.origin.y = lly;
        bbox.size.width = urx - llx;
        bbox.size.height = ury - lly;
        break;
      }
      // Haven't found the BoundingBox comment yet so read a
      // character, advance the position, and scan again.
      if(fread(&ch, 1, 1, fp) != 1)
        break;
    }
    fclose(fp);
  }
  return bbox;
}

static CGImageRef createEPSPreviewImage(CFURLRef url)
{
  char path[PATH_MAX+1];
  if(!CFURLGetFileSystemRepresentation(url, true,
                path, sizeof(path))){
    fprintf(stderr, "Couldn't get the path for EPS file!\n");
    return NULL;
  }

  CGRect epsRect = getEPSBBox(path);
  // Check whether the EPS bounding box is empty.
  if( CGRectEqualToRect(epsRect, CGRectZero) ){
    fprintf(stderr, "Couldn't find BoundingBox comment!\n");
    return NULL;
```

```
}
Boolean wantDisplayColorSpace = false;
Boolean needsTransparentBitmap = true;
// Create a bitmap context to create the preview image. Use the
// routine createRGBBitmapContext from "Creating Bits" (Chapter 12).
CGContextRef bitmapContext = createRGBBitmapContext(
                epsRect.size.width,
                epsRect.size.height,
                wantDisplayColorSpace,
                needsTransparentBitmap);
if(bitmapContext == NULL){
  fprintf(stderr, "Couldn't create bitmap context\n");
  return NULL;
}

epsRect.origin.x = epsRect.origin.y = 0;
// Draw the contents of the preview. The preview consists
// of two diagonal lines and a stroke around the bounding box.
CGContextBeginPath(bitmapContext);
CGContextMoveToPoint(bitmapContext, 0, 0);
CGContextAddLineToPoint(bitmapContext, epsRect.size.width,
                epsRect.size.height);
CGContextMoveToPoint(bitmapContext, epsRect.size.width, 0);
CGContextAddLineToPoint(bitmapContext, 0,
                epsRect.size.height);
CGContextStrokePath(bitmapContext);
// Stroke the bounding rectangle; inset so that the stroke is
// completely contained in the EPS bounding rect.
CGContextStrokeRect(bitmapContext,
                CGRectInset(epsRect, 0.5, 0.5));

// Create an image from the bitmap raster data.
// Use the createImageFromBitmapContext
// from "Creating Bits" (Chapter 12). Calling
// createImageFromBitmapContext gives up ownership
// of the raster data used by the context.
CGImageRef epsPreviewImage =
                createImageFromBitmapContext(bitmapContext);
// Release the bitmap context.
CGContextRelease(bitmapContext);
if(epsPreviewImage == NULL){
  fprintf(stderr, "Couldn't create preview image!\n");
  return NULL;
}
```

```
    return epsPreviewImage;
  }

  static CGImageRef createCGEPSImage(CFURLRef url)
  {
    CGImageRef previewImage = NULL;
    CGImageRef epsImage = NULL;
    CGDataProviderRef epsDataProvider = NULL;

    previewImage = createEPSPreviewImage(url);
    if(previewImage == NULL){
      fprintf(stderr, "Couldn't create EPS preview!\n");
      return NULL;
    }

    // The data provider supplying the EPS data must conform
    // to the Quartz guidelines and must be able to provide the data
    // until the data release function is called.
    epsDataProvider = CGDataProviderCreateWithURL(url);
    if(epsDataProvider == NULL){
      CGImageRelease(previewImage);
      fprintf(stderr, "Couldn't create EPS data provider!\n");
      return NULL;
    }

    // Create the hybrid CGImage that contains the preview image
    // and the EPS data. Note that the data provider isn't
    // called during image creation but at some later point in time.
    epsImage = PMCGImageCreateWithEPSDataProvider(epsDataProvider,
                    previewImage);
    // The preview image and data provider are no longer needed
    // because Quartz retains them and this code doesn't
    // require them further.
    CGImageRelease(previewImage);
    CGDataProviderRelease(epsDataProvider);

    if(epsImage == NULL){
      fprintf(stderr, "Couldn't create EPS hybrid image!\n");
      return NULL;
    }
    return epsImage;
  }
```

```
void drawEPSDataImage(CGContextRef context, CFURLRef url)
{
  // Create a CGImage that has EPS data associated with it.
  CGImageRef epsDataImage = createCGEPSImage(url);
  if(epsDataImage == NULL){
    return;
  }
  // Make a destination rectangle at the location
  // to draw the EPS document where the size is scaled
  // down to 1/2 the size of the EPS data.
  CGRect destinationRect = CGRectMake(100, 100,
                CGImageGetWidth(epsDataImage)/2,
                CGImageGetHeight(epsDataImage)/2);
  // Draw the image to the destination. When the EPS
  // data associated with the image is sent to a PostScript
  // printer, the EPS bounding box is mapped to this
  // destination rectangle, translated and scaled as necessary.
  CGContextDrawImage(context, destinationRect, epsDataImage);

  // Draw the image a second time. This time the image is
  // rotated by 45 degrees and scaled by an additional scaling factor of
  // 0.5 in the x dimension. The center point of this image coincides
  // with the center point of the earlier drawing.
  CGContextTranslateCTM(context,
    destinationRect.origin.x + destinationRect.size.width/2,
    destinationRect.origin.y + destinationRect.size.height/2);
  CGContextRotateCTM(context, DEGREES_TO_RADIANS(45));
  CGContextScaleCTM(context, 0.5, 1);
  CGContextTranslateCTM(context,
    -(destinationRect.origin.x + destinationRect.size.width/2),
    -(destinationRect.origin.y + destinationRect.size.height/2) );
  CGContextDrawImage(context, destinationRect, epsDataImage);

  // Release the image when done.
  CGImageRelease(epsDataImage);
}
```

Figure 16.2 is a screen shot of the onscreen results of the code in Listing 16.3 with a sample EPS file. Figure 16.3 is the result of the same code and sample EPS file sent to a PostScript printer. The screen preview generated by this example is appropriate only for an EPS file that has no available preview. For EPS files that have a PICT or TIFF preview, you should use that preview data to produce better results when viewing onscreen and with raster printing.

Figure 16.2 The EPS preview from Listing 16.3

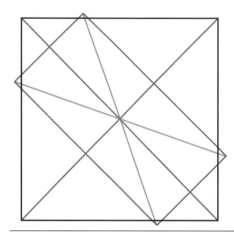

Figure 16.3 The EPS data printed to a PostScript printer

Associating the EPS data with the preview image in a Quartz-produced PDF document is a Quartz-defined extension of the PDF specification. Printing such PDF documents to a PostScript printer using Quartz drawing adds the EPS data to the PostScript stream instead of the preview image. Third-party tools that process PDF documents without using Quartz, such as Adobe Acrobat and some other PDF processing tools, ignore the EPS data associated with the image. Such tools instead produce the preview image rather than the EPS data, even when printing to PostScript printers.

Quartz performs minimal processing of the EPS data as it produces a PostScript data stream for printing. The EPS bounding box data is used to translate and scale the coordinate system prior to streaming the EPS data so that the EPS bounding rectangle is mapped into and clipped to the preview image destination rectangle. No further processing of the EPS data is done. If a given font required by the EPS data is not part of the data stream or available in the printer, the document will likely print with Courier font substitution. Because the EPS data itself is untouched by Quartz, DSC comments and other comments such as OPI comments present in the EPS data are transmitted in the output PostScript data stream Quartz produces when printing to a PostScript printer.

Note The function `PMCGImageCreateWithEPSDataProvider` currently does not utilize the PSConverter capabilities. On Panther and Tiger systems, use of this function behaves as it does on previous systems that do not provide PostScript-to-PDF conversion.

Guidelines for Supporting EPS Data in Your Application

Many users and applications have legacy EPS data they need to support while still using Quartz drawing for the bulk of their drawing needs. There are two distinct approaches available, each described in this chapter. Which approach is appropriate for your application may depend on your needs.

As a general rule, Apple recommends using the functionality of the CGPSConverter available starting in Panther to convert EPS data into a single-page PDF graphic that you can use just as you would any other PDF graphic with Quartz. This approach has the advantage of reproducing the EPS data at full quality for viewing onscreen as well as printing on both PostScript and raster printers. It allows the usage of available installed host fonts when converting the EPS data and printing it. PDF files produced by Quartz that incorporate graphics obtained by converting EPS to PDF data can be viewed and printed at full resolution by Adobe Acrobat and other third-party PDF viewing tools.

There are some drawbacks to using EPS-to-PDF conversion for EPS support. The primary drawback is that this capability is only available on computers that run Panther and later versions. In addition there is a nonnegligible performance overhead when converting EPS to PDF data. One approach to minimizing this overhead is to convert the data as part of your document import of EPS data. This means that the conversion happens only once rather than repeatedly during document processing.

One aspect of EPS-to-PDF conversion that should be considered is the fact that OPI, custom halftone, and other specialized features of PostScript data are not preserved when printing documents converted from EPS to PDF and then sent to PostScript printers. In addition, printing with this method does not currently take advantage of printer-resident fonts. These aspects of EPS data are preserved when using `PMCGImageCreateWithEPSDataProvider` because PostScript printing causes Quartz to simply transmit the EPS data to the printer, allowing any PostScript features present in the EPS data to be executed in the printer or processed by an OPI server, if appropriate. However, the PDF files produced when using `PMCGImageCreateWithEPSDataProvider` do not utilize the EPS data when used by third-party PDF viewers that do not utilize Quartz; they only render the preview image, even when printing to PostScript printers.

There is one additional advantage to converting EPS data to PDF data as part of your document handling. The printing system and other Mac OS X functionality such as the Apple ColorSync Utility provide the ability to use Quartz filters to process PDF files and provide print-time features. These filters cannot operate on EPS data that may be embedded in PDF documents and as such do not apply their effects on EPS data generated using `PMCGImageCreateWithEPSDataProvider`. If you instead convert EPS data to PDF data and draw the resulting PDF graphic with Quartz as part of your PDF creation and printing, Quartz filters can operate on the converted graphic just as they can any other Quartz content.

Summary

Starting in Panther, Quartz provides the ability to convert PostScript and EPS data into PDF data. The conversion process is virtually lossless, resulting in high-quality content. The Quartz functions `CGPSConverterCreate` and `CGPSConverterConvert` perform the conversion using a PostScript interpreter that, although it incurs some startup costs, processes data similarly to other third-party tools. After the data is converted to PDF, you can use it within your application, just as you would any other PDF document.

For working with EPS data prior to Panther, the printing framework provides the ability to print EPS data to PostScript printers using the function `PMCGImageCreateWithEPSDataProvider`. By creating a CGImage object that has EPS data associated with it, you can print EPS data to PostScript printers and use a preview image for printing to raster printers.

See Also

For more information on PostScript and EPS data, see the document

- *Encapsulated PostScript File Format Specification*, which defines the EPS format, including the description of the PC EPS data format:

  http://partners.adobe.com/public/developer/en/ps/5002.EPSF_Spec.pdf

The header files relevant to supporting PostScript and EPS data are

- `CGPSConverter.h`, which contains the functions and definitions needed for using the CGPSConverter routines.

- `PMCore.h`, which contains the `PMCGImageCreateWithEPSDataProvider` function, which is part of the Print Core framework. This header file is located in

  ```
  /System/Library/Frameworks/ApplicationServices.framework/Frameworks/
  PrintCore.framework/Headers/PMCore.h
  ```

The relevant Quartz reference documentation from the ADC Reference Library is

- *CGPSConverter Reference*

The printing system supports the generation of PostScript output from Quartz drawing that you perform during printing. *Carbon Printing Manager Reference* from the ADC Reference Library describes the functions used to set the destination location and output format of a print job, as well as how to execute a print job without any status narration dialogs:

  *http://developer.apple.com/documentation/Carbon/Reference/
  CarbonPrintingManager_Ref/*

The NSView class provides the `dataWithEPSInsideRect:` method, which creates EPS data from the drawing performed by a view. The ADC Reference Library documentation for the NSView class is available at

  *http://developer.apple.com/documentation/Cocoa/Reference/ApplicationKit/
  ObjC_classic/Classes/NSView.html*

Chapter 17

Performance and Debugging

The purpose of this chapter is to help you understand and address many of the issues that affect the graphics performance of your applications. It also provides tips on how to debug your drawing when things aren't working as you expect.

Performance is a dynamic topic. Many of the areas discussed in this chapter evolve and change with each major release of Mac OS X. To understand performance, simply reading this chapter isn't enough. You need to keep up to date with information as it becomes available from Apple. The Apple Developer Connection website and the references at the end of this chapter will help you get the latest information about how to improve not only graphics performance but overall application performance as well.

Optimizing Performance

There are many aspects to achieving excellent performance with drawing code, some of which are related to the system and some of which are under your control. The Quartz Compositor, Quartz object and memory management, and performance measurement are all key to understanding graphics performance.

The Quartz Compositor (which is part of the Mac OS X windowing system) determines how drawing appears in windows on the display. As you've seen, creating and managing Quartz objects is a key aspect of Quartz programming. By understanding the Quartz memory management and object model, you can benefit from any caching of those objects Quartz performs and avoid creating memory leaks or other memory problems. Performance measurement helps you to better understand how your code works and to identify places where the code could be optimized. Apple provides tools that can help, including the Quartz Debug application—a tool that is specifically for analyzing graphics code.

The Quartz Compositor

Quartz consists of several distinct portions, including the Quartz Compositor and the Quartz 2D drawing library. So far you've read a lot about Quartz 2D and not much about the role that the Quartz Compositor plays when drawing graphics. Because the Quartz Compositor plays an important role in window management and getting the graphics you draw onto the display, it is important to understand how it works.

The Quartz Compositor provides the windowing system services that the application frameworks use to supply the onscreen windows your application draws into. Every window has its own **backing store**, a piece of memory into which all drawing to that window is rendered. When your application draws into a given window, even one that is visible on the display, that drawing is not done directly to the display but rather to the backing store offscreen memory. The Quartz Compositor is responsible for moving (or **flushing**) the contents of the backing store into the display frame buffer at an "appropriate time."

The Quartz Compositor composites (or alpha blends) the contents of the backing store to the screen, mixing the contents of each window depending on its opacity. Hence, the name Compositor. In a sense, the Quartz Compositor is a "video mixer," where each pixel on the display has a potential contribution from more than one window—no one window owns a given display pixel. The Exposé feature—where with one keystroke, each onscreen window temporarily appears in miniature form—is also made possible by the windowing system architecture provided by the Quartz Compositor.

The Quartz Compositor does not provide rendering services beyond the compositing of the windows it performs. Instead, you draw using the drawing capabilities provided by the high-level drawing libraries such as Quartz 2D, QuickTime, and OpenGL. Figure 17.1 illustrates the relationship between the drawing libraries and the Quartz Compositor. On systems that have the necessary supporting hardware, the Quartz Compositor makes use of Quartz Extreme, a built-in acceleration layer that significantly improves the performance of the compositing operations it performs by using the capabilities of the graphics card driving a given display.

Providing a backing store for each onscreen window has additional benefits beyond the ability to composite windows together. When windows are resized or moved, other windows become exposed and their newly exposed content needs

Figure 17.1 Graphics system architecture and the Quartz Compositor

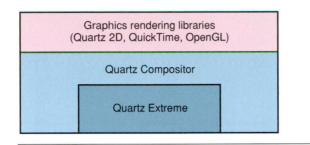

to be drawn. With most other operating systems, this usually involves sending events to applications to redraw the newly exposed content, that is, to repair the damaged area. In Mac OS X, the newly exposed content is already available from each window backing store. Each window backing store contains the full content, unobscured by the way onscreen windows overlap or intersect.

Figure 17.2 shows the relationship between the window backing stores and the screen display. In the figure, the Finder is the only visible application and it has three windows associated with its content. Each window has a backing store that contains the contents of the onscreen window. When you click one window to bring it above another, the Quartz Compositor uses the window backing stores to refresh the display, rather than generating an event that causes a redraw event to be sent to the application.

The Quartz Compositor times its flushing of the window backing store to the display so that it is synchronized with the display beam sweep, avoiding tearing and other artifacts that occur when this synchronization is not performed. On other systems, an application has to perform this kind of careful handling to produce visually smooth results; in Mac OS X, the Quartz Compositor handles this for you.

How Quartz Compositor buffers and flushes windows has implications for the performance of your drawing, as you'll see in the next two sections.

Window Buffering. If you've used graphics drawing programs or have been programming graphics for a number of years, you're probably familiar with the notion of "rubber banding" objects while resizing them. This refers to the animation of a graphical object to produce the effect of interactively changing the size of the object in response to mouse movement. Many developers have historically used an XOR drawing mode to erase previous content prior to drawing new content during graphics resizing. Quartz doesn't have an XOR drawing mode available, but there are two strategies that developers typically use instead of XOR.

Figure 17.2 Every window has a backing store

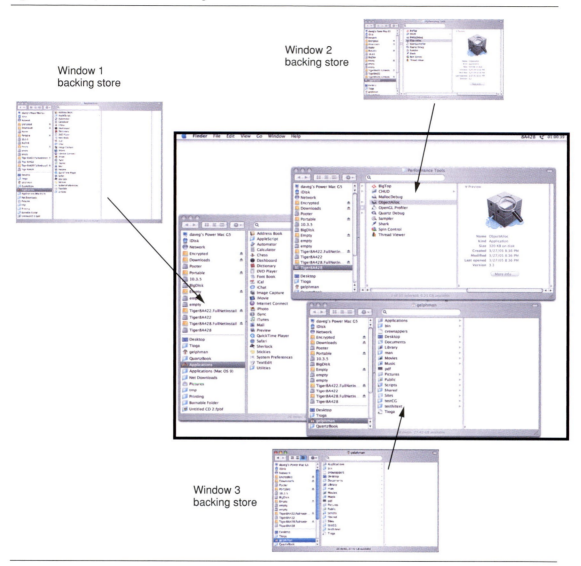

One alternative strategy is to use two buffers for the drawing content along with techniques that allow for straightforward smooth graphics animation. This strategy is referred to as double buffering. Developers who use double buffering in Mac OS X need to take into account that the Quartz Compositor buffers the window contents. This is useful because it allows the application to potentially use the window backing store buffer as one of its buffers when double buffering, allowing the Quartz Compositor to do the final rendering from the backing store buffer to the display. However, applications that utilize double buffering need to be careful to avoid unintentionally *triple* buffering their content. This can happen when porting code from other platforms (or perhaps code written for Mac OS prior to Mac OS X). Instead, use the window backing store buffer as one of your buffers and avoid triple buffering.

An alternative technique to use for the "rubber banding" kind of animation is to take advantage of alpha compositing and the fact that the Mac OS X window system is a compositing window system. Rather than double buffering your content, you can instead use overlay windows, sometimes called transparent windows. By drawing the content you want to animate into a window that is partially transparent and that can be moved, a single graphic element can be drawn, erased, and redrawn, all without adversely affecting content in windows underneath the overlay window.

Cocoa windows have an attibute that determines whether they are opaque or partially transparent. Carbon provides the window class kOverlayWindowClass for creating an overlay window. The references at the end of this chapter point to sample code for Cocoa and Carbon applications that take advantage of this overlay technique.

Window Flushing. The term **flushing** refers to the process of copying the window backing store buffer to the display. As part of your application run loop, the application frameworks together with the Quartz Compositor automatically perform the flushing that is needed by most applications. Your code draws to the window and it appears on the screen, without any additional work on your part. Virtually all the code in this book draws without explicitly flushing the window backing store to the screen; typically, you don't need to. Even the Carbon sample application CarbonSketch uses an overlay window to perform graphics animation and it works just fine without performing an explicit flushing operation.

However, there may be situations where you need to explicitly flush the window backing store to the display. For lengthy drawing operations, you may want to provide incremental display of the drawing. Some types of animation may require you to flush so that the animation appears in a timely way. Without performing flushing, the graphics you draw appear, but not when you expect. For these situations, Quartz provides the function CGContextFlush. (Cocoa provides several instance methods in the class NSWindow that flush window contents. Carbon provides the function HIWindowFlush for use with an HIWindowRef.) Using these functions tells the Quartz Compositor to schedule the window for flushing at the next available update interval. As of Tiger, the only context where CGContextFlush has any effect is a window context.

Explicit flushing can adversely impact the performance of your application in unexpected ways. Because flushing causes the bits from the backing store to be copied to the display frame buffer, by flushing you are requesting an operation that may not need to be performed at that time. Because there is an inherent performance overhead associated with flushing, you always want to perform as much drawing as possible before you explicitly flush so that you flush as much as possible.

Explicit flushing has another side effect that can affect code performance. The Quartz routine CGContextFlush (and the equivalent routines provided by the application frameworks) sends a message to the Quartz Compositor that it should flush the backing store at the next available screen update interval. When you call CGContextFlush, it returns immediately and the backing store flush is performed by the Quartz Compositor at its next screen update. However, Quartz blocks any further attempts to draw to the window backing store until the Quartz Compositor finishes performing the actual compositing of the backing store contents. You can't change the bits in a window backing store while a flush of that backing store is pending. Calling CGContextFlush directly can limit your drawing performance because you are blocked from further drawing until the actual flushing is complete.

For this reason you should be careful not to flush more frequently than the windowing system actually performs its updates, otherwise you are blocking unnecessarily. There is no need to flush faster than the rate at which the Quartz Compositor performs its compositing from the backing store, since the update doesn't actually happen until the next display refresh and flushing blocks additional drawing to the context. The Quartz Compositor flushing occurs at the refresh rate of the hardware; for hardware such as an LCD monitor that has no native beam sync, 60 Hz is used.

Generally, there is no need to call CGContextFlush more frequently than every 1/30 of a second since most users can't perceive updates faster than 30 frames a second. Flushing more frequently than every 1/60 of a second is counterproductive. Not only is this beyond human perception, you don't achieve a faster frame rate and more likely slow down your performance because much of the time you are blocking, waiting for the Quartz Compositor flush to occur.

This kind of behavior shows up in Shark or Sampler profiles in a way that might at first be puzzling. You might find that a Quartz routine or other routine you are using to draw to a Quartz context shows up in a profile as being far more time-consuming than you'd expect. This can happen when you explicitly flush your drawing—the drawing call that *follows* a call to CGContextFlush will block until the next beam sync flush is performed by the Quartz Compositor. For example, you might see the function CGContextFillRect appear in a Shark profile as a hot point of your application, even though you are only calling it to perform an erase-type operation after you draw a scene. If you flush the scene, then call CGContextFillRect on that window context, CGContextFillRect blocks until the flush is complete.

The flushing behavior of the Quartz Compositor has evolved as Mac OS X has evolved and most likely will continue to do so. A full discussion of the topic of flushing behavior in Mac OS X requires more detail and more timely information than can be provided here. See the references for more information from Apple regarding the topic of application flushing and the Quartz Compositor.

Quartz Object and Memory Model

You'll get optimal performance and correct results when using Quartz if you understand its object and memory management model and then use objects appropriately. Doing so ensures the best performance for your application and avoids memory leaks and memory corruption.

Quartz uses the Core Foundation (CF) object and memory management model, in which objects are reference counted. When created or copied, Quartz objects start out with a reference count of 1. You can increment the reference count by calling a function to retain the object and decrement the reference count by calling a function to release the object. When the reference count is decremented to zero, the object is deallocated.

Quartz function names follow the convention introduced in Core Foundation. Functions with Create or Copy in the name create a new reference that you own and are responsible for releasing. Quartz has no automatic reclamation of memory resources (sometimes referred to as "garbage collection").

Most Quartz types have named retain and release routines that are specific to the type. In Jaguar and later versions, Quartz opaque types are true CF objects and you can retain and release an object by using the CF routines CFRetain and CFRelease. Some Quartz types introduced in Panther and later versions don't have explicitly named retain or release routines; those opaque types as well as any opaque Quartz object that you own a reference to can be released with CFRelease. Note that the CGxxxRetain and CGxxxRelease functions (such as CGColorSpaceRetain and CGColorSpaceRelease) ignore a NULL argument, unlike the Core Foundation functions CFRetain and CFRelease, which crash if you pass them a NULL argument.

The fact that Quartz types are Core Foundation types in Jaguar and later versions is useful if you want to add a Quartz type to a CFArray or CFDictionary object. You can use the CFType callbacks when you create one of these CF objects and use the Quartz objects in the same way you use other CFType objects. Another situation where it can be useful to treat a Quartz object as a CF object is when using CFEqual to compare objects. In many cases, this is a comparison of the object references, but in some cases (such as for CGColorSpace objects), the comparison is deeper and examines the color space data and returns equality for equivalent color spaces, even if they are represented by different objects.

Caution Using Core Foundation functions such as CFRetain, CFRelease, and CFEqual with opaque Quartz objects on Mac OS X systems prior to Jaguar will crash your program.

Many Quartz routines that take an opaque Quartz object as a parameter retain the object. Listing 17.1 is an example of a typical pattern of creating an object that you pass to a Quartz function and then release when you are done with it. Quartz CGDataProvider, CGDataConsumer, and CGContext objects you create are generally used for a specific task and then released; they typically do not exist for the duration of a program's execution.

Listing 17.1 The typical pattern of Quartz object creation and release

```
// Create the data consumer.
CGPDFContextRef pdfContext;
CGDataConsumerRef consumer = myDataConsumerCreate();
// ...Error handling if data consumer couldn't be created...

// Use the data consumer to create a PDF context. Quartz
// retains the data consumer so it can write to it as needed.
pdfContext = CGPDFContextCreate(consumer, &mediaRect, NULL);
// Once the code uses the data consumer to create the PDF context,
// it releases the data consumer since it no longer needs it.
CGDataConsumerRelease(consumer);
// ...Error handling if PDF context couldn't be created...

// ...Use of the PDF context...

// When done using the PDF context, release it. On all versions
// of Mac OS X, you can use CGContextRelease. On Jaguar and
// later versions, you can use either CGContextRelease or CFRelease.
CGContextRelease(pdfContext);
```

Some Quartz objects, such as CGColorSpace objects, are typically used repeatedly during program execution and so it makes sense to create them once and make them available thoughout program execution. Listing 17.2 shows one method of obtaining and using a color space. Listing 17.3 shows another, more useful method of creating and repeatedly using a color space. The code demonstrates a best practice; if you obtain a Quartz object and don't own it, you shouldn't release it. (As with Core Foundation, you only own a reference to Quartz objects that you create, copy, or retain.) Additionally, if you created the object but plan to reuse it, don't release it.

Listing 17.2 Code that creates a color space for one-time usage

```
void doColorSpace1(CGContextRef context)
{
  // Create the calibrated generic RGB color space.
  CGColorSpaceRef cs =
              CGColorSpaceCreateWithName(kCGColorSpaceGenericRGB);
  if(cs == NULL){
    // Couldn't create the color space!
    return;
  }
  // Set the fill color space in the context.
  CGContextSetFillColorSpace(context, cs);
  // Release the color space this code created.
  CGColorSpaceRelease(cs);

  // ... Draw to the context ...
}
```

Listing 17.3 Code that creates a color space for repeated usage

```
CGColorSpaceRef getMyRGBColorSpace(void)
{
  static CGColorSpaceRef cs = NULL;
  // Create the color space the first time this code is executed.
  // The expectation is that this function will be called multiple times.
  if(cs == NULL)
  {
    // Create the calibrated generic RGB color space.
    cs = CGColorSpaceCreateWithName(kCGColorSpaceGenericRGB);
  }
  return cs;
}

void doColorSpace2(CGContextRef context)
{
  // Get the calibrated generic RGB color space. This
  // is a 'Get' style function; the reference returned
  // is not owned by the caller.
  CGColorSpaceRef cs = getMyRGBColorSpace();
  if(cs == NULL){
    // Couldn't get the color space!
    return;
  }
```

```
// Set the fill color space in the context.
CGContextSetFillColorSpace(context, cs);
// This code does not release the color space it obtained from
// getMyRGBColorSpace since it doesn't own a reference.

// ... Draw to context ...
}
```

Not releasing an object you created can cause memory leaks. The MallocDebug application is useful for tracking such leaks. If you don't intend to keep the object around, then release it when you are done with it.

Some Quartz objects, such as a CGDataProvider object, have special memory management characteristics. Those variants of CGDataProvider objects that have callbacks have a special data release callback that Quartz calls when the retain count on the object reaches zero and the object is deallocated. Quartz calls the release function when the object itself goes away. Quartz expects the data provided to be invariant and to be available at any time until it calls the data release function. See "Guidelines for Using Data Providers" (page 198) for memory management guidelines that are specific to data providers.

Most Quartz opaque objects, once created, are immutable. (A `CGMutablePathRef` is one exception to this.) As a general rule, you create the object and use it, potentially reusing it many times. Because most Quartz objects are immutable, in many cases Quartz can take advantage of this for caching and other purposes. Some opaque types have a way to create a copy of a given object, modifying some aspect of it. For example, from a given `CGColorRef`, you can create a new `CGColorRef` with the same color space and color components but with a different alpha value using `CGColorCreateCopyWithAlpha`.

There are some situations in which an object is not released when you might expect it to be released, for example, when drawing to a PDF context or during printing. In these situations, Quartz doesn't release many objects until well after you might expect, making it especially important to follow the immutability and data release rules. "Checking for Data Provider Integrity" (page 619) and "Checking for Immutability Violations" (page 620) discuss this in detail.

The memory address for an object reference is not necessarily unique. That is, if an object is released and freed, the memory address of that object reference may be reused for another object reference. However, for the lifetime of a given object, it has a unique memory address.

Improving Performance

You can get the optimum level of performance from your application in several ways. This section discusses some of those that are specific to Quartz. However, there are many other factors that affect your graphics performance beyond those inherent in the Quartz API. For example, your use of memory, the caching behavior of the system CPU(s), your use (or lack of use) of Altivec or SSE in your code, and many other factors affect the performance of your application. The discussion here only scratches the surface of the subject of improving performance. You will want to look at the references at the end of this chapter for detailed information about measuring and improving performance in Mac OS X.

Reusing Quartz Objects and Performance. One way to improve the performance of your application is to appropriately reuse the Quartz objects you create. This applies to many of the Quartz object types, including CGColor, CGImage, CGPath, CGColorSpace, CGPDFDocument, CGPattern, CGFont, CGFunction, and CGShading objects. Reusing objects has a number of benefits both for onscreen drawing and when creating PDF documents. Each of these types represents an immutable object and Quartz can take advantage of that immutability, providing important performance benefits.

Quartz introduced CGColor objects specifically for reusability. Unless you reuse them, they are not a benefit when compared to the Quartz routines `CGContextSetFillColorSpace` and `CGContextSetFillColor` (or their equivalents for setting the stroke color). However, when you reuse CGColor objects, you are setting color in the most efficient way. See "CGColor Objects (Panther)" (page 152) for a discussion about creating and using CGColor objects.

One way you can achieve improved performance is to reuse a CGImage object that corresponds to a given image, rather than creating a new one that represents the same image. This allows you to take advantage of the image caching scheme Quartz implements, allowing for better performance. Quartz potentially caches many types of objects; the only way to take advantage of any caching is to reuse objects rather than creating a new object that is equivalent.

Reusing objects has important benefits when generating PDF documents. When drawing to a PDF context, if you reuse Quartz objects such as CGImage, CGPattern, and so on, then Quartz can store one copy of the resource in the PDF document and reference that one copy, regardless of how many times you use that object. This can dramatically reduce the size of the PDF documents your application produces.

Avoiding Unnecessary Drawing. Drawing is easy to do programmatically, but it has an inherent cost associated with it that you want to avoid if that drawing isn't necessary. For this reason, you want to streamline your drawing code so that it only draws what's necessary and eliminate unnecessary or redundant drawing. Apple provides visual tools to aid you in your efforts to identify and eliminate drawing that is not needed. You can use the Quartz Debug application to observe and analyze your drawing to windows. See "Using Quartz Debug" (page 608) for details.

The Cocoa and Carbon application frameworks each provide mechanisms to help you determine what portions of the drawing canvas need drawing, and you should make sure that you use them. For example, in Cocoa the rectangle passed to your NSView's drawRect: method and the getRectsBeingDrawn:count: method on an NSView allow you to determine the portion of your view that actually needs to be drawn, allowing you to draw only those portions of your graphics that intersect the rectangle or list of rectangles that need painting. For compositing views in Carbon, you can examine the kEventParamRgnHandle or kEventParamShape event parameter passed to your draw event handler.

Consider the scale of the drawing and draw only what can be resolved. That is, if an object (such as a graph) is scaled very small, chances are that you don't need to draw all parts of it. For example, if you are drawing points in a graph and the points are spaced so closely together as to be indistinguishable at the current scale you are drawing, resample your points rather than drawing all of them. This practice can significantly reduce the amount of drawing you perform without adversely affecting the final result. "See Also" (page 627) provides a pointer to sample code from Apple that demonstrates how sampling a data set prior to drawing it can improve performance.

Avoid resizing a window immediately after you create it. Resizing a window requires reallocating the memory for the window backing store. When you create a new window of the size you want, rather than creating it of a fixed size and resizing it, you avoid extra work by the Quartz Compositor and the application frameworks.

It is important to avoid reading from or directly writing to the window backing store—you should not assume the window backing store is in main memory. It may not be, and reading the contents of the window backing store in that case can be quite expensive.

Cocoa provides the "One Shot" attribute on a window that you can set in Interface Builder or by programmatically calling the setOneShot method of the NSWindow class. Windows with this attribute can potentially be disposed of by the system when hidden, releasing the window backing store and thus freeing memory. (You can programmatically hide windows and users can also hide them by minimizing them to the dock.) Marking windows with this attribute makes sense for windows whose contents are not expensive to redraw. Carbon windows are always created as "One Shot" windows.

Performance Tips. One way to improve your graphics performance is to use the Quartz bulk drawing functions when they make sense for your application. The functions CGContextAddRects, CGContextAddLines, CGContextFillRects, and (in Tiger) CGContextStrokeLineSegments each allow you to operate on a large set of data, whereas their singular equivalents (CGContextAddRect, CGContextAddLineTo-

Point, and so forth) are potentially slower when used to produce equivalent results. Use the bulk drawing functions where it makes sense in your application. "See Also" (page 627) provides a pointer to sample code from Apple that demonstrates the advantages of using CGContextStrokeLineSegments.

Consider caching objects that you use frequently and that are expensive to draw into CGLayers or, if running prior to Tiger, into a bitmap context. "Caching Drawing Offscreen" (page 379) discusses strategies for caching content offscreen. For example, shadowed objects can be expensive to render. If you are drawing a given object with a shadow lots of times, consider caching the shadowed object.

You may have drawing in your application that consists of a single complex path that is filled repeatedly in different colors. In this situation, caching the shape in a CGLayer isn't practical, because you need to draw it in different colors rather than simply stamp the same colored object in many locations. A CGPath object is one way to represent such a shape that can be easily used in a repeatable way, potentially simplifying your code and avoiding the cost of building the path over and over. Additionally, CGPath objects are transformed as abstract objects, not as bits, allowing you to use a given CGPath at many sizes and orientations without loss of fidelity, including to contexts that are not bit-based, such as the PDF and printing contexts.

When drawing to bit-based contexts, such as the window and bitmap contexts, you might consider another approach for repeated drawing. If the shape you are drawing is painted repeatedly at a given orientation and scale, you can cache the shape as an alpha mask that can be repainted with the fill color as needed. You can capture drawing as an alpha mask by using the alpha-only context, as shown in "Using an Alpha-Only Bitmap Context (Panther)" (page 366). The code in Listing 12.4 (page 367) shows the overall approach. After you have the alpha mask that corresponds to the drawing of your shape, set the fill color to the color you want to use to paint the shape and draw the mask at the location that you want the shape. This approach only makes sense for shapes that you want to draw many times in various colors, not for content that you can cache in a CGLayer. Because the intermediate representation in this case is bit-based, this approach is not appropriate when drawing to a context that is not bit-based, such as a PDF or printing context.

It is useful to have the ability to conditionally run without your application caches, including the kinds of caches just mentioned, so that you can do performance analysis both with and without them. Quartz caches objects, such as images, and its caching may interact with the caching you perform. This is especially important since Apple has found that as it tunes Quartz, application caches can unintentionally degrade performance rather than enhance it. It's a good idea to measure performance without your application caches and reintroduce them as necessary. Because the caching behavior of Quartz changes over time, make sure you can continue to monitor the effectiveness of your caches as the system evolves.

When drawing to bit-based contexts, drawing on pixel boundaries can avoid anti-aliasing and potentially speed up performance. The best candidates for this alignment are filled shapes and the destination `CGRect` used for drawing images. See "Aligning User Space Coordinates on Pixel Boundaries (Tiger)" (page 139) for more details about how to draw on pixel boundaries.

Whenever you use a bitmap context for drawing content offscreen prior to moving it onscreen, be sure that the color space of the bitmap context matches that of the display. This practice avoids expensive imaging operations and performs a color match only once, during initial drawing, rather than each time you move the content to the display.

The parameters you use when you create a CGImage object using `CGImageCreate` can impact drawing performance. If your image does not contain any alpha information, rather than supplying alpha component values in the image that are fully opaque, you should instead use `kCGImageAlphaNone`, `kCGImageAlphaNone-SkipLast`, or `kCGImageAlphaNoneSkipFirst` when specifying the `CGBitmapInfo` value to `CGImageCreate`. By properly informing Quartz that the image contains no alpha data, the image rendering code can execute code that is optimized for opaque image drawing. For images that contain alpha, Quartz efficiently handles both premultiplied and nonpremultiplied data. There is no need to adjust your image data to supply it in one format or the other; instead, use the data format that is closest to the native format of the data.

When drawing images, the interpolation quality parameter in the graphics state affects drawing performance. The higher the interpolation quality, the greater the potential impact on performance. You should choose the interpolation quality that best suits your needs. For transient drawing, such as that performed during window live resize, low-quality interpolation or no interpolation may be appropriate, followed by better-quality interpolation when drawing the content after the resize operation is complete.

The process of performing text layout has an inherent cost that you want to pay as infrequently as possible. Most applications use the framework text facilities—when doing so you should use the framework text drawing techniques that reuse the text layout, rather than recomputing it each time you draw your text. If you are performing your own text layout, you should cache the layout and only draw the results when you are asked to draw your text, rather than recomputing the layout each time you are asked to draw.

Measuring Performance

Perhaps the most important aspect to measuring performance is to include it as a regular step in your development cycle. Apple is working hard to improve

Quartz drawing performance with each software release. The same is true for the application frameworks; they provide inherent performance improvements as the system is tuned. As Apple optimizes Quartz and the application frameworks, your performance profile may change. You need to continue to look at the performance bottlenecks in your code as Mac OS X evolves. What appears to have no effect on performance today (or may even be a performance benefit) might be revealed as a bottleneck tomorrow.

Apple provides a number of tools to help measure performance, including Shark, Sampler, MallocDebug, ObjectAlloc, and Quartz Debug. Shark is especially useful when looking for bottlenecks in your code and in helping you actually understand where those bottlenecks really are. It's more effective to use Shark than to guess.

The tools MallocDebug and ObjectAlloc help you to find memory leaks (and possibly memory corruption) in your code. Because memory usage has a huge impact on system performance, it's important to ensure that your code be as leak-free as possible, making sure that you aren't using memory unnecessarily. The Quartz Debug application has a number of facilities that you can use to get a view into the drawing you are performing with Quartz. "Using Quartz Debug" (page 608) has detailed information.

Although you might think that you have an intuitive sense about what the performance bottlenecks are in your code, experience shows that intuition can be wrong. Using measurement tools is the most effective way to discover your performance bottlenecks; through that understanding you'll be able to construct ways to minimize or eliminate them.

Because the drawing you perform may be quite complex and make the overall performance profile of your application difficult to analyze, one approach is to simplify your drawing as much as you can for measurement purposes. Then profile the simplified drawing using Shark. (Be sure to explore the different views that Shark provides. By using the Tree view instead of the Heavy view, you will be more likely to recognize your code.) By measuring this simplified drawing, you should have a profile that you can analyze more easily than is possible with more complex drawing. You may find that you can now see bottlenecks in the code, unrelated to rendering, that were previously unknown because they were hidden by the costs of more complex drawing. Apple often finds that application performance bottlenecks that are attributed to the graphics system are instead in other code. Make sure you understand your simplified profile before proceeding. Then progressively add elements into your drawing. Look at the code profile and optimize as you go, until you are happy with the content and performance.

Adding to the excitement of understanding performance is the fact that different configurations can have different performance profiles. The performance of your application on the platform may differ significantly across the spectrum of CPU architectures—from G3- to Intel-based Macintosh computers. The video hardware can also impact performance, especially as Apple optimizes Quartz further.

Depending on your target audience, you will want to measure and optimize on the configurations that are most important to your users. They each have different cache-to-memory ratios and speed differences. As a result, performance can vary appreciably due to how you use memory in your code.

Using Quartz Debug. Apple supplies a number of important performance analysis applications and tools as part of the Developer SDK. The Quartz Debug application is useful for helping to debug your application drawing performance and for eliminating unneeded or redundant drawing that your application performs. When you install the Developer SDK for Tiger, Quartz Debug is installed in the directory /Developer/Applications/Performance Tools.

When you launch Quartz Debug, the first thing you'll notice is the floating window shown in Figure 17.3. Each of the checkboxes in this window controls a special debugging mode of the Quartz Compositor. These debugging modes allow you to visually observe application drawing. Note that these debugging modes don't just apply to *your* application but to *all* drawing done in *every* application. While this can be useful in observing the drawing in applications other than your own, it can also radically slow down system performance and usability, so typically you turn these modes on for observing a given application, then turn them off.

As you can see from the bottom of the Quartz Debug window in Figure 17.3, the hot key combination Control-Option-Command-t turns off and on various debugging modes. To turn on a set of options, check those options in the Quartz Debug window. To toggle that set of options on and off together, you can then use the key combination Control-Option-Command-t. When Quartz Debug is running, this key combination controls the Quartz Debug modes regardless of what application is currently active and frontmost. This is especially useful when you turn on a debugging mode that causes drawing to be time-consuming, making it difficult to switch from the application you are measuring to another application.

Figure 17.3 The Quartz Debug window

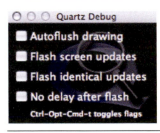

Turning on the "Autoflush drawing" option causes the Quartz Compositor to perform a flush operation after every drawing call that draws to a window. With this checked, you can see virtually every drawing operation as it takes place (with the corresponding dramatic drag on performance). This can be useful in observing the order and kind of each of your drawing operations.

Enabling the "Flash screen updates" option causes the Quartz Compositor to paint with yellow each region of the screen it is about to update, followed by a short pause and then the actual screen update. This allows you to watch the screen updates as they occur. If the "No delay after flash" checkbox is also selected, the short pause between the yellow flash and the screen update is omitted. Typically the pause is useful since otherwise you may not notice the drawing.

Watching the screen updates can help you identify unnecessary drawing. For example, if you find that you are drawing more content than is necessary, you'll notice that the yellow portion flashed before your update is larger than is strictly necessary. You might find ways to eliminate the unnecessary drawing and provide an overall performance win for your application.

Selecting the "Flash identical updates" option causes the Quartz Compositor to paint with red any portion of the update area that is drawn with the same pixels as were already present. This is followed by a pause, then the actual screen update is performed. Drawing preceded by the red flash is redundant. Observing the identical update flashes in your application may provide useful clues as to how to eliminate redundant drawing.

The Quartz Debug application provides some additional controls that can help you to examine application capabilities and performance. The "Show Frame Meter" item in the Tools menu displays a frame rate meter that shows in real time the number of screen updates per second. Recall that frame rates higher than 60 frames per second are almost certainly counterproductive. When performing animations, you should strive to have your frame rates at the lowest value possible to produce smooth results, with 30 frames per second a typical maximum.

The "Show Beam Sync Tools" menu item in the Tools menu opens a window that lets you control the beam syncing update behavior used by the Quartz Compositor. Over time the Quartz Compositor has been updated so that the methods it uses to flush the window backing store buffers to the display potentially produce better-quality results and improve performance. The beam syncing analysis tools allow you to test and measure your code with different beam syncing behavior (automatic, forced, or syncing disabled) and evaluate your application with beam syncing in mind. Apple has written a technical note that discusses beam syncing and how it might impact your application. See the references at the end of the chapter for more information.

Using the Quartz Debug Window List. The Quartz Debug application lets you see how your application uses windows, both those onscreen and those that are hidden. The Quartz Debug Window List window opens when you choose the Show Window List menu item in the Tools menu (see Figure 17.4).

Each window is owned by an application or system process; the connection ID (CID) is unique for each process. In the figure, the windows are sorted by the owning application, but you can sort in other ways by clicking the column title representing your desired sort ordering. In addition, you can drag the columns so that you locate the columns of most interest where you want them.

Each window has a unique window ID (WID), shown in the third column by default. The next column is the kBytes column, representing the amount of memory (in kilobytes) used for the backing store of a given window. As you see in the figure, some windows have a size followed by the letter C, indicating that the backing store of the window is compressed. In addition, a row where the window is compressed appears highlighted in gray in the window list. The backing store for these windows is compressed in order to reduce the amount of memory used. Compressed windows will be discussed further in a moment.

The Origin column has the x,y coordinates, in pixels, of the top-left corner of the window, relative to the top-left corner of the display. The Size column contains the width and height of each window in pixels. The Type column indicates whether a window has a backing store (Buffered) or is another type of window, available in some application frameworks for specialized purposes. The Encoding column indicates the window depth and whether the window allows for alpha data or not. The OnScreen column shows whether a window is visible onscreen or is hidden.

The Fade column shows the opacity of a window; most windows are fully opaque and have a fade value of 100 percent but it is possible to create windows

Figure 17.4 The Quartz Debug window list

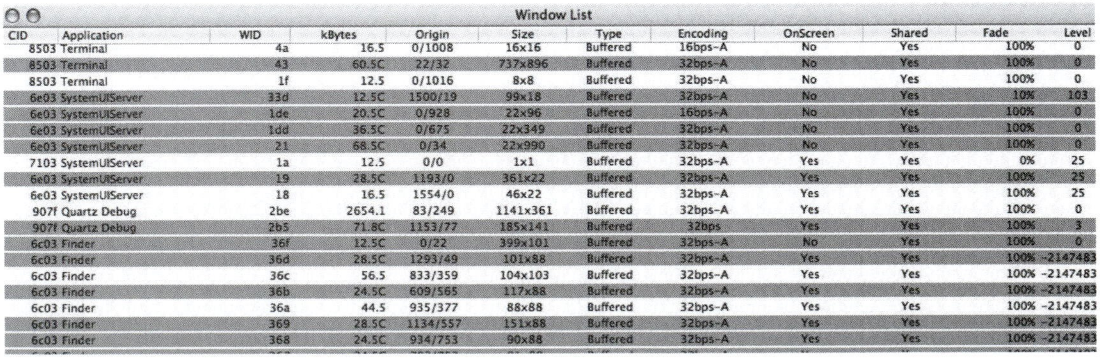

CID	Application	WID	kBytes	Origin	Size	Type	Encoding	OnScreen	Shared	Fade	Level
8503	Terminal	4a	16.5	0/1008	16x16	Buffered	16bps-A	No	Yes	100%	0
8503	Terminal	43	60.5C	22/32	737x896	Buffered	32bps-A	No	Yes	100%	0
8503	Terminal	1f	12.5	0/1016	8x8	Buffered	32bps-A	No	Yes	100%	0
6e03	SystemUIServer	33d	12.5C	1500/19	99x18	Buffered	32bps-A	No	Yes	10%	103
6e03	SystemUIServer	1de	20.5C	0/928	22x96	Buffered	16bps-A	No	Yes	100%	0
6e03	SystemUIServer	1dd	36.5C	0/675	22x349	Buffered	32bps-A	No	Yes	100%	0
6e03	SystemUIServer	21	68.5C	0/34	22x990	Buffered	32bps-A	No	Yes	100%	0
7103	SystemUIServer	1a	12.5	0/0	1x1	Buffered	32bps-A	Yes	Yes	0%	25
6e03	SystemUIServer	19	28.5C	1193/0	361x22	Buffered	32bps-A	Yes	Yes	100%	25
6e03	SystemUIServer	18	16.5	1554/0	46x22	Buffered	32bps-A	Yes	Yes	100%	25
907f	Quartz Debug	2be	2654.1	83/249	1141x361	Buffered	32bps-A	Yes	Yes	100%	0
907f	Quartz Debug	2b5	71.8C	1153/77	185x141	Buffered	32bps	Yes	Yes	100%	3
6c03	Finder	36f	12.5C	0/22	399x101	Buffered	32bps-A	No	Yes	100%	0
6c03	Finder	36d	28.5C	1293/49	101x88	Buffered	32bps-A	Yes	Yes	100%	-2147483
6c03	Finder	36c	56.5	833/359	104x103	Buffered	32bps-A	Yes	Yes	100%	-2147483
6c03	Finder	36b	24.5C	609/565	117x88	Buffered	32bps-A	Yes	Yes	100%	-2147483
6c03	Finder	36a	44.5	935/377	88x88	Buffered	32bps-A	Yes	Yes	100%	-2147483
6c03	Finder	369	28.5C	1134/557	151x88	Buffered	32bps-A	Yes	Yes	100%	-2147483
6c03	Finder	368	24.5C	934/753	90x88	Buffered	32bps-A	Yes	Yes	100%	-2147483

that are partially transparent and are composited on top of other windows. ("Window Buffering" (page 595) discusses transparent windows and the references at the end of this chapter provide pointers to several examples from Apple that demonstrates them.)

The Level column indicates the ordering level of a window. Windows with a level value that is lower than other windows are underneath those windows and cannot be moved above those windows unless the window level value is changed. Windows with the same level value, such as normal application windows, can be placed on top of one another without changing their level value. This mechanism allows for tool windows that float above other windows of your application, even as those windows are reordered amongst themselves. As you see in the screen shot, the Finder owns several windows with a very low window level value. These windows are the desktop icons that appear below any other window on the system, including those of the Dock.

While the origin and size of a window in the window list may help you determine which onscreen window a given entry is, once there are a large number of windows involved, it can be difficult to determine which window corresponds to which entry. If you click on an entry for a given window in the window list and that window is onscreen, the onscreen window itself is alternately highlighted and faded to an unhighlighted state. This gives the appearance of the window "pulsing." This makes it easy to determine which window a given WID corresponds to.

As mentioned previously, some windows in the list are marked as compressed. For windows whose contents haven't changed recently, the Quartz Compositor compresses the backing store so that it minimizes its memory requirements. The compositor can composite the contents from a compressed backing store efficiently. However, if there is any drawing to a window that is compressed, the Quartz Compositor must first decompress the backing store before the drawing is rendered to it.

Notice that in Figure 17.4 there are two entries associated with the Quartz Debug application itself. One window is compressed and the other, larger window, is not. The smaller window is the Quartz Debug window containing the checkboxes controlling the Quartz Compositor flush highlighting behavior. The other window is the window list itself. The smaller window is compressed. This is because there has been no recent interaction with that window that requires it to redraw itself. If you were to click on one of the checkboxes in that window, you would see the window change its status to indicate that it is no longer compressed. After a period of time with no additional interaction, the window will again be compressed and appear in the window list marked accordingly.

You can use the window list to monitor your application windows and verify that they are compressed at the expected times, such as when there is no recent drawing to them. If a window in your application is not compressed, it means there has been recent drawing to the window backing store by either an application framework or your code. Make sure the behavior is what you expect.

You can also use the window list to make sure that the number of your application windows in the list is what you expect. If the window list contains more windows than you expect, it means you are probably inadvertantly holding onto windows you think you have disposed of or released. Since windows take up significant resources, you'll want to make sure you understand your application's usage pattern.

Using Quartz Debug to Explore Resolution Independence. Higher-resolution displays and a high-resolution user interface are an important future direction for Apple. Quartz is built with high resolution in mind; utilizing Quartz properly in your application prepares you for the move to a high-resolution user interface.

In Tiger, the Show User Interface Resolution menu item in the Quartz Debug Tools menu brings up a window that lets you adjust the system-wide user interface resolution scaling factor. In Tiger, by default, the user interface resolution scaling factor is 1.0, meaning that windows are created so that 1 user space unit is 1 pixel. Using Quartz Debug, you can change the user interface resolution to other values to investigate the results you obtain with your application as the user interface resolution changes.

Figure 17.5 shows setting a scaling factor of 1.75 in the User Interface Resolution window, corresponding to a user interface resolution of 126 dpi. This means that if you were to create a window on a display that has a physical resolution of 126 dpi, 72 units in the default Quartz coordinate system would be 126 pixels, or one inch. This kind of control allows a user to choose how to utilize a high-resolution display. A user interface resolution of 1.0 produces windows where each pixel is one Quartz unit. Thus, there is a larger Quartz coordinate space to draw in, albeit at smaller size and potentially reduced visual acuity. Larger values for the scaling factor produce windows with a smaller Quartz coordinate space but with more pixels per coordinate unit. Content drawn in such windows would have better fidelity at the expense of a reduced drawing canvas.

As of Tiger, the high-resolution user interface is a work in progress. The Tiger release notes listed in "See Also" (page 627) are a good source of information about moving your application to a high-resolution user interface. You'll see more up-to-date information on the ADC website as it is available.

Figure 17.5 Setting the resolution for the user interface

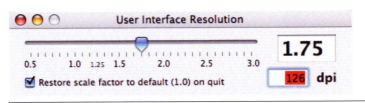

Debugging Your Drawing

One of the advantages of working with graphics systems is that they usually provide visual feedback on the code you write. Most of the time the visual feedback is sufficient to help you track down programming errors and correct them. Of course, there are times when either the visual clues aren't enough or you don't see any drawing! No drawing or incorrect drawing can occur for a number of reasons.

Table 17.1 lists some typical problems and pointers to debugging tips that can help you identify the problem.

Examining the Coordinate System

It is not unusual, particularly when you are new to Quartz programming and coordinate transformations, to sometimes get "lost" in space as you develop an application. Your graphics don't appear where you expect, they might appear deformed, or maybe they don't appear at all. One frequent cause of these problems is that the coordinate system origin, scale, or orientation isn't what you think it is. There are a number of methods that you can use to help debug situations where the drawing coordinate space is different than you expect.

A simple, relatively unobtrusive way to determine where you are in the Quartz coordinate system is to draw a "dot" at a specified user space coordinate. The drawPoint routine in Listing 17.4 draws a 5-unit circle at the point passed to it. Frequently it is useful to draw this dot at the current Quartz origin. By seeing where the origin is relative to your graphics, you can sometimes better determine the current user space origin and why your drawing is not appearing where you expect.

It can also be useful to draw coordinate axes at various points in your code so that you can see the origin, scale, and orientation of the current user space coordinate system. The drawCoordinateAxes routine in Listing 17.4 draws the x and y coordinate axes with tick marks that are 72 units apart and a dot at the origin of coordinates. The x axis and tick marks are drawn in red and the y axis and tick marks are drawn in blue. The coordinate axes make it easy to see the location, scale, and orientation of the current Quartz user space coordinate system.

In some situations, it is helpful to have a debugging routine that strokes a rectangle and puts crosses through it in different colors. This can help determine the location, scale, and orientation of a given user space rectangle. The drawDebuggingRect routine in Listing 17.4 draws such a rectangle. This rectangle drawing is especially helpful when debugging the drawing of images and PDF documents. If

Table 17.1 Drawing Problems and Debugging Tips

Problem	Debugging Tip
Drawing doesn't appear.	See "Examining the Coordinate System" (page 613), "Drawing a Debugging Rectangle" (page 617), "Checking the Clipping Area" (page 617), and "Looking for Console Messages" (page 618).
Drawing appears in the wrong location.	See "Examining the Coordinate System" (page 613) and "Drawing a Debugging Rectangle" (page 617).
Drawing looks deformed.	See "Examining the Coordinate System" (page 613).
Code crashes when drawing to a PDF context or printing.	See "Checking for Data Provider Integrity" (page 619).
Images look identical, but should be different.	See "Checking for Immutability Violations" (page 620).
Drawing contains artifacts.	See "Checking for Immutability Violations" (page 620) and "Checking for Improperly Initialized Contexts" (page 620).
Color is wrong.	See "Checking for Out-of-Sync Color Setting" (page 620).
Images don't appear as expected.	See "Drawing Images to a PDF Context" (page 621) and "Drawing a Debugging Rectangle" (page 617).
Drawing PDF source data doesn't appear as expected.	See "Drawing a Debugging Rectangle" (page 617).
Quartz-generated PDF document can't be opened in any application.	See "Releasing a CGPDFContext Object" (page 621).
Printing fails and Print Preview reports that the PDF is damaged.	See "Releasing a CGPDFContext Object" (page 621).
Acrobat complains about pages with patterns in Quartz-generated PDF documents.	See "Checking Pattern Color Space Usage" (page 622) and "Looking for Console Messages" (page 618).
PostScript printing of patterns produces PostScript errors.	See "Checking Pattern Color Space Usage" (page 622).
Generated PDF files are much larger than expected.	You may not be properly reusing Quartz resources. See "Using PDF Generation as a Debugging Aid" (page 622).

you think there is a problem with your image or PDF drawing code, replace the actual `CGContextDrawImage` or `CGContextDrawPDFPage` (or `CGContextDrawPDFDocument`) call with a call to `drawDebuggingRect`. This helps to narrow down whether the problem you encounter is with the coordinate system transformations or something specific to the type of data you are trying to draw.

Listing 17.4 Helper routines for debugging coordinate system problems

```
void drawPoint(CGContextRef context, CGPoint p)
{
  CGContextSaveGState(context);
    // Set the stroke color to opaque black.
    CGContextSetRGBStrokeColor(context, 0, 0, 0, 1);
    CGContextSetLineWidth(context, 5);
    CGContextSetLineCap(context, kCGLineCapRound);
    CGContextMoveToPoint(context, p.x, p.y);
    CGContextAddLineToPoint(context, p.x, p.y);
    CGContextStrokePath(context);
  CGContextRestoreGState(context);
}

#define kTickLength 5.0
#define kTickDistance 72.0
#define kAxesLength (20*kTickDistance)

void drawCoordinateAxes(CGContextRef context)
{
  int i;
  float t;
  float tickLength = kTickLength;

  CGContextSaveGState(context);

  CGContextBeginPath(context);
  // Paint the x axis in red.
  CGContextSetRGBStrokeColor(context, 1, 0, 0, 1);
  CGContextMoveToPoint(context, -kTickLength, 0.0);
  CGContextAddLineToPoint(context, kAxesLength, 0.0);
  CGContextDrawPath(context, kCGPathStroke);

  // Paint the y axis in blue.
  CGContextSetRGBStrokeColor(context, 0, 0, 1, 1);
  CGContextMoveToPoint(context, 0, -kTickLength);
  CGContextAddLineToPoint(context, 0, kAxesLength);
  CGContextDrawPath(context, kCGPathStroke);

  // Paint the x axis tick marks in red.
  CGContextSetRGBStrokeColor(context, 1, 0, 0, 1);
  for(i = 0; i < 2 ; i++)
  {
```

```
        for(t=0.; t < kAxesLength ; t += kTickDistance){
          CGContextMoveToPoint(context, t, -tickLength);
          CGContextAddLineToPoint(context, t, tickLength);
        }
        CGContextDrawPath(context, kCGPathStroke);
        CGContextRotateCTM(context, M_PI/2.);
        // Paint the y axis tick marks in blue.
        CGContextSetRGBStrokeColor(context, 0, 0, 1, 1);
      }
      drawPoint(context, CGPointZero);
      CGContextRestoreGState(context);
    }


    void drawDebuggingRect(CGContextRef context, CGRect rect)
    {
      CGContextSaveGState(context);
        CGContextSetLineWidth(context, 4.);
        // Draw opaque red from top left to bottom right.
        CGContextSetRGBStrokeColor(context, 1, 0, 0, 1.);
        CGContextMoveToPoint(context, rect.origin.x,
                    rect.origin.y + rect.size.height);
        CGContextAddLineToPoint(context,
                    rect.origin.x + rect.size.width,
                    rect.origin.y);
        CGContextStrokePath(context);
        // Draw opaque blue from top right to bottom left.
        CGContextSetRGBStrokeColor(context, 0, 0, 1, 1.);
        CGContextMoveToPoint(context, rect.origin.x + rect.size.width,
                    rect.origin.y + rect.size.height);
        CGContextAddLineToPoint(context, rect.origin.x,
                    rect.origin.y);
        CGContextStrokePath(context);
        // Set the stroke color to opaque black.
        CGContextSetRGBStrokeColor(context, 0, 0, 0, 1.);
        CGContextStrokeRect(context, rect);
      CGContextRestoreGState(context);
    }


    void printCTM(CGContextRef context)
    {
      CGAffineTransform t = CGContextGetCTM(context);
      fprintf(stderr, "CurrentCTM is a = %f, b = %f, c = %f, d = %f, \
                    tx = %f, ty = %f\n",
                    t.a, t.b, t.c, t.d, t.tx, t.ty);
    }
```

If you get really lost in Quartz user space, you can look directly at the CTM currently in effect. The printCTM routine in Listing 17.4 writes a message to the console that contains the entries of the CTM affine transform. The CTM printed by printCTM for the default Quartz coordinate system in Tiger and earlier versions is the identity transform: a = 1, b = c = 0, d = 1, and tx = ty = 0. This is a coordinate system where the scaling factor is 1, there are no rotations, and the origin is at the default origin, the lower-left corner of the window (or bitmap or PDF document). The tx and ty values correspond to the current Quartz origin, relative to the lower-left corner of the window (or bitmap or PDF document). When b and c are zero, the a and d values specify the scaling in x and y, respectively—negative values indicate a flipped coordinate system. When b and c are nonzero, this indicates a rotation or skew of the coordinate system, relative to the normal orientation where the x axis is horizontal and the y axis is vertical. See "The Quartz Coordinate System and Coordinate Transformations" (page 83) for more information about the Quartz coordinate system and the CTM.

Checking the Clipping Area

You may find that your drawing, or a portion of it, is not appearing at all. One reason your drawing may "disappear" is that the clipping area might be different than what you expect. You may find that your drawing coordinates are correct but the clipping area is causing the drawing to be obscured. The function CGContextGetClipBoundingBox, available in Panther and later versions, returns the bounding rectangle, in current user space coordinates, of the clipping area. By calling drawDebuggingRect with the clipping rectangle returned by CGContextGetClipBoundingBox, you can visually determine the current clipping bounds. In some cases, this approach can be quite revealing. See "Clipping with Paths" (page 129) and "Clipping to a Mask (Tiger)" (page 282) for more information about clipping.

Drawing a Debugging Rectangle

As your drawing gets more complex, it sometimes becomes more difficult to sort out problems. In these situations, it is frequently useful to simplify your drawing to help understand any problems. For example, if you are drawing images or PDF documents and they aren't appearing or are appearing incorrectly, it can be helpful to substitute drawing a simple rectangle (or use the routine drawDebuggingRect in Listing 17.4) to the destination. You know exactly what you should see in the simplified drawing and if you don't see what you expect, the issue isn't with the image or PDF page, but with some other aspect of your setup and drawing.

Looking for Console Messages

The Quartz philosophy on errors and error codes is simple. In the Quartz 2D programming API, Quartz functions do not return an error code. Instead of returning error codes, Quartz functions

- Return NULL for functions that create objects if the object can't be created. For example, when you call CGBitmapContextCreate, if Quartz can't create a bitmap context that represents the set of parameters you supplied to the function, it returns a NULL context.

- Log a message to the console log. The message that Quartz writes to the log is more informative than an error code and indicates the condition that led to the log message.

- Return a bool that indicates success or failure, such as with functions like CGPSConverterConvert or CGPDFDictionaryGetStream. In case of failure, a message may be logged to the console.

In most cases, Quartz returns a NULL object because the parameters to the function are incorrect or unsupported in that version of Mac OS X, rather than due to insufficient resources to satisfy the request. In many cases, Quartz also logs a console or system log message when it returns a NULL object. Quartz logs other messages when it encounters inconsistent usage of its API, such as when setting a colored pattern as the painting color when the current color space is not a pattern color space or if the color space is appropriate for a stencil pattern, *not* a colored pattern.

These kinds of programming errors can, and should, be found during software development, not by end users. It is important during your software development to look in the console log for log messages from Quartz. These messages are frequently a useful way of uncovering problems, especially those problems that you might not detect visually.

Console messages can help identify why your drawing calls produce no drawing or incorrect drawing. As discussed in "Examining the Coordinate System" (page 613), one typical reason for a lack of visible drawing is that prior to drawing, you set up the coordinate system incorrectly. Another reason is that you passed a NULL context to Quartz drawing functions, which can happen if you create a context such as a bitmap context but use incorrect or unsupported parameters. In these cases, the context returned is NULL. (See Table 12.1 (page 348) in "Bitmap Graphics Context" (page 346) for the list of bitmap contexts supported up to and including Tiger.) With most versions of Mac OS X, Quartz logs a message to the console when you pass a NULL context to its drawing routines. Usage of the

NULL context generally doesn't crash. Instead, drawing doesn't take place but warning messages are written to the console. The console log is the first place to look if you don't see the results you expect.

Checking for Data Provider Integrity

As discussed in "Guidelines for Using Data Providers" (page 198) and "Best Practices for Working with Images" (page 241), it is important to ensure that a data provider for an image (or other Quartz object) is prepared to supply its data until the data provider release function is called by Quartz. Failing to follow this guideline can cause your code to crash during printing or drawing to a PDF context. This class of crash typically has a backtrace that includes the Quartz function `CGContextRelease` or `CGContextEndPage`. The problem this kind of crash reveals is a failure to maintain the integrity of a Quartz data provider or other object that has resources associated with it, such as a CGPattern object.

During printing or when generating a PDF document, Quartz typically retains a CGImage or CGPattern object well after you have released it, and uses the data provider or calls the pattern callback when it ends the page or ends the document. If you prematurely release resources or other data that you need for your data provider or other callback that Quartz invokes, Quartz could crash with a memory access violation when it attempts to use the now nonexistent data.

Another symptom of the same problem is an image that appears to be completely corrupted or have damaged data. If the image data is released prior to the time Quartz attempts to access it, the result can be that the memory associated with the data is in use for another purpose.

A similar crash that can occur when you draw to a PDF context (or print) is related to how you allocate the `info` parameter before you pass it to functions such as `CGDataProviderCreate`, `CGFunctionCreate`, and `CGPatternCreate`. You should use `malloc` or another memory allocation function to allocate the `info` parameter; don't allocate it on the stack. CGDataProvider, CGFunction, CGPattern, and other objects are retained by Quartz when you use them and, when drawing to a context, they can be released well after you "think" they have been. Just as image data associated with an image needs to be available until Quartz calls the data provider release function for an image, the `info` data that you supply when creating a data provider, function, pattern, or other similar Quartz object needs to be available until Quartz calls the release function associated with that object.

Checking for Immutability Violations

One aspect of data provider integrity is that the data it provides is immutable. During the lifetime of the data provider, Quartz expects that the underlying data does not change and that it represents the data provided by the data provider.

One way you can accidently violate the immutability of data supplied by a data provider is when that data is the bitmap raster data from a bitmap context or is bitmap data from another drawing system such as QuickDraw. If you draw to the bitmap context that contains the image data after you create the CGImage object, the image data could change and therefore not represent the original image.

In some cases, this problem exists in your code but it isn't apparent until you print or draw to a PDF context. You can diagnose this problem by looking at the PDF document or printed output and observing that the output isn't what you expect. For example, you may have drawn multiple images on the page but one or more of them are identical instead of being distinct. This is typically caused because you violated the immutability of a Quartz object—you drew a CGImage object but changed the image data associated with that object.

You might not observe this problem when drawing to a window, but when drawing to a PDF document or during printing, Quartz only generates a single reference for each CGImage object, even when the object is drawn multiple times. Using a single reference significantly reduces the size of PDF files it produces but can produce unexpected results if you violate the immutability of Quartz objects such as CGImage, CGPattern, CGShading, and CGPDFDocument objects. "Best Practices for Working with Images" (page 241) discusses the notion of object immutability as it applies to images.

Checking for Improperly Initialized Contexts

When you create a bitmap graphics context, Quartz does not initialize the memory you provide as the bitmap raster data. Failing to properly initialize a bitmap context can be a source of drawing artifacts. The UNIX function malloc returns memory that contains unknown values. You should be sure to properly initialize the memory in your bitmap context by using calloc and properly erasing or clearing the context. "Erasing and Clearing a Context" (page 351) discusses this in detail.

Checking for Out-of-Sync Color Setting

If you see incorrect colors in your drawing, check that the color space and color component values in effect at the time you paint your graphics are those you expect. Because you can set the color space and color component values independently, they can get out of sync. Color component values are always interpreted in a color space. If you supply color values for a given color space but use a different color space, you obtain incorrect colors. Depending on the color space and color values, the results may be dramatically incorrect. Using a CGColorRef significantly reduces this possibility because, by setting the color using a CGColor-Ref, you set the color space and color component values simultaneously. (See "CGColor Objects (Panther)" (page 152) for information about creating and using CGColor objects.) You can use the Core Foundation function CFShow to print out a description of a CGColorSpace object. While CFShow doesn't produce useful diagnostic information on many Quartz objects (as of Tiger), it does produce useful information for CGColorSpace objects.

Drawing Images to a PDF Context

You can debug some image drawing problems by creating a PDF context that is the size of the image destination and drawing the image to that context. Drawing an image to a PDF document generally records the image without transforming or modifying the image, allowing you to examine the PDF document to determine what image data you are working with. Other ways to examine image data are to render it to a custom bitmap context and examine those bits or to use the CGImageDestination functionality to a create a TIFF data file for the image.

Releasing a CGPDFContext Object

If you use a PDF context to create a PDF document and the resulting PDF document can't be opened by Preview or Adobe Acrobat, make sure you are calling CGContextRelease on the PDF context you created. The symptom produced by failing to release the PDF context is that the PDF document created is mysteriously incomplete and is considered damaged by applications attempting to use them. Quartz doesn't write out the complete contents of the PDF document associated with a PDF context until the retain count of the context goes to zero. If you create or retain a PDF context and don't release your reference to it, the retain count of the context won't ever reach zero and the document won't be finalized.

You'll see a similar problem when printing fails and a PDF document you save through the print dialog or view by using Print Preview reveals that the PDF document is damaged. This usually means that the PDF context used by the printing system isn't being released properly. The typical reason for this is that you've either retained the printing context in your code and haven't released it, or you've released it but not until after you're finished printing. The printing context associated with a given page should not be retained beyond the scope of that page.

Checking Pattern Color Space Usage

When drawing with colored patterns, you must first set the color space to a pattern color space that has a NULL base color space. If you are drawing with a stencil pattern (that is, one that has no intrinsic color), you must first set the color space to a pattern color space that has a base color space that is not NULL. Failing to follow these guidelines may produce no obvious side effect when drawing to the display but can produce console messages and can cause Quartz to produce PDF documents that don't conform to the PDF specification.

Stencil patterns that you create must not set color or draw objects with intrinsic color in their drawPattern callback. As of Tiger, Quartz doesn't provide any warning or console message if you do this. Failure to observe this requirement can cause Quartz to produce PDF documents that don't conform to the PDF specification.

A PDF document produced when drawing with any of these errors in your drawing code can cause problems for Adobe Acrobat and other third-party PDF utilities. When you open such a malformed PDF document in Adobe Acrobat and navigate to a page in the document that contains the incorrect pattern drawing, you'll see that the drawing is incorrect or missing. Acrobat typically generates warnings and fails to draw a page that contains this type of incorrect drawing. With these errors in your code, printing to a PostScript printer can also fail when you draw these incorrectly formed patterns.

See "Creating and Drawing Colored Patterns" (page 485) and "Creating and Drawing Stencil Patterns" (page 499) for more information about properly creating and drawing patterns.

Using PDF Generation as a Debugging Aid

For debugging purposes, you can use the fact that the Quartz imaging model and the Quartz API map quite well onto the PDF imaging model. By performing your drawing into a PDF context, you produce a recording of your drawing that can be helpful in finding problems.

For example, you can use a PDF representation of your drawing to evaluate appropriate reuse of CGImage and CGPattern objects. If a given image is drawn more than once but, by inspecting the PDF page content stream, you observe multiple image objects in the PDF document rather than a single image referenced multiple times, you are not reusing your objects correctly. Patterns, color spaces, images, PDF document pages, and fonts all benefit from reuse, both when generating a PDF document and potentially when rendering onscreen or to other bit-based contexts. (Note that use of a given pattern but with a different pattern phase generates a new pattern resource during PDF document generation.)

You can examine a PDF document in many ways. "Examining PDF Document Content (Panther, Tiger)" (page 467) introduces the Quartz PDF introspection functions that you can use to write PDF document analysis tools. There are also third-party tools that examine PDF documents; some have the ability to detect duplicate resource usage.

You can also use the PDF page content stream as a debugging tool. By reading it, you can examine a recording of your graphics drawing. Reading the PDF graphics stream isn't a debugging approach for everyone; but it is one way to become more familiar with the PDF file format. Those who already are familiar with the page content stream and PDF file format might find this approach useful.

The contents of the PDF page content stream are not an exact one-to-one mapping with the Quartz drawing calls you make. For example, coordinate transformations are coalesced and the coordinates that are generated into a Quartz PDF page content stream are typically transformed into the default PDF coordinate system, except when explicit changes to the CTM in the PDF stream are necessary. This can be a useful debugging aid since you will see virtually all of your drawing coordinates in default user space with coordinate transformations already applied to them.

The sample application Voyeur in the Tiger Developer SDK lets you browse PDF document structures and their contents. Opening a PDF document in Voyeur presents a view of the document that is similiar to that shown in Figure 17.6. The lower portion of the window presents information about the document, including the PDF document version number, the number of pages, the title and author of the document, and so forth. The top portion of the window presents

Figure 17.6 A PDF document just opened in Voyeur

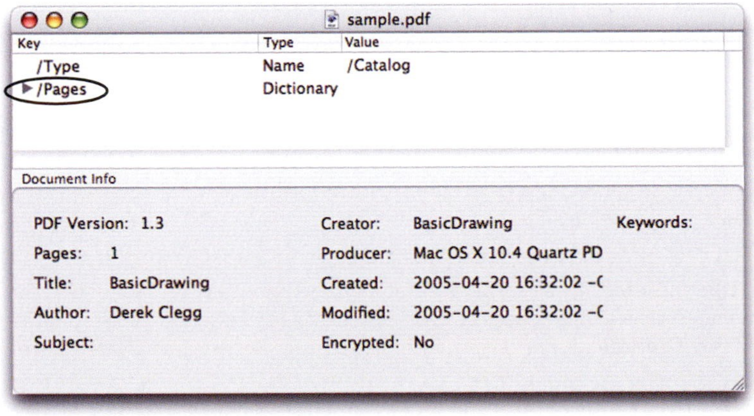

the PDF document catalog, which contains the Pages dictionary that contains the PDF page objects present in the document.

Clicking the disclosure triangle next to Pages reveals the entries in the dictionary. Figure 17.7 shows the results of revealing the Pages dictionary contents. This Pages dictionary contains the entries Type, MediaBox, Count, and Kids. The Kids entry is an array that contains the page objects that each describe a page in the document. Clicking on the disclosure triangle for the Kids array reveals the objects that make up the array. In the case of the PDF document in the figure, there is only one element in the array, the element labeled 0. This PDF document contains only one page so it has only one entry in the Kids array, the Page object for that page. A Page object is a dictionary and its Contents entry is the page content stream. By selecting the Contents entry and choosing the File > Show Info menu item (Command-Shift-I), the Info Window appears, as seen in the inset in Figure 17.7. The text in the Info Window is the page content stream that makes up the PDF document page.

Listing 17.5 shows a simple PDF page content stream for drawing the first example in this book, the code in Listing 2.1 (page 17) that fills a rectangle with red. (Note that the page content stream in the listing is formatted for this discussion.)

Figure 17.7 Using Voyeur to examine the PDF content stream

Listing 17.5 The page content stream for a simple red rectangle

```
q Q
q
/Cs1 cs 1 0 0 sc
20 20 130 100 re f
Q
```

Like the PostScript language, PDF drawing operations use a set of predefined operators that act on objects. The PDF imaging model has a graphics state that is similar to the Quartz graphics state and the PDF specification defines the operator q, which saves the graphics state (similar to the Quartz function CGContext-SaveGState), and Q, which restores the graphics state (similar to the Quartz function CGContextRestoreGState). The first line in the content stream is a q immediately followed by a Q—this saves and restores the PDF graphics state. This initial portion of the content stream generated by Quartz is an artifact of the way Quartz currently generates PDF data and can be ignored; it produces no drawing or persistent changes to the PDF graphics state.

The next operation in the page content stream is the PDF operator q, which saves the PDF graphics state. Quartz generates a PDF content stream that first saves the graphics state before performing any drawing so that it can restore to that graphics state if it needs to do so later. Note that this appears even though the Quartz drawing that produced this PDF page content stream did not explicitly call CGContextSaveGState. As mentioned previously, the PDF content stream is not a one-to-one mapping to the Quartz API calls you make.

The PDF content stream is a postfix language similar to PostScript—arguments (called **operands**) to those PDF operators that take arguments precede the operator in the content stream. The next PDF operator in the content stream in Listing 17.5 is the operator cs, which sets the fill color space. The operand to the cs operator is the name /Cs1. Objects such as color spaces and images appear in the page content stream by named reference—this allows objects to be referenced many times in the document even though the PDF file contains only one copy of the object itself. In this case, the name /Cs1 refers to a color space object that represents an RGB color space.

The definition of the /Cs1 color space is not shown in the listing. The PDF specification requires that objects referenced by name in the page stream, such as color spaces, images, and patterns, have entries in the Resources dictionary of a page on which they appear. You can use Voyeur to examine the Resources dictionary of a page and see the color spaces and other objects that are contained in that dictionary.

Following the setting of the fill color space, the page content stream sets the fill color with the sc operator. The operands to sc are the color components; in the case of an RGB space, they are the red, green, and blue component values. The values 1 0 0 that precede the sc operator represent a pure red, no green, no blue.

Next in the page content stream is the drawing of the rectangle. The PDF operator re creates a rectangular path from coordinates that are the operands to the re operator. In this case, the coordinates are 20 20 130 100, describing a rectangle with its origin at (20,20) and a width of 130 units and a height of 100 units. Once the path is created, the PDF operator f fills the current path. This corresponds to the drawing performed in Listing 2.1 (page 17).

The PDF specification contains a table listing all the PDF operators and describes the syntax of PDF documents. As stated earlier, reading PDF data directly isn't for everyone, but for those who are comfortable with it, it can be a useful way to debug drawing problems, including coordinate system issues.

Summary

Drawing performance is the result of many interacting factors, some tied to your code and others related to the system. The Quartz Compositor, Quartz object and memory management, and performance measurement tools are all key players. The role that the Quartz Compositor plays in moving your drawing to the display is important to understand and utilize to your benefit. Using the Quartz memory and object model properly allows performance gains with object reuse and avoids memory leaks.

Measuring performance is not a one-time task but is something that you will want to perform regularly as you develop your code. Shark and Malloc Debug are important tools that allow you to obtain a performance profile and memory usage information. You can use the visual features of the Quartz Debug application to examine application drawing, enabling you to identify redundant or unnecessary drawing and window usage.

Many Quartz debugging tasks are made simpler by using Quartz as a debugging aid. In some cases, adding code to your drawing can help to identify coordinate system and clipping area problems. Using a PDF context can flush out problems due to data provider integrity and object immutability. Simplifying troublesome drawing can help to pinpoint where problems are cropping up.

Performance and debugging are dynamic topics—you need to keep up to date with information as it becomes available from Apple.

See Also

Apple provides sample code that demonstrates the use of transparent windows. The Cocoa sample code FunkyOverlayWindow shows how to use partially transparent Cocoa windows to overlay content on top of other content and is available from the ADC Reference Library at

*http://developer.apple.com/samplecode/FunkyOverlayWindow/
FunkyOverlayWindow.html*

The Carbon example CarbonSketch is a Quartz-based object drawing application that uses Carbon overlay windows for its resizing and moving of object graphics as a drawing is edited. This example is installed as part of the Tiger Developer SDK and is installed at

```
/Developer/Examples/Quartz/CarbonSketch
```

The Carbon Window Fun sample code demonstrates overlay windows and other window management–related issues in Carbon. It is available at

http://developer.apple.com/samplecode/WindowFun/WindowFun.html

Apple has a number of performance resources available from the ADC Reference Library. Some of those relevant to Quartz drawing are

- The sample program QuartzLines shows how to improve drawing performance by taking advantage of `CGContextStrokeLineSegments` and resampling a data set prior to drawing it:

  http://developer.apple.com/samplecode/QuartzLines/QuartzLines.html

- The sample program QuartzCache compares several techniques for caching drawing and examines the impact excessive flushing can have on performance:

  http://developer.apple.com/samplecode/QuartzCache/QuartzCache.html

- *Performance Overview* is a good starting point for information about looking at your application's performance:

  *http://developer.apple.com/documentation/Performance/Conceptual/
  PerformanceOverview/*

- *Drawing Performance Guidelines* provides information about improving drawing performance in Cocoa and Carbon applications and measuring drawing performance:

  *http://developer.apple.com/documentation/Performance/Conceptual/Drawing/
  index.html*

- Cocoa drawing performance information is available at

  http://developer.apple.com/documentation/Cocoa/Conceptual/DrawViews/
  Tasks/OptimizingDrawing.html

- Carbon drawing performance information is available at

  http://developer.apple.com/documentation/Performance/Conceptual/Drawing/
  Articles/CarbonDrawingTips.html

Because the Quartz object and memory management model is based on that of Core Foundation, the Core Foundation documentation from the ADC Reference Library is a useful guide.

- *Memory Management* provides information about the Core Foundation memory management model:

  http://developer.apple.com/documentation/CoreFoundation/Conceptual/
  CFMemoryMgmt/

- *Design Concepts* provides information about the overall design of Core Foundation:

  http://developer.apple.com/documentation/CoreFoundation/Conceptual/
  CFDesignConcepts/index.html

- A wealth of documentation about Core Foundation can be found at

  http://developer.apple.com/documentation/CoreFoundation/
  CoreFoundation.html

The ADC Reference Library has useful information discussing the measurement of drawing performance and using Quartz Debug at

  http://developer.apple.com/documentation/Performance/Conceptual/Drawing/
  Articles/MeasuringPerformance.html

Apple Technical Note 2133 provides information about how the Quartz Compositor interacts with the display refresh rate.

  http://developer.apple.com/technotes/tn2005/tn2133.html

Information about the resolution-independent user interface is part of the Tiger developer release notes installed as part of the Developer SDK for Tiger.

- The overall concepts of the resolution-independent UI are described in

  ```
  /Developer/ADC Reference Library/releasenotes/GraphicsImaging/
  ResolutionIndependentUI.html
  ```

- Cocoa-specific documentation is available in

  `/Developer/ADC Reference Library/releasenotes/Cocoa/AppKit.html`

  in the section titled "Resolution Independent UI."

- Carbon-specific documentation is available in

  `/Developer/ADC Reference Library/releasenotes/Carbon/`
  `CarbonResolutionIndependence.html`

PDF Reference: Version 1.6, 5th edition, Adobe Systems, Inc. contains a summary table that describes the complete set of PDF operators. This version and other versions of the PDF specification are available at

http://partners.adobe.com/public/developer/pdf/index_reference.html

The Voyeur sample project is installed in

`/Developer/Examples/Quartz/PDF/Voyeur`

Chapter 18

Creating Quartz Tools and Python Scripts

You can use the Quartz API in a number of interesting ways to write UNIX tools and scripts that create graphics and process PDF files, including the following:

- Providing graphics processing capabilities that are useful for creating dynamic web pages that contain Quartz drawing.

- Adding to the capabilities of the printing system through the PDF workflow that is available during printing.

- Providing command line tools that sophisticated users can use for special graphics processing needs, such as PDF manipulation or examination.

- Supplying Automator actions that perform specialized PDF functions. Automator is a tool, introduced in Tiger, that lets users easily assemble scripts (actions).

You don't need to write an application to accomplish any of these tasks. You need only to build a UNIX tool or script; a graphical user interface isn't necessary. This chapter shows two ways to use Quartz from a tool. The first is from a Python script and the second is from a command-line-style tool written using C.

You can use Python with Quartz for a number of tasks, such as to create PDF documents or image files in various file formats. You won't learn how to program in Python in this chapter. Instead, you'll see how to use Quartz in Python scripts that run in Panther and later versions. If you don't know Python already, you'll still be able to read the examples in this chapter and get an idea of how easy it is to use Python with Quartz.

Using the C programming language to write UNIX tools that use Quartz is just as easy as using Python. However, there are some important considerations that you should be aware of and that are discussed in "Using Quartz in UNIX Tools" (page 637).

Python Scripting with Quartz (Panther)

10.3 ▶ The Python scripting language is a good match with Quartz for a number of reasons:

- It's a popular scripting language that makes it easy to perform complex operations with Quartz without writing any C code.

- Python is an object-oriented language and the Quartz Python bindings allow Quartz objects such as contexts and images to be treated as Python objects.

- You can use Python interactively from the command line to experiment with Quartz programming. If you've programmed in PostScript, using Python interactively is reminiscent of typing at the interactive command line of a PostScript interpreter. You might enjoy learning the graphics capabilities of Quartz this way.

Python scripts that use Quartz can't draw to windows but they can draw to PDF and bitmap contexts. Python scripts can create PDF documents by using Quartz to draw to a PDF context. Similarly, they can create a bit-based graphics file by using Quartz to draw to a bitmap context and export those bits to an external file.

The examples in this chapter are relatively simple and are intended as an introduction to what you can do with Quartz from Python. As a Python programmer, you will find that Python and Quartz are a powerful combination.

Getting Started

The best way to get started using Quartz with Python is to look at a simple example (Listing 18.1). You'll see how to create a PDF document that contains a sequence of composited rectangles similar to that shown in Figure 2.10 (page 31) in "Painting with Alpha" (page 30).

Listing 18.1 Python code that draws alpha rectangles

```
#!/usr/bin/python
# Need to import all the attributes of the Core Graphics module.
```

```
from CoreGraphics import *
import math # for pi

# Create a portrait US-letter-size media rectangle.
mediaRect = CGRectMake(0, 0, 612, 792)

# Create a PDF context for the file "alpharects.pdf" using
# the mediaRect.
c = CGPDFContextCreateWithFilename("alpharects.pdf", mediaRect)

# Begin the first page of the PDF document being created.
c.beginPage(mediaRect)

# Compute the drawing to perform. This is the alpha rects
# drawing from Chapter 2, Figure 2.10.
numRects = 6
tintAdjust = 1./numRects
rotateAngle = 2*math.pi/numRects
ourRect = CGRectMake(0., 0., 130., 100.)

# Move the origin so that the drawing fits on the page.
c.translateCTM(2*ourRect.size.width, 2*ourRect.size.height)

# Start at tint value 1 and decrement each time
# through the loop.
tint = 1.
# Loop from 0 to (numRects-1).
for i in range(0, numRects):
  # Set the fill color to the tint of red with an
  # alpha value the same as the tint.
  c.setRGBFillColor(tint, 0., 0., tint)
  c.fillRect(ourRect)
  c.rotateCTM(rotateAngle)
  tint -= tintAdjust

# End the first (and only) page of the PDF document.
c.endPage()
# Finalize the context, emitting any pending output.
# Any calls on the context object after calling
# finish produce undefined results.
c.finish()
```

The script begins with #!/usr/bin/python to indicate that the system Python interpreter should interpret the script. The from statement that follows imports all the attributes from the Core Graphics module, which is built into Mac OS X. Without this statement, you won't be able to use Quartz (Core Graphics) drawing in your Python script.

The script creates a rectangle that is the same size as US-letter-size paper. It uses the function `CGPDFContextCreateWithFilename` defined by the Core Graphics Python module to create a PDF context that corresponds to a PDF document with the file name `alpharects.pdf` in the current directory. The document media box for this PDF document is specified by the media rectangle supplied to the function `CGPDFContextCreateWithFilename`.

After the context is created, the code can draw to it. It first calls the `beginPage` method on the context, which is the same as calling the Quartz function `CGContextBeginPage`, passing in a PDF context. Quartz scripting with Python takes advantage of the object-oriented nature of Python—the `CGContextRef` returned by `CGPDFContextCreateWithFilename` is a Python object with methods that closely correspond to the `CGContext...` methods available in the C-based API.

After calling `beginPage`, the script can draw on that PDF page. It performs the computations needed to perform the drawing and then loops, setting the color and drawing the rectangle each time through the loop. After the script draws the rectangle, it rotates the coordinate system and adjusts the tint value prior to the next iteration through the loop. The `setRGBFillColor`, `fillRect`, and `rotateCTM` methods are equivalent to their `CGContext...` C-based API analogues.

The script indicates the end of drawing on the first page by calling the context `endPage` method. Since there are no more pages to draw in this example, the code is done with the context and calls the context `finish` method, which releases the context and flushes the remaining content to the PDF document. When using Python, the document is not finalized until you call `finish` on a PDF context. Failing to call `finish` on a PDF context in Python produces a corrupt PDF document—this is similar to what happens if you fail to release a PDF context when you use the C-based API. See "Releasing a CGPDFContext Object" (page 621) for more information about this issue.

Although this example doesn't do much drawing with Quartz, it does present the basics. Because a large fraction of the Quartz drawing API is available from Python, you can do much more.

Creating Bits with Python

You can use Quartz and Python to create PNG, JPEG, GIF, or TIFF representations of Quartz drawing by creating a bitmap context, drawing to that context, then exporting the bits in the context to a file. A script that creates bits is useful to serve up data-driven web pages in a format that is recognized by any web browser. Because Quartz can draw PDF content and also convert PostScript data to PDF content it can then draw, you can convert PostScript or PDF data into a graphics file useful on those computing platforms without these built-in capabilities. Listing 18.2 is a Python script that produces a JPEG file for each page of an input PDF file.

Listing 18.2 Python code that creates image files from PDF pages

```python
#!/usr/bin/python

from CoreGraphics import *
import sys, os
from math import ceil

if len(sys.argv) != 2:
  print "usage: %s PDF-FILE" % sys.argv[0]
  sys.exit(1)

pdf_file = sys.argv[1]
out_file_prefix , ext = os.path.splitext(pdf_file)

if not os.path.isfile(pdf_file) :
  print "Input file \"%s\" does not exist!" % pdf_file
  sys.exit(2)

# Create a Quartz data provider from the file.
provider = CGDataProviderCreateWithFilename(pdf_file)

# Create a CGPDFDocumentRef for the file.
pdf = CGPDFDocumentCreateWithProvider(provider)

numPages = pdf.getNumberOfPages()

# Create a color space for the destination bitmap context.
# To run on Panther also, change this to kCGColorSpaceUserRGB.
cs = CGColorSpaceCreateWithName(kCGColorSpaceGenericRGB)

for i in range(1, numPages + 1):
  # Get the media box of the content for this page.
  r = pdf.getMediaBox(i)

  # Set the media box origin to the Quartz origin.
  r.origin.x = r.origin.y = 0
```

```
# Compute an integer width and height value that
# encloses the width and height of the media box.
w = int(ceil(r.size.width))
h = int(ceil(r.size.height))
# Create a bitmap context with the appropriate color space.
# The bits in the bitmap will be initialized with the supplied
# color; in this case opaque white.
ctx = CGBitmapContextCreateWithColor( w, h, cs, (1, 1, 1, 1) )
# Draw the PDF document to the bitmap context.
ctx.drawPDFDocument(r, pdf, i)

# Compute a file name for the output data. Don't serialize
# the output file names if there is only one page.
if numPages is 1 :
  out_file = out_file_prefix + ".jpg"
else :
  out_file = out_file_prefix + "." + str(i) + ".jpg"

# Write the bitmap context data to the output file as
# JPEG format.
ctx.writeToFile(out_file, kCGImageFormatJPEG)

# Finish the context. This is the last statement
# in the loop.
ctx.finish()

# Write a message indicating how many files were written.
print "%s created %d JPEG files from the PDF document" % \
                (sys.argv[0], numPages)
```

The script first imports the modules it needs and processes the arguments to the function. After it has the input file name, it computes the name of the output file prefix to use for the JPEG files it produces. The script creates a data provider that it needs to create a CGPDFDocument object that represents the input PDF document. The script gets the number of pages in the document so that it can loop over all the pages in the document.

For each page in the document, the script obtains the media box and creates a bitmap context that corresponds to that page. The Quartz function CGContext-CreateBitmapWithColor in Python allows you to create a bitmap context of a specific width and height, using a given color space. Quartz uses the color array passed to the function as the initial color of the pixels in the bitmap. In this example, the color is fully opaque white, an appropriate color for initializing the pixels when exporting the bitmap context data as a JPEG file.

After it has created the bitmap context, the code draws the PDF page into the context. Now the bitmap data in the bitmap context contains the rendered content of the PDF page and is ready for exporting to a JPEG file. The script exports the contents of the bitmap raster to the specified file using the bitmap context `writeToFile` method that is available in the Quartz Python bindings. It then finishes the context, which finalizes the file. If there are additional pages, the script loops, creates a new context for the next page, draws the PDF document, and exports the bitmap data to a file.

The Quartz function `CGContextCreateBitmapWithColor` is also useful when exporting to a format that supports transparency, such as TIFF or PNG. If the color space passed to `CGContextCreateBitmapWithColor` is a three-component color space, the alpha value of the color passed to `CGContextCreateBitmapWith-Color` determines whether the context should record alpha. If the alpha value of the color is not 1.0 (fully opaque) and the color space passed to `CGContextCreateBitmapWithColor` is a three-component color space, the context records alpha. Typically, for PNG or TIFF files where you want to record transparency, you pass a color value of (0,0,0,0)—this creates a bitmap context that records alpha and clears the bitmap context as part of its creation.

Using Quartz in UNIX Tools

Some of the previous examples in this book are well suited to build as a UNIX tool, such as the code that stamps a PDF page on top of another PDF document (in Listing 14.6 (page 450)) and code that scans a PDF document for the number and types of images it contains (in Listing 14.11 (page 472)). All you need to do to convert each of these examples to a tool is to add code that takes arguments from the command line. Building command line tools that use Quartz is relatively straightforward, but there are a couple of things that you should be aware of.

The Quartz 2D drawing library is part of the Core Graphics framework that is a subframework of the umbrella framework Application Services. The Application Services framework contains functions that do not generate or require a user interface and can safely be used in tools and other pieces of code that do not present a GUI interface. For application development, you typically don't link explicitly to the Application Services framework since the Cocoa and Carbon frameworks themselves link to it. To access the Quartz APIs from a tool, you aren't required to link to the Cocoa or Carbon frameworks; you can link directly to the Application Services framework.

Listing 18.3 contains a simple `main` routine that calls the routine `dumpPageStreams` from Listing 14.11. You can use this routine together with the code in Listing

14.11 to make a tool that counts the images in a PDF document and writes the result to stdout. As mentioned previously, you need to link only to the Application Services framework to build this tool.

Listing 18.3 A command line tool wrapper for dumpPageStreams

```
int main (int argc, const char * argv[]) {
  const char *inputFileName = NULL;
  char *outputFileName = NULL;
  CFURLRef inURL = NULL;

  if(argc != 2){
    fprintf(stderr, "Usage: %s [inputfile] \n", argv[0]);
    return 1;
  }

  inputFileName = argv[1];
  fprintf(stdout, "Beginning Document \"%s\"\n", inputFileName);

  inURL = CFURLCreateFromFileSystemRepresentation(NULL, inputFileName,
           strlen(inputFileName), false);
  if(!inURL){
    fprintf(stderr, "Couldn't create URL for input file!\n");
    return 1;
  }

  dumpPageStreams(inURL, stdout);

  CFRelease(inURL);

  return 0;
}
```

Security Issues

For security reasons, the Mac OS X window server has restrictions on what a process can do if that process isn't owned by a user who is currently logged into the graphical user interface. For example, such a process can't create and draw to a window or obtain information about the display. This limits what you can do using a UNIX tool that is executed by a user other than one logged into the GUI. If the system detects an illegal access being attempted, the window server logs a console message similar to the following: kCGErrorRangeCheck : Window Server communications from outside of session allowed for root and console user only. `INIT_Processeses()`, could not establish the default connection to the `WindowServer.Abort` trap. For example, if you try to open a GUI application from a remote login to an account other than a user logged in through the graphical user interface, the window server aborts the application and logs the preceding console message.

These restrictions may prevent you from using portions of the Carbon and Cocoa frameworks in your tools, but they don't impact your use of the Quartz 2D drawing API. You can use all of the Quartz 2D drawing APIs from a command line tool. However, because you can't obtain a window context from the Cocoa and Carbon application frameworks, your drawing is restricted to contexts other than the window context, such as the bitmap and PDF contexts.

The PDF Workflow in Printing (Jaguar)

10.2 ▶ As part of the printing process of Mac OS X, application drawing generates a PDF document that is processed by the printing system. Because the printing system generates a PDF representation of the drawing that an application performs during printing, there are many interesting possibilities for postprocessing the generated PDF document. This is where the PDF workflow comes in. The PDF workflow, available since Mac OS X version 10.2.4, is a means of extending the capabilities of the printing system by both users and developers. The PDF workflow menu automatically appears in the print dialog starting in Tiger. Prior to Tiger, a user must install workflow items in order for the PDF workflow menu to appear in the print dialog. Figure 18.1 shows the Tiger print dialog with a sample printing workflow menu.

Workflow items live in a special PDF Services directory in the /Library/ and ~/Library/ directories. They can consist of applications or application aliases, folders or folder aliases, AppleScript scripts, and UNIX executables (a UNIX executable can be a tool, a shell script, or any other executable in UNIX). In Tiger and later versions, an Automator workflow document can be a PDF workflow item. The printing system displays PDF workflow items in a special workflow menu.

When a user chooses a workflow item from the menu in the print dialog, the printing system generates a PDF document from the application's drawing and sends that PDF document to the workflow item. For a workflow item that is an application or an alias to an application, the PDF document opens in the application. The *Open PDF in BBEdit*, *Open PDF in PDFInspector*, and *Open PDF in Mail* workflow items in Figure 18.1 are application aliases for the applications BBEdit, PDFInspector, and Mail. Choosing one of these workflow items opens

Figure 18.1 A sample printing workflow menu in the standard print dialog in Tiger

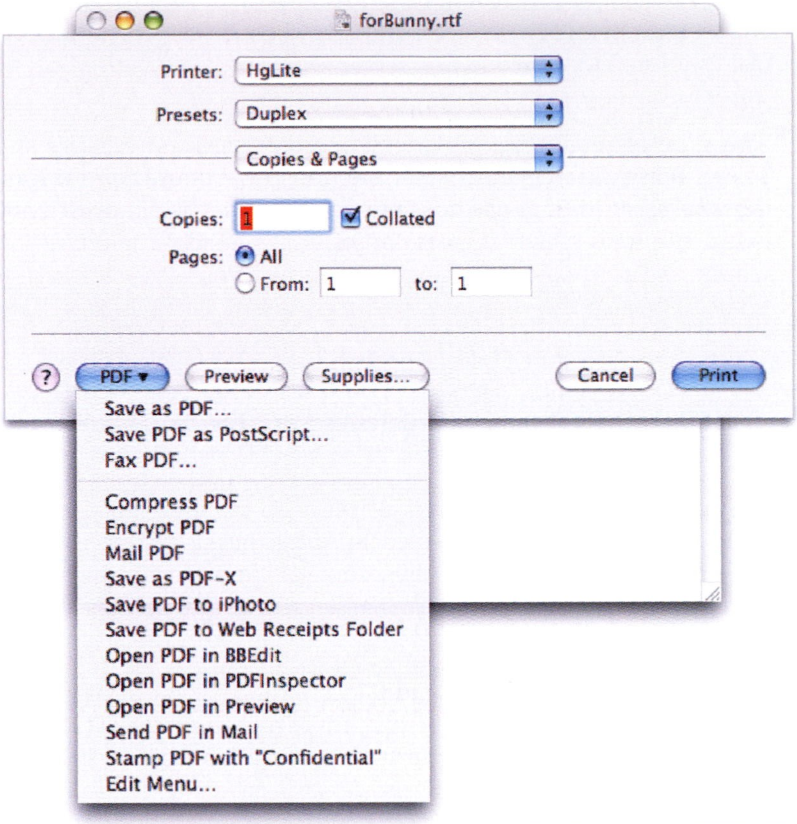

that application with the PDF document generated during printing from any application.

If the chosen workflow item is a UNIX executable, the printing system executes it, passing three arguments. The first argument is a string that corresponds to the print job title, as generated by the printing application. The second argument is a string that contains the requested options for the print job. The last argument is a string that contains the full path to the PDF document passed to the workflow item.

A workflow item can do virtually anything with the PDF file passed to it. A workflow item is run as a process owned by the user performing the print job and can present a user interface for interaction with the user.

The menu item *Stamp PDF with "Confidential"* in the workflow menu in Figure 18.1 is a script that executes when the user chooses that item. This workflow item is the Python script in Listing 18.4. This script creates a new PDF document that contains the same number of pages as the source document and stamps the word "Confidential" on each page of the PDF document generated during printing. After it creates the stamped PDF document, the script opens the new PDF file in Preview.

This Python script is similar to the code in Listing 14.6 (page 450) that stamps each page of an existing PDF document with a graphic that is another PDF file. The primary difference between the previous example and this one is that Listing 18.4 is written in Python and the text that is stamped onto each page is drawn explicitly, rather than as part of drawing a PDF graphic.

The script first imports the modules and functions that it requires, performs some simple argument checking, and creates a temporary file name to use for the output PDF file. Next the script creates a PDF context with a media box that corresponds to the media rectangle of the first page of the document. It then constructs a string that is a short piece of HTML that, when drawn, produces the text "Confidential" in the Gadget typeface at a size of 60 points. It makes a Quartz data provider from the string; this data provider is needed in order to draw the string.

The script loops over each of the pages of the source PDF document, creating a new page in the output PDF document for each page. For each new page, it uses the media box for the source page. On the first page of the document, the script computes the width and height of the string to draw. (This is only done on the first page because the width and height of the string are the same for all pages.) This width and height is used to position the text on the page so that it is centered along a diagonal line from the lower-left corner of the page to the upper-right corner.

Next the script draws the source PDF page. Before drawing the word "Confidential," the script needs to position the text. To do so, it translates the text to the center of the page, computes the angle of the diagonal line between the lower-left and upper-right corners, and rotates by that angle. Next it translates so that the center of the box that contains the text is centered on the page. Before drawing the string, the script sets the global alpha to 30 percent so that the text it draws doesn't completely obscure the contents underneath. The script draws the string using the context method `drawHTMLTextInRect`, which the Quartz Python bindings provide to draw HTML text into a specified rectangle.

For each page in the source PDF, the script creates a new PDF page that contains the contents of the source PDF page, with the "Confidential" text drawn on top of it. The result is a new PDF document that has the same number of pages and the same content but with the "Confidential" watermark on top. After each page is processed, the script calls the `finish` method on the PDF context to finalize the PDF document. Once the source PDF file has been processed, the code deletes it using the Python `unlink` method and opens the output file in Preview.

The computation of the width and height of the text drawn on each page works around a bug that otherwise would produce text that is not centered on the center point of the page. The Quartz Python bindings provide the method `CGContextMeasureHTMLTextInRect` for measuring text without drawing it, but the rectangle returned is not a tight bounding box around the glyphs in the text. To work around this problem, the code takes advantage of the Quartz text drawing mode `kCGTextInvisible`. Drawing with this text mode moves the text position by the width of the text but does not paint any glyphs. To calculate the width and height of the "Confidential" text, the code draws the text with `drawHTMLTextInRect` at the origin of coordinates and uses the x coordinate of the text position after the text is drawn as the width of the text. The height of the text is the height of the rectangle returned by `drawHTMLTextInRect`. (Note that the y coordinate of the text position returned by the `GetTextPosition` method is not reflective of the height of the glyphs but is the y displacement of the text pen when the characters are drawn. Typically this is 0 for fonts that are not vertical writing fonts.) After the code computes the width and height of the text box, it sets the text drawing mode back to the fill text drawing mode.

Listing 18.4 A printing workflow item written in Python

```
#!/usr/bin/python

from CoreGraphics import *
import sys, os
from math import atan

# The arguments to a printing workflow script
# are "title", "options", "path-to-pdf-file".

if len(sys.argv) != 4:
    print >>sys.stderr, "usage: %s title options PDF-FILE" % sys.argv[0]
    sys.exit(1)

in_file = sys.argv[3]

if not os.path.isfile(in_file) :
    print "Input file \"%s\" does not exist!" % in_file
    sys.exit(2)

# Create a temporary file name for the output file.
out_prefix = sys.argv[1] + "."
out_file = os.tempnam(None, out_prefix)

pdf = CGPDFDocumentCreateWithProvider(
            CGDataProviderCreateWithFilename(in_file))
```

```
numPages = pdf.getNumberOfPages()

mediaRect = pdf.getMediaBox(1)
mediaRect.origin.x = mediaRect.origin.y = 0

# Create a PDF context for the output file using
# the mediaRect.
pdfContext = CGPDFContextCreateWithFilename(out_file, mediaRect)

stampString = "Confidential"
font = "Gadget"
fontSize = 60

# This creates an HTML string that draws the word 'stampString'
# in the typeface 'font', at the size 'fontSize'.
htmlString = '<!DOCTYPE html PUBLIC "-//W3C//DTD HTML 4.01//EN" \
      "http://www.w3.org/TR/html4/strict.dtd"> \
  <html> <head> <meta http-equiv=\"Content-Type\" \
    content="text/html; charset=UTF-8\"> \
  <meta http-equiv=\"Content-Style-Type\" content="text/css\"> \
  <style type=\"text/css\"> \
    p.p1 {margin: 0.0px 0.0px 0.0px 0.0px; font: %dpx %s} \
  </style> </head> <body> <p class=\"p1\">%s</p> </body> </html>' \
    % (fontSize, font, stampString)

stringProvider = CGDataProviderCreateWithString(htmlString)

textBoxWidth = -1
textBoxHeight = -1

for i in range(1, numPages + 1):

  # Get the media box of the content for this page.
  mediaRect = pdf.getMediaBox(i)
  mediaRect.origin.x = mediaRect.origin.y = 0

  pdfContext.beginPage(mediaRect)

  # Calculate the box width and height the first time
  # through the loop.
  if(i is 1) :
    # Draw the text to determine the width. Set the drawing mode
    # to invisible so that it doesn't appear.
    pdfContext.setTextDrawingMode(kCGTextInvisible)
    outRect = pdfContext.drawHTMLTextInRect(stringProvider,
            mediaRect, fontSize)
```

```
        # Get the text position.
        newTextPosition = pdfContext.getTextPosition()
        # The width of the text is the ending x pen position minus
        # the starting pen position (which is 0 in this case).
        textBoxWidth = newTextPosition.x
        # The text height is the height of the rectangle returned from
        # drawHTMLTextInRect. Because of a bug in drawHTMLTextInRect,
        # the width of this rectangle is not the correct width.
        textBoxHeight = outRect.size.height
        # Reset the text mode to fill for painting the text.
        pdfContext.setTextDrawingMode(kCGTextFill)


    # Draw the page of the source PDF document to the PDF context.
    pdfContext.drawPDFDocument(mediaRect, pdf, i)

    pdfContext.saveGState()

    # Locate the text. First translate to the center of the page.
    pdfContext.translateCTM(mediaRect.size.width/2,
            mediaRect.size.height/2)

    # Compute the angle along the diagonal and rotate by that angle.
    theta = atan( mediaRect.size.height / mediaRect.size.width)
    pdfContext.rotateCTM(theta)

    # Position so the text will be centered about the center of the page.
    pdfContext.translateCTM(-textBoxWidth/2, -textBoxHeight/2)

    # Set the global alpha to 0.3 so the text is partially transparent.
    pdfContext.setAlpha(0.3)

    # Draw the text on top of the PDF page.
    pdfContext.drawHTMLTextInRect(stringProvider,
            CGRectMake(0,0,textBoxWidth,textBoxHeight), fontSize)

    pdfContext.restoreGState()

    pdfContext.endPage()

pdfContext.finish()

# Delete the input file since it is no longer needed.
os.unlink(in_file)
```

```
# Open the resulting file in Preview.
os.system("/usr/bin/open -a Preview %s" % out_file)
```

The script in Listing 18.4 creates a new PDF document with the stamp on each printed page and opens it in Preview. The user can then specify where to save the PDF document. Of course, the results of a PDF workflow item could be stored to a special folder, queued for printing, served up as web pages, or just about anything you could imagine being useful for users. Figure 18.2 shows the output from running the script on one of the pages of the PDF workflow documentation itself.

Figure 18.2 Results of the Python PDF workflow item

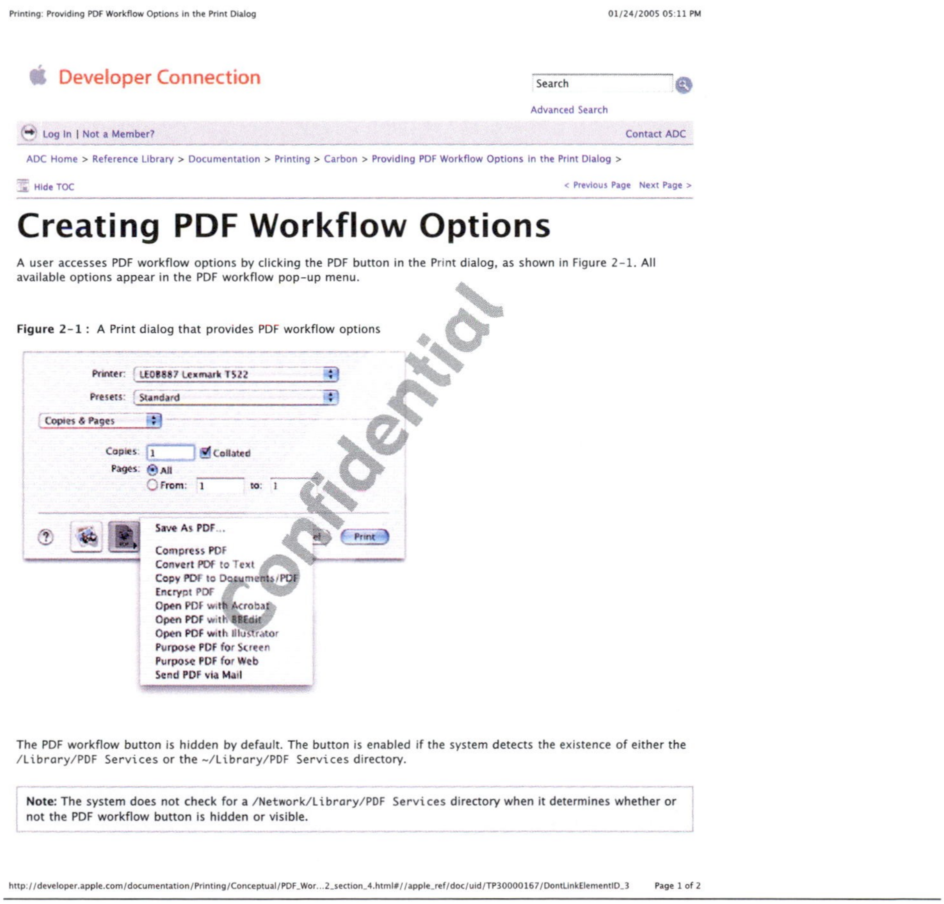

Printing: Providing PDF Workflow Options in the Print Dialog 01/24/2005 05:11 PM

Developer Connection

Search

Advanced Search

Log In | Not a Member? Contact ADC

ADC Home > Reference Library > Documentation > Printing > Carbon > Providing PDF Workflow Options in the Print Dialog >

Hide TOC < Previous Page Next Page >

Creating PDF Workflow Options

A user accesses PDF workflow options by clicking the PDF button in the Print dialog, as shown in Figure 2-1. All available options appear in the PDF workflow pop-up menu.

Figure 2-1 : A Print dialog that provides PDF workflow options

The PDF workflow button is hidden by default. The button is enabled if the system detects the existence of either the /Library/PDF Services or the ~/Library/PDF Services directory.

Note: The system does not check for a /Network/Library/PDF Services directory when it determines whether or not the PDF workflow button is hidden or visible.

http://developer.apple.com/documentation/Printing/Conceptual/PDF_Wor...2_section_4.html#//apple_ref/doc/uid/TP30000167/DontLinkElementID_3 Page 1 of 2

Note that the PDF workflow is available in Mac OS X version 10.2.4 (Jaguar) and later versions, but the Quartz Python bindings are only available in Panther and later versions. Because of this discrepancy, the Python script in Listing 18.4 (page 642) does not work as part of the printing workflow in any version of Jaguar.

Summary

Your code doesn't have to be in a GUI application to take advantage of Quartz. UNIX tools and Python scripts can call Quartz to perform a number of useful drawing tasks. The Quartz Python bindings make it easy for you to write Python scripts that incorporate Quartz drawing. Using the bindings, you can create PDF documents or PNG, TIFF, JPEG, and GIF files that contain Quartz drawing. By combining the scripting power of Python with the graphics capabilities of Quartz, you can generate eye-catching graphics from your input data. UNIX tools can similarly take advantage of Quartz by linking to the Application Services framework.

The PDF workflow available with the printing system lets you integrate your PDF processing tools and scripts in the print dialog where they can provide value to users. Because Quartz can draw existing PDF data, you can add content, rearrange pages, or otherwise process PDF documents generated when the user prints.

See Also

You can find examples of Python scripts that use Quartz in the directory

```
/Developer/Examples/Quartz/Python/
```

You will want to explore these scripts to get a tour of the Quartz functionality available using Python.

The Quartz Python API summary document describes the set of Quartz bindings available when programming with Python:

```
/Developer/Examples/Quartz/Python/API-SUMMARY
```

The PDF workflow documentation is available from the ADC Reference Library:

http://developer.apple.com/documentation/Printing/Conceptual/PDF_Workflow/ index.html

Index

647